QuickBooks 2010

Bonnie Biafore

POGUE PRESS™
O'REILLY®

Beijing · Cambridge · Farnham · Köln · Sebastopol · Taipei · Tokyo

Part Three: Managing Your Business

Part Four: QuickBooks Power

The Missing Credits

About the Author

 **Bonnie Biafore** has always been fascinated with math in its practical and more esoteric forms. As an engineer and project manager, she's thorough and steadfastly attentive to detail but redeems herself by using her sick sense of humor to transform these drool-inducing subjects into entertaining reading. She writes about personal finance, investing, accounting, and project management, although she's working on what she hopes will be a best-selling crime novel with movie rights worth oodles of money. Her *NAIC Stock Selection Handbook* won major awards from the Society of Technical Communication and APEX Awards for Publication Excellence (but the raves she receives from beginning investors mean much more to her).

Bonnie is also the author of O'Reilly's *Online Investing Hacks*, *Quicken 2009: The Missing Manual*, and *Microsoft Project 2007: The Missing Manual*. She writes a monthly column called "WebWatch" for *Better Investing* magazine and is a regular contributor to *www.interest.com*. As a consultant, she manages projects for clients and wins accolades for her ability to herd cats.

When not chained to her computer, she hikes and cycles in the mountains, cooks gourmet meals, and practices saying no to additional work assignments. You can learn more at Bonnie's website, *www.bonniebiafore.com*, or email her at *bonnie.biafore@gmail.com*.

About the Creative Team

Nan Barber (editor) is associate editor for the Missing Manual series. She lives in Massachusetts with her husband and G4 Macintosh. Email: *nanbarber@oreilly.com*.

Nellie McKesson (production editor) currently lives in Brighton, Mass., where she devotes all her free time to her burgeoning t-shirt business (*www.endplasticdesigns.com*). Email: *nellie@oreilly.com*.

Ron Strauss (indexer) specializes in the indexing of information technology publications of all kinds. He has collaborated with Jack Lyon of *www.editorium.com* in the creation of DEXembed, a Microsoft Word template that greatly enhances the process of embedded indexing in Word. Ron is also an accomplished classical violist and lives in northern California with his wife and fellow indexer, Annie, and his miniature pinscher, Kanga.

Lauren Becker (technical reviewer) is a junior at Emory University's Goizueta Business School, pursuing an Accounting concentration (CPA track) and a Persian minor.

Estela Johnson (technical reviewer) is the owner of e-Bookkeeping, LLC (*www.e-Bookkeeping.net*). e-Bookkeeping specializes in remote bookkeeping access and Intuit QuickBooks training. With over ten years of experience, Estela has worked closely with business owners in several industries. Currently, she is working toward an M.A. in Accounting (email: *johnson_estela@yahoo.com*).

Ted Whitby (technical reviewer) is a chef, accountant, Certified QuickBooks ProAdvisor, and a human resource specialist for over 20 years. When not cooking for family, friends, and clients, he specializes in helping businesses from startup to mid-size with their accounting and HR needs. Email: *ted@scaccountingsolutions.com*. Web: *www.SCAcccountingSolutions.com*.

Acknowledgments

Behind the scenes, a throng of folks work hard to make a book (and me) look as good as we do. I am always grateful for the improvements that people make to my writing. My words (and bookkeeping) are better for it. Nan Barber, Peter Meyers, and Dawn Frausto have done their usual fantastic job of piloting this book through the shoals of publishing. Special thanks to Ron Strauss for building an index that helps you find all the information you want (especially important given the complete absence of an index in QuickBooks Help).

I also want to thank the technical reviewers Lauren Becker, Estela Johnson, and Ted Whitby, for their great tips and especially for keeping me honest.

— *Bonnie Biafore*

The Missing Manual Series

Missing Manuals are witty, superbly written guides to computer products that don't come with printed manuals (which is just about all of them). Each book features a handcrafted index; cross-references to specific pages (not just chapters); and RepKover, a detached-spine binding that lets the book lie perfectly flat without the assistance of weights or cinder blocks.

Recent and upcoming titles include:

Access 2007: The Missing Manual by Matthew MacDonald

AppleScript: The Missing Manual by Adam Goldstein

AppleWorks 6: The Missing Manual by Jim Elferdink and David Reynolds

CSS: The Missing Manual, Second Edition by David Sawyer McFarland

Creating a Web Site: The Missing Manual, Second Edition by Matthew MacDonald

David Pogue's Digital Photography: The Missing Manual by David Pogue

Dreamweaver CS4: The Missing Manual by David Sawyer McFarland

Dreamweaver CS5: The Missing Manual by David Sawyer McFarland

eBay: The Missing Manual by Nancy Conner

Excel 2003: The Missing Manual by Matthew MacDonald

Excel 2007: The Missing Manual by Matthew MacDonald

Facebook: The Missing Manual by E.A. Vander Veer

FileMaker Pro 9: The Missing Manual by Geoff Coffey and Susan Prosser

FileMaker Pro 10: The Missing Manual by Susan Prosser and Geoff Coffey

Flash CS4: The Missing Manual by E.A. Vander Veer and Chris Grover

Flash CS5: The Missing Manual by Chris Grover with E.A. Vander Veer

FrontPage 2003: The Missing Manual by Jessica Mantaro

Google Apps: The Missing Manual by Nancy Conner

The Internet: The Missing Manual by David Pogue and J.D. Biersdorfer

iMovie '08 & iDVD: The Missing Manual by David Pogue

iMovie '09 & iDVD: The Missing Manual by David Pogue and Aaron Miller

iPhone: The Missing Manual, Third Edition by David Pogue

iPhoto '08: The Missing Manual by David Pogue

iPhoto '09: The Missing Manual by David Pogue and J.D. Biersdorfer

iPod: The Missing Manual, Eighth Edition by J.D. Biersdorfer and David Pogue

JavaScript: The Missing Manual by David Sawyer McFarland

Living Green: The Missing Manual by Nancy Conner

Mac OS X: The Missing Manual, Tiger Edition by David Pogue

Mac OS X: The Missing Manual, Leopard Edition by David Pogue

Microsoft Project 2007: The Missing Manual by Bonnie Biafore

Netbooks: The Missing Manual by J.D. Biersdorfer

Office 2004 for Macintosh: The Missing Manual by Mark H. Walker and Franklin Tessler

Office 2007: The Missing Manual by Chris Grover, Matthew MacDonald, and E.A. Vander Veer

Office 2008 for Macintosh: The Missing Manual by Jim Elferdink

Palm Pre: The Missing Manual by Ed Baig

PCs: The Missing Manual by Andy Rathbone

Photoshop CS4: The Missing Manual by Lesa Snider

Photoshop Elements 7: The Missing Manual by Barbara Brundage

Photoshop Elements 6 for Mac: The Missing Manual by Barbara Brundage

PowerPoint 2007: The Missing Manual by E.A. Vander Veer

Premiere Elements: The Missing Manual by Chris Grover

QuickBase: The Missing Manual by Nancy Conner

QuickBooks 2009: The Missing Manual by Bonnie Biafore

Quicken 2008: The Missing Manual by Bonnie Biafore

Quicken 2009: The Missing Manual by Bonnie Biafore

Switching to the Mac: The Missing Manual, Tiger Edition by David Pogue and Adam Goldstein

Switching to the Mac: The Missing Manual, Snow Leopard Edition by David Pogue

Wikipedia: The Missing Manual by John Broughton

Windows XP Home Edition: The Missing Manual, Second Edition by David Pogue

Windows XP Pro: The Missing Manual, Second Edition by David Pogue, Craig Zacker, and Linda Zacker

Windows Vista: The Missing Manual by David Pogue

Windows Vista for Starters: The Missing Manual by David Pogue

Word 2007: The Missing Manual by Chris Grover

Your Body: The Missing Manual by Matthew MacDonald

Your Brain: The Missing Manual by Matthew MacDonald

Your Money: The Missing Manual by J.D. Roth

Introduction

Thousands of small companies and nonprofit organizations turn to QuickBooks to keep company finances on track. And over the years, Intuit has introduced editions of QuickBooks to satisfy the needs of different types of companies. Back when milk was simply milk, you either used QuickBooks or you didn't. Now that you can choose milk from soy beans as well as cows and five different levels of fat, it's no surprise that QuickBooks comes in Simple Start, Pro, Premier, Online, and Enterprise editions, which, in some cases, are dramatically different from their siblings, as well as six industry-specific editions. From the smallest of sole proprietorships to burgeoning enterprises, one of the QuickBooks editions is likely to meet your organization's needs *and* budget.

QuickBooks isn't hard to learn. Many of the features that you're familiar with from other programs work just as well in QuickBooks—windows, dialog boxes, dropdown lists, and keyboard shortcuts, to name a few. With each new version, Intuit has added enhancements and new features to make your workflow smoother and faster. The challenge that remains is knowing what to do according to accounting rules, as well as how to do so in QuickBooks.

What's New in QuickBooks 2010

Despite the fluctuating size of the tax code each year, accounting and bookkeeping practices don't change all that much. Although the changes in QuickBooks 2010 tend to be small tweaks and subtle improvements, a few additions might be just what you've been waiting for:

- **Adding and editing multiple list entries.** Suppose you've reworked your customer types and you want to apply the new types to a few dozen customers. The Edit dialog box is too tedious, and importing records is overkill. Enter the new Add/Edit Multiple List Entries command (page 86), which provides welcome shortcuts for adding and updating values in the customer, vendor, and item lists. You can paste information from an Excel spreadsheet directly into a table in the dialog box. Or you can copy or duplicate values between records. (Typing values into cells is OK, too.)

- **Online banking interface choices.** When QuickBooks 2009 introduced a new Online Banking Center, some online banking tasks got easier, but recording multiple transactions became a lot more difficult. Intuit fixed those problems in QuickBooks 2010, but also brought back the QuickBooks 2008–era Online Banking Center for folks who were happy with the way things were. You can switch between Register mode and Side-by-side mode (page 530), although it's best to pick the one you prefer and stick with it.

Note: Switching between the two Online Banking Center styles has some snafus. Side-by-side mode doesn't recognize aliases you create for payees in Register mode. Likewise, Register mode doesn't recognize payee renaming rules you create in Side-by-side mode. Equally annoying, when you switch modes, QuickBooks closes all open windows and leaves it to you to reopen them.

- **Report center.** In QuickBooks 2010, the Report Center (page 498) gives you some great new ways to find the reports you want. You may never have to look further than the Favorites tab. You tell QuickBooks which reports are your favorites, and they all appear on the Favorites tab. Similarly, the Memorized tab lists all the reports you've memorized, and the Recent tab lets you quickly return to and re-run your last several reports.

  The Report Center can display reports in three ways: the Carousel View, a memory-hogging piece of eye candy; Grid view, which displays thumbnails of each report in a category to help you spot the one you want; and List View, which displays report titles and the questions the reports answer in a tidy list. When you select a report in the Report Center, you can preview the report to make sure it's what you want. Even better, you can choose the date range *before* you run the report.

- **The Favorites menu.** The QuickBooks 2010 menu bar includes Favorites (page 609)—an easy-to-access spot to store all your favorite commands, windows, and reports. When you choose Favorites → Customize Favorites, the Customize Your Menus dialog box lists every feature QuickBooks has to offer: every command from every QuickBooks menu and submenu along with every built-in, customized, or memorized report in your company file. To add a command to the Favorites menu, select it in the Available Menu Items list and click Add.

• **Customizing the Company Snapshot.** The Company Snapshot window (page 613) is a great way to see a lot of the key info about your books in one place. In QuickBooks 2010, you can choose from a dozen views, like your income and expense trends, account balances, outstanding invoices and bills, and reminders. You can show or hide views and rearrange them so the most important info is at the top. The downside is you have to choose from the 12 views that Quick-Books offers. If you like to look at your financial status in other ways, you still have to run your customized reports for that.

• **Document management.** You can attach documents to records in your company file—for example, to attach an electronic copy of a job contract to a customer record, or a photo and specifications document to an item you sell. Once you add documents to your document management storage, you can share them with others, too. One downside: The first 100 MB of storage space is free, but you'll pay for more storage after that. Plus, QuickBooks stores your attached documents *on the Internet*, which you may not want to do for security reasons.

• **Electronic signature on checks.** If you have an image of your signature, you can ward off writer's cramp by adding your electronic signature to the checks you print (page 235).

• **Detach the Help window.** Finally, the QuickBooks Help window has learned how to play well with other windows. In QuickBooks 2010, you can detach the Help window from the right side of the QuickBooks main window, position it wherever you want, resize it, and minimize it. It might not sound like much, but this enhancement means you can see reasonably-sized QuickBooks windows and Help topics at the same time. Even better, the QuickBooks main window doesn't change size just because Help is open.

When QuickBooks May Not Be the Answer

When you run a business (or a nonprofit), you track company finances for two reasons: to keep your business running smoothly and to generate the reports required by the IRS, the SEC, and anyone else you have to answer to. QuickBooks helps you perform basic financial tasks, track your financial situation, and manage your business to make it even better. Before you read any further, here are a few things you *shouldn't* try to do with QuickBooks:

• **Work with more than 14,500 unique inventory items or 14,500 contact names.** QuickBooks Pro and Premier company files can contain up to 14,500 inventory items and a combined total of up to 14,500 customer, vendor, employee, and other (Other Names list) names. (QuickBooks Enterprise Solutions version 7.0 and later increases these limits to 1,000,000.)

• **Track personal finances.** Even if you're a company of one, keeping your personal finances separate from your business finances is a good move, particularly when it comes to tax reporting. In addition to opening a separate checking account for your business, track your personal finances somewhere else (like in Quicken). If that somewhere else is QuickBooks, at least create a separate company file for your personal financial information.

- **Track the performance of stocks and bonds.** QuickBooks isn't meant to keep track of the capital gains and dividends you earn from investments such as stocks and bonds. But companies have investments, of course. A machine that costs hundreds of thousands of dollars is an investment that you hope will generate lots of income, and you should track it in QuickBooks. However, in QuickBooks, these types of investments show up as *assets* of the company (page 150).

- **Manage customer relationships.** Lots of information goes into keeping customers happy. With QuickBooks, you can stay on top of customer activities with features like To Do items, Reminders, and Memorized Transactions. But for tracking details like membership, items sold on consignment, project progress, and scheduled events, another program like Microsoft Excel or Access would be a better solution.

Note: Intuit sells an online product called Customer Manager (*http://customermanager.com/*). Also, some third-party customer management products integrate with QuickBooks (page 594).

Choosing the Right QuickBooks Product

QuickBooks comes in a gamut of editions, offering options for organizations at both ends of the small-business spectrum. QuickBooks Simple Start and Online Edition cover the basic needs of very small operations. Enterprise Solutions are the most robust and powerful editions of QuickBooks, boasting enhanced features and speed for the biggest of small businesses.

Warning: QuickBooks for Mac differs *significantly* from the Windows version, and unfortunately you won't find help with that version of the program in this book.

This book focuses on QuickBooks Pro because its balance of features and price make it the most popular edition. Throughout this book, you'll also find notes about features offered in the Premier edition, which is one step up from Pro. Whether you're willing to pay for these advanced features is up to you. Here's an overview of what each edition does:

- **QuickBooks Simple Start** is more of a marketing tool, because you'll quickly outgrow its limitations. (At that point, you can move your data to QuickBooks Pro or QuickBooks Online.) But it's a low-cost option for small businesses with simple accounting needs and only one person using QuickBooks at a time. It's easy to set up and use, but it doesn't handle features like inventory, tracking time, or sharing your company file with your accountant.

- **QuickBooks Online Edition** has most of the features of QuickBooks Pro, but you access it via the Web instead of running it on your PC. It lets you use QuickBooks anywhere, on any computer, so it's ideal for the consultant who's always on the go.

- **QuickBooks Pro is the workhorse edition.** It lets up to five people work in a company file at a time: you can purchase licenses in single- or five-user packs. QuickBooks Pro includes features such as invoicing; entering and paying bills; job costing; creating estimates; saving and distributing reports and forms as email attachments; creating budgets automatically; projecting cash flow; tracking mileage; customizing forms; customizing prices with price levels; printing shipping labels for FedEx and UPS; and integrating with Word, Excel, and hundreds of other programs. All QuickBooks Pro name lists—customers, vendors, employees, and so on—can include up to a combined total of 14,500 entries. Other lists like the Chart of Accounts can have up to 10,000 entries.

- **QuickBooks Premier** is another multi-user edition. For business owners, its big claim to fame is handling inventory items assembled from other items and components. In addition, Premier editions can generate purchase orders from sales orders or estimates and can apply price levels to individual items. You can also track employee information and get to your data remotely. This edition includes a few extra features typically of more interest to accountants, like reversing general journal entries. When you purchase QuickBooks Premier, you can choose from six different industry-specific flavors (see the next section). Like the Pro edition, Premier can handle a combined total of up to 14,500 list entries.

- **Enterprise Solutions 9.0** is the edition for larger operations. It's faster, bigger, and more robust. Up to 30 people can access a company file at the same time, and this simultaneous access is at least twice as fast as in the Pro or Premier edition. The database can handle lots more names in its customer, vendor, employee, and other name lists (1,000,000 versus 14,500 for Pro and Premier). You can have multiple company files, work in several locations, and produce combined reports for those companies and locations. With more people in your company file, this edition has features such as an enhanced audit trail, more options for assigning or limiting user permissions, and the ability to delegate administrative functions to the other people using the program.

The QuickBooks Premier Choices

If you work in one of the industries covered by QuickBooks' Premier, you can get additional features unique to your industry—for about $150 more than QuickBooks Pro. (When you install QuickBooks Premier, you choose the industry version you want to run. If your business is in an industry other than one of the five industry-specific versions, choose General Business.) Some people swear that these customizations are worth every extra penny. Others say the extra features don't warrant the Premier price. On the QuickBooks website (*http://quickbooks.intuit.com*), you can tour the Premier features to decide for yourself. Or, you can purchase the Accountant edition, which can run any QuickBooks edition, from QuickBooks Pro to the gamut of Premier industry-specific versions.

FREQUENTLY ASKED QUESTION

Nonprofit Dilemma

I'm doing the books for a tiny nonprofit corporation. I'd really like to avoid spending any of our hard-raised funds on a special edition of QuickBooks. Can't I just use Quick-Books Pro?

You may be tempted to save some money by using Quick-Books Pro instead of the more-expensive QuickBooks Non-profit Edition, but be prepared to live with some limitations. As long as funding comes primarily from unrestricted sources, the Pro edition fits reasonably well. Your biggest annoyance is using the term "customer" when you mean donor or member, or the term "job" for grants you receive. Throughout this book, you'll find notes and tips about tracking nonprofit finances with QuickBooks Pro (or plain Quick-Books Premier).

However, if you receive restricted funds or track funds by program, you have to manually post them to equity accounts and allocate funds to accounts in your chart of accounts—QuickBooks Pro doesn't automatically perform these staples of nonprofit accounting. Likewise, the program doesn't generate all the reports you need to satisfy your grant providers or the government, though you can export reports (page 599) and then modify them as necessary in a spreadsheet program.

Note: Accountant Edition is designed to help professional accountants and bookkeepers deliver services to their clients. You can run any QuickBooks edition (that is, Pro, or any of the Premier versions). In addition to being compatible with all other editions of QuickBooks, it lets you design financial statements and other documents, process payroll for clients, reconcile client bank accounts, calculate depreciation, and prepare client tax returns.

- The **General Business** version has all the goodies of the Premier Edition like per-item price levels, sales orders, and so on. It also has more built-in reports than QuickBooks Pro, sales and expense forecasting, and a business plan feature (although if you're using QuickBooks to keep your books, you may already have a business plan).

- The **Contractor** version includes special features near and dear to construction contractors' hearts: job cost reports, different billing rates by employee, managing change orders, and other contractor-specific reports.

- **Manufacturing & Wholesale** is targeted to companies that manufacture products. It includes a chart of accounts and menus customized for manufacturing and wholesale operations. You can manage inventory assembled from components and track customer return materials authorizations (RMAs) and damaged goods.

- If you run a nonprofit organization, you know that several things work differently in the nonprofit world, as the box above details. The **Nonprofit** version includes features such as a chart of accounts customized for nonprofits, forms and letters targeted to donors and pledges, help about using QuickBooks for a nonprofit, and the ability to generate the "Statement of Functional Expenses 990" form.

- The **Professional Services** version (not to be confused with QuickBooks Pro) is designed for the company that delivers services to its clients. Unique features include project costing reports, templates for proposals and invoices, billing rates that you can customize by client, billing rate by employee, and professional service-specific reports and help.

- The **Retail** version customizes much of QuickBooks to work for retail operations. It includes a specialized chart of accounts, menus, reports, forms, and help. Intuit offers companion products that you can integrate with this edition to support all aspects of your retail operation. For example, QuickBooks' Point of Sale tracks sales, customers, and inventory as you ring up sales, and it shoots the information over to your QuickBooks company file.

UP TO SPEED

Learning More About Accounting

If you need to learn a lot about QuickBooks and a little something about accounting, you're holding the right book. If bookkeeping and accounting are unfamiliar territory, though, some background training (page 661) may help you use QuickBooks better and more easily (without calling your accountant for help five times a day).

The Accounting and Business School of the Rockies offers an accounting and bookkeeping self-study course that you can play on a VCR or DVD player. The course presents real-life accounting situations, so you'll learn to solve common small-business accounting challenges, and it includes hands-on exercises to help you master the material. It doesn't take long to complete, so you'll be up and accounting in no time. To contact the school, visit *www. usefultraining.com* or call 1-800-772-6885.

Accounting Basics—The Important Stuff

Intuit claims that you don't need to understand most accounting concepts to use QuickBooks. However, the accuracy of your books *and* your productivity will benefit if you understand the following concepts and terms:

- **Double-entry accounting** is the standard method for tracking where your money comes from and where it goes. Following the old saw that money doesn't grow on trees, money always comes from somewhere when you use double-entry accounting. For example, as shown in Table I-1, when you sell something to a customer, the money on your invoice comes in as income and goes into your Accounts Receivable account. Then, when you deposit the payment, the money comes out of the Accounts Receivable account and goes into your checking account. See Chapter 16 for more about double-entry accounting and journal entries.

Note: Each side of a double-entry transaction has a name: debit or credit. As you can see in Table I-1, when you sell products or services, you credit your income account (you increase your income when you sell something), but debit the Accounts Receivable account (selling something also increases how much customers owe you). You'll see examples throughout the book of how transactions equate to account debits and credits.

Table I-1. Following the money through accounts

Transaction	Account	Debit	Credit
Sell products or services	Service Income		$1,000
Sell products or services	Accounts Receivable	$1,000	
Receive payment	Accounts Receivable		$1,000
Receive payment	Checking Account	$1,000	
Pay for expense	Checking Account		$500
Pay for expense	Office Supplies	$500	

- **Chart of Accounts.** In bookkeeping, an *account* is a place to store money, just like your checking account is a place to store your ready cash. The difference is that you need an account for each kind of income, expense, asset, and liability you have. The *chart of accounts* is simply a list of all the accounts you use to keep track of money in your company. (See Chapter 3 to learn about all the different types of accounts you might use.)

- **Cash vs. Accrual Accounting.** Cash and accrual are the two different approaches companies can take to document how much they make and spend. Cash accounting is the choice of many small companies because it's easy. You don't show income until you've received a payment, regardless of when that might happen. And you don't show expenses until you've paid your bills.

  The accrual method follows something known as the *matching principle*, which matches revenue with the corresponding expenses. This approach keeps income and expenses linked to the period in which they happened, no matter when cash comes in or goes out. The advantage of the accrual method is that it provides a better picture of profitability because income and its corresponding expenses appear in the same period. With accrual accounting, you recognize income as soon as you record an invoice, even if you'll receive payment during the next fiscal year. If you pay employees in January for work they did in December, those wages are part of the previous fiscal year.

- **Financial Reports.** You need three reports to evaluate the health of your company (described in detail in Chapter 17). The *income statement*, which QuickBooks calls a *Profit & Loss* report, shows how much income you've brought in and how much you've spent over a period of time. The QuickBooks report gets its name from the difference between the income and expenses, which results in your profit (or loss) for that period.

The *balance sheet* is a snapshot of how much you own and how much you owe. Assets are things you own that have value, such as buildings, equipment, and brand names. Liabilities consist of the money you owe to others (perhaps money you borrowed to buy one of your assets). The difference between assets and liabilities is the *equity* in the company—like the equity you have in your house when the house is worth more than you owe on the mortgage.

The *Statement of Cash Flows* tells you how much hard cash you have. You might think that the Profit & Loss report would tell you that, but noncash transactions, such as depreciation, prevent it from doing so. The statement of cash flows removes all noncash transactions and shows the money generated or spent operating the company, investing in the company, or financing.

About This Book

These days, QuickBooks Help gives more in the way of accounting background and troubleshooting tips, although useful examples are still in short supply. The problem is finding the topics you want. If the Relevant Topics feature (page 654) doesn't answer your question; and the Live Community, which lets you ask your peers and experts for answers (page 656), offers no assistance; and searching with keywords doesn't produce the answer you're looking for; then QuickBooks Help can't help you. Fact is, the Help system doesn't always tell you what you *really* need to know about using QuickBooks for accounting, like *when* and *why* to use a certain feature. QuickBooks Help doesn't let you mark your place, underline key points, jot notes in the margin, or read about QuickBooks sitting in the sun: this book does.

This book takes the place of the manual that should have accompanied Quick-Books 2010. It applies to the *Windows* version of QuickBooks Pro and Premier. (Because the Mac version of the program differs significantly, you won't find answers to QuickBooks for Mac here.)

In these pages, you'll find step-by-step instructions for using every QuickBooks Pro feature, including those you might not have quite understood, let alone mastered: progress invoicing (page 285), making general journal entries (page 421), customizing forms (page 616), writing off losses (page 394), and so on. If you're just starting out with QuickBooks, you can read the first few chapters as you set up your company file. After that, go ahead and jump from topic to topic depending on the bookkeeping task at hand. As mentioned earlier, you'll learn about some of the extra bells and whistles in the QuickBooks Premier edition as well. (All of the features in QuickBooks Pro—and in this book—are also in Premier.) To keep you productive, the book includes evaluations of features that help you figure out which ones are useful and when to use them.

Tip: Although each version of QuickBooks introduces new features and enhancements, you can still use this book if you're keeping your company books with earlier versions of QuickBooks. Of course, the older your version of the program, the more discrepancies you'll run across.

QuickBooks 2010: The Missing Manual is designed to accommodate readers at every technical level. The primary discussions are written for people with advanced-beginner or intermediate QuickBooks skills. But if you're using QuickBooks for the first time, special boxes with the title "Up To Speed" provide the introductory information you need to understand the topic at hand. On the other hand, people with advanced skills should watch for similar boxes called "Power Users' Clinic," which give more technical tips, tricks, and shortcuts for the experienced Quick-Books fan.

About the Outline

QuickBooks 2010: The Missing Manual is divided into five parts, each containing several chapters:

- **Part One: Getting Started**, covers everything you have to do to set up Quick-Books based on your organization's needs. These chapters explain how to create and manage a company file; create accounts, customers, jobs, invoice items, and other lists; and manage QuickBooks files.

- **Part Two: Bookkeeping**, follows the money from the moment you rack up time and expenses for your customers and add charges to a customer's invoice to the tasks you have to perform at the end of the year to satisfy the IRS and other interested parties. These chapters describe how to track time and expenses, pay for things you buy, bill customers, manage the money that your customers owe you, pay for expenses, run payroll, manage your bank accounts, and perform other bookkeeping tasks.

- **Part Three: Managing Your Business**, delves into the features that help you make your business a success—or even more successful than it was before. These chapters explain how to keep your inventory at just the right level, how to build budgets, and how to use QuickBooks reports to evaluate every aspect of your enterprise.

- **Part Four: QuickBooks Power**, helps you take your copy of QuickBooks to the next level. Save time and prevent errors by downloading transactions electronically. Boost your productivity by setting QuickBooks preferences to the way you like to work and integrating QuickBooks with other programs. Customize QuickBooks components to look the way you want. And, most important, set up QuickBooks so your financial data is secure.

- **Part Five: Appendixes**, provides a guide to installing and upgrading Quick-Books and a reference to help resources.

Note: You can find three bonus appendixes online at *www.missingmanuals.com/cds*: Keyboard Shortcuts, Tracking Time with the Standalone Timer, and Advanced Form Customization.

The Very Basics

To use this book (and indeed to use QuickBooks), you need to know a few basics. This book assumes that you're familiar with a few terms and concepts:

- **Clicking.** This book gives you instructions that require you to use your computer's mouse or trackpad. To *click* means to point the arrow pointer at something on the screen and then—without moving the pointer at all—press and release the left button on the mouse (or laptop trackpad). To *right-click* means the same thing, but pressing the *right* mouse button instead. Usually, clicking with the left button selects an onscreen element or presses a button onscreen. A right-click usually reveals a *shortcut menu*, which lists some common tasks specific to whatever you're right-clicking. To *double-click*, of course, means to click twice in rapid succession, again without moving the pointer at all. And to *drag* means to move the pointer while holding down the (left) button the entire time. To *right-drag* means to do the same thing but holding down the right mouse button.

  When you're told to *Shift-click* something, you click while pressing the Shift key. Related procedures, like *Ctrl-clicking*, work the same way—just click while pressing the corresponding key.

- **Menus.** The *menus* are the words at the top of your screen: File, Edit, and so on. Click one to make a list of commands appear, as though they're written on a window shade you've just pulled down. Some people click to open a menu and then release the mouse button; after reading the menu command choices, they click the command they want. Other people like to press the mouse button continuously as they click the menu title and drag down the list to the desired command; only then do they release the mouse button. Either method works, so choose the one you prefer.

- **Keyboard shortcuts.** Nothing is faster than keeping your fingers on your keyboard, entering data, choosing names, triggering commands—without losing time by grabbing the mouse, carefully positioning it, and then choosing a command or list entry. That's why many experienced QuickBooks fans prefer to trigger commands by pressing combinations of keys on the keyboard. For example, in most word processors, you can press Ctrl+B to produce a boldface word. When you read an instruction like "Press Ctrl+A to open the Chart of Accounts window," start by pressing the Ctrl key; while it's down, type the letter A, and then release both keys.

About → These → Arrows

Throughout this book, and throughout the Missing Manual series, you'll find sentences like this one: Choose Lists → Customer & Vendor Profile Lists → Customer Type List. That's shorthand for a much longer instruction that directs you to navigate three nested menus in sequence, like this: Choose Lists. On the Lists menu, point to the Customer & Vendor Profile Lists menu entry. On the submenu that appears, choose Customer Type List. Figure I-1 shows the menus this sequence opens.

Similarly, this arrow shorthand also simplifies the instructions for opening nested folders, such as Program Files → QuickBooks → Export Files.

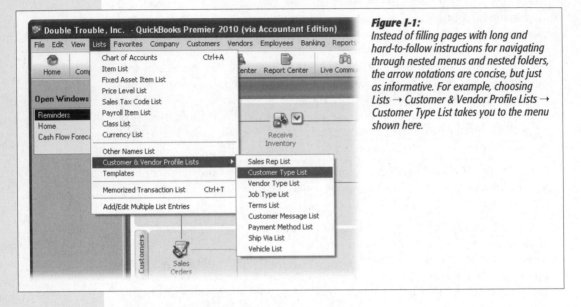

Figure I-1:
Instead of filling pages with long and hard-to-follow instructions for navigating through nested menus and nested folders, the arrow notations are concise, but just as informative. For example, choosing Lists → Customer & Vendor Profile Lists → Customer Type List takes you to the menu shown here.

About MissingManuals.com

At *www.missingmanuals.com*, you'll find articles, tips, and updates to *QuickBooks 2010: The Missing Manual*. In fact, we invite and encourage you to submit such corrections and updates yourself. In an effort to keep the book as up to date and accurate as possible, each time we print more copies of this book, we'll make any confirmed corrections you've suggested. We'll also note such changes on the website, so that you can mark important corrections into your own copy of the book, if you like. (Go to *www.missingmanuals.com/feedback*, choose the book's name from the pop-up menu, and then click Go to see the changes.)

Also on our Feedback page, you can get expert answers to questions that come to you while reading this book, write a book review, and find groups for folks who share your interest in QuickBooks.

We'd love to hear your suggestions for new books in the Missing Manual line. There's a place for that on missingmanuals.com, too. And while you're online, you can also register this book at *www.oreilly.com* (you can jump directly to the registration page by going here: *http://tinyurl.com/yo82k3*). Registering means we can send you updates about this book, and you'll be eligible for special offers like discounts on future editions of *QuickBooks 2010: The Missing Manual*.

Safari® Books Online

Safari® Books Online is an on-demand digital library that lets you easily search over 7,500 technology and creative reference books and videos to find the answers you need quickly.

With a subscription, you can read any page and watch any video from our library online. Read books on your cell phone and mobile devices. Access new titles before they are available for print, and get exclusive access to manuscripts in development and post feedback for the authors. Copy and paste code samples, organize your favorites, download chapters, bookmark key sections, create notes, print out pages, and benefit from tons of other time-saving features.

O'Reilly Media has uploaded this book to the Safari® Books Online service. To have full digital access to this book and others on similar topics from O'Reilly and other publishers, sign up for free at *http://my.safaribooksonline.com*.

CHAPTER 1

Creating a Company File

A *company file* is where you store your company's records in QuickBooks, and it's the first thing you need to work on in the program. You can create a company file from scratch or convert records previously kept in a small business accounting program or Quicken. The easiest approach is to use a file that *someone else* created. If you've worked with an accountant to set up your company, she might provide you with a QuickBooks company file configured precisely for your business so you can hit the ground running.

If you have to create your own company file, this chapter tells you how to use the QuickBooks EasyStep Interview to get started, and points you to the other chapters that explain how to finish the job. If you already have a company file, you'll learn how to open it, update it to a new version of QuickBooks, and modify basic company information.

Opening QuickBooks

Here are the easiest ways to open QuickBooks:

- **Desktop icon.** If you told QuickBooks to create a desktop shortcut during installation (page 648), double-click the shortcut to launch QuickBooks.

- **Quick Launch toolbar.** The fastest way to open QuickBooks is to click its icon on the toolbar (Figure 1-1).

If you have a QuickBooks desktop shortcut, right-drag (that's dragging while holding down the right mouse button) the desktop shortcut onto the Quick Launch toolbar and then choose Copy Here to create a second shortcut on the toolbar. (If you're trying to clean up your desktop, choose Move Here instead.) You can also use the right-drag technique to copy or move a shortcut in Windows Explorer or from the Start menu.

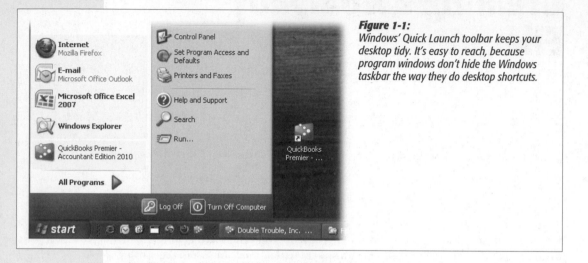

Figure 1-1:
Windows' Quick Launch toolbar keeps your desktop tidy. It's easy to reach, because program windows don't hide the Windows taskbar the way they do desktop shortcuts.

Note: If you don't see the Quick Launch toolbar, in the Windows taskbar, right-click an empty area and then choose Toolbars → Quick Launch. When a checkmark appears to the left of the Quick Launch menu entry, the toolbar should appear in the Windows taskbar.

- **Programs menu.** Without a desktop icon, you can launch QuickBooks from the Start menu. Click Start → QuickBooks Pro 2010 (or QuickBooks Premier Edition 2010). If QuickBooks isn't already listed on the menu, choose All Programs → QuickBooks → QuickBooks Pro 2010 (or QuickBooks Premier Edition 2010).

The first time you launch QuickBooks, you're greeted by the "Welcome to Quick-Books" window. You have to create or open a company file, and then you're ready to dive into bookkeeping. Later, if you close a company file, the No Company Open window appears (Figure 1-2). The rest of this chapter tells you how to create or open company files, no matter which window is open.

About the EasyStep Interview

Keeping books requires accuracy, attention to detail, and persistence, hence the customary image of spectacled accountants hunched over ledgers. QuickBooks can help you keep your books without ruining your vision or your posture—as long as you start your QuickBooks company file with good information.

UP TO SPEED

The Fastest Way to a New Company File

The proud owners of brand-new businesses face a dilemma: They have more important things to do than muddle around setting up a company file in QuickBooks, but money is usually as short as free time. If you don't know much about bookkeeping or accounting, the price of a few hours of your accountant's time is a valuable investment. You'll not only save untold hours of tedium and confusion, but you'll also feel confident that your books are set up properly. Accountants well-versed in QuickBooks can create a flawless company file without breaking a sweat.

If you plan to do without an accountant but you want some help setting up your company file, once you get past the Welcome to QuickBooks screen, you can choose Help → Find A Local Expert. By answering a few questions on the QuickBooks Find-a-ProAdvisor website (*www.proadvisor. intuit.com/referral*), you can locate someone in your area to help you get started.

The EasyStep Interview tries to make creating a company file as painless as possible, but the process isn't pain *free*. The EasyStep Interview is kind of like a family reunion, where you're asked lots of questions you don't want to answer. But unlike the reunion, you can skip parts of the Interview, leave it at any time (once QuickBooks creates the company file), or return to it when you're better prepared for the interrogation.

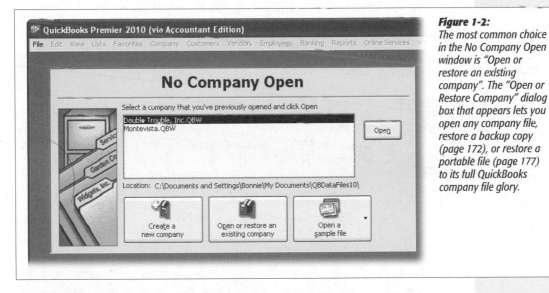

Figure 1-2:
The most common choice in the No Company Open window is "Open or restore an existing company". The "Open or Restore Company" dialog box that appears lets you open any company file, restore a backup copy (page 172), or restore a portable file (page 177) to its full QuickBooks company file glory.

In QuickBooks 2010, the Interview is relatively short and sweet; it takes about 30 minutes. All it wants to know is some company information, the industry you're in, and the features you want to use. The Interview sets your preferences and creates a few accounts (like basic income and expense accounts and your checking account), but you have to do the bulk of the setup work later.

Experimenting with a Sample File

You don't have to use your real company file as a guinea pig for QuickBooks features you've never used. QuickBooks comes with several sample files: one for a basic product-based business, another for a basic service-based business, and several more for more specialized pursuits like contracting, consulting, manufacturing, law firms, and so on.

To experiment with QuickBooks features before you put them in production, in either the "Welcome to QuickBooks" window or the No Company Open window, click "Open a sample file", and then choose the sample file you want. (If your company file is open, choose File → Close to display the No Company Open window.) If you botch your experiment, you can always reinstall the sample files from the QuickBooks CD.

Don't try to use these sample files as your company file. They come with accounts, customers, vendors, and transactions (such as checks, invoices, and purchase orders). Besides, QuickBooks sets the date in these files to 12/15/2012, which makes transactions later than you or your vendors would like.

Before You Create Your Company File

If you've just started a business and want to inaugurate your books with Quick-Books, your prep work will be a snap. On the other hand, if you have existing books for your business, you have a few small tasks to complete before you jump into QuickBooks' setup. Whether your books are paper ledgers or electronic files in another program, gather your company information *before* you open Quick-Books. That way, you can hunker down in front of your computer and crank out a company file in record time. Here's a guide to what you need to create your company file in QuickBooks.

Start Date

To keep your entire financial history at your fingertips, you need every transaction and speck of financial information in your QuickBooks company file. But you have better things to do than enter years' worth of checks, invoices, and deposits, so the comprehensive approach is practical only if you just recently started your company.

The more realistic approach is to enter your financial state as of a specific date and from then on, add all new transactions in QuickBooks. The date you choose is called the *start date*, and you shouldn't choose it randomly. Here are your start date options and the ramifications of each:

- **The last day of the previous fiscal year.** If you're setting up QuickBooks during the first half of the year, bite the bullet and fill in your records for the entire year. Choose the last day of your company's previous fiscal year as the Quick-Books start date. That way, the account balances on your start date are like the ending balances on a bank statement, and you're ready to start bookkeeping fresh on the first day of the fiscal year.

Yes, you have to enter checks, credit card charges, invoices, and other transactions that happened since the beginning of the year, but that won't take as much time as you think. You'll regain those hours when tax time rolls around, as you nimbly generate the reports you need to complete your tax returns. During the second half of the year, the best approach is to be patient and postpone your QuickBooks setup until the next fiscal year. Intuit releases new versions of QuickBooks in October or November for just that reason.

Tip: For practice, you can set the start date for your company file to the starting date from the bank statement closest to your company start date. Then you can enter transactions for the month and practice reconciling your bank account to those transactions.

- **The first day of a fiscal period.** The next best start date is the first day of a fiscal quarter (or fiscal month at the very least).

Waiting until next year isn't always an option, particularly if your old accounting system vendor wants a truckload of cash for an upgrade. Starting in the middle of a fiscal year makes the entire year's accounting more difficult. Even if you fill in year-to-date values for all your accounts, since your company file doesn't contain a full year's worth of detail, you'll have to switch between QuickBooks and your old filing cabinets to prepare your tax returns and look up financial information. Starting at the beginning of a fiscal period mitigates this hassle but doesn't eliminate it.

Account Balances

Unless you begin using QuickBooks when you start your business, you need to know your account balances as of the start date to get things rolling. For example, if your checking account has $342 at the end of the year, that value goes into QuickBooks during setup. Here are the balances you need to know and where you can find them in your records:

- **Cash balances.** For each bank account you use in your business (checking, savings, money market, petty cash, and so on), find the bank statements with statement dates as close to—but *earlier* than—the start date for your QuickBooks file.

Gather deposit slips and your checkbook register to identify the transactions that haven't yet cleared in your bank accounts. You'll need them to enter transactions, as described in the upcoming chapters. If you have petty cash lying around, count it and use that number to set up your petty cash account.

- **Customer balances.** If customers owe you money, pull the paper copy of every *unpaid* invoice or statement out of your filing cabinet so you can give QuickBooks what it needs to calculate your Accounts Receivable balance. If you didn't keep copies, you'll have to figure out how much you sold in services and products, the discounts you applied, what you charged for shipping and other charges, and the amount of sales tax. As a last resort, you can ask your customers for copies of the invoices they haven't paid or create invoices in QuickBooks to match the payments you receive.

- **Vendor balances.** If your company thinks handing out cash early is more painful than data entry, find the bills you haven't paid and get ready to enter them in QuickBooks. If you'd rather reduce the transactions you have to enter, simply pay those outstanding bills and record the payments in QuickBooks.

- **Asset values.** When you own assets such as buildings or equipment, the value of those assets depreciates over time. If you've filed a tax return for your company, you can find asset values and accumulated depreciation on your most recent tax return (yet another reason to start using QuickBooks at the beginning of the year). If you haven't filed a tax return for your company, the asset value is typically the price you paid for the asset, and you won't have any depreciation until you file that first return.

- **Liability balances.** Unpaid vendor bills that you enter in QuickBooks generate the balance for your Accounts Payable liability account. However, you have to find the current balances you owe on any loans or mortgages.

- **Inventory.** For each product you stock, you need to know how many items you had in stock as of the start date, how much you paid for them, and what you expect to sell them for.

Note: The basic QuickBooks editions like QuickBooks Pro or QuickBooks Premier aren't very good at working with inventory that you assemble from components or raw materials. See page 115 to learn how to track inventory you assemble.

- **Payroll.** Payroll services are a great value for the money, which you'll grow to appreciate as you collect the information you need for payroll (including salary and wages, tax deductions, benefits, pensions, 401(k) deductions, and other stray payroll deductions you might have). You also need to know who receives withholdings, such as tax agencies or the company handling your 401(k) plan. Oh yeah—and you need payroll details for each employee. Chapter 14 explains the ins and outs of payroll in QuickBooks.

Tip: If you have outstanding payroll withholdings such as employee payroll taxes, send in the payments so you don't have to enter those open transactions in QuickBooks.

Other Important Information

If you're starting at the beginning of the fiscal year, you need every transaction that's happened since the beginning of the year—sales you've made, expenses you've incurred, payroll and tax transactions, and so on—to reestablish your asset, liability, equity, income, and expense accounts. So dig that information out of your existing accounting system (or shoebox). Federal tax returns and payroll tax returns (federal and state) include all sorts of information that QuickBooks setup wants to know, like your federal tax ID number. And the balance sheet that goes with the return is a great starting point for your account balances.

Starting the EasyStep Interview

You can create a brand-new company file by clicking "Create a new company" from either the Welcome to QuickBooks window or the No Company Open window. What Intuit considers an "easy" interview seems to change with every new version of QuickBooks. Although the EasyStep Interview wizard doesn't provide hints about which step comes next, the interview covers the basics of creating and customizing a company file to fit your business. After you start the Interview, click Next or Back to move from screen to screen.

The Get Started screen assures you that you'll be ready to start using QuickBooks in about 30 minutes. Start by choosing one of the following three buttons:

- **Convert Data.** If you have existing records in Quicken or another accounting program, you're in luck. Converting your books (page 33) is easier than starting from scratch.

- **Skip Interview.** If you're something of a QuickBooks expert, this option lets you set up a company file without a safety net. It opens the "Enter your company information" window, followed by a few screens of data entry. If you need help during the process, you can always click the "Get answers" link. (Choose Help → Learning Center Tutorials for some fast training on accounting with QuickBooks.)

- **Start Interview.** If you don't fit into either of the previous categories, this one's for you. The following sections take you through the process step by step, from start to finish. If you leave the interview before QuickBooks creates the company file, QuickBooks won't save any of the information you entered. So make sure you have at least 10 minutes to complete the first set of steps.

Company Information

The first setup screen asks you for the basic 411 about your company, such as legal name and tax ID, as you can see in Figure 1-3. If any of the fields are confusing, try clicking "Get answers" in the upper-right corner. Click Next when you're done.

After you complete the basics, the EasyStep Interview walks you through several screens of questions. Here's what the EasyStep Interview wants to know before it creates your company file:

- **Your industry.** Choose carefully on the "Select your industry" screen. The list of industries is robust, so chances are good you'll find one that's close to what your company does. Based on your choice, QuickBooks adjusts its settings and the chart of accounts it creates to match how your business operates. For example, the program creates income and expense accounts for your type of business or turns on features like sales tax and inventory if your industry typically uses them. If QuickBooks makes assumptions you don't like, you can change preferences (page 547) and accounts (page 58) later.

  If you don't see an obvious choice in the Industry list, scroll to the bottom and choose either General Product-based Business or General Service-based Business.

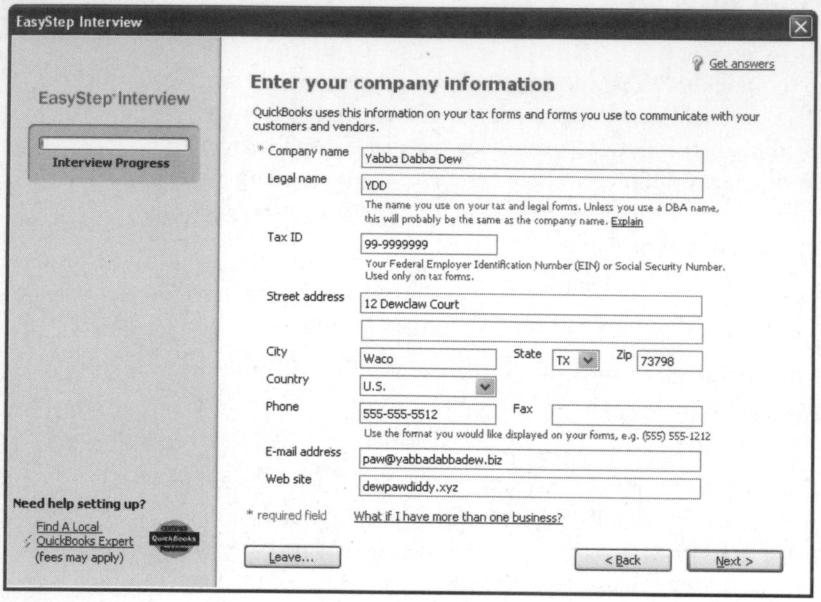

Figure 1-3:
In the "Company name" field, type the name you want to appear on invoices, reports, and other forms. In the "Legal name" field, type the company name as it should appear on contracts and other legal documents. The company name and the legal name are usually the same unless you use a DBA (doing business as) company name. If you own a corporation, the legal name is what appears on your Certificate of Incorporation. The Tax ID box is for the federal tax ID number you use when you file your taxes—your Social Security Number or Federal Employer Identification Number.

- **The type of company.** The tax form you use depends on the type of business entity you choose. The "How is your company organized?" screen lists the most common types from sole proprietorships and partnerships, to corporations and nonprofits. When you select an option for the type of company, QuickBooks assigns the corresponding tax form to your company file. To see the tax form, choose Company → Company Information (to see what it looks like, peek ahead to Figure 1-6). The Income Tax Form Used box at the bottom of the Company Information window shows the tax form for your company type.

- **The first month of your fiscal year.** When you start your company, you choose a fiscal year. QuickBooks automatically sets the "My fiscal year starts in" box to January, because so many small businesses stick with the calendar year for simplicity. If you start your fiscal year in another month, choose it in the drop-down menu.

- **The Administrator password.** The administrator can do absolutely anything in your company file: set up other users, log in as other users, and access any area of the company files. Surprisingly, the administrator password is optional. QuickBooks lets you click Next and skip right over it, but this is no time for shortcuts, as the box on page 23 explains. Type the password you want to use in both the "Administrator password" and "Retype password" boxes. Keep the login name and password in a safe but memorable place.

TROUBLESHOOTING MOMENT

Safe Login Practices

Don't even think about having everyone who works with a company file share one login. You don't want everyone to have access to payroll data, and you wouldn't know which person to fire if you found any less-than-legal transactions in the company file. Even if you run a small business from home, an administrator password prevents the chimney sweep from swiping your business credit card number. Chapter 26 has much more about keeping your Quick-Books files secure, but here are some password basics:

• Set a password that's at least eight characters long and has a combination of letters and numbers.

• Pay attention when you set the administrator password. If you forget the administrator login and password

or lose the paper they're written on, you won't be able to open your company file without some fancy footwork (page 631). Passwords are case-sensitive, so make sure that Caps Lock isn't turned on by mistake.

• *Type* the administrator's password in both the "Administrator password" and "Retype password" boxes. If you copy and paste the password from the "Administrator password" box into the "Retype password" box, you could copy a typo and not be able to access the company file you just created.

If you've tried everything and your administrator password is still missing in action, see page 633 for how you can reset it.

Creating Your Company File

After you set the administrator password and click Next, the "Create your company file" screen appears. If you're new to QuickBooks, click the "Where should I save my company file?" link, which opens a QuickBooks Help window that explains the pros and cons of storing files in different places. QuickBooks veterans can click Next to specify the filename and location.

QuickBooks opens the "Filename for New Company" dialog box, which is really just a Save File dialog box. Navigate to the folder where you want to store your company file (page 650 explains why you should). Initially, the program sets the "File name" box to the company name you entered and the "Save as type" box to "QuickBooks Files (*.QBW,*.QBA)". But you're free to change the file name. Here are some guidelines:

• QuickBooks fills in the "File name" field with the company name that you entered earlier in the Interview. Keep this name or type one that's shorter or that better identifies the company's records within.

• Consider storing your company file in a folder with the rest of your company data so that it gets backed up along with everything else. For example, you could create a Company Files folder in My Documents—if you're the only person who uses QuickBooks. See page 650 for some background on choosing a location for your company files.

When you click Save in the "Filename for New Company" dialog box, Quick-Books may take a minute or so to create the new file. In the meantime, a message box with a progress bar appears. Go grab a coffee, because when the company file is ready, the EasyStep Interview displays the "Customizing QuickBooks for your business" screen. Click Next to dig in.

Note: At this point, the progress bar in the left margin of the EasyStep Interview window is depressingly short because you still have to do the bulk of company file setup. If you need a break before continuing, click Leave. The EasyStep Interview continues where you left off the next time you open that company file.

Customizing Your Company File

The next several screens in the EasyStep Interview ask questions about your business to help QuickBooks decide which features to turn on, what to include on your QuickBooks Home page, and so on. The wizard displays "(recommended for your business)" next to the options that are typical for a company in your industry, as you can see in Figure 1-4.

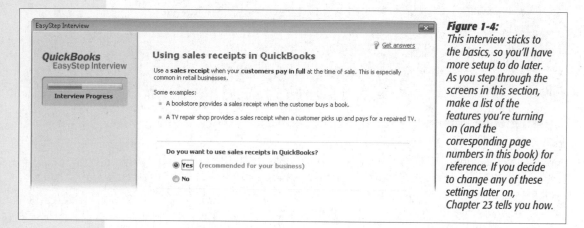

Figure 1-4:
This interview sticks to the basics, so you'll have more setup to do later. As you step through the screens in this section, make a list of the features you're turning on (and the corresponding page numbers in this book) for reference. If you decide to change any of these settings later on, Chapter 23 tells you how.

Here are some guidelines for answering the questions on the screens that follow:

- The **What do you sell?** screen is where you tell QuickBooks whether you sell services, products, or both. When you choose one of these options, Quick-Books knows which types of income accounts you need. If you select "Products only" or "Both services and products", the Interview asks about whether you track inventory later.

- The **Do you sell products online?** screen appears if your business sells things. Whether you want to sell online or not, you can bypass Intuit's marketing pitch for their add-on sales services by selecting the "I don't sell online and I am not interested in doing so" option.

- The **Do you charge sales tax?** screen has only Yes or No options. If you're one of the unfortunate souls who has to navigate the rocky shoals of sales tax, select Yes. If you don't charge sales tax, select No and breathe a sigh of relief. For detailed instructions on dealing with sales tax in QuickBooks, see page 124.

- On the **Do you want to create estimates in QuickBooks?** screen, select Yes or No to turn the estimate feature on or off. If you prepare quotes, bids, or estimates for your customers and want to do so in QuickBooks (page 280), select Yes.

Note: If you use QuickBooks Premier, the "Tracking customer orders in QuickBooks" screen asks whether you want to use sales orders to track backorders (page 276) or other orders that you plan to fill at a later date.

- The **Using sales receipts in QuickBooks** screen is targeted to retailers who provide sales receipts when customers purchase or pick up products and pay in full. Simply select Yes if you want to create sales receipts in QuickBooks (see page 349).

- **Using statements in QuickBooks** is where you tell the program whether you generate statements to send to your customers (page 299). For example, your wine-of-the-month club might send monthly statements to your members. Or, a consultant could send invoices for work performed and then send a statement that summarizes the fees, payments, and outstanding balance.

- The **Using progress invoicing** screen asks whether you invoice customers based on the percentage you've completed on a job. To learn why (and how) you might use this feature, see page 285.

- **Managing bills you owe** asks whether you plan to write checks to pay bills immediately (select No) or enter bills in QuickBooks and then pay them later (select Yes). You can read about bill preferences on page 553 and payment preferences on page 571.

Note: It's more work to enter bills in QuickBooks than just writing checks, but there's a benefit if you do: QuickBooks can remind you when bills are due or qualify for timely payment discounts, and it can keep track of the total you owe.

- The **Do you print checks?** screen asks whether or not you print checks. If you want a sales pitch about the benefits of printing checks, select the "I don't currently print checks, but I would like to" option.

- **Tracking inventory in QuickBooks** is the screen where you tell QuickBooks whether you keep track of the products you have in stock. This screen provides a few examples of when to track or bypass inventory, but page 101 includes more guidelines for whether tracking inventory makes sense for your business.

- The **Do you accept credit cards?** screen lets you tell QuickBooks whether you take credit cards for payment (and whether you want to get a sales pitch about Intuit's card).

- If you bill by the hour, **Tracking time in QuickBooks** is ideal. Select Yes to track the hours people work and create invoices for their time. Read Chapter 8 to learn how to set time tracking up properly.

- **Do you have employees?** is where you specify whether you want to use QuickBooks' payroll and 1099 features (select Yes). If you use non-Intuit services to run payroll or generate contractors' 1099s, select No.

- The **Tracking multiple currencies in QuickBooks?** screen lets you tell Quick-Books whether you buy or sell in more than one country (and currency). You can't turn off multiple currencies once you've turned them on, so select No unless you're sure you need multiple currencies. You can turn this preference on later (page 570).

When you click Next on the "Tracking multiple currencies in QuickBooks?" screen, you see the "Using accounts in QuickBooks" screen and the progress bar indicating that you're about three-quarters of the way through the Interview. With a few more steps, you'll have your start date and most of the accounts you want to use. Here are the last things you set up during the Interview:

- The **Select a date to start tracking your finances** screen gives you a summary of what you learned about start dates on page 18. To start at the beginning of this fiscal year (which QuickBooks can figure out using the current calendar year and the starting month you selected), select the "Beginning of this fiscal year: 01/01/10" option. (The year that you see depends on the current calendar year.) If you've already decided which start date to use, select the "Use today's date or the first day of the quarter or month" option, and then type or choose that date in the box.

- The **Add your bank account** screen asks if you'd like to add an existing bank account. Select Yes if you'd like QuickBooks to walk you through setting up the bank account. If you're comfortable setting up the account on your own (page 51), select "No, I'll add a bank account later."

  If you select Yes, the next screen asks for the bank account name, bank account number, bank routing number, and when you opened the account. Click Next again. If the opening date for the bank account is before the start date for your company file, another screen asks for the statement ending date and ending balance prior to your company file's start date. If you opened the bank account after your company file starting date, QuickBooks creates the account with a zero opening balance. After you create that account, you can add additional bank accounts, or select No to add the rest after you finish the Interview.

- The **Review income and expense accounts** screen lists the accounts typically used by companies in your industry, as shown in Figure 1-5.

When you click Next, you'll see a bright orange, but premature, "Congratulations!" You still have a few more steps before you can open your company file, as the next section explains.

Beginning to Use QuickBooks

When your company file first opens, you'll see the QuickBooks Home page (page 35) with the QuickBooks Coach pane front and center. If you click Start Working, you can get down to bookkeeping and dock the QuickBooks Coach pane at the upper right of the QuickBooks main window. You may also see the QuickBooks Learning Center window with links to tutorials and Help topics about new features (page 658). At this point, you have four choices:

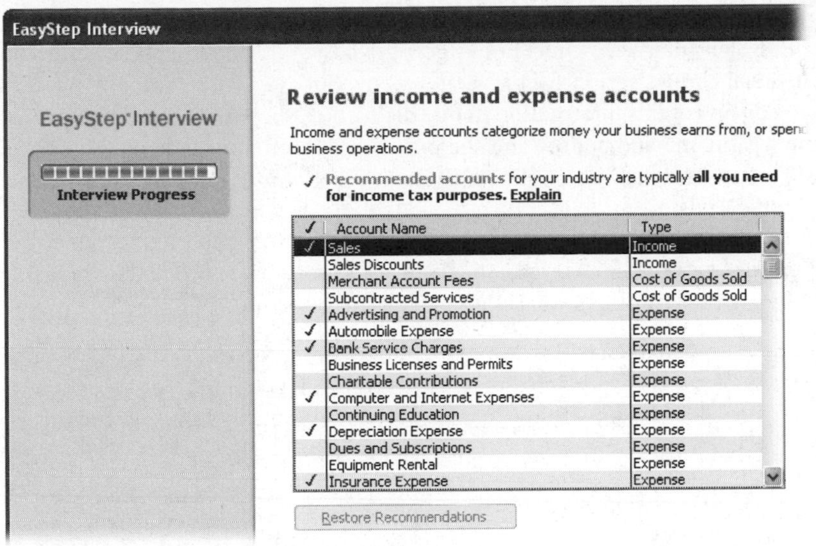

Figure 1-5:
QuickBooks places a checkmark in front of the accounts that are typical for your industry. Click the checkmark cell for an account to add one that the program didn't select, or click a cell with a checkmark to turn that account off. You can also drag the pointer over checkmark cells to turn several accounts on or off.

- **Watch a tutorial.** Click "View the Tutorial" to have the coach walk you through QuickBooks.

- **Setup and Training.** Click this button if you want to pay Intuit to help you get set up. A browser window opens to the Intuit QuickBooks Set-up & Training Services web page (*http://quickbooks.intuit.com/product/training/setup-training-services.jsp*). A quick ramp-up costs $99, while setup and training goes for $249.

Note: To ask a question in the QuickBooks Live Community, choose Help → Live Community. The "Have a Question?" window opens with a box where you type your question. Page 656 explains how to use this feature.

- **Get coaching as you work.** When you create a new company, QuickBooks automatically turns on the coach. With the coach running, you see coach icons (blue circles with an "i" inside); click them to find out about any part of the QuickBooks workflow. See page 41 for the full scoop on the QuickBooks Coach.

- **Use QuickBooks without any assistance.** To start working with QuickBooks without a coach or tutorial, click the icon for the bookkeeping task you want to perform. Initially, QuickBooks displays coach icons in the Home page. To hide the Coach Tips, in the QuickBooks Coach pane, click the Hide Coach Tips button (it's below the "View the Tutorial" and "Setup and Training" buttons).

Tip: See page 559 to learn how to turn the coach off completely.

Modifying Company Information

In the EasyStep Interview, QuickBooks gets the basic information about your company in small chunks spread over several screens. But after your company file exists, you can edit any of this information in one dialog box, shown in Figure 1-6. Remember, the legal name and address are the ones you use on your federal and state tax forms. To open this dialog box, choose Company → Company Information.

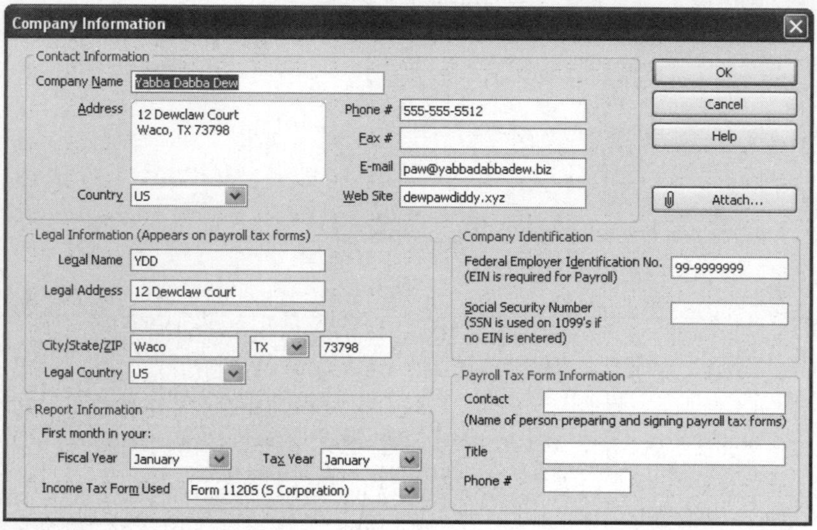

Figure 1-6:
Some company information changes more often than others. For instance, you might relocate your office or change your phone number, email, or website. But information like your legal name and address, Federal Employer Identification Number, and business type (corporation, sole proprietor, and so on) usually stay the same.

What's Next?

The EasyStep Interview doesn't tell you what to do next. The Interview completes quite a bit of setup for you, but you may need guidance for the rest. Look no further than the book in your hands. Here are the ways you can flesh out your company file:

- **Set up your users and passwords.** See "Assigning the Administrator User Name and Password" on page 630.

- **Review and/or change the preferences that QuickBooks set.** See "An Introduction to Preferences" on page 548.

- **Set up or edit the accounts in your Chart of Accounts.** If you didn't set up all your accounts in the EasyStep Interview, you can create them now. See "Creating Accounts and Subaccounts" on page 51.

- **Create a journal entry to specify account opening balances.** See "Creating General Journal Entries" on page 421.

- **Create items for the products and services you sell.** See "What Items Do" on page 99.

- **Set up sales tax codes.** See "Setting Up Sales Tax" on page 124.

- **Set up your 1099 tracking.** See "Tax: 1099" on page 583.

- **Sign up for Intuit Payroll Service if you want help with payroll.** See "Choosing a Payroll Service" on page 361.

- **Enter your historical transactions.** For invoices, see "Creating an Invoice" on page 255; for bills, see "Entering Bills" on page 206; for payroll, see Chapter 14.

- **Create a backup copy.** See "Backing Up Files" on page 163.

- **Customize your forms.** See "Customizing Forms" on page 616.

Tip: QuickBooks has several videos that show you how to perform basic bookkeeping tasks. To watch, choose Help → Learning Center Tutorials.

UP TO SPEED

Setting Up an Intuit Account

If you want to use some of QuickBooks' online services, you have to set up a special Intuit account. (The account is free; some of the services aren't.) This Intuit account gives you access to Live Community, where you can get answers to your questions from experts or your peers (page 656). With an Intuit account, you can also create a website for your company hosted on Intuit Websites. (Your company's URL is *http://<your company name>.intuitwebsites.com*.) The Intuit Website Services site gives advice about online marketing and has an option for setting up email for your company. Your Intuit account also gets you to the documents you store in QuickBooks using document management (page 307).

When you first try to use a feature that requires an Intuit account (Live Community or Document Management, for example), a browser window opens and you'll see a page that asks you to create an account or sign in with your existing Intuit account. Here are the steps for setting up your Intuit account:

1. Click Create Account.

2. On the "Get started with your Intuit Account" screen, enter your email address, the password you want to use, your name, and a security question that gives you a second way into your account if you forget your password.

3. Turn on the "I have read and agree to the Terms and Conditions" checkbox and then click Create Account. You'll know that the creation of your Intuit account succeeded when the browser window proceeds to the service you want to use (Live Community, for example).

4. If you've already created an account using the email address you typed, you'll see a warning that a user with the same email address exists. That usually means that you already created an account. In that case, click Sign In. In the Sign-in dialog box that appears, click the Forgot User ID or Forgot Password link to receive an email with the information you forgot.

Opening an Existing Company File

After you've opened a company file in one session, QuickBooks kicks off your next session by opening the same company file. If you keep the books for only one company, you might never have to manually open a QuickBooks company file again.

For irrepressible entrepreneurs or bookkeepers who work on several companies' books, you don't have to close one company file before you open another. You can open another company file in QuickBooks any time you want. The following sections describe the different ways to do so.

Opening a Recently Opened Company File

If you work on more than one file, you may frequently switch between them. The easiest way to open a recent file is to choose File → Open Previous Company, and then choose the file you want to open on the submenu, as shown in Figure 1-7. If the Open Previous Company menu doesn't list the company file you want to open, follow the steps in the next section instead.

Click to open company file   Double-click to open company file

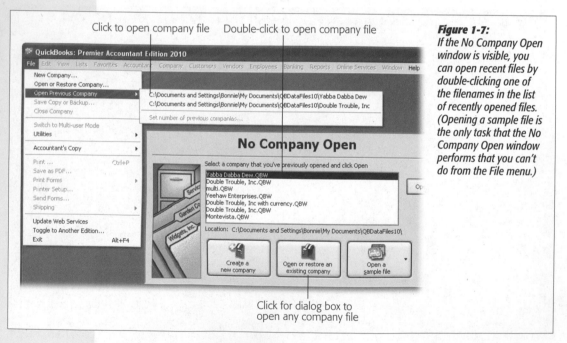

Figure 1-7:
If the No Company Open window is visible, you can open recent files by double-clicking one of the filenames in the list of recently opened files. (Opening a sample file is the only task that the No Company Open window performs that you can't do from the File menu.)

Click for dialog box to open any company file

Opening Any Company File

Sometimes, a company file you want to open falls off the recent file list. Say your bookkeeping business is booming and you work on dozens of company files every month. (You can tell QuickBooks how many companies to list on the Open Previous Company submenu, as the box on the next page explains.) Or maybe you want to upgrade a file from a previous version (see the box on page 32). Here are the steps to open any company file, no matter how long it's been:

1. **Choose File → "Open or Restore Company".**

   If you're in the No Company Open window, you can click "Open or restore an existing company".

2. **In the "Open or Restore Company" dialog box, select the "Open a company file" option and click Next.**

   The "Open a Company" dialog box opens.

3. **Navigate to the folder with the company file you want and double-click the filename.**

   You can also click the filename and then click Open.

4. **If the QuickBooks Login window appears (which it will if you've assigned a password to the Admin account or set up multiple users), type your user name and password, and then click OK.**

   The company file opens and you're ready to keep the books.

ORGANIZATION STATION

Fast Access to Several Companies

If you work on several sets of company books at the same time, choosing File → Open Previous Company is the quickest way to hop between company files. Out of the box, Quick-Books shows up to 20 companies on the Open Previous Company submenu. If you work with fewer companies, the submenu may have company files that you'd rather forget.

You can change the number of companies QuickBooks shows on the submenu to match the number of companies you work on. With a clever workaround, you can also clear out old entries that you don't want to see.

Here's how to change the number of companies on the Open Previous Company submenu:

1. Choose File → Open Previous Company → "Set number of previous companies". (A company file has to be open for this command to be active.)

2. In the "Set Number of Previous Companies" dialog box, type the maximum number of companies you want to see on the menu, and then click OK. Quick-Books can show up to 20, which it lists starting with the most recent.

To clear old entries off the menu, reset the number of entries to *1*. Then, QuickBooks lists only the most recent company file, clearing all the others off the list. If you want to see more than one company, reset the number of entries a second time, this time to a higher number.

Restoring a Backup File

Backup files are the answer to the adrenaline rush you get when you do something dumb with your company file, your hard drive crashes, or a plume of smoke wafts up from your computer. To restore a backup file, choose File → "Open or Restore Company". In the "Open or Restore Company" dialog box, select the "Restore a backup copy" option and click Next. To learn how to create backup files in the first place, as well as the details on restoring them, see page 172.

FREQUENTLY ASKED QUESTION

Upgrading a Quickbooks File

How do I upgrade a company file to the newest version of QuickBooks?

If you've used a previous version of QuickBooks, your company file is set up to work with that version of the program. When you upgrade to QuickBooks 2010, the program has to make some changes to the format of your company file. Fortunately, updating a company file is easy. All you have to do to update a company file is open it in the new version of QuickBooks. Here are the steps:

1. Choose File → "Open or Restore Company".

2. In the "Open or Restore Company" dialog box, select the "Open a company file" option, and then click Next.

3. In the "Open a Company" dialog box, double-click the company file.

4. In the "Update Company File for New Version" dialog box, turn on the verbose "I understand that my company file will be updated to this new version of QuickBooks" checkbox, and then click Update Now.

5. Click OK to create a backup before the upgrade. Follow the steps to create a backup copy of your company file. The program warns you that backup copies created by QuickBooks 2010 won't work with earlier versions of the program. To convert a QuickBooks 2010 backup file to any earlier version, choose File → Utilities → Restore Backup For Earlier QuickBooks Versions.

6. When the Update Company message box appears, click Yes to start the upgrade. Keep in mind that updating could take a while if your company file is large or you're updating from several QuickBooks versions back.

When the update is complete, the QuickBooks Learning Center (page 658) opens in case you want to learn more about what's new in QuickBooks 2010.

Once you upgrade the company file, your coworkers won't be able to open it until you upgrade the QuickBooks program on their computers. To prevent work disruption, plan to upgrade all copies of QuickBooks and the company file during downtime.

Opening a Portable Company File

Portable files are a special file format that makes QuickBooks company files more compact, so you can email them more easily. Opening a portable file is similar to opening a regular file. Here are the steps:

1. **Choose File → "Open or Restore Company".**

   The "Open or Restore Company" dialog box opens.

2. **Select the "Restore a portable file" option and click Next.**

   The Open Portable Company File dialog box appears.

3. **Navigate to the folder with the portable file and double-click the filename.**

   QuickBooks automatically changes the "Files of type" box to QuickBooks Portable Company Files (*.QBM).

Converting from Another Program to QuickBooks

If you launched your small business from your basement and kept your records with Quicken Home & Business Edition, your accountant has probably recommended that you make the leap to using QuickBooks. On the other hand, you may have used another accounting program like Peachtree or Microsoft Small Business Accounting and have decided to move to QuickBooks. Regardless of which other program you used, the command to convert your records to QuickBooks is the same. Choose File → Utilities → Convert. Then, choose From Quicken, From Peachtree, or From Microsoft Small Business Accounting or Microsoft Office Accounting.

Converting from Quicken Home & Business

Quicken doesn't report your business performance in the way that most accountants want to see, nor does it store your business transactions the way QuickBooks does. If you want the conversion to proceed as smoothly as possible, do some cleanup in your Quicken file first.

For example, you have to record overdue scheduled transactions and send online payments before you convert your Quicken file. Delete accounts you don't want in QuickBooks, because once they're in QuickBooks you can't delete accounts that have any transactions. Make sure that customer names are consistent and unique. QuickBooks doesn't support repeating online payments, so you also have to send an instruction in Quicken to delete any repeating online payments you've set up. In addition, you need complete reports of your past payroll because Quicken payroll transactions don't convert to QuickBooks.

Intuit publishes a detailed guide to help you prepare for a Quicken conversion. The easiest way to find this info is to point your browser to *http://quickbooks.com/ support*. On the Intuit QuickBooks Support web page, you'll see a Search box front and center. If the label doesn't show the QuickBooks edition you use, click the "Choose a different product" link to choose your edition. In the Search box, type *Quicken convert*, and then press, Enter. Click the "Convert data to QuickBooks from other programs" link. On the article web page, under the heading "Is your data already in QuickBooks or Quicken format?" click the "Converting or upgrading between different versions of QuickBooks or Quicken" link.

Note: If you run into problems converting from Quicken to QuickBooks, Intuit technical support just intensifies your headache. You're likely to get bounced back and forth between Quicken and QuickBooks technical support, with neither one being particularly helpful. If you've already cleaned up your Quicken file and run into conversion problems in QuickBooks, check the QuickBooks company file for errors by choosing File → Utilities → Verify Data, described on page 178. Another potential solution is to remove transactions prior to the current fiscal year and then try to convert the file. If nothing you try works *and* you're willing to send your financial data to Intuit, QuickBooks technical support may agree to convert the file for you.

When your Quicken file is ready for conversion to QuickBooks, you have two options in QuickBooks:

• Choose File → New Company. In the EasyStep Interview window, click Convert Data and then choose Quicken.

• Choose File → Utilities → Convert → From Quicken.

Converting from a Non-Intuit Program

To convert files created in other accounting programs like Peachtree or Microsoft Small Business Accounting, you have to download a conversion tool from the QuickBooks website. Choose File → Utilities → Convert and then choose the product you want to convert from. In the dialog box that opens, click Yes to tell Quick-Books to go online to download the QuickBooks Conversion Tool. The web page that opens tells you a little bit about the tool. Scroll to the bottom of the page, fill in the boxes for your name and email address, and then click Submit.

Getting Around in QuickBooks

You have enough to do running your business, so you don't want bookkeeping to take any longer than necessary. The QuickBooks Home page is a visual roadmap to the bookkeeping tasks you use regularly. It has panels for tasks related to vendors, customers, and employees, giving you quick access to the commands and financial info you use most often. Click an icon, and the corresponding window or dialog box appears. The Home page has other icons in the Company and Banking panels that open the windows you use most often. The Vendors, Customers, and Employees buttons on the left side of the window open centers that let you manage those groups. This chapter explains how to use the workflow icons and the centers.

You'll also learn how to review your company finances in the Company Snapshot window and access QuickBooks commands from the menu bar and icon bar. Finally, you'll learn how to work with all the windows you open during a rousing bookkeeping session.

Getting Around the QuickBooks Home Page

The QuickBooks Home page (Figure 2-1) is a slick way to work through your company's bookkeeping tasks. When you create your company file with the EasyStep Interview (page 21), you tell QuickBooks what you want to see on the Home page. For example, if you invoice customers and send statements, the Customers panel can show the tasks for invoicing and preparing statements. But if you run a one-person shop and don't have employees, you can make sure the Employees panel is nowhere to be seen.

The Home page also has icons for other must-do tasks—like Chart of Accounts (Company section) to open the Chart of Accounts window and Check Register (Banking section) to open your checking account register window. This section shows you how to use the Home page to best advantage.

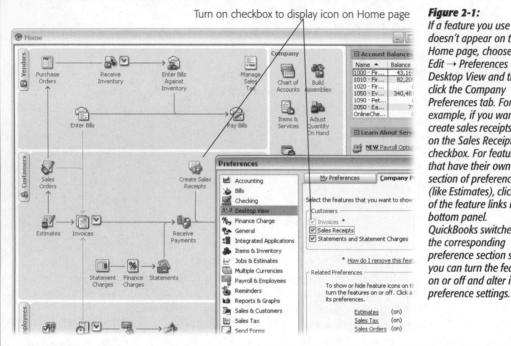

Turn on checkbox to display icon on Home page

Figure 2-1:
If a feature you use doesn't appear on the Home page, choose Edit → Preferences → Desktop View and then click the Company Preferences tab. For example, if you want to create sales receipts, turn on the Sales Receipts checkbox. For features that have their own section of preferences (like Estimates), click one of the feature links in the bottom panel. QuickBooks switches to the corresponding preference section so you can turn the feature on or off and alter its preference settings.

Tip: To make sure the Home page appears each time you log in, click the My Preferences tab and turn on the "Show Home page when opening a company file" checkbox. If you prefer to choose commands from menus and want to keep the Home page hidden, turn this checkbox off.

The Home page gives you an overview of your bookkeeping tasks. It lets you see how everything fits together so you can follow your money from start to finish. Vendors, customers, and employees each have their own panel of activities. The bookkeeping tasks for each group are laid out like breadcrumbs you can follow from beginning to end. Each company is different, so you don't *have* to use every icon you see. This section outlines the tasks in each panel and where you can find detailed instructions elsewhere in this book.

Vendors

Whether you order products and services to run your company or to sell to your customers, the Vendors panel steps you through purchasing and paying for the goods and services you use (as you can see at the top of Figure 2-2), all of which are described in detail in Chapter 9. The Vendors button on the left side of the panel opens the Vendor Center, where you can set up or edit vendors. The Vendor Center is the best place to create, edit, and view what's going on with the vendors you work with. On the left side of the Home page, click Vendors or choose Vendors → Vendor Center to open the Vendor Center window.

Here's what you can do in the Vendor Center and where to find detailed instructions in other chapters:

- **Create a new vendor.** In the Vendor Center toolbar, click New Vendor. The New Vendor window opens so you can create a new vendor record, as described on page 135.

- **Find a vendor.** If you have a bazillion vendors, you can shorten the vendor list that you see. The View drop-down list is initially set to Active Vendors. Choose "Vendors with Open Balances" if you want to see only the vendors you owe money to. Choose Custom Filter to specify exactly the criteria you want. On the other hand, if you want to see active and inactive vendors alike, choose All Vendors.

  For a quick search of vendor records, type part of the vendor name in the Find box and then click the Find button (the icon looks like a magnifying glass).

- **Review a vendor record.** When you select a vendor on the Vendors tab, shown in Figure 2-2, basic info about the vendor appears on the right side of the window.

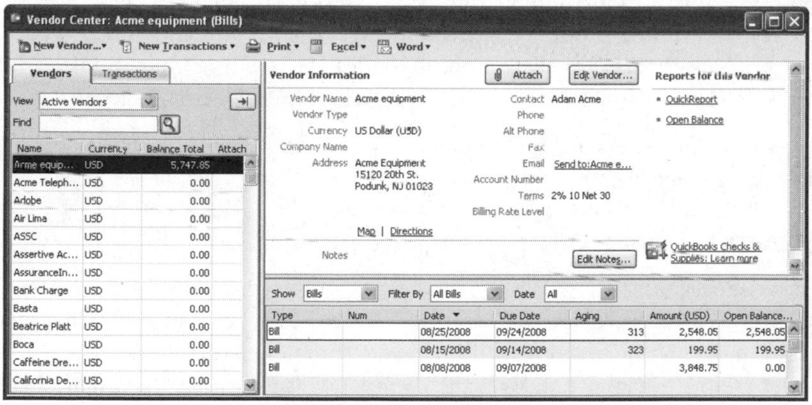

Figure 2-2:
The Vendor Center puts all vendor-related tasks in a single window. When you choose a vendor, the right pane displays info about that vendor and its transactions. To attach an electronic vendor document like a bill to the vendor's record, click the Attach button on the right pane. If the vendor record includes an email address, you can click the "Send to" link next to the Email label to email the vendor. You can even click the Map or Directions links to find out how to get to your vendor's location.

- **Edit an existing vendor's record.** To change a vendor's record, on the Vendors tab, right-click the vendor name and then choose Edit Vendor. The Edit Vendor window opens with the same fields you filled in when you created the record. If you've selected the vendor in the list, you can also click the Edit Vendor button on the right pane.

- **Attach an electronic document to a vendor record.** You can attach electronic documents to a vendor record (and even scan them right in QuickBooks). See page 307 to learn more about this new QuickBooks 2010 feature.

- **Create transactions for a vendor.** In the Vendor Center toolbar, click New Transactions to display a drop-down menu of vendor-related commands like Enter Bills, Pay Bills, and Receive Items. (These do the same thing as the icons in the Vendors panel of the Home page.)

- **Review transactions for a vendor.** When you select a vendor on the Vendors tab, the table at the bottom-right of the Vendor Center lists that vendor's transactions. By filtering the transactions, you can find out which purchase orders are still open, whether any bills are overdue, or the payments you've made. To limit the transaction list to only a specific type of transaction, in the Show drop-down list, choose the transaction type like Bills or Bill Payments.

  The Filter By drop-down list lets you restrict the transactions you see by their status, such as Open Bills or Overdue Bills. To track down transactions within a date range, choose the date range in the Date drop-down list. (The date range options in this menu are the same as the ones available in reports; see page 508.)

Tip: Double-click a transaction in the list to open the corresponding window to that transaction.

- **Print or export vendor information.** In the Vendor Center toolbar, click Print or Excel to print or export vendor info (page 599). If you click Excel, you can choose "Import from Excel" to import vendor records into QuickBooks, which works similarly to importing customer records as described on page 80.

- **Prepare vendor letters.** In the Vendor Center toolbar, click Word to create letters to vendors (page 586).

Customers

Like its vendor sibling, the Customers panel has icons for customer-oriented commands for creating invoices, statements, sales receipts, and so on. (Chapter 10 describes in detail how to work with invoices, estimates, sales orders, refunds, and customer credits. Chapter 11 covers the commands for creating statement charges and statements. Receiving payments and sales receipts for cash sales are both described in Chapter 13.) The Customers button on the left side of the panel (or choose Customers → Customer Center) opens the Customer Center, which lets you create new customer records and transactions, edit existing ones, or check on their status. Here are customer tasks you can perform from the Customer Center:

- **Create a new customer or job.** In the Customer Center toolbar, click New Customer & Job. On the drop-down menu, choose New Customer to create a new customer record (page 72). If you want to add a job to a customer, first select the customer on the Customers & Jobs tab. Then, choose New Customer & Job → Add Job (page 90).

- **Find a customer.** You can filter the customer list to show active customers, only customers with open balances (those who owe you money), or all customers. Choose Custom Filter to specify criteria for the customers you want to see. To search for a specific customer, type part of the customer name in the Find box, and then click the Find button (the icon looks like a magnifying glass).

- **Review a customer record.** When you select a customer on the Customers & Jobs tab, the right side of the window displays the basic 411 about the customer. In the Customer Information section, shown in Figure 2-3, you can send an email to the customer, attach electronic documents, get directions to their location, add notes to the record, or run reports about the customer.

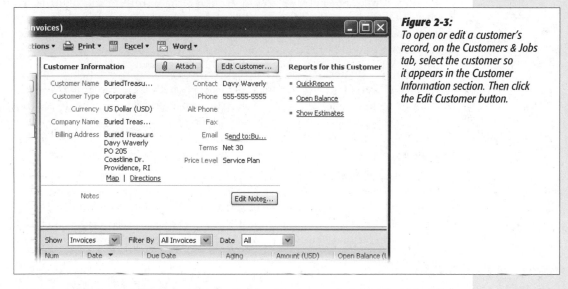

Figure 2-3:
To open or edit a customer's record, on the Customers & Jobs tab, select the customer so it appears in the Customer Information section. Then click the Edit Customer button.

- **Edit an existing customer's record.** On the Customers & Jobs tab, right-click the customer name and then choose Edit Customer. The Edit Customer window opens, filled in with the values you entered when you created the record.

- **Attach an electronic document to a customer record.** You can attach electronic documents to a customer record (or scan them right in QuickBooks). See page 307 to learn more about this new QuickBooks 2010 feature.

- **Create transactions for a customer.** In the Customer Center toolbar, click New Transactions and then choose one of the commands from the drop-down menu, such as Estimates, Invoices, or Receive Payments. The commands on the drop-down menu are the same as the icons in the Customers panel of the Home page.

- **Review transactions for a customer.** The table at the bottom-right of the Customer Center lists the transactions for the customer you select on the Customers & Jobs tab. You can filter the transactions you see (page 329) by type (estimates or invoices, for example), status, and date. Double-click a transaction in the list to open the corresponding window to that transaction.

- **Print or export customer information.** In the Customer Center toolbar, click Print or Excel to print or export customer and job info (page 599). If you click Excel, you can choose Import from Excel to import customer records into QuickBooks (page 80).

- **Prepare customer letters.** In the Customer Center toolbar, click Word to create letters to customers (page 586).

Employees

The Employees panel has only a few icons. The devilish details arise when you click one of the icons to enter time, set up paychecks, or pay payroll tax liabilities. The Employee Center works the same way as the Vendor and Customer Centers. To see it, click Employees on the left side of the Home page or choose Employees → Employee Center. (See Chapter 8 to learn how to record the time that employees work. Chapter 14 walks you through paying employees and other payroll expenses.)

In the Employee Center, you can create new records for employees, update info for existing employees, and view transactions like paychecks. On the Employees tab, you can filter the employee list to view active employees, released employees (the ones that no longer work for you), or all employees.

Company Features

The Company section appears on the right side of the Home page. The two icons that you'll probably click often are Chart of Accounts and Items & Services, which open the Chart of Accounts (page 53) and Item List (page 107) windows, respectively. If you track inventory, the Adjust Quantity On Hand icon lets you change the quantity and value of your inventory (page 474).

Banking

The Banking section is a one-stop-shop for banking tasks. Whether you visit this section frequently or almost never depends on how you like to record transactions. For example, you can click the Write Checks icon to open the Write Checks window (page 238) or simply press Ctrl+W to do the same thing. Or, if you prefer to record checks in a check register window, you might prefer to double-click your bank account in the Chart of Accounts window. Similarly, the Enter Credit Card Charges icon opens the Enter Credit Card Charges window (page 241), but you can record credit card charges directly in a credit card register (page 384).

The Record Deposits icon opens the "Payments to Deposit" dialog box, so you can record bank deposits (page 354) in QuickBooks. The Reconcile icon opens the Begin Reconciliation dialog box, so you can reconcile your QuickBooks records to those of your bank (page 396). The Print Checks icon opens the Select Checks to Print dialog box, so you can select the checks you want to print and send them to the printer loaded with your checks.

Note: The far right side of the Home page shows account balances and a link to display reminders. However, the new Company Snapshot window (page 613) shows this information and more.

The QuickBooks Coach

The QuickBooks Coach can help you learn how to use the program. When you first install QuickBooks, the Coach is turned on, which means that the QuickBooks Coach section appears at the top-right of the Home page, as shown in Figure 2-4. To see tips that help you decide what to do, click the blue circle with an "i" inside. A pop-up box tells you what the Home page steps do and shows the order in which you perform them.

Tip: When you grow tired of the Coach's assistance, choose Edit → Preferences and then click the Desktop icon. Turn the "Show Coach window and features" checkbox off.

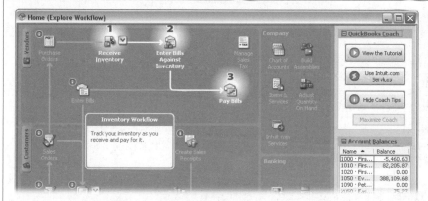

Figure 2-4:
You can still click an icon, Receive Inventory in the figure, to launch the command. If you need more assistance, in the QuickBooks Coach section, click View the Tutorial to watch an animated tutorial with sound.

The Company Snapshot

The Company Snapshot window (choose Company → Company Snapshot) is a financial dashboard that can show important aspects of your company's financial state like account balances, income breakdown (by top-level income accounts), customers who owe money, and best-selling items, as you can see in Figure 2-5. In QuickBooks 2010, you can choose from 12 different financial views (page 613) so the Company Snapshot can show the financial information you care about most.

Using Menus and the Icon Bar

Although the QuickBooks Home page guides you through bookkeeping tasks, QuickBooks' veterans may still prefer the menu bar (Figure 2-6) to launch the program's tools for different financial activities. Unlike other navigation features, the menu bar is always available, and it serves up every command that QuickBooks has to offer.

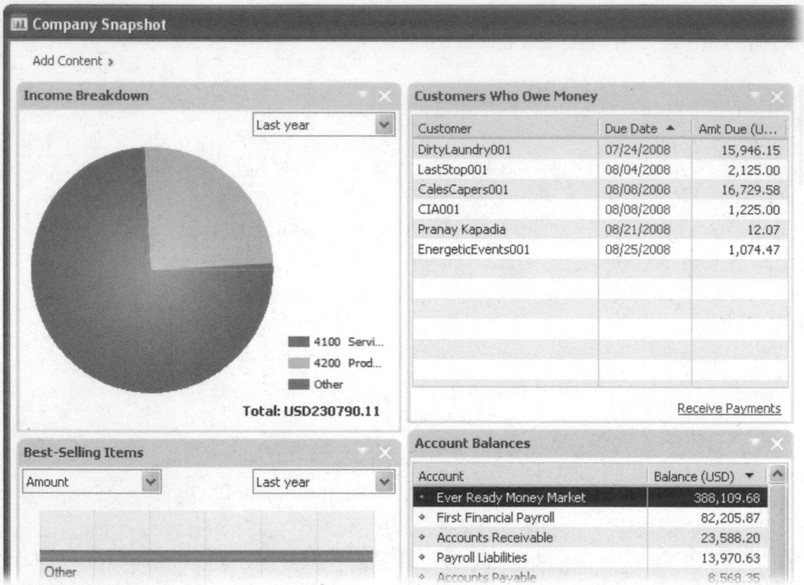

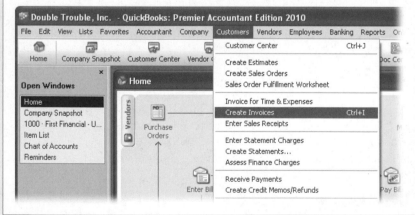

Figure 2-5:
*Not only can you quickly
scan your company's
financial status, you can
double-click entries in the
window to dig into the
details. In QuickBooks
2010, you can add or
remove items from the
Snapshot or drag items
to rearrange them, as
described on page 613.*

After shortcut menus and keyboard shortcuts (see Appendix C at *www.
missingmanuals.com/cds*), the QuickBooks icon bar is the fastest way to launch
your favorite commands. You can add your favorite commands, memorized
reports, or windows you open often. You can also remove commands that you no
longer use. Page 609 tells you how to add icons for all these items to the icon bar
and how to change their appearance.

Figure 2-6:
*Every command that
QuickBooks has is always
within reach on the menu
bar. Choose a top-level
menu like Customers and
then choose a command
from the drop-down menu
or a submenu. For one-click
access to your favorite
commands, use the
QuickBooks icon bar, which
you can customize to show
the features and reports you
use the most (page 609).*

Switching Between Open Windows

If you tend to work on one bookkeeping task for hours on end, you can set Quick-Books up to display one full-size window at a time (page 557). If you open additional windows, they stack on top of each other so you see the last one you opened. With the one window approach, you can view another window by choosing it in the Open Window List, on the left in Figure 2-7. (Or on the menu bar, choose Window and then choose the name of the window you want to display.) If the Open Window List isn't visible, choose View → Open Window List.

When you flit between bookkeeping tasks like a honey bee in an alfalfa field, you probably want several windows open at a time. QuickBooks can display several windows at the same time, as shown on the right in Figure 2-7. Like windows in other programs, you can click a window to bring it to the front, reposition windows by dragging their title bars, or resize windows by dragging their edges and corners.

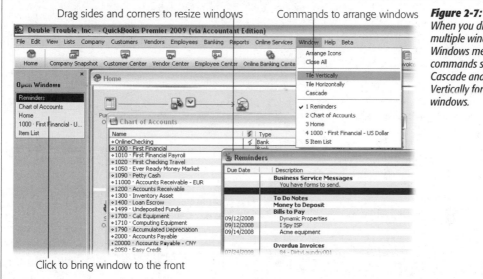

Figure 2-7:
When you display multiple windows, the Windows menu has commands such as Cascade and Tile Vertically for arranging windows.

Tip: Everyone who uses QuickBooks can work with windows the way they want. To tell QuickBooks how you want the desktop to look when you run the program, see page 558.

CHAPTER 3

Setting Up a Chart of Accounts

If you've just started running a business and keeping books, all this talk of accounts, credits, and debits might have you flummoxed. Accounting is a cross between mathematics and the mystical arts that records and reports the financial performance of an organization. The end result of bookkeeping and accounting is a set of financial statements (page 429), but the starting point is the chart of accounts.

In accounting, an *account* is more than an account you have at a financial institution; it's like a bucket for holding money. When you earn money, you document those earnings in an income account, just as you might toss the day's take at the lemonade stand into the jar on your desk. When you buy supplies for your business, that expense shows up in an expense account like the pocket of receipts you carry around. If you buy a building, its value ends up in an asset account. And if you borrow money to buy that building, the mortgage owed shows up in a liability account.

Accounts come in a variety of types to reflect whether you've earned or spent money, whether you own something or owe money to someone else, as well as a few other financial situations. The chart of accounts is a list of all the accounts you use to track money in your business and what type each one is.

Neophytes and experienced business folks alike will be relieved to know that no one has to build a chart of accounts from scratch in QuickBooks. This chapter explains how to get a ready-made chart of accounts for your business and what to do with it once you've got it. If you want to add or modify accounts in your chart of accounts, you'll learn about that, too.

Acquiring a Chart of Accounts

The easiest—though probably not the cheapest—way to get a chart of accounts is from your accountant. Accountants understand the accounting guidelines set by the Financial Accounting Standards Board (FASB—pronounced "faz bee"—a private-sector organization that sets standards with the SEC's blessing). When your accountant builds a QuickBooks chart of accounts for you, you can be reasonably sure that you have the accounts you need to track your business and that those accounts conform to accounting standards.

Note: Don't worry—getting an accountant to build a chart of accounts for you probably won't bust your budget, since your accountant won't start from scratch either. Many financial professionals maintain spreadsheets of accounts and build a chart of accounts by importing a customized account list into Quick-Books. Or, they may keep QuickBooks company files around to use as templates for new files.

Using a QuickBooks Chart of Accounts

If you've opted to work without an accountant, QuickBooks tries to help you do the right thing accounting-wise. If you use QuickBooks' EasyStep Interview (page 21) to create your QuickBooks file, you can tell the program to create income, expense, and bank accounts for you. When you choose an industry during the Interview, QuickBooks selects accounts typical for that industry, which you can use as a starting point for your chart of accounts.

If the Chart of Accounts window is devoid of accounts after you've completed the EasyStep Interview, there's no need for concern. At the bottom of the Chart of Accounts window (press Ctrl+A to open it), turn on the "Include inactive" checkbox. If an X appears to the left of an account that you want to use, click the X to reactivate the account (see page 59 for more about hiding and reactivating accounts).

With your QuickBooks chart of accounts in place, you can add more accounts, hide accounts you don't need, merge accounts, or edit the accounts on the list—all of which are described in the rest of this chapter.

Note: Intuit offers QuickBooks Premier editions for several different business types: accounting, construction, manufacturing, nonprofit, professional services, retail, and wholesale. With an industry-specific Premier edition, QuickBooks provides a chart of accounts, an item list, payroll items, and preferences already tuned to your industry. The industry-specific editions also have features unique to each industry, like enhanced job costing in the Contractor Edition. You have to decide whether these features are worth a few hundred dollars more than the QuickBooks Pro price tag.

Importing a Chart of Accounts

If you don't like the chart of accounts that QuickBooks delivers, how about one built by experts and available at no charge? A quick search on the Web for "Quick-Books chart of accounts" returns links to sites with predefined charts of accounts.

For example, a chart of accounts (and item list, other lists, customized forms and reports) for the construction industry is available at no charge from *www.powertoolssoftware.com*. At *www.rrgconsulting.com/restaurant_coa.htm*, you can download a free .iif file with a restaurant-oriented chart of accounts that you can import into QuickBooks.

In the not-for-profit world, the National Center for Charitable Statistics website (*http://nccs.urban.org/projects/ucoa.cfm*) includes downloadable QuickBooks files that contain the Unified Chart of Accounts for nonprofits (known as the UCOA). You can download a QuickBooks backup file of a nonprofit company file complete with chart of accounts, an .iif file that you can import (see the next section) into QuickBooks, or a backup file for the Mac version of QuickBooks.

Importing a Downloaded Chart of Accounts

Once you download an .iif file with a chart of accounts, you can import that file into a QuickBooks company file. Because you're importing a chart of accounts, you want to create your company file with basic info about your company and as few accounts as possible in the Chart of Accounts list. Here's how you set up a QuickBooks company file to import a chart of accounts from an .iif file:

1. **Choose File → New Company. In the EasyStep Interview window, click Skip Interview.**

   The "Enter your company information" window appears. As described on page 21, enter the company name, legal name, tax ID, and other 411 about your company.

2. **Click Next.**

   QuickBooks takes you through data entry screens where you select the type of business entity (LLC, corporation, and so on), and the start of your fiscal year.

3. **When the "Select your industry" screen appears, scroll to the bottom of the list, and then choose Other/None. Click Next.**

   Choosing Other/None tells QuickBooks to create a company file with only a handful of accounts. The .iif file you import (step 6) creates the rest of your accounts.

4. **In the "Create your company file" screen that appears, click Finish to create your company file.**

   The "Filename for New Company" dialog box appears.

5. **Choose the folder and filename for the company file as described on page 23, and then click Save.**

   QuickBooks creates the company file and opens it. Now you're ready to import your chart of accounts.

6. **Choose File → Utilities → Import → IIF Files.**

   QuickBooks opens the Import dialog box to the folder where you stored your company file. It also sets the "Files of type" box to IIF Files (*.IIF).

7. **Navigate to the folder that contains the .iif file and double-click the filename.**

   A message box appears that displays progress for the import. If all goes well, QuickBooks then displays a message box that tells you that it imported the data successfully. Click OK. If the Chart of Accounts window is open (Ctrl+A), you'll see it blossom with imported accounts. If QuickBooks ran into other problems with the data in your .iif file, it tells you that it didn't import the data successfully.

Account Naming and Numbering

Accountants and bookkeepers tend to refer to accounts by both numbers *and* names. This section explains why you should set up naming and numbering conventions—and suggests some rules you can follow—but it won't explain the meaning of all the different names you'll find in your chart of accounts. If you accept the accounts that QuickBooks recommends in the EasyStep Interview, your accounts already have assigned account numbers, as shown in Figure 3-1. You might think that lets you off the hook. But by taking the time to learn standard account numbers and names, you'll find working with accounts more logical, and you'll understand more of what your accountant and bookkeeper say.

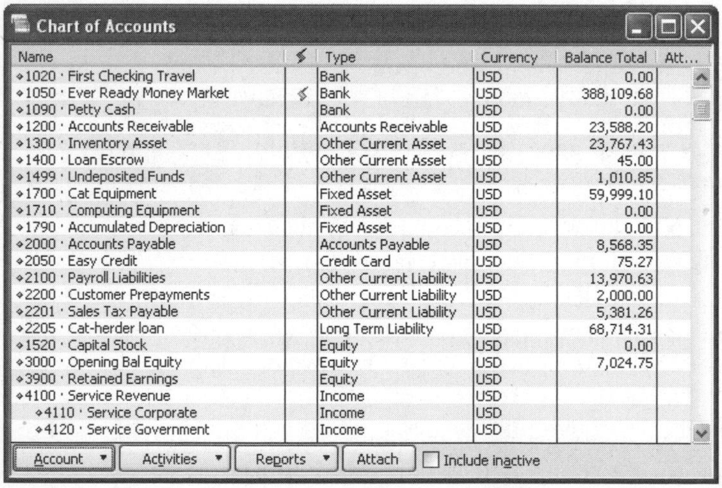

Name		Type	Currency	Balance Total	Att...
◆1020 · First Checking Travel		Bank	USD	0.00	
◆1050 · Ever Ready Money Market	✓	Bank	USD	388,109.68	
◆1090 · Petty Cash		Bank	USD	0.00	
◆1200 · Accounts Receivable		Accounts Receivable	USD	23,588.20	
◆1300 · Inventory Asset		Other Current Asset	USD	23,767.43	
◆1400 · Loan Escrow		Other Current Asset	USD	45.00	
◆1499 · Undeposited Funds		Other Current Asset	USD	1,010.85	
◆1700 · Cat Equipment		Fixed Asset	USD	59,999.10	
◆1710 · Computing Equipment		Fixed Asset	USD	0.00	
◆1790 · Accumulated Depreciation		Fixed Asset	USD	0.00	
◆2000 · Accounts Payable		Accounts Payable	USD	8,568.35	
◆2050 · Easy Credit		Credit Card	USD	75.27	
◆2100 · Payroll Liabilities		Other Current Liability	USD	13,970.63	
◆2200 · Customer Prepayments		Other Current Liability	USD	2,000.00	
◆2201 · Sales Tax Payable		Other Current Liability	USD	5,381.26	
◆2205 · Cat-herder loan		Long Term Liability	USD	68,714.31	
◆1520 · Capital Stock		Equity	USD	0.00	
◆3000 · Opening Bal Equity		Equity	USD	7,024.75	
◆3900 · Retained Earnings		Equity	USD		
◆4100 · Service Revenue		Income	USD		
◆4110 · Service Corporate		Income	USD		
◆4120 · Service Government		Income	USD		

Account ▼ | Activities ▼ | Reports ▼ | Attach | ☐ Include inactive

Figure 3-1:
Accounts that QuickBooks adds to your chart of accounts during the EasyStep Interview come with account numbers assigned. If you don't see account numbers in the Chart of Accounts window, choose Edit → Preferences. In the Preferences window, click Accounting and then click the Company Preferences tab. When you turn on the "Use account numbers" checkbox and click OK, the numbers appear in the Chart of Accounts window.

Setting Up Account Numbers

Companies reserve ranges of numbers for different types of accounts, so you can identify the *type* of account by its account number alone. Business models vary, so you'll find account numbers carved up in different ways depending on the business. Think about your personal finances: You spend money on lots of different things, but your income derives from a precious few sources. Businesses and nonprofits are no different. You might find income accounts from 4000 to 4999 and expense accounts using numbers anywhere from 5000 through 9999 (see Table 3-1).

Table 3-1. *Typical ranges for account numbers*

Number Range	Account Type
1000–1999	Assets
2000–2999	Liabilities
3000–3999	Equity
4000–4999	Income
5000–5999	Sales, cost of goods sold, or expenses
6000–6999	Expenses or other income
7000–7999	Expenses or other income
8000–8999	Expenses or other expenses
9000–9999	Other expenses

Note: The account-numbering scheme is consistent for most types of businesses until you reach the number 4999. Some companies require more income accounts, but in most businesses, expense accounts are the most plentiful.

Account numbering conventions don't end with number ranges for account types. If you read annual reports as a hobby, you know that companies further compartmentalize their finances. For example, assets and liabilities get split into *current* and *long-term* categories. Current means something happens in the next 12 months, such as a loan that's due in 3 months. Long-term is anything beyond 12 months. Typically, companies show assets and liabilities progressing from the shortest to the longest term, and the asset and liability account numbers follow suit. Here's one way to allocate the asset account numbers for current and progressively longer-term assets:

- **1000–1099.** Immediately available cash, such as a checking account, savings account, or petty cash.

- **1100–1499.** Assets you can convert into cash within a few months to a year, including accounts receivable, inventory assets, and other current assets.

- **1500–1799.** Long-term assets, such as land, buildings, furniture, and other fixed assets.

- **1800–1999.** Other assets.

Companies also break down expenses into smaller categories. Many companies keep an eye on whether the sales team is doing its job by tracking sales expenses separately and monitoring the ratio of sales to sales expenses. Sales expenses often appear in the number range from 5000 through 5999. QuickBooks reinforces this standard by automatically creating a "Cost of Goods Sold" account with the account number 5001. Other companies assign overhead expenses to accounts in the 7000 to 7999 range, so they can assign a portion of those expenses to each job performed.

Tip: When you add new accounts to your chart of accounts, increment the account number by 5 or 10 to leave room in the numbering scheme for similar accounts that you might need in the future. For example, if your checking account number is 1000, assign 1005 or 1010, not 1001, to your new savings account.

In QuickBooks, an account number can be up to seven digits long, but Quick-Books sorts numbers beginning with the leftmost digit, as shown in Figure 3-2. If you want to categorize in excruciating detail, slice your number ranges into sets of 10,000. For example, assets range from 10000 to 19999; income accounts span 40000 to 49999, and so on.

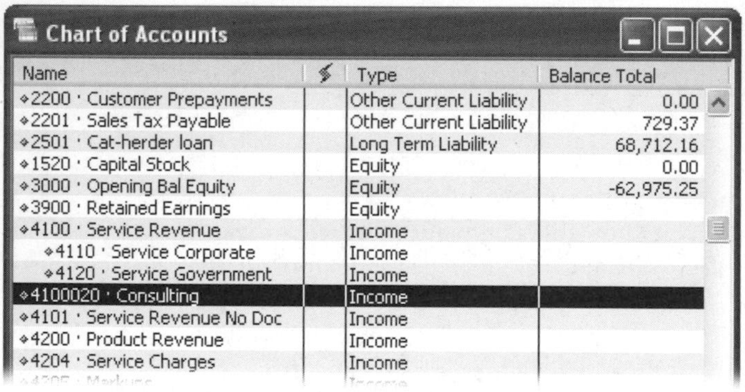

Figure 3-2:
QuickBooks sorts accounts by account type and then by account number. By looking at the income account numbers, you can see that QuickBooks sorts numbers beginning with the leftmost digit, so account 4100020 appears before account 4101. The box on page 52 lists account types in the order in which they appear in the QuickBooks Chart of Accounts window.

Standardizing Account Names

Accounts should be unique in name and function because you don't need two accounts for the same type of income, expense, or financial bucket. For example, if you consider advertising and marketing as two distinctly different activities, create an account for each. But if advertising and marketing blur in your eyes, create one account with a name like Marketing & Advertising.

Naming Rules for Accounts

If you haven't used QuickBooks before, you probably don't know all the different ways that account names can cause trouble. Here are some rules you can apply to introduce consistency into your account names:

- **Word order.** Decide whether to include the account type in the name: Postage or Postage Expense. If you include the account type in the name, append it to the end of the name. You'll spot Postage Expense more easily than Expense Postage.

- **Consistent punctuation.** Choose "and" or "&" for accounts that cover more than one item, like "Dues and Subscriptions." And decide whether to include apostrophes, as in "Owners Draw" or "Owners' Draw."

- **Spaces.** Decide whether to include spaces for readability or to eliminate spaces for brevity; for example, "Dues and Subscriptions" vs. "Dues&Subscriptions."

- **Abbreviation.** If you abbreviate words in account names, choose a standard abbreviation length. If you choose a four-letter abbreviation, for example, Postage would become "Post." With a three-letter abbreviation, you might choose "Pst."

Someone might conclude that an account for postage doesn't exist if the account is named Mail Expense or Expense-postage. If that person creates a postage account, you're on your way to inconsistency and confusion. A naming standard can help you keep expenses in their proper accounts.

QuickBooks does its part to enforce unique account names. Suppose you try to create a new expense account with the name Samovar Rental, but an account by that name already exists. QuickBooks displays the message "This name is already in use. Please use another name." What QuickBooks *can't* do is ensure that each account represents a unique category of money. Without a naming standard, you could end up with multiple accounts with unique names, each representing the same category, as shown by the following names for an account used to track postage:

    Expense-postage
    Postage
    Postage and delivery
    Shipping

Warning: QuickBooks won't enforce your naming standards. After you set the rules for account names, write them down so that you don't forget what they are. A consistent written standard encourages everyone (yourself included) to trust and follow the naming rules. Also, urge everyone to display inactive accounts (page 60) and then scan the chart of accounts, using synonyms to see if such an account already exists, before creating a new one. These rules are easier to enforce if you limit the number of people who can create and edit accounts (page 637).

Creating Accounts and Subaccounts

Different types of accounts represent dramatically different financial animals, as described in the box on page 52. The good news is that accounts of every type share most of the same fields, so you have to remember only one procedure for creating accounts.

If you look closely at the chart of accounts list in Figure 3-2, you'll notice that accounts fall into two main categories: those with balances and those without. If you're really on your toes, you might also notice that accounts with balances are the ones that appear on the Balance Sheet report. Accounts without balances appear on the Profit & Loss report. To learn more about financial statements and the accounts they reference, see Chapter 17.

UP TO SPEED

Making Sense of Account Types

If QuickBooks' account types are unfamiliar, rest assured that they're standard types used in finance. Here's a quick introduction to the account types and what they represent:

- **Bank.** An account that you hold at a financial institution, such as a checking, savings, money market, or petty cash account.

- **Accounts Receivable.** The money that your customers owe you, such as outstanding invoices or goods purchased on credit.

- **Other Current Asset.** Things you own that you'll use or convert to cash within 12 months, such as prepaid expenses.

- **Fixed Asset.** Fixed assets are things your company owns that decrease in value over time (depreciate), such as equipment that wears out or becomes obsolete.

- **Other Asset.** If you won't convert an asset to cash in the next 12 months, and it isn't a depreciable asset it's—you guessed it—an Other Asset. A long-term note receivable is one example.

- **Accounts Payable.** This is a special type of current liability account (money you owe in the next 12 months), in which QuickBooks calculates the balance from the amounts you owe each of your vendors.

- **Credit Card.** A credit card account.

- **Current Liability.** Money you owe in the next 12 months, such as sales tax and short-term loans.

- **Long-term Liability.** Money you owe after the next 12 months, like mortgage payments you'll pay over several years.

- **Equity.** The owners' equity in the company, including the original capital invested in the company and retained earnings. (Money that owners withdraw from the company shows up in an Equity account, but the values are negative.)

- **Other Income.** Money you receive from sources other than business operations, such as interest income.

- **Income.** The revenue (that is, money) you generate through your main business functions, such as sales or consulting services.

- **Cost of Goods Sold.** The cost of products and materials that you held originally in inventory but then sold.

- **Expense.** The money you spend to run your company.

- **Other Expense.** Money you pay out for things other than business operations, like interest.

- **Non-posting Account.** QuickBooks creates non-posting accounts automatically when you use features such as estimates and purchase orders. When you create an estimate (page 280), you don't want that money to appear on your financial reports, so QuickBooks stores those values in non-posting accounts.

Creating an Account

After you've had your business for a while, you won't add new accounts very often. However, you might need a new account if you start up a new line of income, take on a mortgage for your new office building, or want a new expense account for the emu infertility insurance you took out for your bird farm. The procedure for creating accounts is simple, which is a refreshing change from many accounting tasks.

Before you can create an account, you have to open the Chart of Accounts window. Because the chart of accounts is central to accounting, QuickBooks gives you several ways to open this window:

- The easiest way is by pressing Ctrl+A (which you can do from anywhere in the program).

- At the top right of the Home page, in the Company section, click Chart of Accounts.

- In the menu bar, choose Lists → Chart of Accounts.

- On the icon bar, click Acct. (If you don't see the Acct icon, you may need to add the icon to the icon bar or reorder the icons so the Acct icon is visible.) See page 609 to learn how to customize the icon bar.

Tip: You can create accounts on the fly by clicking *<Add New>* in any account drop-down list. Suppose you create a new service item (in the Item List window, press Ctrl+N) and want a new income account for what you earn with the service. In the New Item dialog box, scroll to the top of the Account drop-down list and choose *<Add New>*. Fill in the info and then click Save & Close. QuickBooks fills in the Account box with the new account, and you can finish creating your item.

Once you've opened the Chart of Accounts window, here's how to create an account:

1. **To open the Add New Account dialog box, press Ctrl+N.**

   Alternatively, on the menu bar at the bottom of the Chart of Accounts window, click Account, and then choose New. Or, right-click anywhere in the Chart of Accounts window, and then choose New from the shortcut menu.

   QuickBooks opens the Add New Account dialog box, shown in Figure 3-3.

2. **Select the option for the type of account you want to create, and then click Continue.**

   The Add New Account window lists the most common types of accounts. If the type you want isn't listed—Other Current Liability, for example—select the Other Account Types option, and then choose the type from the drop-down menu (Figure 3-3).

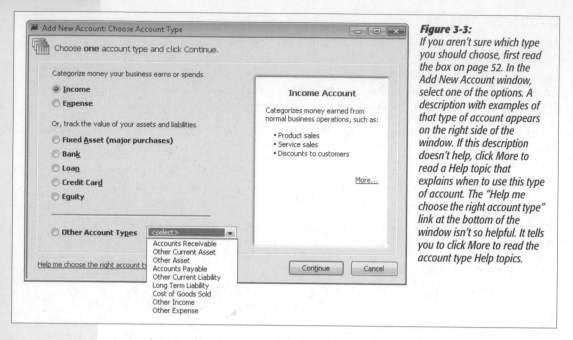

Figure 3-3:
If you aren't sure which type you should choose, first read the box on page 52. In the Add New Account window, select one of the options. A description with examples of that type of account appears on the right side of the window. If this description doesn't help, click More to read a Help topic that explains when to use this type of account. The "Help me choose the right account type" link at the bottom of the window isn't so helpful. It tells you to click More to read the account type Help topics.

3. **In the Number box, type the chart of accounts account number you want to use.**

If you keep the chart of accounts in view while you create new accounts, as in Figure 3-4, review the account numbers for similar types of accounts. Then, when you generate your new account number by incrementing an existing account number by 5 or 10, the new account snuggles in nicely with its compatriots in the chart of accounts.

Note: If the Number box doesn't appear, you haven't turned on account numbers in QuickBooks preferences. To turn on account numbers, choose Edit → Preferences. In the Edit Preferences dialog box, click the Accounting icon, and then click the Company Preferences tab. Turn on the "Use account numbers" checkbox.

---

4. **In the Account Name box, type the name for the account.**

See the box on page 51 for tips on effective account names. If you create an account and don't see one of the fields mentioned here, it simply doesn't apply to that account type.

5. **If you want to turn an account into a subaccount (see the box on page 55), turn on the "Subaccount of" checkbox. Then, in the drop-down list, choose the account that you want to act as the parent.**

In the chart of accounts, subaccounts are indented to differentiate them from parent accounts.

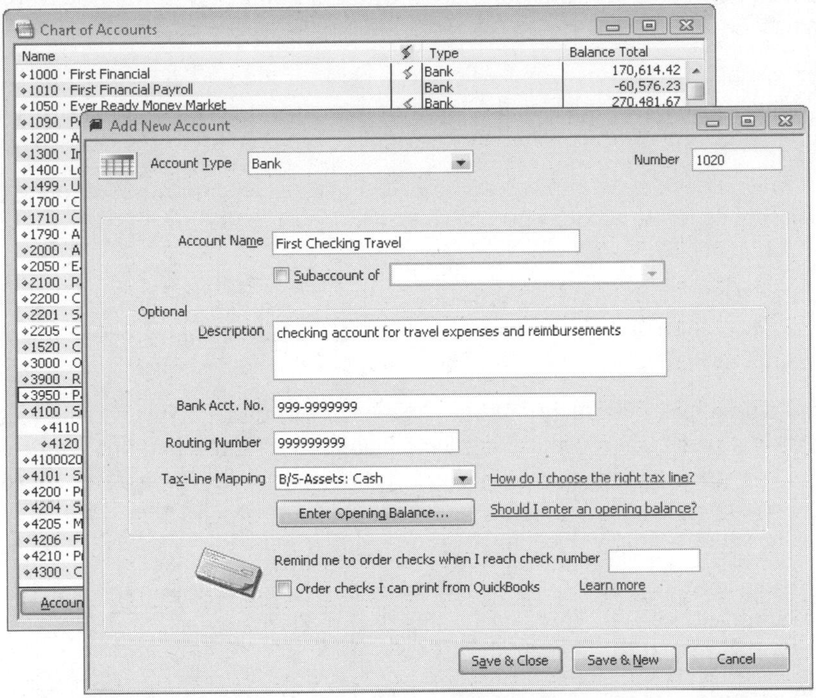

Figure 3-4:
The Bank account type includes every account field except for the Note field. It also includes one field that you won't find on any other account type: If you want QuickBooks to remind you to order checks, in the "Remind me to order checks when I reach check number" box, type the check number you want to use as a trigger. If you want the program to open the browser to the Order Supplies web page, turn on the "Order checks I can print from QuickBooks" checkbox and save the account. If you get checks from somewhere else, just reorder checks the way you normally do.

Adding Detail with Subaccounts

Your company's travel expenses are sky-high and you want to start tracking what you spend on different types of travel, such as airfare, lodging, and limousine services. You could try creating reports that categorize expenses by vendor, but subaccounts are easier to use, and they produce more dependable results. Subaccounts are nothing more than further partitions within a higher-level account (a parent account).

When you post transactions to subaccounts only (not the parent account), your reports show the subtotals for the subaccounts and a grand total for the parent account, such as the Travel account (say, number 6336) and its subaccounts Airfare (6338), Lodging (6340), and Limousine (6342), for example.

Subaccounts help categorize transactions with more precision, but they're indispensable for assigning similar expenses to different lines on a tax form. For example, the IRS doesn't treat all travel expenses the same. You can deduct only half of your meal and entertainment expenses, while other travel expenses are fully deductible. Meals and Entertainment are separate subaccounts from Travel for this very reason.

---

6. **If you've turned on QuickBooks' multiple currency preference, the Currency box appears below the "Subaccount of" checkbox. If the currency for the account is different from the one that QuickBooks fills in, choose the currency in the drop-down list.**

   If you do business in more than one currency, you can turn on multiple currencies in QuickBooks, as described on page 570.

7. **To add a more meaningful description of the account, fill in the Description box.**

   For example, you can define whether a bank account is linked to another account or give examples of the types of expenses that apply to a particular expense account. The account Description field can hold up to 100 characters.

   For several types of accounts, you'll see a field for an account number (one that corresponds to the account number assigned by a financial institution). You'll fill that in next.

8. **In the Bank Acct. No. box, type the account number for your real-world account at your financial institution, like a checking account, money market account, or mortgage.**

   This field appears for Bank, Other Current Asset, Other Asset, Credit Card, Other Current Liability, and Long-term Liability account types, but the field's label changes depending on the account type. For example, the label for a credit card account is Credit Card Acct. No, while the label for an Other Current Liability account is simply Account No.

   When an account type doesn't include a field for an account number, you'll see the Note field instead. You can use this field to store any additional information you want to document about the account.

9. **In the Routing Number box, type the routing number for your bank.**

   The routing number is a nine-digit number in funny-looking digits at the bottom of your checks.

10. **To associate the account with a tax form and a specific line on that tax form, in the Tax-Line Mapping drop-down menu, choose the entry for the appropriate tax form and tax line.**

    The Tax-Line Mapping field is unassigned if you haven't specified the tax form that your company files with the IRS. To see QuickBooks tax line assignments, start by choosing Company → Company Information. In the Company Information dialog box, in the Income Tax Form Used field, choose the appropriate tax form for your business, such as Form 1120S (S Corporation).

    If QuickBooks hasn't assigned a tax line for you, you can scan the entries in the drop-down list for a likely match. If you don't find an entry that seems right, or if QuickBooks tells you the one you chose isn't compatible with the account type, your best bet is to call your accountant or the IRS. You can also get a hint for an appropriate tax line for the account you're creating by examining one of QuickBooks' sample files (page 18).

    To remove a tax line from an account, in the drop-down list, choose *<Unassigned>*.

Note: For a brand-new account, the value for the Opening Balance field is easy—it's zero. But if you're setting up QuickBooks with accounts that existed prior to your QuickBooks start date, those accounts *do* have opening balances. Even so, you should leave the Opening Balance field blank. Check out the box below to learn how to specify opening balances for all your accounts in just a few steps.

Doing Opening Balances Right

When I add an account to my company file, can I just type the balance I want to start with in the Opening Balance field? That seems the most logical place for it.

You can, but your accountant may not be too happy about it. Filling in the Opening Balance field in the Add New Account dialog box (or the Edit Account dialog box, for that matter) automatically adds the opening balance to the Opening Bal Equity account, which accountants consider sloppy bookkeeping. Instead, they usually recommend creating a general journal entry from your trial balance for most of your accounts. The only exceptions are your Accounts Receivable (AR) and Accounts Payable (AP) accounts. Because QuickBooks requires customer names and vendor names in journal entries that contain AR and AP accounts, you're better off creating invoices and bills to define your AR and AP opening balances. If you work with an accountant, ask her how she'd like you to enter opening balances—or better yet, have her do it.

Whoa! What's a general journal entry? What's a trial balance?

Here's the deal: *General journal entries* (page 421) are a mechanism for moving money between accounts—on paper, that is. A *trial balance* (page 446) is a report that lists all your accounts with their balances in either the Debit or Credit column. In the days of paper-based ledgers, bean counters totaled the Debit and Credit columns. If the totals weren't equal, the accountant had to track down the arithmetic error. QuickBooks' digital brain does the math automatically, and without error. But it's up to you to set up the journal entry properly in the first place.

Your trial balance report (from your accountant or your old accounting system), as of your company file start date, shows account balances as debits or credits. If you begin your QuickBooks company file on the first day of your fiscal year, your trial balance is quite simple—it includes balances only for your balance sheet accounts, not income and expense accounts.

You can use these values to fill in a general journal entry to assign all your accounts' opening balances. For each account, add a line in the general journal entry with the account name and the balance from your trial balance report in either the debit or credit column. Omit your Accounts Receivable and Accounts Payable accounts in the general journal entry. Then, create invoices and bills to define the opening balances for those accounts. You can download a QuickBooks company file that includes an opening balance general journal entry from *www.missingmanuals.com/cds*.

11. **Click Save & New to save the current account and begin the next one.**

    If you want to save the account you just created and close the Add New Account dialog box, click Save & Close; or click Cancel to discard the account in progress and close the Add New Account dialog box.

12. **If the Set Up Online Services dialog box appears, click Yes if you want to set up a bank account for online services.**

    If you want to set up the account for online banking later—or never—click No. If you click Yes, QuickBooks' windows close while you go through the setup. (See Chapter 22 to learn about online services and QuickBooks.)

Viewing Account Names and Numbers

Perhaps it's the nature of accounting, but financial professionals put great store in account numbers. You can earn the eternal gratitude of your bookkeeper or accountant by assigning and displaying account numbers in QuickBooks.

Turning on the "Use account numbers" preference (page 550) displays account numbers in the Chart of Accounts window, account drop-down lists, and account fields. With the "Use account numbers" checkbox turned on, the Add New Account and Edit Account dialog boxes display the Number box, so you can add or modify an account's number.

Note: Turning off the "Use account numbers" checkbox doesn't remove account numbers you've already added. You can see them again by simply turning the checkbox back on. However, you can't add account numbers to any accounts that you create while the checkbox is turned off. If you create an account anyway, you can edit it (page 58) to add the account number.

When you use subaccounts, QuickBooks displays both the parent account name and the subaccount name in account fields, which often makes it impossible to tell which account a transaction uses, as Figure 3-5 shows. If you use account numbers and want to see only the lowest-level subaccount in Account fields, turn on the "Show lowest subaccount only" checkbox (page 558).

Modifying Accounts

If you stick to your account numbering and naming conventions, you'll have few reasons to edit accounts. In the Edit Account dialog box, you can tweak an account name or description, adjust an account number to make room for new accounts, or change an account's level in the chart of accounts hierarchy.

You're not likely to change the Type field unless you chose the wrong type when you created the account. If you do want to change the account type, back up your QuickBooks file first (see page 163), in case the change has effects that you didn't anticipate. QuickBooks has several restrictions on changing account types. You can't change account types under the following conditions:

- An account has subaccounts.

- You try to change an Accounts Receivable or Accounts Payable account to another account type, or vice versa.

- QuickBooks automatically created the account, like Undeposited Funds.

To modify an account, in the Chart of Accounts window, select the account you want to edit and press Ctrl+E. In the Edit Account dialog box, make the changes you want, and then click OK when you're done. You can also open the Edit Account dialog box by clicking Account at the bottom of the Chart of Accounts window and then choosing Edit Account from the drop-down menu.

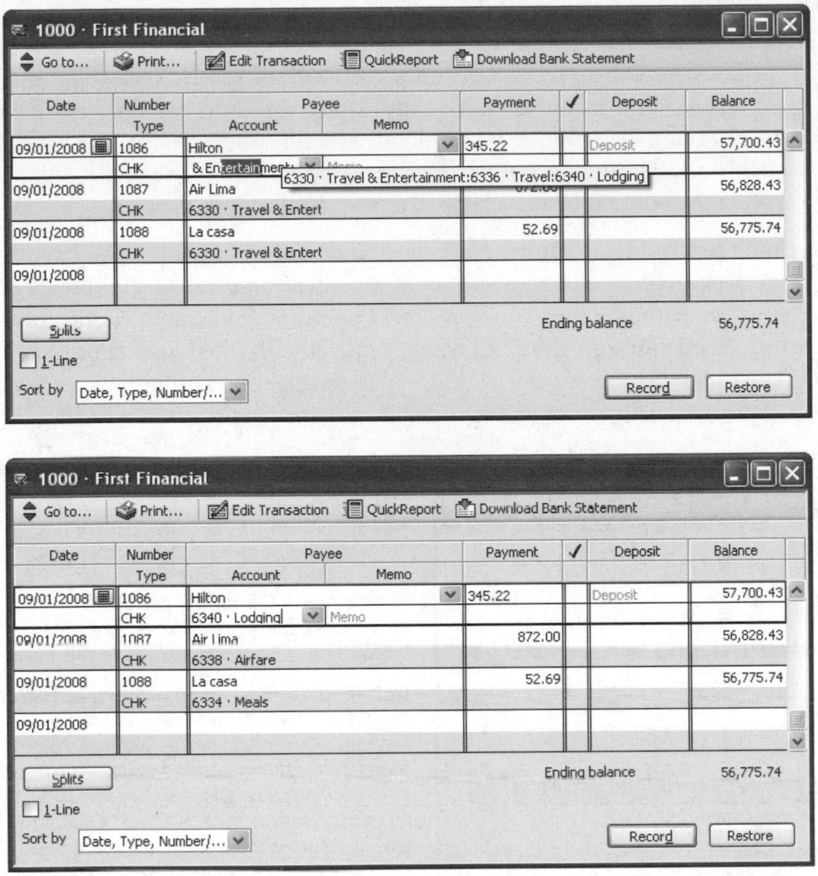

Figure 3-5:
Top: QuickBooks combines the name of the parent account and the name of the subaccount as one long name in Account fields and drop-down lists. In many instances, only the top-level account is visible unless you scroll within the Account field.

Bottom: When you turn on the "Show lowest subaccount only" checkbox, the Account field shows the subaccount number and name, which is exactly what you need to identify the assigned account.

Tip: The Chart of Accounts window works much like other list windows. For example, you can sort the account list by different columns or drag accounts in the list to a different location. See page 157 to learn how to sort and rearrange lists.

Hiding and Deleting Accounts

If you create an account by mistake, you can delete it. However, because Quick-Books drops your financial transactions into account buckets and you don't want to throw away historical information, you'll usually want to hide accounts that you don't use anymore instead of deleting them. For example, you wouldn't delete your Nutrition Service income account just because you've discontinued your nutrition consulting service to focus on selling your new book, *The See Food Diet*. The income you earned from that service in the past needs to stay in your records.

Hiding Accounts

The records of past transactions are important, whether you want to review the amount of business you've received from a customer or the IRS is asking unsettling questions. Hiding accounts doesn't mean you withhold key financial information from prying eyes. When you hide an account, the account continues to hold your historical transactions, but it doesn't appear in QuickBooks' account lists, so you can't choose it by mistake with a misplaced mouse click.

Hiding and reactivating accounts (Figure 3-6) also comes in handy when you use QuickBooks' predefined charts of accounts, explained on page 46. If QuickBooks overwhelms you with accounts you don't think you need, hide the accounts for the time being. When you find yourself saying, "Gosh, I wish I had an account for the accumulated depreciation of vehicles," the solution might be as simple as reactivating a hidden account.

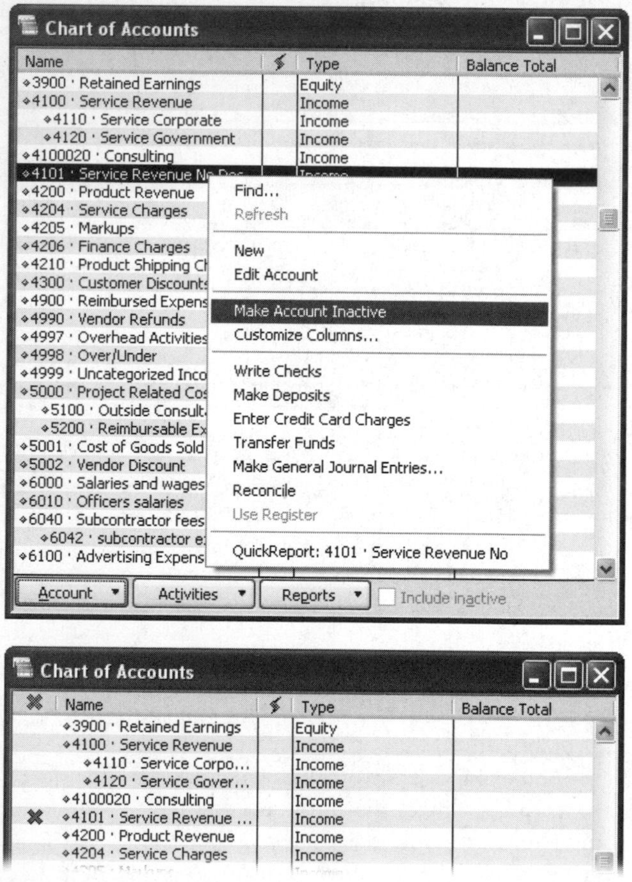

Figure 3-6:
Top: To hide an account, in the Chart of Accounts window, right-click the account and choose Make Account Inactive from the shortcut menu. The account and any subaccounts disappear from the chart of accounts.

Bottom: To reactivate an account, first view all accounts: At the bottom of the Chart of Accounts window, turn on the "Include inactive" checkbox. QuickBooks adds a column with an X as its heading and displays an X in that column for every inactive account in the list. Click the X next to the account name. If the account has subaccounts, in the Activate Group dialog box, click Yes to reactivate the account and any subaccounts.

Deleting Accounts

You can delete an account only if nothing in QuickBooks references it in any way. An account with references within QuickBooks is a red flag that deleting it might not be the right choice. If that red flag isn't enough to deter you, the sheer tedium of removing references to an account should nudge you toward hiding the account instead. If you insist on deleting an account, here are the conditions that prevent you from doing so and what you have to do to remove the constraints:

- **An item uses the account.** If you create any items that use the account as an income account, an expense account, cost of goods sold account, or inventory asset account, you can't delete the account. Edit the items to use other accounts, as described on page 127.

- **The account has subaccounts.** You have to delete all subaccounts before you can delete the parent account.

- **Payroll uses the account.** You can't delete an account if your payroll setup uses it. See Chapter 14 to learn how to modify your payroll and payroll liabilities accounts.

- **At least one transaction references the account.** If you create a transaction that uses the account, either edit the transaction to use a different account or consider hiding the account if you want to keep the transaction the way it is.

- **The account has a balance.** An account balance comes from either an opening balance transaction or other transactions that reference the account. You remove an account balance by deleting all the transactions in the account (or reassigning them to another account).

To delete transactions, in the Chart of Accounts window, double-click the account name. For bank accounts and other accounts with balances, QuickBooks opens a register window, where you can select a transaction and then press Ctrl+D to delete that transaction.

For accounts without balances, QuickBooks opens an Account QuickReport window. To delete a transaction that appears in the report, double-click the transaction. QuickBooks opens a dialog box (for instance, the Write Checks dialog box appears if the transaction is a check). Choose Edit → Delete Check or the corresponding delete command for the type of transaction you chose.

After you've deleted all references to the account, in the Chart of Accounts window, select the account you want to delete, and then press Ctrl+D or, on the QuickBooks menu bar, choose Edit → Delete Account. If references to the account are indeed gone, QuickBooks asks you to confirm that you want to delete the account; click Yes.

Merging Accounts

Suppose you find multiple accounts for the same purpose—Postage and Mail Expense, say—lurking in your chart of accounts. Rather than punishing your QuickBooks experts, it's more productive to merge the accounts into one and then remind everyone who creates accounts in QuickBooks about your account naming conventions. (You haven't gotten around to setting up account naming conventions? See page 51 for some guidelines.)

Tip: Before you merge accounts, see what your accountant thinks. There's no going back once you've merged two accounts–they're merged for good. And the QuickBooks audit trail (page 640) doesn't keep track of this kind of change.

When you merge accounts, QuickBooks sweeps all the transactions from both accounts into the account that you keep. Each type of account has a distinct purpose, so you can merge accounts only if they're the same type. As an experienced manager, you can imagine the havoc that merging income and expense accounts would cause in your financial statements.

Note: If you find two accounts with similar names but different types, those accounts might not represent the same thing. For instance, a Telephone Ex. expense account probably represents what you pay for your monthly telephone service, while the Telephone Eq. asset account might represent the big telephone switch that your mega-corporation owns. In this situation, the accounts should be separate, although more meaningful names and descriptions would help differentiate them.

Here's how to eliminate an extraneous account:

1. **Switch to single-user mode, as described on page 161.**

   You have to be in single-user mode to merge accounts. Be nice to your fellow QuickBooks workers by making these changes outside of working hours. If you have to merge accounts during the workday, remember to tell your coworkers they can log into the program after you've switched the company file back to multi-user mode.

2. **To open the Chart of Accounts window, press Ctrl+A. Then, in the chart of accounts list, select the name of the account that you want to eliminate and press Ctrl+E.**

   The Edit Account dialog box opens.

3. **In the Edit Account dialog box, change the account number and name to match the values for the account you want to keep.**

   As long as you get the letters and numbers right, QuickBooks takes care of matching uppercase and lowercase for you.

If you don't remember the number and name of the account you're keeping, drag the Chart of Accounts window and the Edit Account dialog box so you can see both at the same time. If QuickBooks won't let you do that, you might have the One Window preference set. See page 557 to learn how to change your window display to show multiple windows.

4. **Click OK.**

   QuickBooks displays a message informing you that the name is in use and asks if you want to merge the accounts.

5. **Click Yes to merge the accounts.**

   In the chart of accounts list, the account you renamed disappears and any transactions for that account now belong to the account you kept.

Setting Up Customers and Jobs

You may be fond of strutting around your sales department proclaiming, "Nothing happens until somebody *sells* something!" As it turns out, you can quote that tired adage in your accounting department, too. Whether you sell products or services, the first sale to a new customer can initiate a flurry of activity, including creating a new *customer* in QuickBooks, assigning a *job* for the work, and the ultimate goal of all this effort—*invoicing* your customer (sending a bill for your services and products and how much the customer owes) to collect some income.

The people who buy what you sell have plenty of nicknames: customers, clients, consumers, patrons, patients, purchasers, donors, members, shoppers, and so on. QuickBooks throws out the thesaurus and applies one term—customer—to every person or organization that buys from you. In QuickBooks, a *customer* is a record of information about your real-life customer. The program takes the data you enter for customers and fills in invoices and other sales forms with your customers' names, addresses, payment terms, and other information. If you play it safe and define a credit limit, QuickBooks even reminds you when orders put customers over their limits.

To QuickBooks, a *job* is a record of a real-life project that you agreed (or perhaps begged) to perform for a customer—remodeling a kitchen, designing an advertising campaign, or tracking down the safety deposit box that matches your customer's key. Regardless of how your organization works, customers and jobs are inseparable in QuickBooks. Both the New Customer dialog box and the Edit Customer dialog box, which you'll meet in this chapter, include tabs for customer information *and* job information. When you create a customer, in effect, you get one job built in automatically.

Some organizations don't track jobs, and if your company is one of those, you don't have to create jobs in QuickBooks. For example, retail stores sell products, not projects. Even consultants who usually work on projects sometimes work on retainer, which provides a steady income that isn't related to one specific project. In these situations, you simply create your customers in QuickBooks and move on to invoicing them for their purchases without assigning the income to a job.

Real-world customers are essential to your success, but do you need customers in QuickBooks? Even if you run a primarily cash business, creating customers in QuickBooks could still be a good idea. For example, setting the repeat customers at your store up as customers in QuickBooks not only saves you time by automatically filling in their information on each new sales receipt, it also gives you time to help them become even better customers. And, because your retail business isn't job-oriented, you can just pretend the fields for job information aren't there. See the box on page 91 to learn more. (If you have a point-of-sale system, like QuickBooks POS, you can track customer sales there and leave customers out of QuickBooks completely.)

On the other hand, when your business revolves around projects, you can create a job in QuickBooks for each project you do for a customer. Suppose you're a plumber and you regularly do work for a general contractor. You might create several jobs, one for each place you plumb: Smith house, Jones house, and Winfrey house. In QuickBooks, you can track income and expenses by job and gauge each one's profitability. This chapter guides you through customer and job creation and helps you decide how to apply customer and job fields in your business.

Before You Create Customers and Jobs

QuickBooks doesn't care if you create customers and jobs without any forethought, but it pays to take the time to set them up properly. If you want to report and analyze your financial performance to see where your business comes from and which type is most profitable, categorizing your QuickBooks customers and jobs is the way to go. For example, customer and job types can help you produce a report of kitchen remodel jobs that are in progress for residential customers. With that report, you can order catered dinners to treat those clients to customer service they'll brag about to their friends.

If you take the time to plan your customers and jobs in QuickBooks in advance, you'll save yourself hours of effort later, when you need information about your business. You can add customer and job *categories* (as well as customers and jobs) at any time. If you don't have time to add categories now, come back to this section when you're ready to learn how.

Categorizing Customers and Jobs

Categorizing your customers and jobs is one way to slice and dice your business reports to show what parts of your business are doing well and what parts need closer attention. For a construction company, knowing that your commercial customers cause fewer headaches *and* that doing work for them is more profitable than residential jobs is a strong motivator to focus your future marketing efforts on commercial work. Organize your customers and jobs by type, and you'll easily get some insightful analysis. The box below explains how you can analyze your business even more.

GEM IN THE ROUGH

Categorizing with Classes

The Class Tracking feature, explained in detail on page 138, is a powerful and often misunderstood way to categorize business. When you turn on Class Tracking, *classes* appear in an additional field in your transactions so you can classify your business in various ways. Their power derives from their ability to cross income, customer, and job boundaries. Say you want to track how much each sales region actually sells to figure out who gets to host your annual sales shindig. Your income accounts show sales by products and services, even if each region sells all those items. Customer types won't help if some large customers buy products from several of your sales regions. The same goes if a job requires a smorgasbord of what you sell.

To solve this sales-by-region dilemma, you can create a class for each region. When you turn on Class Tracking, every transaction includes a Class field. Unlike the Customer Type and Job Type fields, which you assign when you create a customer or job, a transaction's Class field starts out blank. For each invoice, sales receipt, and so on, choose the class for the region that made the sale. By doing so, you can produce a report sorted by class that totals each region's productivity.

As you'll learn on page 138, classes can track information that spans multiple customers and jobs, such as business unit, company division, and office location. But don't expect miracles—classes work best when you stick to only one use of class. Mixing business unit and location classes tend to render the classes ineffective.

Understanding customer types

Business owners often like to look at the performance of different segments of their business. Say your building supply business has expanded over the years to include sales to homeowners, so you probably want to know how much you sell to homeowners versus professional contractors. You could designate each customer as Homeowner or Contractor to make this comparison, and then sort invoices by Customer Type, as shown in Figure 4-1. As you'll learn on page 145, categorizing a customer is as easy as choosing a customer type from the aptly named Customer Type List.

Note: As you'll see throughout this book, QuickBooks lists make it easy to fill in information in most QuickBooks dialog boxes by choosing from a list instead of typing.

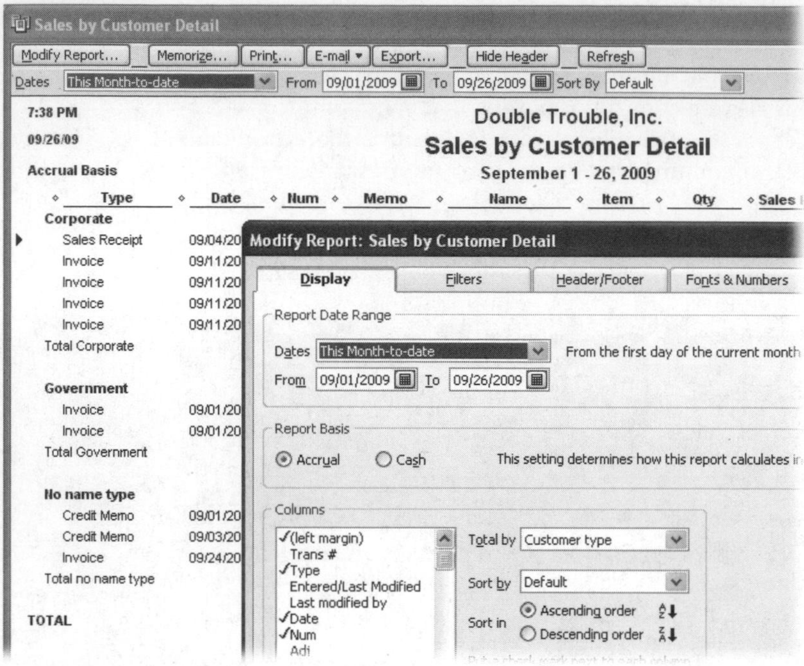

Figure 4-1:
The "Sales by Customer Detail" report initially totals income by customer. To subtotal income by customer type (corporate and government customers as shown here), click Modify Report. On the Display tab, choose "Customer type" in the "Total by" drop-down list, and then click OK.

Customer types are yours to mold into whatever categories help you analyze your business. A healthcare provider might classify customers by their insurance, because reimbursement levels depend on whether a patient has Medicare, major medical insurance, or pays privately. A clothing maker might classify customers as custom, retail, or wholesale, because the markup percentages are different for each. And a training company could categorize customers by how they learned about the company's services.

When you create your company using industry-specific editions of QuickBooks or with the EasyStep Interview (page 21), QuickBooks fills in the Customer Type List with a few typical types of customers for your industry. If your business sense is eccentric, you can delete QuickBooks' suggestions and replace them with your own entries. As a landscaper, you might include customer types such as Lethal, Means Well, and Green Thumb, so you can decide whether Astroturf, cacti, or orchids are most appropriate.

Tip: A common beginners' mistake is creating customer types that don't relate to customer characteristics. For example, if you provide consulting services in several areas—like financial forecasting, investment advice, and reading fortunes—your customers might hire you to perform any or all of those services. If you classify your customers by the services you offer, you'll wonder which customer type to choose when someone hires you for two different services.

Here are some suggestions for applying customer types and other QuickBooks features to analyze your business in different ways.

- **Customer business type.** Use customer types to classify your customers by their business sector, such as corporate, government, and small business.

- **Nonprofit "customers."** For nonprofit organizations, customer types such as Member, Individual, Corporation, Foundation, and Government Agency can help you target fundraising efforts.

- **Location or region.** Customer types also help track business performance when your company spans multiple regions, offices, or business units.

- **Services.** To track how much business you do for each service you offer, set up separate income accounts in your Chart of Accounts, as outlined on page 53.

- **Products.** To track product sales, create one or more income accounts in your Chart of Accounts.

- **Marketing.** To identify the income you earned based on how customers learned about your services, create classes such as Referral, Web, Newspaper, and Blimp. With these categories, you can create a report that shows the revenue you've earned from different marketing efforts—and whether each marketing strategy is worth the money.

- **Customer support.** You may find it handy to use classes to categorize customers by their headache factor, such as High Maintenance, Average, and Easy To Please (as long as you're careful to keep the class designation off of the invoices you send out).

Creating a customer type

You can create the types of customers you want when you set up your QuickBooks company file or at any time after setup is complete. To create a customer type, follow these steps:

1. **If the company file isn't already open, choose File → Open Previous Company, and then choose the company file you want to open.**

   Page 30 describes the different methods you can use to open company files.

2. **Choose Lists → Customer & Vendor Profile Lists → Customer Type List.**

   The Customer Type List window opens, displaying the customer types that already exist.

3. **To create a new customer type, press Ctrl+N or, at the bottom of the Customer Type List window, click Customer Type, and then choose New.**

   The New Customer Type dialog box opens, shown in Figure 4-2.

4. **Type a name for the customer type in the Customer Type box, and then click OK.**

   You can set up a customer type as a subtype of another, such as Federal, State, and Local subtypes within the Government customer type. Figure 4-2 shows you how.

5. **To create another customer type, click Next and add another type.**

   Lather, rinse, and repeat.

When you close the New Customer Type dialog box, the new customer type appears in the Customer Type List.

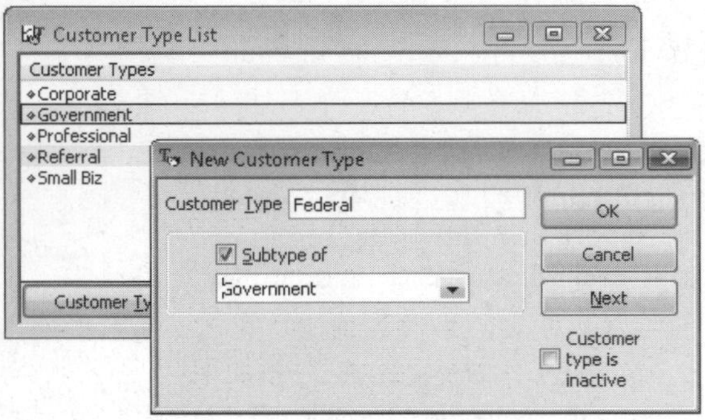

Figure 4-2:
To define a customer type as a subtype of another, turn on the "Subtype of" checkbox in the New Customer Type dialog box. Then, in the drop-down list, choose the top-level customer type. For example, if you sell to different levels of government, the top-level customer type could be Government and contain subtypes Federal, State, County, and Local.

Categorizing jobs

Jobs are optional in QuickBooks, so job types matter only when you track your work by job. If your sole source of income is selling organic chicken fat ripple ice cream to health-obsessed carnivores, jobs and job types don't matter. Your relationship with your customers is one long run of selling and delivering products. On the other hand, for project-based businesses, job types add another level of filtering to the reports you produce. If you're a writer, then you can use job types to track the kinds of documents you produce (Manual, White Paper, and Marketing Propaganda, for instance) and filter the Job Profitability Report by job type to see which types of writing are the most lucrative.

Creating a job type is similar to creating a customer type, described in the previous section. With the company file open, choose Lists → Customer & Vendor Profile Lists → Job Type List. With the Job Type List window open, press Ctrl+N to open the New Job Type window. As you do for customer types, type a name for the job type. For a subtype, turn on the "Subtype of" checkbox and choose the job type to which you want to add this subtype.

Creating Customers in QuickBooks

If bringing in business were as easy as creating customers in QuickBooks, sales of QuickBooks would propel Intuit past Microsoft as the largest software company. Face facts—you still have to convince customers to work with your company. But once you've cleared *that* hurdle, creating those customers in QuickBooks is easy. The box below provides some hints on keeping customers straight in QuickBooks.

WORD TO THE WISE

Making Customers Easy to Identify

In QuickBooks, the Customer Name field isn't the name that appears on invoices; it's a code that uniquely identifies each of your customers and makes it easy to tell them apart.

If you own a small company with only a few customers, you're not likely to create multiple records for the same customer. Your customer list is short, so you know which ones you've created and you can see them without scrolling in the Customer Center. Even so, it's a good idea to define a standard for customer names. Perhaps you hide customers you haven't worked with in a while, or you have so many customers that it takes all day to scroll through the list.

Consistent naming can help you avoid multiple records for the same customer by preventing you from creating slightly different values in the Customer Name field for that customer. For example, you could end up with three customers in QuickBooks, such as Cales's Capers, Cales Capers, and CalesCapers, all representing the same events organizer.

QuickBooks doesn't enforce naming conventions. After you define rules that work for your business, you have to discipline yourself and apply those rules each time you create a new customer. You're free to choose from alphanumeric characters and punctuation. Here are a few of the more common naming conventions:

- The first few letters of the customer's company name followed by a unique numeric identifier. This standard is easy to apply and differentiates customers as long as their names don't all begin with the same words. For example, if most of your customers are wine stores with unimaginative owners, your customer names could end up as Wine001, Wine002, and Wine003. But if your customers are Zinfandels To Go, Merlot Mania, and Cabernet Cabinet, this system works nicely.

- For individuals, the last name followed by the first name and a numeric ID to make the name unique. Although unusual names such as Zaphod Beeblebrox render a numeric ID unnecessary, using this standard ensures that all customer names are unique.

- The actual company name with any punctuation and spaces omitted. Removing spaces and punctuation from company names helps eliminate multiple versions of the same name. If you choose this convention, capital letters at the beginning of each word (called *camel caps*) make the customer name more readable. For instance, Icantbelieveitsyogurt is a headache waiting to happen, but ICantBelieveItsYogurt looks much like its spaced and punctuated counterpart.

- A unique alphanumeric code. Customer:Job drop-down menus and reports sort customers by the Customer Name field. Codes like X123Y4JQ use only a few characters to produce unique identifiers, but cryptic codes make it difficult to pick out the customer you want from drop-down lists or to sort reports in a meaningful way. Stick with using part of the customer name whenever possible.

The Customer Center (Figure 4-3) is your starting point for creating, modifying, and viewing customers and jobs. QuickBooks provides four easy ways to open the Customer Center window:

- From anywhere in the program, press Ctrl+J.

- On the left side of the QuickBooks Home page, click Customers.

- On the icon bar, click Customer Center.

- On the QuickBooks menu bar, choose Customers → Customer Center.

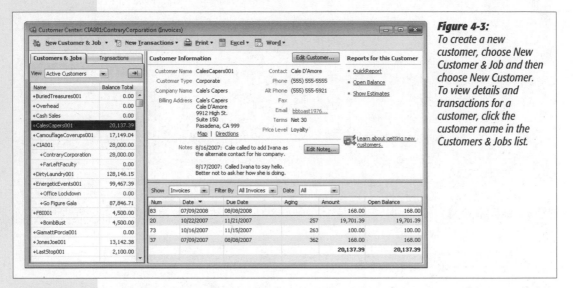

Figure 4-3:
To create a new customer, choose New Customer & Job and then choose New Customer. To view details and transactions for a customer, click the customer name in the Customers & Jobs list.

Creating a New Customer

QuickBooks is quite accommodating when it comes to creating customers. If you run a mom-and-pop shop and don't add new customers very often, you can create a customer when you create the customer's first invoice. The handy *<Add New>* menu command in every drop-down list of customer and job types is your ticket to just-in-time customer and job type creation. For larger outfits that sign new customers up all the time, creating customers in batches is much more efficient. Without closing and reopening the New Customer dialog box, you can create several customers in one session. Or you can use the Add/Edit Multiple List Entries feature (page 86), which is new in QuickBooks 2010, to paste data from Microsoft Excel or copy values from customer to customer.

The box on page 73 tells you how to prevent your QuickBooks' customer list from growing out of control.

In the Customer Center tool bar, create a new customer by clicking New Customer & Job → New Customer. The New Customer dialog box opens, as shown in Figure 4-4. Customer Name is the only field you need to fill in. Type the unique name or code for your new customer, following the customer naming convention you've chosen, as described in the box on page 71.

TROUBLESHOOTING MOMENT

How Many Names?

If you're a big fish in the small business pond, limitations on the number of names can cause problems. In QuickBooks Pro and Premier Editions, the maximum number of names (including customers, vendors, employees, and other names) is 14,500 and the maximum number of customer names is 10,000. To make matters worse, once you reach the limit, not only can you not add more names, deleting existing names doesn't even free up slots in the lists.

Here are a few techniques you can use to avoid this maddening situation:

- **Conserve customer names.** You can be frugal with names by creating one customer to represent many individual sales. For example, you can aggregate all your cash sales under one customer, Cash Sales. Mind you, by doing so, you can't produce sales reports by customer name. You can add the buyer's name to the Bill To field in sales forms so you and the buyer have a record of their purchase.

- **Keep an eye on how many names you have.** Press F2 at any time to view the number of entries you have in each list. They appear in the List Information box in the middle-right of the window.

- **Upgrade.** If there's no getting around your company's gluttony for names, QuickBooks Enterprise Solutions 7.0 and more recent versions let you add up to one million names. *Caveat emptor*: if your company has tens of thousands of customers, congratulations! But honestly, you shouldn't be reading this book. You need an accounting program other than QuickBooks that can handle the accounting needs of a large company.

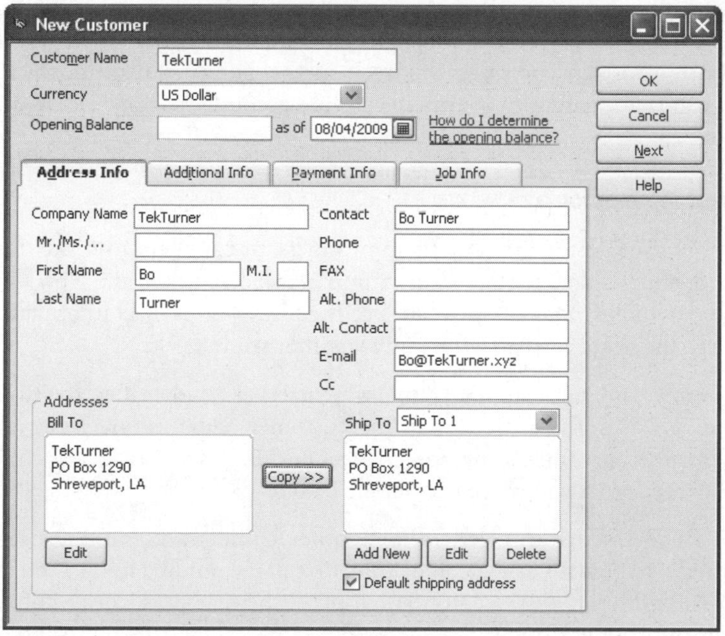

Figure 4-4:
Although the Opening Balance box beckons from below the Customer Name in the New Customer dialog box, it's better to leave it blank. The box on page 57 explains the best way to define a customer's opening balance.

Tip: After you create one customer, you can click Next to save that customer record and start a new one. On the other hand, to create a job for a customer, you must first close the New Customer dialog box and then open the New Job dialog box. Unless opening and closing the New Customer and New Job dialog boxes gives you a feeling of accomplishment, create all your customers first and then add the jobs for each customer.

FREQUENTLY ASKED QUESTION

Opening Act

Should I add an opening balance for new customers?

Since the Opening Balance and As Of fields are always visible at the top of the New Customer dialog box, you might think these fields are incredibly important. Actually, you're better off skipping them altogether.

Entering an opening balance as of a specific date is a shortcut that eliminates having to create the invoices that generate the customer's current balance. But that shortcut comes at a price: If customers haven't paid, then you might have a hard time collecting the money, especially if you can't tell them what services and products you delivered, how much

they cost, the invoice numbers, and when the invoices were due. In addition, when your customers *do* pay, you can't accept those payments against specific invoices to track your accounts receivable.

The best way to build your customer's balance is to create QuickBooks invoices for the invoices that the customer hasn't paid yet. That way, you'll have complete documentation about those sales and detailed records in your Accounts Receivable account. Also, you can apply the payments that come in to settle those invoices.

If you turn on the multiple currency option (page 570), the Currency box appears below the Customer Name box. QuickBooks automatically fills in the Currency box with your home currency, so you usually don't have to change this value. If the customer pays in a foreign currency, choose it in the Currency drop-down list. QuickBooks creates a separate Accounts Receivable account (page 332) for each currency you use.

Entering address information

If you plan to bill your customers, ship them products, or call them to make them feel appreciated, address and contact information is important. On the New Customer dialog box's Address Info tab, you can specify address and contact information. Here's a guide to the fields you can enter and what they're good for:

- **Company Name.** Unlike Customer Name, which acts as an identifier, the Company Name field is nothing more than the customer name as you want it to appear on invoices and other forms you create. QuickBooks automatically copies the company name that you type into the Bill To box.

- **Contact.** To address invoices, letters, and other company communications, enter the primary contact's salutation or title, first name, middle initial, and last name in the appropriate fields. As often happens, the first person you contact isn't the person who gets things done day after day. If this turns out to be the case, you can always make this dependable resource the primary contact and assign the figurehead as the alternate contact. QuickBooks automatically copies the salutation and name that you type to the Bill To box and the Contact box.

- **Bill To address.** To complete the address for invoices, type the street address, city, state, country, and postal code, or copy the information from another program (page 79).

  To view or enter address information as separate fields, including Address, City, State/Province, Zip/Postal code, and Country, click the Edit button below the Bill To section. In the Edit Address Information dialog box, QuickBooks automatically turns on the "Show this window again when address is incomplete or unclear" checkbox, which tells the program to notify you when you forget a field like the city or when the address is ambiguous. For example, if the address for your biggest toy customer is Santa Claus, North Pole, QuickBooks opens the Edit Address Information dialog box so that you can fatten the address up a bit with a street, city, and arctic postal code.

- **Ship To address.** If the billing address and the shipping address are the same, click Copy>> to replicate the contents of the Bill To field in the Ship To field. (The greater-than symbols on the button indicate the direction that Quick-Books copies the address.) If you don't ship products to the customer, skip the Ship To field altogether.

Note: You can define more than one Ship To address, which is perfect for a single customer with multiple locations. To add another Ship To address, click Add New and fill in the boxes. Once you have shipping addresses created, you can choose the one you want in the Ship To drop-down list. When the shipping address you use most often is visible, turn on the "Default shipping address" checkbox to tell QuickBooks to pick that address automatically. Click the Edit or Delete buttons to modify or remove a shipping address, respectively.

- **Additional contact information.** QuickBooks gets you started by copying the contents of the First Name and Last Name fields into the Contact field. If you plan to look up contact information such as phone number and email in Quick-Books rather than in your contact program (Outlook, for example), fill in the other fields on the Address Info tab to specify the contact's phone number, fax number, alternate phone number like a cellphone number, email address, an email address to carbon copy, and an alternate contact.

Specifying additional customer information

The New Customer dialog box's Additional Info tab (Figure 4-5) serves up several fields that categorize your customers and simplify your bookkeeping. Although they're optional, some fields speed up entering transactions down the road by storing the values you use most frequently. Other fields appear or disappear depending on the preferences you choose (preferences are the topic of Chapter 23). For example, if you charge sales tax, you need to turn on QuickBooks Sales Tax preferences if you want the Additional Info tab to include the Tax Code, Tax Item, and Resale Number fields.

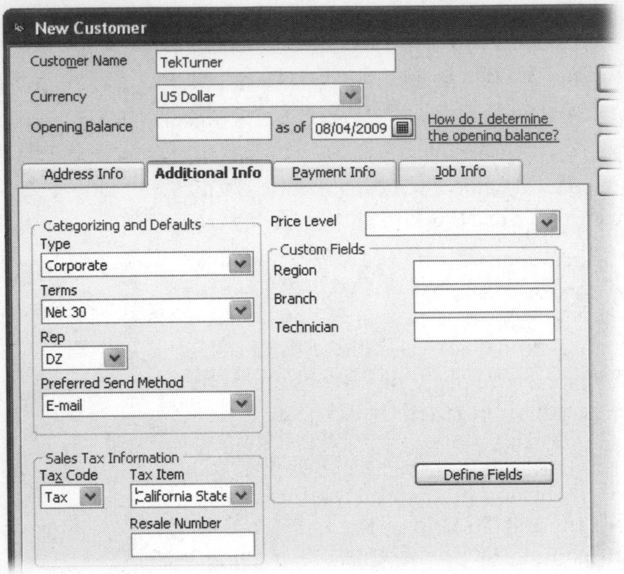

Figure 4-5:
Most of the fields on the Additional Info tab use QuickBooks' lists. To jump directly to the entry you want in long lists, in any text box with a drop-down list, type the first few characters of that entry. QuickBooks selects the first entry that matches the characters you've typed and continues to reselect the best match as you continue typing. You can also scroll to the entry in the list and click to select it. If the entry you want doesn't exist, click <Add New> to create it.

Here are the fields you might see on the Additional Info tab and some ways you can use them:

- **Type.** Categorize the customer (see page 145) by choosing a type from the Type drop-down list, which displays the entries from your Customer Type List, such as government, health insurance, or private pay, if you run a healthcare company.

- **Terms.** The choice you select in the Terms field represents the payment terms the customer has agreed to. The entries you see in the Terms drop-down menu come from the Terms List (page 147), which represents payment terms for your customers *and* the ones you accept from your vendors. QuickBooks provides several of the most common payment terms, such as Due on Receipt and Net 30, but you can choose *<Add New>* at the top of the drop-down list to define additional payment terms in the Terms List. If you leave the Terms field blank in a customer record, you have to choose the payment terms every time you create an invoice for that customer.

- **Rep.** Choosing a name in the Rep field links a customer to a sales representative, which is helpful if you want to track sales representatives' results. But reps don't have to be sales representatives. One of the best ways to provide good customer service is to assign a customer service representative to a customer. When you choose *<Add New>* to create a new Rep entry (page 144), you can select existing names from the Employee List, Vendor List, and the Other Names List.

- **Preferred Send Method.** Choose None, Mail, or E-mail to identify the method that your customer prefers for receiving documents. Choose None if you typically print documents and mail them the old-fashioned way instead of using

QuickBooks' add-on mail feature (page 316). If you choose E-mail, Quick-Books automatically turns on the E-mail checkbox when you create forms such as invoices for the customer. The Mail method uses an add-on QuickBooks service to mail invoices. You can't add a new entry to the Preferred Send Method list, so if you use carrier pigeons to correspond with your incarcerated customers, you'll just have to remember that preference.

• **Sales Tax Information.** The Sales Tax Information area appears only if you turn on the Sales Tax preference (page 580). If the customer pays sales tax, choose an entry in the Tax Item drop-down list, which specifies the tax rate percentage. See page 124 for instructions on setting up sales tax items and page 263 for the full scoop on charging sales tax.

Customers who buy products for resale usually don't pay sales tax because that would tax the products twice. (Who says tax authorities don't have hearts?) To bypass the sales tax, choose Non (for "nontaxable sales") in the Tax Code drop-down list, and then type the customer's resale number in the Resale Number field. That way, if tax auditors pay you a visit, the resale number tells them where the burden of sales tax should fall.

• **Price Level.** More often than not, customers pay different prices for the same product. Consider the labyrinth of pricing options for seats on airplanes. In QuickBooks, price levels represent discounts or markups that you apply to transactions. For example, you might have one price level called Top20, which applies a 20 percent discount for your best customers, and another price level called AuntMabel that extends a 50 percent discount to your Aunt Mabel because she fronted you the money to start your business. See page 141 to learn how to define price levels.

Note: In QuickBooks Pro, your only choice is fixed percentage price levels, which means the price levels you define increase or decrease prices on all items by fixed percentages. On the other hand, QuickBooks Premier adds the Per Item price level type as an option. Per item price levels open the door to setting the dollar amount of individual items you sell for different customers or jobs.

• **Custom Fields.** QuickBooks provides 15 custom fields, which you can use to store important information that QuickBooks didn't see fit to give you out of the box. Because custom fields don't use drop-down lists, you have to type your entries and take care to enter values consistently. Learn more about custom fields on page 155.

Designating payment information

That's right: The New Customer dialog box has still more fields for storing customer information. The Payment Info tab, shown in Figure 4-6, is the place to say how the customer pays and how much credit you're willing to extend.

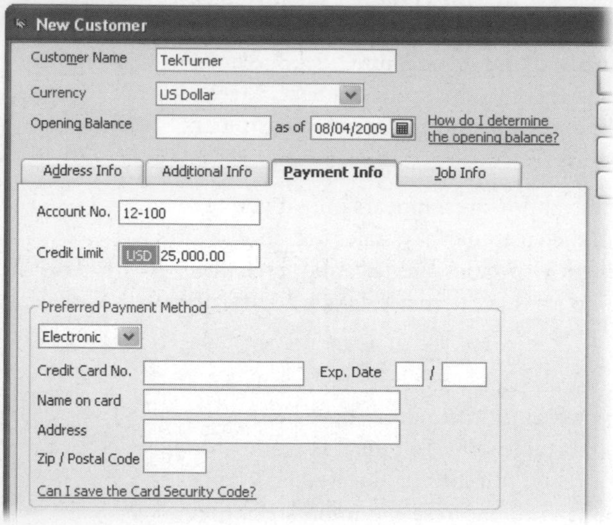

Figure 4-6:
On the Payment Info tab, only one field has a drop-down menu of commonly used values. You have to type the values you want in all the fields except the Preferred Payment Method field, whose drop-down menu displays the Payment Method List (page 149).

You can use the following fields to specify the customer's payment information:

- **Account No.** Account numbers are optional in QuickBooks. Large accounting programs often assign unique account numbers, which greatly reduce the time it takes to locate a customer record. In QuickBooks, the Customer Name field works like an identifier, so the Account No. field is best reserved for an account number generated by one of your other business systems. You can use account numbers or the codes in the Customer Name field to both identify and classify your customers. For example, R402 could represent one of your retail customers, whereas W579 could represent a wholesale customer.

- **Credit Limit.** You can specify a dollar value of credit that you're willing to extend to the customer. If you do, QuickBooks warns you when an order or invoice exceeds the customer's credit limit, but that's as far as it goes. It's up to you to reject the order or ship your products COD. If you don't plan to enforce the credit limits you assign, don't bother entering a value in this field.

- **Preferred Payment Method.** Choose the payment method that the customer uses most frequently. The Payment Method List includes several common payment methods such as Cash, Check, and Visa, but you can add others by choosing <Add New>. The payment method you specify for the customer appears automatically in the Receive Payments window (page 332) when you choose the customer. If a regular customer forgets her checkbook and pays with cash, you can simply replace Check with Cash as you create the sales receipt in QuickBooks.

- **Credit card information.** For credit card payments (see page 605 for info on QuickBooks' credit card processing service), you can specify the customer's credit card number, the name that appears on the card, the billing address for the card, the Zip code, and the expiration date. But before you enter this sensitive and valuable information into your QuickBooks file, check for government and merchant card provider restrictions on storing credit card numbers. For example, QuickBooks doesn't let you store the card security code (the three digit code on the back of a credit card) as a security precaution. Even if you can legally store the numbers, consider whether your security procedures are sufficient to protect your customers' credit card information.

ALTERNATE REALITY

Tracking Donors for Nonprofits

For nonprofit organizations, any individual or organization that sends money is a donor (as well as generous), but the term *donor* doesn't appear in most QuickBooks editions. The Premier Nonprofit Edition of QuickBooks talks about donors, pledges, and other nonprofit terms, but QuickBooks Pro focuses single-mindedly on customers, so you may have to get used to mentally saying "donor" whenever you see "customer" in QuickBooks.

Likewise, a job in QuickBooks is the equivalent of a contract or grant. If you need to report on a grant or contract, add a separate job for it to the customer (er, donor) who donated the funds.

Entering members or individual donors as separate customers can max out QuickBooks' customer name limit or increase your company data file to a size that makes QuickBooks' response time slower than your great-grandmother's driving. True, the Enterprise Solutions Edition of QuickBooks provides a larger number of customers, but most nonprofits would choke at that edition's price tag.

To solve this dilemma, create customers in QuickBooks to represent generic pools, such as donors and members, reserving the details of your membership and donor names for a separate database or spreadsheet. For example, create a customer called Unrestricted and post all unrestricted donations to that customer.

Note: The New Customer window includes a Job Info tab, which has fields for job-related information. If you don't track jobs, you could use the Job Status field to store the overall status of your work for the customer, although a contact management or project management program is probably more useful. If you work on more than one job for a customer, skip the Job Info tab, since you'll create separate jobs, as described on page 90.

Customer Data Entry Shortcuts

If you add or edit more than one customer a time, filling in the New Customer dialog box isn't only mind-numbingly tedious, it also wastes time you should spend on more important business tasks like selling, managing cash flow, or finding out who has the incriminating pictures from the Christmas party. Chances are you store customer information in programs other than QuickBooks, such as a customer relationship management (CRM) program to track customer interactions or a word processing program to produce mailing labels. (Page 4 tells you how you can learn about Intuit's CRM product.) If your other programs can create *Excel-compatible files or delimited text files*, you can avoid data entry grunt work by transferring data to or from QuickBooks. Delimited text files are nothing more than files that separate each piece of data with a comma, space, tab, or other character. In both type of files, the same kind of information appears in the same position in each line or row, so QuickBooks (along with other programs) can pull the information into the right places.

When you want to transfer a *ton* of customer information between QuickBooks and other programs, importing and exporting is the way to go. By creating a map between QuickBooks fields and the other program's fields, you can quickly transfer hundreds, even thousands, of records in no time.

Sometimes, though, you want to add (or edit) more than one, but less than a gazillion records. QuickBooks 2010 introduces the perfect tool: the Add/Edit Multiple List Entries command. When you're working with the customer, vendor, or item list, you can use the Add/Edit Multiple List Entries dialog box to paste data from Excel into QuickBooks. Or, to edit existing records, you can filter or search the list to show just the customers (or vendors or items) you want to update and then paste Excel data, type values, or use shortcut commands to copy values between records.

This section covers it all: importing, exporting, and working with multiple entries.

Importing Customer Information

Salespeople learn a lot about companies long before they become customers. For example, knowing who the decision makers are and what they want is at the heart of most sales strategies. If your sales team stores contact names, phone numbers, email addresses, and other information in a program that exports data to delimited files or Excel spreadsheets, why not import the relevant data into QuickBooks when that company finally decides to buy from you?

Tip: You don't have to import every field you've captured so far. Salespeople build relationships with clients by remembering spouses' and kids' names or favorite sports teams, but much of that information doesn't belong in QuickBooks.

To import data into QuickBooks, you first have to export a delimited text file or a spreadsheet from the other program (page 599). The data is compartmentalized by separating each piece of information with commas or tabs, or by cubbyholing them into columns and rows in a spreadsheet file.

An exported delimited file isn't necessarily ready to import into QuickBooks, though. Headings in the delimited file or spreadsheet might identify the field names in the program that held the information, but QuickBooks has no way of knowing the correlation between the other program's fields and its own.

QuickBooks looks for keywords in the import file to tell it what to do, as shown in Figure 4-7. As a result, you'll need to rename some headings to transform an export file produced by another program into an import file that QuickBooks can read. QuickBooks' customer keywords and the fields they represent appear in Table 4-1. Fortunately, Excel and other spreadsheet programs make it easy to edit the headings in cells. The box on page 83 describes how to use spreadsheets for other data tasks. When your exported file looks something like the file in Figure 4-7, save it in Excel 2007 by clicking the Office button and then choosing Save (in Excel 2003, choose File → Save).

Tip: To see how QuickBooks wants a delimited file to look, export your current QuickBooks customer list to an .iif file (page 83) and then open it in Excel.

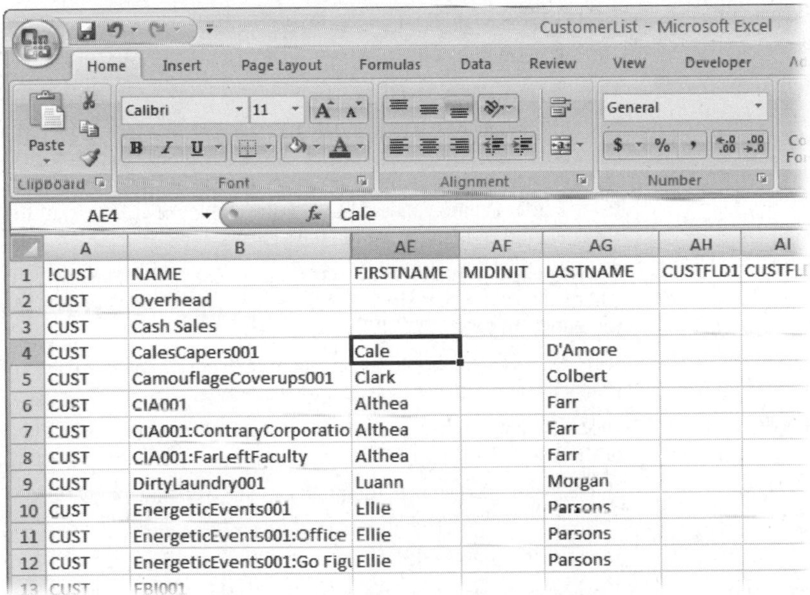

Figure 4-7:
The imported file has to use field names that match QuickBooks field names. For example, replace a Last_Name heading with LASTNAME, which is the keyword for the last name field in QuickBooks. The first column has to include the keywords QuickBooks looks for to identify customer records. And the first cell in the first row of a customer import file has to contain the text !CUST.

Table 4-1. *Customer keywords and their respective fields*

Keyword	Field contents
NAME	(Required) The Customer Name field, which specifies the name or code that you use to identify the customer.
BADDR1 – BADDR5	Up to five lines of the customer's billing address.
SADDR1 – SADDR5	Up to five lines of the customer's shipping address.
PHONE1	The number stored in the Phone Number field.
PHONE2	The customer's alternate phone number.
FAXNUM	The customer's fax number.

Table 4-1. *Customer keywords and their respective fields (continued)*

Keyword	Field contents
EMAIL	The customer's email address.
NOTE	Despite the keyword, this field is the name or number of the account, stored in the Account No. field. To set up a customer as an online payee, you have to assign an account number.
CONT1	The name of the primary contact for the customer.
CONT2	The name of an alternate contact for the customer.
CTYPE	The customer type category. If you import a customer type that doesn't exist in your Customer Type List, QuickBooks adds the new customer type to the list.
TERMS	The payment terms by which the customer abides.
TAXABLE	Y or N indicates whether you charge sales tax to the customer.
SALESTAXCODE	The code that identifies the sales tax to charge.
LIMIT	The dollar amount of the customer's credit limit with your company.
RESALENUM	The customer's resale number.
REP	The representative who works with the customer. The format for a rep entry is *name:list ID:initials*, such as "Saul Lafite:2:SEL." *Name* represents the name of the representative; the list ID equals 1 if the rep name belongs to the Vendor List, 2 for the Employee List, or 3 for the Other Names List. *Initials* are the rep's initials.
TAXITEM	The name of the type of tax you charge this customer. The name you enter has to correspond to one of the sales tax items on your Item list (described on page 127).
NOTEPAD	This field is your chance to wax poetic about your customer's merits or simply document details you want to remember.
SALUTATION	The salutation or title to prefix to the contact's name, such as Mr., Ms., or Dr.
COMPANYNAME	The name of the customer's company, as you want it to appear on invoices or other documents.
FIRSTNAME	The primary contact's first name.
MIDINIT	The primary contact's middle initial.
LASTNAME	The primary contact's last name.
CUSTFLD1-CUSTFLD15	Custom field entries for the customer, if you've defined any. To learn how to create custom fields, see page 155.
HIDDEN	This field is set to N if the customer is active in your QuickBooks file. Inactive customers are set to Y.
PRICELEVEL	The price level for the customer.

Note: QuickBooks also exports the fields for job information into six columns with the keywords JOBDESC, JOBTYPE, JOBSTATUS, JOBSTART, JOBPROJEND, and JOBEND.

POWER USERS' CLINIC

The Easy Way to View Data

Data is easier to examine when you view an export or import file with a spreadsheet program like Excel, as described in Chapter 24. Most programs can open or import delimited text files, but Excel is a master at reading the records stored in these text files. When you export data to a delimited text file and then open it in Excel, the program pigeonholes the data into cells in a spreadsheet. Because records and fields appear in rows and columns, respectively, you can quickly identify, select, and edit the data you want.

Furthermore, in spreadsheet programs, you can eliminate entire rows or columns with a few deft clicks or keystrokes. The following steps explain how to open a delimited text file with Excel:

1. In Excel 2007, click the Office button and then choose Open. In Excel 2003, choose File → Open (as you would to open any workbook).

2. The delimited text files won't appear in the Open dialog box at first because they're not Excel workbooks. Delimited text files come with a range of file extensions (the three characters that follow the last period in the filename). Because of this, the only way to be sure you'll see your delimited file is to choose All Files in the "Files of type" drop-down list.

3. To open the file, navigate to the folder that contains the delimited text file and double-click the filename. The Text Import Wizard dialog box appears.

4. As you tell the wizard which characters act as delimiters and what type of data appears in each column, the wizard shows you what the data will look like after it's imported into Excel. When the interpretation of the data is correct, click Finish.

5. Now, you can use Excel's commands to rename column headings or delete the columns or rows you don't want to import.

Exporting Customer Information

QuickBooks lets you do lots of cool things with customer information, but say you have a mail merge already set up in FileMaker Pro, or you want to transfer all of your customer records to Access to track product support. You have to export your customer data out of QuickBooks into a file that the other program can read and import.

To extract customer information from QuickBooks, you have three choices:

- **Export your customer information directly to Excel** if you're not sure what information you need, and you'd rather delete and rearrange columns in a spreadsheet program. QuickBooks exports every customer field. Then, you can edit the spreadsheet all you want and transfer the data to yet another program when you're done. (The one downside to this approach is that the spreadsheet includes blank columns between each field column.)

- **Create a report** when you want control over exactly which fields to export. By creating a customized version of the Customer Contact List report, you can export the same set of records repeatedly, creating delimited files, spreadsheets, and so on.

• **Export a text file** of your customer data if you need a delimited text file to load into another program. The delimited file lists each customer in its own row with each field separated by tabs.

Exporting to Excel

In QuickBooks, exporting the Customer List to Excel is a snap, as Figure 4-8 shows. To export all the customer data stored in QuickBooks to an Excel file, in the Customer Center icon bar, click Excel, and then choose Export Customer List to open the Export dialog box. The Excel menu also contains commands for exporting transactions and for importing and pasting spreadsheet data into QuickBooks.

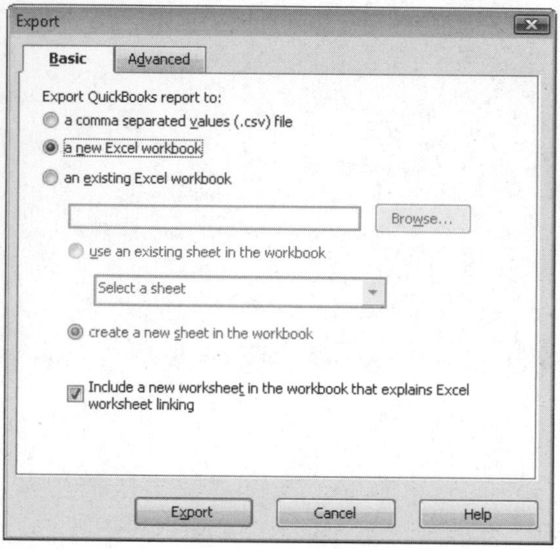

Figure 4-8:
The Export dialog box that appears is already set up to create a new spreadsheet. Click Export at the bottom and you'll be looking at the Customer List in Excel in seconds. If you'd rather give QuickBooks more guidance on creating the spreadsheet, click the Advanced tab and specify options like Autofit to set the column width so you can see all your data, before clicking Export.

Customized exports using the Contact List report

By modifying the settings for the Contact List report, you can export exactly the fields you want for specific customers. For example, storing email addresses in QuickBooks is perfect when you email invoices to customers, but you probably also want them in your email program for the steady stream of communication you exchange with customers about the work you're doing for them. Exporting the entire Customer List is overkill when all you want is the contact name and email address; that's where exporting a report shines.

Out of the box, QuickBooks' Customer Contact List report includes the Customer Name, Bill To address, Contact, Phone, FAX, and Balance fields. Here's how you transform the Contact List report into an export tool:

1. **Choose Reports → Customers & Receivables → Customer Contact List.**

   The Customer Contact List report window opens.

2. **In the report window tool bar, click Modify Report.**

The Modify Report:Customer Contact List dialog box that appears lets you customize the report to filter the data that you export. See page 506 to learn about other ways to customize the report.

3. **To choose the report fields to export, select the Display tab. In the Columns section, choose the fields you want to export in the report.**

The Contact, Phone, and FAX fields might be a good start for the fields you want to export. Then again, they might not. You can add or remove a few fields in the report or make wide-scale changes to the list of fields.

To change the fields that appear in the report, you need to click every field you want to add or remove from the list. Clicking a field in the Columns list toggles the field on and off. If there's a checkmark in front of the field name, that field appears in the report. If there's no checkmark, the report doesn't include a column for that field.

4. **To produce a report for only the customers you want, select the Filters tab. In the Filter list, choose Customer. In the Customer drop-down list, choose "Multiple customers/jobs" to select the customers you want to export.**

In the Select Customer:Job dialog box, the Manual option is selected automatically, which is what you want.

5. **In the name list, click each customer you want to export, and then click OK. Then, in the Modify Report dialog box, click OK.**

You see the report with the modifications you've made.

6. **In the report window toolbar, click Export.**

The Export Report dialog box opens. To create a new Excel workbook, simply click Export. Excel launches and displays the report in a workbook.

Tip: Saving the modified report reduces the number of steps you have to take the next time you export. Page 518 describes the steps for memorizing a report.

Exporting a text file

To create a delimited text file of the entire Customers & Jobs List (or any other QuickBooks list), choose File → Utilities → Export → "Lists to IIF Files". The first Export dialog box that appears includes checkboxes for each QuickBooks list, as described in detail on page 597. Turn on the checkboxes for the lists you want to export. If you want to export *only* customer names and addresses to a tab-delimited file, choose File → Utilities → Export → "Addresses to Text File".

Adding and Editing Multiple Customer Records

The new Add/Edit Multiple List Entries command lets you add or update values in the customer, vendor, and item lists by pasting information from an Excel spreadsheet directly into a table in the dialog box. Additional commands for copying or duplicating values between records make short work of changes like updating the new billing contact for a customer who sends you job after job. Typing values into cells is OK, too, if you notice a typo in one of the records in the list. You can customize the table in the dialog box to show only the customers you want to edit and only the fields you want to modify.

The command goes by different names depending on where you find it in QuickBooks 2010. Choose the command in any of these locations to open the Add/Edit Multiple List Entries dialog box to the customer list:

• On the Lists menu, choose Add/Edit Multiple List Entries.

• In the Customer Center toolbar, choose New Customer & Job, and then choose Add Multiple Customer:Jobs.

• In the Customer Center toolbar, choose Excel, and then choose Paste from Excel.

Selecting the list to work with

QuickBooks automatically selects Customers in the List drop-down list (unless you open the Add/Edit Multiple List Entries dialog box from the Vendor Center or the Item List window). You can switch lists by choosing Customers, Vendors, or Items in the List drop-down list.

To make editing existing list entries easier, you can display only the entries you want to edit. Here are the methods you can use to restrict the customers that appear in the table:

• **Filter the entries that appear in the table.** The View drop-down list includes several choices for filtering the customer list. Choose Active Customers if you want to make changes to only active customers in your company file. Inactive Customers displays customers that you've changed to inactive status (page 97). To filter the customer list to your exact specifications, choose Custom Filter, illustrated in Figure 4-9. For example, if you want to divide your government customers into local, state, and federal customers, you can filter the list to show only records with Government in the Customer Type field.

List entries display only if they exactly match what you filter for. For example if you type *(555)* to look for the 555 area code, records that don't have parentheses around the area code won't show up.

Because QuickBooks doesn't save the changes you make in the dialog box until you click Save Changes, you can select Unsaved Customers to see all the entries

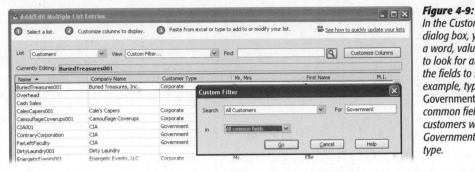

Figure 4-9:
In the Custom Filter dialog box, you can type a word, value, or phrase to look for and specify the fields to search. For example, type Government *and search common fields to find customers with the Government customer type.*

you've edited but not yet saved. Choosing "Customers with errors" displays entries that contain invalid values, like a customer type or tax code that doesn't exist in your company file. In fact, if you click Save Changes when there are records with errors, the dialog box automatically filters the list to the "Customer with errors" view, so you can see what you must correct before you save your changes. See page 89 to learn how to spot and fix errors.

- **Find entries.** Typing a word, value, or phrase in the Find box is similar to applying a custom filter to the list, except that QuickBooks searches all fields. For example, if you type *555* in the Find box and click the Search button (which looks like a magnifying glass), QuickBooks will display records that contain 555 somewhere in the record, whether it appears in the company name, telephone number, address, or account number fields.

Note: The entries you see exactly match what you typed in the Find box. For example, if you type *New York,* QuickBooks displays customer records that contain New York, but won't display records if New York is abbreviated to NY.

- **Customize the columns that appear in the table.** To paste data from Excel in a jiffy, you can customize the columns in the table to match the columns and column order in your Excel spreadsheet. (Or if you're an Excel wiz, you may prefer to rearrange the columns in your spreadsheet before pasting data.) Click Customize Columns to open the Customize Columns dialog box. The tools for customizing columns are straightforward, as Figure 4-10 illustrates. To add a column, select the field you want in the Available Columns list and click Add. To remove a column, select the field in the Chosen Columns list and click Remove.

- **Sort the list entries.** To sort the entries in the table, click the column heading for the field you want to sort by. QuickBooks initially sorts the records in ascending order (from A to Z or from low to high numbers). Click a second time to sort by descending order.

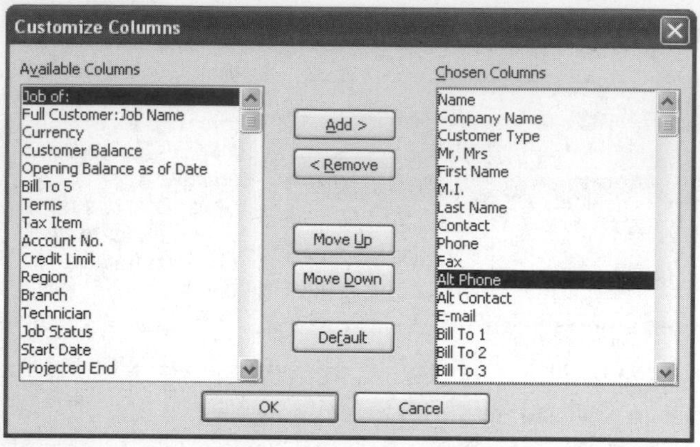

Figure 4-10:
In addition to adding and removing columns, you can change the position of a column by selecting the field in the Chosen Columns list and clicking Move Up or Move Down. If you completely mangle the columns, click Default to restore the preset columns.

Adding or editing list entries

Whether you want to add new entries or edit existing ones, you can paste data from Excel, type values, or use commands like Copy Down to copy values between records. The only difference when you want to add a new record is that you must first click the first empty row at the bottom of the list before you enter any data. Here are the methods you can use to enter values in records:

- **Type values in cells.** Click the cell for a field and make changes using the usual text editing commands. Click within text to select the text up to where you clicked. Click a second time to position the cursor at that location. Click the right end of a cell to select all the text in it. Drag over text to select part of an entry.

- **Copy and paste values.** If you're a fan of copying and pasting (and who isn't?), you can copy and paste data from one cell, row, or column in the table to another. For example, if a customer with several jobs has relocated its main office, you can copy the Bill To cells and paste them into the cells for the customer's jobs. Or you can copy values from billing address cells into shipping address cells.

  You can also copy data from an Excel spreadsheet (a single cell, a range of cells, a row, or a column) and paste it into the table, as long as the columns in the dialog box table and the columns in the Excel spreadsheet contain the same information in the same order. You can customize the columns either in the dialog box or in the spreadsheet, whichever you prefer. When you paste Excel data into existing records in the Add/Edit Multiple List Entries dialog box, QuickBooks overwrites the existing values in the cells. To paste Excel data into new records, be sure to select the first empty row in the Add/Edit Multiple List Entries dialog box and then paste the data.

- **Insert line.** If you want to insert a blank line in the table (for example, to create a new job for a customer), right-click the record where you want the blank line, and then choose Insert Line on the shortcut menu (or press Ctrl+Ins).

- **Delete line.** If you created a record by mistake, you can remove it by right-clicking anywhere in the row and then choosing Delete Line from the shortcut menu.

- **Copy values down a column.** You can quickly fill in several cells in a column with the Copy Down shortcut command. Right-click a cell and choose Copy Down on the shortcut menu. QuickBooks copies the value in the selected cell to the cells below it in the column, overwriting any existing data. For example, if you want to change the contact name for all the jobs for one customer, filter the list to show all the records for that customer (in the Find box, type the customer name, and then click the Find icon). Type the new contact in the first Contact cell. Then, right-click the cell and choose Copy Down from the shortcut menu.

- **Duplicate a row.** To create a new record that has many of the same values as an existing record, right-click in the row you want to duplicate and choose Duplicate Row from the shortcut menu. The new record appears in the next row and contains all the same values as the existing record, except for one. The value in the first field begins with "DUP" to differentiate from the existing record.

- **Clear column.** If you want to clear all the values in a column, right-click in the column and then choose Clear Column from the shortcut menu.

Saving changes

After you have completed the additions and modifications you want, click Save Changes to save those list entries. QuickBooks saves all the entries that have no errors and tells you how many records it saved. If any entries contain errors, like a value that doesn't exist in the Terms list, the dialog box displays only the entries that contain errors and changes the incorrect values to red text. Fix the errors and then click Save Changes once more.

Tip: If you don't know what the problem is, you can select the incorrect value and delete it by pressing Ctrl+X. When you figure out what the value should be, you can edit the record in the Edit Customer or Add/Edit Multiple List Entries dialog boxes.

Creating Jobs in QuickBooks

Project-based work means that your current effort for a customer has a beginning and an end, even if it sometimes seems like your project will last forever. Whether you build custom software programs or apartment buildings, you can use QuickBooks' job tracking to analyze financial performance by project.

If you sell products and don't give a hoot about job tracking, you can simply invoice your customers for the products you sell without ever creating a job in QuickBooks. On the other hand, suppose you want to know whether you're making more money on the mansion you're building or the bungalow remodel. What's more, you want to know the percentage of profit you made on each project. These financial measures are the reason you create jobs for each project you want to track.

In QuickBooks, jobs cling to customers like baby possums to their mothers. A QuickBooks job *always* belongs to a customer. In fact, if you try to choose the Add Job command before you create a customer, you'll see a message box telling you to create a customer first.

Creating a New Job

Because jobs belong to customers, you have to create a customer before you can create any of that customer's jobs. Once the customer exists, follow these steps to add a job to the customer's record:

1. **In the Customer Center, right-click the customer you want, and then choose Add Job from the shortcut menu.**

   You can also select the customer in the Customers & Jobs tab, and then, in the Customer Center toolbar, choose New Customer & Job → Add Job.

   The New Job dialog box appears.

2. **In the Job Name box, type a name for the job.**

   The name that you type appears on invoices and other customer documents. You can type up to 41 characters in the Job Name box. The best names are short but easily recognizable by both you *and* the customer.

   QuickBooks fills in most of the remaining job fields with the information you entered for the customer who owns the job. You can skip the fields on these tabs unless the information on the Address Info, Additional Info, and Payment Info tabs is different for the job. For example, if materials for the job go to a different shipping address than the one stored with the customer, type the job shipping address in the fields on the Address Info tab.

3. **If you want to add information about job type, dates, or status, in the New Job dialog box, click the Job Info tab and enter values in the fields.**

   If you add job types, you can analyze jobs with similar characteristics, no matter which customer hired you to do the work. Fill in the Job Status field so you can see what's going on by scanning the Customer Center, as shown in Figure 4-11. If you want to see whether you're going to finish the work on schedule, you can document your estimated and actual dates for the job in the Date fields. (The box on page 91 tells you more about these fields.)

Note: To change the values for Job Status, modify the status text in Preferences (see page 569).

---

4. **After you've filled in the job fields, click Next to create another job for the same customer, or click OK to save the job and close the New Job dialog box.**

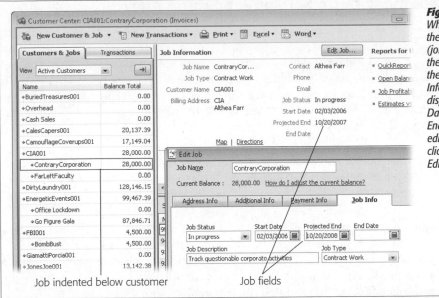

Job indented below customer Job fields

Figure 4-11:
When you select a job in the Customer Center (jobs are indented below the customers to whom they belong), the Job Information section displays Job Status, Start Date, Project End, and End Date. If you want to edit job fields, double-click a job to open the Edit Job dialog box.

POWER USERS' CLINIC

Specifying Job Information

The fields on the Job Info tab are optional—you can invoice a customer even if every Job Info field is blank. However, Job Status and Job Type both help you analyze your business performance, past and future. You don't even have to use the terms that QuickBooks provides for status. Defining the text that appears for each phase isn't a matter of creating a QuickBooks list. Instead, you set them with Jobs and Estimates preferences as described on page 569.

Here's a guide to the Job Info fields and how you can put them to use:

- **Job status.** The Job Status field can indicate trends in your business. If several jobs are set to Pending status, a resource crunch might be headed your way.

- **Start date.** When you start the job, in the Start Date box, select the actual start date on the calendar.

- **Projected end.** If you've estimated when you'll complete the job, in the Projected End box, select that date on the calendar.

- **End date.** By comparing the actual end date with your projection, you can improve future projections or change how you work in order to finish jobs on time. When you complete the job, in the End Date box, select the actual end date on the calendar.

- **Description.** Type a more detailed description of the job to remind you about the work when the job name doesn't ring any bells.

- **Job type.** If you categorize your jobs, choose the job type (page 147) from the Job Type drop-down menu.

Modifying Customer and Job Information

As long as you enter a customer name when you create a new customer, it's fine to leave the remaining customer fields blank. You can change customer information at any time to add more data or to change what's already there. Similarly, you can create a job with only the job name and come back later to edit or add more. To modify a customer or job, open the Customer Center and then double-click the customer or job you want to edit. See page 86 to learn how to modify multiple customer and job records at once.

Note: If you don't like double-clicking, select the customer or job you want to edit and then press Ctrl+E. If you can't remember keyboard shortcuts, right-click the customer or job and then choose Edit Customer: Job on the shortcut menu. Or, on the right side of the Customer Center, click Edit Customer (or Edit Job).

In the Edit Customer dialog box, you can make changes to all customer fields—except for the customer balance, that is. QuickBooks pulls the customer balance from the opening balance (if you provide one) and shows any unpaid invoices for that customer. Once a customer exists, creating invoices (page 255) is your only way of reproducing the customer's current balance.

Similarly, all the fields in the Edit Job dialog box are editable, except for the customer balance. Remember that the changes you make to fields on the Address Info, Additional Info, Payment Info, and Job Info tabs apply only to the job, not the customer.

You can't change the currency assigned to a customer if you've recorded at least one transaction for that customer. If the customer moves from Florida to France and starts using euros, you need to close the customer's current balance (by receiving payments for outstanding invoices). Then, you can create a new customer in QuickBooks and assign the new currency to it. After the new customer record is ready to go, you can make the old customer record inactive (page 97).

Warning: Unless you've revamped your naming standard for customers, don't edit the value in a customer's Customer Name field. Because this field uniquely identifies your customers, you might customize QuickBooks based on that field. For example, if you created a customized report filtered by a specific customer name, the report isn't smart enough to take on the new customer name. If you do modify the Customer Name, make sure to modify any customization to use the new name.

Adding Notes About Customers

Attention to detail. Follow through. These are a few of the things that keep customers coming back for more. Following up on promises or calling if you can't make your meeting is good business. But sending reorder brochures after customers have made purchases can just make them mad. If you use another program for customer relationship management, you can track these types of details there. But if you prefer

to use the smallest number of programs, QuickBooks' notes can help you stay in customers' good graces by tracking personal information and customer to-do lists.
When you select a customer on the left side of the Customer Center window, that
customer's information appears on the right side of the window.

To add a note to a customer or job record, follow these steps:

1. **In the Customers & Jobs tab in the left pane of the Customer Center, select the
   customer or job to which you want to add a note.**

   The customer's or job's information appears in the right pane of the Customer
   Center.

2. **In the right pane, click Edit Notes.**

   The Notepad window appears and displays all the notes you've added for the
   selected customer, as shown in Figure 4-12. The insertion point is at the beginning of the text box, ready for you to type.

3. **To keep track of when conversations happen, click Date Stamp before you
   begin typing a note.**

   If you're adding a note about something that happened on a day other than
   today, you have to type in the date.

4. **Type the note you want to add.**

   If you want to add information somewhere else in the notes, first click to position
   the insertion point where you want to type.

5. **When you've added the note, click OK.**

   QuickBooks adds the note to the Notes area in the Customer Information (or
   Job Information) pane on the right side of the Customer Center window.

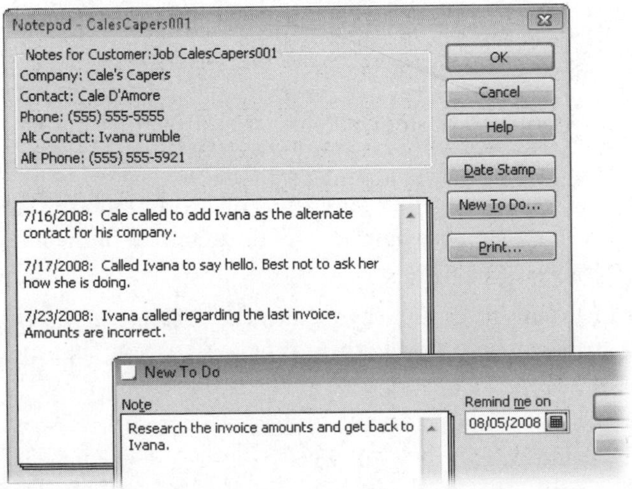

Figure 4-12:
*To add a reminder of what you want to do for
a customer and when, in the Notepad window,
click New To Do. In the New To Do dialog box,
type your to-do item. Choose a date in the
"Remind me on" box. Then, the to-do item
shows up on the QuickBooks Reminder List on
the date you asked QuickBooks to remind you.
Of course, QuickBooks reminders work only if
you open QuickBooks on that day and you
remember to look at the Reminders List.*

Merging Customer Records

Suppose you remodeled buildings for two companies run by brothers: Morey's City Diner and Les' Exercise Studio. The brothers conclude that their businesses have a lot of synergy—people are either eating or trying to lose weight, and usually doing both. To smooth out their cash flow, they decide to merge their companies into More or Less Body Building and All You Can Eat Buffet. You have to figure out how to create one customer in QuickBooks from the two businesses, and you also want to retain the jobs, invoices, and other transactions that you created when the companies were separate.

If you don't use a standard naming convention as recommended on page 71, you could end up with multiple customer records representing one real-life customer, such as Les's Exercise Studio and LesEx. You can merge these doppelgangers into one customer just as you can merge two truly separate companies into one.

When you merge customer records in QuickBooks, one customer retains the entire transaction history for the two original customers. You don't so much merge two customers as turn one customer's records into those of another's.

Merging customers in QuickBooks won't win any awards for best intuitive process. You merge two customers by renaming one customer to the same name as another. But that's not all: The customer you rename can't have any jobs associated with it. If your customers have jobs associated with them, you have to move all the jobs to the customer you intend to keep *before* you start the merge. Subsume the customer with fewer jobs so you don't have to move as many jobs. If you don't use jobs, subsume whichever customer you want.

Note: If you work in multi-user mode, you have to switch to single-user mode for the duration of the merging operation. See page 161 to learn how to switch to single-user mode and back again after the merge is complete.

To merge customers with a minimum of angry outbursts, follow these steps:

1. **Open the Customer Center.**

   In the QuickBooks icon bar, click Customer Center or, on the left side of the QuickBooks Home page, click Customers.

2. **If the customer you're going to merge has jobs associated with it, on the Customers & Jobs tab, position the mouse pointer over the diamond to the left of the job you want to reassign.**

   Jobs appear indented beneath the customer to which they belong. If you have hundreds of jobs for the customer, moving them is tedious at best—but move them you must.

3. When the pointer changes to a two-headed arrow, drag the job under the customer you plan to keep after the merge, as shown at left in Figure 4-13.

   Repeat steps 2 and 3 for each job that belongs to the customer you're going to merge.

4. On the Customers & Jobs tab, right-click the name of the customer you're going to merge and, on the shortcut menu, and choose Edit Customer:Job.

   You can also edit the customer by selecting the customer name on the Customer & Jobs tab. Then, when the customer information appears on the right side of the Customer Center, click the Edit Customer button.

   Either way, the Edit Customer dialog box opens.

5. In the Edit Customer dialog box, change the name in the Customer Name field to match the name of the customer you intend to keep. Click OK.

   QuickBooks displays a message letting you know that the name is in use and asks if you want to merge the customers.

6. Click Yes to merge the customers.

   In the Customer Center, shown in Figure 4-13, the customer you renamed disappears and any customer balances now belong to the remaining customer.

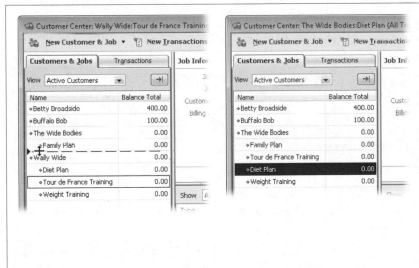

Figure 4-13:
Left: The mouse pointer changes to a two headed arrow that you can drag within the Customers & Jobs tab. A horizontal line between the two arrowheads shows you where the job will go when you release the mouse button.

Right: After you reassign all the jobs to the customer you intend to keep, you can merge the now-jobless customer into the other. When the merge is complete, you see only the customer you kept.

Hiding and Deleting Customers

Hiding customers isn't about secreting them away when the competition shows up to talk to you. Because you can delete customers only in very limited circumstances, hiding customers keeps your list of customers manageable and your financial history intact.

Deleting Customers

You can delete a customer only if there's no activity for that customer in your QuickBooks file. If you try to delete a customer that has even one transaction, QuickBooks tells you that you can't delete the record.

If you create a customer by mistake, you can remove it, as long as you first remove any associated transactions—which are likely to be mistakes as well. But Quick-Books doesn't tell you which transactions are preventing you from deleting this customer. To delete transactions that prevent you from deleting a customer, do the following:

1. **View all the transactions for the customer by selecting that customer in the Customer Center, and then setting the Show box to All Transactions and the Date box to All, as shown in Figure 4-14.**

   You can also view transactions by running the "Transaction List by Customer" report (Reports → Customers & Receivables → Transaction List by Customer).

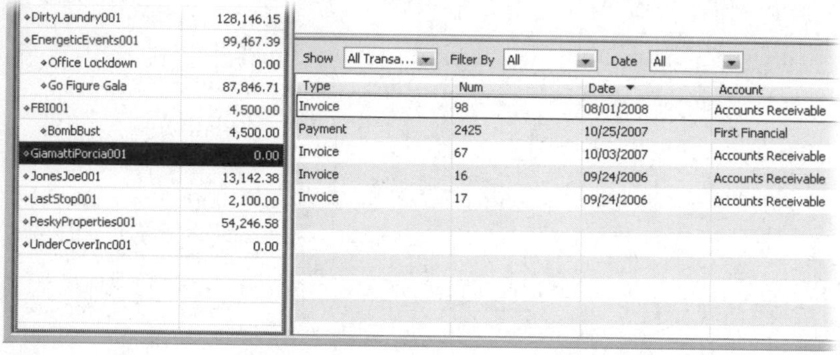

Figure 4-14:
When you select a customer in the Customer Center, the transaction pane on the lower-right shows that customer's transactions. To see them all, in the Show drop-down list, choose All Transactions, and in the Date drop-down list, choose All.

2. **In the Customer Center or the report, open the transaction you want to delete by double-clicking it.**

   The Create Invoices window (or the corresponding transaction window) opens to the transaction you double-clicked.

3. **Choose Edit → Delete Invoice (or Edit → Delete Check, or the corresponding delete command).**

   In the message box that appears, click OK to confirm that you want to delete the transaction. Repeat steps 2 and 3 for every transaction for that customer.

4. **Back on the Customers & Jobs tab, select the customer you want to delete. Press Ctrl+D or choose Edit → Delete Customer:Job.**

   If the customer has no transactions, QuickBooks asks you to confirm that you want to delete the customer. Click Yes. If you see a message telling you that you can't delete the customer, go back to steps 2 and 3 to delete any remaining transactions.

Hiding and Restoring Customers

Although your work with a customer might be at an end, you still have to keep records about your past relationship. But old customers can clutter up your Customer Center, making it difficult to select your active customers. Hiding customers is a better solution than deleting them. It retains the historical transactions for a customer, so you can reactivate them if they decide to work with you again. And hiding removes customer names from all the lists that appear in transaction windows so you can't select them by mistake.

To hide a customer, in the Customer Center, right-click the customer and, from the shortcut menu, choose Make Customer:Job Inactive. The customer and any associated jobs disappear from the list. Figure 4-15 shows you how to hide and reactivate customers.

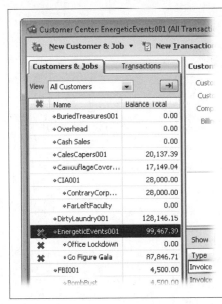

Figure 4-15:
To make hidden customers visible, in the View drop-down list, choose All Customers. QuickBooks displays an X to the left of every inactive customer in the list. Click that X to restore the customer to active duty.

CHAPTER 5

Setting Up Invoice Items

Whether you build houses, sell gardening tools, or tell fortunes on the Internet, you'll probably use *items* in QuickBooks to represent the products and services you sell. But to QuickBooks, things like subtotals, discounts, and sales tax are items, too. In fact, *nothing* appears in the body of a QuickBooks sales form (such as an invoice) unless it's an item.

Put another way, when you want to create invoices in QuickBooks (Chapter 10), you need customers *and* items to do so. So, now that you've got your chart of accounts and your customers set up, it's time to dive into items.

This chapter begins by helping you decide whether your business is one of the few that doesn't need items at all. But if your organization is like most and uses business forms like invoices, sales receipts, and so on, the rest of the chapter will teach you how to create, name, edit, and manage the items you add to forms. You'll learn how to use items in invoices and other forms in the remaining chapters of this book.

What Items Do

For your day-to-day work with QuickBooks, items save time and increase consistency on your sales forms. Here's the deal: Items form the link between what you sell (and buy) and the income, expense, and other types of accounts in your chart of accounts. When you create an item, you specify what the item is, how much you pay for it, how much you sell it for, and the accounts to which you post the corresponding income, expense, cost of goods sold, and asset value. For example, you might charge $75 an hour for the bookkeeping service you provide, and you want the income to show up in your Financial Services income account. When you add that bookkeeping item to a sales form, QuickBooks multiplies the price per hour by the number of hours to calculate the full charge, and posts the income to your Financial Services account.

You can work out which accounts to assign items to on your own or with your accountant (a good idea if you're new to bookkeeping), and then specify the accounts in your items, as shown in Figure 5-1. QuickBooks remembers these assignments from then on.

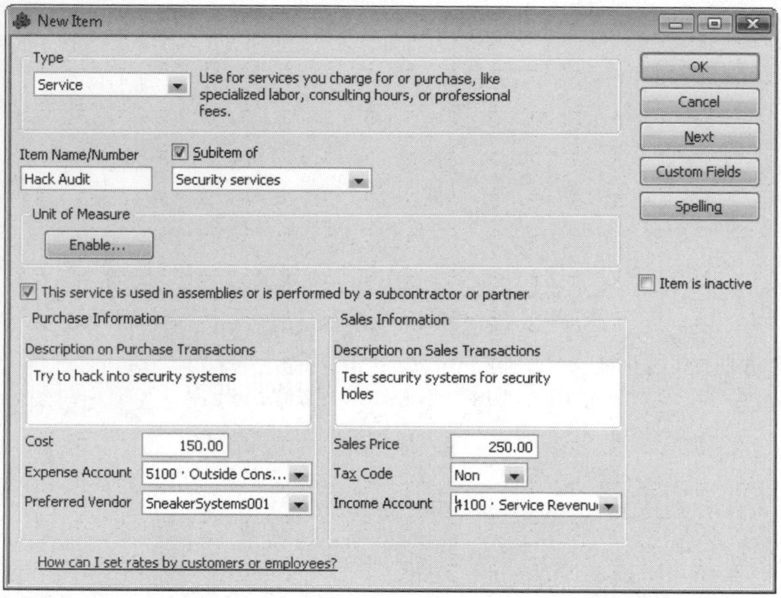

Figure 5-1:
You'd be bound to make mistakes if you had to enter item details each time you added an entry to an invoice. By setting up an item in the New Item dialog box, you can make sure you use the same information on sales forms each time you sell that item. When the inevitable exception to the rule arises, you can edit the item information that QuickBooks fills in on the invoice by selecting portions of the text for replacement or clicking in the text to position the cursor.

When it's time to analyze how your business is doing, items shine. QuickBooks has built-in reports based on items, which show the dollar value of sales or the number of units of inventory you've sold. To learn how to use inventory reports, see page 468. Other item-based reports are described in chapters throughout this book.

When You Don't Need Items

Bottom line: Without items, you can't create any type of sales form in QuickBooks, which includes invoices, statements, sales receipts, credit memos, and estimates. Conversely, if you don't use sales forms, you don't need items. Not many organizations operate without sales forms, but here are a few examples:

- Old Stuff Antiques sells junk—er, antiques—on consignment. Kate, the owner, doesn't pay for the pieces; she just displays them in her store. When she sells a consignment item, she writes paper sales receipts. When she receives her cut from the seller, she deposits the money in her checking account.

- Tony owns a tattoo parlor specializing in gang insignias. He doesn't care how many tattoos he creates and—for safety's sake—he doesn't want to know his customers' names. All Tony does is deposit the cash he receives upon completing each masterpiece.

- Dominic keeps the books for his charity for icebergless penguins. The charity accepts donations of money and fish, and it doesn't sell any products or perform services to earn additional income. He deposits the monetary donations into the charity's checking account and enters the checking account deposit in QuickBooks. Dominic does keep track of the donors' contributions and fish inventory in a spreadsheet.

Should You Track Inventory with Items?

If your business is based solely on selling services, you can skip this section entirely. But if you sell products, you can handle them in two ways: by stocking and tracking inventory or by buying products only when work for your customers requires them. The system you use affects the types of items you create in Quick-Books. When you use QuickBooks' inventory feature, the program keeps track of how many products you have on hand, increasing the number as you purchase them and decreasing the number when you sell them to customers. When you buy products specifically for customers, you still need items, but there's no need to track the quantity on hand. In this case, you can create Non-inventory Part items, which you'll learn about shortly.

For example, general contractors rarely work on the same type of project twice, so they usually purchase the materials they need for a job and charge the customer for those materials. Because general contractors don't keep materials in stock, they don't have to track inventory and can use Non-inventory Part items. On the other hand, specialized contractors like plumbers install the same kinds of pipes and fittings over and over. These contractors often purchase parts and store them in a warehouse, selling them to their customers as they perform jobs. These warehoused parts should be set up as Inventory Part items in QuickBooks.

Tracking inventory requires more effort than buying only the materials you need. Use the following questions to determine whether your business should track inventory:

- **Do you keep products in stock to resell to customers?** If your company stocks faux pony bar stools to resell to customers, those bar stools are inventory. By tracking inventory, you know how many units you have on hand, how much they're worth, and how much money you made on the bar stools you've sold.

  On the other hand, the faux pony mouse pads you keep in the storage closet for your employees are business supplies. Most companies don't want the overhead of tracking inventory for supplies they consume in the course of their business.

- **Do you want to know when to reorder products so you don't run out?** If you sell the same items over and over, keeping your shelves stocked means more sales (because the products are ready to ship out as soon as an order comes in). QuickBooks can remind you when it's time to reorder a product.

- **Do you purchase products specifically for jobs or customers?** If you special order products for customers or buy products for specific jobs, you don't need to track inventory. After you deliver the special order or complete the job, your customer has taken and paid for products, and you only have to account for the income and expenses you incurred.

- **Do you rent equipment to customers?** If you rent or lease equipment, you receive income for the rental or lease of assets you own. In this case, you can show the value of the for-rent products as an asset in QuickBooks and the rental income with a Service item, so you don't need Inventory items.

Your business model might dictate that you track inventory. However, QuickBooks' inventory-tracking feature has some limitations. For example, it lets you store up to 14,500 items, and then you're stuck. If you answer yes to any of the following questions, QuickBooks isn't the program to use to handle the products you sell:

- **Do you sell products that are unique?** In the business world, tracking inventory is meant for businesses that sell commodity products, such as electronic equipment, and stock numerous units of each product. If you sell unique items, such as fine art or compromising Polaroid photos, you'd eventually use up the 14,500 items that QuickBooks can store. For such items, consider using a spreadsheet to track the products you have on hand. When you sell your unique handicrafts, you can record your sales in QuickBooks using more generic items. For example, use an item called Oil Painting on the sales receipts for the artwork you sell and fill in more specific information about the painting in the sales receipt Description field.

- **Do you manufacture the products you sell out of raw materials?** QuickBooks inventory can't follow materials as they wend through a manufacturing process or track inventory in various stages of completion.

Note: QuickBooks Premier and Enterprise editions can track inventory for products that require light assembly. For instance, if you create Wines from Around the World gift baskets using the wine bottles in your store, you can build an Inventory Assembly item out of wine and basket Inventory items. The box on page 115 explains another way to track assembled inventory.

- **Do you value your inventory by a method other than average cost?** QuickBooks calculates inventory value by average cost. If you want to use other methods, like last in, first out (LIFO) or first in, first out (FIFO), you can export inventory data to a spreadsheet and calculate inventory cost outside of QuickBooks (page 476).

• **Do you use a point-of-sale system to track inventory?** Point-of-sale inventory systems often blow QuickBooks inventory tracking out of the water. If you forego QuickBooks' inventory feature, you can periodically update your Quick-Books file with the value of your inventory from the point-of-sale system.

Note: If you like the point-of-sale idea but don't have a system yet, Intuit offers QuickBooks Point of Sale, an integrated, add-on product for retail operations that tracks store sales, customer information, and inventory.

You don't have to use QuickBooks' inventory feature at all if you don't want to. For example, if you perform light manufacturing, you can track the value of your manufactured inventory in a database or other program. Periodically, you can then add journal entries (page 421) to QuickBooks to show the value of in-progress and completed inventory.

Note: The answer to your inventory dilemma could be an add-on program that tracks inventory *and* keeps QuickBooks informed. One of the best is FishBowl Inventory (*www.fishbowlinventory.com*).

Planning Your Items

Setting up items in QuickBooks is a lot like shopping at a grocery store. If you need only a few things, you can shop without a list. Similarly, if you use just a few QuickBooks items, you don't need to write the list out before you start creating items. But if you use dozens or even hundreds of items, planning your item list can save you from experiencing all sorts of unpleasant emotions.

If you jumped feet first into this section, now's the time to read "Should You Track Inventory with Items?" on page 101. Those sections help you with your first decision: whether to use items that represent services, inventory, or non-inventory products.

By deciding how to name and organize your items before you create individual items, you won't waste time editing and reworking existing items to fit your new naming scheme. Read on to learn what you should consider before creating your items in QuickBooks.

Generic or Specific?

Conservation can be as important with QuickBooks' items as it is for the environment. QuickBooks Pro and Premier can hold no more than 14,500 items, which is a problem if you sell unique products, such as antiques, or products that change frequently, such as the current clothing styles for teenagers. Once you use an item in a transaction, you can't delete that item, so your item list could fill up with items you no longer use (see page 130).

By planning how specific your items will be, you can keep your QuickBooks list lean with generic items. For instance, a generic item such as Top can represent a girl's black Goth t-shirt one winter and a white poplin button-down shirt the next summer.

Generic items have their limitations, though, so use them only if necessary. You can't track inventory properly when you use generic items. QuickBooks might show that you have 100 tops in stock, but that doesn't help when your customers are clamoring for white button-downs and you have 97 black Goth t-shirts. In addition, the information you store with a generic item won't match the specifics of each product you sell. So, when you add generic items to an invoice or sales form, you'll have to edit a few fields, such as description or price, as you can see in Figure 5-2.

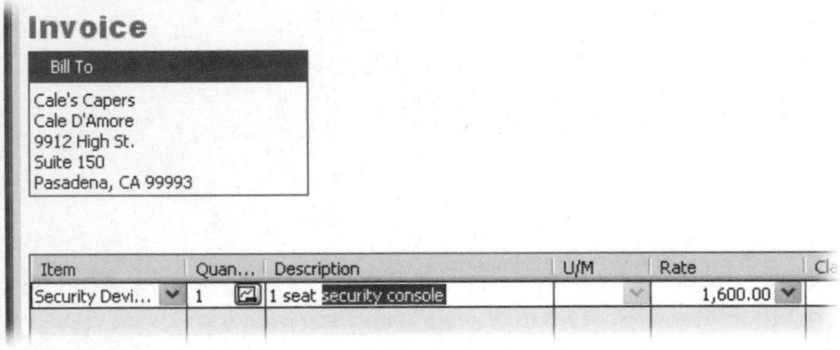

Invoice

Bill To

Cale's Capers
Cale D'Amore
9912 High St.
Suite 150
Pasadena, CA 99993

Item	Quan...	Description	U/M	Rate	Cl
Security Devi...	1	1 seat Security console		1,600.00	

Figure 5-2:
QuickBooks automatically fills in fields like description and price with values you've saved in item records. But you can edit those fields once you add an item to an invoice, whether you use generic or specific items to describe what you sell. Just click a field in a sales form, select the text you want to change, and type the new value.

Naming Items

Brevity and recognizability are equally desirable characteristics when naming items. On the one hand, short names are easier to type and manage, but they can be unintelligible. Longer names take more effort to type and manage, but are easier to read. Decide ahead of time which type of naming you prefer and stick with it as you create items.

QuickBooks encourages brevity by allowing no more than 31 characters in an item's name. If you sell only a handful of services, you can name your items as you would when you're talking. For a tree service company, names like Cut, Limb, Trim, Chip, and Haul work just fine. If your item list runs in the hundreds or thousands, some planning is in order. Here are some factors to consider when naming your items:

- **Abbreviation.** If you have to compress a great deal of information into an item name, you'll have to abbreviate. For example, suppose you want to convey all the things you do when you install a carpet, including installing tack strips, padding, and carpet; trimming carpet; vacuuming; and hauling waste. That's more than the 31 characters you have to work with. Poetic won't describe it, but something like "inst tkst, pad, cpt, trim, vac, haul" says it all in very few characters. The box on the next page describes two other ways to identify items.

- **Aliases.** Create a pseudonym to represent the item. For the carpet job, "Standard install" can represent the installation with vacuuming and hauling waste, while "Deluxe install" includes the standard installation plus moving and replacing furniture. You can include the details in the item description.

- **Sort order.** In the Item List, QuickBooks lists items first by item type and then in alphabetical order. If you want your items to appear in some logical order on drop-down lists (like an invoice item table, for instance), pay attention to the order of characteristics in your item names. Other service items beginning with the intervening letters of the alphabet would separate "Deluxe install" and "Standard install." If you name your installation items "Install deluxe" and "Install standard," they'll show up one after the other in your item list.

POWER USERS' CLINIC

Other Ways to Identify Items

If you want to keep item names lean but still include detailed information, look to these two item features:

- **Descriptions.** Items have fields for both *names* and *descriptions*. When you create an invoice, you choose the item name from a drop-down list. But the invoice that the customer sees shows the item description. Keep your item names brief by placing text for the details in the Description field, which is, for all practical purposes, unlimited in length.

- **Group.** Instead of creating one item that represents several phases of a job, you can create separate items for each phase and create a Group item to include those phases on an invoice. For instance, create one item for installing the tack strips, padding, and carpet. Create additional items for vacuuming, hauling, and moving and replacing the furniture. Then, when you add a Group item to the invoice, QuickBooks adds each item to a line in the invoice.

Note: Construction companies in particular can forego long hours of item data entry using third-party estimating programs. Construction estimating programs usually include thousands of entries for standard construction services and products. If you build an estimate with a program that integrates with QuickBooks, you can import that estimate into QuickBooks and then sit back and watch as it automatically adds all the items in the estimate to your item list. To find such programs that integrate with QuickBooks, go to *http://marketplace.intuit.com*. On the menu bar, click Find Software and then choose Find Solutions by Industry on the drop-down menu. In the By Industry tab's drop-down menu, choose Construction/Contractors.

Subitems

If you keep all your personal papers in one big stack, you probably have a hard time finding everything from birth certificates to tax forms to bills and receipts. If you've got one big list of items in QuickBooks, you're in no better shape. To locate items more easily, consider designing a hierarchy of higher-level items *(parents)* and one or more levels of subitems, as shown in Figure 5-3. The box on page 106 explains how to make sure you have items for every purpose.

For example, a landscaping business might create top-level items for trees, shrubbery, cacti, and flower bulbs. Within the tree top-level item, the landscaper might create items for several species: maple, oak, elm, sycamore, and dogwood. Additional levels of subitems can represent categories such as size (seedling, established, and mature, for example).

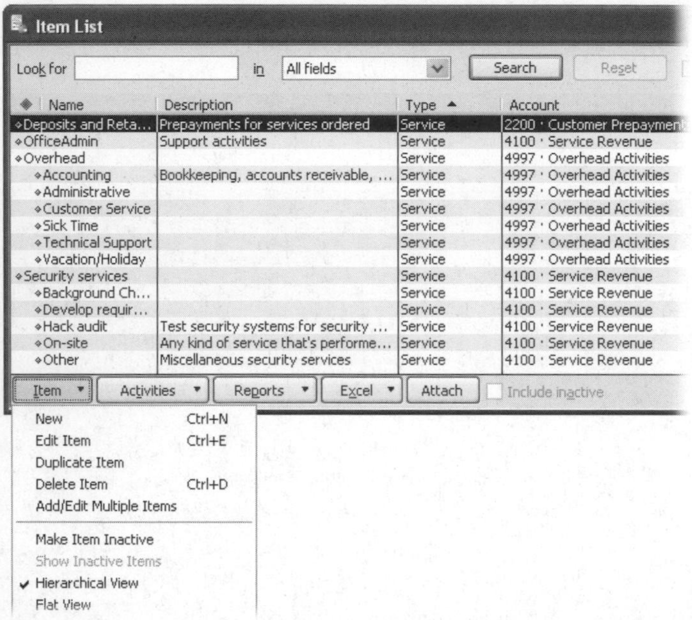

Figure 5-3:
In the Item List window, the Hierarchical View indents subitems, making it easy to differentiate the items that you use to categorize the list from the items you actually sell. If you work with long lists of subitems, the parent might scroll off the screen. To keep the hierarchy of items visible at all times, in the menu bar at the bottom of the window, click Item and then choose Flat View. QuickBooks uses colons to separate the names of each level of item and subitem.

WORD TO THE WISE

Catch-All Items

When you develop a hierarchy of parent items and subitems, eventually someone in your company will run across a service or product that doesn't fit any of your existing subitems. For every parent item, create a catch-all subitem to give these outcasts a home. "Other" is a popular name for these catch basins. For example, if you use a parent item called Security Services, be sure to add a subitem like Security Services-Other.

Catch-all items also act as holding pens while you figure out which item you should use. You can create a transaction using the Security Services-Other item, and then change the item in the transaction later (page 292) when you've identified (or created) the correct item.

Creating Items

The best time to create items is *after* you've created your accounts but *before* you start billing customers. Each item links to an account in your chart of accounts, so creating items goes quicker if you don't have to stop to create an account as well.

Similarly, you can create items while you're in the midst of creating an invoice, but you'll find creating items goes much faster when you create one item after the other. How long it takes to create items depends on how many items you need. If you sell only a few services, a few minutes should be sufficient. On the other hand, construction companies that need thousands of items often forego hours of data entry by importing items from third-party programs (page 594). In QuickBooks 2010, the Add/Edit Multiple List Entries feature is another time-saving method for adding several items to the Item List. The feature lets you paste data from Excel or copy values between entries to populate entries. It works the same way for customer, vendor, and item lists, so page 86 in Chapter 4 describes how to use it.

Each type of item has its own assortment of fields, but the overall process for creating an item is the same for every type. With the following procedure under your belt, you'll find that you can create many of your items without further instruction.

If you *do* need help with fields for a specific type of item, read the sections that follow to learn what each field does.

1. **In the QuickBooks Home window, click Items & Services to open the Item List window. Or, choose Lists → Item List.**

   When you first display the Item List, QuickBooks sorts entries by item type. The sort order for the item types isn't alphabetical—it's the order that item types appear in the Type drop-down list, as shown in Figure 5-4. You can change the sort order of the list by clicking a column header.

2. **Open the New Item dialog box by pressing Ctrl+N. Alternatively, on the menu bar at the bottom of the window, click Item, and then choose New.**

   QuickBooks opens the New Item dialog box and highlights the Service item type (page 109) in the Type drop-down list.

3. **To create a Service item, just press Tab to proceed to naming the item. If you want to create any other type of item, choose the type in the Type drop-down list.**

   Some item types won't appear in the list if you haven't turned on the corresponding feature. For example, the Inventory Item type doesn't appear if you haven't turned on inventory tracking, as described on page 567.

4. **In the Item Name/Number box, type a unique identifier for the item.**

   For example, if you opt for long and meaningful names, you might type *Install carpet and vacuum*. For a short name, you might type *Inst Carpt*.

5. **To make this item a subitem of another item, turn on the "Subitem of" checkbox and choose the item that you want to act as the parent.**

   You can create the parent item in the midst of creating a subitem, but creating the parent first puts much less strain on your brain. When the parent item already exists, simply choose it from the "Subitem of" drop-down list. To create

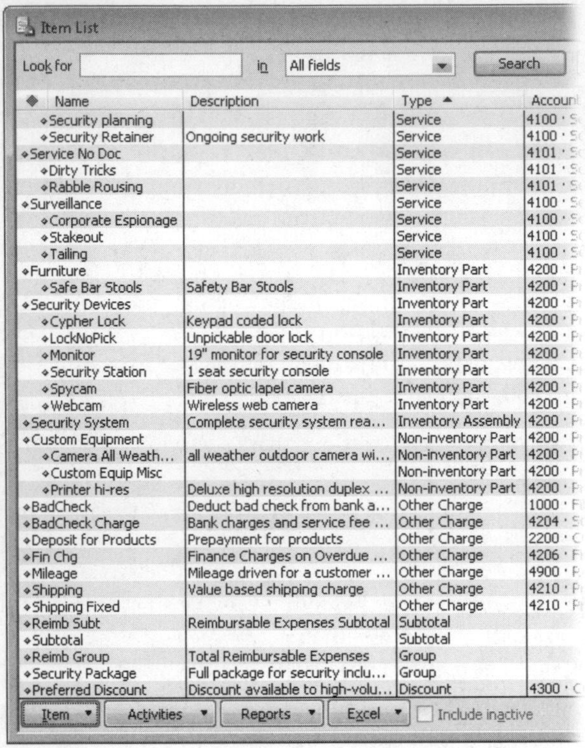

Figure 5-4:
QuickBooks lists items in alphabetical order within each item type. You can change the sort order of the Item List by clicking a column heading. If you click it again, QuickBooks toggles the list order between ascending and descending order. To return the list to sort by item type, click the diamond to the left of the column headings (which appears any time the list is sorted by a column other than Type).

the parent *while* creating the subitem, choose *<Add New>* on the "Subitem of" drop-down list, and jump to step 3 to begin the parent creation process. Subitems and parents have to be the same type. (You can't create subitems for Subtotal, Group, or Payment items.)

You have to assign an account to every item, whether it's a parent or not. However, you need Rate or Price values only if you plan to use items on invoices or other sales forms.

6. **Complete the other fields as described in the following sections (page 109, page 112, and so on) for the type of item that you're creating.**

You can enter information that QuickBooks uses later to fill in fields on sales forms. For example, you can type in the sales price, and QuickBooks uses that price on an invoice when you sell some units. If the sales price changes each time, simply leave the item's Sales Price field at zero. In this case, QuickBooks doesn't fill in the price, so you can type the price each time you sell the item. Even if you set up a value for an item, you can overwrite it whenever you use the item on a sales form.

7. **When you have additional items to create, simply click Next to save the current item and begin another. If you want to save the item you just created and close the New Item dialog box, click OK.**

If you've made mistakes in almost every field or need more information before you can complete an item, click Cancel to throw away the current item and close the New Item dialog box.

Service Items

Services are less tangible things that you sell, like time or the output of your brain. For example, you might sell consulting services, Internet connection time, magazine articles, or Tarot card readings. In construction, services represent phases of construction, which makes it easy to bill customers based on progress and to compare actual values to estimates.

Suppose you provide a telephone answering service. You earn income when your customers pay you for the service. You pay salaries to the people who answer the phones, regardless of whether you have 2 service contracts or 20. For this business, you earn income with your service, but your costs don't link to the income from specific customers or jobs.

In some companies, such as law practices, the partners get paid based on the hours they bill, so the partners' compensation is an expense associated directly with the firm's income. Services that you farm out to a subcontractor work similarly. If you offer a 900 number for gardening advice, you might have a group of freelancers who field the calls and whom you pay only for their time on the phone. You still earn income for the service you sell, but you also have to pay the subcontractors to do the work. The subcontractors' cost relates to the income for that service. QuickBooks displays different fields depending on whether a service has costs associated with income.

The mighty Service item single-handedly manages all types of services, whether you charge by the hour or by the service, with associated expenses or without. This section describes the fields you fill in when you create service items.

The "This service is used in assemblies or is performed by a subcontractor or partner" checkbox, as shown in Figure 5-5, is the key to displaying the fields you need when you purchase services from someone else.

Here's how the service fields work when you *don't* purchase services from someone else (that is, when you turn off the "This service is used in assemblies or is performed by a subcontractor or partner" checkbox):

- **Description.** Type a detailed description for the service in this box. This description appears on invoices and sales forms, so use terms your customers can understand.

- **Rate.** Type how much you charge your customers for the service. You can enter a flat fee or a charge per unit of time. For example, *you* might charge $9.95 for unlimited gardening advice per call, but Intuit telephone support charges by the minute.

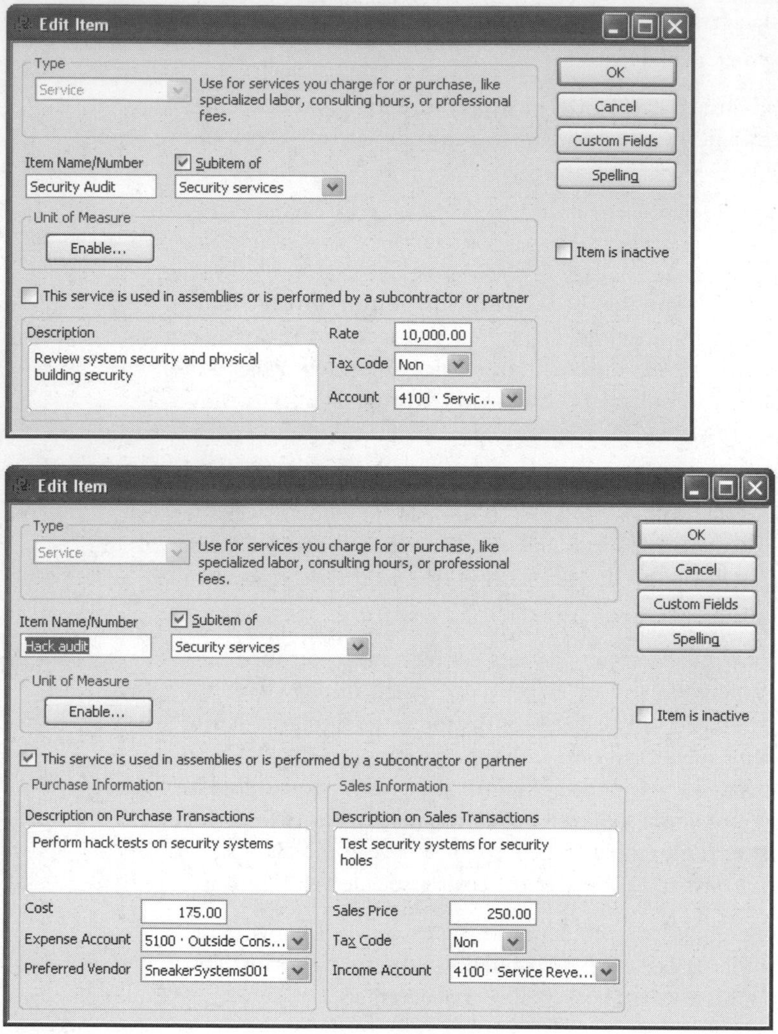

Figure 5-5:
Top: If a service doesn't have costs directly associated with it, you define only the rate, tax code, and income account for the service.

Bottom: If subcontractors or partners perform the service and get paid for their work, a Service item has to contain information for both the sales and purchase transactions. QuickBooks uses the information in the Purchase Information section of the Create Item or Edit Item dialog box to fill out purchase orders or track owners' earned compensation. The information in the Sales Information section goes into fields on invoices.

When you add the item to an invoice, QuickBooks multiplies the quantity by the sales price to calculate the total charge. If the cost varies, type *0* in the Rate or Sales Price field. You can then enter the price when you create an invoice or other sales form. If the rate or price is often the same, you can also type the most common rate. Then, when you add the item to an invoice, you can modify the rate if you want to use a different amount. For services that carry a flat fee, use a quantity of *1* on your invoices.

Note: QuickBooks multiplies the cost and sales prices by the quantities you add to sales forms. Be sure to define the cost and sales price in the same units so that QuickBooks calculates your income and expenses correctly.

- **Tax Code.** Most service items are nontaxable, so you'll choose Non more often than not. (This field appears only if you've turned on the sales tax feature, as described on page 580.)

- **Account.** Choose the income account to which you want to post the income for this service, whether it's a catch-all income account for all services or one you create specifically for the service.

If you purchase services from someone else and have associated costs, you have to provide information about your purchase from the other party and your sales transaction to your customer. Here are the service fields you fill in when you *do* have associated costs for an item:

- **Description on Purchase Transactions.** Type the description that you want to appear on the purchase orders you issue to subcontractors.

- **Cost.** Enter what you pay for the service, which can be an hourly rate or a flat fee. For example, if a subcontractor performs the service and receives $100 for each hour of work, type *100* in this field. If the cost varies, type *0* in the Cost field. You can then enter the actual cost when you create a purchase order.

- **Expense Account.** Choose the account to which you want to post what you pay for the service. If a subcontractor does the work, choose an expense account for subcontractor or outside consultants' fees. If a partner or owner performs the work, choose an expense account for job-related costs.

- **Preferred Vendor.** If you choose a vendor in this drop-down list, QuickBooks selects the preferred vendor for a purchase order when you add this Service item. This behavior is helpful only if you almost always use the same vendor for this service *and* you add the service item to a purchase order before you choose the vendor.

- **Description on Sales Transactions.** QuickBooks copies the text from the "Description on Purchase Transactions" box to the "Description on Sales Transactions" box. However, if your vendors use technical jargon that your customers wouldn't recognize, you can change the text in the "Description on Sales Transactions" box to something more meaningful.

- **Sales Price.** Type how much you charge your customers for the service, as you would in the Rate field for a service item that you don't purchase from someone else.

- **Tax Code.** Most service items are nontaxable, so you'll choose Non more often than not. (This field appears only if you've turned on the sales tax feature, as described on page 580.)

- **Income Account.** Choose the income account to which you want to post the income for this service, whether it's a catch-all income account for all services or one you create specifically for the service.

ALTERNATE REALITY

Subitems for Nonprofits

Service items are the workhorses of nonprofit organizations. Donations, dues, grants, and money donated in exchange for services all fall into the Service item bucket. The only time you'll need another type of item is if you raise money by selling products from inventory (calendars and note cards, for instance).

For nonprofits without heavy reporting requirements, you can make do with one item for each type of revenue you receive (grants, donations, dues, fundraising campaigns), with a link to the corresponding income account. For example, a Service subitem called Donation would link to an income account called Donations.

But subitems come in handy for categorizing the money you receive for different types of services, particularly when donors give money and want to see detailed financial reports in return.

You don't make the big subitem-related decision yourself, the organizations that contribute do. If your organization receives money from the government or a foundation with specific reporting requirements, you can set up subitems and classes (see page 138) to track the details you need for the reports they require. Here's an example of an item list that differentiates type of income and different donors:

Grant
> Government
> Corporate

Donation
> Regular
> Matching

Membership Dues
> Individual
> Corporate
> Contributing
> Platinum Circle

Product Items

Products you sell to customers fall into three categories: products you keep in inventory, products you special order, and products you assemble. QuickBooks can handle inventory as long as your company passes the tests on page 101. Likewise, products purchased specifically for customers or jobs are no problem. As explained on page 114, QuickBooks can handle lightly assembled products like gift baskets or gizmos made from widgets—but you'll need QuickBooks Premier Edition to do even that.

In QuickBooks, choose one of these three item types for the products you sell:

- **Inventory Part.** Use this type for products you purchase and keep in stock for resale. Retailers and wholesalers are the obvious examples of inventory-based businesses, but other types of businesses like building contractors may track inventory, too. You can create Inventory Part items only if you turn on the inventory feature as described on page 567. With inventory parts, you can track how many you have, how much they're worth, and when you should reorder. The box on page 113 explains how you account for all these details.

- **Non-inventory Part.** If you purchase products specifically for a job or a customer and you don't track how many products you have on hand, use Non-inventory Part items. Unlike an Inventory Part item, the Non-inventory Part item has at most two account fields: one for income you receive when you sell the part, and the other for the expense of purchasing the part in the first place.

- **Inventory Assembly.** This item type (available only in QuickBooks Premier and Enterprise editions) is perfect when you sell products built from your inventory items. For example, you stock wine bottles and related products like corkscrews and glasses, and you assemble them into gift baskets. With an Inventory Assembly item, you can track the number of gift baskets you have on hand as well as the individual inventory items. You can assign a different price for the gift basket than the total of the individual products, as described in the box on page 114.

The box on page 115 describes an easier approach to tracking products you build from other items.

ACCOUNTING CONCEPTS

Following the Inventory Money Trail

Inventory Part items are the most complicated items because, in accounting, the cost of inventory moves from place to place as you purchase, store, and finally sell your products. Table 5-1 and the following steps show the path that the inventory money trail takes:

1. You spend money to purchase faux pony bar stools to sell in your store and that money buys something of value. Your checking or credit card account shows the money you pay going out the door.

2. Because inventory has value, it represents an asset of your company. Hence, the value of the inventory you purchase appears in an inventory asset account in your chart of accounts.

3. When you sell some bar stools, QuickBooks posts the sale to an income account (such as Product Sales)

and the money your customer owes you shows up in Accounts Receivable.

4. The stools leave inventory, so QuickBooks deducts the cost of the stools you sold from the inventory asset account. As accounting aficionados already know, the cost of the sold stools has to go somewhere. QuickBooks posts the cost to a *cost of goods sold account*.

In the financial reports you create, the gross profit of your company represents your income minus the cost of goods sold. As soon as you turn on the QuickBooks preference for tracking inventory (page 567), QuickBooks adds cost of goods sold and inventory asset accounts to your chart of accounts.

Table 5-1. *Following inventory money through accounts*

Transaction	Account	Debit	Credit
Buy inventory	Checking Account		$500
Buy inventory	Inventory Asset	$500	
Sell inventory	Product Income		$1,000
Sell inventory	Accounts Receivable	$1,000	
Sell inventory	Inventory Asset		$500
Sell inventory	Cost of Goods Sold	$500	

Tip: Many companies don't bother with purchase orders—forms that record what you order from a vendor—to buy office supplies. But if you want to track whether you receive the supplies you bought, you can create purchase orders for them (page 215). Then use Non-inventory Part items for supplies you add to purchase orders but don't track as inventory.

Assembling Products

In the Premier and Enterprise editions of QuickBooks, you can create an Inventory Assembly item (page 113) that gathers Inventory Part items into a new item that you sell as a whole.

As shown in Figure 5-6, the New Item dialog box for an assembled item is similar to the one for an Inventory Part.

The main difference is that you select other inventory items or Inventory Assembly items as the building blocks of your new item. In the Bill of Materials section, you specify the components and the quantity of each. QuickBooks calculates the total cost of the bill of materials. Moreover, you set the price you charge for the entire ball of wax in the Sales Price field, regardless of the cost of the individual pieces.

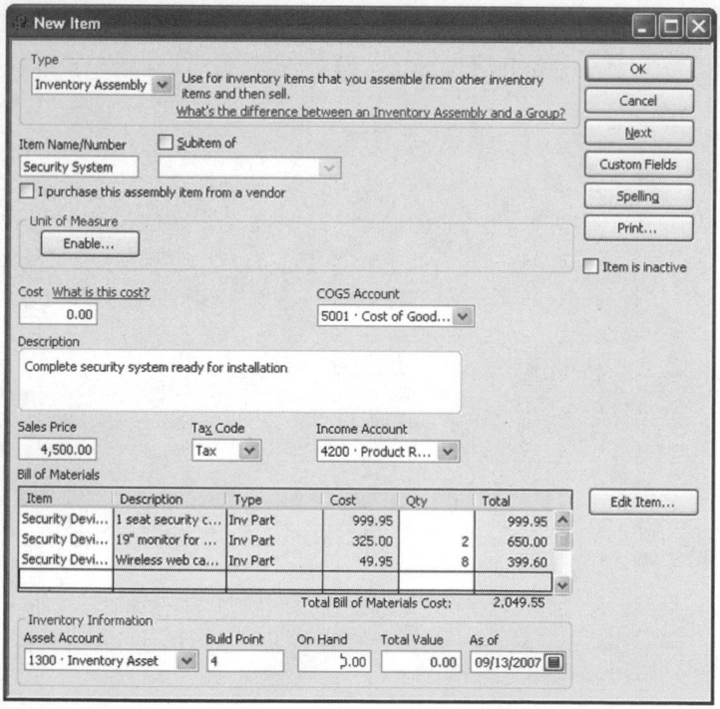

Figure 5-6:
An Inventory Assembly item includes a Build Point field instead of the Reorder Point field that Inventory items have. Because you assemble this type of item, you need to tell QuickBooks when to remind you to build more.

Turning Parts into Products

QuickBooks' Inventory Assembly item is a bit clunky to use, since it doesn't reflect the way many manufacturers treat assembled items. Manufacturers and distributors often pool manufacturing costs and then assign a value to the resulting batch of products that goes into inventory. To take this approach, you track the parts you use to build products (Non-inventory items) as *assets* instead of Inventory Assembly items. Here's how it works:

1. As you buy ingredients for a batch, assign the costs (via bills and so on) to an asset account specifically for inventory you build (often referred to as WIP for "work in progress").

2. When the batch is complete, make an inventory adjustment to add the items you made to inventory. Choose Vendors → Inventory Activities → Adjust Quantity/Value On Hand.

3. In the "Adjust Quantity/Value on Hand" dialog box, turn on the Value Adjustment checkbox (below the item table).

4. In the Adjustment Account drop-down list, choose the asset account for your work in progress.

5. In the New Qty box, type the number of items you built from your pool of parts. In the New Value box, type the value of the parts you used.

6. Click Save & Close to save the adjustment. The adjustment places the value of the new inventory in your inventory asset account. Because the inventory value matches what you paid for parts, the value adjustment also reduces the work in progress asset account balance to zero, in effect moving the value of your parts from work in progress asset account to your inventory asset account.

You have to know how many units you got out of the parts pool, so this approach works only if you build products in batches. If you constantly manufacture products, you need a program other than QuickBooks to track your inventory. Go to *http://marketplace.intuit.com*. On the menu bar, click Find Software and then choose Find Solutions by Industry on the drop-down menu. Then choose Manufacturing → Inventory and Order Management.

Inventory Part Fields

As described in the box on page 113, dollars move between accounts as you buy and sell inventory. Here's how you can use the fields for an Inventory Part item (shown in Figure 5-7) to define your company's inventory money trail and, at the same time, keep track of how much inventory you have:

- **Manufacturer's Part Number.** If you want your purchase orders to include the manufacturer's part number or unique identifier for the product, add it here.

Note: If you use QuickBooks Premier or QuickBooks Enterprise, you'll see the Unit of Measure section. You specify the units the inventory parts come in (bottles, cases, tons, and so on) and those units appear on invoices, sales forms, and reports.

- **Description on Purchase Transactions.** Any description you type here appears on the purchase orders you issue to purchase inventory items. Describe the product in terms that the vendor or manufacturer understands, because you can use a different and more customer-friendly description for the invoices that customers see.

- **Cost.** Enter what you pay for one unit of the product. QuickBooks assumes you sell products in the same units that you buy them. For example, if you purchase four cases of merlot but sell wine by the bottle, enter the price you pay per bottle in this field.

- **COGS Account.** Choose the account to which you want to post the costs *when you sell the product.* (COGS stands for "cost of goods sold," which is an account for tracking the underlying costs of the things you sell in order to calculate your gross profit.)

Note: If you don't have a cost of goods sold account in your chart of accounts, QuickBooks creates a Cost of Goods Sold account for you as soon as you type the name for your first inventory item in the New Item dialog box.

- **Preferred Vendor.** If you choose a vendor in this drop-down list, QuickBooks selects the preferred vendor when you add this Inventory Part item to a purchase order.

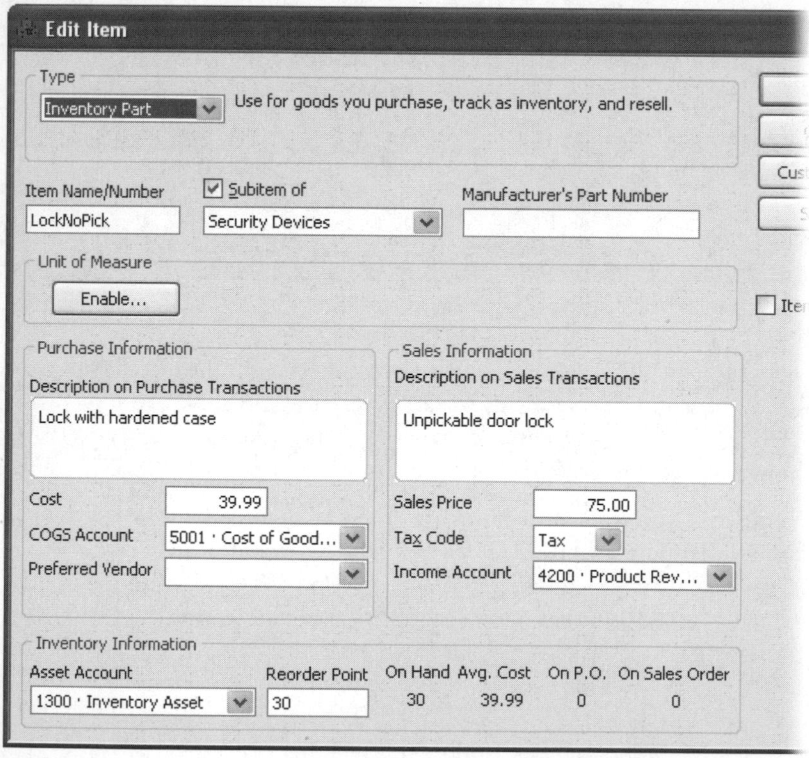

Figure 5-7:
When you create a new Inventory Part item, QuickBooks includes fields for purchasing and selling the item. The fields in the Purchase Information section show up on purchase orders. The Sales Information section sets the values you see on sales forms, such as invoices and sales receipts. The program simplifies building your initial inventory by letting you type the quantity you have on hand and their value.

- **Description on Sales Transactions.** When you type a description in the "Description on Purchase Transactions" box, QuickBooks copies that description into the "Description on Sales Transactions" box. If your customers wouldn't recognize the description you use to buy the product, type a more customer-friendly description in this field.

- **Sales Price.** In this field, type how much you charge for the product. Make sure that the Cost field uses the same units. For example, if you sell a bottle of merlot for $15, type *15* in this field and type the price you pay *per bottle* in the Cost field.

- **Tax Code.** When you add an item to an invoice, QuickBooks checks this code to see whether the item is taxable. (QuickBooks comes with two tax codes: Non for nontaxable items and Tax for taxable items.) Most products are taxable, although groceries are the most familiar exception.

- **Income Account.** This drop-down list includes all the accounts in your chart of accounts. Choose the *income* account for the money you receive when you sell one of these products.

- **Asset Account.** Choose the asset account for the value of the inventory you buy. Suppose you buy 100 bottles of merlot, which are worth the $8-a-bottle you paid. QuickBooks posts $800 into your inventory asset account. When you sell a bottle, QuickBooks deducts $8 from the inventory asset account and adds that $8 to the COGS Account.

- **Reorder Point.** Type the quantity on hand that would prompt you to order more. When your inventory hits that number, QuickBooks notifies you to reorder the product on the Reminders List (page 573).

Tip: If you can receive products quickly, use a lower reorder point to reduce the money tied up in inventory and prevent write-offs due to obsolete inventory. When products take some time to arrive, set the reorder point higher. Start with your best guess and edit this field as business conditions change.

- **On Hand.** If you already have some of the product in inventory, type the quantity in this field. From then on, if you use QuickBooks' inventory feature (Chapter 19) to record inventory you receive, you can rely on it to accurately post inventory values in your accounts.

- **Total Value.** If you filled in the On Hand field, fill in *this* field with the total value of the number of the products on hand. QuickBooks increases the value of your inventory asset account accordingly.

- **As of.** The program uses this date for the transaction it creates in the inventory asset account.

Note: You can enter values for the last three fields only when you create a new item. From then on, QuickBooks calculates how many you have on hand based on the number you've sold and the number you've received.

Non-Inventory Part Fields

You'll need Non-inventory Part items if you use purchase orders to buy supplies or other products that you don't track as inventory. For example, suppose you're a general contractor and you purchase materials for a job. When you use Non-inventory Part items, QuickBooks posts the cost of the products to an expense account and the income from selling the products to an income account. You don't have to bother with the inventory asset account because you transfer ownership of these products to the customer almost immediately. See page 225 to learn how to charge your customer for these reimbursable expenses.

The good news about Non-inventory Part items is that they use all the same fields as Service items. The bad news is the few subtle differences you need to know. Take the following disparities into account when you create Non-inventory Part items:

- **"This item is used in assemblies or is purchased for a specific customer:job" checkbox.** The checkbox goes by a different name than the one in Service items, but its behavior is the same. Turn on this checkbox when you want to use different values on purchase and sales transactions, that is, for items you resell. If the Non-inventory Part item is for office supplies you want to place on a purchase order, turn this checkbox off because you won't have sales values.

    When you turn this checkbox on, QuickBooks displays an Income Account field and an Expense Account field, like the fields you saw in Figure 5-5 (bottom). For Non-inventory Part items, the accounts that you choose are income and expense accounts specifically for products. Read the next bullet point to find out what happens when you turn this checkbox off.

- **Account.** If you don't resell this product and you thus turn off the "This item is used in assemblies or is purchased for a specific customer:job" checkbox, you see only one Account field. QuickBooks considers the account in this field an expense account for the purchase.

- **Tax Code.** The Tax Code field works exactly the same way as the Tax Code field for a Service item. Choose Non if the products are nontaxable (like groceries), and Tax if the products are taxable.

Other Types of Items

If a line on a sales form isn't a service or a product, read through this section to find the type of item you need.

Other Charge

The Other Charge item is aptly named because you use it for any charge that isn't quite a service or a product—for instance, shipping charges, finance charges, or bounced check charges. Other Charge items can be percentages or fixed amounts. For example, you can set up shipping charges as the actual cost of shipping, or estimate shipping as a percentage of the product cost.

If a customer holds back a percentage of your charges until you complete the job satisfactorily, create an Other Charge item for the retainer (that is, the portion of your invoice that the customer doesn't pay initially). In this case, when you create the invoice, enter a negative percentage so QuickBooks deducts the retainer from the invoice total. When your customer approves the job, create another invoice, this time using another Other Charge item, called Retention, to charge the customer for the amount she withheld.

Tip: Progress invoices (page 285) are another way to invoice customers for a portion of a job. They're ideal if you invoice the customer based on the percentage of the job you've completed or on the parts of the job that are complete.

For Other Charge items, the checkbox for hiding or showing cost fields comes with the label "This item is used in assemblies or is a reimbursable charge". For example, turn on this checkbox when you want to set the Cost field to what you pay and set the Sales Price field to what you charge your customers. You'll see the same sets of fields for purchases and sales as you do for Service and Non-inventory Part items.

Alternatively, you can create charges that don't link directly to expenses by turning off this checkbox. You can create a percentage, which is useful for calculating shipping based on the value of the products being shipped, as shown in Figure 5-8. When you turn off the "This is used in assemblies or is a reimbursable charge" checkbox, the Cost and Sales Price fields disappear, and the "Amount or %" field takes their place. If you want to create a dollar charge (like the dollar value charge for a country club's one-time initiation fee), type a whole or decimal number in this field.

Note: When you add a percentage-based Other Charge item to an invoice, such as shipping, Quick-Books applies the percentage to the previous line in the invoice. If you want to apply the Other Charge percentage to several items, add a Subtotal item to the invoice before the Other Charge item.

Subtotal

You'll need Subtotal items if you charge sales tax on the products you sell, or if you discount only some of the items on a sales form. You need only one Subtotal item, because a Subtotal item does only one thing—it totals all the amounts for the preceding lines up to the last subtotal. That means you can have more than one subtotal

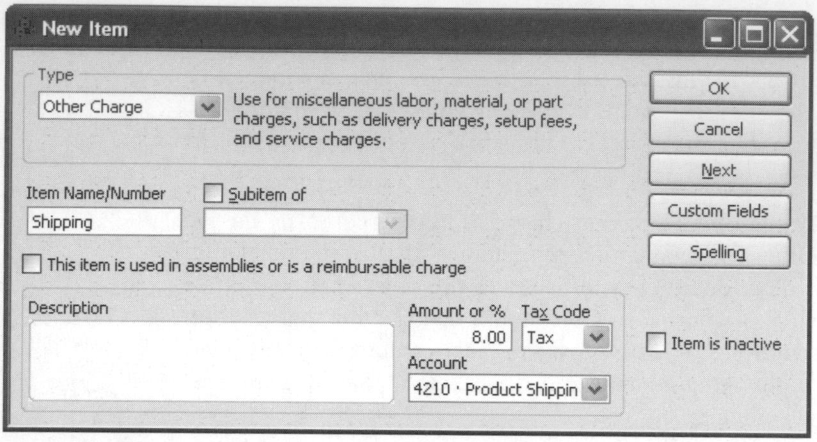

Figure 5-8:
To create a percentage-based charge, type a number followed by % in the "Amount or %" field. To set a dollar value, type a number as shown here.

on an invoice. For example, you can use one Subtotal item to add up the services you sell before applying a preferred customer product discount and a second Subtotal for product sales when you have to calculate sales tax. Because you can't change a Subtotal item's behavior in any way, a Subtotal item has just two fields: Item Name/Number and Description. You can type any name and description you wish in these fields, but in practically every case, Subtotal says it all.

Group

The Group item is a great timesaver, and it's indispensable if you have a tendency to forget things. Create a Group item that contains items that always appear together, such as each service you provide for a landscaping job. As shown in Figure 5-9, you can show or suppress the individual items that a Group item contains. When you add this Landscaping Group item to an invoice, QuickBooks automatically adds the Service items for phases, such as Excavation, Grading, Planting, and Cleanup.

You can also use a Group item to *hide* the underlying items, which is useful mainly when you create fixed-price invoices (page 264) and you don't want the customer to know how much profit you're making. Here's how you set up a Group item to do these things:

- **Group Name/Number.** Type a name for the group that gives a sense of the individual items within it, such as Landscaping Project.

- **Print items in group.** To show all the underlying items on your invoice, turn on the "Print items in group" checkbox. Figure 5-9 shows examples of both showing and hiding the items within a group.

- **Item.** To add an item to a group, click a blank cell in the Item column, as shown in Figure 5-10, and choose the item you want.

Invoice

	Date	Invoice #
	07/13/2008	88

Bill To
Pesky Properties, LLC
25 1st Ave. Suite 10
Peoria, IL
61601

P.O. No.	Terms
	2% 10 Net...

Item	Quantity	Description	Rate	Amount	Tax
Security Package					
Security services...	1	Review system security and physical building security	12,000.00	12,000.00	Non
Security services...	8	Install custom-designed security system	180.00	1,440.00	Non
Security Devices:...	1	1 seat security console	2,400.00	2,400.00	Tax
Security Devices:...	2	19" monitor for security console	660.00	1,320.00	Tax
Security Devices:...	5	Wireless web camera	119.94	599.70	Tax

Customer Message

Tax Colorado Sal... (3.8%) 164.15
Total 17,923.85

Bill To
Pesky Properties, LLC
25 1st Ave. Suite 10
Peoria, IL
61601

P.O. No.	Terms	Project
	2% 10 Net 30	

Quantity	Description	Rate	Amount
	Full package for security including audit, install, basic equipment		17,759.70
	Sales Tax	3.80%	164.15

Figure 5-9:
Top: When you add a Group item to an invoice (Security Package in this example), QuickBooks replaces that one item with all of the individual items, along with their prices, descriptions, and whatever else you've defined. To show these items on the invoice you send to your customer, turn on the "Print items in group" checkbox when you create the Group item.

Bottom: For fixed-price invoices, which you use when you charge the customer a fixed amount—regardless of how much or little it costs you to deliver—you don't want to show the underlying prices for each item you deliver. If you turn off the "Print items in group" checkbox when you create the Group item, you still see the individual items in the Create Invoices window, but the invoice you print to send to the customer shows only the Group item itself, along with the total price for all of the items in the Group.

- **Qty.** When you create a Group item, you can include different quantities of items, just like a box of note cards usually includes a few more envelopes than cards. For each item, type how many you typically sell as a group. If the quantity of each item varies, type *0* in the Qty cells. You can then specify the quantities on your invoices after you've added a Group item.

Discount

As a bookkeeper, you know that a discount is an amount you deduct from the standard price you charge. Volume discounts, customer loyalty discounts, and sale discounts are examples, and QuickBooks' Discount item calculates deductions like these. By using both Subtotal and Discount items, you can apply discounts to some or all of the charges on a sales form.

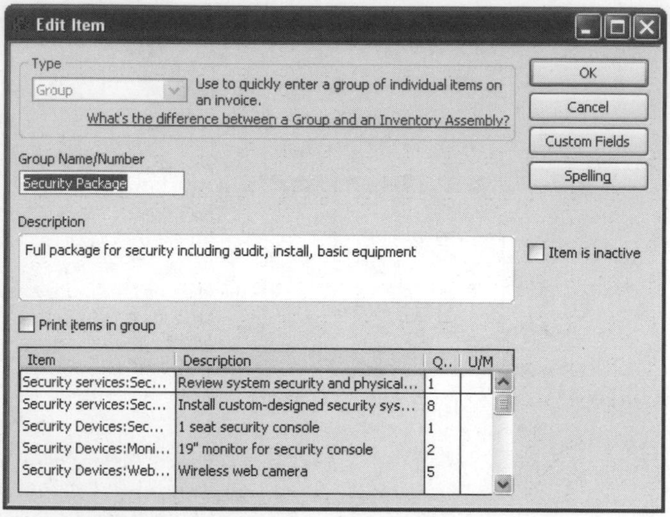

Figure 5-10:
When you add a Group item to an invoice and display all the underlying items, QuickBooks fills in the Description cells for each individual item with the contents of its Description field. In the New Item or Edit Item dialog boxes when you work on a group item, the background of the Description column is a different color to indicate that you can't edit these cells.

The Discount item deducts either a dollar amount or a percentage for discounts you apply at the time of sale, such as volume discounts, damaged goods discounts, or the discount you apply because your customer has incriminating pictures of you.

Note: Early payment discounts don't appear on sales forms because you won't know that a customer pays early until long after the sales form is complete. You apply early payment discounts in the Receive Payments window, described on page 337.

The fields for a Discount item are similar to those of an Other Charge item with a few small differences:

- **Amount or %.** This field is always visible for a Discount item. To deduct a dollar amount, type a positive number (whole or decimal) in this field. To deduct a percentage, type a whole or decimal number followed by %, like 5.5%.

- **Account.** Choose the account to which you want to post the discounts you apply. You can post discounts to either income accounts or expense accounts.

  When you post discounts to an income account, they appear as negative income, so your gross profit reflects what you actually earned after deducting discounts. Posting discounts to expense accounts, on the other hand, makes your income look better than it actually is. The discounts increase the amounts in your expense accounts, so your net profit is the same no matter which approach you use.

- **Tax Code.** When you choose a taxable code in the Tax Code field, QuickBooks applies the discount before it calculates sales tax. For instance, if customers buy products on sale, they pay sales tax on the sale price, not the original price.

When you choose a nontaxable code in the Tax Code field, QuickBooks applies the discount after it calculates sales tax. You'll rarely want to do this because you'll collect less sales tax from your customers than you have to send to the tax agencies.

Payment

When your customers send you payments, you can record them in your Quick-Books file using the Receive Payments command. If you're in the middle of creating invoices when the checks arrive, it's easier to record those payments by adding a Payment item to the customers' sales forms. A Payment item does more than reduce the amount owed on the invoice (see Figure 5-11).

Beyond the Type, Item Name/Number, and Descriptions fields, the Payment item boasts fields unlike those for other items. The fields for a Payment item designate the method of payment that a customer uses and whether you deposit the funds to a specific bank account or group them with other undeposited funds. For example, if your customers send checks, you save up the checks you receive each week and make one trip to deposit them in your bank. Banks sometimes transfer credit card payments into a bank account individually and sometimes group all the charges for the same day.

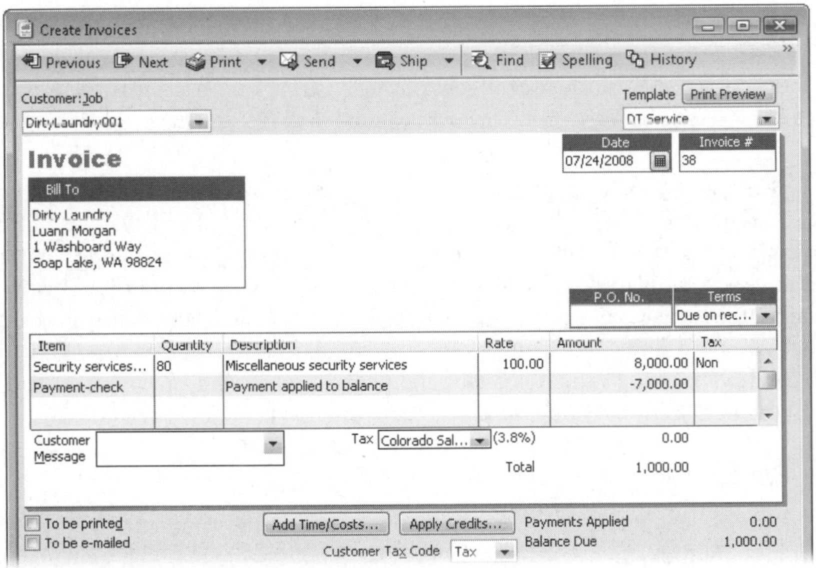

Figure 5-11:
A Payment item (here, a check) reduces the balance on an invoice by the amount the customer paid. That Payment item also executes the equivalent of a Receive Payments command: it deposits the funds into a bank account, or groups the payment with other undeposited funds.

Here's what the payment fields do:

- **Payment Method.** Choose the payment method, such as cash, check, or brand of credit card. In the Make Deposits window (page 354), you can filter pending deposits by the payment method.

- **Group with other undeposited funds.** Choose this option if you want to add the payment to other payments you received. When you add the Payment item to a sales form, QuickBooks adds the payment to the list of undeposited funds. To actually complete the deposit of all your payments, choose Banking → Make Deposits (page 354).

- **Deposit To.** If payments flow into an account without any action on your part, such as credit card or electronic payments, choose this option and then choose the bank account in the drop-down list.

Setting Up Sales Tax

If you don't have to collect and remit sales tax, skip this section and give thanks. Sales taxes aren't much more fun in QuickBooks than they are in real life. Confusingly, QuickBooks has two features for dealing with sales tax: *codes* and *items*. If you sell taxable and nontaxable products or services, Sales Tax codes specify whether or not an invoice item is taxable. Sales Tax items let you calculate and organize sales taxes charged by state and local authorities for the items on your invoices or other sales forms. This section describes both features and how to use each. If you sell products in a location burdened with multiple sales taxes (state, city, and local, say), you can use a Sales Tax Group item to calculate the total sales tax you have to charge. Your sales form shows the total, but QuickBooks keeps track of the tax you owe to each agency.

Note: Before you can dive into the details of setting up sales tax, you need to turn the sales tax feature on. Page 580 explains how.

For most product sales in most areas, you have to keep track of the sales taxes you collect and then send them to the appropriate tax agencies. Labor usually isn't taxable, whereas products usually are. Creating separate items for labor and materials makes it easy to apply sales tax to the right items or subtotals on your invoices. Separating the items you've identified as taxable or nontaxable can help you decide whether you need one or more items for a particular service or product. You can assign a sales tax code to the items you create for services and products. As you'll learn in the next section, QuickBooks has two built-in tax codes: Tax and Non.

Sales Tax Codes

Sales tax codes are QuickBooks' way of letting you specify whether to apply sales tax. Out of the box, the Sales Tax Code List comes with two self-explanatory options: Tax and Non. If you'd like to further refine taxable status, for example, to specify why a sale isn't taxable, you can add more choices.

You can apply tax codes in two places: to customers or to individual sales items. For example, nonprofit organizations and government agencies are usually tax-exempt (Non). In many states, food and services aren't taxable, although some states tax almost everything.

Assigning tax codes to customers

To tell QuickBooks whether a customer pays sales tax, open the Edit Customer dialog box (page 92) and click the Additional Info tab. Here's how QuickBooks interprets a customer's tax-exempt status:

- **Nontaxable customer.** When you assign Non or another nontaxable sales tax code to customers (page 77), QuickBooks doesn't calculate sales tax on *any* items you sell to them.

- **Taxable customer.** When you assign Tax or any taxable sales tax code to a customer, the program calculates sales tax only on the taxable items on their invoices.

Assigning tax codes to items

Some items aren't taxable whether or not a customer pays sales tax. As mentioned earlier, most services and non-luxury goods like food don't get taxed in most states. If you look carefully at the top invoice in Figure 5-9, you'll notice Non or Tax to the right of some of the amounts, which indicates nontaxable and taxable items, respectively. QuickBooks applies the sales tax only to taxable items to calculate the sales taxes on the invoice.

Items include a Tax Code field, so you can designate each item as taxable or nontaxable. In the Create Item or Edit Item dialog box (page 107), choose the code in the Tax Code drop-down list. (Taxable and nontaxable items can live together peacefully assigned to the same income account. QuickBooks figures out what to do with sales taxes based on tax codes, tax items, and whether a customer has to pay sales tax.)

Creating additional sales tax codes

Built-in tax codes aren't QuickBooks' most powerful feature: They let you mark customers and items as either taxable or nontaxable, and that's it. So, the two built-in options, Tax and Non, pretty much cover all possibilities. The only reason you may want to create additional sales tax codes is to classify nontaxable customers by their *reason* for exemption (nonprofit, government, wholesaler, out-of-state, and so on).

With that caveat in mind, here are the steps for creating additional sales tax codes in QuickBooks:

1. **Choose Lists → Sales Tax Code List.**

   The Sales Tax Code List window opens.

2. **To create a new code, press Ctrl+N. Or, at the bottom of the list window, click the Sales Tax Code drop-down menu and choose New.**

   The New Sales Tax Code dialog box opens.

3. **In the Sales Tax Code box, type a one- to three-character code.**

   For example, type *Gov* for a nontaxable sales tax code for government agencies, *Whl* for wholesalers who resell your products, or *Oos* for out-of-state customers, and so on.

4. **In the Description box, add some helpful details about the code.**

   For example, type a description that explains the purpose for the code, like *Government* for Gov.

5. **Choose the Taxable or Non-taxable option.**

   Sales tax codes are limited to taxable or nontaxable status.

6. **Click Next to add another code.**

   The code you created appears in the Sales Tax Code List window.

When you've added all the codes you want, click OK to close the New Sales Tax Code dialog box.

As you can see, QuickBooks' sales tax codes sport only a three-code ID, a description, and a taxable or nontaxable setting. They don't let you specify a sales tax percentage or note which tax office to send the collected sales taxes. That's where Sales Tax items (described next) come to the rescue.

Sales Tax Items

QuickBooks' built-in sales tax codes are fine for turning taxable status on and off at will, but you also have to tell QuickBooks the sales tax rate and which tax authority levies the tax. If you sell products in more than one state, Sales Tax items are the way to deal with varying tax regulations. Like the IRS, each tax agency wants to receive the taxes it's due. To track the taxes you owe to each agency, create a Sales Tax item for *each* agency. Also, if you sell products through direct mail, you'll need a Sales Tax item for each state you ship to, as described on page 126.

For example, suppose *both* local and state taxes apply to products you sell in your store. And, for customers to whom you ship goods in *other* states, sales taxes for those other states apply as well. You can create separate Sales Tax items for your local tax and the state sales taxes for each state in which you do business. Or, if one tax authority collects several sales taxes, QuickBooks has its Sales Tax Group feature (page 128) to help you collect them all in one shot.

Unlike sales tax codes, which can apply to both customers and products, Sales Tax items apply only to customers, which makes sense when you think about it, since sales tax rates usually depend on the customer's location. If the customer is in the boonies, you might assign the state Sales Tax item because the customer pays only that one tax. Alternatively, a customer smack in the middle of downtown might have to pay state tax, city tax, and a special district tax. If you assign Sales Tax items to customers (page 129), QuickBooks automatically fills in the Sales Tax item on your invoices to show the customer the sales taxes they pay.

To create a Sales Tax item, in the New Item dialog box, from the Type drop-down list, choose Sales Tax Item. Then fill in the fields (see Figure 5-12) as follows:

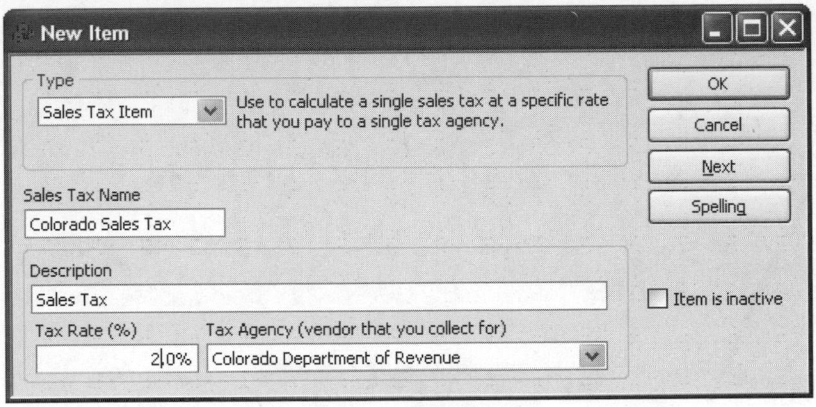

Figure 5-12:
The Tax Name field can include up to 31 characters—more than enough to use the 4- or 5-digit codes that many states use for sales taxes. The Tax Rate (%) field sets the percentage of the sales tax. The Tax Agency drop-down list shows the vendors you've set up, so you can choose the tax agency to which you remit the taxes. If a tax authority collects the sales taxes for several government entities, a Sales Tax group is the way to go. (See the box on page 128.)

- **Sales Tax Name.** Fill in this box with a name for the sales tax. You can use the identifiers that the tax authority uses, or a more meaningful name like Denver City Tax.

- **Description.** If you want QuickBooks to display a description of the sales tax on your invoices or sales forms, type the description that you want to appear.

- **Tax Rate (%).** In this box, type the percentage rate for the sales tax. Quick-Books automatically adds the percent sign (%), so simply type the decimal number—for example, *4.3* for a 4.3% tax rate.

- **Tax Agency.** In this drop-down list, choose the tax authority that collects the sales tax. If you haven't created the vendor for the tax authority, choose *<Add New>*.

Modifying Items

You can change information about an item even if you've already used the item in transactions. The changes you make don't affect existing transactions. When you create *new* transactions using the item, QuickBooks grabs the updated information to fill in fields.

In the Item List window (click Items & Services in the QuickBooks Home page), double-click the item you want to edit. QuickBooks opens the Edit Item dialog box. Make the changes you want and then click OK. Or if you want to modify several items at once, use the new Add/Edit Multiple List Entries feature (see page 86).

Sales Tax Groups

A Sales Tax Group item calculates the total sales tax for multiple Sales Tax items—perfect when you sell goods in an area rife with state, city, and local sales taxes. The customer sees only the total sales tax, but QuickBooks tracks how much you owe to each agency. This item works in the same way as the Group item, except that you add Sales Tax items to cells instead of items such as Service, Inventory, and Other Charges.

As shown in Figure 5-13, a Sales Tax Group item applies several Sales Tax items at once. The program totals the individual tax rates into a total rate for the group, which is what the customer sees on the invoice. For example, businesses in Denver charge a combined sales tax of 7.6%, which is made up of a Denver sales tax, the Colorado sales tax, an RTD tax, and a few special district taxes. Before you can create a sales tax group, you first need to create each of the Sales Tax items that you plan to include.

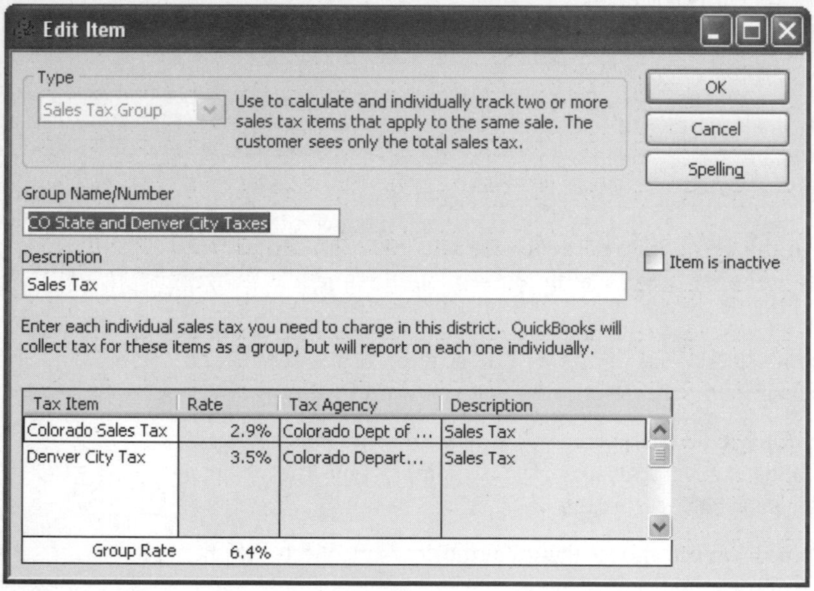

Figure 5-13:
After you type the name or number of the sales tax group and a description, click the Tax Item drop-down list to choose one of the individual Sales Tax items to include in the group. QuickBooks fills in the rate, tax agency, and description from the Sales Tax item.

Note: If you change an account associated with an item (like the income account to which sales post), the Account Change dialog box appears when you save the edited item. This dialog box tells you that all future transactions for that item will use the new account. If you also want to change the account on all *existing* transactions using the item, click Yes. Click No to keep the old account on existing transactions using the item.

Be particularly attentive if you decide to change the Type field. You can change only Non-inventory Part or Other Charge items to other item types, and they can morph into only certain item types: Service, Non-inventory Part, Other Charge, Inventory Part, or Inventory Assembly (this last type is available only in QuickBooks

Premier and Enterprise). If you conclude from this that you can't change a Non-inventory Part item back once you change it to an Inventory part, you're absolutely correct. To prevent type change disasters, back up your QuickBooks file before switching item types (see page 163).

Tip: Parts that you keep in inventory have value that shows up as an asset of your company, but non-inventory parts show up simply as expenses. If you change an item from a Non-inventory Part to an Inventory Part, be sure to choose a date in the "As of" field that's *after* the date of the last transaction using the item in its Non-inventory Part guise.

UP TO SPEED

Assigning Sales Tax Items to Customers

Once you've created Sales Tax items, you associate them with customers. To do so, follow these steps:

1. In the New Customer or Edit Customer dialog box, click the Additional Info tab.

2. In the Tax Code box, choose a sales tax code (page 124).

3. In the Tax Item box, choose the corresponding Sales Tax item or Sales Tax Group item.

If you prefer to assign Sales Tax items as you go, on an invoice or other sales form, choose the Sales Tax item or group you want to assign to the customer. When you save the form, QuickBooks asks if you want to change the customer record to use that item. Click Yes. QuickBooks adds the Sales Tax item or group to the customer record, which means it'll automatically appear in the Tax box the next time you create an invoice or other sales transaction for that customer.

Hiding and Deleting Items

Deleting items and hiding them are two totally different actions, although the visible result is the same—QuickBooks doesn't display the items in the Item List window. The only time you'll delete an item is when you create it by mistake and want to eliminate it permanently from the Item List. As you might discover when you attempt to delete an item, deleting an item is possible only if you've never used it in a transaction.

Hiding items doesn't have the same restrictions as deleting them, and offers a couple of advantages to boot. First, when you hide items, they don't appear in your Item List, which prevents you from selecting the wrong item as you create an invoice or other sales form. And unlike deleting, hiding is reversible: You can switch items to active status if you start selling them again. Suppose you hid the item for bell-bottom hip-huggers in 1974. Decades later, when '70s retro becomes cool again, you can reactivate the item and use it on sales forms. (Of course, you'll probably want to edit the cost and sales price to reflect today's higher prices.)

Hiding Items

If you've sold an item in the past, then the only way to remove it from the Item List is to hide it. Hiding items means that your Item List shows only the items you currently use. You'll scroll less to find the items you want and you're less likely to pick the wrong item by mistake. If you start selling an item again, you can reactivate it so that it appears on the Item List once more. If you're wondering how you make an item reappear if it isn't visible, here's a guide to hiding and reactivating items in your Item List:

- **Hide an item.** In the Item List, right-click the item and choose Make Item Inactive from the shortcut menu. The item disappears from the Item List.

- **View all items, active or inactive.** At the bottom of the Item List window, turn on the "Include inactive" checkbox. QuickBooks displays a column with an X as its heading and shows an X in that column for every inactive item in the list. The "Include inactive" checkbox is grayed out when all the items are active.

- **Reactivate an item.** First, turn on the "Include inactive" checkbox to display all items. To reactivate the item, click the X next to its name. When you click the X next to a parent item, QuickBooks opens the Activate Group dialog box. If you want to reactivate all the subitems as well as the parent, click Yes.

If you find that you're constantly hiding items that you no longer sell, your item list might be too specific for your constantly changing product list. For example, if you create 100 items for the clothes that are fashionable for teenagers in May, those items will be obsolete by June. Consider creating more generic items, such as pants, shorts, t-shirts, and bathing suits. You can reuse these items season after season, year after year, without worrying about running out of room on the Item List, which is limited to 14,500 items.

Tip: To see how many items you have, press F2 to open the Product Information window. Then, head to the List Information section in the lower-right corner of the window and look for Total Items.

Deleting Items

If you improperly create an item and catch your mistake immediately, deleting the offender is no sweat. Use any one of these methods to delete an item:

- In the Item List window, select the item you want to delete and press Ctrl+D.

- In the Item List window, select the item, and then choose Edit → Delete Item (if commands on menus are more to your liking).

- In the menu at the bottom of the window, click Item and then choose Delete Item.

If you try to delete an item that's used in even one transaction, QuickBooks warns you that you can't delete it. Say you created an item by mistake and then compounded the problem by inadvertently adding the item to an invoice. When you realize your error and try to delete the item, QuickBooks refuses to oblige. If you used the item in one or two recent transactions, you can probably find those transactions and replace the item without thinking too hard. (Open the Item List by choosing Lists → Item List. Right-click the item and choose QuickReport on the shortcut menu. QuickBooks displays a report with all the transactions using that item.) When you've removed the item from all transactions, use one of the methods above to delete it.

If you blasted out a bunch of transactions, it's easier to find the transactions with the "Sales by Item Detail" report, which includes a heading for each item you sell, and groups transactions underneath each heading. If you sell lots of items, you probably want the report to show the transactions only for the item you want to delete. Here's how you modify the "Sales by Item Detail" report and then edit the transactions:

1. **To create a "Sales by Item Detail" report, choose Reports → Sales → "Sales by Item Detail".**

   QuickBooks opens the "Sales by Item Detail" report in its own window.

2. **To modify the report, in the report window tool bar, click Modify Report.**

   QuickBooks opens the "Modify Report: Sales by Item Detail" dialog box. To produce a report with transactions for one item, modify the date range and filter the report based on the item's name, as shown in Figure 5-14.

   If you know when you first used the item in a transaction, type or click that date in the From box. QuickBooks sets the date in the To box to the current date, which is perfect for this situation. Alternatively, in the Dates drop-down list, choose a predefined date range, such as "This Fiscal Year-to-date".

3. **To edit a transaction to remove an item, in the "Sales by Item Detail" window, double-click the transaction.**

   Based on the type of transaction you double-click, QuickBooks opens the corresponding dialog box or window. For example, if you double-click an invoice, QuickBooks opens the Create Invoices window and displays the invoice you chose.

   In the Item Code column, click the cell containing the item you want to delete, click the downward-pointing arrow in the cell, and then choose the correct item from the Item drop-down list.

4. **To save the transaction with the revised item, click Save & Close.**

   You'll know that you've successfully eliminated the item from all sales transactions when the report in the "Sales by Item Detail" window shows no transactions.

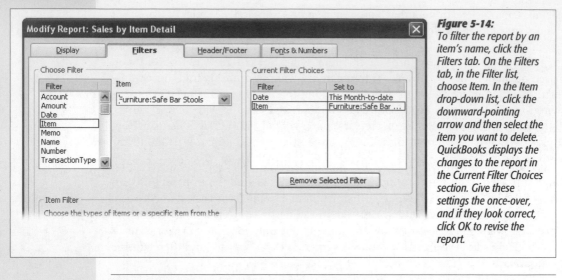

Figure 5-14:
To filter the report by an item's name, click the Filters tab. On the Filters tab, in the Filter list, choose Item. In the Item drop-down list, click the downward-pointing arrow and then select the item you want to delete. QuickBooks displays the changes to the report in the Current Filter Choices section. Give these settings the once-over, and if they look correct, click OK to revise the report.

Tip: To be sure that you've removed all links to the item, in the menu bar at the top of the report window, click Refresh to update the report based on the current data in your QuickBooks file.

5. **Finally, back in the Item List window, select the item you want to delete and press Ctrl+D. In the Delete Item message box, click Yes to confirm the deletion of the item.**

The item disappears from your Item List for good.

6. **To close the report window, click the Close box at the upper-right.**

The item is gone and you're ready to get back to work.

CHAPTER 6

Setting Up Other QuickBooks Lists

Open any QuickBooks window, dialog box, or form, and you're bound to bump into at least one QuickBooks list. These drop-down lists make it easy to fill in transactions and forms. Creating an invoice? If you pick the customer and job from the Customer:Job List, QuickBooks fills in the customer's address, payment terms, and other fields for you. Selecting the payment terms from the Terms List tells QuickBooks how to calculate the due date for the invoice. If you choose an entry in the Price Level List, QuickBooks calculates the discount you extend to your customers for the goods they buy. Even the products and services you sell to your customers come from the Item List, which you already learned about in Chapter 5.

In this chapter, you'll discover what the different lists actually do for you and whether you should bother setting them up for your business. Because some lists have their own unique fields (such as the Price Level Type for a Price Level entry), you'll also learn what the various fields do and how to fill them in. If you already know which lists and list entries you want, you can skip to "Creating and Editing List Entries" on page 152 to master the techniques that work for most lists in QuickBooks, such as creating and editing entries, hiding entries, and so on. Once you learn how to work with one QuickBooks list, the doors to almost every other list open as well.

Note: The Customer, Vendor, and Employee lists are the exceptions. Although you'll learn about the Vendor List in this chapter, here are the other chapters that provide instructions for working with a few of the QuickBooks lists:

- The **Chart of Accounts**, which is a list of your bookkeeping accounts, is covered in Chapter 3.

- The **Customer:Job List**, which includes entries for both customers and their jobs, is the topic for Chapter 4.

- The **Item List** helps you fill in invoices and other sales forms with services and products you sell and is described in Chapter 5. (Although the Sales Tax Code List appears on the Lists menu, sales tax codes are inextricably linked to how you handle sales tax. Details for setting up the Sales Tax Code List are described in Chapter 5, on page 125.)

- Chapter 12 shows you how to have QuickBooks **memorize transactions** to reuse in the future.

- If you turn on the payroll feature (page 571), the Lists menu shows the **Payroll Item List** command, which covers the deposits and deductions on your payroll. Payroll Items are quite specialized, and QuickBooks has tools to help you set them up, which are explained in detail in Chapter 14 on page 364.

- Chapter 24 describes how to create or modify **templates** for your QuickBooks business forms.

The Vendor List

There's no way around it: You're going to work with vendors and pay them for their services and products. The telephone company, your accountant, and the subcontractor who installs Venetian plaster in your spec houses are all vendors. You can create vendors in QuickBooks one at a time, whenever you get the first bill from a new vendor. But if you already know who most of your vendors are, it's easier to create those entries all at once so that you can write checks or enter bills without interruptions.

The Add/Edit Multiple List Entries feature, new in QuickBooks 2010, lets you paste data from Microsoft Excel or copy values from vendor to vendor. It works the same way for customer, vendor, and item lists, and you can read how to use it on page 86.

Importing vendor information into QuickBooks is the fastest way to create oodles of vendor records. After you create a map between QuickBooks fields and fields in another program, you can transfer all your vendor information with one command. In this section, you'll see what fields QuickBooks uses for vendor information. Use the instructions on page 80 in conjunction with the vendor fields in Table 6-1 to import vendor records into QuickBooks.

Creating, editing, and reviewing your vendors in QuickBooks is a breeze with the Vendor Center. Like the Customer Center (page 38), the Vendor Center lists the details of your vendors and their transactions in one easy-to-use dashboard. To open the Vendor Center window, use any of the following methods:

- Choose Vendors → Vendor Center.

- On the left side of the QuickBooks Home page, click Vendors.

- In the icon bar, click Vendor Center.

Create a new vendor from the Vendor Center window by pressing Ctrl+N (or, in the Vendor Center menu bar, clicking New Vendor). The New Vendor dialog box opens.

Many of the fields that you see should be familiar from creating customers in QuickBooks. For example, the Vendor Name field corresponds to the Customer Name field, which you might remember is actually more of a code than a name. Use the same sort of naming convention for vendors that you use for customers (see the box on page 71). As with customer records, you're better off leaving the Opening Balance field empty and building your current vendor balance by entering the invoices or bills they send.

Entering Address Information

If you print checks and envelopes to pay your bills, you'll need address and contact information for your vendors. The Address Info tab in the New Vendor dialog box (which you opened in the previous section) has fields for the vendor's address and contact information, which are almost identical to customer address and contact fields, so see page 74 if you need help filling them in. The one additional vendor field on the Address Info tab is "Print on Check as", which QuickBooks automatically fills in with the name you enter in the vendor's Company Name field. When you print checks, QuickBooks fills in the payee with the name in the "Print on Check as" field, so to use a different name, simply edit the name in this box.

Additional Info

The Additional Info tab, shown in Figure 6-1, has fields that are a bit different than the ones you see for customers. The following list describes what they are and what you can do with them.

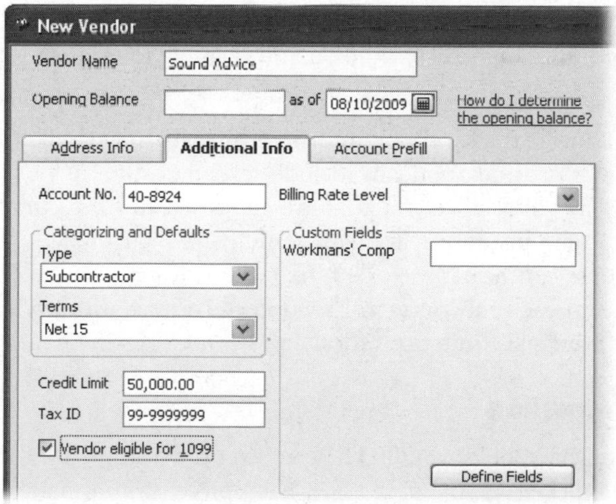

Figure 6-1:
The fields on the Additional Info tab are easy to fill in—just remember that they pertain to your account with the vendor. For example, the Account No. field holds the account number that the vendor assigned to your company, and the Credit Limit field represents how much credit the vendor extends to your company.

- **Account No.** When you create customers, you can assign an account number to them. When it's your turn to be a customer, your vendors return the favor and assign an account number to *your* company. If you fill in this box with the account number that the vendor gave you, QuickBooks prints it in the memo field of the checks you print. Even if you don't print checks, keeping your account number in QuickBooks is handy if a question arises about one of your payments.

- **Type.** If you want to classify vendors or generate reports based on types of vendors, choose a type in the Type drop-down list or create a new type in the Vendor Type List (page 147) by choosing *<Add New>*. For example, if you assign a Tax type to all the tax agencies you remit taxes to, you can easily prepare a report of your tax liabilities and payments.

- **Terms.** Choose the payment terms that the vendor extended to your company. The entries in the Terms drop-down list (page 147) apply to both vendors and customers.

- **Credit Limit.** If the vendor has set a credit limit for your company (like $45,500 for your credit card), type that value in this box. That way, QuickBooks warns you when you create a purchase order that pushes your credit balance above your credit limit.

- **Tax ID.** You have to fill in this field with the vendor's Employer Identification Number (EIN) or Social Security number *only if* you're going to create a 1099 for the vendor.

Note: When you hire subcontractors to do work for you, you first ask them to fill out a W-9 form, which tells you the subcontractor's taxpayer identification number (Social Security number or Federal Employer Information Number, for example). Then, at the end of the year, you fill out a 1099 tax form telling them how much you paid them.

- **Vendor eligible for 1099.** Turn on this checkbox if you're going to create a 1099 for the vendor.

- **Custom fields.** If you want to track vendor information that isn't handled by the fields that QuickBooks provides, you can include several custom fields (see the box on page 155). Say your subcontractors are supposed to have current certificates for workers' comp insurance, and you could be in big trouble if you hire a subcontractor whose certificate is expired. If you create a custom field to hold the expiration date for each subcontractor's workers' comp certificate, you can generate a report of workers' comp expiration dates.

Importing Vendor Information

To import vendor data into QuickBooks, you first have to export a delimited text file or a spreadsheet from the other program (page 600). Each piece of information is separated with commas or tabs, or into columns and rows in a spreadsheet file.

QuickBooks looks for keywords in the import file to tell it what to do, so you usually have to rename some headings to transform an export file produced by another program into an import file that QuickBooks can read. QuickBooks' vendor keywords and the fields they represent appear in Table 6-1. Fortunately, Excel and other spreadsheet programs make it easy to edit the headings in cells.

Tip: To see how QuickBooks wants a delimited file to look, export your current QuickBooks vendor list to an .iif file (page 597) and then open it in Excel.

Table 6-1. Vendor keywords and their respective fields

Keyword	Field contents
NAME	(Required) The Vendor Name field, which specifies the name or code that you use to identify the vendor.
PRINTAS	The name you want to appear as the payee when you print a check to the vendor.
ADDR1 – ADDR5	Up to five lines of the vendor's billing address.
VTYPE	The vendor type category. If you import a vendor type that doesn't exist in your Vendor Type List, QuickBooks adds the new type to the list.
CONT1	The name of the primary contact for the vendor.
CONT2	The name of an alternate contact for the vendor.
PHONE1	The number stored in the Phone Number field.
PHONE2	The vendor's alternate phone number.
FAXNUM	The vendor's fax number.
EMAIL	The vendor's email address.
NOTE	Despite the keyword, this field is the name or number of the account, stored in the Account No. field. To set up a vendor as an online payee, you have to assign an account number.
TAXID	The vendor's tax ID, which you will need to produce a 1099 for the vendor at the end of the year.
LIMIT	The dollar amount of your credit limit with the vendor.
TERMS	The payment terms the vendor requires.
NOTEPAD	This field is your opportunity to document details you want to remember.
SALUTATION	The title that goes before the contact's name, such as Mr., Ms., or Dr.
COMPANYNAME	The name of the vendor's company as you want it to appear on documents and transactions.
FIRSTNAME	The primary contact's first name.
MIDINIT	The primary contact's middle initial.
LASTNAME	The primary contact's last name.
CUSTFLD1- CUSTFLD15	Custom field entries for the vendor, if you've defined any. To learn how to create custom fields, see page 155.

Table 6-1. *Vendor keywords and their respective fields (continued)*

Keyword	Field contents
1099	Y or N to indicate whether you produce a 1099 for the vendor at the end of the year.
HIDDEN	This field is set to N if the vendor is active in your QuickBooks file. Inactive vendors are set to Y.

Filling in Expense Accounts Automatically

When you write checks, record credit card charges, or enter bills for a vendor, you have to fill in the expense account to which you want to assign the payment.

QuickBooks is happy to fill in expense account names for you if you tell it which ones you typically use. Then all you do is type the amounts that go with each account. Here are the steps:

1. **In the New Vendor dialog box, click the Account Prefill tab.**

   The Account Prefill tab includes three drop-down lists, so you can assign up to three expense accounts for each vendor. (Each drop-down list shows *all* the accounts in your chart of accounts, not just expense accounts.)

2. **In each drop-down list, choose the expense account you want.**

   For example, if you get office equipment and supplies from one vendor, choose Office Equipment in the first drop-down list and Office Supplies in the second.

Tip: To remove the account assignments, click Clear All.

---

3. **Click OK to save the vendor record.**

   When you choose the vendor name in the Write Checks, Enter Credit Card Charges, or Enter Bills dialog box, QuickBooks fills in the Expenses tab with any prefill expense accounts you assigned. If you record a transaction directly in the register, the expense accounts appear automatically in the split transaction Account fields (if you assign more than one expense account) as soon as you choose the vendor's name.

   You don't have to use the prefill accounts. Instead, you can simply click an Account field and choose a different account or leave the amounts blank and add new accounts below the prefilled entries.

Categorizing with Classes

Classes are the only solution if you want to classify income and expenses by business unit, department, location, partner, consultant, or other categories that span multiple accounts in your chart of accounts or multiple types of customers, jobs, and vendors. They also come in handy for tracking the Allocation of Functional Expenses that nonprofit organizations have to show on financial statements. Not everyone needs classes, so don't feel that you *have* to use them. The box below can help you decide.

Tip: Before you decide to turn on classes, use QuickBooks without them for a few weeks or months. If you can generate all the reports you need without classes, don't burden yourself with another field to fill in. For example, if you run restaurants in a couple of locations, you don't necessarily need classes to track your business for each restaurant. You could create income accounts for each location instead. However, to separately track expenses for each restaurant, classes for each location are a lot easier than creating multiple sets of expense accounts. If you work *without* classes and then decide to use them after all, you'll have to go back and edit past transactions to assign classes to them. Or, you can start using classes at the beginning of a new fiscal period (and not run class-based reports prior to that date).

UP TO SPEED

Do You Need Classes?

You can call on several QuickBooks features (such as accounts, customer and job types, and classes) to help you track your business. Each tracking feature has its advantages, so how do you decide which ones to use to evaluate your performance? Here's a brief description of each feature and the best time to use it:

- **Accounts.** You can use accounts to segregate income and expenses in several ways. For instance, keep income from your physical store separate from your website sales by creating two separate income accounts. Accounts are the fastest way to see performance because Profit & Loss reports built into QuickBooks (page 494) automatically include results by account.

- **Customer, job, and vendor types.** To analyze income by wholesale, retail, online, and other types of customers, use customer types to classify your customers. Types are more limited in scope than accounts—customer types apply only to customers (page 145). When you assign customer types, you can filter the reports you generate to show results for a specific type of customer. Likewise, job types and vendor types (page 147) help you categorize only by job and vendor, respectively.

- **Classes.** Classes cut across accounts, customers, jobs, and vendors because you assign a class to an individual transaction, such as a check, bill, or invoice. Classes are perfect for categories that span accounts and types. Suppose the partners in your company help customers implement technology and tighten their security. You've decided to use separate income accounts to track technology sales and security sales, and you use customer types to track work for the government versus the private sector. You also want to track income and expenses by partner—but each partner works on any type of service for any type of customer. You can create classes to track partners' sales and expenses, regardless of which service the partner delivers or the type of customer. A Profit & Loss report by class (page 435) tells you how each partner is performing.

If you choose to work with classes, be sure to follow these guidelines to get the most out of them:

- **Pick one use for your classes.** QuickBooks has only one list of classes, and every class should represent the same type of classification. Moreover, you can assign just one class to a transaction, so classes add only one additional way to categorize your transactions. For example, once you assign a class for a business unit to a transaction, there's no way to assign another class—to identify the office branch, say—to the same transaction.

- **Use classes consistently.** Make sure to use classes on *every* transaction. Otherwise, your class-based reports won't be accurate.

Tip: QuickBooks can remind you to enter a class for a transaction if you forget. Choose Edit → Preferences, click the Accounting icon, click the Company Preferences tab, and then turn on the "Prompt to assign classes" checkbox. If you try to save a transaction without an entry in the Class field, QuickBooks gives you a chance to add the class or save the transaction without one.

- **Create a catch-all class.** Set up a class like Other so that you can still classify transactions even if they don't fit into any of the specific classes you've defined.

Here's how to set up classes:

1. **Turn on the class-tracking feature (page 551).**

   If class tracking is turned off, the Lists menu won't display the Class List command. To turn on class tracking, you need to be a QuickBooks administrator, because classes affect everyone in your organization who uses the program. If you aren't a QuickBooks administrator, you'll have to convince someone who is to turn on classes. To do so, choose Edit → Preferences, click the Accounting icon, click the Company Preferences tab, and then turn on the "Use class tracking" checkbox. QuickBooks automatically turns on the "Prompt to assign classes" checkbox. Click OK to close the dialog box.

2. **Choose Lists → Class List.**

   The Class List window opens.

3. **In the Class List window, press Ctrl+N (or click Class and then choose New on the drop-down menu).**

   The New Class dialog box opens. You can create all of your classes at once by filling in the fields for one class and then clicking Next to create another one.

4. **In the Class Name box, type the name of the class.**

   If you want to create classes that are subclasses to a parent (say to set up subclasses for each region within a business unit), turn on the "Subclass of" checkbox. Then, in the drop-down list, choose the parent class you want.

5. **Click Next to create another class, or click OK to close the New Class dialog box.**

   If you realize you need another class while working on a transaction, you can create an entry by choosing *<Add New>* in the Class drop-down list, as you can see in Figure 6-2.

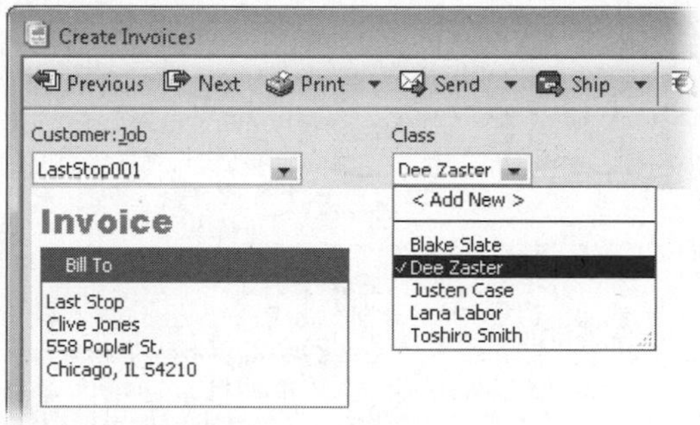

Figure 6-2:
After you turn on class tracking, every transaction you create includes a Class field. To assign a class to a transaction, choose one of the classes from the drop-down list or choose <Add New>.

Price Levels

Whether you give your favorite customers price breaks or increase other customers' charges because they keep asking for "just one more thing," you can apply discounts or markups when you create invoices. Remembering who gets discounts and what percentage you apply is tough when you have a lot of customers, and it's bad form to mark up a favorite customer's prices by mistake. Say hello to QuickBooks' Price Level list. When you define price levels and assign them to customers, QuickBooks takes care of adjusting the prices on every invoice you create. You can also apply a price level to invoice lines to mark up or discount individual items.

Creating a Price Level

To create a price level, do the following:

1. **If the Price Level preference isn't turned on already, do that now.**

   Choose Edit → Preferences, click the Sales & Customers icon, and then click the Company Preferences tab. Turn on the "Use price levels" checkbox, and then click OK. (If you don't turn on the Price Level preference, the Price Level List command doesn't appear on the Lists menu.)

2. **Choose Lists → Price Level List.**

   The Price Level List window opens.

3. **In the Price Level List window, press Ctrl+N (or click Price Level, and then choose New on the drop-down menu).**

   The New Price Level dialog box opens.

4. **In the Price Level Name box, type a name for the price level.**

If you have a fixed set of discounts, you might name the price levels by the percentage, like Discount 10 and Discount 20, for example. An alternative is to name price levels by their purpose, like Customer Loyalty or User Group Discount.

5. **In the "This price level will" box, choose "increase" or "decrease" based on whether you want the price level to mark up or discount prices.**

In QuickBooks Pro, the Price Level Type box is automatically set to Fixed % because you can create price levels only with fixed percentage increases or decreases, as shown in Figure 6-3. A fixed percentage price level does one thing: increases or decreases a price by a fixed percentage.

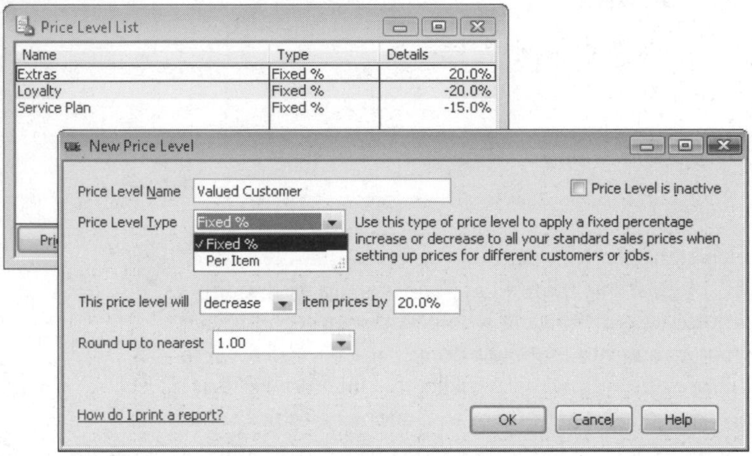

Figure 6-3:
Think of fixed percentage price levels as standard discounts or markups. For example, you can create a price level called Extras to boost prices by 20 percent. Then, assign that price level in the customer record (page 77) for every nitpicker you work for. (Although price level names don't appear on your customer invoices, it's still a good idea to choose names that are meaningful without being rude.)

In QuickBooks Premier and Enterprise, you can create price levels that apply to individual items in your Item List. In the Price Level Type drop-down list, choose Per Item. The New Price Level dialog box immediately displays a table containing all your items. In the Custom Price column, type the price for an item at that price level. Suppose you sell calendars to retail stores for $5 each. The Standard Price column would show 5.00 for the calendar item. If you're creating a price level for nonprofit organizations, you could type 3.50 in the item's Custom Price cell so that a nonprofit would pay only $3.50 for a calendar.

If you want to apply percentages to several items in the list, there's a shortcut for calculating custom prices. Turn on the checkboxes for the items that use the same percentage increase or decrease. Then, in the "Adjust price of marked items to be" box, type the percentage. In the drop-down list, choose "lower" or "higher". You can set the price level to calculate based on the standard price, the cost, or the current custom price. When you click Adjust, QuickBooks fills in the Custom Price cells for the marked items with the new custom prices.

To apply different percentages to another set of items, clear any checkmarks and then select the next set of items. Repeat the steps to define the percentage adjustment.

Note: If you work with more than one currency and use QuickBooks Premier or Enterprise, you can set up price levels for individual items to set their prices in a different currency. In the New Price Level dialog box, choose the currency in the Currency drop-down list. Then, in the Custom Price cell, type the price for the item in the foreign currency. When you add the item to an invoice, choose the currency price level in the Rate drop-down list.

6. **For percentage price levels, in the "Round up to nearest" drop-down list, choose the type of rounding you want to apply.**

   The "Round up to nearest" feature is handy if the percentages you apply result in fractions of pennies or amounts too small to bother with. This setting lets you round discounts to pennies, nickels, dimes, quarters, 50 cents, and even whole dollars (if you *really* hate making change). The box on page 144 explains fancier rounding you can apply.

7. **Click OK to close the New Price Level dialog box.**

   To create another price level, repeat steps 3–7.

Note: You can't create price levels on the fly while you're creating an invoice. The easiest solution to a missing price level is to adjust the price on the invoice manually. Then, after the invoice is done, add the price level to your Price Level List.

Applying a Price Level

You can apply price levels to invoices in two ways:

- **Applying a price level to a customer record** (page 77) tells QuickBooks to automatically adjust all the prices on a new invoice for that customer by the price level percentage (page 142).

- You can **apply a price level to line items in an invoice** whether or not a customer has a standard price level. In the Create Invoices dialog box, click an item's Rate cell, click the down arrow that appears, and then choose the price level you want from the drop-down list.

Note: If you use the Contractor, Professional Services, or Accountant edition of QuickBooks, the Billing Rate Level is another list that lets you set up custom billing rates for employees and vendors. The Billing Rate Level helps you price the services you sell the same way a Price Level helps you adjust the prices on products you sell. Say you have three carpenters: a newbie, an old timer, and a finish carpenter. You can set up Billing Rate Levels for each level of carpentry experience. Then, when you create an invoice based on your carpenters' billable time, QuickBooks automatically applies the correct rate to each carpenter's hours.

Rounding Price Level Values

When you use percentages to calculate markups and discounts, the resulting values may not be what you want. The basic choices in the "Round up to nearest" drop-down menu take care of the most common rounding—to the nearest penny, dime, quarter, dollar, and so on. Other entries on the drop-down list let you give QuickBooks more complex rounding instructions. These additional entries are easy to understand with a bit of study.

The bottom seven entries help you position prices at magic marketing prices like $29.99 or $1.95. For example, the ".10 minus .01" entry ensures that the price always ends in 9 cents. With this rounding choice, if the discounted price comes out to be $8.74, QuickBooks rounds up to the nearest 10 cents ($8.80) and then subtracts 1 cent, so the rounded value is $8.79.

If you like to undercut your competitors with unusual price points, in the "Round up to nearest" drop-down menu, choose "user defined". QuickBooks displays several boxes and options for defining your own rounding:

- **The "nearest" drop-down menu.** In the unlabeled drop-down menu below "user defined" you can choose "to nearest", "up to nearest", or "down to nearest". "To nearest" rounds in whichever direction is closest (for example, rounding from 1.73 to 1.70 or from 1.77 to 1.80).

- **The $ box.** Type the value you want to round to like .01, .25, or 1.00.

- **Plus or Minus.** Select the Plus or Minus option if you want to add or subtract some money after you've rounded the value. In the last box, type the amount of money you want to add or subtract from the rounded value.

Customer and Vendor Profile Lists

Filling in fields goes much faster when you can choose info from drop-down lists instead of typing values. The lists that appear on the Customer & Vendor Profile Lists menu pop up regularly, whether you're creating an invoice, paying a bill, or generating reports. For example, when you create an invoice, QuickBooks fills in the Payment Terms field with the payment terms you assigned to the customer's record (page 76), but you can choose different payment terms from the drop-down list to urge your customer to pay more quickly.

For many of these lists, creating entries requires no more than typing an entry name and specifying whether the entry is a subentry to another. This section describes the information you add to entries in each list and how to put these lists to work for you.

Sales Rep List

If you pay sales reps on commission or want to assign employees as points of contact for your customers, you can assign people as sales reps to your customers (page 76) and then generate reports by sales rep (page 509). But first you have to add the names of your sales reps and contacts to the Sales Rep List.

Note: QuickBooks can't help you calculate sales commissions, even if you assign sales reps to your customers. To find a third-party program that does, go to *http://marketplace.intuit.com*. In the Find Apps box, type "sales commission" and press Enter.

To add a name to the Sales Rep List:

1. **Choose Lists → Customer & Vendor Profile Lists → Sales Rep List. In the Sales Rep List window that opens, press Ctrl+N (or click Sales Rep and choose New from the drop-down menu).**

   The New Sales Rep List dialog box opens.

2. **In the Sales Rep Name drop-down list, choose a name. In the Sales Rep Initials box, type the person's initials.**

   When you create a sales rep entry, you can choose only names that are on the Employee List (page 368), the Vendor List (page 134), or the Other Names List (page 146). If the name you want doesn't exist, choose *<Add New>* at the top of the drop-down list.

   QuickBooks automatically fills in the Sales Rep Type with Employee, Vendor, or Other Name, depending on which list the name came from. The box on page 146 gives hints about when to use the Other Names List.

3. **Click Next to add another sales rep, or click OK to close the New Sales Rep dialog box.**

   If you select a name and realize that it's misspelled, you can edit the name from the New Sales Rep dialog box. Click Edit Name, and QuickBooks opens the Edit Employee, Edit Vendor, or Edit Name dialog box so you can change the name.

Customer Type List

Customer types help you analyze your income and expenses by customer category (page 67). For example, a healthcare provider might create Govt and Private customer types to see how much a change in government reimbursement might hurt revenue. You first create customer types in the Customer Type List and then assign one of those types in each customer's record.

Creating all your customer types up front is fast—as long as you already know what your entries are:

1. **Choose Lists → Customer & Vendor Profile Lists → Customer Type List. In the Customer Type List dialog box that opens, press Ctrl+N.**

   The New Customer Type dialog box (Figure 6-4) opens.

2. **Create the customer type.**

   A Customer Type entry includes a name (in the Customer Type field) and whether the customer type is a subtype of another.

When to Use the Other Names List

If you have more than a few names in your Other Names List, you're probably not getting the most out of Quick-Books. In fact, unless you're a sole proprietor or several partners share ownership of your company, you can run QuickBooks without *any* names in the Other Names List.

The problem with Other Names is that QuickBooks doesn't track activity for them. You can't invoice someone or enter a bill for what you owe to someone if they're in your Other Names List. Sure, the entries in the Other Names List show up in the drop-down lists for a few types of transactions, such as checks and credit card charges (page 238). But they're conspicuously absent when you create invoices, purchase orders, sales receipts, or any other type of transaction.

What are Other Names good for? The perfect use for the Other Names List is for *your* name as sole proprietor or the names of company partners. When you write owners' draw checks to pay partners, you can choose the names from the Other Names List.

To create an entry on the Other Names List, do the following:

1. Choose Lists → Other Names List.

2. In the Other Names List window, press Ctrl+N.

3. Fill in the fields in the New Name and Edit Name dialog boxes with contact information, similar to the fields found in the New Customer and Edit Customer dialog boxes (see page 72).

If you aren't sure which name list to use, add someone to the Other Names List. When you figure out which list the person should belong to, you can move Other Names entries to another list. Because QuickBooks needs to close all open windows to do this, it's best to save this task for a lull in your work day. Click Activities (at the bottom of the Other Names window) and then choose Change Other Name Types. In the Change Name Types dialog box, click the cell in the Customer, Vendor, or Employee column to reset Other Name to a new type. Click OK to complete the makeover.

3. **After you create one type, click Next to create another or click OK if you're done.**

   You can also create entries as you work. If you're creating or modifying a customer in the New Customer or Edit Customer dialog boxes, click the Additional Info tab. In the Type drop-down list, choose *<Add New>*, which opens the New Customer Type dialog box. Then, you can create a new customer type, as shown in Figure 6-4.

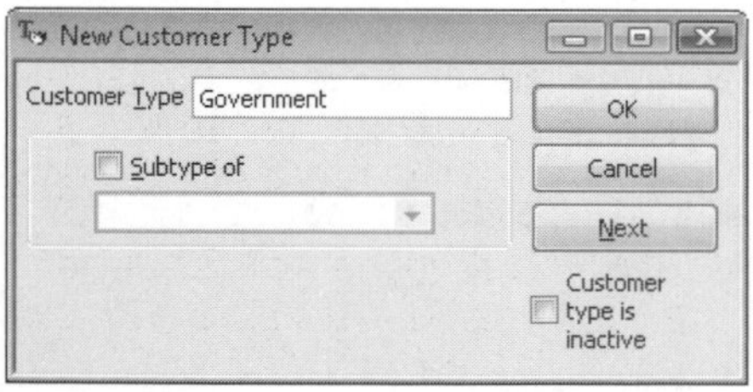

Figure 6-4:
In the New Customer Type dialog box, the only thing you have to provide is a name in the Customer Type field. If the customer type represents a portion of a larger customer category, turn on the "Subtype of" checkbox and choose the parent customer type. For example, if you have a parent customer type of Utilities, you might create subtypes for Water Utility, Electric Utility, Gas Utility, and so on.

Vendor Type List

Vendor types work similarly to customer types—you can filter reports or subtotal your expenses by different types of vendors. For example, if you create a Communications vendor type, you could generate a report of the expenses you've paid to your telephone, Internet, and satellite communications providers.

You create Vendor Type entries the way you create Customer Type entries. Choose Lists → Customer & Vendor Profile Lists → Vendor Type List. With the Vendor Type List window open, press Ctrl+N to open the New Vendor Type dialog box.

Tip: To create a new vendor type while you're creating a vendor, in the New Vendor dialog box, click the Additional Info tab, and in the Type drop-down list, choose *<Add New>* to open the New Vendor Type dialog box.

Job Type List

Job types also follow the customer type lead. For instance, you can filter a Profit & Loss report to show how profitable your spec house projects are compared to your remodeling contracts. You create Job Type entries the way you create Customer Type entries (page 145). Open the Job Type List window by choosing Lists → Customer & Vendor Profile Lists → Job Type List.

Terms List

The Terms List (Lists → Customer & Vendor Profile Lists → Terms List) holds both the payment terms you require of your customers and the payment terms your vendors ask of you. When you assign terms in a customer record, QuickBooks automatically fills in the Terms box on the invoices you create for that customer. Likewise, filling in terms in a vendor record means that QuickBooks fills in the Terms box on bills you create.

The fields that you fill in to create Terms (Figure 6-5) are different from those in other Customer & Vendor Profile lists.

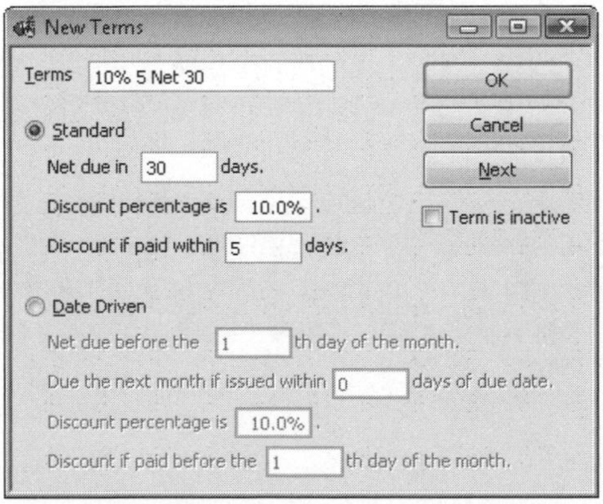

Figure 6-5:
Because payment terms apply to vendors and customers, consider using generic names that say something about the payment terms themselves. For example, the "10% 5 Net 30" entry is an enticement for early payments because it means that the amount is due 30 days from the invoice date, but you can deduct 10 percent from your bill if you pay within 5 days.

Setting up terms using elapsed time

The Standard option is ideal when the due date is a specific number of days after the invoice date (or the date you receive a bill, if you're the customer). If you send invoices whenever you complete a sale, choose the Standard option so that payment is due within a number of days of the invoice date. Here's an explanation of what the Standard option fields do:

- **Net due in _ days.** Type the maximum number of days after the invoice date that you or a customer can pay. For example, if you type *30*, customers have up to 30 days to pay an invoice or you have up to 30 days to pay a bill. If you charge penalties for late payments, QuickBooks can figure out whose payments are late, so you can assess finance charges (page 347).

- **Discount percentage is.** If you offer a discount for early payments, type the percentage discount in this box.

- **Discount if paid within _ days.** Type the number of days after the invoice date within which a customer has to pay to receive the early payment discount.

Note: When you use terms that reduce a customer's bill for early payments, QuickBooks deducts these discounts in the Receive Payments window (page 332), which is when the program can tell if the customer paid early.

Setting up date-driven terms

The Date Driven option sets up terms for payments that are due on a specific date, regardless of the date on the invoice. This option is handy if you send invoices on a schedule—say, on the last day of the month. For example, your home mortgage might assess a late fee if your payment arrives after the 15th of the month.

Here's what the Date Driven option fields do:

- **Net due before the _ th day of the month.** Type the day of the month that the payment is due. For example, if a payment is due before the 15th of the month, no matter what date appears on your statement, type *15* in the box.

- **Due the next month if issued within _ days of due date.** Your customers might get annoyed if you require payment by the 15th of the month and send out your invoices on the 14th. They would have no way of paying on time, unless they camped out in your billing department.

  You can type a number of days in this box to automatically push the due date to the following month when you issue invoices too close to the due date. Suppose payments are due on the 15th of each month and you type 5 in this box. For invoices you create between August 10th and August 15th, the program changes the due date to September 15th.

- **Discount percentage is.** If you extend a discount for early payments, type the percentage discount in this box.

- **Discount if paid before the _ th day of the month.** Type the day of the month before which a customer receives the early payment discount.

Customer Message

When you create an invoice, you can add a short message to the form, such as "If you like the service we deliver, tell your friends. If you don't like our service, tell us." Save time and prevent embarrassing typos by adding your stock messages to the Customer Message List. The New Customer Message dialog box has only one field—the Customer Message field—which can hold up to 101 characters (including spaces).

Don't use the Customer Message List for messages that change with every invoice, like one that specifies the calendar period that an invoice covers. You'll fill your Customer Message List with unique messages and won't be able to add any more. If you want to include unique information, do so in the cover letter (or email) that accompanies your invoice.

Payment Method List

You can choose to process all the payments you've received via a specific payment method when you select Banking → Make Deposits. For example, you can deposit all the checks and cash you received into your checking account, but you might deposit the payments you receive via credit cards to a dedicated merchant checking account. QuickBooks starts the Payment Method List for you with entries for cash, check, and credit cards (such as American Express and Visa).

If you want another payment method—for payments through PayPal, for example—you can create a new Payment Method entry. Choose Lists → Customer & Vendor Profile Lists → Payment Method List, and then press Ctrl+N. In the New Payment Method dialog box, type a name for the payment method, and then choose a payment type. For instance, if you use two Visa credit cards, you can create two entries with a Visa payment type. Other payment types include Discover, Debit Card, Gift Card, and E-Check.

Ship Via List

When you include the shipping method that you use on your invoices, your customers know whether to watch for the mailman or the UPS truck. QuickBooks creates several shipping methods for you, including DHL, Federal Express, UPS, and U.S. Mail. If you use another shipping method, like a bike messenger in New York City or your own delivery truck, simply create additional entries in the Ship Via List. In the Shipping Method field (the only field in the New Ship Method dialog box), type the name of the method you want to add.

Tip: If you use one method of shipping most of the time, you can have QuickBooks fill in the Shipping Method with that entry automatically. See page 579 to learn about this and other shipping preferences, such as the "Usual Free on Board" location.

Vehicle List

If you want to track mileage (page 198) on the vehicles you use for your business, create entries for your cars and trucks in the Vehicle List (Lists → Customer & Vendor Profile Lists → Vehicle List). Use the Vehicle box to name the vehicle: Ford Prefect 1982 Red, for example. The Description field holds up to 256 characters, so you can use it to store the VIN, license plate, and even the insurance policy number. If you want to charge your customers for your mileage, see page 269.

Fixed Asset Items

Assets that you can't convert to cash quickly—such as backhoes, buildings, or supercomputers—are called *fixed assets*. If you track information about your fixed assets in another program or have only a few fixed assets, there's no reason to bother with the Fixed Asset Item List. As you can see in Figure 6-6, Fixed Asset items track information such as when you bought the asset and how much you paid. But in QuickBooks, *you* have to calculate depreciation (see the box on page 151) for each asset at the end of the year and create journal entries to adjust the values in your asset accounts.

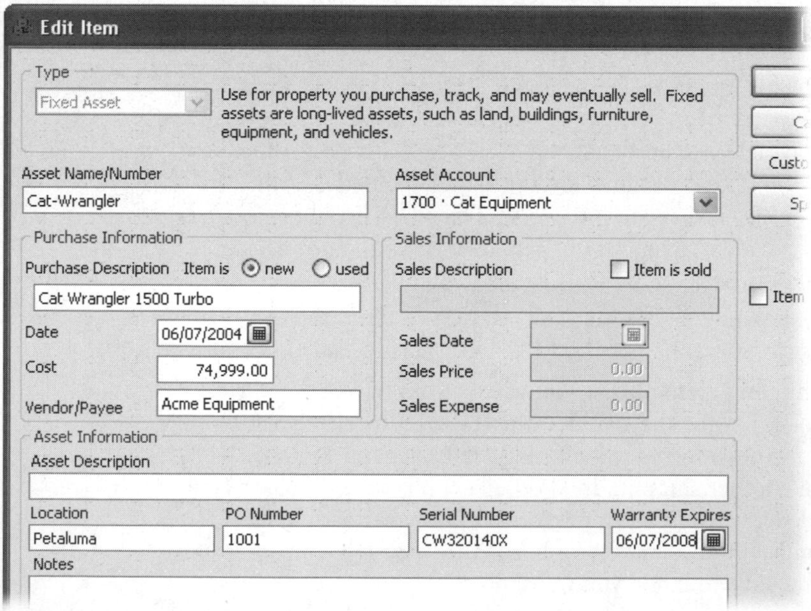

Figure 6-6:
When you buy a fixed asset, you can create a Fixed Asset item and enter its name and purchase information, where you keep it, the item's serial number, and when the warranty expires. When you create a Fixed Asset item, QuickBooks doesn't automatically add the purchase price to the Asset Account you choose. The account you choose in your purchase transaction (check or credit card charge, for instance) is what adds the purchase price to the Fixed Asset account in your chart of accounts.

How Depreciation Works

When your company depreciates assets, you add dollars here, subtract dollars there, and none of the dollars are real. Sounds like funny money, but depreciation is nothing more than an accounting concept, which actually presents a more realistic picture of financial performance. To see how it works, here's an example of what happens when a company depreciates a large purchase.

Suppose your company buys a Deep Thought supercomputer for $500,000. You spent $500,000, and you now own an asset worth $500,000. Your company's balance sheet moves that money from your bank account to an asset account, but your total assets remain the same.

The problem arises when you sell the computer, perhaps 10 years later when it would make a fabulous boat anchor. The moment you sell, the asset's value plummets from $500,000 to your selling price—say $1,000. The drop in value shows up as an expense, putting a huge dent in your profits for the 10th year. Shareholders don't like it when profits spike from year to year—up *or* down. With depreciation, though, you can spread the cost of a big purchase over several years, which does a better job of matching revenue and expenses. As a result, shareholders can see how well you use assets to generate income.

Depreciation calculations come in several flavors: straight-line, sum of the years' digits, and double declining balance. Straight-line depreciation is the easiest and most common.

To calculate annual straight-line depreciation, subtract the *salvage* value (how much the asset is worth when you sell it) from the purchase price, and then divide by the number of years of useful life, like so:

- Purchase price: $500,000

- Salvage value after 10 years: $1,000

- Useful life: the 10 years you expect to run the computer

- Annual depreciation: $499,000 divided by 10, which equals $49,900

Every year, you use the computer to make money for your business, and you show $49,900 as that income's associated equipment expense. On your books, the value of the Deep Thought computer drops by another $49,900 each year, until the balance reaches the $1,000 salvage value at the end of the last year. This decrease in value each year keeps your balance sheet (page 448) more accurate and avoids the sudden drop in asset value in year 10.

The other, more complex methods depreciate your assets faster in the first few years (called *accelerated depreciation*), making for big tax write-offs in a hurry. Page 427 explains how to record journal entries for depreciation, but your best bet is to ask your accountant how to post depreciation in your QuickBooks accounts.

When you sell an asset, open the Edit Item dialog box (with the Fixed Asset Item List window open, select the item and press Ctrl+E), and then turn on the "Item is sold" checkbox. When you do so, the sales fields come to life so that you can specify when you sold the asset, how much you sold it for, and any costs associated with the sale.

Note: QuickBooks Premier Accountant Edition and QuickBooks Enterprise Edition include the Fixed Asset Manager, which not only figures out the depreciation on your assets, but posts depreciation to QuickBooks with a click of the mouse.

If you decide to track the details about your fixed assets outside QuickBooks, you still need the *value* of your fixed assets in your financial reports. Simply create Fixed Asset accounts (page 52) to hold the value of your assets. Each year, you'll add a general journal entry to each Fixed Asset account (page 427) to reduce the asset's value by the amount of depreciation.

Creating and Editing List Entries

Every list in QuickBooks responds to the same set of commands. As your business changes, you can add new entries, edit existing ones, hide entries that you no longer use, and, in some lists, merge two entries into one. If you make a mistake creating an entry, you can delete it. You can also print your QuickBooks lists to produce a price list of the products you sell, for example. With the following techniques, you'll be able to do what you want with any list or entry you might need.

Creating Entries

If you're setting up QuickBooks, creating all the entries for a list at the same time is fast and efficient. Open the New dialog box for the type of list entry you want (New Vendor, for example), and you'll soon get into a rhythm creating one entry after another.

You can also add new list entries in the middle of bookkeeping tasks without too much of an interruption. If you launch a new line of business selling moose repellent, you can add a customer type for burly men in the middle of creating an invoice. But don't rely on this approach to add every entry to every list—you'll spend so much time jumping from dialog box to dialog box that you'll never get to your bookkeeping.

Each list has its own collection of fields, but the overall procedure for creating entries in lists is the same:

1. **Open the window for the list you want to work on by choosing Lists and then selecting the list you want on the submenu.**

   For example, to open the Class List window, choose Lists → Class List. Several lists are tucked away one level deeper on the Lists menu. For lists that include characteristics for your customers or vendors, such as Vendor Type or Terms, choose Lists → Customer & Vendor Profile Lists, and then choose the list you want, as shown in Figure 6-7.

2. **To create a new entry, press Ctrl+N or, at the bottom of the list window, click the list name, and then choose New.**

   For instance, to create an entry in the Class List, make sure that the Class List is the active window and then press Ctrl+N. Or, at the bottom of the Class List window, click Class and then choose New. QuickBooks opens the New Class dialog box.

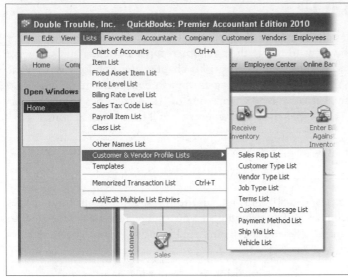

Figure 6-7:
Many of the QuickBooks lists appear directly on the Lists menu, but some lists are one level lower on the Customer & Vendor Profile Lists submenu. To boost your productivity, take note of the keyboard shortcuts for lists you're likely to access most often. Ctrl+A opens the Chart of Accounts window. To see customer, vendor, or employee lists, in the QuickBooks Home page, click Customers, Vendors, or Employees to open the corresponding center.

3. After you've completed one entry, simply click Next to save the current entry and begin another. To save the entry you just created and close the dialog box, click OK.

Note: Unlike all the other New dialog boxes for lists, the New Price Level dialog box doesn't include a Next button.

To toss an entry that you botched, click Cancel to throw it away and close the dialog box. A few of the lists on the Customer & Vendor Profile Lists menu can include subentries, as shown in Figure 6-8.

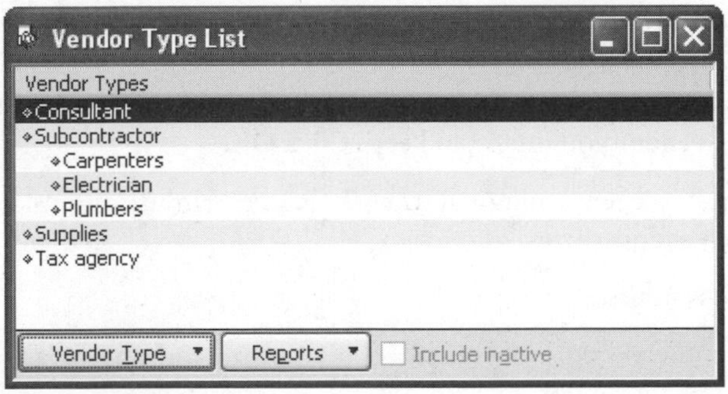

Figure 6-8:
You can create multiple levels of entries in the Customer Type, Job Type, and Vendor Type lists. For example, you might create top-level types for vendors who require 1099 forms and those that don't. Then, you can create subentries for types such as electricians, plumbers, and carpenters.

Editing Entries

To modify an entry, open the window for the list. Select the entry you want to edit and press Ctrl+E. When the Edit dialog box opens, make the changes you want, and then click OK when you're done.

Merging List Entries

Over time, your lists collect detritus. For example, two of your suppliers for copper pipes merge, and you want to merge their vendor records as well. You can merge entries on only two of the lists discussed in *this* chapter: the Vendor List and the Other Names List. (You can't undo merging entries, so make sure merging is what you want to do. The alternative is to change one of the two entries to inactive, as described on page 154, and then use the other entry for all future transactions.)

Note: Merging accounts on your chart of accounts is described on page 62. Merging customers is covered on page 94.

When you merge entries, QuickBooks puts all the transactions from both entries into the one that you keep. For example, if you merge Financial Finesse into Fuggedaboudit Financial, all your payments to Financial Finesse become payments to Fuggedaboudit Financial.

Here's how you can merge two entries, using the Vendor List as an example:

1. **Switch to single-user mode.**

   If you work in multi-user mode, choose File → "Switch to Single-user Mode". (When you're done, be sure to switch back to multi-user mode and tell your colleagues they can work in QuickBooks again.)

2. **Open the Vendor Center.**

   On the QuickBooks Home page, click Vendors, or choose Vendors → Vendor Center. (If you want to merge names on the Other Names List, choose Lists → Other Names List.)

3. **In the Vendors tab, right-click the name of the vendor you're going to merge and, on the shortcut menu, choose Edit Vendor.**

   The Edit Vendor dialog box opens.

4. **In the Edit Vendor dialog box, change the name in the Vendor Name field to match the name of the vendor you intend to keep. Click OK.**

   QuickBooks displays a message warning you that the name is in use and asks if you want to merge the vendors.

5. **Click Yes to merge the vendors.**

   In the Vendor Center, the vendor you renamed disappears and any balances now belong to the remaining vendor.

Don't forget to switch back to multi-user mode so your coworkers can use QuickBooks again.

Hiding and Deleting List Entries

Deleting entries is only for discarding entries that you create by mistake. If you've already used list entries in transactions, hide the entries you don't use anymore so your historical records are complete. For example, you wouldn't delete the "Net 30" payment term just because you're lucky enough to have only Net 15 clients right now; you may still extend Net 30 terms to some clients in the future.

Hiding Entries

Hiding list entries that you no longer use does two things:

- Your previous transactions still use the entries you've hidden, so your historical records don't change.

- When you create new transactions, the hidden entries don't appear in drop-down lists, so you can't choose an old entry by mistake.

The methods for hiding and reactivating list entries are exactly the same regardless of which list you're working on:

- **Hide an entry.** In the list window (or the list in Vendor Center), right-click the entry and choose "Make *<list name>* Inactive" from the shortcut menu, where *<list name>* is the list that you're editing. The entry disappears from the list.

GEM IN THE ROUGH

Defining Custom Fields for Lists

QuickBooks provides numerous fields for customer, vendor, employee, and item records, but those fields may not cover all the information you need. For example, you might add a custom field for the branch office that services a customer. For employees, you could set up a custom field to track whether they make charitable contributions that your company matches.

QuickBooks' answer to this issue is custom fields. Unfortunately, these fields are pretty feeble compared to what some of QuickBooks' built-in fields can do. After you create a custom field and apply it to a list, QuickBooks does nothing more than add the custom field label and a text box to the Additional Info tab (see Figure 4-5 on page 76). You have to type your entries each time; there's no drop-down list or even a way to compare it to text you entered in other records. It's up to you to make sure that your data entry is correct and consistent.

If you still want to set up a custom field, follow these steps:

1. In the Create dialog box or Edit dialog box, click the Additional Info tab.

2. Click the Define Fields button. The "Set up Custom Fields for Names" dialog box opens, as shown in Figure 6-9.

3. In one of the 15 Label boxes, type a name for the field.

4. If you're associating a custom field with a customer, vendor, or employee record, click the cell for the appropriate list to turn on a checkmark. For example, the Region custom field could apply to both the Customer:Job List and the Vendors List.

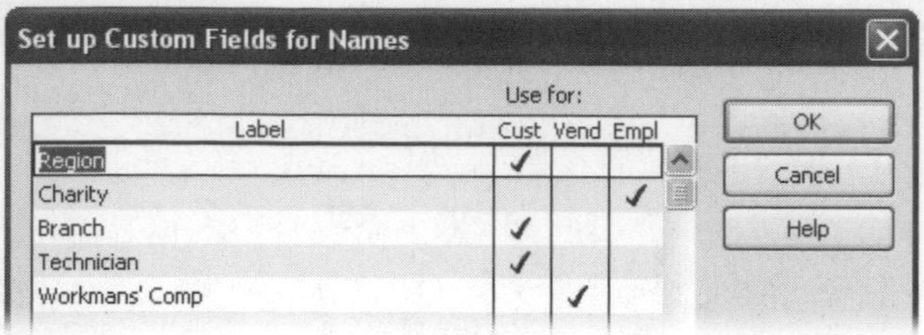

Figure 6-9:
When you edit an item in the Items List, click Custom Fields in the Edit Item dialog box. In the Custom Fields dialog box, click Define Fields to create labels for up to five custom fields for your items. Unlike names in name lists, items can have only up to 5 custom fields.

- **View all the entries in a list.** At the bottom of the window, turn on the "Include inactive" checkbox to show both active and hidden entries. In the Vendor Center, in the View drop-down list, choose All Vendors. QuickBooks adds a column with an X as its heading and displays an X in that column for every inactive entry in the list.

- **Reactivate an entry.** First, view all the entries, and then click the X next to the entry that you want to reactivate. If the entry has subentries, in the Activate Group dialog box, click Yes to reactivate the entry and all its subentries.

Deleting Entries

You can delete an entry only if nothing in QuickBooks references it in any way. If you create a list entry by mistake, your only hope is to catch it quickly. To delete a list entry, open the appropriate list window and select the entry you want to delete. Press Ctrl+D or choose Edit → Delete *<list name>*. If you haven't used the entry in any records or transactions, QuickBooks asks you to confirm that you want to delete the entry. Click Yes.

Finding List Entries in Transactions

If QuickBooks won't let you delete a list entry because a transaction is still using it, don't worry. It's easy to find transactions that use a specific list entry. Here's how:

1. **Open the list that contains the entry you want to find. In the list window, select the entry.**

2. **At the bottom of the list window, click the list name, and then choose "Find in Transactions".**

   The Find dialog box opens already set up to find transactions that use the list entry you selected.

3. **Click Find.**

   The table at the bottom of the Find dialog box displays all the transactions using that entry.

4. **To modify the list entry a transaction uses, select the entry in the table, and then click Go To.**

QuickBooks opens the window or dialog box that corresponds to the type of transaction. If you're trying to eliminate references to a list entry so you can delete it, choose a different list entry and then save the transaction.

Sorting Lists

QuickBooks sorts lists alphabetically by name, which is usually what you want. The only reason to sort a list another way is if you're having trouble finding the entry you want to edit. For example, if you want to find equipment you bought within the last few years, you could sort the Fixed Asset List by purchase date to find the machines that you're still depreciating. Sorting in the list window doesn't change the order that entries appear in drop-down lists.

Figure 6-10 shows you how to change the sort order—and how to change it back.

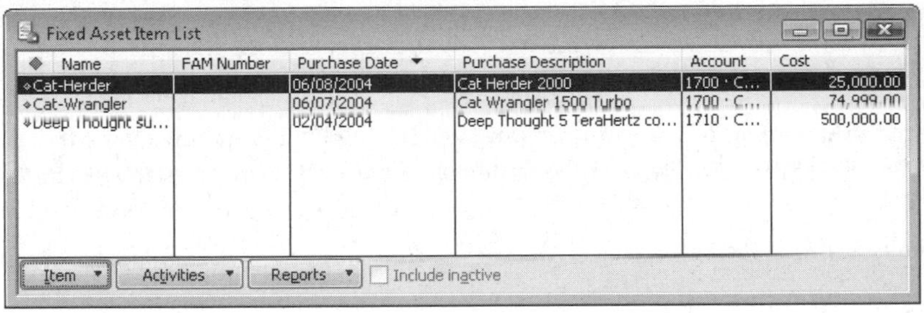

Figure 6-10:
To sort a list by a column, click the column heading, such as Purchase Date. The first time you click a column heading, QuickBooks sorts the list in ascending order. To toggle between ascending and descending order, click the heading again. The small black triangle in the column heading points up when the list is sorted in ascending order and points down when it's sorted in descending order.

Note: If you use a different column to sort a list, QuickBooks displays a gray diamond to the left of the column heading that it uses to sort the list initially. For example, the Fixed Asset Item List shows items in alphabetical order by Name. If you sort the list by Purchase Date instead, a gray diamond appears to the left of the Name heading. To return the list to the order that QuickBooks uses, click the diamond.

Printing Lists

After you spend all that time building lists in QuickBooks, you'll be happy to know that it's much easier to get those lists back out of the program. For instance, suppose you want to print a price list of all the items you sell. Or, you want a text file of your customer information to import into your email program. QuickBooks makes short work of printing your lists or turning them into files that you can use in other programs.

Blasting Out a Quick List

Here's the fastest way to produce a list, albeit one that doesn't give you any control over report appearance:

1. **At the bottom of the list window, click the button containing the list name—Price Level, for example—and then, in the drop-down menu, choose Print List.**

   QuickBooks might display a message box telling you to try list reports if you want to customize or format your reports. That method is covered in the next section. For now, in the message box, click OK. The Print Lists dialog box opens.

Note: To print customer, vendor, or employee lists, in the Customer Center, Vendor Center, or Employee Center tool bar, click Print and choose Customer & Job List, Vendor List, or Employee List, respectively.

---

2. **To print the list, select the "Printer" option and choose the printer in the drop-down list. If you want to output the list to a file, choose the File option and then select the file format you want.**

   You can create ASCII text files, comma-delimited files, or tab-delimited files (page 597). You can also specify printer settings, as you can in many other programs. Choose landscape or portrait orientation, the pages to print, and the number of copies.

3. **Click Print.**

   QuickBooks prints the report.

Customizing a Printed List

If the Print List command described in the previous section scatters fields over the page or produces a comma-delimited file that doesn't play well with your email program, QuickBooks might provide a report closer to what you have in mind. For example, a vendor phone list and employee contact list are only two menu clicks away. To access the reports that come with QuickBooks, choose Reports → List and then choose the report you want. If these reports fall short, you can modify them to change the fields and records they include, or you can format them in a variety of ways.

Chapter 21 explains how to customize reports, but if you click Modify Report in the report window toolbar, you can make the following changes to a list report before you print your list or create a file of your list information:

- **Choose fields.** The Columns box (on the Display tab) includes every field for a list entry. When you click a field, QuickBooks adds a checkmark before its name and adds that field to the report.

- **Sort records.** Choose the field you want to sort by (on the Display tab) and whether you want the report sorted in ascending or descending order.

- **Filter the report.** Filters (on the Filters tab) limit the records in a report. For example, you can produce an employee report for active employees, which refers to their employment status—not the level of effort they devote to their jobs. You can also filter by employee name or values in other fields.

- **Set up the report header and footer.** On the Header/Footer tab, you can choose the information that you want to show in the report's title and the footer at the bottom of each page. A report's title identifies the information in the report, and the footer can include the date the report was prepared so you know whether the list is current.

- **Format text and numbers.** On the Fonts & Numbers tab, choose the font that QuickBooks uses for different parts of the report. For instance, labels should be larger than the lines in the report. You can also choose how to display negative numbers: The In Bright Red checkbox controls whether red ink truly applies to your financial reports. You can also divide numbers by 1,000 before displaying them in a report so that it's easier to differentiate thousands from millions.

Managing QuickBooks Files

When company ledgers were made of paper, you had to be careful not to tear the pages or spill coffee on them. Today's electronic books require their own sort of care and feeding. Protecting your QuickBooks files is essential, not only because your books tell the financial story of your company, but because computers are notorious for chewing up data in all sorts of ways.

QuickBooks files have a few advantages over their paper-based relatives. Most importantly, you can make copies of your company files for safekeeping. (Quick-Books can also create a *special* copy of your company file so you and your accountant can both work on it at the end of the year; see page 451 to learn how.) If several people work on your QuickBooks file simultaneously, you'll learn when and how to switch from multi-user mode to single-user mode so you can perform the file housekeeping tasks that require dedicated access. This chapter focuses on the most important things you can do with your QuickBooks files: backing up and copying them. It also explains why and how to verify, condense, and delete your files, which you'll do less often, if ever.

Switching Between Multi-User and Single-User Mode

In QuickBooks, some maintenance tasks require that only one person have access to the company file. For these tasks, you change a company file to *single-user mode*. You have to be in single-user mode to merge or delete accounts and items, export data from a company file, and save or open an accountant's copy of your company file. Single-user mode can also speed up time-consuming tasks like running humongous reports.

Some tasks that required single-user mode in QuickBooks 2008 and earlier versions, such as backups, now run contentedly while several people work in a company file. You can verify data (page 178) while a company file is in multi-user mode, but others can't work on the file, and the verification isn't as thorough as one running in single-user mode.

The good news is you don't have to remember which tasks demand single-user mode. QuickBooks advises you to switch modes if you try to perform a single-user mode task when the company file is chugging away in multi-user mode. Because everyone else has to close the company file before you can switch it to single-user mode, you may find it easiest to wait until no one else is working on the company file (early in the morning or after work, say).

Here's how you switch from multi-user mode to single-user mode:

1. **If your single-user task can't wait until off-hours, ask everyone else to close the company file you want to work on.**

   Exiting QuickBooks is another way to close a company file.

2. **When everyone else has closed the company file, open it in QuickBooks. (Choose File → Open Previous File, and then choose the company file in the submenu.)**

   If the company file doesn't appear on the Open Previous File submenu, choose File → "Open or Restore Company". In the "Open or Restore Company" dialog box, select the "Open a company file" option, and then click Next. In the "Open a Company" dialog box, navigate to the folder where you store the company file, and double-click the file name.

3. **Choose File → "Switch to Single-user Mode". In the message box that appears telling you the file is in single-user mode, click OK.**

   QuickBooks closes all open windows before it switches to single-user mode. After you click OK, it reopens the windows and you're ready to work solo on the company file.

4. **After you finish your single-user task, switch back to multi-user mode by choosing File → "Switch to Multi-user Mode". When the message box appears telling you the file is in single-user mode, click OK.**

   You'll see all the windows in QuickBooks close. After you click OK, the windows reappear and the company file is back in multi-user mode.

5. **Don't forget to tell your colleagues that they can log back into the company file.**

Backing Up Files

If you already have a backup procedure for *all* your company data, the Quick-Books Backup command might seem at first glance as useful as your appendix. Your companywide backups regularly squirrel your data files away in a safe place, ready to rescue you should disaster strike. Still, the QuickBooks Backup command can complement even the most robust backup plan. And if you run a mom-and-pop business, online backups let you back up all of your data without hiring an IT staff. Here are some ways you can put QuickBooks Backup to work:

- **Backing up one QuickBooks company file.** Before you experiment with a new QuickBooks feature, you don't want to back up *all* your data—just the company file. If the experiment goes terribly wrong, you can restore your backup and try a different approach. You can also call on the QuickBooks Backup command when you've worked hard on your company file, say by entering hundreds of inventory items in one long session, and the thought of losing that work makes you queasy. In both of these situations, running a QuickBooks *manual backup* creates a backup file immediately.

- **Scheduling backups of your QuickBooks data.** If you have trouble remembering to back up your work, QuickBooks' automatic backups have your back. You can set QuickBooks up to automatically back up a company file after you've opened it a certain number of times. If you mangle your data or it gets corrupted in some way, you can use one of these backups to recover. If QuickBooks is the only program on your computer—so your company file is the only data that you want to back up—the program can run company file backups automatically according to the schedule you specify. For example, QuickBooks can automatically back up your company file Tuesdays through Saturdays at 2:00 a.m.

- **Backing up your data online.** Online backups are a handy alternative to setting up your own backup plan—scheduling regular backups, rotating backup media, storing backups offsite, and so on. You can select which data you want to back up and when. When the backups run, your backup files are encrypted and stored at secure data centers managed by IT professionals. If you don't have IT staff to back up your data and keep it secure, the price you pay may be worth every penny. See the box on page 166 to learn more.

Tip: QuickBooks 2010 packs more backup into smaller files than earlier versions of the program. But even in QuickBooks 2010, backup files still aren't much smaller than company files—20 to 25 percent, depending on what you store in your company file.

Whether you want to set up options for your backups, schedule backups, or run a backup immediately, open the QuickBooks Backup dialog box using either of the following methods:

- **Choose File → "Save Copy or Backup".**

- **On the icon bar, click Backup.** (If you don't see the Backup icon, which looks like a floppy disk, click the double right arrows on the right end of the icon bar, and then choose Backup on the drop-down menu that appears. If the Backup command is nowhere to be found on the icon bar, choose Customize Icon Bar on the drop-down menu. See page 609 to learn how to add commands to the icon bar.)

Note: What and how often you back up are up to you (or your company's system administrators). It depends on what information you feel you can't afford to lose and how much data you're willing to recreate in case of a disaster.

Choosing Standard Settings for Your Backups

For each company file that you back up, you can choose settings for when, where, and how many backups QuickBooks creates. These standard settings are great timesavers and make for more consistent backups. For example, you can tell QuickBooks to ask you about backing up your data after you've closed the company file a specific number of times. Or, you can automatically append the date and time that you run the backup to the name of the backup file. You choose these settings once for each company file, and QuickBooks uses them for every backup of that file until you change the settings.

To choose the backup settings you want, choose File → "Save Copy or Backup". In the "Save Copy or Backup" dialog box, select the "Backup copy" option, and then click Next. In the "Do you want to save your backup copy locally or online?" screen, click Options. The Backup Options dialog box, shown in Figure 7-1, lays out your choices for backing up the current company file.

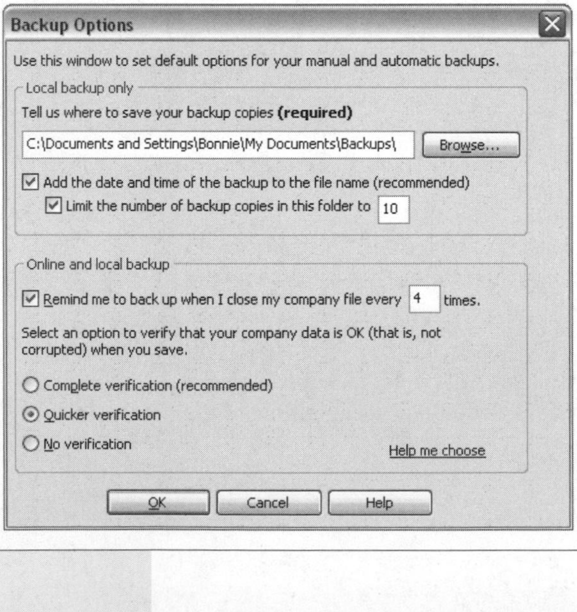

Figure 7-1:
The Backup Options dialog box has a section for settings that apply only to local backups, like the location and the number of backup copies you want to save. The settings in the "Online and local backup" section apply whether you create a backup on your computer or use Intuit's Online Backup Service. For example, you can specify how thoroughly you want the program to verify that your data isn't corrupted.

Here are the settings and what they're good for:

- **Where to save backup copies.** If you'd rather not search for backups accidentally saved to unconventional locations, choose a location for your backups. To tell QuickBooks to store the backup file in the same folder each time, click Browse. QuickBooks opens the "Browse for Folder" dialog box. Navigate to the folder or removable media device on your computer or network, and then click OK.

    The "Browse for Folder" dialog box doesn't let you create a new folder. If you want to save your backups in a folder that doesn't exist, click Cancel and create the new folder in Windows Explorer. Then, in the Backup Options dialog box, click Browse.

Note: Saving a backup file to the same hard drive where your company file is stored won't help you if your hard disk crashes. To protect your data from human error *and* hardware failure, back up your file to a *different hard drive* or to removable media like a CD, DVD, or USB thumb drive. If you choose a location on the same hard drive as your company file and click OK in the Backup Options dialog box, QuickBooks asks you if you want to change the location. When a company-wide backup transfers data to removable media every night, backing up your company file to a hard drive is fine for protection during the day. In this case, click "Use this location". To choose another location, click Change Location, which throws you back into the Backup Options dialog box. Click Browse, and then choose another hard disk or another location on your network.

- **Append a timestamp to the filename.** If you want to make sure that you *never* overwrite a backup file, turn on the "Add the date and time of the backup to the file name (recommended)" checkbox. When QuickBooks creates the backup file, it tacks on a timestamp to the end of the filename prefix; for example *Double Trouble, Inc (Backup Sep 25, 2010 11 30 PM).qbb*. Unless you make multiple backups within a minute of each other, you can be sure that your filenames are unique.

- **Limit the number of backup copies.** Regular backups can consume a lot of disk space. By turning on the "Limit the number of backup copies in this folder to" checkbox and typing a number, QuickBooks takes care of deleting older backup files. If you back up your files to an insatiable hard disk, you can save as many as 99 backup files before QuickBooks starts deleting older ones.

- **Get a reminder to back up.** If you want QuickBooks to remind you to back up your file every so often, in the "Online and local backup" section, turn on the "Remind me to back up when I close my company file every _ times" checkbox. When you've closed the company file the number of times you specified, QuickBooks displays the Automatic Backup message box. If you decide to bypass this automatic backup, click No. To create a backup of your company file, click Yes, which takes you to the QuickBooks Backup dialog box so you can run a manual backup.

Note: The "Remind me to back up when I close my company file every _ times" checkbox in the Backup Options dialog box sounds a lot like the "Save backup copy automatically when I close my company file every _ times" checkbox that goes with scheduled backups (page 170), but the two do different things. The checkbox in the Backup Options dialog box tells QuickBooks to *ask* you if you want to back up your file after you've closed it that many times. On the other hand, the checkbox for scheduled backups tells QuickBooks to create a back up automatically—*without asking*—after you close the file that many times.

- **Choose how thoroughly to verify.** In the "Online and local backup" section, QuickBooks automatically selects the "Complete verification (recommended)" option, which scrutinizes your backup file to make sure that the data you save isn't corrupt. You can speed up the verification process (at the risk of some corrupted data slipping through) by selecting the "Quicker verification" option. For high speed—and higher risk—select "No verification".

POWER USERS' CLINIC

Backing Up Online

Yes, this service costs money. But as long as your Internet connection is relatively fast, an online backup service may be a worthwhile investment. You can back up your company files, databases, documents, email—all your data, not just QuickBooks. Your backups reside in a data center managed by IT experts who live, eat, and breathe effective backup procedures.

Intuit's Online Backup Service works hand in hand with QuickBooks. But it isn't the only game in town. If the benefits of backing up online sound good, look at other services before you make your decision. Intuit's service has only two plans: backing up 1 GB (for $4.95 a month or $49.95 a year) or 10 GB (for $14.95 a month or $149.95 a year). You can check it out with a 30-day free trial. If you buy an Intuit support plan, you get a subscription to Online Backup Service as part of the deal. But even small businesses can rack up more than 10 GB of data.

On the other hand, Carbonite (*www.carbonite.com*) is a popular online backup service that gives unlimited storage space for $54.95 a year. Dropbox (*www.getdropbox.com*) acts as a backup and synchronization service, perfect for financial professionals on the go. When you store files in a special folder on your computer, Dropbox copies them to your online account. If you hit the road with your laptop, Dropbox downloads the files onto your laptop when you go online. 2 GB of storage is free. 50 GB or 100 GB of data

costs $9.99 or $19.99 a month, respectively. Mozy (www. mozy.com) also provides 2 GB of storage for free. After that, you pay $4.95 per month for unlimited storage.

Another option with a different approach is CrashPlan (*www.crashplan.com*). With this service, you can back up your files to the destination of your choice: another hard disk on your computer, from your laptop to your desktop computer, a computer in another location, even from a Mac to a PC. CrashPlan compresses your files, so backups take no time at all. Even better, you purchase a one-time software license ($60) for each computer you want to back up: no monthly or annual fees.

The one thing Intuit's Online Backup Service does well is back up company files. When you run the QuickBooks backup command and select online backup, the Online Backup Service software steps in. Any time you're connected to the Internet, you can select the files you want to back up or restore, schedule backups, or download your backups to your computer, as Figure 7-2 shows. To learn more about this service, choose Help → Add QuickBooks Services. In the QuickBooks Products and Services window, click Online Backup. Then, click the Learn More link. A browser window opens the QuickBooks Online Backup Service web page.

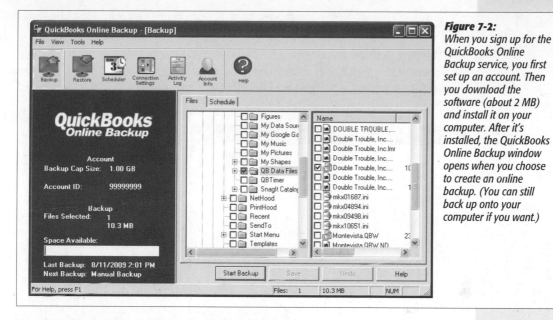

Figure 7-2:
When you sign up for the QuickBooks Online Backup service, you first set up an account. Then you download the software (about 2 MB) and install it on your computer. After it's installed, the QuickBooks Online Backup window opens when you choose to create an online backup. (You can still back up onto your computer if you want.)

Backing Up to Your Computer Right Away

If you just spent four hours of tedious typing to create a few dozen new customers in QuickBooks, you definitely want to save that work. To run a backup right away, here's what you do:

1. **If you want to back up your file to removable media like a CD, DVD, or tape, put the disc or tape in the drive now.**

   Although you don't have to put the media in until just before you click Save, you may as well do it now so you don't forget.

2. **Choose File → "Save Copy or Backup".**

   The "Save Copy or Backup" dialog box opens with a trio of options for the different types of copies you can make. QuickBooks selects the "Backup copy" option automatically, which is what you want. (You'll learn about the "Portable company file" option later in this chapter. See page 451 for more on accountant's copies.)

3. **With the "Backup copy" option selected, click Next.**

   The next screen has options for saving your backup online or on your computer.

4. **Select the "Local backup" option and then click Next.**

   You can select the "Online backup" option to create an online backup immediately. QuickBooks' online backup service isn't free, but it has its advantages, as you learned on page 166.

5. In the "When do you want to save your backup copy?" screen, select the "Save it now" option, and then click Next.

The Save Backup Copy dialog box opens. QuickBooks chooses the folder you specified in QuickBooks' backup options (page 164), as Figure 7-3 shows. If you want to save the file somewhere else, browse to the folder.

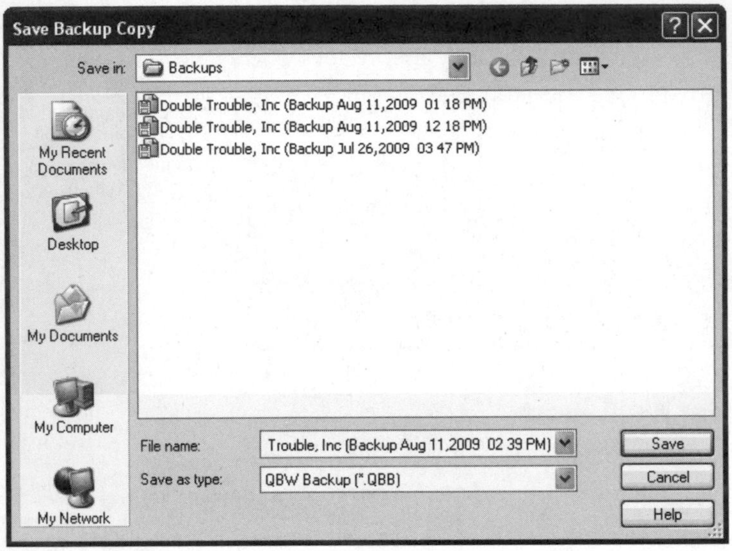

Figure 7-3:
QuickBooks automatically fills in the "File name" box with the same filename prefix as your company file and adds a timestamp to show when you made the backup. For example, if you're backing up your DoubleTrouble.qbw file, the backup file prefix is something like "DoubleTrouble (Backup Aug 09,2008 05 28 PM)". In the "Save as type" box, the program automatically fills in QBW Backup (*.QBB).

Note: QuickBooks backup files aren't merely copies of your company files. They're compressed files that take up less space, which is helpful whether you back up to floppy disks, CDs, another hard drive, or somewhere online.

6. Click Save.

The Working message box shows progress as QuickBooks verifies the data and creates the backup. You know the backup is complete when the QuickBooks Information dialog box shows you the file that you backed up and the backup file you created. Click OK to close the dialog box.

Automated QuickBooks Backups

QuickBooks can back up your data without your help in two different ways—automatically or scheduled. This section explains the differences and how you set each one up:

- **Automatic backup.** An automatic backup runs after you close a company file a specific number of times, which is great for protecting the work you do in a few back-to-back QuickBooks sessions. You simply close the company file at the end of a session and QuickBooks immediately creates a backup if this session hit the magic number.

- **Scheduled backups.** You can also schedule QuickBooks backups to run at a specific date and time (typically when you aren't around). A scheduled backup for a single company file is ideal when your QuickBooks data is the *only* data on your computer or you want to backup your books more often than your other data. Otherwise, you're better off using your operating system's backup utility (or an online backup service) to schedule a backup that captures *all* your data.

Setting up automatic backups

Automatic backups require a bit of upfront setup. You tell QuickBooks where you want to store the automatic backup files and the number of sessions between backups. From then on, they spawn themselves quietly in the background. Here's how you set this up:

1. **Choose File → "Save Copy or Backup". In the "Save Copy or Backup" dialog box, select the "Backup copy" option, and then click Next.**

   The "Do you want to save your backup copy locally or online?" screen appears.

2. **Select the "Local backup" option, and then click Next.**

   The "When do you want to save your backup copy?" screen appears.

3. **To set up a backup schedule, select the "Only schedule future backups" option, and then click Next.**

   The screen displays the settings to define both automatic backups and scheduled backups, as shown in Figure 7-4.

4. **Turn on the "Save backup copy automatically when I close my company file every _ times" checkbox. In the text box, type the number of sessions you want in between automatic backups.**

   For example, if you type 5, QuickBooks creates an automatic backup when you close the company file the fifth time since the last backup.

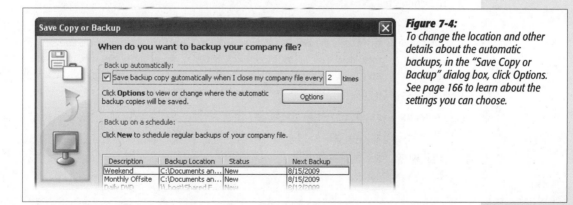

Figure 7-4:
To change the location and other details about the automatic backups, in the "Save Copy or Backup" dialog box, click Options. See page 166 to learn about the settings you can choose.

5. **Click Finish.**

   QuickBooks starts counting. After you've completed the number of sessions you specified, the QuickBooks Automatic Backup message box appears telling you that it's creating the automatic backup as promised.

The file naming convention that QuickBooks uses for automatic backup files is:

ABU_0_<company name> <date stamp> <time stamp>

For example, the first automatic backup file might be *ABU_0_Double Trouble, Inc Sep 22, 2010 05 17 PM* (ABU stands for "automatic backup"). However, when QuickBooks creates the next automatic backup, QuickBooks renames the file that begins with ABU_0 to start with ABU_1, (*ABU_1_Double Trouble, Inc Sep 22, 2010 05 17 PM*, for example) and renames the ABU_1 file to start with ABU_2. With this system, you always know that the file that starts with ABU_0 is the most recent automatic backup.

Scheduling backups for a single company file

Although most companies back up all of their computers on a regular schedule, you can set up a scheduled backup for your QuickBooks company file for an extra layer of safety. If you back up your data only every other day, for example, you may want to back up your company file every night, and a QuickBooks scheduled backup is the ideal way to do it. Here's how you schedule backups:

1. **Choose File → "Save Copy or Backup". In the "Save Copy or Backup" dialog box, select the "Backup copy" option, and then click Next.**

   The "Do you want to save your backup copy locally or online?" screen appears.

2. **Select the "Local backup" option, and then click Next.**

   The "When do you want to save your backup copy?" screen appears.

3. **To set up a backup schedule, select the "Only schedule future backups" option, and then click Next.**

   If you want to make a backup right away as well as set up the schedule, select the "Save it now and schedule future backups" option. Either way, the screen includes a table showing scheduled backups you've already set up, plus each backup's description, storage location, status, and next occurrence, as shown in Figure 7-5.

4. **To set up a schedule, below the table, click New.**

   QuickBooks opens the Schedule Backup dialog box with all the options you need to set up a regularly scheduled backup.

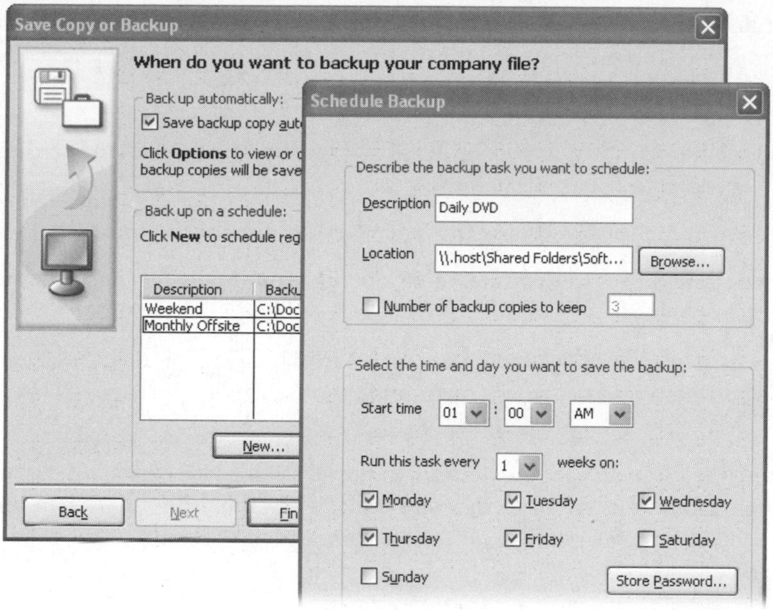

Figure 7-5:
You won't need more than a few scheduled backups. For instance, you can create one scheduled backup to save your data every weeknight from Monday through Thursday; a second scheduled backup might save a weekly backup every Saturday night. Finally, you could set up a third scheduled backup to run once a month on Saturday to create a backup on a DVD that you can store offsite.

5. In the Description box, type a meaningful name for the scheduled backup, like Monthly.

   When you finish defining the schedule, the description appears in the table in the "Save Copy or Backup" dialog box. Consider including the frequency of the backup and where to find the backup (such as the network drive or offsite location).

6. **The easiest way to specify the backup location is to click Browse.**

   QuickBooks opens the "Browse for Folder" dialog box. To choose a folder, hard drive, or other location on your computer, expand the My Computer entry, and then choose the backup location you want. If you want to store the backup on another computer on your network, expand the My Network Places entry, and then choose the backup location.

Warning: If you've scheduled backups, don't turn off your computer when you go home, or your backup won't work. If you back up to a hard drive on another computer, you have to leave that computer running, too. If you back up to any kind of removable media, be sure to place a blank disk or tape in the drive before you leave the office.

---

7. **If you back up your company file to a hard drive and don't want to overwrite your last backup each time the scheduled backup runs, turn on the "Number of backups to keep" checkbox and, in the box to the right of the label, type the number of previous backups you want to keep.**

   When you turn on this checkbox, QuickBooks uses the filename *SBU_0_<company name> <date stamp> <time stamp>*. For example, a scheduled backup file might be *SBU_0_Double Trouble, Inc Sep 24, 2008 01 00 AM* (SBU stands for "scheduled backup"). Each time QuickBooks creates a new scheduled backup file, it renames the previous backups to the next number in the list, and then replaces the SBU_0 file with the new backup. For example, if you keep four backups, the SBU_2 backup becomes the SBU_3 file; the SBU_1 file becomes the SBU_2 file; the SBU_0 backup file becomes the SBU_1 file; and the new backup becomes the new SBU_0 file.

8. **In the "Start time" boxes, choose the time you want the backup to run.**

    The "Start time" boxes work on a 12-hour clock, so you specify the hour, minutes, and a.m. or p.m.

    It's easy to confuse midnight and noon on a 12-hour clock: midnight is 12 a.m.; noon is 12 p.m. Avoid this gotcha by running your scheduled backups at 11 p.m., 1 a.m., or later.

9. **To set up the frequency for the backup, in the "Run this task every _ weeks on" box, type the number of weeks that you want between backups, and then turn on the checkboxes for each day of the week on which you want the backup to happen.**

    For example, for your daily backups, in the "Run this task every _ weeks on" box, type *1*, and then turn on the checkbox for each weekday.

10. **Click Store Password, and then type your Windows user name and password.**

    With your user name and password stored, QuickBooks can log into the computer to run the backup.

When you're done, click OK. QuickBooks adds the scheduled backup to your list of scheduled backups.

Restoring Backups

Having backup files can reduce your adrenaline level in a number of situations:

- You merge two customers into one by mistake or make another type of major faux pas that you want to undo.

- Your company file won't open, which can happen if the file's been damaged by a power outage or power surge.

- Your hard disk crashes and takes all your data with it.

- You recently assigned a password to your administrator login and can't remember what it is.

QuickBooks 2010 includes a utility that restores backup files to a format you can use in earlier versions of the program—for example, if you decide to switch back to QuickBooks 2009. The box on the next page tells you why and how to use the Restore Backup File For Earlier QuickBooks Version command.

DON'T PANIC

Restoring to an Earlier QuickBooks Version

When you upgrade to QuickBooks 2010, the program converts any existing company file you open to work with the new version. As part of the conversion process, QuickBooks backs up your company file so you can restore it in case you run into trouble. But the QuickBooks 2010 backup command uses a new and improved method to compress backup files that doesn't happen to play well with earlier versions of QuickBooks. So if you switch back to an earlier version of QuickBooks, you can't restore the QuickBooks 2010 backup file directly in your earlier version. Here's what to do instead:

1. In QuickBooks 2010, choose File → Utilities → Restore Backup For Earlier QuickBooks Version.

2. In the "Select the backup file you want to restore" section, click the Ellipsis button (…). The Open Backup Copy dialog box appears and displays the contents of the folder in which you last saved backup files.

3. Select the QuickBooks backup file you want to restore, and then click Open.

4. In the "Where do you want to save the restored file", click the Ellipsis button (…). The "Save Company File as" dialog box appears and displays the contents of the back up folder.

5. Navigate to the folder where you want to save the restored company file, for example, in the folder you use to store your company files (page 650).

6. In the "File name" box, type a unique name for the restored file, and then click Save.

7. Click OK. A QuickBooks Information message box appears telling you that the file has been restored and the folder in which you restored it. Click OK to close the message box.

Now, you can open that file as a regular company file in your earlier version of QuickBooks.

Warning: Hard disk crashes used to be dramatic events accompanied by impressive grinding noises. With today's smaller hard disks, crashes can be deceptively quiet. If you hear odd sounds emanating from your computer—little chirps or squeaks, for instance—stop what you're doing immediately. Take it to a computer repair shop to see if they can fix it or recover your data. If you shut down your computer and it won't reboot because of a disk crash, a data recovery company can sometimes recover some of your data, but the price is usually in the thousands of dollars. If smoke wafts from your computer, don't bother with shutting down. Just pull the plug and get that puppy to a repair shop.

Here's how to restore a QuickBooks backup when you need to recover from a mistake or damaged data:

1. **If you backed up your data to removable media, put the disk containing your backup in the appropriate drive.**

   If you backed up your data to another hard drive on your computer or on a network, you need access to that drive. For example, if the shared network drive that you used is offline, you'll have to reconnect to it before restoring your backup. If you need some guidance on how to reconnect an offline drive, consult your operating system's online help or refer to a copy of *Windows XP Pro: The Missing Manual* or *Windows Vista: The Missing Manual*.

2. Choose File → "Open or Restore Company".

If the No Company Open window is visible, you can also click "Open or restore an existing company".

Either method opens the "Open or Restore Company" dialog box, as shown in Figure 7-6.

3. In the "Open or Restore Company" dialog box, select the "Restore a backup copy" option, and then click Next.

The "Is the backup copy stored locally or online?" screen appears.

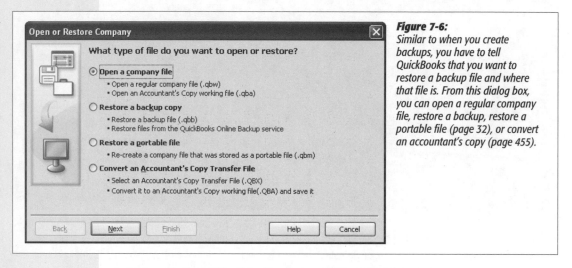

Figure 7-6:
Similar to when you create backups, you have to tell QuickBooks that you want to restore a backup file and where that file is. From this dialog box, you can open a regular company file, restore a backup, restore a portable file (page 32), or convert an accountant's copy (page 455).

4. Select the "Local backup" option, and then click Next.

The Open Backup Copy dialog box opens to your standard backup folder.

Note: If you select the "Online backup" option, and then click Next (and you subscribe to QuickBooks Online Backup), the online backup window opens. In the window icon bar, click Restore.

---

5. Double-click the name of the backup file you want to restore.

You can navigate to the folder or removable media where your backup file is saved and double-click the filename. Or, select the filename in the list, and then click Open.

6. Back in the "Open or Restore Company" dialog box, the "Where do you want to restore the file?" screen makes it clear that you need to choose the location carefully. Click Next. In the "Save Company File as" dialog box, choose the folder where you want to restore the file.

If you restore the backup to your regular company file folder, you run the risk of overwriting your existing company file. If that's what you want, fine. If it's not, that file may be gone for good.

7. **In the "File name" box, type a new name, as shown in Figure 7-7.**

The dialog box opens to the folder where you store your company files (page 650). QuickBooks fills in the "File name" box with the company file's name (minus the timestamp). If you want to replace a company file that's corrupt or has evidence of your big gaffe, you can keep the file name the program fills in.

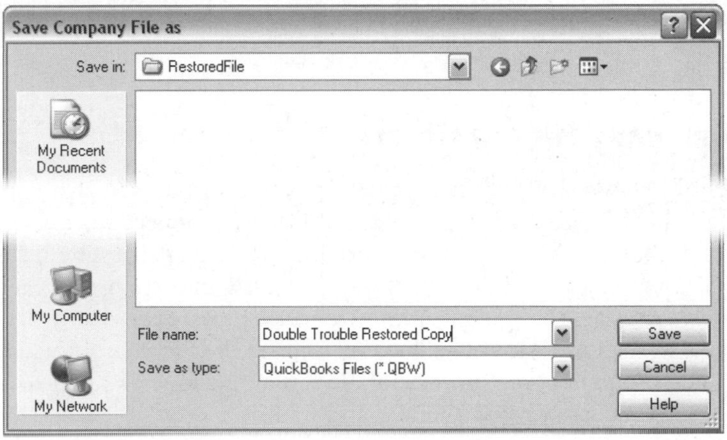

Figure 7-7:
To restore the file without overwriting the existing company file, choose another folder. In the "File name" box, consider adding unique text like Try 2 or Restore Sept 20 to the end of the name.

Tip: If you give a restored file a different name as a precaution—Double Trouble Copy, for example—you can trick QuickBooks into renaming the file after you're sure it's the one you want. Create a manual backup of the file. Then, immediately restore it with the company file name you want (Double Trouble in this example).

8. **Click Save.**

If you're restoring a backup of a company file that already exists, QuickBooks warns you that you're about to overwrite an existing file. If the original file is corrupt or won't open for some reason, click Yes because that's exactly what you want to do. You'll have to type *Yes* once more to confirm that you want to delete the file. It's better to take these precautions than to overwrite the wrong file and have to dig out yet another backup.

If the restored file has a password, you have to log in, just as you do in a regular company file. When you see the message that says your data has been restored successfully, click OK to open the company file and reenter any transactions that the backup doesn't have.

Note: If restoring a backup copy from removable media (CD, DVD, USB thumb drive, Zip disk, or floppy) doesn't work, try copying the contents of the backup media to your hard drive and restoring the backup file from there. If the restore still doesn't work, your backup file is probably damaged. Try restoring the next most recent backup.

If none of your backups work, Intuit offers data recovery services to extract data from your backup files. The service isn't free, but it might be cheaper than rebuilding your entire company file. To arrange for this service, choose Help → Support. On the QuickBooks Support web page, click Contact Us in the menu bar. Follow the instructions on the page to submit a request for technical support.

Sending Company Files to Others

In the past, QuickBooks company files were unwieldy to transport. To give a copy to your accountant, you needed a lightning-fast Internet connection, a CD or DVD, or a forklift. But QuickBooks now has portable company files, a slim file format that flies through the email ether and slips effortlessly into removable media like USB thumb drives and CDs. You can now email a portable company file to your accountant so she can take a quick look or transfer the file to a colleague in another office before you head out on vacation. If you intend to work on the company file at the same time as your accountant and want to merge her changes into your copy, create an Accountant's Copy (page 451) instead of a portable copy. But, before you transmit your file electronically, be sure you've added a password to it so nobody else can intercept it and access your financial data.

For example, a company file that's 10 MB in size turns into a portable company file of less than 1 MB. Portable company files come with a .qbm file extension, but QuickBooks converts them to regular company files with a .qbw file extension when you open them.

Note: If the person you send the file to is going to make any changes and send the file back, she needs a login or the administrator password. Remember that this password lets her use any and every QuickBooks feature on your file, so don't give it out to just anybody.

Creating a Portable Company File

Creating a portable company file is just a wee bit more complicated than saving a file. Here are the steps:

1. **Choose File → "Save Copy or Backup".**

   You can also click Backup in the icon bar, but the "Save Copy or Backup" command may be easier to remember because it has the word "Copy" in its name.

2. In the "Save Copy or Backup" dialog box, select the "Portable company file" option, shown in Figure 7-8, and then click Next.

QuickBooks fills in the "File name" box with the name of your company file followed by "(Portable)", and fills in the "Save as type" box with QuickBooks Portable Company Files (*.QBM).

3. If you want to use a different filename, change the name in the "File name" box, and then click Save.

The "Close and reopen" dialog box tells you that you need to close and reopen your company file to create a portable file.

4. Click OK to create the file.

A QuickBooks Information message box lets you know when QuickBooks finishes creating the portable company file. Click OK to reopen your company file in QuickBooks.

Feel free to view the portable company file in Windows Explorer and admire its sleek size.

Opening a Portable Company File

Opening a portable company file is almost identical to restoring a backup file, except for a few different label names. QuickBooks essentially converts the portable format file into a full-size, bona fide company file. Here's what you do:

1. Choose File → "Open or Restore Company".

If the No Company Open window is visible, you can click "Open or restore an existing company." Either method opens the Open or Restore Company dialog box.

2. In the "Open or Restore Company" dialog box, select the "Restore a portable file" option, and then click Next.

QuickBooks opens the Open Portable Company File dialog box to the last folder you selected for portable company files.

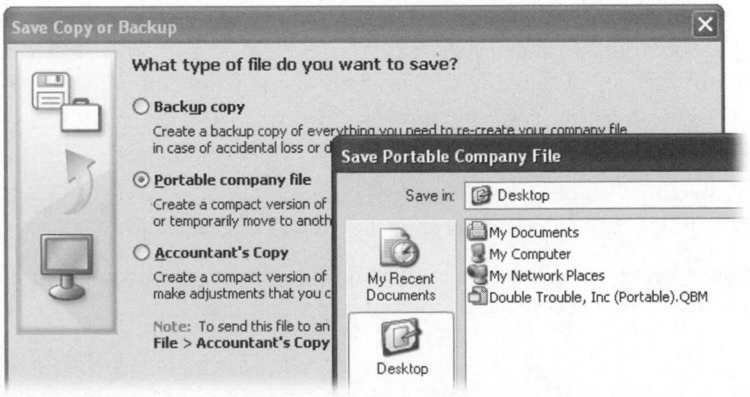

Figure 7-8:
Unlike the Save Backup Copy dialog box, the Save Portable Company File dialog box opens to your computer's desktop the first time around. If you want to save the file to a folder, choose the folder. From then on, QuickBooks opens the Save Portable Company File dialog box to the last folder you selected.

3. **Double-click the portable file you want to restore (or select the filename and then click Open).**

   QuickBooks sets the "Files of type" box to QuickBooks Portable Company Files (*.QBM) so the dialog box list shows only portable company files.

4. **Back in the "Open or Restore Company" dialog box, the "Where do you want to restore the file?" screen makes it clear that you should choose the location carefully. Click Next.**

   If you restore the portable file to your regular company file folder, you'll overwrite your existing company file. If that's what you want, fine. Otherwise, be sure to choose another folder or another filename.

5. **In the "Save Company File as" dialog box, choose the folder to which you want to restore. In the "File name" box, type a new name.**

   The dialog box opens to the folder you last chose for portable files. If you want to replace your company file, choose the folder that holds your everyday company file. QuickBooks fills in the "File name" box with the last restored file name you used.

6. **Click Save.**

   If you're restoring a portable file for a company file that already exists, QuickBooks warns you that you're about to overwrite an existing file. If that's what you want, click Yes. You'll have to type *Yes* once more to confirm that you want to delete the existing file.

   The Working message box shows its progress (restoring a portable file can take several minutes). When the file is ready, the QuickBooks Login dialog box appears (or the file opens if you don't use a password).

Verifying Your QuickBooks Data

QuickBooks files hiccup now and then. Perhaps you worked through a spectacular thunderstorm and a power spike zapped a bit of your company file. Fortunately, the QuickBooks Verify Data utility can scan your company files and tell you whether your file has suffered any damage. It's a good idea to run the Verify Data utility every so often, just to make sure that your company file is OK. How often you run this utility depends on how hard you work your company file, but monthly verifications are in order for most companies. The utility is indispensable, though, if you notice any of the following symptoms:

- **Invalid Protection Faults or Fatal Errors.** If these types of errors appear when you run QuickBooks, you almost certainly have a damaged data file.

- **Discrepancies on reports.** Your Balance Sheet doesn't show all your accounts, or transactions show negative values instead of positive ones.

Tip: If the totals in your reports don't seem right, first check that the report dates are correct and that you're using the correct cash or accrual accounting setting (see page 577).

- **Missing transactions and names.** Transactions or names that you're sure you entered don't appear in reports or lists.

Running the Verify Data Utility

Whether you're just giving your company file a checkup or you see signs of problems, the Verify Data utility is easy to use. To run the utility, choose File → Utilities → Verify Data. (If any windows are open, click OK to give QuickBooks permission to close them.) When the utility's done, you'll see one of two possible outcomes:

- If QuickBooks displays a message that it detected no problems with your data, your file is healthy.

- If you see the message "Your data has lost integrity," your company file has some problems. QuickBooks displays instructions for running the Rebuild Data utility, which tries to repair the damage. Read on to learn what to do.

Reviewing Problems

If your company file has "lost integrity," the Verify Data utility writes any errors it finds to a file named *QBWIN.log*. Before you run the Rebuild Data utility, take a look at this log file to review your company file's problems. You need a map to find the folder that contains these log files. Fortunately, you can open the file with the Windows Notepad program. Here's how:

1. **In Windows Explorer, go to the folder where QuickBooks stores QBWIN.log.**

   In Windows Vista, it's *C:\Users\<your user name>\AppData\Local\Intuit\ QuickBooks\log\20.0.*

   In Windows XP, it's *C:\Documents and Settings\<your user name>\Local Settings\ Application Data\Intuit\QuickBooks\log\20.0.*

2. **To open the log file, double-click its name.**

   The file opens in Windows Notepad, and you can use Notepad commands to move around the file, as shown in Figure 7-9. If the file doesn't open, launch Notepad, choose File → Open, and double-click the *QBWIN.log* filename. The most recent addition to the file is at the very end.

Note: Windows initially hides application data folders. If you don't see the folder, in the Windows Explorer window's menu bar, choose Tools → Folder Options. Click the View tab. In the "Advanced settings" list, under "Hidden files and folders", select "Show hidden files and folders".

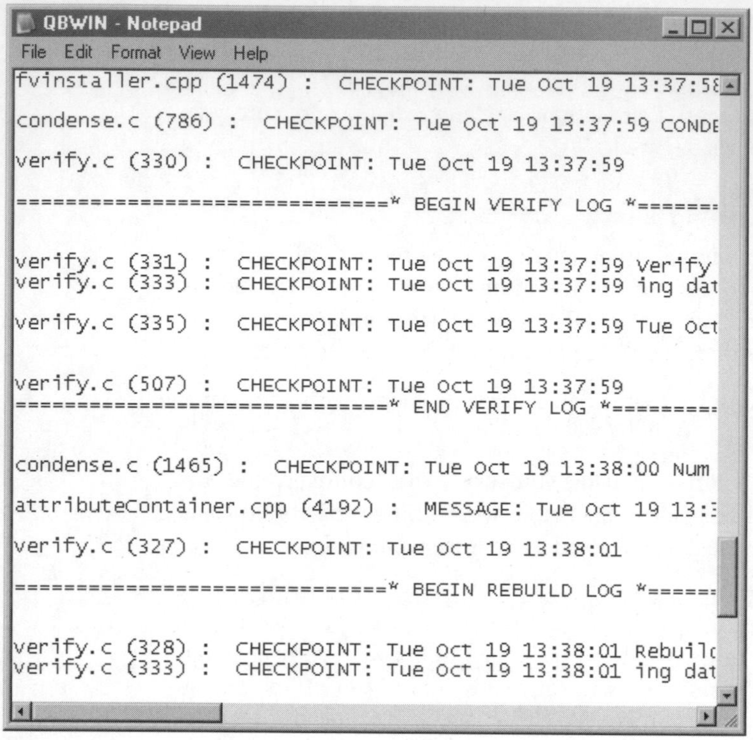

Figure 7-9:
*When you verify data,
QuickBooks automatically
renames the previous QBWIN.log
file to QBWin.log.old1 so that the
QBWIN.log file contains
information for only the most
recent verification. It also
renames other old files,
changing QBWIN.log.old1 to
QBWin.log.old2, and so on.*

Running the Rebuild Data Utility

If your file is damaged, the Rebuild Data utility tries to fix it. Unfortunately, it can also make matters worse. Intuit recommends that you run the Rebuild Data utility *only if* an Intuit technical support person tells you to. *Always* make a backup of your company file before trying to rebuild it. Take extra care to prevent overwriting your previous backups—those files might be your only salvation if the rebuild doesn't work.

To run the Rebuild Data utility, choose File → Utilities → Rebuild Data. When the utility finishes, close your company file and reopen it, which refreshes the lists in your data file so you can see if the problems are gone.

Run the Verify Data utility once more after you run the Rebuild Data utility to see if any damage remains. If this second Verify Data run still shows errors, restore a recent backup of your company file.

Cleaning Up Data

As you add transactions and build lists in QuickBooks, your company file gets larger. Although larger company files aren't too big of a hassle, you might be alarmed when your company file reaches hundreds of megabytes. Plus, if you use CDs to back up your file, your backups will start to take up too much valuable time and storage space. The Clean Up Company Data command creates an archive file and deletes obsolete list items and transactions prior to the date you choose.

Warning: The Clean Up Company Data wizard removes the audit trail information for transactions that the cleanup deletes. So if you're watching transaction activity, print an Audit Trail report *first*, and, as always, back up your company file.

When QuickBooks cleans up data, it replaces the detailed transactions prior to your specified date with general journal entries that summarize the deleted transactions by month. As a result, some of your financial detail is no longer available for running reports, filing taxes, and other accounting activities. Still, there are a couple of compelling reasons to do a data cleanup:

- **You no longer refer to old transactions.** If you've used QuickBooks for years, you probably *don't* need the finer details from eight or more years ago. And if you ever do need details from the past, you can open an archive file to run reports.

- **You have obsolete list items.** Cleaning up a company file can remove list items that you don't use, like customers you no longer sell to. This option comes in handy if you're nearing the limit on the number of names (page 73).

Note: If the Clean Up Company Data command isn't the housekeeper you hoped for, you can always start a fresh company file. That way, you can export all the lists from your existing company file (page 597) and import them (page 602) into the new file, so you start with lists but no transactions. Set your account opening balances (page 57) to the values for the start date of the new file. If you want to copy transactions from the old file to the new, try the QIF to IIF Convertor for QuickBooks (*www.bigredconsulting. com*) to transfer transactions from one QuickBooks file to another.

An archive file created by the Clean Up wizard is a regular company file that contains all of your transactions, but it's read-only, so you can't inadvertently enter new transactions. If QuickBooks runs into trouble cleaning up your file, it automatically pulls transaction details from the archive file.

Note: It's counterintuitive, but an archive copy is not a backup file, so it won't let you use the QuickBooks Restore command to replace a corrupt company file. Even with an archive copy, you still need to back up your data.

If you decide to clean up your company file, here's what you can expect to find afterward:

- **General journal entries summarize deleted transactions.** QuickBooks replaces all the deleted transactions that happened during each month with one general journal entry. For example, instead of 20 separate invoices for the month of June, you'll see one journal entry transaction with the total income for June for each income account.

Note: If you see other transactions for the same month, QuickBooks wasn't able to delete those transactions for some reason. For example, QuickBooks won't delete unpaid invoices or other transactions with an open balance, nor will it delete any transactions marked "To be printed" (page 267) or ones that you haven't reconciled (page 399).

- **Inventory adjustments reflect the average cost of items.** QuickBooks removes inventory transactions that are complete, such as invoices that have been paid in full. When QuickBooks finds an inventory transaction that it can't condense (perhaps because the payment is outstanding), it keeps all the inventory transactions from that date forward. Because inventory transactions use the average cost of inventory items, QuickBooks also adds an inventory adjustment to set the average cost of the inventory items as of that date.

- **Reports might not include the details you want.** You can still generate summary reports using condensed data because QuickBooks can incorporate the information in the monthly general journal entries. Likewise, sales tax reports still include the information about your sales tax liabilities. However, detailed reports won't include transaction details before the cutoff date you choose for condensing the file (see below). Cash accounting reports (see page 8) aren't accurate because they need the dates for detailed transactions.

- **Payroll for the current year remains.** QuickBooks keeps payroll transactions for the current year and the previous year regardless of the cutoff date you choose for condensing the file.

- **QuickBooks deletes estimates for closed jobs.** If a job has any status other than Closed, QuickBooks keeps the estimates for that job.

- **QuickBooks keeps time data that you haven't billed.** QuickBooks keeps any time you've tracked that's billable but that you haven't yet billed to your customers. Also, if you pay employees by the time they work, QuickBooks keeps data for time for which you *haven't* compensated your employees.

Running the Clean Up Company File Tool

If you're ready to clean up your company file, first consider *when* to do it. The cleaning process can take several hours for a large company file, and a slow computer or a small amount of memory exacerbates the problem. You might want to clean your company file at the end of a workday so it can run overnight.

Here's how to condense a company file:

1. **Choose File → Utilities → Clean Up Company Data.**

   If you've created budgets in QuickBooks, you'll see a message that the clean up might remove budget data. You can export your budget before you clean up your data and then import the budget back into your company file after cleanup (page 488). If the loss of some budget data doesn't scare you, click Yes. The Clean Up Company Data dialog box opens.

2. **Select the "Remove transactions as of a specific date" option.**

   The "Remove transactions as of a specific date" option removes old transactions and other things like unused accounts and items. The "Remove ALL transactions" option removes transactions but keeps your preferences, lists, and service subscriptions—such as payroll—intact. You won't use this option often, but it comes in handy if, for example, you wanted to offer your clients a template company file that contains typical list entries, but without any transactions.

3. **In the "Remove closed transactions on or before" box, type or select the ending date for the period you want to condense.**

   If you use a QuickBooks Payroll Service for your payroll (page 362), you can't clean up data for the current year. Besides, QuickBooks won't let you clean up transactions that are later than the closing date on your company file (page 552). Choosing a date at least two years in the past ensures that you can compare detailed transactions for the current year and the previous year. For example, if it's March 1, 2010, consider using December 31, 2007 or earlier as your cutoff date.

4. **Click Next to advance to the "Select Additional Criteria for Removing Transactions" screen. If you want QuickBooks to remove transactions that the clean up process would normally leave alone, turn on the appropriate checkboxes. Click Next.**

   Figure 7-10 shows your choices. Before you turn on these checkboxes, carefully review your company file to make sure you won't delete transactions that you want to keep. Click Next.

5. **In the "Select Unused List Items To Remove" screen, turn on the appropriate checkboxes if you want QuickBooks to delete list items no longer referenced in the cleaned up file. Then click Next.**

   Accounts, customers, vendors, other names, and invoice items might become orphans when you delete old transactions they're linked to. You can neaten your file by removing these list items, which now have no links to the transactions that still remain. But keep in mind that you might still work with one of these vendors or customers later.

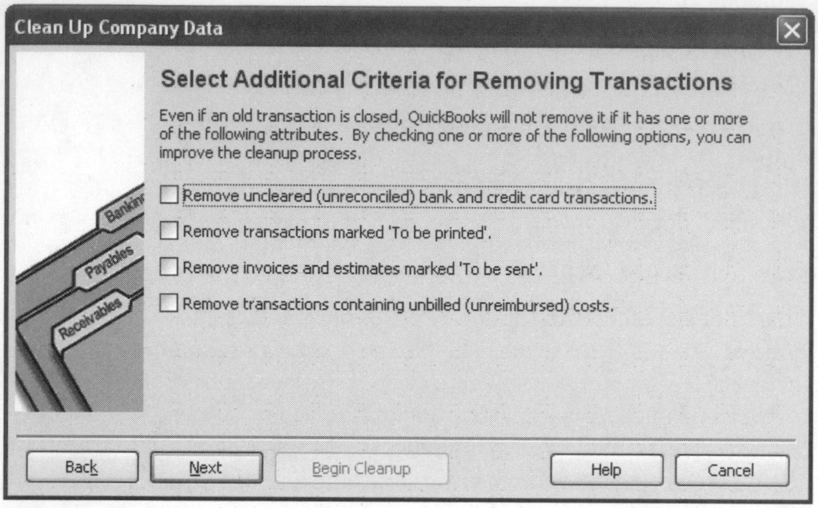

Figure 7-10:
The Clean Up Company File tool includes settings to remove transactions that it would normally leave alone—like transactions marked "To be printed" that you don't need to print. If you have very old, unreconciled transactions, invoices, or estimates marked "To be sent," or transactions with unreimbursed costs, turn on these checkboxes to remove them during the cleanup.

If seeing all the To Do notes you've completed gives you a sense of accomplishment, leave the "'Done' To Do notes" checkbox turned off. But to show only To Do notes that you *haven't* completed, turn this checkbox on.

6. **On the "Proceed with cleanup?" screen, click Begin Cleanup.**

   If you're not sure of the options you chose, or if you have any doubts about cleaning up your file, click Back to return to a previous screen, or click Cancel to exit without taking any action.

When you click Begin Cleanup, QuickBooks tells you that it'll back up your file before condensing the transactions. Click OK when you're ready to back up *and* clean up your data. QuickBooks first creates a backup file of your data. Then, it creates the archive file (a QuickBooks company file, not a backup file; see page 181) in the same folder as your original company file. The file name for the archive copy has the format "Archive Copy mm-dd-yyyy <company name>.qbw", where "mm" represents the month, "dd" the day, and "yyyy" the year that you created the file.

As QuickBooks proceeds with the cleanup process, it scans your data *three* times. You might see dialog boxes wink on and off in rapid succession; then again, you might not see anything happen for a while if your file is large. But if your hard disk is working, the cleanup process is still in progress. Be patient and resist clicking Cancel. When the cleanup is complete, QuickBooks displays a message telling you so.

Cleaning Up After Deleting Files

Although QuickBooks lets you delete transactions (which is risky because doing so makes it easier for people to embezzle), the program *doesn't* give you a command for deleting company files. If someone else takes over responsibility for your non-profit's accounting, or if you want to get rid of a practice file you no longer use, you can easily delete the company file right in Windows. But you'll still have some housekeeping to do to remove all references to that file from QuickBooks. A deleted company file will still appear in the list of previously opened files (Figure 7-11), but QuickBooks won't be able to find the file if you choose that entry. Here's how you eliminate those stale entries:

1. **In Windows Explorer, navigate to the folder where your QuickBooks company files are stored. Right-click the company file you want to delete.**

   What you look for depends on how you've set up your folder view. If your folder shows the full names of your files, look for a file with a .qbw file extension, such as *DoubleTrouble, Inc.qbw*. If the folder includes a Name column and a Type column, the type you want is QuickBooks Company File.

   Files with .qbx extensions represent accountant's copies. Files with .qbb file extensions are backup copies of your company files. If you delete the company file, go ahead and delete the backup and accountant's copies as well.

2. **On the shortcut menu, choose Delete.**

   Windows displays the Confirm File Delete message box. Click Yes to move the file to the Recycle Bin. If you have second thoughts, click No to keep the file.

Tip: If you find that you always seem to need a file the day after you delete it, get in the habit of backing up files before you delete them.

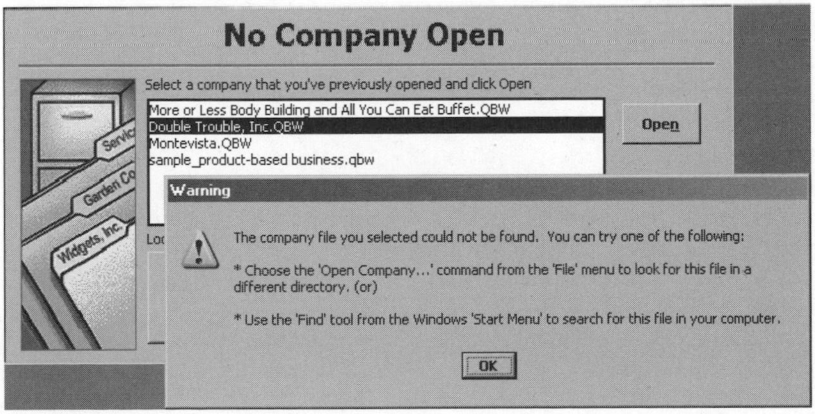

Figure 7-11:
*If you double-click the name of a file that QuickBooks can't find, the program suggests that you choose File →
Open Company and then look for the file in another directory, or that you use Windows' Find command. If you know that the file doesn't exist, simply click OK, and then select another file.*

3. In QuickBooks, to eliminate the deleted company file from the list that you see when you choose File → Open Previous Company, you first have to open another company file.

   If QuickBooks displays the No Company Open window, open the company file that you typically work with by double-clicking it.

4. **To clear out old companies in the previously opened file list, you need to reset the number of companies displayed in the No Company Open window. To do this, choose File → Open Previous Company → "Set number of previous companies".**

   In the "How many companies do you want to list (1 to 20)?" box, type *1*, and then click OK. When you choose File → Open Previous Company again, you'll notice that only one company appears—the company file you opened last. In the No Company Open window, the "Select a company that you've previously opened and click Open" list also contains only the last file you opened.

5. **Now that you've removed the deleted company file from these lists, you can reset the number of previously opened companies. With a company file open, choose File → Open Previous Company → "Set number of previous companies".**

   In the "How many companies do you want to list (1 to 20)?" box, type the number of companies you'd like to see in the list, and then click OK.

As you open different company files, QuickBooks displays these files in the No Company Open window and on the Open Previous Company menu.

CHAPTER 8

Tracking Time and Mileage

When customers pay for your services, they're really buying your knowledge of how to get the job done the best and fastest possible way. That's why a carpenter who can barely hit the nail on the head charges $15 an hour, whereas a master who hammers faster and straighter than a nail gun charges $80 an hour. When you come right down to it, time is money, so you want to keep track of both with equal accuracy. Product-based companies track time, too. For example, companies that want to increase productivity often start by tracking the time that employees work and what they work on.

There are hordes of off-the-shelf and homegrown time-tracking programs out there, but if your time tracking needs are fairly simple, you can record time directly in QuickBooks or use its companion Timer program, which you can provide to each person whose work hours you want to track. If you have to track the billable hours of lots of employees or contractors, Intuit has Time Tracker, a for-a-fee online timesheet service. The advantage of QuickBooks time tracking is that the time you record is ready to attach to an invoice (see page 269) or payroll (see page 367). In this chapter, you'll learn how to record time in QuickBooks itself and with the help of the online Time Tracker. Appendix D explains the ins and outs of the stand-alone Timer program.

Mileage is another commodity that many businesses track—or should. Whether your business hinges on driving or merely requires the occasional jaunt, the IRS lets you deduct vehicle mileage, *but* it requires documentation of the miles you deduct. The QuickBooks mileage tracking feature helps you track the mileage of company vehicles, which you can use not only for tax deductions, but to charge customers for mileage.

Setting Up Time Tracking

For many businesses, *approximations* of time worked are fine. For example, employees who work on only one or two tasks each day can review the past week and log their hours in a weekly timesheet. But for people with deliciously high hourly rates, you want to capture every minute you work on an activity from the time you start to the time you finish. QuickBooks can help you track time whether you take a conscientious approach or a more cavalier one. In fact, you can choose from three different ways to record time in QuickBooks:

- **Enter time data in QuickBooks.** When QuickBooks is running, you can enter time for individual activities or in a weekly timesheet. If you enter time for a single activity, the Time/Enter Single Activity dialog box has a stopwatch of its own, so you can either time the task or simply type the number of hours.

- **Use Time Tracker and download online timesheets.** Intuit's online time tracking service lets people fill out timesheets online. You review the submitted timesheets online and download those timesheets into your company file. The box on page 194 tells you more.

- **Use the QuickBooks Timer stopwatch.** This program, which comes free with QuickBooks, lets you time activities as you work so you can track your time to the second—as long as you remember to start and stop the Timer at the right moments. (If you forget to turn the Timer on or off, you can edit time entries to correct them.) The best thing about the Timer program is that you can record time without QuickBooks running. Moreover, you can give a copy of the Timer program to all your employees and subcontractors so they can send you time data to import into QuickBooks.

No matter which technique you use to capture time, the setup in QuickBooks is the same: You tell QuickBooks that you want to track time and then set up the people who have to track their time (employees and outside contractors alike). You use the customers and items you've set up in QuickBooks to identify the billable time you work. If you want to track nonbillable time, you need a few more entries in QuickBooks, which you'll learn about in the following sections.

Turning on Time Tracking

If you created your company file with the QuickBooks EasyStep Interview (page 21) and told QuickBooks that you want to track time, the preferences and features for time tracking should be ready to go. Only a QuickBooks administrator can turn time tracking on or off (which is why time tracking preferences are on the Company Preferences tab). You have to switch the company file to single-user mode (page 161) to change Company preferences. To see if time tracking is turned on, choose Edit → Preferences. Click the Time & Expenses icon, and then click the Company Preferences tab, shown in Figure 8-1.

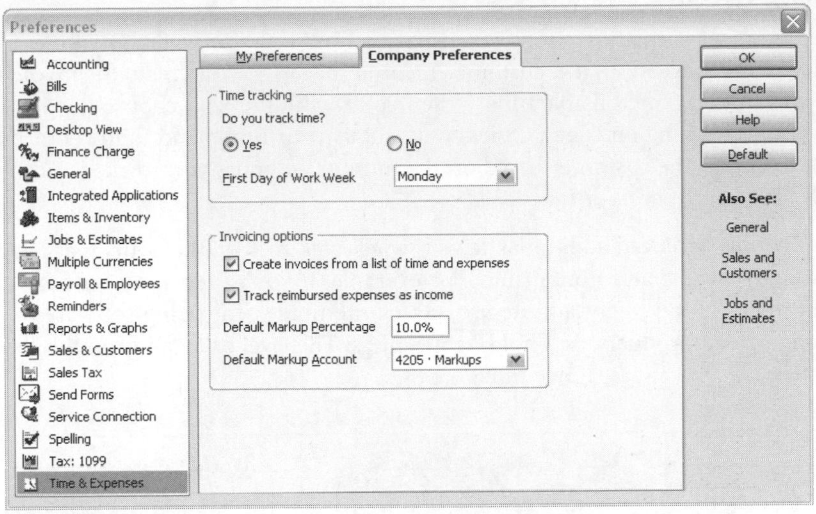

Figure 8-1:
If you use this feature to generate hours for payroll, the QuickBooks work week should end on the same day of the week as your pay periods. For example, if you pay employees on Friday, in the "First Day of Work Week" drop-down list, choose Saturday, so that the work week ends on Friday like your payroll.

If the Yes option isn't selected, click it. The only other time tracking preference is the first day of the work week. QuickBooks sets this preference to Monday to match the Monday through Friday work week of so many businesses. For round-the-clock services, self-employed people, and workaholics, choose whichever day of the week feels most like the beginning of the week. For example, many companies on a seven-day work week start the week on Sunday.

Setting Up the People Who Track Time

You can't enter or import people's time into QuickBooks unless their names appear in one of your name lists (Employee List, Vendor List, or Other Name List). If a person whose time you want to track doesn't belong to a name list yet, here's how you decide which list to use:

- **Employee List.** Use this list *only* for the people you pay using QuickBooks' payroll features.

- **Vendor List.** Add subcontractors and outside consultants (people or companies that send you bills for time), whether or not their time is billable to customers. (Undoubtedly, their time is billable to you.)

- **Other Names List.** By process of elimination, anyone who isn't a vendor and isn't paid via QuickBooks' payroll belongs on the Other Names List. For example, employees paid using a third-party payroll service or owners who take a draw instead of a paycheck (page 146) qualify for this list.

People who track time *directly* in QuickBooks (with a weekly timesheet or in the Time/Enter Single Activity dialog box, not with the standalone Timer program) need the program's permission to do so. When you set up QuickBooks users, you can set their permissions so they can enter time as described on page 639.

Setting Up Items and Customers for Time Tracking

The good news is that your setup for what you bill time on is already done. The Service items (page 109) and customer records (page 72) you create for invoicing also work for tracking billable time. When you track time, you choose the Service item you're working on. Then QuickBooks totals your hours and figures out how much to charge the customer based on the number of hours you worked and how much you charge per hour for the service.

The only time you need additional items is when you track *all* the hours that people work, both billable and nonbillable. For example, if you're trying to reduce your overhead costs, you might add items to track the time spent fixing software bugs, exchanging bad products, and holding meetings. The level of detail for nonbillable activities is up to you, as shown in Figure 8-2.

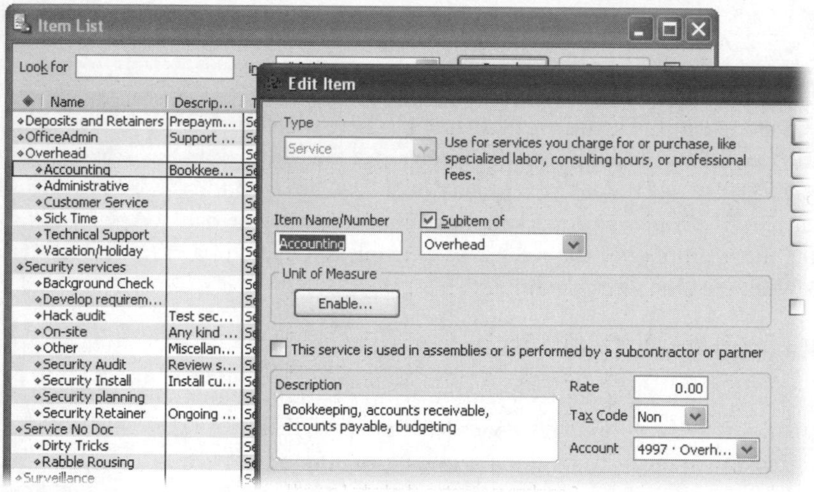

Figure 8-2:
If you want to capture nonbillable activities in one big pot, create a single Service item called Overhead. For greater detail about nonbillable time, you can create a top-level item, such as Overhead, and then create subitems for each type of nonbillable work you want to track. Be sure to create one catch-all item, such as Administrative, to capture the time that doesn't fit in any other nonbillable category.

Here is how you fill in item fields when you create items to track time that you don't bill to a customer:

- **Type.** Use the Service item type (page 109) because that's the only item type that QuickBooks time tracking recognizes.

- **Rate.** In the New Item or Edit Item dialog box, the Rate box represents how much you charge your customers for the service. Because no money changes hands for nonbillable time, leave the Rate box blank.

- **Account.** You can't create an item without assigning it to an account. Go ahead and create an income account and call it something like Nonbillable Work or Overhead. If you number accounts, assign a number that places the account near the end of your Income type accounts (like 4997, because QuickBooks uses 5000 for the first Cost of Goods Sold account [page 431]). Because nonbillable time doesn't bring in any income, the account balance remains zero no matter how much nonbillable time you assign to it.

• **This service is performed by a subcontractor, owner, or partner.** Leave this checkbox blank for nonbillable items performed by owners and partners. However, if a subcontractor performs nonbillable work, create a separate item for nonbillable time with this checkbox turned on. Then you can assign the subcontractor's costs to an expense account and use time tracking to make sure the subcontractor's bills are correct.

Entering Time in Timesheets

In QuickBooks, you can enter and view time for a single activity or through a weekly timesheet. If you record time after the fact, the weekly timesheet is the fastest way to enter time. If you already have one timesheet filled in, you can use it to speed up time entry, as the box below explains. To time work as you perform it, the Time/Enter Single Activity dialog box (explained in the section that begins on page 194) is the place to go.

UP TO SPEED

Copying Timesheets

People often work on the same tasks from week to week. Filling in row after row of customer, Service item, Payroll item, and Class when you filled in the same things the week before is bound to generate grumbling from employees who already have enough to do.

QuickBooks can reduce tedium by copying the entries from a person's last timesheet. Copying timesheets not only saves time for whoever enters time, but also helps prevent mistakes or omissions. Here's how you copy a timesheet:

1. In the Weekly Timesheet dialog box in the Name field, choose the person's name.

2. Click Previous or Next, or click the calendar icon to display the weekly timesheet you want to copy into.

3. Click Copy Last Sheet. If the current timesheet is empty, the program fills in all the rows with the entries from the person's last timesheet, including the customer, service item, class, notes, and hours.

4. If the timesheet already has values, QuickBooks asks whether you want to replace the entries or add entries to the timesheet. Click Yes to replace the entries with the ones from the last timesheet you opened. Click No to append the entries from the last timesheet as additional rows in this week's timesheet. To keep the current timesheet just the way it is, click Cancel.

Filling in Weekly Timesheets

The weekly timesheet is the fastest way to enter time for several activities or work that spans several days:

1. Choose Employees → Enter Time → Use Weekly Timesheet.

   QuickBooks opens the Weekly Timesheet dialog box.

Note: Although you can track time for people other than employees, you still access time tracking from the Employees menu or the Employee Center. To open the Weekly Timesheet window from the Employee Center, on the Home page, click Employees. Then, in the Employee Center's menu bar, choose Enter Time → Use Weekly Timesheet.

2. **In the Name drop-down list, choose the name of the person who performed the work.**

   Because time tracking is rarely limited to only the people with permission to run QuickBooks, you can enter time for yourself or anyone else. After you choose a name, the program displays the weekly timesheet for the current week and shows any time already entered for the week, as shown in Figure 8-3.

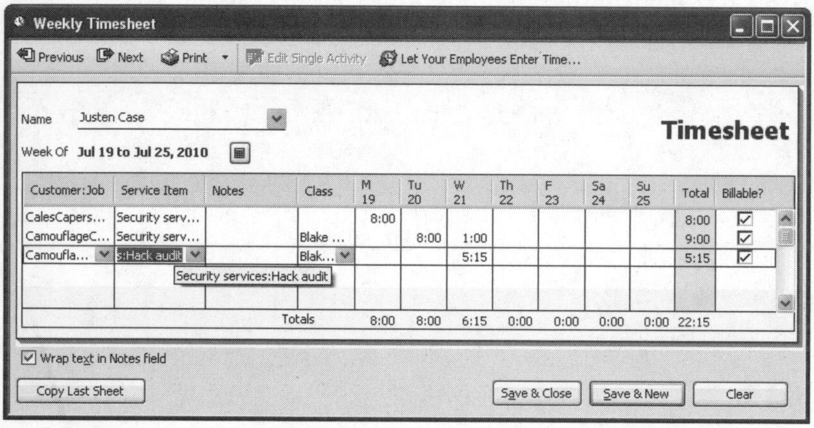

Figure 8-3:
The weekly timesheet doesn't provide much room to display customer names, job names, or more than a few letters of the Service item for the task performed. To see the full contents of a cell in a pop-up screen tip, position the mouse pointer over the cell.

3. **If you want to enter time for a different week, in the window toolbar, click Previous or Next until the week you want appears.**

   To choose a week further in the past, click the calendar icon to the right of the week's date range. In the Set Date window that appears, click the arrows to the left or right of the month heading to move to a past or future month. Click any date during the week to choose that work week. For example, choosing 22 in the July 2010 calendar switches the weekly timesheet to the week beginning July 19, 2010.

4. **To add a billable activity to the timesheet, in the first blank Customer:Job cell (the first column of the timesheet table), choose the customer or job associated with the work performed.**

   If the work is billable, choose the customer or job that pays for it. If the time isn't billable, you can leave the customer field blank. Depending on whether you keep your hands on the keyboard or the mouse, you can move to the Service Item cell by pressing Tab or clicking the Service Item cell.

5. **In the Service Item cell, choose the item that represents the work the person performed.**

   If you use QuickBooks payroll and pay employees by the hours they work, you fill in the Service Item and the Payroll Item. The Payroll Item column appears to the right of the Service Item column. In the Payroll Item column, you can choose the payroll-related item (page 364) that applies to the time worked. For example, for billable work, choose a payroll item such as Salary or Employee Income. If the hours are for vacation or sick time, choose the payroll item you've created for that time.

6. **In the Notes cell, type additional information about the work.**

   For example, if someone receives comp time but your company doesn't formally track it, you might use a Service Item such as Administrative and use the Notes cell to identify the comp time taken. If your customers require detail about the work performed, store that information in the Notes cell, which then appears on the invoices you create (see page 273).

Tip: To see the entire contents of Notes cells, turn on the "Wrap text in Notes field" checkbox. Each row in the Timesheet table takes up more space, but you won't have to position the pointer over every Notes cell to see what it contains.

---

7. **If you use classes to track income (page 67), in the Class column, choose one for the work.**

   For example, if you track income by partner, choose the class for the partner who handles the customer. If you use classes to track office branches, choose the class for the branch where the person works.

8. **To enter time for a day during the week, click the cell for that day or press Tab until you reach the right day.**

   You can enter time in several ways. If you know the number of hours, type the hours as a decimal or as hours and minutes. For example, for seven and a half hours, type either *7.5* or *7:30*. QuickBooks displays the hours in the timesheet based on the preference you set for time (page 565). If you know the starting and ending time, QuickBooks can calculate the hours for you. For example, if you type 9-5 in a cell, the program transforms it into eight hours when you move away from the cell (by pressing Tab or clicking another cell).

   As you enter time for each day of the week, the Total column on the *right side* of the table shows the total hours for each activity. The numbers in the Totals row *below* the table show the total hours for each day and for the entire week.

Note: A row in a weekly timesheet represents one service item and one customer or job. If you perform the same type of work for two different customers, you have to enter that time in two separate rows.

---

9. **If you aren't billing the customer for the work, in the Billable? column, click the checkmark to turn it off.**

   QuickBooks adds a checkmark to the Billable? column automatically. When you click the billable cell, the checkmark disappears to indicate that the time isn't billable.

Note: Adding billable time to customer invoices is easy, as described in detail on page 273.

---

10. **To save the timesheet, click Save & Close or Save & New.**

   If you enter time for a number of people, click Save & New to save the current weekly timesheet and open a new blank one. Clicking Save & Close saves the timesheet and closes the weekly timesheet dialog box.

POWER USERS' CLINIC

Tracking Time Online

Time Tracker is an add-on service that works with Quick-Books. Anyone who you set up to track time with the service logs into a website, fills in a timesheet, and submits it to you. You don't have to do their data entry for them. And they can submit their time from any computer that has Internet access, so you don't have to wait for an employee to get back from a trip to fill in a timesheet. The service even handles reminding people to submit their time.

You review the timesheets online and then download them all into QuickBooks in one fell swoop. You can even look at unsubmitted timesheets if, for instance, someone's hours are nearing a limit set by your customer.

The bad news is this service isn't free, although Intuit offers a 30-day free trial. (There had to be a catch.) The price per month for a single person is $10 (that's $120 a year). For up to five employees, the price is $25 per month. If you have more than 50 employees, the price jumps to $150 per month.

To get the full details, choose Employees → Enter Time → Let Your Employees Enter Time. (On the QuickBooks Home page, click Enter Time and then choose Let Employees Enter Time on the shortcut menu.) Or, in your browser, go directly to the Time Tracking Software web page (*http://quickbooks.intuit.com/product/add-ons/time-tracking-software.jsp*).

Entering Time for One Activity

Entering time in a weekly timesheet is quick, but the width of the columns makes it hard to see which customer and service item you're tracking. If you prefer readability to speed, the Time/Enter Single Activity window is a better choice. The Time/Enter Single Activity window also lets you start and stop a stopwatch if you want to time work as you go.

You have to fill in every field for every activity in the Time/Enter Single Activity window. If you grow tired of this form of time entry, in the window's toolbar, click Timesheet to switch to the Weekly Timesheet window. The weekly timesheet that appears is for the person you selected in the Time/Enter Single Activity window and the week that includes the selected day.

Here's how you enter time for one activity at a time:

1. **Choose Employees → Enter Time → Time/Enter Single Activity.**

   The Time/Enter Single Activity window opens to today's date.

   If the person with time to report is an employee, you can get QuickBooks to fill in the Name box automatically. On the Home page, click Employees to open the Employee Center. On the Employees tab, select the employee whose time you want to enter and then, in the Employee Center's menu bar, choose Enter Time → Time/Enter Single Activity.

2. **If you want to record time for another day, in the Date field, click the Calendar icon and choose the date on which the work took place.**

   When you first open the Time/Enter Single Activity window, QuickBooks selects all the text in the Date box. You can replace the date by simply typing the new date, like *6/07/10*.

3. **In the Name drop-down list, choose the name of the person who performed the work.**

   The Name drop-down list includes vendors, employees, and names from the Other Names List. If you choose an employee who isn't set up for sending time data to payroll, QuickBooks asks whether you want to change the employee's setup (page 368). If you want to use the time entered to generate paycheck data—for instance, when employees are paid by the hour—click Yes, which links the employee's time records to paycheck data.

Note: When you first open the Time/Enter Single Activity window you may see the Payroll Item label. If you set up employees so that their time data generates the values on their paychecks (page 367), you can select the payroll item to which the time applies. However, if you choose the name of a person who isn't paid based on their time, the Payroll Item entry disappears. If you use classes, the Class entry takes its place.

---

4. **In the Customer:Job drop-down list, choose a customer or job.**

   If someone performs work for a real customer or job, choose that customer or job whether or not you bill the time. To track overhead time, choose the customer you created for nonbillable work.

5. **If the hours aren't billable to a customer, turn off the Billable checkbox.**

   The Billable checkbox isn't the next field that QuickBooks chooses if you press Tab; it's located in the upper-right corner of the window. But choosing a customer is a reminder for whether the hours are billable. QuickBooks automatically turns on the Billable checkbox, so you have to worry about this checkbox only if the hours *aren't* billable.

6. **In the Service Item drop-down list, choose the item that represents the work performed.**

   Choose this item whether it's one you use to invoice customers or a nonbillable item you created to track overhead activities.

7. **Press Tab to move to the Duration box. QuickBooks automatically selects the contents of the box, so you can simply type the hours worked. If you click the Duration box, drag to select its contents.**

   Type hours as a decimal or as hours and minutes, such as *5.5* or *5:30*. Or, if you know the starting and ending time, type the time range to have QuickBooks calculate the hours. For example, if you type *11-5* in a cell, the program fills in the box with *6:00* when you tab or click away from the box.

   If you work in QuickBooks almost all the time, you can time a task that you're working on in the Time/Enter Single Activity window, as shown in Figure 8-4.

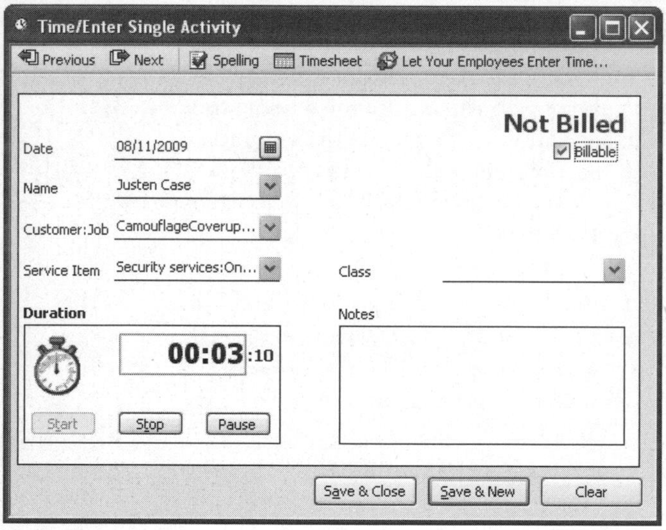

Figure 8-4:
To time your current activity, the Date field has to have today's date. To start the stopwatch, click Start. You'll see the seconds that are passing to the right of the Duration box to show that it's timing your work. If you want to pause the stopwatch to take a break or a phone call, click Pause; simply click Start to start timing again. When you finish the task, click Stop. (Unless you have special time-travel powers, you can't run a stopwatch for work performed on a different day.)

Note: If you click Previous to display another single activity and then click Start, the stopwatch feature starts adding additional time to what you've already recorded.

8. **If you track classes, in the Class field, choose the appropriate one. To add notes about the activity, type text in the Notes box.**

   These notes appear in the Notes column in the Weekly Timesheet dialog box and, for billable work, appear on invoices you generate from time worked.

9. **To save the transaction, click Save & New or Save & Close.**

When you click Save & New, the saved activity represents time for only one day. To record time for another day's work even if it's for the same worker, customer, and Service item, you have to create a new activity.

Running Time Reports

Customers don't like being charged for too many hours, and workers are quick to complain if they're paid for too few. Before you use time records either for billing customers or feeding your payroll records, it's a good idea to generate time reports to make sure your time data is correct. (The box below explains how to set up employees in QuickBooks so their reported time links to your QuickBooks payroll.)

GEM IN THE ROUGH

Building Paychecks from Time Worked

If you pay your employees by the hour *and* use QuickBooks payroll to generate employee payroll checks, time tracking can automate your payroll process a bit.

The people you pay via QuickBooks payroll have to be in your QuickBooks Employee List. But when you link your employees to their QuickBooks timesheets, the program takes care of calculating how much they've earned.

Here's how you link employees and timesheets to gain this small payroll improvement:

1. On the left side of the Home page, click Employees to open the Employee Center.

2. On the Employees tab, double-click the employee you want to pay.

3. When the Edit Employee dialog box opens, click the "Change tabs" drop-down menu and choose "Payroll and Compensation Info".

4. Turn on the "Use time data to create paychecks" checkbox.

5. Click OK to save the record.

Employees can still track time without this checkbox turned on, which is ideal if you *don't* need a connection between the hours worked and the employee's paycheck. For example, turn the checkbox *off* if you bill customers for employee time but pay those employees a straight salary.

To generate a time report in QuickBooks, choose Reports → Jobs, Time & Mileage, and then choose the report you want. Here are the reports you can choose from and what they're useful for:

- **Time by Job Summary.** If you bill by the job, the "Time by Job Summary" report shows hours by customer or job, broken down by Service items. Overly high or low hours—or Service items that don't belong on a job—are red flags for data entry errors. Review the total hours worked on a job during a period. Because of the high-level view in this report, it's perfect for spotting time charged to inappropriate Service items or hours that exceed job limits. If hours seem too high or low, you can drill down with the "Time by Job Detail" report to investigate.

- **Time by Job Detail.** If you want to verify that hours were correctly set as billable or nonbillable, use this report. It's grouped by job and Service item, but each time entry shows the date the hours were worked, who performed the work, and whether the work is billable (the Billing status is Unbilled for billable hours not yet invoiced, Billable for invoiced billable hours, or Not Billable).

- **Time by Name.** This report shows the hours worked by person, with the hours worked for each customer or job, as shown in Figure 8-5. QuickBooks sets the date range to This Fiscal Year-to-Date, but if you want to check timesheets for accuracy, you can change the date range to Last Week or Last Month. If a person reports too many or too few hours for a period, use the Weekly Timesheet dialog box to look for signs of inaccurate or missing time reports.

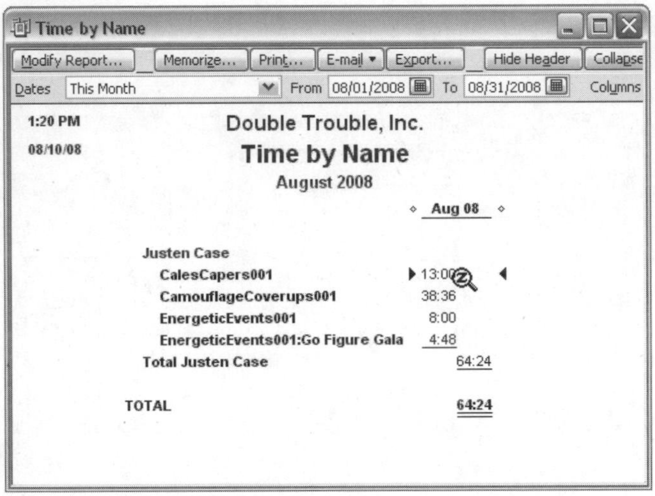

Figure 8-5:
The "Time by Name" report summarizes the hours someone works for each customer or job. To see the dates and times for the work, hover the cursor over an hourly total. When you see the magnifying glass, double-click the time to open a "Time by Name Detail" report.

- **Time by Item.** This report groups hours by Service item and then by customer or job. You can use this report to analyze where your billable and nonbillable time is spent, either to cut unproductive activities or to determine staffing needs.

Tracking Mileage

If you charge your customers for mileage, keeping track of the billable miles you drive helps you get all the reimbursements you're due. But *all* business-related mileage is tax-deductible, so tracking nonbillable business mileage is important, too. Customers and the IRS alike want records of the miles you drive, and QuickBooks can help you produce that documentation.

The mileage tracking feature in QuickBooks tracks only the miles you drive using company vehicles, not other vehicle expenses, such as fuel or tolls. Likewise, you don't use QuickBooks mileage tracking to record miles driven by employees, vendors, or subcontractors, which instead go straight to an expense account. For example, if a vendor bills you for mileage, when you enter the bill in QuickBooks (page 206), you assign that charge to an expense account, such as Travel-Mileage. When you write a check to reimburse an employee for mileage driven, you assign that employee reimbursement to the expense account for mileage.

Adding a Vehicle

To track mileage for a company vehicle, you first have to add the vehicle to the QuickBooks Vehicle List. Here's how:

1. **To open the Vehicle List window, choose Lists → Customer & Vendor Profile Lists → Vehicle List.**

   The Vehicle List window opens.

2. **To add a new vehicle, press Ctrl+N or click Vehicle and then choose New from the drop-down menu.**

   The New Vehicle dialog box opens, as shown in Figure 8-6.

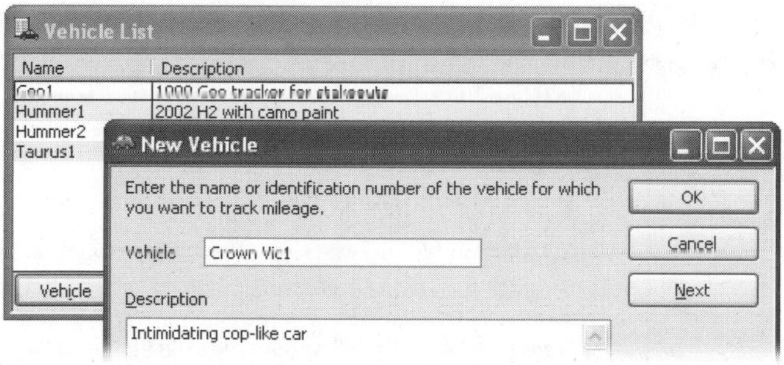

Figure 8-6:
QuickBooks doesn't want to know much about company vehicles. Specifying a name in the New Vehicle dialog box will do. You can add any details you want in the Description box. After you click OK, the vehicle takes its place in the Vehicle List (shown in the background).

3. **In the Vehicle box, type a name for the vehicle.**

   To easily identify your company cars and trucks, include the type of vehicle and a way to differentiate it from others. For instance, if your company cars are all white Jeeps, the license plate number is a better method of identification than make and color.

4. **In the Description box, type additional information such as the year, make, model, license plate number, or Vehicle Identification Number (VIN).**

   To change vehicle information later, in the Vehicle List window, double-click the vehicle name, and then, in the Edit Vehicle dialog box, edit the name or description.

5. **Click OK.**

   That's it. The name and description appear in the Vehicle List window.

Setting the Mileage Rate

For tax purposes, you can deduct mileage expenses based on a standard mileage rate or by tracking the actual costs of operating and maintaining your vehicles. Using a standard mileage rate is convenient—simply multiply the miles you drove by the standard rate to calculate your vehicle deduction.

If you own an expensive car with expensive maintenance needs, actual costs might provide a larger deduction. But you have to keep track of what you spend on gas, tires, repairs, insurance, and so on, and deduct those costs on your tax return. As usual, the tax rules for deducting operating and maintenance costs are, well, taxing. Before you choose this approach, ask your accountant or the IRS if you can deduct actual costs and whether it's the best approach.

Note: You can deduct either the standard rate amount or your actual costs, but not both.

QuickBooks stores multiple mileage rates along with their effective dates, because standard mileage rates usually change at the beginning of each calendar year. To set a mileage rate, first open the Enter Vehicle Mileage window (choose Company → Enter Vehicle Mileage). Then, in the dialog box's tool bar, click Mileage Rates, which opens the Mileage Rates window shown in Figure 8-7.

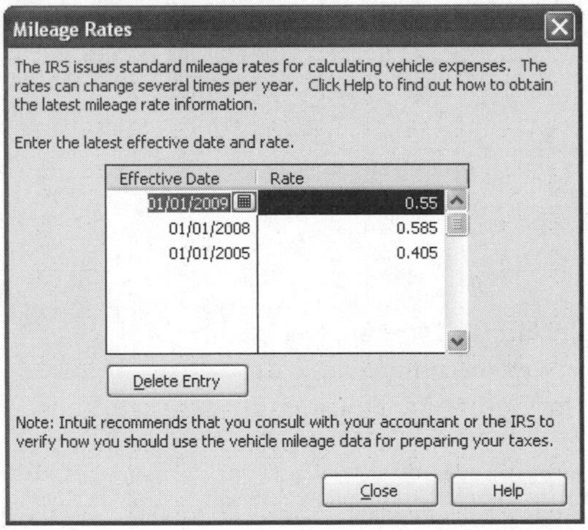

Figure 8-7:
QuickBooks displays the standard mileage rates with the most recent rate at the top and the other rates going backward in time, so that the most recent rate appears at the top of the list. To add a new rate, scroll down if necessary until you see a blank line in the rate table. In the first blank Effective Date cell, choose the date that the new mileage rate becomes effective, such as 1/1/2010. In the Rate cell, type the rate in dollars (.55 per mile beginning July 1, 2009 as documented on the IRS website, www.irs.gov). Click Close when you're done.

Recording Mileage Driven

Once you've added a vehicle to the Vehicle List, you're ready to record mileage. (You don't have to set the mileage rates to record the miles you drive, but you'll need that rate in place before you bill a customer for mileage.) Here's how you fill in the Enter Vehicle Mileage window to record billable and nonbillable miles you've driven:

1. **Open the Enter Vehicle Mileage window (choose Company → Enter Vehicle Mileage). In the Vehicle box, choose the vehicle that you drove.**

   If you forgot to add the vehicle to the list, you can create it now by choosing *<Add New>* from the drop-down menu.

2. **In the Trip Start Date box and the Trip End Date box, choose the days you started and completed the trip, respectively.**

   If you're recording mileage for one day of onsite work, choose the same day in both boxes. On the other hand, if you used a company car to drive to another city for several days, the Trip Start Date is the day you headed out of town and the Trip End Date is the day you returned.

3. **In the Odometer Start box and Odometer End box, type the vehicle mileage before you began driving and the mileage when you returned, as shown in Figure 8-8.**

   QuickBooks automatically calculates the miles you drove and plops that number in the Total Miles box.

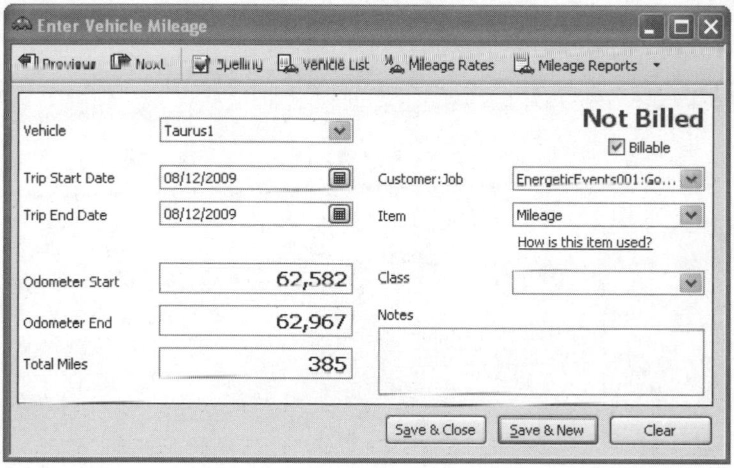

Figure 8-8:
From the Enter Vehicle Mileage toolbar, you can generate reports of the mileage you've driven. Click Mileage Reports (page 203).

If you usually forget to check the starting mileage, you can ignore the Odometer Start and Odometer End boxes entirely. Instead, in the Total Miles box, type the mileage you drove. For example, if you know that a round-trip to your customer is 72 miles, in the Total Miles box, just type *72*. You can type the mileage with or without commas (*1,500* or *1500*).

The drawback to this approach is that your mileage record doesn't include the odometer readings that the IRS wants to see. But if every mile you drive is for business, you can prove your deduction by showing the IRS an odometer reading at the beginning of the year and one at the end of the year.

4. **If your mileage is billable to a customer or job, turn on the Billable checkbox. Then, in the Customer:Job box, choose the customer or job to whom you want to assign the mileage. In the Item drop-down list, choose the item you created for mileage.**

   If the mileage isn't billable to a customer, choose the faux customer you created to track time spent on administrative activities (page 190). For tips on creating an item for mileage, see the box below.

5. **If you track classes, in the Class box, choose the appropriate one.**

   For example, if you use classes to track branch performance, choose the class for the branch. However, if you track partner income with classes and the mileage is nonbillable, you don't need a class assignment.

6. **To further document the reason for the mileage, type text in the Notes box. Then, to save the mileage and close the dialog box, click Save & Close.**

   If you want to enter additional mileage for other customers and jobs, click Save & New.

FREQUENTLY ASKED QUESTION

Mileage Rates and Invoice Items

What if the IRS rate is different than the rate I charge customers for mileage?

The rates you enter in the Mileage Rates dialog box are the standard rates set by the IRS for tax purposes. The IRS doesn't care one whit what you charge your customers for miles.

For the reimbursable miles that you drive, you need to create a Service or Other Charge type item in your Item List. (In the Enter Vehicle Mileage window, the Item drop-down list includes only these two types of items.) When you create

the item, you can assign the rate per mile that you charge customers or leave the rate at zero if you charge variable mileage rates.

For an Other Charge item, the "Amount or %" box is the place to enter the mileage rate, as shown in Figure 8-9. (For a Service type item, use the Rate box.) In the Account box, choose the income account you use for reimbursable mileage, whether it's specific to mileage or an overall reimbursable expense account.

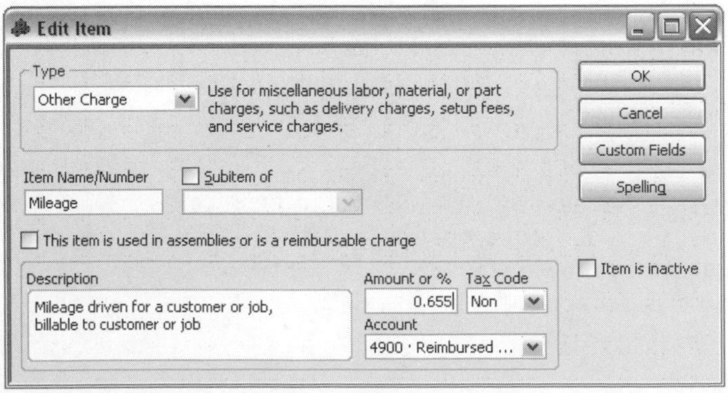

Figure 8-9:
You can enter whatever rate per mile you want. When you add the mileage to an invoice, QuickBooks multiplies the number of billable miles driven by the rate you set in the mileage item.

Generating Mileage Reports

Mileage records come in handy when you prepare your taxes or if your customers question their mileage charges. The reports are simple, mainly because you don't track that much mileage information. You can generate mileage reports by choosing Reports → Jobs, Time & Mileage and then choosing the report. To generate a report, in the Enter Vehicle Mileage window's toolbar, click the down arrow to the right of the Mileage Reports command.

Here are the reports you can choose and what they're useful for:

- **Mileage by Vehicle Summary.** For your tax backup, this report shows the total miles you drove each vehicle and the corresponding mileage expense (which QuickBooks calculates using the standard mileage rate in effect at the time). The date range is set initially to This Tax Year, which is perfect for generating the data you need for your tax return, as shown in Figure 8-10.

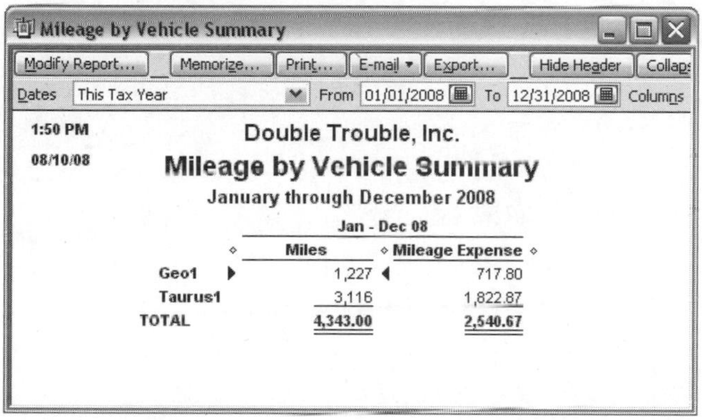

Figure 8-10:
If you wait until after January 1st to gather your tax documentation, in the Dates box, choose Last Tax Year.

- **Mileage by Vehicle Detail.** This report shows each trip that contributed to a vehicle's mileage. For each trip made, the report includes the trip end date, total trip miles, mileage rate, and mileage expense. If you have questions about your deductions, double-click a trip entry to open the Enter Vehicle Mileage window for that transaction.

- **Mileage by Job Summary.** If you charge customers for mileage, run this report both for total miles driven and the billable mileage by customer and job.

- **Mileage by Job Detail.** If a customer has a question about mileage charged, this report is the quickest way to find the charges in question. The report groups mileage by customer or job, but lists each trip in its own line. The report shows the trip start date, trip end date, miles driven, billing status, mileage rate, and billable amount, so you can answer almost any mileage-related question a customer might have.

Paying for Expenses

Although most small business owners sift through the daily mail looking for the envelopes that contain checks, they usually find more envelopes containing *bills*. One frustrating aspect of running a business is that you often have to pay for the items you sell before you can invoice your customers for the goods.

When you use QuickBooks, paying bills is a multistep process. If you want your financial records to be right, you have to tell the program about the expenses you've incurred. And, if you want your vendors to leave you alone, you have to pay the bills they send.

Handling expenses can take several forms. QuickBooks is up to the challenge and, aside from a few idiosyncrasies that drive accountants wild, it succeeds. This chapter explains your choices for paying bills (now or later) and describes how to enter bills and your payments. If you pay bills right away, you'll learn how to write checks, use a credit card, or pay with cash in QuickBooks. If you enter bills in QuickBooks for payment later, you'll learn how to handle the easy ones, such as rent, as well as reimbursable expenses and inventory.

QuickBooks is happy to help you through every step of the process: entering bills you receive, setting up bill payments, and even printing the checks you mail to vendors. But for modest enterprises with few expenses, writing checks by hand and entering them in the program works just as well.

When to Pay Expenses

When it comes to handling expenses, QuickBooks gives you a choice—pay now or pay later. (You can choose to *not* pay bills, but QuickBooks can't help you with collection agencies or represent your company in bankruptcy court.) If bills arrive about as often as shooting stars, paying each bill immediately is a snap, and you'll know your bills are paid on time. In QuickBooks, paying immediately means writing a check, entering a credit card charge, making an online payment, or using some money from petty cash—all of which are described in this chapter.

But when bills arrive as steadily as coffee orders at the local Starbucks, you'll probably want to set aside time to pay bills all at once when it won't interfere with delivering services or selling products. What's more, most companies don't pay bills until just before they're due—unless there's a good reason. Setting up vendor bills for later payment is known as *using accounts payable* because you store your unpaid expenses in an Accounts Payable account.

In QuickBooks, entering bills for later payment delivers all the advantages of convenience and good cash management. You can tell the program when you want to pay bills—for instance, to take advantage of an early payment discount or the grace period that a vendor allows. Then, you can go about your business without distraction, knowing that QuickBooks will let you know when bills are on deck for payment.

Tip: For the infectiously forgetful, QuickBooks can add bills to your Reminders List (page 573). Choose Edit → Preferences and, in the Edit Preferences dialog box, click the Reminders icon. Click the Company Preferences tab. For the Bills to Pay option, choose Show Summary or Show List and then specify the number of days of lead time you want before bills are due.

Once you decide whether you're going to pay bills now or later, you're better off using that method consistently. Otherwise, you could pay for something twice by entering a bill in QuickBooks and then, a few days later, writing a paper check for the same expense. If you take the Accounts Payable path (paying later), you can still charge expenses to your credit card and write checks by hand when you're out of the office, and enter those transactions in QuickBooks without a corresponding bill. To prevent duplicate payments, though, always enter bills you receive as bills in QuickBooks and pay them using the Pay Bills command (page 226).

Entering Bills

At first glance, entering bills and then paying them might *seem* like more work than just writing a check. But as you'll learn in this chapter, after you enter bills in QuickBooks, the program makes it incredibly easy to pay them.

To enter bills in QuickBooks, open the Enter Bills window using any of the following methods:

- On the Home page, click Enter Bills (it's in the Vendors panel).

- In the Vendor Center icon bar, click New Transactions → Enter Bills.

- Choose Vendors → Enter Bills.

The fields on a vendor's bill are similar to the ones you see on the invoices you create. In fact, if your vendors use QuickBooks, the bills you receive are just another company's QuickBooks invoices (see Chapter 10) or statements (see Chapter 11).

With the Enter Bills window open, here's how to enter a bill in QuickBooks:

1. **In the Vendor drop-down list, choose the vendor who billed you.**

   QuickBooks automatically chooses the Bill option so that you can record a vendor bill. (You'll learn about recording a credit from a vendor on page 242.) The program also turns on the Bill Received checkbox because you rarely enter a bill you haven't received. Turn off this checkbox only if you receive a shipment of inventory without a bill, which you'll learn about on page 220.

   If you set up any pre-fill accounts in the vendor's record (page 138), QuickBooks automatically adds those accounts to the table on the Expenses tab.

2. **In the Date box, type or select the date you received the bill.**

   If you set up payment terms in the vendor's record (page 136), QuickBooks figures out when the bill is due and fills in the Bill Due box, as you can see in Figure 9-1. For example, if the bill date is 8/24/2009 and the vendor's payment terms are Net 30, the bill is due 30 days (one month) after the bill date, which is 9/23/2009.

   If QuickBooks fills in a date that doesn't match the due date on the bill you received, in the Bill Due field, enter the date printed on the vendor's bill—it's the one you want to go by.

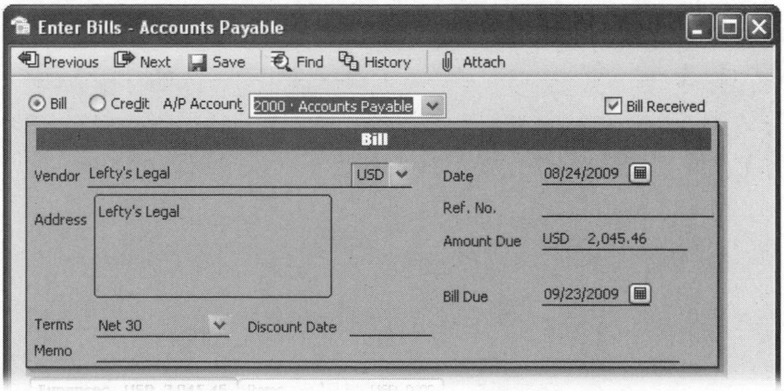

Figure 9-1:
The Terms field shows the payment terms from the vendor record. If you haven't assigned payment terms to a vendor, you can do so right in the Enter Bills window. In the Terms drop-down list, choose the terms that the vendor requires. When you save the bill, QuickBooks asks if you want the new terms to appear the next time. The program is trying to ask if you want to save the terms to the vendor's record; click Yes.

3. **In the Ref. No. box, type the vendor's invoice number, statement date, or other identifying feature of the bill you're paying.**

   The Ref. No. box accepts any alphanumeric characters, so you can type reference numbers such as "1242," "Invoice 1242," or "Statement 1/6/2010."

   If you want to include additional notes about the bill, type a description in the Memo box.

4. **In the Amount Due box, type the total from the bill.**

   The only time you'd change the amount is when you take a discount that the vendor forgot to apply or deduct a portion of the bill because the goods were defective. QuickBooks displays the Expenses tab initially, which is where you enter information about expenses such as utility bills, office supply bills, and your attorney's fees. If you assign only one pre-fill account (page 138) to the vendor, QuickBooks automatically fills in the first cell in the Amount column with the Amount Due value.

Note: The box below tells you what to do when you receive a bill from a vendor who uses a different currency.

FREQUENTLY ASKED QUESTION

Bills and Foreign Currencies

How do I enter a bill that has values in a foreign currency?

If you've turned on multiple currencies (page 570), the Enter Bills window shows currency in several places. The currency you apply to a vendor appears in the title bar and to the right of the vendor name, as shown in Figure 9-2. The Amount Due box shows the foreign currency above the line, with the corresponding value in your home currency below the line. The Expenses and Items tabs both show the foreign currency, indicating that the values you enter are in the foreign currency. See page 444 to learn how to enter or download currencies into the Currency List.

Here's how you fill out a bill a vendor submitted in a foreign currency:

1. In the Amount Due box, type the bill's value (in the foreign currency).

2. On the Expenses and Items tabs, type the amounts in the foreign currency.

3. Below the Expenses and Items table, in the "Exchange Rate 1 <currency> = " box, type the exchange rate from the foreign currency to your home currency (Chinese Yuan Renminbi to U.S. dollars in this example).

4. Click Recalculate to calculate the bill total in your home currency.

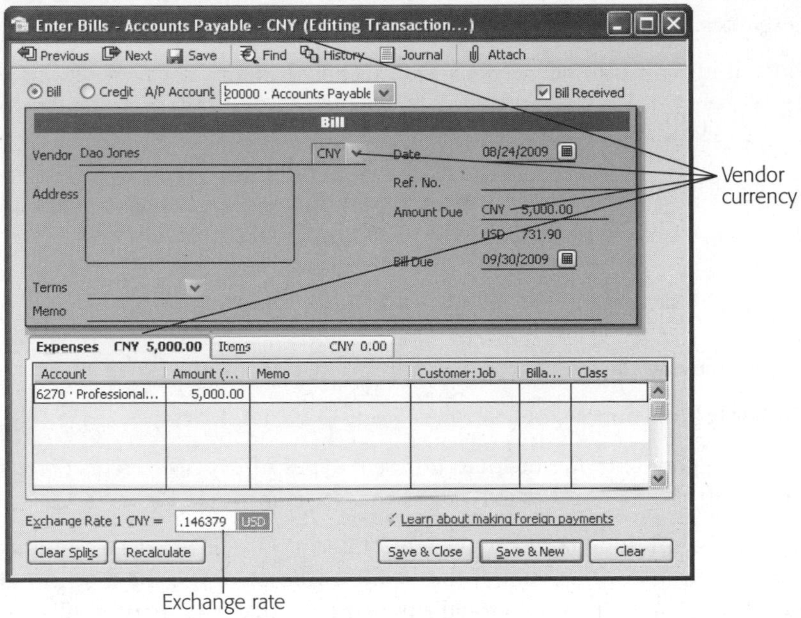

Figure 9-2:
You can't change a vendor's currency after you've recorded your first transaction for that vendor. To switch to a different currency, you have to create a new vendor record using the new currency. The alternative is to calculate the bill's values in your home currency based on the going exchange rate and enter the bill in QuickBooks with those converted values.

5. **In the first cell in the Account column, choose the expense account from your chart of accounts that corresponds to the first expense on the bill.**

   When you click a cell in the Account column, a down arrow appears. Clicking the down arrow displays a drop-down list of every account in your chart of accounts, but the program automatically highlights the first expense account in the list. To choose a different expense account—the account for your legal fees, say—scroll in the drop-down list and select the account you want.

   If you set up any pre-fill accounts in the vendor's record, QuickBooks automatically fills in cells in the Account column with those accounts.

6. **If the bill covers several types of expenses (such as airfare and your travel agent's fees), in the first Amount cell, type the amount that belongs to the expense account in the first row.**

   If you assign more than one pre-fill account to a vendor, QuickBooks doesn't make any assumptions about how the amount due should be divided. You have to type the amounts in each row's Amount cell.

Tip: You can increase or decrease the width of drop-down lists (to see the full names of the accounts in your chart of accounts, for example). When the drop-down list is open, position your cursor over the lower-right corner of the list. When it changes to a two-headed arrow, drag to adjust the width and height. In addition, you can change the width of the columns on the Expenses and Items tabs. Position your cursor over the vertical line between two column headings and drag to the left or right to respectively shrink or widen the column on the left.

---

7. **If an expense relates to a job, in the Customer:Job cell, choose the customer or job.**

   If you fill in the Customer:Job cell, QuickBooks turns on a checkmark in the Billable? column. If you don't want to charge the customer for the expense, click the checkmark to turn it off.

Tip: If you're recording reimbursable expenses, which eventually appear on a customer invoice (page 270), be sure to type a meaningful description in each Memo cell. QuickBooks uses the text in the Memo cell as the description of the expense on your invoice. If there's no Memo text, your invoice includes charges without descriptions, which is bound to generate a call from the customer.

---

8. **If you're tracking classes, choose the appropriate class for the expense.**

   The Class column appears only if you're using QuickBooks' classes (page 138).

9. **If the bill you're entering includes different types of expenses, repeat steps 5 through 8 to add a row for each type of expense, as shown in Figure 9-3.**

   As soon as you finish one row in the table, QuickBooks fills in the Amount cell in the next row with the amount that's still unallocated. For the first through the next to last line, you have to edit the amount that the program fills in to match your expense. The amount that QuickBooks enters for the last line should be correct if you haven't made any typos.

   If the multiple accounts and amounts are hopelessly mangled, click Clear Splits to clear the table so you can start over.

10. **Click Save & Close to save the bill and close the window.**

    Or, if you haven't had enough, click Save & New to save the bill and then display a blank bill.

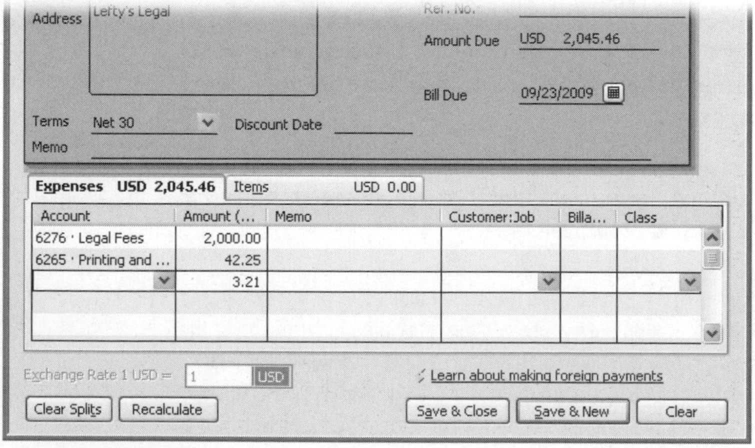

Figure 9-3:
If you change the value in the Amount Due box, QuickBooks doesn't automatically adjust the values on the Expenses or Items tab to match. Click Recalculate to automatically modify the last entry amount so that the Amount Due and the total in the table are the same. If you change a value in one or more Amount cells, click Recalculate to update the Amount Due.

Automating Recurring Bills

Many of your bills are due the same time every month, and some are even the same *amount* every month. For example, your $1,000 rent check is due the first of every month. Your electric bill is due the 19th of the month, but the amount varies each time. Each time you reorder office supplies or inventory, the items you buy are often the same. These sorts of bills are perfect for QuickBooks' memorized transactions.

In QuickBooks, you can memorize bills and reuse them. You can even create a group of bills so that you can process all the bills due on the same day of the month. Even when some fields change, recalling a transaction with *most* of the fields filled in saves you time.

Tip: If you get the same bill only once in a blue moon, memorizing it might be overkill. Instead, just create a duplicate using the Vendor Center whenever you need it. Go to the Transactions tab and then click Bills. Double-click the bill you want to reuse to open it in the Enter Bills window. Then, right-click and choose Duplicate Bill from the shortcut menu. Make any changes you want, like the date and the amount, and then click Save & Close.

Memorizing a Bill

Here's how to memorize a bill:

1. **On the Home page, click Enter Bills (or choose Vendors → Enter Bills).**

   QuickBooks opens the Enter Bills window.

2. **Fill in all the fields that will be the same on each bill, as shown in the background in Figure 9-4.**

   If a field changes for each bill, such as the Amount Due, simply leave that field blank (or 0.00 for amount fields). When you use the memorized bill, fill in the empty fields with the values on the bill that your vendor sent.

3. **When the bill is set up the way you want, press Ctrl+M to open the Memorize Transaction dialog box (in the foreground in Figure 9-4). In the Name box, type a name for the memorized bill.**

   QuickBooks automatically fills in the Name box with the vendor name, but you can type a more meaningful name. For example, naming a memorized bill "Rent" is more helpful than using the landlord's name.

4. **If you want QuickBooks to remind you when it's time to pay the bill, choose the Remind Me option and tell the program when to remind you.**

   If bills don't arrive on a regular schedule (like the ones for snowplowing), choose the Don't Remind Me option. Then, when you receive a bill, you can call up the memorized transaction as described on page 320.

For bills that you receive regularly, in the How Often box, choose the frequency, such as Monthly. In the Next Date, choose the next due date. For example, if the bill you memorized is set for 2/5/2010, choose 3/5/2010.

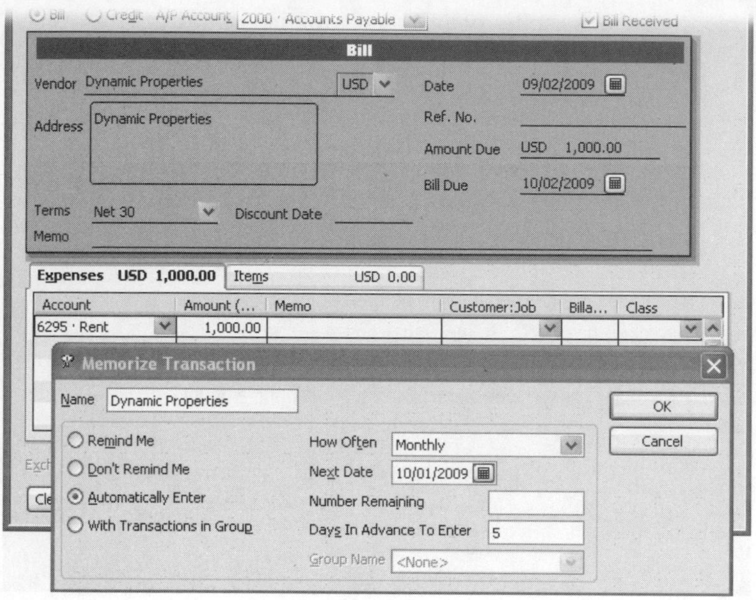

Figure 9-4:
For bills that are identical from month to month, such as rent, choose the Automatically Enter option. You can tell QuickBooks how many days before the due date to enter the bill, as shown here. When that date arrives, the program tacks the bill onto the list of bills waiting to be paid (see page 573). When you choose Automatically Enter, the Number Remaining box becomes active, so you can type how many payments remain, which is ideal for loan payments that—thankfully—don't go on forever.

5. **To memorize the bill, click OK.**

   QuickBooks adds the bill to the Memorized Transaction List, closes the Memorize Transaction dialog box, and returns to the Enter Bills window.

   If you want to add the bill to the queue of bills to be paid, click Save & Close. If you created the bill *only* to memorize it, click the dialog box's Close button (the red X in the top-right corner), and then click No when QuickBooks asks if you want to save the transaction.

Using a Memorized Bill

How you generate a bill from a memorized transaction in QuickBooks depends on whether you've opted for total automation, a reminder, or no reminder:

- **Automatically Enter.** If you create a memorized bill with the Automatically Enter option, that's exactly what the program does. When the next scheduled date for the bill arrives, QuickBooks creates a new bill and adds it to the list of bills waiting to be paid.

- **Remind Me.** When you ask QuickBooks to remind you and the scheduled date arrives, the program adds the bill to the Reminders List. In the Reminders List, below the "Bills to Pay" heading, double-click a bill to open the Enter Bills window. The bill that you see contains only the memorized information. Make any changes you want, fill in the empty fields, and then click Save & Close.

Tip: For reminders that are hard to miss, tell QuickBooks to display the Reminders List each time you open the company file. As soon as you log into the file, you'll see the tasks awaiting you. To set this behavior, choose Edit → Preferences and, in the icon bar, click Reminders. Click the My Preferences tab and turn on the only checkbox there: "Show Reminders List when opening a Company file".

- **Don't Remind Me.** When you memorize a bill that you use only occasionally or for bills that occur on an irregular schedule, choosing Don't Remind Me stores the bill in the Memorized Transaction List in case you need it. When you want to use the memorized bill, click it in the Memorized Transaction List, and then click Enter Transaction.

Creating Memorized Groups of Bills

The first day of the month is the nemesis of bill payers everywhere because so many bills are due then. QuickBooks can't ease the pain of watching your money go out the door, but it can at least ease the burden of entering all those bills in the program. Memorized bills are a start, but why enter individual memorized bills when you can enter several at once?

You can set up memorized transaction *groups* that act like their individual memorized counterparts—to remind you about all the bills due on a specific day or enter all the recurring transactions automatically.

Most QuickBooks features let you create new list entries whenever you need them by choosing *<Add New>* from a drop-down list, but memorized groups break the mold. When you first open the Memorize Transaction dialog box, the With Transactions in Group option and the Group Name box are tantalizingly visible, but they stay grayed out no matter what you click.

That's because, to add a memorized transaction to a group, you have to first create a *memorized group*. The steps are easy, once you know the right order:

1. **Press Ctrl+T to open the Memorized Transaction List.**

   The Memorized Transaction List window opens.

2. **In the Memorized Transaction List menu bar, click Memorized Transaction and then, on the shortcut menu, choose New Group.**

   QuickBooks opens the New Memorized Transaction Group dialog box—identical to the Memorize Transaction dialog box except that it doesn't have the "With Transactions in Group" option and Group Name box.

3. **Name the group something meaningful like Monthly Bills. Fill in the other fields as you would for a memorized transaction (page 318).**

   Tell QuickBooks how and when you want to be reminded.

4. **Click OK to save the group.**

   Now that the group exists, you can add individual transactions to it.

5. **To add an existing memorized transaction to the group, in the Memorized Transaction List window, select the transaction you want to add, and then press Ctrl+E to edit it.**

The Schedule Memorized Transaction dialog box opens.

6. **Select the "With Transactions in Group" option. In the Group Name box, choose the group you just created, and then click OK.**

When you add a memorized transaction to a group, you'll see that QuickBooks tucks the transaction underneath the memorized group in the Memorized Transaction List, as shown in Figure 9-5.

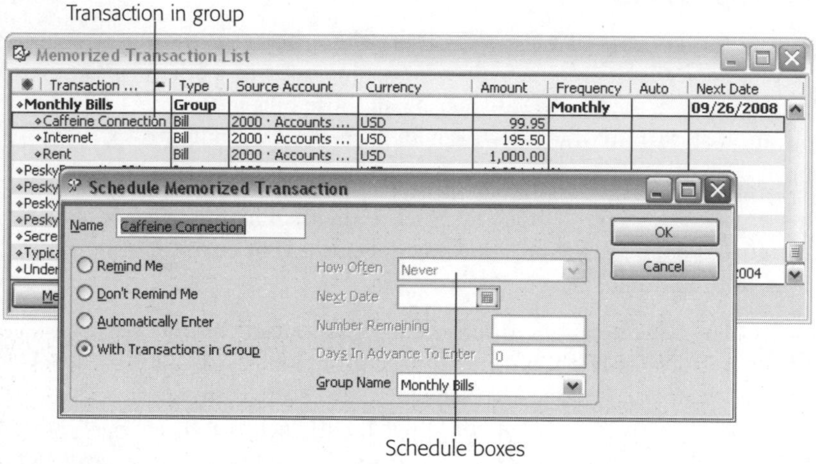

Transaction in group

Figure 9-5:
Individual memorized transactions take on the schedule and reminder characteristics of the memorized group. If you edit a memorized transaction that belongs to a group, the How Often, Next Date, Number Remaining, and Days In Advance To Enter boxes are grayed out.

Schedule boxes

Tip: Create separate memorized groups for bills with consistent amounts and those whose amounts vary. That way, you can set up the unvarying memorized group with the Automatically Enter option, so QuickBooks simply adds all the bills to your list of bills to be paid without any intervention from you. Then, you can set the second memorized group to use the Remind Me option, so you can go through each bill and fill in the amount before you record it.

Purchasing Inventory

Purchasing and paying for inventory items is *mostly* the same as paying for other expenses. But as you learned in Chapter 4, inventory always seems more complicated than the other things you sell.

Part of the problem with inventory is that you have to keep track of how much you have. As inventory wends its way from your warehouse to your customers, it also hops between accounts in your chart of accounts (see page 113). An income account tracks the money you make from selling inventory; a second account tracks the costs of the inventory you've sold; and a third asset account tracks the value of the inventory you still own.

Purchasing inventory involves three transactions in QuickBooks:

• Adding the inventory you purchase to a QuickBooks inventory asset account.

• Entering the bill you receive for the inventory you bought.

• Paying the bill for the inventory.

What's tricky is that you don't know whether the bill or the inventory will arrive first. In many cases, the bill arrives with or after the shipment. But Samurai Sam could email you a bill while you wait weeks for your swords to arrive. You don't want to pay for products you haven't received—nor do you have to. (If you decide to pre-pay, see the box below to learn how to do so in QuickBooks.) In the following sections, you'll learn how to use QuickBooks commands to handle any order of bill and inventory arrival.

If you want to track inventory in QuickBooks, your first task is turning on the preference for inventory and purchase orders (page 567). Although the program turns on purchase order features as part of tracking inventory, you can skip purchase orders if you don't use them in your business. As soon as you turn on inventory, QuickBooks adds icons for purchase orders and inventory to the Home page; the Vendors menu picks up inventory-related commands like Create Purchase Orders and Receive Items; and the chart of accounts gains a non-posting account called Purchase Orders.

WORKAROUND WORKSHOP

Paying for Inventory Before It Arrives

QuickBooks doesn't provide a command for paying for inventory before you receive it. In the business world, you don't *have to* pay bills for inventory you haven't received. But anything is possible in business, including prepaying for inventory that you order.

Here's what you have to do to prepay for inventory:

1. Write a check to the vendor (page 237) or enter a credit card charge (page 241) to pay for the items. If you have an open purchase order for the inventory, QuickBooks displays a message box about it. Click No because it's too early to use the purchase order.

2. In the Write Checks or Enter Credit Card Charges window, click the Expenses tab.

3. In the first Account cell, choose the Accounts Payable account.

4. Save the transaction. Now you have a credit for that vendor in Accounts Payable.

5. When you receive the inventory items, you can apply your vendor credit to the bill you receive (page 228).

Creating Purchase Orders

Before you get to receiving inventory and paying the corresponding bills, it's a good idea to make sure that you actually *receive* the inventory you ordered. If you ordered corsages for Mother's Day, but the box that shows up contains corsets, the mistake is obvious. Remembering what you ordered is tougher when products and quantities vary. Most businesses address this problem by creating *purchase orders* for the inventory they buy. When the order arrives, comparing the shipment to the purchase order can confirm that the items and quantities are correct. Because purchase orders are typically the first step in purchasing, the QuickBooks Home page places the Purchase Orders icon in the pole position in the Vendors workflow.

Note: You can create all the purchase orders you want without altering the balances in your income, expense, and asset accounts; and the purchase orders won't appear in your Profit & Loss or Balance Sheet reports.

Purchase orders are known as *non-posting* transactions. No money changes hands (or accounts), so there's nothing to post in your chart of accounts. In QuickBooks, the first posting for purchased inventory happens when you either receive the inventory or the bill.

The Create Purchase Orders dialog box is like a mirror-image of the Create Invoices dialog box that you'll meet in Chapter 10. You choose a vendor instead of a customer, and the Ship To address is your company's address, as shown in Figure 9-6.

Here's how you create a purchase order:

1. **On the Home page, click Purchase Orders (or choose Vendors → Create Purchase Orders).**

   In the Create Purchase Orders window, QuickBooks fills in the current date, and there's no reason to change that because purchase orders are a paper trail of what you order. The program also fills in the Ship To box with your company's address. If you're ordering inventory that you want shipped directly to one of your customers, choose that customer (or job) in the Ship To drop-down list at the top of the window, which changes the shipping address that appears in the Ship To box.

2. **In the Vendor box, choose the vendor you're ordering your inventory from.**

   QuickBooks fills in the Vendor box in the header area with the vendor name and address (from the vendor record you created on page 135) as shown in Figure 9-6.

Note: If you use multiple currencies, the vendor's currency appears to the right of the vendor's name. The "Exchange Rate 1 <unit> =" box becomes active below the item table if the vendor is set up to use a currency different from your home currency.

---

3. **If you use classes to categorize income and expenses (page 138), choose a class for the purchase order.**

   If you use classes and skip this box, QuickBooks politely reminds you that the box is empty when you try to save the purchase order. Click Cancel to return to the purchase order so you can choose a class, or click Save Anyway to save the purchase order without a class.

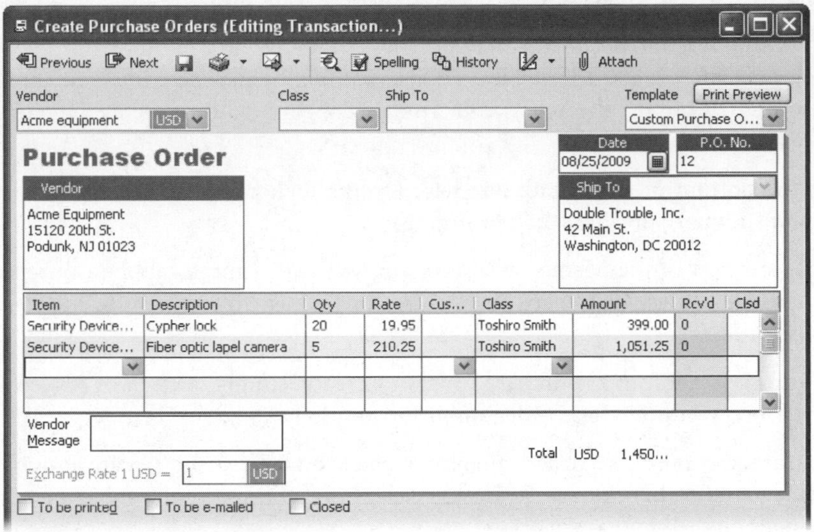

Figure 9-6:
QuickBooks has one predefined template for purchase orders, confusingly called Custom Purchase Order. If you want to customize your purchase order form (page 621), click the customize icon (it looks like a pencil and a ruler) at the upper-right of the Create Purchase Orders window.

4. **When you create your first purchase order, in the P.O. No. box, type the number that you want to start with.**

   From then on, QuickBooks increments the number in the P.O. No. box by one. If you order your products over the phone or through an online system and the vendor asks for your purchase order number, give them this number.

5. **In the drop-down list for the first Item cell in the table, choose the item that corresponds to the first product you're purchasing.**

   The Item drop-down list shows all the entries in your Item List, even though companies usually create purchase orders only for inventory items. (As you type the first few letters of an item's name, QuickBooks displays matching entries. You can keep typing or click the item you want as soon as you see it.)

   When you choose an item, QuickBooks fills in other cells in the row with information from the item record (see Chapter 4). The Description cell gets filled in with the item record description, which you can keep or edit. The Rate cell grabs the value from the Cost field of the item record (that's the price you pay for the item).

6. **In the cell in the Qty column, type the quantity you want to purchase.**

   QuickBooks fills in the Amount cell with the total purchase price for the item: the quantity multiplied by the rate.

7. **If you're purchasing inventory specifically for a customer or job, choose the customer or job in the drop-down list.**

   The Create Purchase Orders dialog box doesn't include a column for designating purchases as billable. Don't worry: You tell QuickBooks that an item is billable when you create a bill or receive the item into inventory.

8. **Repeat steps 5 through 7 for each product you're purchasing.**

    You can insert and delete lines in a purchase order as you can on invoices (page 263) and other forms with tables. To insert a line, right-click a line and choose Insert Line from the shortcut menu. To delete the line, choose Delete Line from the shortcut menu.

9. **At the bottom of the Create Purchase Orders dialog box, in the Memo box, type a summary of what you're ordering.**

    The contents of the Memo field show up when it's time to apply a purchase order to a bill (as you'll learn shortly), making it easy to identify the right purchase order.

10. **If you have additional purchase orders to create, simply click Save & New to save the current purchase order and begin another.**

    To save the purchase order you just created and close the Create Purchase Orders window, click Save & Close. Click Clear to throw out your choices or changes on the purchase order.

Receiving Inventory and Bills Simultaneously

For many orders, you'll find your bill tucked into one of the boxes of your shipment like a bonus gift. Although a bill isn't the most welcome of gifts, receiving a bill and inventory simultaneously is a bonus because you can record your inventory and the accompanying bill at the same time in QuickBooks. Here's how you process a shipment and bill at the same time:

1. **On the Home page, click Receive Inventory and then choose Receive Inventory with Bill (or choose Vendors → "Receive Items and Enter Bill").**

    QuickBooks opens the Enter Bills window that you first met on page 207 and automatically turns on the Bill Received checkbox as it does when you create a regular bill. The difference in the Enter Bills window comes to light when you choose a vendor, as described in Figure 9-7.

2. **If any open purchase orders exist for that vendor and you want to apply the shipment you received to one of them, in the Open POs Exist message box, click Yes. Click No if the items you received don't go with any open purchase orders.**

    QuickBooks opens the Open Purchase Orders dialog box (in the foreground in Figure 9-7). You can also open the Open Purchase Orders dialog box from the Enter Bills window by clicking Select PO (below the items table).

    In the Open Purchase Orders dialog box, you'll see only purchase order dates, purchase order numbers, and memos. If the vendor's bill includes the purchase order number, picking the correct purchase order is easy.

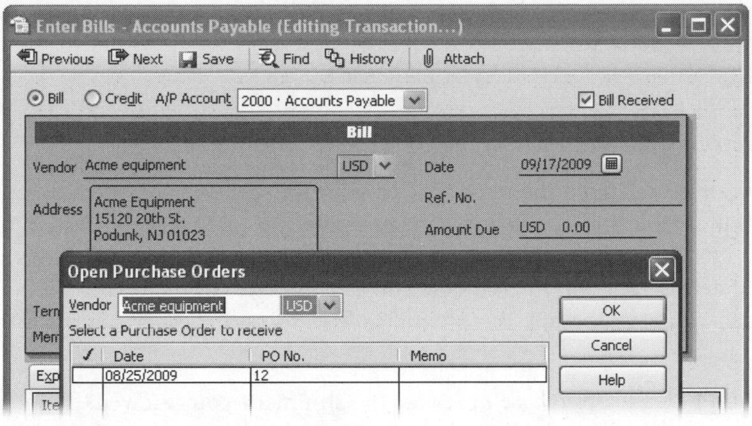

Figure 9-7:
In the Enter Bills window, when you choose the vendor who shipped the items you've received from the Vendor drop-down list, QuickBooks checks for any open purchase orders for that vendor. If it finds any open purchase orders, it displays the Open POs Exist message box, so you can apply the items you've received to a purchase order.

If you filled in the Memo box when you created the purchase order, that note may help you identify which purchase order to choose. But if you don't know which one to pick, click Cancel to close the Open Purchase Orders dialog box. To view a report of open purchase orders, choose Reports → Purchases → Open Purchase Orders. Double-click a purchase order to view its details.

3. **If you want to apply the shipment to an existing purchase order, in the "Select a Purchase Order to receive" table, click the checkmark column (the first column) for the purchase order you want. Click OK.**

QuickBooks displays a checkmark in the purchase order's checkmark cell. When you click OK, the program closes the Open Purchase Orders dialog box and fills in the bill fields with purchase order information, like the amount and the items ordered, as shown in Figure 9-8.

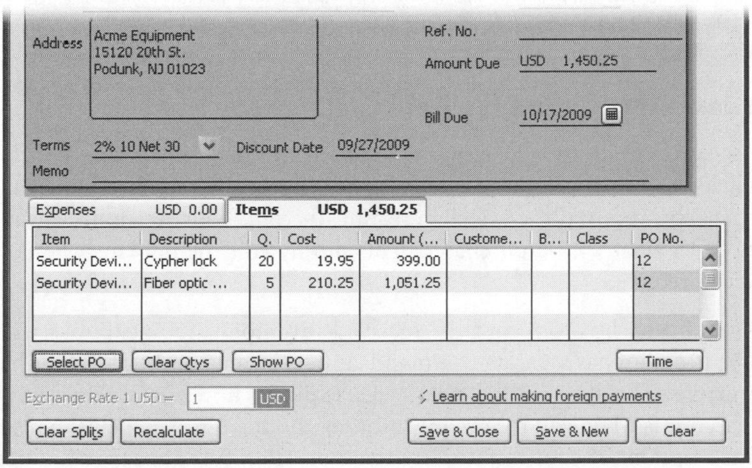

Figure 9-8:
When you choose an open purchase order, QuickBooks uses the information from the purchase order to fill in fields in the Enter Bills window, such as the Amount Due field in the header as well as the Items tab with most of the information about the items you ordered. When you work from a purchase order, QuickBooks displays the purchase order number in the PO No. column.

Note: Compare the quantities you received in the shipment to the quantities on your purchase order. If you received fewer items than you ordered, in the Qty cell for the item, enter the number you actually received and adjust the amount due to match what you received.

---

4. **In the Date box, fill in the date when you received the bill.**

If you've already defined the payment terms in the vendor record (page 135), QuickBooks fills in the Terms box and automatically calculates the date in the Bill Due box. If the bill you received shows different terms or a different due date, update the values in the Bill Due and Terms boxes to match the vendor's bill. When you save the bill, the program offers to save the new terms in the vendor's record.

5. **If you didn't create a purchase order for the shipment you received, fill in the fields as you would for a regular bill.**

In the Amount Due field, type the amount due from the vendor's bill. You'll also have to fill in the Items tab manually with the items you received. For each item you receive, in a blank line on the Items tab, specify the item, quantity, customer or job, and class. QuickBooks fills in the Description and Cost cells using the values in the item record (see Chapter 4) and then calculates the Amount by multiplying the quantity by the item cost.

6. **Click Save & New or Save & Close.**

When you save a combination inventory/bill transaction, QuickBooks goes to work behind the scenes. For the inventory you received, QuickBooks first debits your inventory account for the amount you paid for the inventory items. The program also updates the quantity on hand for the item (page 469). The amount of the bill also increases the balance in your Accounts Payable account.

Note: If you want to see how many of a particular product you have on hand, on the Home page, click Items & Services. In the Item List window, look at the On Hand column for the item you're interested in.

Receiving Inventory Before the Bill

When you receive inventory, you want to record it in QuickBooks so you know that it's available to sell. If you receive inventory without a bill, the best solution is to *pretend* that you received the bill. By creating the bill, your Accounts Payable stays in sync with what you've purchased. You simply edit the bill later to match the real one you receive.

An alternative approach is to record the received inventory in QuickBooks without a bill. The program has separate commands to receive inventory and enter bills when they arrive. The box on the next page explains how QuickBooks posts amounts to accounts when you receive inventory without a bill. The fields that you specify and the options at your disposal are the same, they just appear in different windows:

TROUBLESHOOTING MOMENT

Posting Inventory Received

When you receive inventory before the bill arrives, your accountant might squawk about how QuickBooks posts inventory to your accounts. In standard accounting practice, only bills show up as credits to the Accounts Payable account. But QuickBooks credits the Accounts Payable account when you receive inventory items.

When you use Receive Items, in the Accounts Payable register, QuickBooks adds an entry for the items you received. (To view the register, press Ctrl+A to open the Chart of Accounts window, and then double-click the Accounts Payable account name.) The program fills in the Type cell with ITEM RCPT to indicate that the entry isn't a bill. Later, when

you enter the bill, QuickBooks overwrites the same transaction, replacing the ITEM RCPT type with BILL.

Although the result in your company file is correct after you both receive inventory and enter bills, accountants typically complain about incomplete audit trails when they see a transaction change without some kind of record. Unfortunately, there's no workaround for keeping track of items received without bills or bills received without shipments. If you want to track inventory, bills, and price differences between your purchase orders and the final bills, you'll have to do so outside of QuickBooks.

1. **To receive inventory in your company file, on the Home page, click Receive Inventory and then choose Receive Inventory without a Bill (or choose Vendors → Receive Items).**

    QuickBooks opens the Create Item Receipts window, which is a close relative to the Enter Bills window. In fact, other than the title of the dialog box, only three things are different, all of which are shown in Figure 9-9.

Tip: If you choose "Receive Inventory without a Bill" (or Vendors → Receive Items) and then realize that you *do* have the bill, there's no need to close the window and choose a different command. In the Create Item Receipts window, simply turn on the Bill Received checkbox in the top-right corner of the window. The window changes to the Enter Bills window, so you can receive the items and create the bill at the same time (page 218).

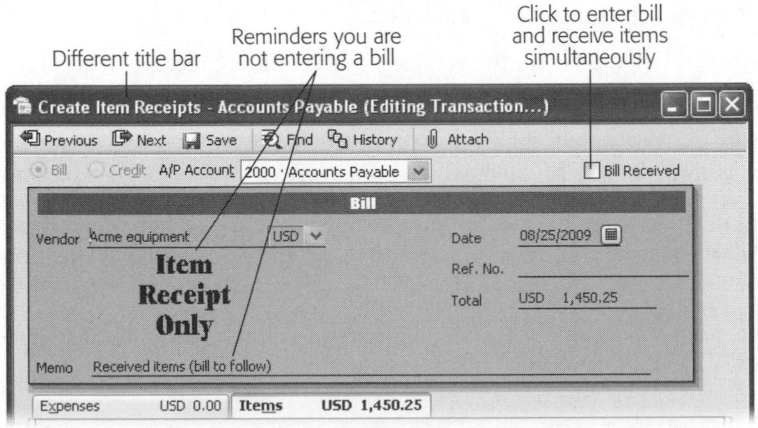

Figure 9-9:
Because you're only adding inventory to your company file, QuickBooks automatically turns off the Bill Received checkbox in the Create Item Receipts window. To make it crystal clear that you aren't creating a bill, the program displays the words Item Receipt Only and, in the Memo box, adds the message "Received items (bill to follow)".

Similar to receiving inventory and a bill at the same time, the Create Item Receipts window reminds you about open purchase orders that you can select to fill in the items received automatically. The rest of the fields behave like the ones in the Enter Bills window.

2. **When you've added all the items you received and updated any quantities that differ from those on your purchase order, click Save & Close.**

   QuickBooks records the inventory in your company file, as described in the box on page 221.

3. **When the bill arrives, choose Vendors → "Enter Bill for Received Items" (or on the Home page, click Enter Bills Against Inventory).**

   The box below tells you how to recover if you choose Vendors → Enter Bills by mistake.

TROUBLESHOOTING MOMENT

Double (Posting) Trouble

When you want to enter a bill for items you received earlier, be particularly careful to choose Vendors → "Enter Bills for Received Items" (or Enter Bills Against Inventory on the Home page). If you choose Vendors → Enter Bills instead, you'll end up with *two* postings for the same items in your Accounts Payable account. The first posting appears when you receive the items in QuickBooks (the one identified with the type ITEM RCPT); the second posting is for the bill.

If this double entry happens, delete the bill. (In the Chart of Accounts window, double-click the Accounts Payable account. In the Accounts Payable register, select the bill and then choose Edit → Delete Bill or right-click the bill and then choose Delete Bill on the shortcut menu.) Then, recreate the bill using the "Enter Bills for Received Items" command. Another option is to create a journal entry to reverse the second Accounts Payable entry (page 421).

---

4. **In the Select Item Receipt dialog box (Figure 9-10), choose the vendor that sent the shipment. Then choose the shipment that corresponds to the bill you just received and click OK.**

   QuickBooks opens the Enter Bills window and fills in the fields with the information from your Receive Items transaction.

5. **If the prices and quantities on the vendor's bill are different from those Quick-Books used, on the Items tab, you can update the prices and quantities.**

   When prices and quantities differ, don't take the vendor's bill as the final word. Check your record to see where the discrepancy arose.

6. **If the bill includes sales tax and shipping that you didn't include on your purchase order, click the Expenses tab, and then fill in additional lines for those charges.**

   If you changed anything on the Items or Expenses tab, click Recalculate to update the Amount Due field with the new total.

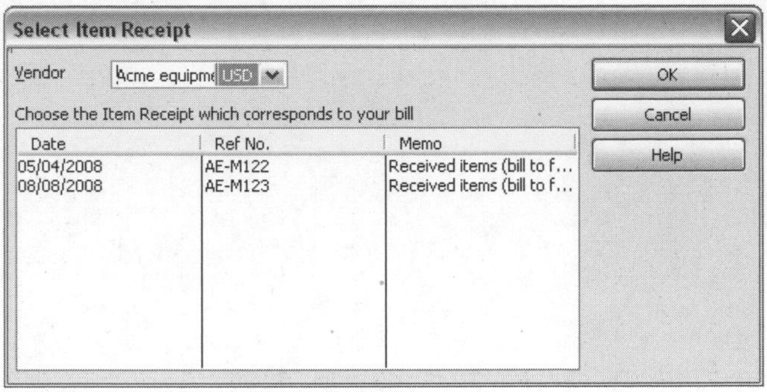

Figure 9-10:
The Ref. No. and Memo cells identify the shipments you've received. If those fields are blank, the Date cell won't be enough to select the right item receipt, so click Cancel and then choose Vendors → Receive Items. In the Create Item Receipts dialog box's menu bar, click Previous or Next to display the item receipt you want, and then fill in its Ref. No. field with the purchase order number for the shipment or the carrier's tracking number. After you save the item receipts with identifying reference numbers, choose Vendors → "Enter Bill for Received Items" once more.

7. **Click Save & Close.**

   You'll see a message box that asks if you want to save the changes you made—even if you didn't make any. QuickBooks asks this question because it has changed the item receipt transaction to a bill in your Accounts Payable account as the box on page 221 explains. Click Yes to save the changes.

Handling Reimbursable Expenses

Reimbursable expenses are costs you incur that a customer subsequently pays. For example, you've probably seen telephone and photocopy charges on your attorney's statements. Travel costs are another common type of reimbursable expense. Products you purchase specifically for a customer or a subcontractor you hire for a customer's job are all costs you pass on to your customers.

In accounting, as in QuickBooks, there are two ways to track reimbursable expenses:

- **As income.** With this method, QuickBooks posts the expenses on a bill you pay to the expense account you specify. When you invoice your customer, QuickBooks posts the reimbursement as income in a separate income account. Your income is higher, but it's offset by higher expenses. This approach is popular because it lets you compare income from reimbursable expenses to the reimbursable expenses themselves to make sure that they match. (The box on page 224 describes income accounts you need for tracking reimbursable expenses this way.)

- **As expense.** Tracking reimbursements as expenses doesn't change the way QuickBooks handles bills—expenses still post to the expense accounts you specify. But, when your customer pays you for the reimbursable expenses, QuickBooks posts those reimbursements right back to the expense account. The expense account balance looks as if you never incurred the expense in the first place.

Accounts for Reimbursable Expenses

QuickBooks won't let you assign the same income account to more than one reimbursable expense account. You have to create a separate income account (see Chapter 3) for each type of reimbursable expense.

To keep your chart of accounts neat, create a top-level income account called something like Reimbursed Expenses. Then create an income subaccount for each type of reimbursable expense. When you're done, your income accounts will look like this:

- 4100 Service Revenue
- 4200 Product Revenue
- 4900 Reimbursed Expenses—Income

Subaccounts for account 4900:

- 4910 Reimbursed Telephone
- 4920 Reimbursed Postage
- 4930 Reimbursed Photocopies

Setting Up Reimbursements As Income

If you want to track your reimbursable expenses as income, you have to turn on the Track Reimbursed Expenses As Income preference (page 583). Choose Edit → Preferences and, in the Edit Preferences icon bar, click Time & Expenses. On the Company Preferences tab, turn on the "Track reimbursed expenses as income" checkbox.

With this preference turned on, whenever you create or edit an expense account (in the Add New Account or Edit Account windows), QuickBooks adds a "Track reimbursed expenses in Income Acct." checkbox and drop-down list at the bottom of the dialog box, as shown in Figure 9-11.

Here's what happens as you progress from paying your bills to invoicing your customers:

- When you assign an expense on a bill as reimbursable to a customer, Quick-Books posts the money to the expense account you specified.

- When you create an invoice for the customer, the program reminds you that you have reimbursable expenses.

- When you add the reimbursable expenses to the customer's invoice, they post to the income account you specified for that type of expense. See the box above to learn more about creating income accounts for reimbursable expenses.

Note: If you track reimbursable expenses as expenses, you don't have to set up anything in QuickBooks. When you pay a bill, the expenses post to the expense account. When you invoice a customer, Quick-Books posts the reimbursements back to the same account.

That way, the expense won't show up on the customer's invoice.

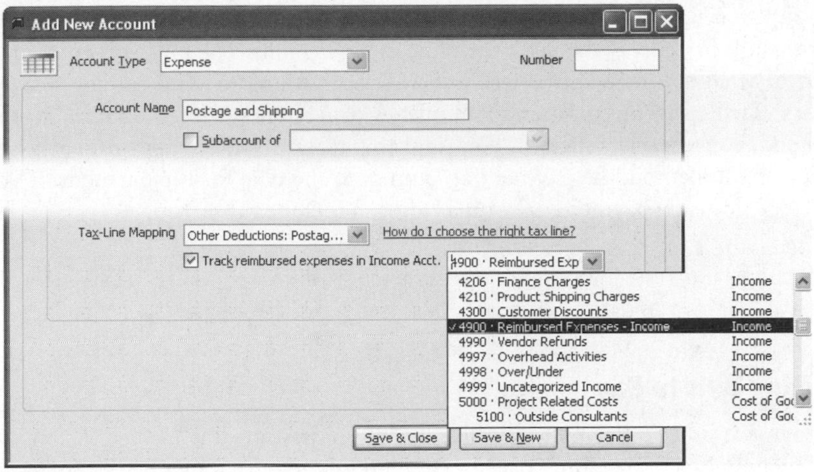

Figure 9-11:
To track the expense as reimbursable income, in the Edit Account window, turn on the checkbox and then, in the drop-down list, choose the income account to use. Since you've already created your expense accounts, you'll have to edit each one that's reimbursable (travel, telephone, equipment rental, and so on) and add the income account to the record.

Recording Reimbursable Expenses

As you enter bills (page 206) or make direct payments with checks or credit cards, you add designated expenses as reimbursable, as shown in Figure 9-12.

When you choose a customer or Job in the Customer:Job column, QuickBooks automatically adds a checkmark to the Billable? cell. Be sure to type a note in the Memo cell to identify the expense to you and your customer. QuickBooks uses the text in the Memo field as the description of the reimbursable expense on your invoice.

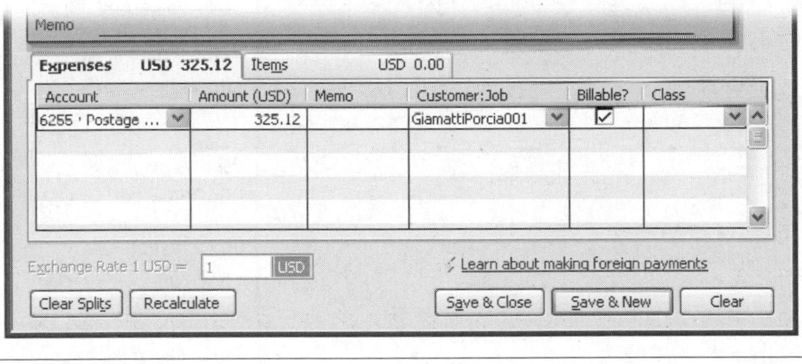

Figure 9-12:
The tables in the Enter Bills, Write Checks, and Enter Credit Card Charges windows all include columns to designate reimbursable expenses and the customers or jobs to which they apply. (You can click Splits in an account register to access these columns.)

Note: Sometimes you want to track expenses associated with a customer or job, but you dont want the customer to reimburse you—such as for fixed-price contracts. In this situation, click the Billable? cell for that expense to remove the checkmark from the cell.

Paying Your Bills

Entering bills in QuickBooks isn't the same as *paying* bills. The bills you enter are a record of what you owe and when, but they do nothing to send money to your vendors. Pay Bills is the command that pushes your money out the door. With this command, you can select the bills you want to pay, how much to pay for each one, your payment method, the payment account, and the date for the payment. If you have credits or early payment discounts, you can include those, too.

Tip: If you want to evaluate all your unpaid bills before you pay them, the Unpaid Bills Detail report displays the bills due up to the current date, grouped by vendor, as described on page 244.

Selecting Bills to Pay

The payment process begins with choosing the bills you want to pay. When you choose Pay Bills (on the Home page or the Vendors menu), QuickBooks opens the Pay Bills window and shows the bills due within the next two weeks. As Figure 9-13 shows, you can change the bills that appear, view bill details, or apply credits and discounts.

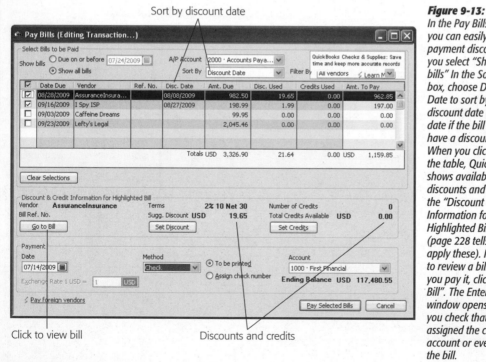

Sort by discount date

Click to view bill

Discounts and credits

Figure 9-13:
In the Pay Bills window, you can easily spot early payment discounts when you select "Show all bills" In the Sort Bills By box, choose Discount Date to sort by the discount date (or the due date if the bill doesn't have a discount date). When you click a bill in the table, QuickBooks shows available discounts and credits in the "Discount & Credit Information for Highlighted Bill" section (page 228 tells how to apply these). If you want to review a bill before you pay it, click "Go to Bill". The Enter Bills window opens and lets you check that you assigned the correct account or even revise the bill.

Here are the ways you can select bills to pay:

- **Clicking Select All Bills** below the table is the easiest way to select bills. Quick-Books selects all the bills displayed in the Pay Bills table and fills in the Amt. To Pay cells with the total due on each bill. You can choose individual bills for payment by turning on their checkboxes. (The button label changes to Clear Selections when at least one bill is selected.)

Note: When you select more than one bill from the same vendor, QuickBooks automatically combines those bills onto one check when you pay them (page 226).

- **To use different payment methods** (check and credit card, for example), make two passes through the Pay Bills window. On the first pass, choose all the bills that you pay by check and, in the Payment Method box, choose Check. During the second pass, in the Payment Method box, choose Credit Card.

- **To pay bills submitted in different currencies,** you have to make a pass through the Pay Bills window for each currency. QuickBooks creates an Accounts Payable account for each currency you assign to vendors. To pay bills from vendors using a specific currency, choose the corresponding Accounts Payable account in the A/P Account drop-down list. The Pay Bills window displays the bill amounts in the foreign currency, and the amount you have to pay in your home currency.

Modifying Payment Amounts

Whether you select individual bills or QuickBooks selects them for you, the program automatically fills in the Amt. To Pay cells with the total amounts that are due. Paying bills in full means you don't have to worry about the next due date or paying late fees. But making partial payments can stretch limited resources to appease more of your unpaid vendors, as the box below explains. To pay only part of a bill, in a bill's Amt. To Pay cell, type how much you want to pay.

When Cash Is Tight

If your cash accounts are dwindling, you may face some tough decisions about whom you pay and when. To help keep your business afloat until the hard times pass, here are a few strategies to consider:

- Pay government obligations (taxes and payroll withholdings) first. In the Sort Bills By box, choose Vendor to easily spot all your government bills.

- Pay the vendors whose products or services are essential to your business.

- Make partial payments to all your vendors rather than full payments to some and no payments to others. If you want to pay small bills in full, in the Sort Bills By box, choose Amount Due to see your outstanding bills sorted by dollar value.

Tip: If you keep your cash in an interest-bearing account until you need it, you'll want to know how much money you need to transfer to your checking account to pay the bills. In the Pay Bills window, QuickBooks shows two totals: one for all the bills displayed, and another for what you've entered in the Amt. To Pay column. Initially, the two totals are the same. If you change a value in an Amt. To Pay cell, click another cell to update the total Amt. To Pay.

Applying Discounts and Credits to Payments

Most companies like to use their discounts and credits as soon as possible. By far, the easiest way to deal with discounts and credits you receive from vendors is to let QuickBooks automatically handle them. Here's how you delegate application of early payment discounts and available credits to QuickBooks:

1. **Choose Edit → Preferences. In the Preferences dialog box icon bar, click Bills. Then click the Company Preferences tab.**

   The setting you choose here applies to every person who logs into your company file. Because the preference appears on the Company Preferences tab, you have to be a QuickBooks administrator to change this setting.

2. **Turn on the "Automatically use discounts and credits" checkbox.**

   QuickBooks turns on the Default Discount Account box.

3. **In the Default Discount Account box, choose the account you use to track your vendor discounts.**

   If you don't have an account set up for vendor discounts yet, choose *<Add New>* at the top of the Default Discount Account drop-down list. Create a new account (page 53) called something like Vendor Discounts.

Note: Whether you create an income account or expense account for vendor discounts is neither an accounting rule nor QuickBooks requirement, but a matter of how you view vendor discounts. If you think of vendor discounts as expenses you've saved by paying early, create an expense account. If you view vendor discounts as money you've made, create an income account.

Either way, vendor discounts are different from discounts you extend to your customers. So, in the Default Discount Account box, choose an account specifically for vendor discounts, not your customer discount account.

As you'd expect, turning on the "Automatically use discounts and credits" checkbox tells QuickBooks to apply early payment discounts and available credits to bills without further instructions from you. The program uses your payment terms to figure out the discount you've earned, and it adds all available credits to their corresponding bills.

Whether the "Automatically use discounts and credits" preference is on or off, you can control the discounts and credits QuickBooks applies to your bills, as you'll learn on the following pages. For example, you might want to delay a large credit until the following year. The delay increases your expenses in the current year, which, in turn, decreases this year's taxable income.

Applying discounts manually

If you want to apply discounts manually or change the discount that QuickBooks added, here's what you do:

1. **Open the Pay Bills window.**

   On the Home page, click Pay Bills, or choose Vendors → Pay Bills.

2. **To select a bill that isn't already selected for payment, turn on its checkbox in the table. If the checkbox is already turned on, select the bill by clicking anywhere in the bill's row.**

   In the "Discount & Credit Information for Highlighted Bill" section, Quick-Books shows the discount and credits that are available for the bill. More importantly, the program turns on the Set Discount and Set Credits buttons, which you click to apply discounts and credits, respectively. (If the check-marked cell is turned off, QuickBooks shows the suggested discount and available credits, but the Set Discount and Set Credits buttons are dimmed.)

Tip: When you apply discounts manually, you can use the Disc. Date column to identify bills that qualify for early payment. If the date in a Disc. Date cell is in the future, the bill qualifies for an early payment discount.

---

3. **To apply or modify a discount to the selected bill, click Set Discount.**

   QuickBooks opens the "Discount and Credits" dialog box (Figure 9-14). If you've turned on multiple currencies, the currency you set for the vendor appears to the left of the Suggested Discount label and in the "Amount of Discount" box.

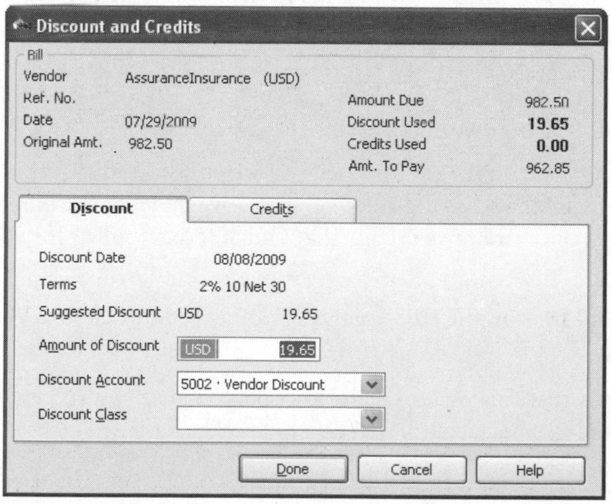

Figure 9-14:
In the "Discount and Credits" dialog box, QuickBooks automatically selects the Discount tab and displays your payment terms, the discount date, and the amount of discount you deserve. If the suggested discount is worth an early separation from your money, click Done to deduct the discount from your bill. Otherwise, click Cancel. If you also want to work on credits (page 230), when you're done modifying the discount, click the Credits tab.

4. **In the "Amount of Discount" box, QuickBooks fills in the suggested discount. If you want to apply a different discount, type the new value.**

   Many companies try to save money by taking early payment discounts when they haven't paid early. Some companies apply discounts regardless of what their payment terms are, and most vendors honor these undeserved discounts in the name of goodwill.

5. **In the Discount Account drop-down list, choose the account you use to track your vendor discounts.**

   If your vendor discount account is an income account, discounts appear as positive numbers and increase the balance of the income account. In vendor discount expense accounts, discounts appear as negative numbers because they reduce how much you spend on expenses.

Tip: If you want to track discounts on inventory separately, create a Cost of Goods Sold account specifically for inventory discounts. For example, if QuickBooks created account 5000 for Cost of Goods Sold, you can create two subaccounts: 5005 for Cost of Inventory Sold and 5010 for Inventory Discounts. In your financial reports, the two subaccounts show your original cost and the discounts you receive. Account 5000 adds the two subaccounts together to show your net cost of goods sold.

---

6. **If you track classes, choose the class for the discount.**

   Typically, you'll choose the same class for the discount that you used for the original expense.

7. **Click Done.**

   QuickBooks closes the "Discount and Credits" dialog box. Back in the Pay Bills window, the program adds the discount you entered in the bill's Disc. Used cell and recalculates the value in the Amt. To Pay cell by subtracting the discount from the amount due.

Applying credits manually

When you select a bill in the Pay Bills window, the "Discount & Credit Information for Highlighted Bill" section shows the credits that are available for the bill. To apply available credits to a bill or remove credits that QuickBooks applied for you, follow these steps:

1. **Open the Pay Bills window. (On the Home page, click Pay Bills, or choose Vendors → Pay Bills.)**

   If the "Discount and Credits" dialog box is already open because you've applied a discount, just click the Credits tab and then continue with step 4.

2. **Select a bill by turning on its checkbox in the table.**

In the Discount & Credit Information for Highlighted Bill section, QuickBooks shows the credits available for the vendor, if any. The program turns on the Set Credits button.

3. **To apply a credit to the selected bill, click Set Credits.**

QuickBooks opens the "Discount and Credits" dialog box, and displays the Credits tab, shown in Figure 9-15. Credits that are already applied to the bill are checkmarked.

4. **Turn on the checkmark cell for each credit you want to apply. Click Done.**

QuickBooks closes the dialog box and applies the credits.

Setting the Payment Method and Account

After you've selected the bills to pay and applied any discounts and credits, you still have to tell QuickBooks how and when you want to pay your bills. At the very bottom of the Pay Bills window, these settings are the last choices you have to make before paying your vendors:

- **Payment Date.** QuickBooks fills in the current date automatically. To predate or postdate your payments, choose a different date. Page 556 tells you how to get QuickBooks to date checks using the day you print your checks.

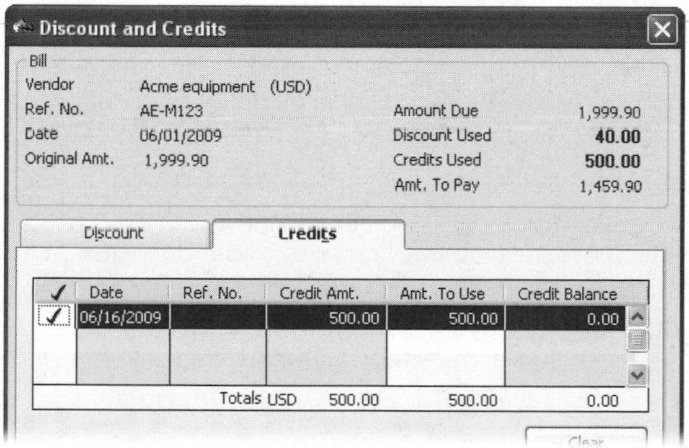

Figure 9-15:
In the table section of the "Discount and Credits" dialog box, click a credit's checkmark cell to toggle between applying the credit and removing it from the bill. QuickBooks updates the Credits Used value to show the amount of credit applied to the bill. The Amt. To Pay value is the amount you have to pay based on both applied discounts and credits.

- **Payment Method.** In the drop-down list, choose how you want to pay the bills. QuickBooks offers Check, Credit Card, and Online Bank Pmt (if you subscribe to QuickBooks online bill payment).

If you pay bills by check and print your checks within QuickBooks, choose the "To be printed" option. The program automatically adfsds the bills you selected to the queue of checks to be printed. You'll learn about printing these checks on page 236.

If you write checks by hand, choose the "Assign check number" option. When you click Pay Selected Bills, the program opens the Assign Check Numbers dialog box. To assign check numbers starting with the next unused check number, choose the "Let QuickBooks assign check numbers" option. If you want to specify the check numbers for each check you write, choose the "Let me assign the check numbers below" option.

- **Payment Account.** If you specified a default account for the Pay Bills window to use (page 555), QuickBooks automatically fills in the account. To use a different account, in the Account drop-down list, choose the account you use to pay the bills, such as a checking or credit card account.

Pay Selected Bills

When you're done setting up bills to pay, click Pay Selected Bills. QuickBooks closes the Pay Bills window, displays a Payment Summary dialog box showing the payments you've made, and adds those payments to your bank account register. In the Enter Bills window, QuickBooks adds a PAID stamp to bills you've paid. Here are your choices, depending on how you produce checks:

- **If you write paper checks for your bills,** click Done and your QuickBooks work is complete. But you still have to sign your John Hancock to the checks you send out.

- **For checks you print in QuickBooks,** click Print Checks. See page 236 to learn how to print checks for the bills you pay. If you aren't ready to print checks just yet, click Done.

- You can **create another batch of bill payments** (for example, to pay bills using another method) by clicking Pay More Bills in the Payment Summary dialog box.

Producing Checks

When you use Check as the payment method, your bank account register shows check transactions, but you still have to generate checks to send to your vendors. For companies that produce lots of checks, printing checks in QuickBooks can prevent carpal tunnel syndrome. For a sole proprietorship that generates a few checks each month, writing checks by hand is easy enough. QuickBooks accepts either approach with equal aplomb.

Writing Checks by Hand

Writing checks by hand doesn't require any work in QuickBooks. But you still have to keep your company file in sync with your paper checks. Whether you're writing checks for bills you've paid in QuickBooks or scratching out a spur-of-the-moment check to the fortune-teller for this week's corporate horoscope, you want to make sure that the check numbers in your bank account register match your paper checks.

If check transactions already exist in QuickBooks, synchronizing check numbers is as simple as writing the paper checks in the same order as you entered them in QuickBooks. Open the checking account register window and use the check transactions to guide your check writing, as shown in Figure 9-16.

Note: If the next check number in QuickBooks isn't the one on your next paper check, you should figure out why they don't match. The answer might be as simple as a voided check that you forgot to enter in QuickBooks or a check you wrote earlier that was out of sequence. But if someone is walking off with blank checks, you need to take action.

Until you find the reason for the mismatched check number, editing the check numbers that QuickBooks assigns in the checking account register is the easiest way to get checks into the mail. In the register window, double-click an incorrect check number and type the number that's on your paper check.

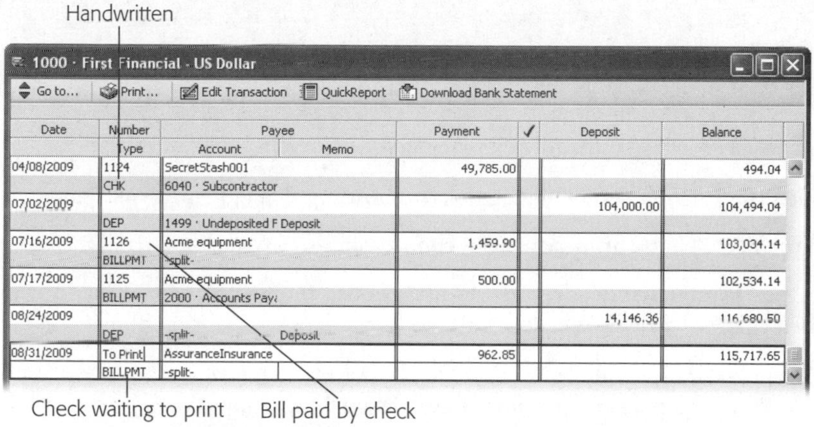

Figure 9-16:
To open the checking account register, first press Ctrl+A to open the Chart of Accounts window. Then, double-click the checking account (or right-click the checking account, and then choose Use Register). In a register window, the code CHK in the Type cell indicates a check transaction. The code BILLPMT along with a check number indicates a bill paid by check.

Setting Up QuickBooks to Print Checks

If you have scads of checks to generate, printing on preprinted computer checks is well worth the small amount of setup you have to do. If you dedicate a printer to check printing and keep it stocked with checks, setup is truly a one-time event.

Tip: Lock up your preprinted checks and any printer stocked with them. Otherwise, you might discover checks missing, which can lead to money missing from your bank account.

The first step is telling QuickBooks which printer to print to and the type of checks you use. The program remembers these settings, so you need to go through this process just once. After you've specified your check printing settings, QuickBooks fills them in automatically in the Print dialog box. You can always change those options before you print.

Here's how you set up QuickBooks to print checks:

1. **Open the "Printer setup" dialog box by choosing File → Printer Setup.**

   In the Form Name drop-down list, choose Check/Paycheck.

2. **In the "Printer name" drop-down list, choose the printer you want to use to print checks.**

   If you choose a printer brand that QuickBooks recognizes (there are only a few it doesn't), the program automatically fills in the "Printer type" box. If you use a very old or very odd printer, you'll have to choose the type of printer. "Page-oriented (Single sheets)" refers to printers that feed one sheet at a time. Choose Continuous (Perforated Edge) when the printer feeds a roll of paper.

Note: If you print to checks on continuous-feed paper, the alignment of the paper in the printer is critical. You can save time and a lot of wasted checks by aligning the paper *before* you print batches of checks, as described on page 309.

---

3. **In the Check Style section, choose the option that represents the style of checks you purchased. (The box above tells you where you can buy your checks.)**

   The "Printer setup" dialog box displays examples of each check style it can deal with, making it easy to choose the right one, as shown in Figure 9-17. See the box on page 236 to learn how to tell QuickBooks how you want to print partial pages of checks.

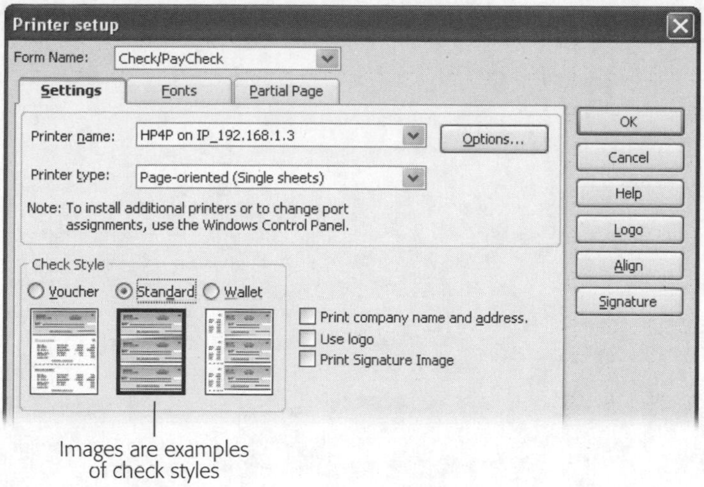

Figure 9-17:
The Standard option sets up QuickBooks to print to checks that fit in a #10 business envelope. These checks typically come three to a page. The Voucher option represents one-page forms that include both a check and a detachable stub for payroll or check information. Wallet checks are smaller than business checks. Because they're narrower than standard business checks, these forms have a perforation on the left for tearing the check off, leaving a stub containing check information that you can file.

4. **If the company you buy checks from wants too much money to print your company info and logo on the checks, turn on the "Print company name and address" and "Use logo" checkboxes.**

   When you turn on the "Print company name and address" checkbox, Quick-Books prints on your checks the company name and address you filled in when you created the company file (page 21). If you turn on the "Use logo" check-box, the program opens the Logo dialog box. Click File. In the Open Logo File dialog box, choose a graphic image of your logo. (QuickBooks can handle BMP, GIF, JPG, PNG, and TIFF formats.)

   If your company info and logo are preprinted on your checks, leave the check-boxes for printing your company name, address, and logo turned off.

5. **If you have an image of your signature, you can print it on your checks by turning on the Print Signature Image checkbox (new in QuickBooks 2010).**

   The program opens the Signature dialog box. Click File. In the Open Logo File dialog box, locate and double-click the graphic image of your signature. (One way to create a graphic file of your signature is by signing a piece of paper and scanning it to your computer.)

Note: If you want to change the fonts on the checks you print, click the Fonts tab. You can change the font for the entire check form (click Font) or designate a special font for the company name and address (click Address Font).

---

6. **Click OK to save your check printing settings.**

   The next section tells you how to print your checks.

Using Leftover Checks

When you print to single sheets of paper, you might print only one or two of the checks on the last sheet, leaving one or two left over. QuickBooks includes a printer setting so that you can print to the orphaned checks.

Choose File → Printer Setup, and then choose Check/Paycheck in the Form Name drop-down list. Click the Partial Page tab, choose the option (Side, Center, or Portrait) that corresponds to how your printer feeds envelopes, and then click OK to save the setting. The Side and Portrait options are the most common methods. If you select Side, you insert the partial page of checks into the envelope feed sideways with the top of the first check lined up with the side of the envelope feed. With the Portrait option, you feed the top of the first check straight into the envelope feed. (Whether you insert pages face up or down depends on the type of printer you have. Print a sample page of checks to

determine which direction you have to feed a page. Then, tape a note to the printer with instructions like "print side down, top edge in first" so you don't misprint any pages in the future.)

When you start printing, first feed the pages with orphaned checks into the envelope feed on your printer.

If you have an old dot-matrix printer taking up space in a junk closet, consider putting it to work printing checks. The continuous feed mechanism on a dot-matrix printer means you can stop printing anywhere and resume right where you left off. You won't need the Partial Page printing feature. An added bonus is that you don't have to worry about printing reports on preprinted checks or printing checks to blank paper by mistake.

Printing Checks

In the Pay Bills window, if you choose the "To be printed" option, QuickBooks adds the checks you've selected for payment to a print queue when you click Pay Selected Bills. After you confirm that your preprinted checks are in your printer and that the checks are aligned properly, you can print checks right from the Payment Summary dialog box by following these steps:

1. **In the Payment Summary dialog box, click Print Checks. If the Payment Summary dialog box isn't open, choose File → Print Forms → Checks.**

   QuickBooks opens the "Select Checks to Print" dialog box and selects all the unprinted checks, as shown in Figure 9-18.

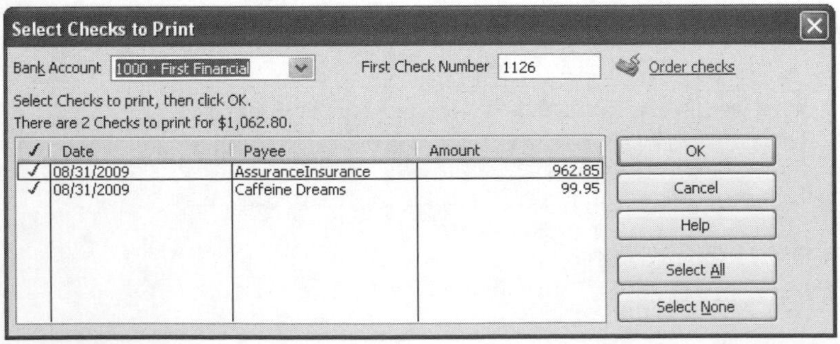

Figure 9-18:
The first time you print checks, QuickBooks sets the first check number to 1. If necessary, in the First Check Number box, type the number of the first check number loaded in your printer. If you want to prevent a check from printing, turn off its checkbox.

Note: If you aren't ready to print checks, click Done in the Payment Summary dialog box. You can print checks whenever convenient for you by choosing File → Print Forms → Checks. (The "Select Checks to Print" dialog box opens and you can continue with the next step.)

2. **After you select the checks you want to print (by turning on their checkmark cells), click OK.**

   QuickBooks opens the Print Checks dialog box, which looks much like the Printer Setup dialog box for checks (Figure 9-17).

3. **If the first page of checks in your printer is a partial page, in the "Number of checks on first page" box, type how many checks you have on the first page.**

   In the Print Checks dialog box, the "Number of checks on first page" box lets you use leftover checks from previous print runs when you have a page-oriented printer. Type the number of leftover checks on the page from which one or more checks have been printed and insert that page in the envelope feed of your printer. After the program prints checks to that page, it begins feeding sheets of checks from the paper tray.

4. **Click Print.**

   QuickBooks anticipates the problems that can happen during printing (paper jams, low toner, or an ill-timed margarita spill). After the program prints checks, it opens the Print Checks - Confirmation dialog box.

5. **If there was a problem, in the Print Checks - Confirmation dialog box, click the Reprint cell for each check that didn't print correctly.**

   If the whole batch is a loss, click Select All.

6. **Click OK to reprint the checks.**

   In addition to printing the checks, QuickBooks also removes the words To Print for those checks in your checking account register, replacing them with the check numbers it used.

Writing Checks Without Entering Bills

You might enter bills for the majority of your vendor transactions, but you're still likely to write a quick check from time to time. For example, when the person who plows your parking lot knocks on the door and asks for payment, he won't want to wait while you step through the bill entering and paying process in QuickBooks—he just wants his $100. And if you write only a couple of checks a month, there's nothing wrong with writing checks to pay your vendors without entering a bill in QuickBooks.

When you first use QuickBooks and want some guidance, use the Write Checks dialog box to make sure you enter everything you need. In no time, you'll grow tired of all the clicking and handholding. At that point, you can switch to recording your checks in the QuickBooks checking account register.

Note: Entering checks in the register is best reserved for paper checks that you write. But you can print a check you enter in the register. First, record the check. Then, right-click it and choose Edit Check to open the Write Checks window. In the window's menu bar, click Print.

Using the Write Checks Window

The Write Checks window is like a trimmed-down Enter Bills window. There's no need for fields such as Bill Due or Terms because you're paying immediately. But bills in QuickBooks take care of allocating costs to expense and inventory accounts. So, for a payment without a bill, you have to provide that information, which is why the Write Checks window has tabs for Expenses and Items. Quick-Books fills in a few fields for you, and the rest of the fields are like the ones you've met already in the Enter Bills window (page 206).

Note: The Enter Bills window is no place to write checks for sales tax, payroll, payroll taxes and liabilities, or bills you've paid immediately. See page 244 for how to pay sales tax. Chapter 14 explains how you pay employees, payroll taxes, and other payroll liabilities.

To write a check in the Write Checks window, follow these steps:

1. **Press Ctrl+W for fast access to the Write Checks window (or choose Banking → Write Checks).**

   You can also click Write Checks on the Home page. As you can see in Figure 9-19, QuickBooks tries to flatten the learning curve by making the first part of the Write Checks window look like a paper check. If you use multiple currencies, the Write Checks window tacks on the currency for your checking account in the Bank Account box, the currency for the vendor on the right side of the "Pay to the Order of" box, and the currency for the check to the left of the check amount.

   If you set up regular account preferences (page 555), such as the bank account to use when you open the Write Checks window, the program automatically chooses your bank account for you and positions the cursor in the "Pay to the Order of" field.

2. **QuickBooks automatically fills in the No. box with the next check number for the selected bank account. If the number that the program fills in doesn't match the check you're writing by hand, type the number from your paper check.**

   If you type a check number that's already been used, QuickBooks warns you about the duplicate number when you try to save the check. In the warning message box, click Cancel, and then, in the Write Checks window, edit the value in the No. field.

Tip: If you suspect that there's more than one check number awry, open the checking account register to review multiple checks at the same time. To renumber the checks in the register window, double-click a transaction's Number cell and type the new number. Press Enter to save the change. It's perfectly accept-able to save a duplicate check number, as long as you keep editing check numbers until all the duplicates are gone.

3. **If you want to print the check, turn on the "To be printed" checkbox just above the right end of the Expenses table.**

   When you turn on the "To be printed" checkbox, the words To Print appear to the right of the No. label. This setting adds the checks you create to a print queue. When you print those checks (page 236), QuickBooks replaces To Print with check numbers. To write checks by hand, be sure to leave the "To be printed" checkbox turned off.

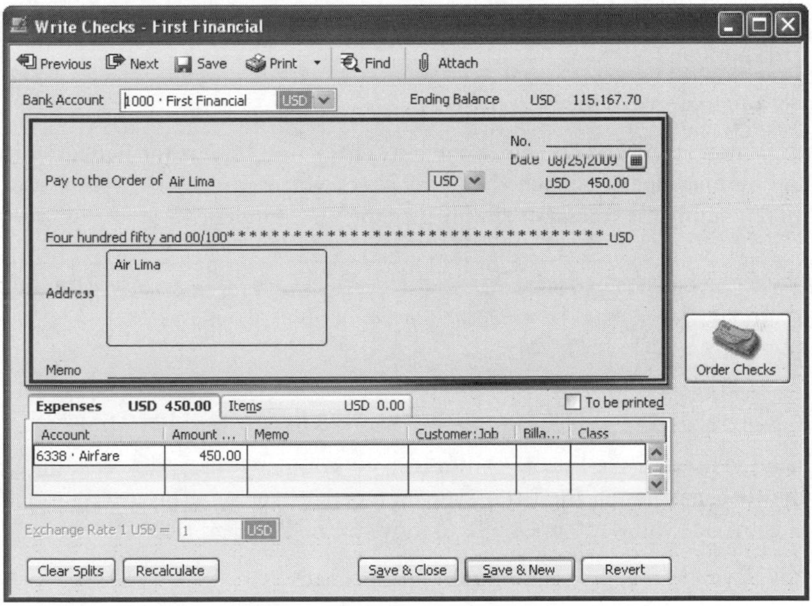

Figure 9-19:
Choosing a vendor fills in not only the "Pay to the Order of" field, but also the Address box, which is perfect for printing checks for mailing in window envelopes. Even though the vendor name appears in the "Pay to the Order of" field, the Address box displays the company name to show you what it prints on checks. If you include account numbers in your vendor records, QuickBooks adds the account number to the Memo field.

4. **Add entries to the Expenses and Items tabs for the things the check is paying for, just like you do when you enter a bill (page 206).**

   QuickBooks calculates the check amount as you add entries on the Expenses and Items tabs. If you fill in the check amount and then start adding expenses and items, you'll know that the check total and the posted amounts match when no unallocated dollars remain. If you've mangled the entries on the Expenses or Items tab, you can start over by clicking Clear Splits.

5. **Click Save & Close to record the check. To write another check, click Save & New. To throw away any values in the window and start over, click Revert.**

Adding Checks to an Account Register

Entering checks in a bank account register is fast, easy, and—for the keyboard aficionado—addictive. By combining typing and keyboard shortcuts, such as tabbing from cell to cell, you can make short work of entering checks.

Here's how you create checks in a register window:

1. **Press Ctrl+A to open the Chart of Accounts window, and then double-click your bank account.**

   If you have only one bank account, you can open your register with one click: On the icon bar, click Reg to have QuickBooks open the account register window and position the cursor in the Date cell of the first blank transaction. (If you don't see the Reg icon, see page 609 to learn how to add it.)

2. **If you want to adjust the check date by a few days, press + or – until the date is what you want.**

   See Appendix C at *www.missingmanuals.com/cds* for more date-related keyboard shortcuts.

3. **Press Tab to move to the Number cell.**

   QuickBooks automatically fills in the next check number for the bank account. If the number doesn't match the paper check you want to write, press + or – until the number is correct or simply type the new number.

Note: If you make a payment without using a check or credit card, you can type a code in the Number cell to identify the payment method. For example, if you ask the bank to create a bank check for you, in the Number cell, type a code like *Bk Draft*.

---

4. **Press Tab to move to the Payee cell. Start typing the name of the payee.**

   QuickBooks scans the lists of names in your company file and selects the first name that matches all the letters you've typed so far. As soon as QuickBooks selects the one you want, press Tab to move to the Payment cell.

5. **In the Payment cell, type the amount for the check.**

   Press Tab to jump past the Deposit cell to the Account cell.

6. **If the check applies to only one expense account, in the Account drop-down list, choose the account you want.**

   You can also choose an account by typing the account number or the first few letters of the account name. As you type, QuickBooks selects the first account that matches what you've typed. When the account is correct, press Tab to move to the Memo cell.

   If your check covers more than one type of expense, you can allocate the payment among several accounts, as you can see in Figure 9-20.

7. To add a reminder about the check, in the Memo cell, type your notes. When you've filled in all the fields you need, click Record to save the check.

Lather, rinse, repeat.

Paying with Cash

If you carry company cash around in your wallet (called *petty cash*, and described in detail on page 214), or if you receive a cash advance toward travel expenses, you eventually have to record the details of your cash transactions in QuickBooks. For example, on a business trip, you might pay cash for meals, parking, tips, and tolls. When you return with your receipts, your bookkeeper can enter a transaction documenting those expenses in the petty cash account.

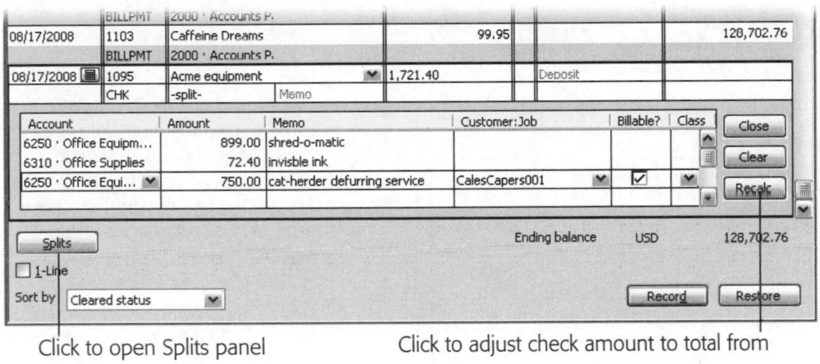

Figure 9-20:
To allocate a check to multiple accounts or to specify a customer, job, or class in the check register, click Splits, which opens a panel where you can assign them. For each allocation, specify the account, amount, memo, customer, and class, and then click Close. If you modify the value in the Payment cell or any values in the allocation Amount cells, click Recalc to change the check payment amount to the total of the splits.

Click to open Splits panel

Click to adjust check amount to total from

Entering cash transactions in the petty cash account register is even easier than entering checks in the checking account register (page 240). For cash transactions, the key fields are the amount and the account. You can skip the Payee field altogether to keep your Vendor List concise. If you want a record of where you spent the cash, type the business name in the Memo cell. QuickBooks assigns a check number to a cash transaction, which you might as well keep. If you hand out petty cash receipts that have receipt numbers, you can type that value in the Number cell.

Paying with Credit Cards

When you make credit card purchases, the easiest way to record those charges in your company file is by signing up for online banking (page 525) and downloading your transactions (page 531). But you can also enter credit charges manually.

Tip: Whether you download charges or not, entering charges manually is a great way to catch erroneous or fraudulent charges that appear on your statement. For example, after entering your charges manually, you can download the charges from your credit card company. If you see additional charges that don't match the ones you entered, either you forgot a charge or there's an error in your account.

Entering credit card charges is similar to writing checks except that you work in the Enter Credit Card Charges window, shown in Figure 9-21. To open it, choose Banking → Enter Credit Card Charges. You can also enter charges directly in the credit card account register, just as you do checks.

Note: To enter a refund for a credit card charge, in the Enter Credit Card Charges window, choose the Refund/Credit option and fill in the rest of the fields based on the refund you received.

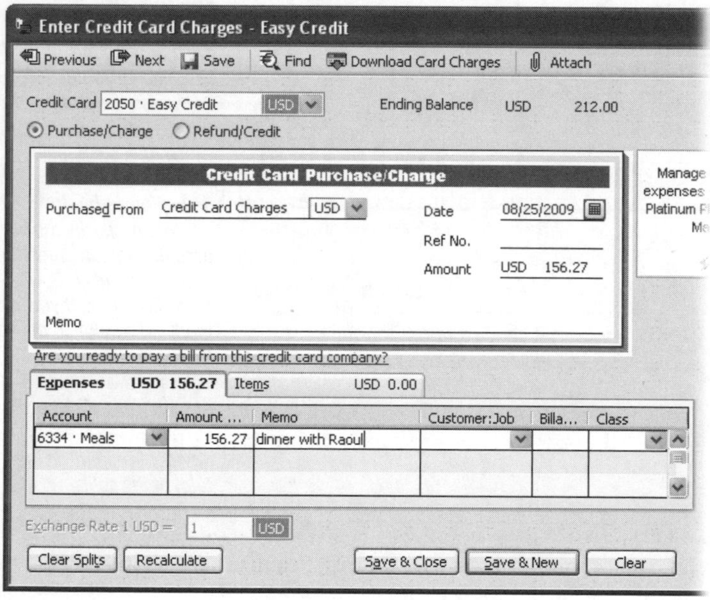

Figure 9-21:
Unless you want your Vendor List awash with every pizza parlor, gas station, and toll booth you patronize, consider creating a vendor called Credit Card Charges (or create several generic vendors such as Gas, Restaurant, and Parking). If you want to track the specific vendors, type their names in the Memo field. In the Ref. No. field, you can type your receipt number. Allocating a charge to multiple accounts or to a customer works the same as for checks (page 209).

Recording Vendor Credits

You ordered 30 dozen lightweight polypropylene t-shirts for your summer Death Valley marathon, but your vendor mistakenly silk-screened the logo on long-sleeved cotton t-shirts heavy enough to survive a nuclear blast. Despite your complaints, the vendor insists on issuing a credit instead of a refund check. The only good thing about this situation is how easy it is to record a credit in QuickBooks:

1. **On the Home page, click Enter Bills (or choose Vendors → Enter Bills).**

   QuickBooks opens the Enter Bills window as if you're going to enter a bill.

2. **Just below the window's menu bar, choose the Credit option.**

   QuickBooks changes the heading in the window to Credit, and the Amount Due label switches to Credit Amount. The other fields stay the same.

3. **On the Expenses and Items tabs, fill in the cells with the items for which you're receiving credit.**

   You can enter positive numbers just as you did when you entered the original bill. QuickBooks takes care of posting the credit amounts to your accounts. Your inventory account decreases due to the inventory items you return. Expense accounts decrease due to expense credits. And the total credit amount reduces the balance in your Accounts Payable account as well.

4. **Click Save & Close.**

That's it! See page 230 for the steps to apply a credit.

Running Expense-Related Reports

Vendors & Payables reports tell you how much you owe each vendor and when the bills are due. Choose Reports → Vendors & Payables, and then choose the report you want to run. The reports in the Purchases category focus on how much you've bought from each vendor you work with. This section tells you how to put these two categories of reports to work.

A/P Aging and Vendor Balance Reports

If your company is flush with cash and you pay bills as soon as they appear in the Pay Bills window, your A/P Aging reports and Vendor Balance reports will contain mostly zeroes. In fact, because the Pay Bills window lets you sort bills by due date, discount date, vendor, and amount (page 226), you might not find any reason to run these reports. For example, if you juggle payments to vendors to conserve cash, you can easily pay the oldest bills first by sorting bills by due date. But if you want an overview of how much you owe to each vendor and how much is overdue, use one of the following reports:

- **A/P Aging Summary.** This report shows all the vendors you owe money to, and how old your balances are for each one. Double-click a value to see a report of the transactions that produced the amount owed, for example, to look at a bill that's more than 90 days overdue.

- **A/P Aging Detail.** Run this report to see each unpaid bill sorted by the billing date and grouped by bills that are current, and those that are 1 to 30 days overdue, 31 to 60 days overdue, 61 to 90 days overdue, and more than 90 days late.

- **Unpaid Bills Detail.** If you want to evaluate all your unpaid bills before you pay them, the Unpaid Bills Detail report displays the bills due up to the current date, grouped by vendor. To include bills due in the future, in the Dates box, choose All. If you want to inspect a bill more closely, double-click anywhere in that bill's line; the Enter Bills window opens with the bill's information.

- **Vendor Balance Detail.** Run this report to see the bills and payments grouped by vendor.

Purchases Reports

When you run the "Purchases by Vendor Summary" report and see high dollar values, you might want to negotiate volume discounts or faster delivery times. These summary reports can also show when you rely too heavily on one vendor—a big risk should that vendor go out of business.

The "Purchases by Item Summary" report shows how many inventory items you've purchased and the total you paid. The "Purchases by Item Detail" report shows each purchase transaction with the quantity, cost, and vendor. If your supplies are dwindling, the Open Purchase Orders report shows when more items are due, as shown in Figure 9-22.

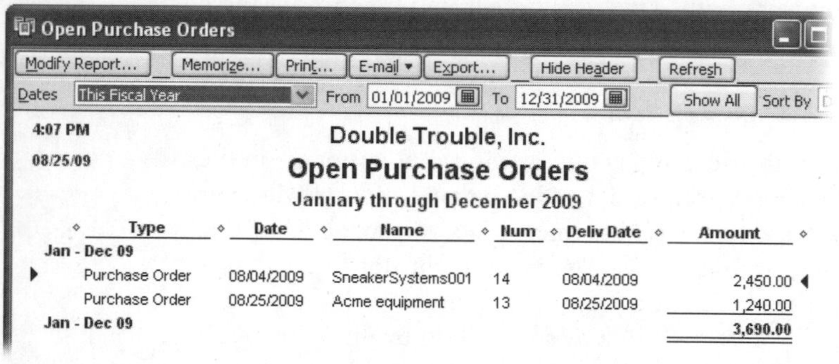

Figure 9-22:
For a report of open purchase orders, choose Reports → Purchases → Open Purchase Orders. The report shows only the date, vendor name, purchase order number, and delivery date. Double-click a purchase order to open the Create Purchase Orders window, which shows the products on the order.

Paying Sales Tax

Sales tax can be complicated, particularly in states where the number of tax authorities has exploded. You might have to pay sales taxes to several agencies, each with its own rules about when and how much. QuickBooks sales tax features can't eliminate this drudgery, but they can help you pay the right tax authorities the right amounts at the right time—something to be thankful for.

After governmental paperwork, the chief aggravation of sales tax is that setup spans several areas of QuickBooks. If you're new to collecting sales tax for your products, make sure you've completed the following tasks so you're collecting and tracking sales taxes properly. Only then can you pay the sales taxes you owe:

- **Sales tax preferences.** If you're liable for sales tax, be sure to turn on the sales tax feature in QuickBooks. Choose Edit → Preferences, and, in the Edit Preferences dialog box's icon bar, click Sales Tax. On the Company Preferences tab, in the Do You Charge Sales Tax? section, choose Yes.

Note: When you turn on the sales tax preference, QuickBooks automatically creates a liability account in your chart of accounts called Sales Tax Payable. If the sales tax preference is turned off, QuickBooks creates this account for you the first time you add sales tax to an invoice.

To help QuickBooks fill in tax-related fields for you, you can set preferences for the tax codes you use most often for taxable and nontaxable sales. If you sell predominantly in your own state, in the "Your most common sales tax item" drop-down list, choose the sales tax item or sales tax group for your state.

- **Customer records.** When you create a customer in the Customer:Job List, you can assign tax codes and tax items to the customer record (page 77). If you do, QuickBooks automatically applies the correct sales tax items to taxable sales on the customer's invoices.

- **Items.** When you create items in your Item List, you can specify whether they're taxable or not (page 125). When you add these items to invoices or other sales forms, QuickBooks automatically applies the correct tax status. (See pages 124–127 to learn how to set up sales tax items and sales tax groups. When you add these to invoices, QuickBooks calculates the sales taxes you need to remit.)

- **Invoices and other sales forms.** QuickBooks calculates sales tax on invoices and other sales forms based on whether items are taxable and customers are tax exempt.

Note: On the Home page, the Manage Sales Tax icon appears at the right end of the Vendors panel. The Manage Sales Tax window includes links to several sales tax-related tasks, like setting sales tax preferences and viewing the sales tax items you've set up. However, you can get to all the same commands by choosing Vendors → Sales Tax, and then choosing a command. Also, remember that you don't have to close the Manage Sales Tax window when you're done.

Sales Tax Payment Preferences

The preference settings you choose for paying sales taxes aren't up to you. Tax agencies decide when your sales taxes are due, usually based on how much sales tax you collect. When you receive a notice about your required payment interval from the state or other tax authority, be sure to update your QuickBooks preferences to match.

To set your sales tax preferences, choose Edit → Preferences, and, in the Edit Preferences dialog box's icon bar, click Sales Tax. On the Company Preferences tab, QuickBooks provides two sets of payment options to satisfy the tax agencies you're beholden to:

- **When do you owe sales tax?** If your tax agency deems sales taxes due when you add them to customer invoices (known as *accrual basis payment*), choose the "As of invoice date" option. If your tax agency says sales taxes are due when your customers pay them (known as *cash basis payment*), choose the "Upon receipt of payment" option. When you generate sales tax reports (next section), QuickBooks uses these options to calculate the sales taxes that you have to remit.

- **When do you pay sales tax?** Tax agencies determine how frequently you have to remit sales taxes based on how much sales tax you collect. If your sales taxes are only a few dollars, you might pay only once a year. But if you collect thousands of dollars of sales tax, you can be sure that the tax agency wants its money more quickly, such as quarterly or monthly. When your tax agency informs you of your remittance frequency, choose Monthly, Quarterly, or Annually, as appropriate.

Producing Reports of the Sales Tax You Owe

Tax agencies are renowned for their forms. You have to fill out these forms to tell the agencies how much sales tax you've collected and how much you're required to remit to them. Fortunately, QuickBooks can take *some* of the sting out of your tax paperwork with reports that collate the sales tax information you need. Here are the reports you can generate:

- **Sales Tax Liability report.** This report summarizes the sales taxes you've collected for each tax agency. Choose Reports → Vendors & Payables → Sales Tax Liability. QuickBooks automatically sets the dates of the report to match the payment interval preference you chose, as you can see in Figure 9-23.

- **Sales Tax Revenue Summary.** This report shows how much of your sales are taxable. Choose Reports → Vendors & Payables → Sales Tax Revenue Summary.

Remitting Sales Taxes

You don't have to enter a bill to pay sales taxes. QuickBooks not only keeps records of the sales taxes you owe, but also provides a dialog box especially for sales tax payments. Here's how you keep the tax agency off your back:

1. **Choose Vendors → Sales Tax → Pay Sales Tax.**

   QuickBooks opens the Pay Sales Tax dialog box and fills in the sales taxes you owe for the last collection period (as defined in your Sales Tax preferences), as shown in Figure 9-24.

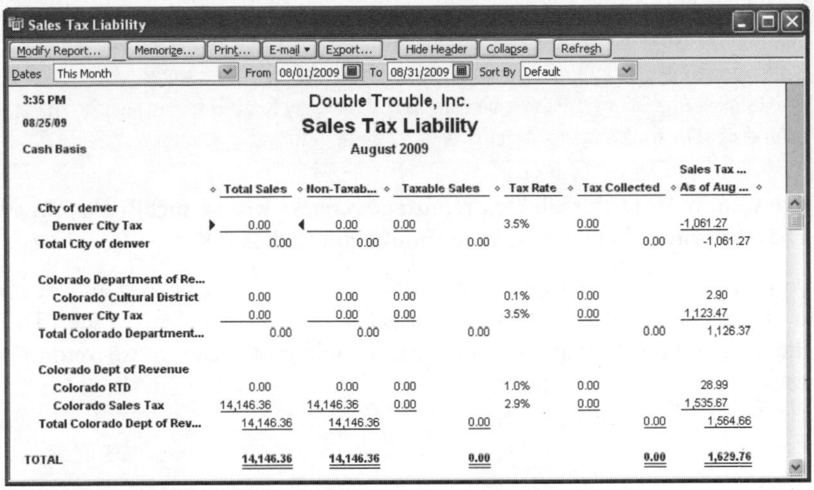

Figure 9-23:
If you remit sales taxes to several tax agencies, each with its own payment interval, you can rerun the report with a different interval to calculate the sales tax you owe to other agencies. In the Dates drop-down list, choose another interval, such as Last Calendar Quarter.

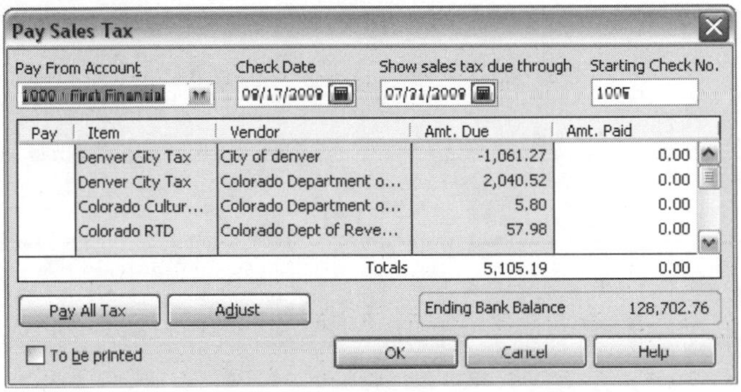

Figure 9-24:
If you remit sales taxes to only one tax agency, or all your sales tax payments are on the same schedule, you can click Pay All Tax to select all the payments in the table. Chances are that you make payments on different schedules to different agencies—in which case, select all the agencies on the same schedule. You'll have to repeat these steps for agencies on a different timetable.

Note: Make sure that the date in the "Show sales tax due through" box is the last day of the current sales tax reporting period. For example, if you pay sales taxes quarterly, choose a date like 6/30/2010.

---

2. **If you use more than one checking account, in the Pay From Account drop-down list, choose the account you want to use for payment.**

   QuickBooks fills in the Pay from Account box automatically if you set the "Open the Pay Sales Tax form with _ account" preference (page 555).

3. **In the Pay column, click cells to select the tax payments you want to make.**

   QuickBooks adds a checkmark to indicate that a payment is selected, and it adds the amount of the remittance in the Amt. Paid cell.

Note: In some states, you may need to adjust the payment you make to a tax agency; for example, to apply a discount for timely payment. Click Adjust to open the Sales Tax Adjustment dialog box. You can increase or decrease the sales by a dollar value, and you have to specify the account to which you want to post the adjustment (the Sales Tax Payable account, say). If the Entry No. box seems vaguely familiar, it's because this dialog box actually creates a journal entry for the adjustment.

4. **If you want to print the sales tax remittance checks from QuickBooks, turn on the "To be printed" checkbox. When you're done, click OK.**

   If you set up the checks to print in QuickBooks, you'll see them the next time you choose File → Print Forms → Checks. If you didn't turn on the "To be printed" checkbox, whip out your checkbook and write those remittance checks.

CHAPTER 10

Invoicing

Telling your customers how much they owe you (called *accounts receivable*) and how soon they need to pay is an important step in accounting. After all, if money isn't flowing into your organization from outside sources, eventually you'll close up shop, closing your QuickBooks company file with it.

Although businesses use several different sales forms to bill customers, the *invoice* is the most popular, and, unsurprisingly, customer billing is often called *invoicing*. This chapter begins by explaining the difference between invoices, statements, and sales receipts—each of which is a way of billing customers in QuickBooks—and when each is most appropriate.

In this chapter, you'll learn how to fill in the QuickBooks versions of invoices, whether you're invoicing for services, products, or both. If you track billable hours with QuickBooks, now's when you tell the program to add your billable hour charges to invoices. Similarly, when you designate expenses as billable to customers, QuickBooks can chuck them into the invoices you create, too.

This chapter also explains how to handle a few special billing situations, like creating invoices when products you sell are on backorder. You'll also learn how to create estimates for jobs in QuickBooks and then use them to generate invoices as you perform the work. And occasionally, you have to give money back to customers (like when they return the lime-green polyester leisure suits that suddenly went out of style), so you'll also learn how to assign a credit to a customer's account, which you can then deduct from the next invoice, or refund by cutting a refund check.

Note: Chapter 11 continues the billing lesson with instructions for producing statements that show your customers' account status. It also explains how to create sales receipts when customers pay you right away. Chapter 12 explains how to get any kind of sales form into your customers' hands, along with a few other time-saving techniques like finding transactions or memorizing them for reuse.

Choosing the Right Type of Form

In QuickBooks, you can choose from three different sales forms to document what you sell, and each form has its own strengths and limitations. Invoices can handle any billing task you can think of, so an invoice is the best choice if you have any doubts about which one to use. Table 10-1 summarizes what each of the sales forms can do. The sections that follow explain each form's capabilities in detail and when to choose each one.

Table 10-1. Sales receipts and statements have limitations, but an invoice always works

Action	Sales receipt	Statement	Invoice
Track customer payments and balances		Yes	Yes
Accept payments in advance		Yes	Yes
Accumulate charges before sending sales form		Yes	Yes
Collect payment in full at time of sale	Yes	Yes	Yes
Create summary sales transaction	Yes	Yes	Yes
Apply sales tax	Yes		Yes
Apply percentage discounts	Yes		Yes
Use group items to add charges to form	Yes		Yes
Add long descriptions for items	Yes		Yes
Subtotal items	Yes		Yes
Include customer message	Yes		Yes
Include custom fields on form	Yes		Yes

Sales Receipts

The sales receipt is the simplest sales form that QuickBooks offers and it's also the shortest path between making a sale and having money in the bank (at least in QuickBooks). But the sales receipt is suitable only if your customers pay the full amount at the time of the sale—for example, in a retail store, restaurant, or beauty salon. Because sales receipts don't include a field for customer payments that have been applied toward the total balance, you can't use them to keep track of how much your customers owe (called accounts receivable and explained in detail on page 328).

When you create and save a sales receipt in QuickBooks, the program immediately posts the money you receive to the Undeposited Funds account or the bank account you choose. As you'll learn in this chapter and the next, invoices and statements take several steps to move from billing to bank deposits.

Despite their shortcomings in the customer payment department, sales receipts *can* handle sales tax, discounts, and subtotals—in fact, any item in your Item List. But when you operate a cash business, creating a sales receipt in QuickBooks for each newspaper and pack of gum your newsstand sells is *not* good use of your time. Instead, consider creating a sales receipt that summarizes a day's or week's sales, using a customer named Cash Sales created specifically for that purpose (see page 351).

Statements

Suppose you're a lawyer and you spend 15 minutes here and 15 minutes there working on a client's legal problem over the course of a month. Each time you spend some time, that's another charge to the client's account. In QuickBooks, each of those charges is called a *statement charge*, and you enter them individually (page 296). If you track time in QuickBooks, though, it's actually easier to add your time to an invoice (page 270).

Businesses often turn to statements when they charge the same amount each month, such as a fixed monthly fee for full-time work as a contract programmer. But memorized invoices (page 317) are just as easy.

Where statements really shine is summarizing a customer's account. Behind the scenes, a statement adds up all the accounts receivable transactions for the customer over a period of time, which includes statement charges, payments, and invoices. A statement shows the customer's previous balance, any payments that have been made, overdue invoices that haven't been paid, and any new charges on the account. From all that information, QuickBooks calculates the last number on a statement, which is the most important—how much money is outstanding, and whether or not it's overdue.

Note: Although statements can track customer payments and balances, they *don't* handle the following billing tasks:

- Tracking sales tax.
- Using Group items to add several items.
- Typing multi-paragraph descriptions of services or products.
- Subtotaling items.
- Applying percentage discounts to items sold.
- Including a customer message.
- Including custom fields.
- Summarizing the services and products sold. (On statements, each separate service or product you sell has to appear as a separate statement charge.)

Invoices

The bottom line: If statements or sales receipts don't work, don't be afraid to use invoices. They accept any item you've created in your Item List (see Chapter 5) without complaint, *and* they track what your customers owe you.

Besides the features in Table 10-1, an invoice is the only type of sales form that you can generate from an estimate (page 284). If you're a general contractor and prepare a detailed estimate of the services and products for a job, you'll save a huge chunk of time by turning that estimate into an invoice for billing.

Note: QuickBooks Premier and Enterprise editions include one more type of sales form: the sales order. In those editions, when you create a sales order for the products that a customer wants to buy, you can create an invoice for the items that are in stock and keep track of out-of-stock items that you'll need to ship to your customer when a new shipment arrives (page 276).

Sales Forms and Accounts

An invoice or other sales form is the first step in the flow of money through your company, so now's a good time to look at how QuickBooks posts income and expenses from your invoices to the accounts in your chart of accounts. Suppose your invoice has the entries shown in Figure 10-1.

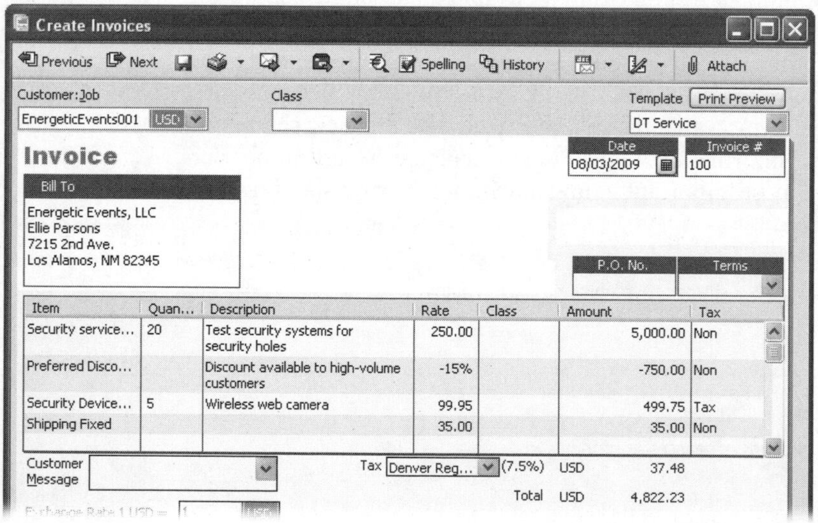

Figure 10-1:
If you're still getting used to double-entry accounting, balancing the debit and credit amounts for an invoice is a brainteaser. For example, the items for services and products in the invoice shown here turn up as credits in your income accounts, as in Table 10-2. The discount reduces your income so it's a debit to the Sales Discounts income account. Although the debits and credits appear in different accounts, the total debit has to equal the total credit.

Table 10-2 shows how the amounts on the invoice post to accounts in your chart of accounts.

Table 10-2. Debits and credits have to balance

Account	Debit	Credit
Accounts Receivable	4822.23	
Services Revenue		5000.00
Product Revenue		499.75
Sales Discounts	750	
Sales Tax Payable		37.48
Shipping		35.00
Cost of Goods Sold	249.78	
Inventory		249.78
Total	5822.01	5822.01

And, here's why the amounts post the way they do:

- You sold $5,000 of services and $499.75 of products, which is income. The income values appear as credits to your Services Income and Product Revenue accounts to show that you sold something. In this example, the discount is in an income account, so the discount is in the Debit column to *reduce* your income.

- The sales tax you collect is a credit to the Sales Tax Payable account. Your shipping charge reduces your shipping expense account.

- All those credits need to balance against a debit. Because your customer owes you money, the amount owed belongs in the Accounts Receivable account, indicated by the debit.

- You also sold some products from inventory. You credit the Inventory account with the cost of the products, which decreases the Inventory account balance. You offset that credit with a debit to the Cost of Goods Sold account, which is an income statement account.

Creating Invoices

In QuickBooks, you have two ways to create invoices:

- **Create Invoices** used to be your only option (QuickBooks 2007 and earlier) for creating invoices. It can still handle everything you throw at it: services, products, billable time, and billable expenses. This command is available in QuickBooks Pro, QuickBooks Premier, and QuickBooks Enterprise.

• **Invoice for Time & Expenses,** available only in QuickBooks Premier and Enter-prise editions, can do everything that the Create Invoices window can do, but it's a real time-saver when you usually invoice for billable time and expenses. As you'll learn in detail on page 269, you specify a date range and QuickBooks shows you all the customers who have billable time and expenses during that period. When you choose the customer or job and tell the program to create an invoice, it opens the Create Invoices window, fills in the usual fields, and auto-matically fills in the invoice table with the customer's billable time and expenses. Once you're in the Create Invoices window, you can add any other items you want, like products you sold or discounts you're offering.

Invoices tell your customers everything they need to know about what they pur-chased and the payment they're about to make. If you created your customers and jobs with settings such as payment terms and sales rep (page 76), filling in an invoice is almost effortless. As soon as you choose a customer and job in the Customer:Job field, QuickBooks fills in most of the fields for you.

Some fields on an invoice are more influential than others, but they all come in handy at some point. To understand the purpose of the fields on an invoice more easily, you can break an invoice up into three basic sections, as shown in Figure 10-2. Because the invoices you create for product sales include a few more fields than the invoices for services only, the following sections use a product invoice to explain how to fill in each field you might run into on the invoices you create. If the information that QuickBooks fills in for you is incorrect, these sec-tions also tell you how to correct the problem.

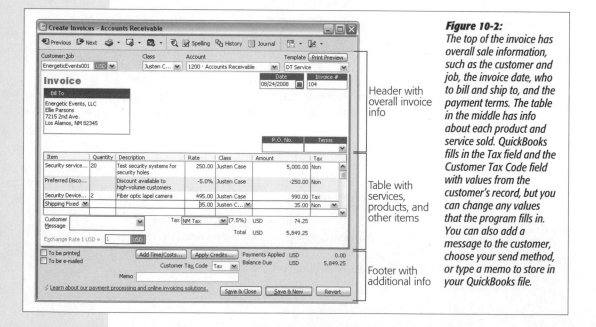

Figure 10-2:
The top of the invoice has overall sale information, such as the customer and job, the invoice date, who to bill and ship to, and the payment terms. The table in the middle has info about each product and service sold. QuickBooks fills in the Tax field and the Customer Tax Code field with values from the customer's record, but you can change any values that the program fills in. You can also add a message to the customer, choose your send method, or type a memo to store in your QuickBooks file.

Note: If you charge your customers based on the progress you've made, invoices are a *little* more complicated, but you'll learn how to handle this situation on page 285.

Creating an Invoice

In the sections that follow, you'll find details about filling in all the fields on an invoice. For now, here's the basic procedure for creating and saving one or more invoices using the Create Invoices command:

1. **On the QuickBooks home page (in the Customer panel), click Invoices (or press Ctrl+I).**

   The Create Invoices window opens.

   If you use QuickBooks Premier and you've turned on the preference to invoice for time and expenses (page 583), clicking Invoices on the Home page displays a shortcut menu with both invoicing commands. Choose Create Invoices from the shortcut menu. See page 271 to learn how to use the other command on the shortcut menu, "Invoice for Time & Expenses". If the preference for invoicing time and expenses isn't turned on, clicking Invoices opens the Create Invoices window immediately.

2. **In the Customer:Job box, choose the customer or job associated with the invoice.**

   When you choose a customer or job, QuickBooks fills in many of the invoice fields with values from the customer record (see page 72), job record (page 90), and the preferences you set for them (page 578). For example, QuickBooks pulls the data for the Bill To address, Terms, and Rep fields from the customer or job record. Your Sales & Customers preferences provide the values for the Ship Via and FOB (which stands for "free on board" or the physical point at which the customer becomes responsible for damage to or loss of the shipment) fields come from.

Note: In QuickBooks Premier, if the preference for invoicing time and expenses is turned on and the customer or job has associated time or expenses, the Billable Time/Costs dialog box opens with the "Select the outstanding billable time and costs to add to this invoice" option selected. If you don't want to add the time and expenses to this invoice, select the option whose label begins with "Exclude", and then click OK. To learn more about invoicing for time and expenses, see page 270.

3. **For each product or service sold, in the line-item table, enter the information for the item, including the quantity and price (or rate).**

   If you want, fill in the boxes below the line-item table, such as Customer Message and Memo.

   You can also turn on the checkboxes below the line-item table to specify how to send the invoice. You'll rarely need to change the sales tax rate associated with the customer, but you can if you need to.

4. **Maintain your professional image by checking for spelling errors before you send your invoice.**

   To run the QuickBooks spell checker, in the Create Invoices window's icon bar, click Spelling. If you checked spelling when you created your customers and invoice items, the main source of spelling errors is edits you've made to item descriptions. If the QuickBooks spell checker doesn't work the way you want, change your Spelling preferences (page 582).

5. **If you have additional invoices to create, simply click Save & New to save the current invoice and begin another.**

   To save the invoice you just created and close the Create Invoices window, click Save & Close. If you're unhappy with the choices you made in the current invoice, click Clear to start over with a fresh, blank invoice.

Tip: In QuickBooks 2007 and earlier, you could print an invoice and then *not* save it by either clicking Clear, which erases the current invoice; Revert if you're editing an existing invoice; or the Close button, which closes the Create Invoices window without saving the current invoice. If you create or modify an invoice and click the Print icon in QuickBooks 2008 or later, the program saves the invoice before printing it.

Filling in Invoice Header Fields

If you fill in all the fields in your customer and job records (see Chapter 4), Quick-Books takes care of filling in most of the invoice header section. Here's what the header fields do and where QuickBooks gets the values it fills in automatically.

Choosing the customer or job

The selection you make in the Customer:Job field is your most important choice for any invoice. In addition to billing the correct customer for your work, Quick-Books uses the settings from your customer and job records to fill in many of the invoice fields.

To choose a customer or job, in the Customer:Job drop-down list, choose the customer or job you want, as shown in Figure 10-3.

Note: If you've turned on the preference for multiple currencies, the last column in the customer drop-down menu shows the currency for the customer.

After you choose a customer, the "Price level" box appears to the right of the Customer:Job box if you've assigned a price level to the customer record (page 77). When you add an invoice item and the price isn't what you expect, the price level (which applies a discount or markup) may be the culprit. You can change a customer's price level by editing the customer record (page 92), or you can choose existing price levels to change the price you charge as you add items to your invoice (see the box on page 266).

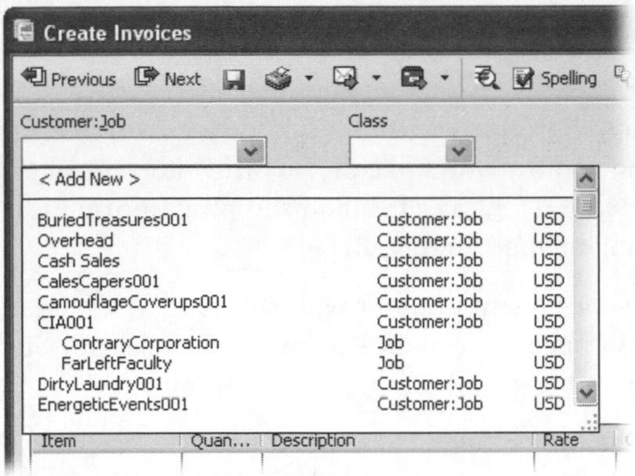

Figure 10-3:
If you work on different jobs for a customer, click the name of the job, which is indented underneath the customer's name. If your work for a customer doesn't relate to jobs, click the customer's name. The column to the right of the customer and job names provides another way to differentiate customers and jobs. You'll see Customer:Job for a customer entry, whereas the second column displays Job for a job entry.

Choosing an invoice template

The template you choose in the Template drop-down list (at the top right of the Create Invoices window) determines which fields appear on your invoices and how they're laid out. For example, you might have two templates: one for printing on your company letterhead and the other for invoices you send electronically. Choosing a template before doing anything else is the best way to prevent printing the wrong invoice to your expensive stationery.

QuickBooks remembers the template you chose when you created your last invoice. If you use only one invoice template, choose it on your first invoice and the program chooses it for you from then on.

Note: Templates aren't linked to customers. If you pick a template when you create an invoice for one customer, QuickBooks chooses that same template for your next invoice, regardless of which customer it's for.

You can switch templates any time you want. When you choose a template, the Create Invoices window displays the fields and layout for the new template. If you've already filled in an invoice, changing the template doesn't throw out the data; QuickBooks simply displays the data in the new template. However, QuickBooks won't display settings like your company logo, fonts, and other formatting until you print or preview your invoice (page 311).

Many small companies are perfectly happy with the invoice templates that Quick-Books provides. When you create your first invoice, you might not even think about the layout of the fields on the invoice. But if you run across a billing task that the current template can't handle, don't panic: You can choose from more than one built-in invoice template. And if you want your invoices to reflect your company's style and image, you can create your own templates (see page 626).

Before you accept the template that QuickBooks chooses, in the Template drop-down list, quickly select and review each of the following templates to see whether you like them better:

- **Intuit Product Invoice.** If you sell products with or without services, the Intuit Product Invoice is set up to show information like the quantity, item code, price for each item, total charge for each item, sales tax, and shipping information—including the ship date, shipping method, and FOB.

- **Intuit Service Invoice.** This invoice doesn't bother with shipping fields because services are performed, not shipped. The template includes fields for item, description, quantity, rate, amount, tax, and purchase order number.

- **Intuit Professional Invoice.** The only difference between this template and the Intuit Service Invoice is that this template doesn't include a purchase order number field, and the quantity (Qty) column follows the Description column.

- **Progress Invoice.** If you bill your customers based on the progress you've made on their jobs, the Progress Invoice has columns for your estimates, prior charges, and new totals. It appears in the Template drop-down list only if you turn on the preference for progress invoicing (see page 569).

Note: The Packing Slip template also appears in the Template drop-down list, but it isn't an invoice template. When you ship products to customers, you can print an invoice *and* packing slip from within the Create Invoices window (see page 314).

- **Fixed Fee Invoice.** This invoice drops the quantity and rate fields, since the invoice shows only the total charge. The template includes the date, item, description, tax, and purchase order number.

- **Time & Expense Invoice.** If you bill your customers by the hour, this template includes a column for hours and hourly rate, and it calculates the resulting total. The Attorney's Invoice template is identical to this one except in name.

The other header fields

As you can see in Figure 10-4, QuickBooks can fill in most of the remaining header fields for you. Although the following fields don't appear on every template, here's what you do to fill in any empty fields or change the ones that QuickBooks didn't complete the way you want:

- **Class.** If you turned on the class tracking feature (page 551) to categorize your income and expenses in different ways, choose a class for the invoice. If you skip this box, QuickBooks reminds you that the box is empty when you try to save the invoice. Although you *can* save the invoice without a class, it's important to assign classes to every transaction if you want your class-based reports to be accurate. For example, if you use classes to track income by partner and save an invoice without a class, the partner who delivered the services on the invoice might complain about the size of her paycheck.

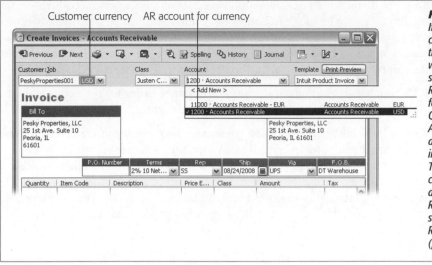

Customer currency   AR account for currency

Figure 10-4:
If you work with multiple currencies, at the top of the Create Invoices window, the Account box shows the Accounts Receivable (AR) account for the invoice's income. QuickBooks uses the Accounts Receivable account to store income in your home currency. To store income in other currencies, it creates additional Accounts Receivable accounts, such as Account Receivable-EUR (page 332).

- **Date.** QuickBooks fills in the current date, which is fine if you create invoices when you make a sale. But service businesses often send invoices on a schedule—the last day of the month is a popular choice. If you want to get a head start on your invoices, type or choose the invoice date you want. QuickBooks uses the same date for every subsequent invoice, making your end-of-month invoicing a tiny bit easier.

- **Invoice #.** When you create your first invoice, type the number that you want to start with. For example, if you'd rather not reveal that this is your first invoice, type a number such as 245. Each time you create a new invoice, QuickBooks increases the number in the Invoice # box by one: 246, 247, and so on.

Tip: Press the plus (+) key or the minus (–) key to increase or decrease the invoice number by one, respectively. When you save the current invoice, QuickBooks considers its invoice number the starting point for subsequent numbers.

If your last invoice was a mistake and you delete it (page 293), you'll end up with a gap in your invoice numbers. For example, when you delete invoice number 203, QuickBooks has already set the next invoice number to 204. Your invoice numbers don't *have* to be sequential, but it's easier to spot missing payments and other issues when your invoice numbers are in numeric order. If you notice the gap, in the Invoice # box, type the invoice number you want to use to get QuickBooks back on track.

- **Bill To.** The Bill To field is essential when you mail your invoices. When the customer record includes a billing address (page 75), QuickBooks uses that address to fill in this field. If you email invoices, a billing address isn't necessary—the customer name in the Bill To field identifies the customer on the emailed form.

- **Ship To.** If you sell services, you don't need an address to ship to, which is why the Intuit Service Invoice template doesn't show the Ship To box. But when you sell products, you need a shipping address to send the products to your customer. When you use a template like Intuit Product Invoice, QuickBooks uses the shipping address from the customer record to fill in the Ship To field.

- **P.O. Number.** If your customer issued a purchase order for the goods and services on your invoice, type that purchase order number.

- **Terms.** Typically, you set up the payment terms when you create customers, which you then use for every invoice. When the customer record includes payment terms (page 76), QuickBooks uses those terms to fill in this field. However, if you decide to change the payment terms—perhaps due to the customer's failing financial strength—choose a different term, such as "Due on receipt". When you save the invoice, QuickBooks offers to save that change to the customer record.

Note: If QuickBooks fills in fields with incorrect values, make the corrections on the invoice. You can't lose: When you save the invoice, QuickBooks asks if you'd like the new values to appear the next time, as shown in Figure 10-5.

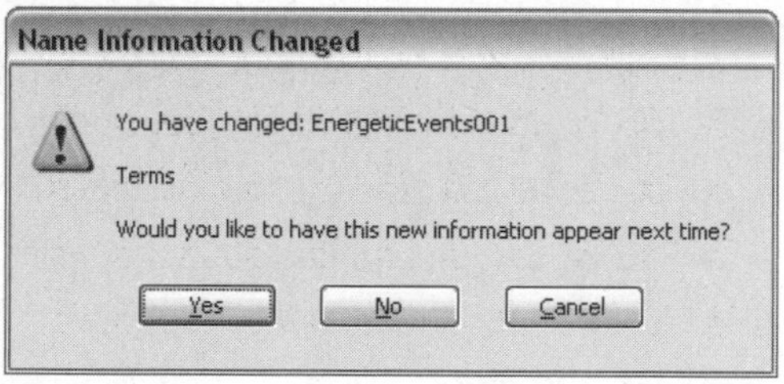

Figure 10-5:
If you click Yes, QuickBooks changes the corresponding fields in the customer and job records. If you click No, QuickBooks changes the values only on the invoice.

- **Rep.** If you assigned a sales rep in the customer record (page 76), QuickBooks fills in this field for you. If the sales rep changes from invoice to invoice (for instance, when the rep is the person who takes a phone order) and you left the Rep field in the customer record blank, choose the right person.

- **Ship Date.** QuickBooks fills in the current date. If you plan to ship on a different date (when the products arrive from your warehouse, for example), type or choose the ship date.

- **Ship Via.** If you set the Usual Shipping Method preference (page 579), QuickBooks uses that value to fill in the Ship Via box. To choose a different shipping method for this invoice—for instance, when your customer needs the order right away—in the invoice Ship Via box, choose the shipping method you want.

• **FOB.** This stands for "free on board" and signifies the physical point at which the customer becomes responsible for the shipment. That means that if the shipment becomes lost or damaged beyond the FOB point, it's the customer's problem. If you set the Usual FOB preference, QuickBooks uses that preference to fill in the FOB box. To choose a different location for this order, you have to type the FOB location you want.

Note: Unlike many of the other fields in the invoice header, the FOB box doesn't include a drop-down list. QuickBooks doesn't keep a list of FOB locations because most companies pick one FOB location and stick with it.

POWER USERS' CLINIC

Adding Group Items to Invoices

If you find the same items frequently appearing together on your invoices, you can add those items in one step by creating a Group item (page 120).

For example, customers who buy your deluxe vinyl sofa covers also tend to purchase the dirt-magnet front hall runner and the faux-marble garage floor liner. A Group item, perhaps called the Neat Freak Package, can include the items for the sofa cover, runner, and liner. You can create a Group item with the quantity you typically sell of each item. Any type of item is fair game for a Group item, so you can include service items, discounts, subtotals, and other charges as well.

To add a Group item to an invoice, in the Create Invoices window, in the Item drop-down list, choose the Neat Freak Package Group item you created. QuickBooks fills in the first line by adding the name of the Group item in the Item field. Then, the program adds additional lines (including quantity, description, and price) for the sofa cover, runner, and liner.

Entering Invoice Line Items

If you dutifully studied Chapter 5, you already know about the different types of items you can add to an invoice. This section describes how to fill in a line in the line-item table to charge your customers for the things they buy. (The box on page 120 explains a shortcut for speeding up filling in invoice items.)

Note: The order in which you add items to an invoice is important. For example, when you add a Subtotal item, QuickBooks subtotals all the preceding items up to the previous Subtotal item (if there is one). QuickBooks does nothing to check that you add items in the correct order. You can add a Subtotal item as the first line item, even though that does nothing for your invoice. See page 265 for info on adding Subtotal, Discount, and Sales Tax items in the right order.

The column order in the line-item table varies from template to template, but this section and Figure 10-6 show the columns in the order they appear on the Intuit Product Invoice template:

• **Quantity.** For products, type the quantity. For services you sell by the hour (or other unit of time), type the number of time units. (See page 273 to learn how to select hours from a timesheet.) If you sell services at a flat rate, you can leave the Quantity cell blank and simply fill in the Amount cell.

Note: If you type a quantity for a product that exceeds how many you have on hand, QuickBooks Pro simply warns you that you don't have enough. QuickBooks Premier displays the warning, and also tells you how many you have on hand, how many are on sales orders (page 276), and the total you have available.

When you use the Intuit Product Invoice, the Quantity column comes first. After you choose an item, make sure to check the value in the Amount field. If the number looks too large or too small, the quantity you entered might not match the units for the item. For example, if you charge for developing training materials by the *hour*, but charge for teaching a training class by the *day*, the quantity for developing training materials has to be in hours and the quantity for teaching has to be in days.

Quantity doesn't apply if the item is a discount, subtotal, or sales tax. If you choose one of these items after entering a quantity, QuickBooks removes the value in the Quantity field.

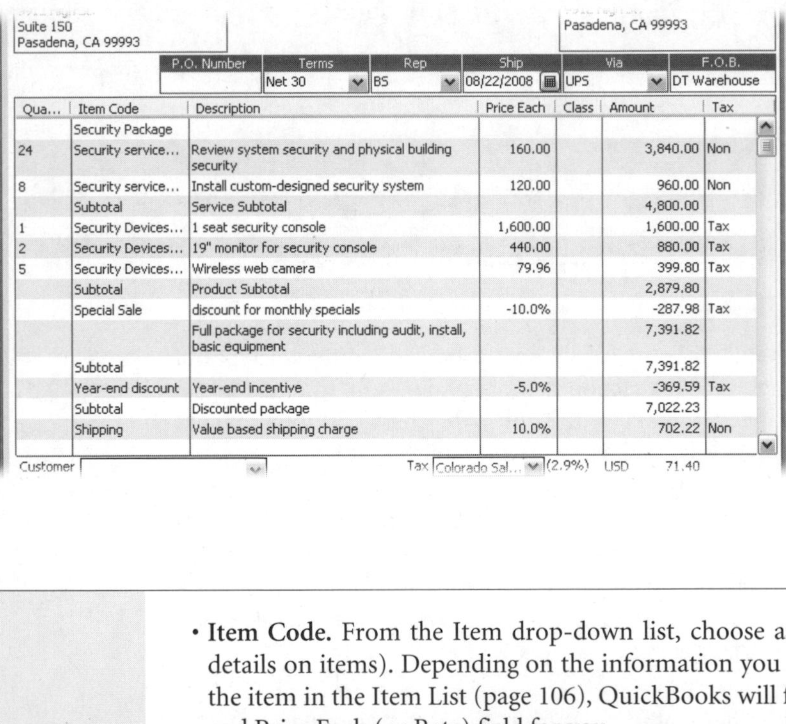

Figure 10-6:
It seems odd to set the quantity before you choose an item, but that's how the Intuit Product Invoice works. (You can customize an invoice to place the columns in the order you want; see page 624.) If you realize that you entered the wrong quantity after you pick an item, simply double-click the Quantity field and type the correct quantity. After you've added your first line item, start another line item by clicking any field in the next empty line of the table.

- **Item Code.** From the Item drop-down list, choose an item (see Chapter 5 for details on items). Depending on the information you entered when you created the item in the Item List (page 106), QuickBooks will fill in the Description field and Price Each (or Rate) field for you.

- **Description.** You can keep the description that comes from the item record or you can edit it. For example, when you set up your inventory items with standard descriptions, you don't have to change the description on the invoice. On the other hand, you can add detail to a generic description—like changing the description "Security service" to "Nightly rounds every two hours."

- **Price Each (or Rate).** Depending on the type of item you're adding to the invoice, QuickBooks uses the value in the Sales Price field or Rate field in the item record (see Chapter 5). For example, an inventory part always uses the Sales Price field. Service items use the Rate field, unless a partner or subcontractor performs the work, in which case they use the Sales Price field.

    If multiple currencies are turned on and you set up the customer to use a foreign currency, QuickBooks automatically applies the current exchange rate for that currency to item prices and service rates. To use a specific exchange rate in an invoice, fill in the "Exchange Rate 1 <currency> =" box with the exchange rate *before* you add items to the invoice. (If you didn't change the exchange rate, delete the lines in the invoice, set the exchange rate, and then add the line items again.)

Note: Don't forget that different items can use different units for their price. If you charge for a service by the hour, the value in the Rate or Price Each field is the price per hour and the value you type in the Quantity field should be the number of hours. Conversely, if you charge a fixed fee for your "How to Hack-Proof Your Business" seminar, leave the Quantity field blank (or type *1*). Or, if you use the Time & Expense or Fixed Fee templates (page 258), you don't have to remember these rules.

- **Amount.** QuickBooks calculates the total in this field by multiplying the quantity by the value in the Price Each (or Rate) field. Nothing stops you from simply typing a value in this field, which is exactly what you want for a fixed-fee contract.

- **Tax.** If you set up the taxable status of your customers (page 77) and the items you sell (page 111), QuickBooks automatically handles sales tax on your invoices. For example, when an item is taxable *and* the customer is liable for paying sales tax, the program calculates the total sales tax that appears below the table (see Figure 10-2 on page 254) by totaling all the taxable items on your invoice and multiplying by the tax rate set in the Tax box. (QuickBooks fills this box in with the sales tax item you set in the customer's record.)

Tip: If you notice that the taxable status isn't correct, don't change the value in the Tax field. You're better off correcting the customer's or the item's tax status so QuickBooks can calculate tax correctly in the future.

Inserting and deleting line items

Sometimes, you forget to add line items you need. For example, you've added several services and inventory items to your invoice, and then you realize that you need Subtotal items following the last service and last inventory items so that you can apply a shipping charge only to the inventory items.

Here's how you insert and delete lines in the line-item table:

- **Insert a line.** Right-click the line above which you want to insert a line, and then choose Insert Line from the shortcut menu. If you prefer keyboard shortcuts, press Ctrl+Insert instead.

- **Delete a line.** Right-click the line you want to delete and choose Delete Line from the shortcut menu, or press Ctrl+Delete.

As shown in Figure 10-7, QuickBooks adjusts the invoice's lines accordingly.

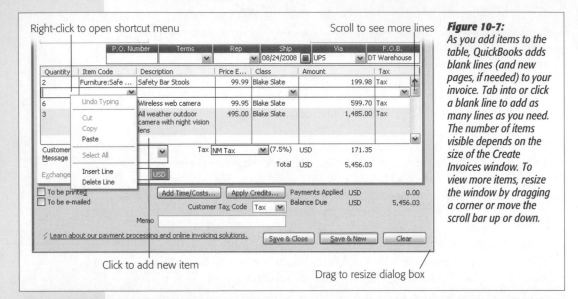

Right-click to open shortcut menu   Scroll to see more lines

Click to add new item

Drag to resize dialog box

Figure 10-7:
As you add items to the table, QuickBooks adds blank lines (and new pages, if needed) to your invoice. Tab into or click a blank line to add as many lines as you need. The number of items visible depends on the size of the Create Invoices window. To view more items, resize the window by dragging a corner or move the scroll bar up or down.

Invoicing Fixed-Price Contracts

Fixed-price contracts are risky for contractors because they have to swallow any cost overruns. But if you've sharpened your skills on similar projects in the past and can estimate the costs with reasonable accuracy, a fixed-price contract provides opportunity for better-than-average profit.

Once you and your customer agree on the fixed price, that price is all that matters to the customer. Even if *you* track the costs of performing a job, your customer never sees those numbers. In QuickBooks, you can invoice fixed-price contracts two different ways:

- If you use the same sets of services and products for multiple jobs, create a Group item that includes each service and product you deliver and set up the

Group item to hide the details of the underlying services and products (page 120). After you add the Group item to your invoice, change the price of the Group item to your fixed price.

- If every fixed-price job is different, create a Service item (page 103) called something like Fixed Fee. When you create the item, fill in the Rate field with the full amount of the fixed-price contract. Then, when you reach a milestone that warrants a payment, create a progress invoice. In the quantity column, type the decimal that equates to the percentage completed (.25 for 25 percent, for example). QuickBooks calculates the payment by multiplying the quantity by the fixed-price amount.

Applying Subtotals, Discounts, and Percentage Charges

Services, Inventory Parts, and Non-inventory Parts (see Chapter 5) are standalone items. When you add them to the line-item table, they don't affect their neighbors in any way. However, with percentage discounts on what you sell or Other Charge items that calculate shipping as a percentage of price, the order in which you add items becomes crucial. And, if you want to apply a percentage to several items, you'll also need one or more Subtotal items to make the calculations work.

You first learned about Subtotal, Discount, and Other Charge items in Chapter 5. Figure 10-8 shows how to combine them to calculate percentage discounts and add markups to the items on your invoice.

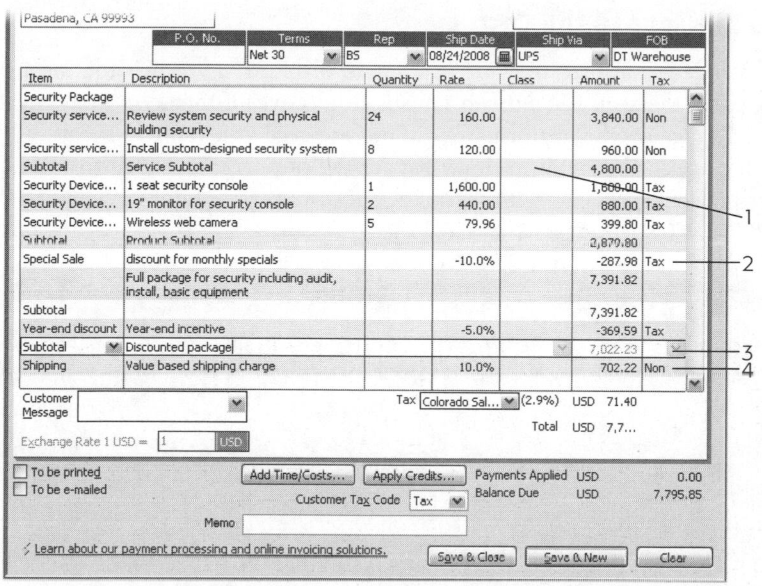

Figure 10-8:
1: A Subtotal item adds up the values of all the items up to the previous Subtotal item. For example, if you want to keep the Service items out of the product subtotal, add a Subtotal item after the last Service item. 2: For Discount items and Other Charge items created as percentages, QuickBooks multiplies the percentage by the total on the preceding line. If the discount applies only to one item, add the Discount item immediately below the item you want to discount. 3: If you want to apply a percentage discount to several items, use a Subtotal item to total their cost. 4: Add a percentage Discount or Other Charge item on the line following a Subtotal.

Here are the steps for arranging Subtotal, Discount, and Other Charge items to calculate percentages on invoice items:

1. **If you want to discount several items on your invoice, add all the items you want to discount one after the other.**

   Even though the Balance Due field shows the total of all items, to apply a discount to all of them, you first need to add a Subtotal item to the line-item table.

2. **Add a Subtotal item after the last item you want to discount, as shown by the Product Subtotal item in Figure 10-8.**

   The Subtotal item adds up all the preceding line items up to the previous Subtotal. For example, in Figure 10-8, the Services Total item is a subtotal of the

Service items on the invoice. The Product Subtotal item adds up all items between the Services Total and the Product Subtotal items.

3. **To apply a percentage discount or charge to the subtotal, simply add the Discount or Other Charge item to the line immediately below the Subtotal item.**

   If you've already added other items to your invoice, right-click the line immediately below the Subtotal item and choose Insert Line from the shortcut menu.

4. **If you have additional items that you don't want to include in the discount or charge, add those below the Discount or Other Charge item.**

Note: These steps also work for Other Charge items that you set up as percentages, such as shipping.

Adding a Message to the Customer

You can include a message to your customers on your invoices—for instance, reminding them that you'll send your cousin Guido over if they don't pay. In the Customer Message drop-down list, choose the message you want to include. The messages that appear in the drop-down list are the ones you've added to the Customer Message List (page 149). If the message you want to use doesn't exist, in the drop-down list, click *<Add New>* to open the New Customer Message dialog box.

FREQUENTLY ASKED QUESTION

Adjusting Price Levels

I run a doggie spa, and one of my Service items is Deluxe Spa Day, which costs $300. But when I was creating a customer invoice, the Price Each came up as $250. What's going on?

Before you rush to correct that Service item's price, look near the top of the Create Invoices window, immediately to the right of the Customer:Job label. If you see text in square brackets, such as [Preferred], you'll know that you set up your customer with a price level (page 77). Instead of a mistake, this price adjustment on your invoice is actually a clever and convenient feature.

Price levels are percentages (either increases or decreases) that you can apply to the prices you charge. For example, you can set up price levels to give discounts to your high-volume customers or mark up prices for customers well-known for their frequent use of your customer service line.

If you apply a price level to a customer, QuickBooks automatically applies the price level percentage to every item you add to invoices for that customer. The only indication you'll see is the price level name next to the Customer:Job label. To use price levels, you first have to turn on the Price Level preference (page 579).

You can also apply price levels to individual items in an invoice. For example, suppose you offer a 20 percent discount on a different item each month. When an item is the monthly special, you can apply the Monthly Special price level to just that item, as shown in Figure 10-9.

When you use price levels, your customers don't see that the price increases or decreases, which could mean that they could take your discounts for granted. If you want to emphasize the discounts you apply, use a Discount item instead to visibly reduce prices on your invoices (see page 265).

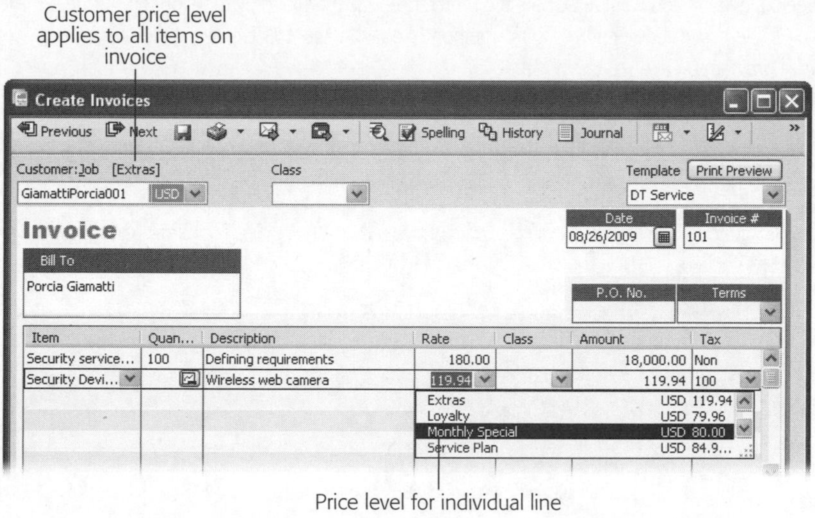

Customer price level applies to all items on invoice

Price level for individual line

Figure 10-9:
To apply a price level to a single item, click the Price Each (or Rate) field for the item that's on special. When QuickBooks displays a down arrow to indicate that a drop-down list is available, click the arrow and then choose the price level you want to apply.

Choosing How to Send the Invoice

Below the line-item table, you'll find two checkboxes that simplify sending your invoices to your customers: "To be printed" and "To be e-mailed". But these checkboxes don't tell the whole story because you actually have five options for sending invoices:

- **Print immediately.** If you create only the occasional invoice and send it as soon as it's complete, turn off both checkboxes. Instead, in the Create Invoices window icon bar, click the Print icon and follow the instructions on page 311.

- **Print later.** If you want to add the invoice to a queue to print later, turn on the "To be printed" checkbox. Then, you can print all the invoices in the queue, as described on page 311.

- **Email immediately.** In the Create Invoices window's toolbar, click the Send icon (it looks like an envelope with a green arrow) and follow the instructions for emailing invoices on page 315.

- **Email later.** If you want to add the invoice to a queue to email later, turn on the "To be e-mailed" checkbox. You can send all the invoices in the queue via email, as described on page 315.

- **Print and email later.** You can turn on both checkboxes if you want to email invoices to get the ball rolling and then follow up with paper copies.

If you're sending an invoice for products you've sold, you also have to ship those products to your customer. See the box on page 268 for a convenient and money-saving way to ship products.

Tip: See page 581 if you want to activate the preference that automatically turns on the "To be e-mailed" checkbox if the customer's preferred send method is email. Page 315 explains how QuickBooks works with email programs.

Shipping Products

If you sell products, making regular runs to the FedEx or UPS office gets old quickly. But sitting quietly within QuickBooks is a free service that could change the way you ship packages.

Shipping Manager is already built into QuickBooks, so you can sign up for shipping services and start sending out your packages right away. You can print FedEx and UPS shipping labels, schedule pickups, and track package progress right in QuickBooks. Shipping Manager fills in shipping labels with customer addresses from your QuickBooks invoices, sales receipts, or customer records. All you pay are the FedEx or UPS charges on your shipment.

Using Shipping Manager isn't just about convenience. By setting up a FedEx account through Shipping Manager, you get discounts of up to 16 percent on FedEx Express and 12 percent on FedEx Ground service. (Discounts don't apply if you use QuickBooks Online or QuickBooks for the Mac.)

In case you haven't noticed Shipping Manager, here's where it's hiding in QuickBooks:

- If you're creating an invoice for products you plan to ship, in the Create Invoices window toolbar, click the Ship icon, shown in Figure 10-10.

- The Sales Receipt window toolbar also includes a Ship icon.

- Choose File → Shipping, and then choose Ship FedEx Package or Ship UPS Package.

To set up Shipping Manager and an account with FedEx, UPS, or both, you'll need your QuickBooks Registration Number (for QuickBooks 2004 and earlier) or QuickBooks License and Product Number (QuickBooks 2005 and later). If you don't memorize these crucial numbers, press F2 or choose Help → About QuickBooks to open a window that displays them.

The first time you launch Shipping Manager, the program steps you through setup and creating an account with either FedEx or UPS.

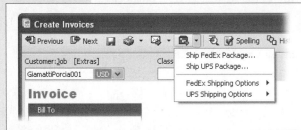

Figure 10-10:
On the QuickBooks Shipping Manager drop-down menu, click the downward-pointing arrow to display a drop-down menu with commands for shipping packages or choosing shipping options to schedule a pick-up or track a package that's already on its way.

Adding a Memo to Yourself

The Create Invoices window includes a Memo box, which works just like Memo boxes throughout QuickBooks. You can use this box to remind yourself about something special on the invoice or to summarize the transaction. For example, if the invoice is the first one for a new customer, you can note that in the Memo box. The memo appears in your sales reports, although it won't print on the invoices you send to your customers.

Invoicing for Nonprofits

When you sell products and services for a living, you create invoices when someone buys something. For nonprofits, however, invoices record the pledges, donations, grants, or other contributions you've been promised.

Invoicing for nonprofits differs from the profit world's approach. First of all, many nonprofits don't bother sending invoices to donors. Nonprofits might send reminders to donors who haven't sent in the pledged donations, but they don't add finance charges to late payments.

Moreover, because some donors ask for specific types of reports, nonprofits often use several Accounts Receivable accounts to track money coming from grants, dues, pledges,

and other sources. When you use multiple Accounts Receivable accounts, the Create Invoices window includes an Account field where you can choose the Accounts Receivable account (just like when you work with multiple currencies, as described on page 332). For example, if you create an invoice for pledges, you'll choose the Pledges Receivable account.

To compensate for this additional field, QuickBooks provides a handy feature when you use multiple Accounts Receivable accounts: The program remembers the last invoice number used for each account, so you can create unique invoice numbering schemes for each account.

Note: The Open Invoices report (choose Reports → Customers & Receivables → Open Invoices) is perfect when you want to see all the invoices for which you haven't yet received payment. The report shows all the invoices for each customer and job, when they're due, and the open balance. If the invoices are overdue, the Aging column shows just how late the invoices are.

Invoicing for Billable Time and Costs

When you work on a time-and-materials contract, you charge the customer for labor costs plus job expenses. Cost-plus contracts are similar except that you charge a fee on top of the job costs. Contracts like these are both low-risk and low-reward—in effect, you're earning an hourly wage for the time you work. For these types of contracts, it's critical that you capture all the expenses associated with the job or you'll lose the profit that the contract offers.

QuickBooks helps you get those billable items into your invoices. You have to tell QuickBooks about every hour you worked and every expense you incurred for a job. But once you enter those things into QuickBooks, it's easy to build an invoice that captures them. You can add billable time and costs to an invoice whenever the Create Invoices window is open. When you open the Create Invoices window in QuickBooks Pro or Premier, it reminds you about outstanding billable time and costs. QuickBooks Premier also has a separate command specifically for creating invoices for billable time and costs. The following sections tell you how to perform all these tasks.

Setting Up Invoicing for Time and Cost

In some industries, like consulting and law, invoicing for time and expenses is the norm. Other industries, like retail, never invoice for time and expenses.

Before you can pop your billable time and expenses into your invoices, you first need to record them as billable items and assign them to the correct customer or job. If you regularly invoice for billable time and expenses, you can also set up QuickBooks to include a special command for that task.

Here are the billable items you can add to your invoices and the chapters where you'll learn how to track them:

- **Billable time.** Chapter 8 (page 191) describes how to track your billable time and assign your hours to a customer or job.

- **Mileage.** Chapter 8 (page 200) describes how to track mileage and assign mileage to a customer or job.

- **Purchases and expenses related to a customer or job.** Reimbursable expenses include products you purchase specifically for a job, services you get from a subcontractor, and other expenses such as shipping and postage. Chapter 9 describes how to make items and expenses reimbursable to a customer or job (page 210) as you enter bills, checks, or credit card charges in QuickBooks.

If you use QuickBooks Premier or Enterprise, to set the preference for invoicing time and expenses, choose Edit → Preferences. In the icon bar, click Time & Expenses. On the Company Preferences tab, turn on "Create invoices from a list of time and expenses" checkbox. Leave this checkbox turned off if invoicing for time and expenses is the exception rather than the rule. (You can still add time and other costs to an invoice in the Create Invoices window. After you choose the customer or job, click Add Time/Costs below the line-item table.)

Adding Billable Time and Costs to Invoices

In QuickBooks Pro and QuickBooks Premier, you can add billable time and costs directly in the Create Invoices window. Here's how:

1. **Press Ctrl+I or choose Customers → Create Invoices to open the Create Invoices window. In the Customer:Job drop-down list, choose the customer or job you want to invoice.**

   If the customer or job has outstanding billable time or expenses, the Billable Time/Costs dialog box opens and automatically selects the "Select the outstanding billable time and costs to add to this invoice?" option.

2. **In the Billable Time/Costs dialog box, click OK.**

   The "Choose Billable Time and Costs" dialog box opens.

Note: If the Create Invoices window is already open, you can open the "Choose Billable Time and Costs" dialog box by clicking the Add Time/Costs button below the invoice line-item table.

3. To select the time and costs you want to add to the invoice, follow the instructions that begin with step 1 on page 273.

Using the Invoice for Time and Expenses Command

The QuickBooks Premier "Invoice for Time & Expenses" command shows you every customer with billable time and expenses waiting to be invoiced and how much there is of each type, so it's hard to miss outstanding billable hours and reimbursable expenses.

Here's how to put the "Invoice for Time & Expenses" command to use:

1. **Choose Customers → "Invoice for Time & Expenses". (Or, on the Home page, click the Invoices icon, and then choose "Invoice for Time & Expenses" on the drop-down menu.)**

   QuickBooks opens the "Invoice for Time & Expenses" window, which lists the customers and jobs that have billable time and expenses associated with them. The table shows the amount of billable time, expenses, and mileage for each customer and job. The Items column shows the reimbursable amount for products that you purchased specifically for the customer or job.

2. **In the Date Range From and To boxes, type the starting and ending dates for the time and expenses you want to invoice for.**

   For example, if you want to invoice for billable time and expenses for the previous month, type the first and last day of the month, like 3/1/2010 and 3/31/2010. To invoice for all outstanding time and expenses up to a certain date, leave the Date Range From box blank, as shown in Figure 10-11.

3. **To select a customer or job for invoicing, click anywhere in its row.**

   QuickBooks highlights the customer or job you select, as shown in Figure 10-11.

4. **To choose specific billable time and costs to add to the invoice, turn on the "Let me select specific billable costs for this Customer:Job" checkbox.**

   Nothing happens until you click Create Invoice.

5. **Click Create Invoice.**

   If you turned on the "Let me select specific billable costs for this Customer:Job" checkbox, QuickBooks opens the "Choose Billable Time and Costs" dialog box shown in Figure 10-12, which includes tabs for time, expenses, mileage, and products (items). This dialog box is the same one you see if you click Add Time/Costs in the Create Invoices window. Proceed to the next section to learn how to add billable time and costs to an invoice.

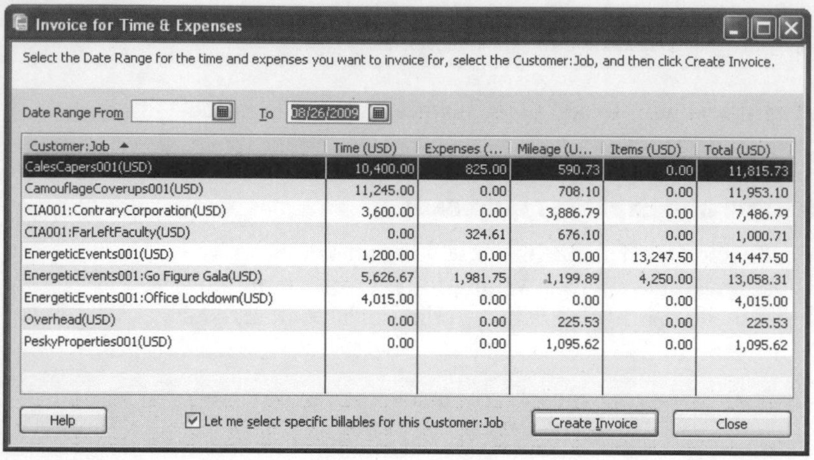

Figure 10-11:
To invoice for all billable costs, leave the "Let me select specific billable costs for this Customer: Job" checkbox turned off in the "Invoice for Time & Expenses" dialog box. With that setting, when you click Create Invoice, QuickBooks immediately opens the Create Invoices window filled in with all the billable time and expenses for that customer or job.

If you turned off the "Let me select specific billable costs for this Customer:Job" checkbox, the Create Invoices window opens with your invoice already filled out. All you have to do is save the invoice by clicking Save & Close.

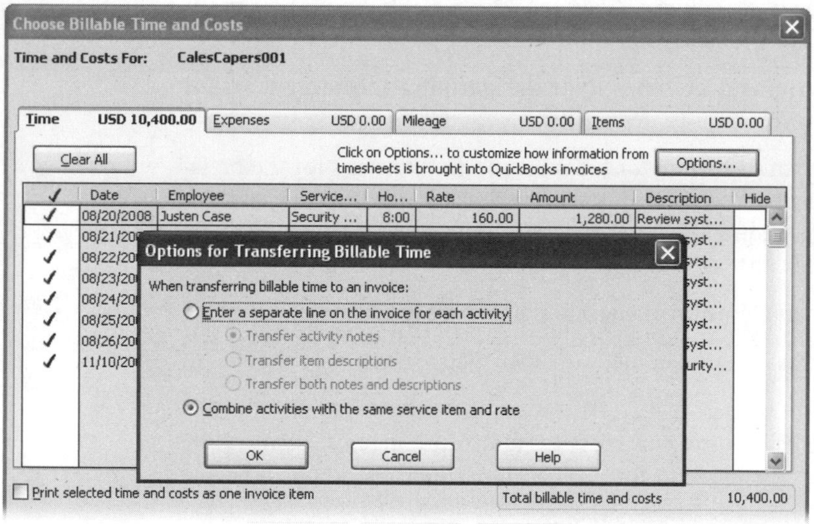

Figure 10-12:
On the Time tab, click Options to tell QuickBooks how to handle different activities. In the "Options for Transferring Billable Time" dialog box (foreground), the program automatically selects the option that includes the total hours for each service item. However, you can tell the program to add a separate line for each activity, to show the hours worked each day, for instance. If each activity is on its own line, you can transfer activity descriptions, notes, or both to the invoice.

Selecting Billable Time and Costs

Regardless how you open the "Choose Billable Time and Costs" dialog box, the steps for selecting the billable time and costs to invoice are the same. Here's what you do:

1. **In the "Choose Billable Time and Costs" dialog box, to select all the entries on the Time tab, click Select All.**

   QuickBooks adds a checkmark in the checkmark column for every activity. To add or remove a row, click its checkmark cell to toggle it on or off.

   Each tab in the dialog box shows the total value of the entries you've selected on that tab. The "Total billable time and costs" value below the table is the total of all the selected items on all four tabs.

2. **If you want the invoice to include only one line for all the time and expenses you've selected, turn on the "Print selected time and costs as one invoice item" checkbox (below the table).**

   The Create Invoices window shows the separate entries so you can verify that the invoice is correct. The printed invoice shows only one line labeled Total Reimbursable Expenses.

Note: If you've created the invoice with one line for time and costs, it takes several steps to recreate it showing individual costs. To change an invoice back to a line-by-line listing, in the Create Invoices window, delete the Total Reimbursable Expenses line item. Click Add Time/Costs to open the "Choose Billable Time and Costs" dialog box and reselect all the entries you want. Turn off the "Print selected time and costs as one invoice item" checkbox and then click OK.

---

3. **On the "Choose Billable Time and Costs" dialog box's Expenses tab, click the checkmark cell for each expense (like meals, airfare, and other costs) you want to add to the invoice.**

   If you mark up expenses, such as phone calls and postage, the Expenses tab lets you track your markups. In the "Markup Amount or %" box, type the markup's dollar value or percentage. Choose the income account for the markup. (The box on page 275 tells you how to apply different markups to different expenses.)

   To have QuickBooks calculate the sales tax, turn on the "Selected expenses are taxable" checkbox. If the customer is tax exempt, QuickBooks doesn't add sales tax no matter what.

Note: On the Expenses tab, the Memo column displays what you typed in the Memo field for the original vendor bill, check, or credit card charge. QuickBooks uses the entries in this column as the description on the invoice, so don't leave these fields blank. If you didn't enter a Memo in the original expense transaction, you'll have to type the description for each expense once it's added to the invoice.

---

4. Click the Mileage tab and select the mileage you want to add to the invoice.

   Like you did on the Time tab, click Options to tell QuickBooks whether to show one line for mileage or a separate line for each activity.

5. **On the Items tab, select any products that you bought specifically for the customer or job.**

   Click an item's checkmark cell to add it to the invoice.

6. **When you've selected all the billable items you want to add from every tab, click OK.**

   QuickBooks adds all the billable items you selected to the invoice, as shown in Figure 10-13. If it has everything you want to invoice, click Save & Close.

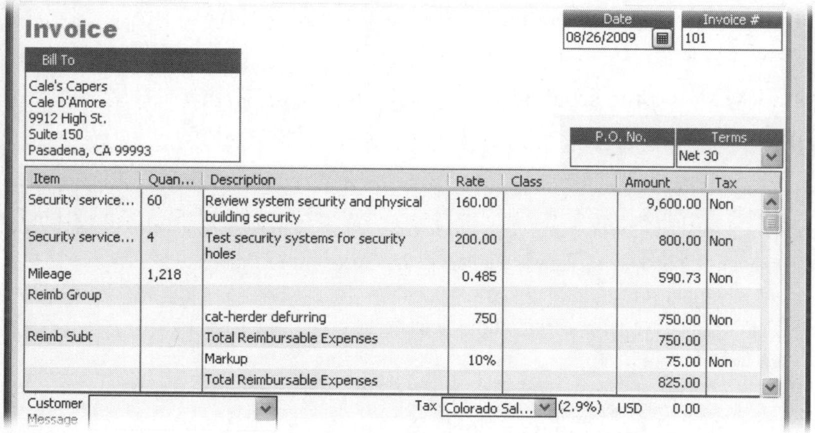

Figure 10-13:
If you didn't type memos in the original expense transactions, you have to type the descriptions for billable expenses directly into the invoice. Because the invoice is open in the Create Invoices window, you can add additional line items to the invoice before you save it.

Checking for Unbilled Costs

Most Customers & Receivables reports focus on charges you've already invoiced. If you invoice customers for reimbursable expenses, forgetting to invoice for reimbursable costs takes a bite out of your profits. Be sure to regularly run the "Unbilled Costs by Job" report (choose Reports → Customers & Receivables → "Unbilled Costs by Job") to look for job expenses that you've forgotten to invoice. This report shows costs that you designated as billable to a customer or job that haven't yet been added to an invoice.

Invoicing for Backordered Products

Placing a product order to fulfill your customers' orders is known as a *backorder*. If backorders are a regular part of your business day, you should consider finding suppliers who deliver more quickly, and maybe upgrading to QuickBooks Premier, which has a built-in sales order form for tracking backordered items. By combining a few of QuickBooks Pro's features, you can also handle backorders.

WORKAROUND WORKSHOP

Adding Different Markups to Billable Expenses

The Expenses tab has only one "Markup Amount or %" box, which is frightfully inconvenient if you add markup to some, but not all, of the billable expenses. But there's nothing stopping you from adding these expenses to your invoice in more than one batch with a different markup amount or percentage for each batch. Here's how it works:

1. In the "Choose Billable Time and Costs" dialog box, click the Expenses tab.

2. In the "Markup Amount or %" box, type the markup for the first batch of expenses.

3. Turn on the checkmark cell for each expense that you want to mark up at the current markup.

4. Click OK to add the selected expenses to the invoice.

5. Below the Create Invoices window's item table, click Add Time/Costs.

6. In the "Choose Billable Time and Costs" dialog box, click the Expenses tab.

7. Change the value in the "Markup Amount or %" to the next markup and turn on the checkmark cell for the expenses at this markup. Click OK to close the dialog box.

8. Repeat steps 5 through 7 for each additional markup.

This technique works just as well when some of the expenses are taxable while others aren't. Choose the taxable items, turn on the "Selected expenses are taxable" checkbox, and add the taxable expenses to the invoice. Reopen the "Choose Billable Time and Costs" dialog box, choose the nontaxable items, turn off the "Selected expenses are taxable" checkbox, and add the nontaxable expenses to the invoice.

When you tell your customers that a product is out of stock, they might ask you to handle the backorders in different ways. Here are the most common requests for backorders:

- **Remove the backordered items from the order.** Customers in a hurry ask you to fill the order with only the products you have in stock. If they can't find the backordered products anywhere else, they can call in a new order.

- **Ship all items at once.** If convenience is more important than delivery date, you can hold the customer order until the backordered products arrive and ship the entire order at once.

- **Ship backordered items when they arrive.** Many customers request that you process their orders for the products you *do* have in stock and then send the backordered products when you receive them.

If you remove backordered items from an order, you can ship the entire order and invoice the customer immediately. But when customers ask you to hold all or part of their orders until backordered products arrive, they usually expect you to invoice them for backordered products only when you ship them. You don't want the income appearing in your account balances until the order ships.

Tip: If you need help remembering *how* customers want you to handle their backorders, store back-order preferences in a custom field in the customer record (page 155). An alternative approach is to add a note in the Customer Center (select the customer and click Edit Notes). Any information you add to the customer Notepad appears front and center whenever you select the customer on the Customers & Jobs tab.

Using Pending Invoices for Backorders

In QuickBooks, setting an invoice status to Pending places it in a holding pattern with no income or expenses posting to your accounts. But they're easy to spot in the Create Invoices window—QuickBooks adds a Pending stamp to the form. If you don't use QuickBooks Premier, a pending invoice is the way to track backorders.

To set an invoice to Pending status, follow these steps:

1. **Press Ctrl+I to open the Create Invoices window.**

   Fill in the invoice fields as usual (page 258).

2. **Choose Edit → Mark Invoice As Pending (or right-click the Create Invoices window and choose Mark Invoice As Pending on the shortcut menu). After QuickBooks adds the "Pending (non-posting)" stamp to the invoice, as shown in the background in Figure 10-14, click Save & Close.**

   The invoice is ready for action, but none of the values post to income or expense accounts.

3. **When the backordered products arrive, open the invoice in the Create Invoices window, choose Edit → "Mark Invoice as Final", and then click Save & Close.**

   When you save the invoice, QuickBooks posts its values to the appropriate income and expense accounts.

Using Sales Orders for Backorders

QuickBooks Premier and Enterprise have a Sales Order form, which is perfect for backorders. The Create Sales Orders window looks like the Create Invoices window, except that the item table includes an Ordered column, which holds the number of items the customer ordered but that you haven't yet invoiced. In effect, it's a record of how much stock you need to have on hand to fill the order.

Tip: To see all your sales orders at once, choose Reports → Sales and then select either "Open Sales Order by Customer" or "Open Sales Orders by Item".

If you try to add more items to an invoice than you have in stock, you'll see an error message warning of the shortfall. In QuickBooks Premier, this message tells you how many you have on hand, how many are on other sales orders, and the remaining quantity available. Because the products aren't in stock, the remaining

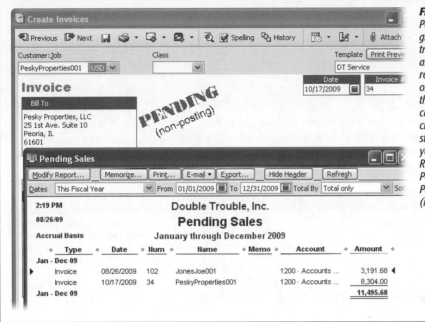

Figure 10-14:
Pending invoices are also great for entering transactions ahead of time and holding them until you receive approval for a sale or reach the milestone that the invoice represents. You can set sales receipts and credit memos to Pending status as well. To see all your pending sales, choose Reports → Sales → Pending Sales to run the Pending Sales report (in foreground).

quantity is either zero or a negative number. (QuickBooks Pro simply warns you that you don't have enough.) You can then cancel the invoice and create a sales order instead.

If you already know that your inventory is woefully low or nonexistent, simply create a sales order for the customer's order. Then, if a review of your inventory shows that some items are in stock, you can create a partial invoice for the items you have and use the sales order to track the backordered items. Since the sales orders keep a running balance of backordered items, you can easily create a purchase order to restock the products you need. (See Chapter 19 to learn more about managing inventory.) Here are the steps (available only if you have QuickBooks Premier or Enterprise):

1. **If you haven't turned on the preference for using sales orders, do so now.**

   Choose Edit → Preferences. In the Preferences dialog box, click the Sales & Customers icon and click the Company Preferences tab. In the Sales Orders section, turn on the Enable Sales Orders checkbox.

2. **On the Home page, click Sales Orders (or choose Customers → Create Sales Orders).**

   The Create Sales Orders window opens.

3. **Fill in the fields for the sales order as you would the fields in an invoice (page 258).**

   The only difference is that the column where you record the quantity of items ordered is the Ordered column, instead of an invoice's Quantity column.

4. **In the toolbar, click Create Invoice.**

The aptly named "Create Invoice Based on Sales Order(s)" dialog box opens.

5. **To create a partial invoice for the items you have in stock, select the "Create invoice for selected items" option and then click OK.**

The "Specify Invoice Quantities for Items on Sales Order(s)" dialog box (Figure 10-15) appears. Turn on the "Show quantity available instead of quantity on hand" checkbox to see how many items are *really* available to ship. Quantity available is the quantity on hand minus the quantity on other sales orders or already used in assembly items.

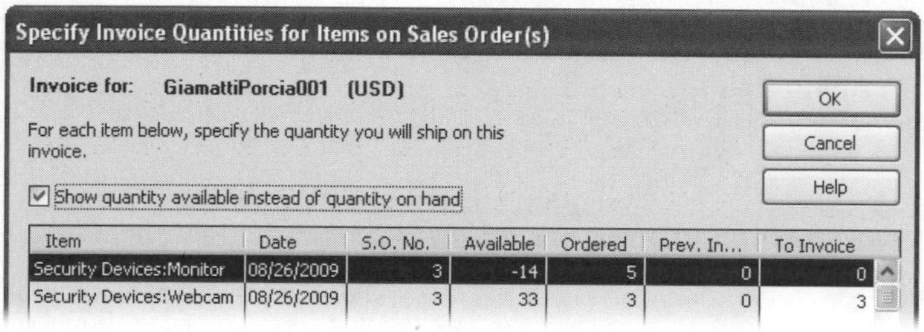

Figure 10-15:
The "Specify Invoice Quantities for Items on Sales Order(s)" dialog box lists each item on the sales order and shows how many items you have in stock. QuickBooks automatically fills in the To Invoice column with the number of items on hand because you usually invoice for only the products you can ship, but you can edit the quantity if you want to invoice for the full order.

6. **Click OK to create the invoice for the in-stock items.**

QuickBooks opens the Create Invoices window and fills in the invoice. Click Save & Close.

7. **Open the Create Sales Orders window again and click Previous until you see the sales order on which you based the invoice.**

The quantity of backordered items appears in the Ordered column. It's a good idea to place an order for the backordered items while it's still fresh in your mind.

8. **In the toolbar, click the down arrow to the right of Create Invoice, and then choose Purchase Order, as shown in Figure 10-16.**

The "Create Purchase Order Based on the Sales Transaction" dialog box appears.

9. **Select the "Create purchase order for selected items" option, and then click OK.**

The "Specify Purchase Order Quantities for Items on the Sales Transaction" dialog box opens. QuickBooks automatically fills in the Preferred Vendor with the vendor you designated in the item record (page 111) and the Qty cells with how many items you have to order to fulfill the backorder. If you purchase the items from multiple vendors, select only the items you want to purchase from one vendor and create the purchase order. You'll have to create separate purchase orders for each vendor.

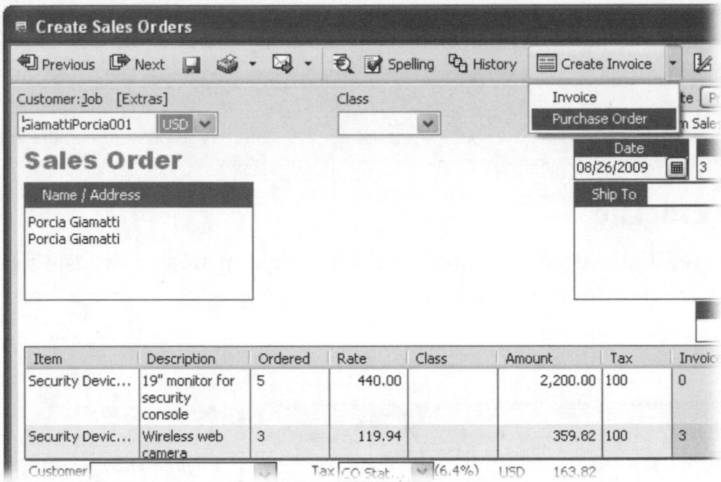

Figure 10-16:
The Create Invoice drop-down menu has two commands. Choose Invoice to create a customer invoice for the items you have on hand to ship. Choose Purchase Order to order items that customers have purchased but you don't have on hand to ship.

10. Click the checkmark cell for each item you want to order. If you want to order some spare inventory, edit the values in the Qty cells. Click OK when you're done.

   The Create Purchase Orders window appears already filled in with the items you're ordering. Although QuickBooks fills in the Vendor box with the preferred vendor, you can choose a different vendor in the drop-down list.

11. When the Purchase Order is filled out the way you want, click Save & Close and send the purchase order to the vendor.

   After you receive the items you ordered to replenish your inventory, return to step 4 to create a final invoice from the sales order.

Estimating Jobs

Many customers ask for an estimate before hiring you. If you're good with numbers, you might tot up the costs in your head and scribble the estimate on a napkin. But creating estimates in QuickBooks not only generates a more professional-looking estimate, it also feeds numbers into your customer invoices as you perform the work. When you create an estimate in QuickBooks, you add the items you'll sell or deliver and set the markup on those items.

QuickBooks estimates make short work of pricing small time and material jobs. But QuickBooks estimating isn't for every business. Particularly in construction, where you might require hundreds or even thousands of items for a major project, you definitely don't want to enter all the data you'd need to build the Item List for your project. That's why most construction firms turn to third-party estimating packages, which come with databases of the services and products you need. Many of these estimating packages integrate with QuickBooks, which means you can import an estimate you created in another program and use it to produce your invoices (see Chapter 24).

Note: The totals on estimates don't post to accounts in your chart of accounts. After all, an estimate doesn't mean that your customer has committed to going ahead with the job. The estimates show the *potential* value of a job without showing up in your financial reports, like the Profit & Loss report. When you turn on the preference for estimates (page 569), QuickBooks creates a *non-posting* account, called Estimates, which is where it stores estimate values. (If you use account numbers, its account number is 4.)

Creating an Estimate

If you've mastered QuickBooks invoices, you'll feel right at home with the fields that appear in a QuickBooks estimate. Figure 10-17 shows the Create Estimates window.

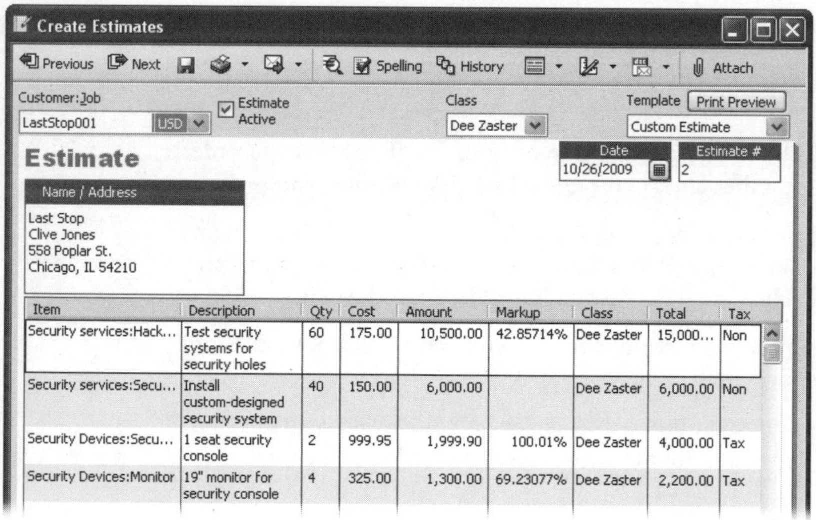

Figure 10-17:
QuickBooks turns on the Estimate Active checkbox (to the right of the customer name) for every estimate you create, which means you can experiment with several and then build your invoices from the one your customer approves. You may wonder where QuickBooks gets the percentages you see in Markup column, especially when they're off the wall, like 42. 85714%. The percentage you see is the markup based on the cost you pay for an item and the sales price you set in the item record (page 117).

Here's how you create an estimate and handle the small differences between invoices and estimates:

1. **On the Home page, click Estimates (or choose Customers → Create Estimates).**

   QuickBooks opens the Create Estimates window and automatically chooses the Custom Estimate template in the Template box. If you've created your own estimate template (page 620), choose your custom template from the Template drop-down list (QuickBooks automatically uses your custom template from then on).

2. **As you do for an invoice, build your estimate by adding items to the line-item table (page 261).**

   In a blank line in the line-item table, in the Item drop-down list, choose the item that you want to add to the estimate. When you fill in the quantity, Quick-Books uses the cost and sales price from the item record to fill in the Cost, Amount, Markup, and Total fields.

   The markup percentage is based on how much you pay for the item and the sales price you charge. If you want to apply a different markup percentage, click the item's Markup cell. Either type the percentage you want to use or choose a price level (page 266) from the drop-down list. (The markup you add is only visible while you work on the estimate. When you print it or email it to your customer, only the cost and total columns appear in the form.)

Note: The calculated value in an item's Total cell isn't set in stone. If you change the Total value, Quick-Books recalculates the markup percentage for you. Likewise, if you change the percentage in the Markup cell, QuickBooks recalculates the value in the Total cell.

---

3. **To email the estimate to your customer, turn on the "To be e-mailed" checkbox.**

   QuickBooks queues up the estimate to be emailed later (page 316). For reasons unknown, you can't queue up an estimate to *print* later. If you want to print an estimate, in the Create Estimates window's toolbar, click the Print icon.

4. **When the estimate is complete, click Save & Close to save the estimate and close the Create Estimates window.**

   After you've created an estimate and printed it or emailed it to your customer, you don't do much with it until the customer gives you the nod for the job.

Creating Multiple Estimates

Whether you're creating a second estimate because the customer thought the first price was too high, or creating separate estimates for each phase of a multiyear job, it's easy to build and manage several estimates for the same job. You've got the following methods at your disposal:

- **Creating an estimate.** You can create additional estimates for a job simply by creating a new estimate (as described in the previous section). When you create additional estimates, QuickBooks makes them active so they appear in the Available Estimates dialog box (page 284) when you choose the corresponding customer in the Create Invoices window. Active estimates also appear in the Estimates by Job report, shown in Figure 10-18.

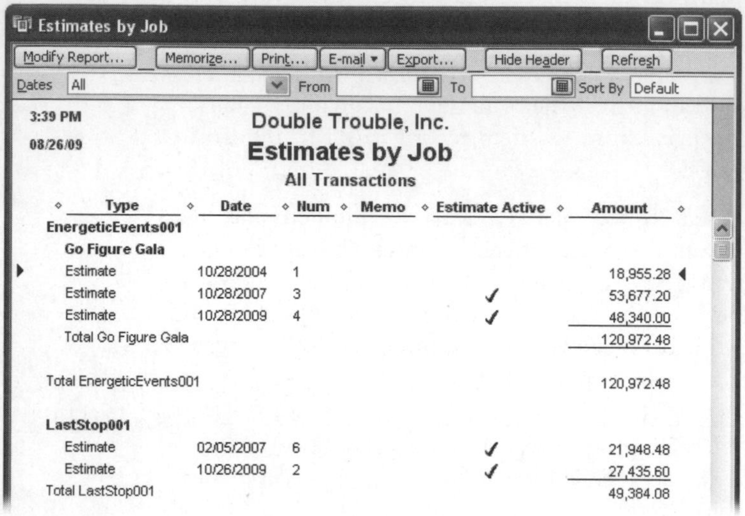

Figure 10-18:
If you have too many estimates to click Previous and Next in the Create Estimates window, try looking at the "Estimates by Job" report. To display it, choose Reports → Jobs, Time & Mileage → "Estimates by Job". This report includes an Estimate Active column, which displays a checkmark if the estimate is active. Double-click anywhere in the line to open that estimate in the Create Estimates window.

- **Duplicating an estimate.** If you want to play what-if games with an existing estimate, duplicate it and then make your adjustments. In the Create Estimates window, display the estimate you want to copy and then choose Edit → Duplicate Estimate or right-click the estimate and choose Duplicate Estimate from the shortcut menu. QuickBooks pulls everything from the existing estimate onto a new one, and it uses the next estimate number in sequence. After you make the changes you want, click Save & Close or Save & New. The box on page 283 tells you how to create boilerplate estimates, which is faster if you intend to duplicate the estimate frequently.

- **Finding an estimate.** When you know the estimate you want exists, you can search for it based on the customer or job, when you created it, the estimate number, or the amount. Choose Edit → Find Estimates or right-click the Create Estimates window and then choose Find Estimates from the shortcut menu. In the Find Estimates dialog box, fill in what you know about the estimate and then click Find. If you click Advanced, QuickBooks opens the full-blown Find window, so you can set up more specific criteria (page 325).

- **Making an estimate inactive.** When you create several estimates for the same work, eventually you and your customer will pick one to run with. Once you've picked an estimate, make the other estimates inactive by turning off their Estimate Active checkboxes. QuickBooks won't display inactive estimates in the Available Estimates dialog box (page 284), but you still have a record of your other attempts, which you can see by clicking Next or Previous in the Create Estimates window or by running the "Estimates by Job" report.

POWER USERS' CLINIC

Building Boilerplate Estimates

Suppose you've put a lot of thought into the typical tasks you perform and the materials you need for different types of jobs. You can capture this information in QuickBooks estimates so that you can quickly produce an estimate that takes into account your performance on similar jobs in the past. Your new customer will be impressed by your speedy response, and you'll be confident that you haven't forgotten anything.

To create a boilerplate estimate, build an estimate with all the information you reuse and then memorize that estimate. Here's how:

1. In the Create Estimates window, fill in all the fields and line items you want in the boilerplate estimate. If you want to capture the items you use but not the quantities, in the line-item table, leave the quantity (Qty) cells blank.

2. To memorize the transaction, press Ctrl+M (or right-click the estimate and choose Memorize Estimate from the shortcut menu).

3. QuickBooks tells you that it removes the Customer: Job so you can use the memorized estimate for any customer. Click OK to dismiss the message.

4. In the Memorize Transaction dialog box, type a name for the memorized transaction. For example, if you're creating a boilerplate estimate for fire mitigation, use a name like Fire Mitigation Estimate.

5. Because you'll recall this estimate only when you get a similar job, choose the Don't Remind Me option.

6. Click OK to add the estimate to your Memorized Transaction List.

7. When you bid on a similar job, press Ctrl+T to open the Memorized Transaction List window.

8. Double-click the memorized estimate to open the Create Estimates window with the memorized estimate information.

9. In the Customer:Job box, choose the new customer. Make any other changes you want.

10. Click Save & Close.

To make an estimate inactive, in the Create Estimates window, display the estimate and then turn off the Estimate Active checkbox. Click Save & New to save the estimate while keeping the Create Estimates window open. If you want to make another estimate inactive, click Previous or Next until the estimate appears, and then repeat the steps.

• **Deleting an estimate.** Deleting an estimate isn't the no-no that deleting an invoice is. Your only risk is that you'll realize you wanted to keep the estimate as soon as you delete it. In the Create Estimates window, display the estimate and then choose Edit → Delete Estimate or right-click the estimate in the Create Estimates window and then choose Delete Estimate from the shortcut menu. In the Delete Transaction dialog box, click OK to complete the deletion.

Note: To protect profit margins from being nibbled away by small changes, many businesses keep track of every change that a customer requests (called *change orders*). The Contractor and Accountant Editions of QuickBooks let you track change orders on estimates.

Creating an Invoice from an Estimate

Whether you create one estimate for a job or several, you can generate invoices from your estimates. In fact, if you choose a customer or job for which estimates exist in the Create Invoices window, QuickBooks displays the Available Estimates dialog box, which lists all the active estimates for that customer or job. This section gives the steps for turning an entire estimate into an invoice. See page 285 to learn how to use estimates to generate progress invoices when you reach milestones on large projects.

To use an estimate to create an invoice, do the following:

1. **Press Ctrl+I to open the Create Invoices window. In the Customer:Job drop-down list, choose the customer or job you want to invoice.**

   If one or more estimates exist for the customer or job, the Available Estimates dialog box opens, showing the active estimates for that customer or job, as shown in Figure 10-19. You don't have to use your estimate to create your invoice if, say, you want to invoice for your actual time and materials. In this situation, click Cancel. The Available Estimates dialog box closes, and the Create Invoices window is ready for you to fill in the line-item table.

2. **In the Available Estimates dialog box, click anywhere in the row for the estimate you want, and then click OK.**

   The Create Invoices window opens with the information from the estimate filled in.

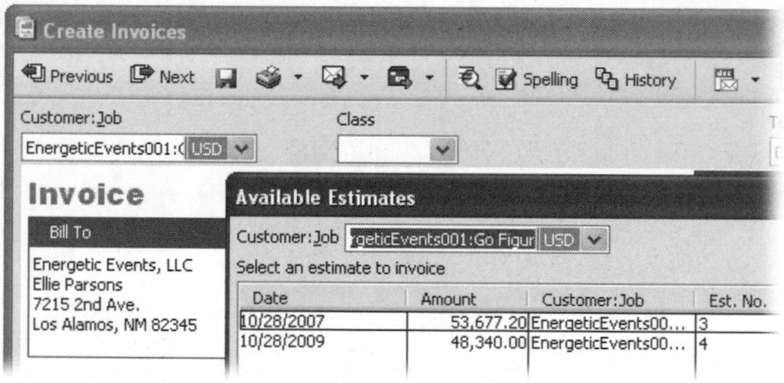

Figure 10-19:
To keep your customer happy, be sure to choose the estimate that the customer accepted. The Available Estimates dialog box shows the date, amount, and estimate number. Usually, the amount is the field you use to choose the agreed upon estimate. Alternatively, when you and the customer have agreed on an estimate, you can delete all the other estimates for that customer or make them inactive, so you have only one estimate to choose.

3. **Make any changes you want and then click Save & Close.**

   You're done.

Comparing Estimates to Actuals

Customers who write you a blank check for a job are rare, so most jobs require estimates of what the work will cost. When you finish a job that you estimated, take some time to run the "Job Estimates vs. Actuals Summary" report to see how you did compared to your estimate. Do this a few times and the accuracy of your estimates should improve dramatically.

If you invoice jobs based on the progress you've made (next section), run the "Job Progress Invoices vs. Estimates" report. This report compares your estimate to actual performance through your most recent progress invoice.

Creating Progress Invoices

When you work on jobs and projects that take more than a few days, you probably don't want to wait until the job is completely finished to charge for some of your work. *Progress invoices* include charges based on your estimate *and* the progress you've made on the job. These invoices are common for jobs that are broken into phases or when payments are made when you reach milestones. Since most large jobs start with an estimate, you won't have to start from scratch when it's time to invoice your customer. QuickBooks can convert your estimates into progress invoices with only a few additional pieces of information.

Note: To produce progress invoices, you first have to turn on the preferences for creating estimates and progress invoicing (page 569).

Progress Invoicing Options

Progress invoices are still invoices; they just happen to link to estimates you've created for a job. In the Create Invoices window, when you choose a customer or job, QuickBooks checks to see if an estimate exists. If there's at least one estimate for the customer or job, QuickBooks opens the Available Estimates dialog box so you can choose an estimate to invoice against.

When you create your first progress invoice (select an estimate in the Available Estimates dialog box and then click OK), you can choose to invoice the entire estimate or only a portion, as shown in Figure 10-20. Following are the options that appear in the Create Progress Invoice Based On Estimate dialog box and when you might use them.

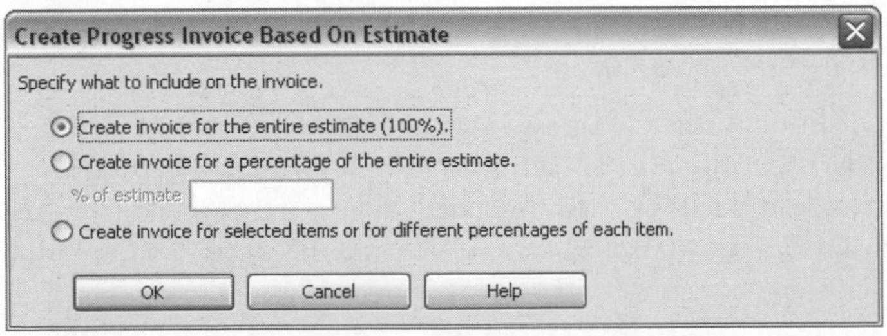

Figure 10-20:
The first progress invoice for an estimated job is the only time the "Create invoice for the entire estimate (100%)" option is available. After the first progress invoice, you have to invoice based on a percentage of the entire estimate, by picking individual items, or for the remaining amounts on the estimate.

- **Create invoice for the entire estimate (100%).** This option is perfect if you prepared an estimate to get approval before starting a job, and you completed the job in a short period of time. QuickBooks takes care of the grunt work of transferring all the services, products, and other items from the estimate to the invoice.

Note: You can edit the invoice amounts that come from an estimate, which is handy if your actual costs were higher than your estimates, for instance. However, the contract you signed determines whether your customer will actually pay the revised amounts!

- **Create an invoice for the remaining amounts of the estimate.** For every progress invoice *after* the first one for a job, you'll see this option instead of "Create invoice for the entire estimate (100%)". Use this option when you're ready to create your last invoice for the job. Its sole purpose is to save you the hassle of calculating the percentages that haven't yet been billed.

- **Create invoice for a percentage of the entire estimate.** Choose this option if you negotiated a contract that pays a percentage when you reach a milestone, such as 15 percent when the house's foundation is complete. (Of course, you and the customer have to agree that a milestone is complete; QuickBooks can't help you with that.) This option is also handy if your contract specifies a number of installment payments. In the "% of estimate" box, type the percent you've completed.

  Suppose your contract includes a clause that covers cost overruns, and the job ended up costing 20 percent more than the estimate. You might wonder how you can charge for that extra 20 percent. The trick is noticing that the "% of estimate" box doesn't limit the percentage to 100 percent. In this example, type 120 percent for the last invoice to reflect the costs that exceeded the estimate.

- **Create invoice for selected items or for different percentages of each item.** This option is the most flexible and a must if you bill your customers only for the work that's actually complete. For example, if you're building an office complex, one building might be complete while another is still in the framing phase. When you select this option, you can choose the services and products to include on the invoice and specify different percentages for each one.

  When you select this option and click OK, the "Specify Invoice Amounts for Items on Estimate" dialog box appears, initially showing your estimated amounts and any previously invoiced amounts. The next section tells you how to fill in this dialog box.

Fine-Tuning a Progress Invoice

When you click OK in the Create Progress Invoice Based On Estimate dialog box (or the "Specify Invoice Amounts for Items on Estimate" dialog box when you choose items to invoice), QuickBooks automatically fills in the estimate items, percentages, and amounts, as shown in Figure 10-21. You don't have to stick with the numbers that QuickBooks comes up with—you can reconfigure the charges on the invoice any way you want. (However, it's always a good idea to review the customer's contract and get approval before you make any increases or additions not covered by the contract.)

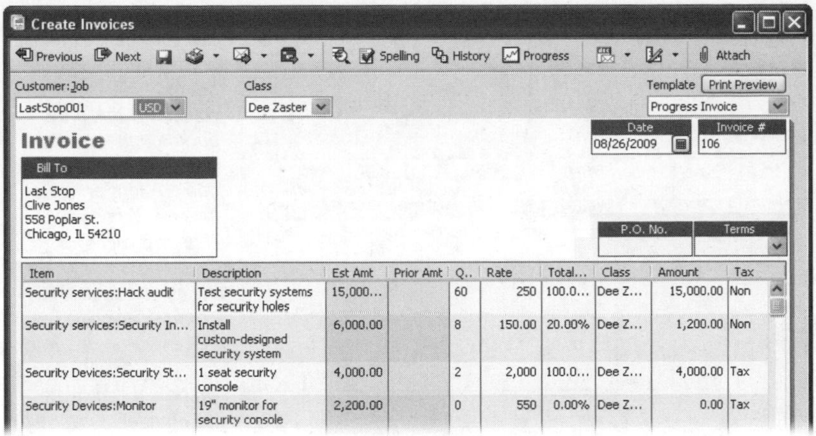

Figure 10-21:
When you provide materials for a job, they're either onsite or not. Assigning 50 percent to materials only makes sense if half the boxes made it. If you created an invoice for 25 percent of the job, you can change the invoice to cover 100 percent for materials by editing the values in the Total % column. Changing a Total % cell also solves the problem of one task that's far behind—or far ahead.

You can modify line items directly in a QuickBooks invoice, but that approach doesn't create a history of your changes. If you want to keep a record of the changes you make between estimate and progress invoice, follow these steps instead:

1. **Open the progress invoice in the Create Invoices window (press Ctrl+I and then click Previous until the progress invoice you want appears).**

   You can also open an invoice from the Customer Center. On the Customers & Jobs tab, select the customer you want. Then, in the Show drop-down list above the transactions table, choose Invoices. Double-click the invoice you want to open.

2. **In the Create Invoices window's icon bar, click Progress.**

   QuickBooks opens the "Specify Invoice Amounts for Items on Estimate" dialog box.

3. **Before you begin changing values, make sure that the correct columns are visible. Turn on the "Show Quantity and Rate" checkbox or the Show Percentage checkbox.**

   QuickBooks remembers the checkboxes you turn on and turns the same ones on the next time you open the "Specify Invoice Amounts for Items on Estimate" dialog box.

4. **To change a value for the progress invoice, click the cell that you want to change, as shown in Figure 10-22.**

   Changing a rate is a rare occurrence. However, it might happen, if, say, you have a contract that bumps your consulting rate by 10 percent for the next calendar year. If the job runs into the next calendar year, you can increase the rate for the hours worked in January.

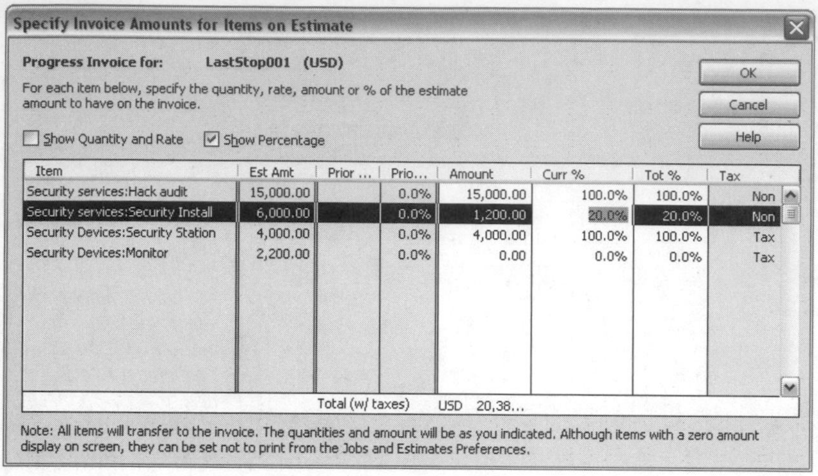

Figure 10-22:
You can change the cells in columns with a white background. The columns with a gray background show the values from the estimate and previous progress invoices. When you change a value, QuickBooks recalculates the other columns. For example, if you type a percentage in a Curr % (current percentage) cell, QuickBooks calculates the amount to invoice by multiplying your estimated amount by the current percentage. The Tot % column shows the total percentage including previously invoiced amounts and the current amount.

5. **To apply the changes, click OK.**

   The "Specify Invoice Amounts for Items on Estimate" dialog box closes, taking you back to the now modified progress invoice.

6. **Save the progress invoice by clicking Save & New or Save & Close.**

Handling Refunds and Credits

If a customer returns a product or finds an overcharge on their last invoice, you have two choices: issue a credit against the customer's balance, or issue a refund by writing a check. In the bookkeeping world, the documents that explain the details of a credit are called *credit memos*. On the other hand, when a customer doesn't want to wait to get the money she's due or she isn't planning to purchase anything else from you, a refund check is the logical solution. In either case, refunds and credits both begin with a credit memo, as shown in Figure 10-23.

Creating Credit Memos

Here's how to create a credit memo:

1. **On the Home page, click Refunds & Credits, or choose Customers → Create Credit Memos/Refunds.**

   QuickBooks opens the Create Credit Memos/Refunds window. If you stay on top of your invoice numbers, you'll notice that the program automatically uses the next invoice number as the credit memo number.

2. **As you would for an invoice, choose the Customer:Job.**

Choose a class if you use classes; and, if necessary, choose the credit memo template you want to use.

3. **In the line-item table, add a line for each item you want to credit.**

Be sure to include all the charges you want to refund, including shipping charges and taxes.

Note: If you want to include a customer message, in the Customer Message box, choose the message from the list.

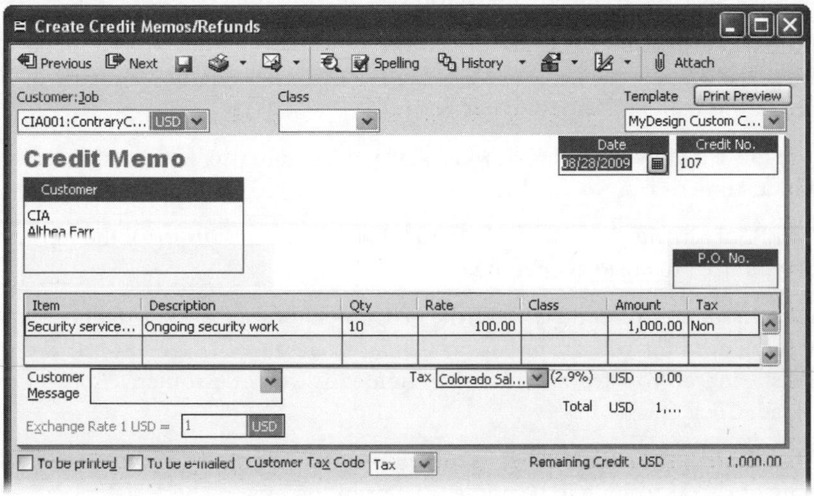

Figure 10-23:
A credit memo is like an invoice except that the items you add represent money flowing from you to the customer instead of the other way around. Don't enter negative numbers—QuickBooks takes care of calculating the money due based on the value of the items.

4. **If you want to print or email the credit memo, turn on the "To be printed" or "To be e-mailed" checkbox.**

5. **Click Save & Close when you're done.**

When you save a credit memo with an available credit balance, the Available Credits dialog box appears with three options for handling the credit, as shown in Figure 10-24.

Creating Refund Checks

If your customer is dreadfully disgruntled, you'll probably want to write a refund check. If you didn't do that when the Available Credit dialog box appeared (see the previous section), here's how to do it now.

1. **Open the Customer Center and select the disgruntled customer. In the Show drop-down list, choose Credit Memos.**

The list of open credit memos for the customer appears.

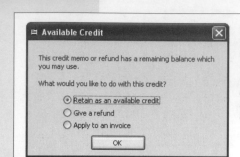

Figure 10-24:
When you save a credit memo with available credit, QuickBooks displays the Available Credit dialog box. If you choose "Give a refund", QuickBooks opens the Write Checks window so you can write the refund check. Choosing "Apply to an invoice" works only if you have an open invoice for the customer. To keep the credit around and apply it (page 290) to the next invoice you create for the customer, choose "Retain as an available credit".

2. **Double-click the credit memo that you want to refund as a check.**

   The Create Credit Memos/Refunds window opens to that credit memo.

3. **In the window's toolbar, find the icon on the right that looks like a dollar bill with a hand above it. To create a refund check, click the down arrow to the right of this icon and choose "Give refund".**

   The icon is Intuit's way of showing that you're going to give money back to your customer.

   QuickBooks opens the "Issue a Refund" dialog box and fills in all the information you need to create the refund.

4. **In the "Issue this refund via" box, the program chooses Check, and chooses the checking account you set in your checking preferences (page 554). If the red face staring at you from across the counter is your customer, choose Cash instead. Click OK.**

   If the "To be printed" checkbox is turned on, QuickBooks adds the check to the queue of checks waiting to be printed. To print the refund check right away, you need to find the check in your checking account register and open it in the Write Checks window (right-click the check transaction and choose Edit Check from the shortcut menu). Then, in the Write Checks window's toolbar, click Print.

Note: If you've signed up for the QuickBooks Merchant Service (page 605) and accept credit card payments, you can also refund money via credit card.

Applying Credits to Existing Invoices

If a customer has an unpaid invoice or statement, you can apply a credit to that invoice or statement and reduce the amount that the customer owes. Applying a credit to an invoice is almost like receiving a payment, so when you choose a customer or job in the Receive Payments window, QuickBooks tells you if the customer has available credits and discounts. Here's how to apply that credit to an invoice:

1. **On the Home page, click Receive Payments.**

   QuickBooks opens the Receive Payments window.

2. **In the Received From drop-down list, choose the customer whose credit you want to apply.**

   Below the invoice table, QuickBooks displays a message that the customer has available credit and shows the amount of the credit.

3. **To select the invoice or statement to which you want to apply the credit, click anywhere in the line for the invoice or statement except the Checkmark column (Figure 10-25).**

   Clicking the Checkmark column chooses the invoice to receive a real payment from the customer.

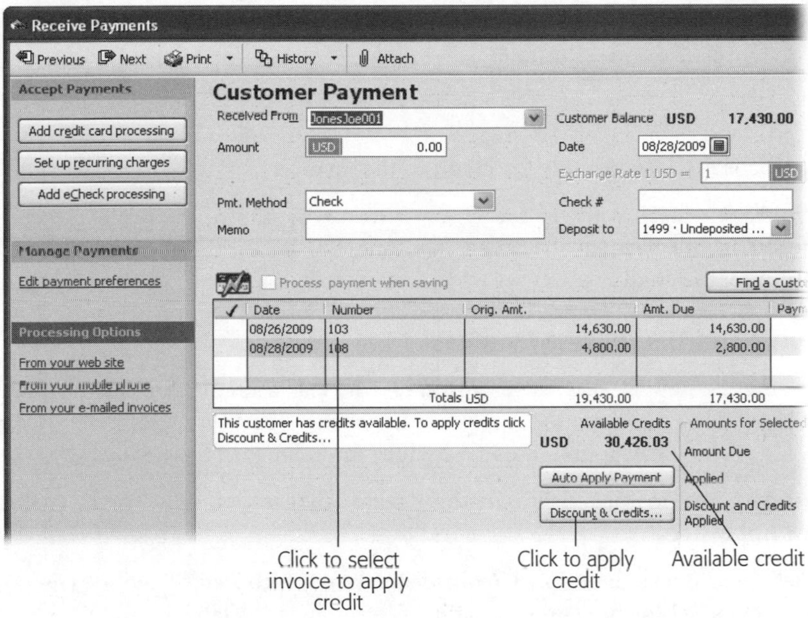

Figure 10-25:
If you didn't choose a job in the Received From drop-down list, the Available Credits value represents the total credits available for all jobs for that customer. To select an invoice for a credit, click anywhere in the invoice row—except the Checkmark cell, which selects the invoice for payment.

4. **Click Discount & Credits.**

   QuickBooks opens the "Discount and Credits" dialog box, as shown in Figure 10-26. If you don't see the credit you expect, it might apply to a different job or to the customer only. To apply one of the customer's credits, click the checkmark for that credit to turn it on.

5. **In the "Discount and Credits" dialog box, click Done.**

   After all this, the Receive Payments window doesn't look very different, but there's one important change: In the Credits column for the open invoice, you'll see the value of the credit. The amount due won't change until you receive the actual payment.

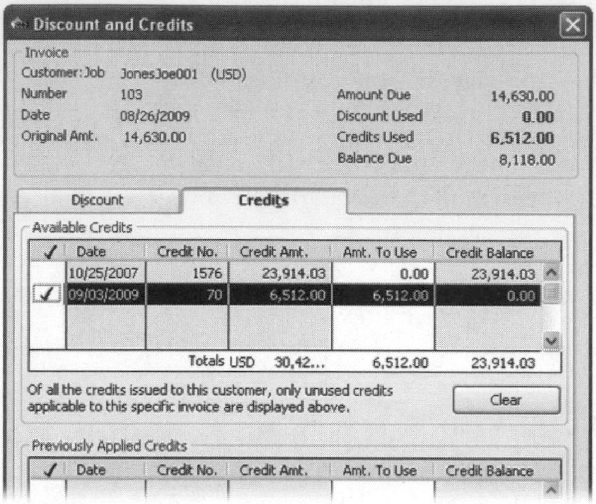

Figure 10-26:
When you turn on credit checkmarks, the Credits Used value shows the total amount of credit you applied. Balance Due shows how much is still due on the invoice. If the original invoice balance is less than the available credit, QuickBooks applies only enough of the credit to set the invoice balance to zero. You can apply the remaining credit to another invoice by repeating the steps in this section.

6. Click Save & Close to apply the credit to the invoice.

   If you open the invoice in the Create Invoices window, you'll see the credit amount in the Payments Applied field and the Balance Due reduced by the amount of the credit.

Applying Credits to New Invoices

If you create a new invoice for a customer who has a credit due, in the Create Invoices window, you'll see the Apply Credits button (below the item table) come to life. Here's how you apply a credit to reduce the balance of the invoice:

1. **With the new invoice visible in the Create Invoices window (press Ctrl+I), click Apply Credits.**

   QuickBooks opens the Apply Credits dialog box, which looks like the "Discount and Credits" dialog box, except that it has only a Credits tab.

2. **Turn on the checkmarks for each credit you want to apply to the invoice, and then click Done.**

   In the Create Invoices window, you'll see the credit amount in the Payments Applied field and the Balance Due reduced by the amount of the credit.

Editing Invoices

If you're still in the process of creating an invoice or sales receipt, you can jump to any field and change its value, delete lines, or insert new ones. Even after you've saved an invoice, editing is easy. Any time an invoice is visible in the Create Invoices window, you can click any field and make any change you want. If you've already printed the invoice, turn on the "To be printed" checkbox so that you don't forget to reprint the form with the changes you made.

If you've received a payment against an invoice, editing that invoice is *not* the way to go, because the edits can disrupt the connections between payment, invoice, and accounts to the point that you'll never straighten it out. If you undercharged the customer, simply create a new invoice with the missing charges on it. If you charged the customer for something she didn't buy, issue a credit memo or refund (see page 288).

Voiding and Deleting Invoices

Sometimes, you want to eliminate an invoice—for instance, when you create an invoice by mistake and want to remove its values from your accounts. Quick-Books provides two options, but for your sanity's sake, you should *always* void invoices that you don't want rather than deleting them.

When you void an invoice, QuickBooks resets the dollar values to zero so that your account balances show no sign of the transaction. However, it also marks the transaction as void, so you know what happened to it when you stumble upon it in the future.

If you delete an invoice, QuickBooks truly deletes the transaction, removing the dollar values from your accounts and deleting any sign of the transaction. All that remains is a hole in your numbering sequence of invoices and an entry in the audit trail that says you deleted the transaction (page 640). If your accountant or the IRS looks at your books a few years down the road, your chances of remembering what happened to the transaction are slim. If an invoice has a payment attached to it, deleting the invoice is even more problematic: You have to delete the bank deposit first, followed by the customer's payment, and finally the invoice.

To void an invoice, do the following:

1. **In the Customer Center, find the transaction you want to void (page 322), and then double-click it to open its window.**

   The window that opens depends on the type of transaction you double-clicked. For example, Create Invoices opens for an invoice, and Enter Sales Receipts opens for sales receipts.

2. **When you see the invoice in its window, right-click in the window and then choose Void Invoice from the shortcut menu. (Or, choose Edit → Void Invoice.)**

   All the values in the form change to zero and QuickBooks adds the word "VOID:" to the Memo field. As a reminder of the reason that you voided the transaction, type the reason after "VOID:" in the Memo field.

3. **Click Save & Close.**

Note: If you open the Accounts Receivable register window, you might get nervous when you see the word Paid in the Amt Paid column of a voided transaction. Don't get excited. Notice that the amount paid is zero. You'll also see the word Void in the Description field. The word Paid in the Amt Paid column is QuickBooks' somewhat skewed way of telling you the invoice is no longer open.

CHAPTER 11

Producing Statements

Statements are the perfect solution for businesses that charge for time and other services in bits and pieces, such as law offices, wireless telephone services, or astrology advisors. Statements summarize the statement charges racked up during the statement period (usually a month). This type of sales form is also great for showing payments and outstanding balances, the way your cable bill shows the charges for your monthly service, the Pay-Per-View movies you ordered, your last payment, and your current balance. So even if you invoice your customers, you can send statements to show them their previous balances, payments received, new charges, and overdue invoices. (To learn about the limitations of statements, see page 251.)

In this chapter, you'll learn how to produce statements, whether you accumulate charges over time or simply summarize your customers' account status.

Producing Statements

You don't fill in a QuickBooks statement in one fell swoop the way you do invoices and sales receipts. Think of a statement as a report of all the charges and payments during the statement period that you then send to your customer. A statement's previous balance, charges, and customer payments all depend on the dates you choose for the statement. Businesses typically send statements out once a month, but you can generate statements for any time period you want.

In QuickBooks, creating statements is a two-step process:

1. **Enter the statement charges, which are the services or other items you delivered to your customers. (If you use statements simply to show invoices, payments, and the resulting balance, you can skip this step.)**

2. **After all the statement charges are complete, generate statements for your customers.**

Creating Statement Charges

Statement charges look like the line items you see in an invoice, except for a few small but important omissions. When you select an item for a statement charge, you won't see any sales tax items, percentage discounts, subtotals, or groups in your item list, because QuickBooks doesn't let you use those features in statements. You don't see payment items either, because QuickBooks automatically grabs any payments that have been made when you generate the statement.

Here are the types of items in your Item List that you can use to create statement charges:

- Service items

- Inventory Part items

- Non-inventory Part items

- Other Charge items

Unlike invoice line items, you create statement charges directly in the Accounts Receivable register for the customer or job that has racked up charges, as shown in Figure 11-1. A statement charge has fields much like those for a line item in an invoice, although they're scrunched into two lines in the Accounts Receivable register.

Entering statement charges is the first step in preparing *billing statements* to send to customers. The charges land in the customer's Accounts Receivable register, just as the total for a customer's invoice does. Here's how to create a statement charge:

1. **Choose Customers → Enter Statement Charges or on the Home page, click Statement Charges.**

   The Accounts Receivable window opens. (Or you can press Ctrl+A to open the Chart of Accounts window and then double-click the Accounts Receivable account.)

2. **In the Customer:Job drop-down list, choose the customer to whom you want to assign the statement charge.**

   The Accounts Receivable window filters the transactions to show only accounts receivable for the customer or job you choose.

Note: If you set up the customer or job to use a foreign currency, you can't record statement charges directly in the Accounts Receivable register. Instead, in the Accounts Receivable window's toolbar, click Edit Transaction. The Make General Journal Entries window opens so you can record the charge there.

3. **In a blank line in the Accounts Receivable register, in the Item drop-down list, choose the item you want to charge for.**

   When you choose an item, QuickBooks fills in the Rate and Description fields with the rate and description from the item record (page 109). QuickBooks sets the Type to STMTCHG to denote a charge that appears on a statement rather than an invoice. The program initially copies the value in the Rate field to the Amt Chrg field (the total amount for the charge).

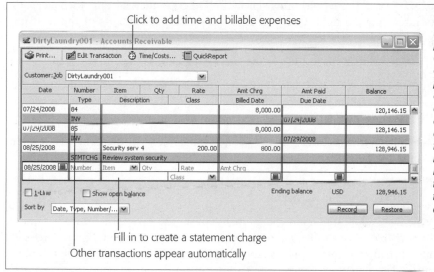

Click to add time and billable expenses

Fill in to create a statement charge

Other transactions appear automatically

Figure 11-1:
Because invoices and payments post to your accounts receivable account, statements can pull those transactions automatically from your accounts receivable account register. To create statement charges for billable time, costs, or mileage, in the Accounts Receivable window's toolbar, click Time/Costs to add statement charges for those items.

Note: If you track billable time, costs, or mileage, you can create statement charges for those items in one fell swoop. In the Accounts Receivable window's toolbar, click Time/Costs to add statement charges for those items. The "Choose Billable Time and Costs" dialog box that opens is the same one you see when you add billable time and costs to an invoice (page 270).

4. **Press Tab to move to the Qty field, and then type the quantity for the item. (If you don't use a quantity and rate, type the amount charged directly in the Amt Chrg field.)**

   Just as you do for invoice line items, enter the quantity based on the units for the item (page 261). When you move to another field (by pressing Tab or clicking the field), QuickBooks updates the total amount charged (in the Amt Chrg field) to the rate multiplied by the quantity.

Tip: If the item you add has a fixed price, you can skip the Qty field. QuickBooks fills in the Rate field and copies that value to the Amt Chrg field.

5. **If you want to change the rate, press Tab to move to the Rate field, and type the value you want.**

   When you change the value in the Rate field, QuickBooks recalculates the amount in the Amt Chrg field.

6. **If you want to revise the description for the charge (which appears on the statement you create later), edit the text in the Description field.**

   QuickBooks automatically fills in the Description field with the first paragraph of the Sales description from the item record, but you can see only a smidgeon of it. To see the whole thing, click the Description field and then keep the pointer over the field. QuickBooks displays the full contents of the field in a pop-up tooltip just below the field.

7. **If you use classes (page 138), in the Class field, choose the one you want.**

   You can skip the Class field, but when you try to save the statement charge, QuickBooks asks if you want to save it without a class. Click Save Anyway to omit the class, or click Cancel to return to the transactions so you can add the class.

8. **To control which statement the charge appears on, in the Billed Date field, choose the date for the charge.**

   If you don't choose a Billed Date, QuickBooks uses the date in the Date field to gather the charge onto a statement.

   When you add a statement charge that you want to save for a future statement, be sure to choose a Billed Date within the correct time period. For example, if a membership fee comes due in April, choose a Billed date during the month of April. The statement charge won't show up until you generate the customer's April statement. On the other hand, if you forgot a charge from the previous month, set its Billed date to a day in the current month so the charge appears on this month's statement.

9. **If you plan to assess finance charges for late payments, in the Due Date field, choose the date when payment is due.**

   QuickBooks uses the date in the Due Date field along with your preferences for finance charges (page 561) to calculate any late charges due. (The due date is based on the terms you apply to the customer [page 76].) But late charge calculations don't happen until you generate statements.

10. **To save the statement charge, click Record.**

Tip: If you charge the same amount every month, memorize (Ctrl+M) the first statement charge and set its recurrence schedule to the same time each month (page 319). QuickBooks then takes care of entering your statement charges for you, so all you have to do is generate customer statements once a month.

Generating Customer Statements

QuickBooks is a smart program, but it can't read your mind. The statements you generate include only the statement charges and other transactions you've entered. Before you produce your monthly statements, double-check that you've entered all customer payments, credits, or refunds that your customers are due, and all new statement charges for the period.

As Figure 11-2 shows, everything about the statements you generate appears in the Create Statements window, including the date range for the statements, the customers you want to send statements to, the template you use, printing options, and finance charges. To begin creating statements, on the Home page, click Statements (or choose Customers → Create Statements). The sections that follow explain the choices you can make and the best way to apply them.

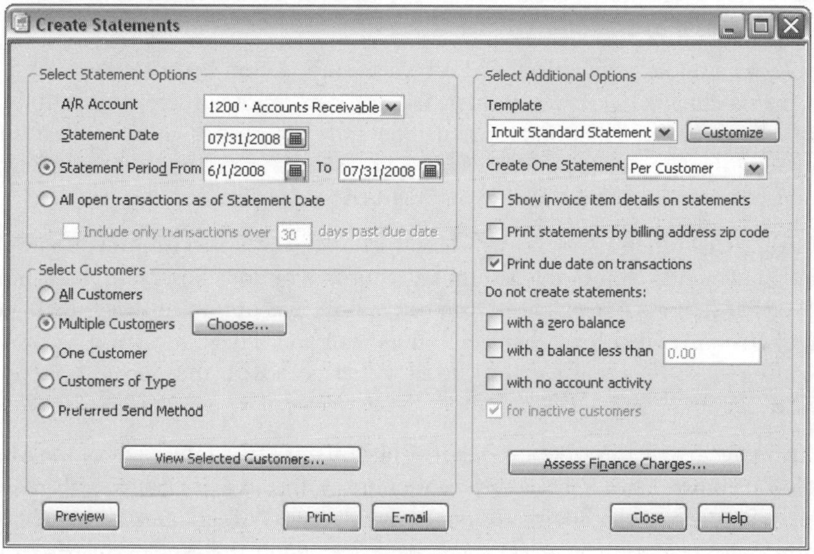

Figure 11-2:
Usually, you'll create statements for all your customers. But you can also generate statements for just a subset. For example, if you send statements to some customers by email and to some by U.S. mail, you can generate statements based on the send method. You'll create two sets: one for email and the other for paper. You might also create a statement for a single customer if you made a mistake and want a corrected version.

Choosing the date range

Statements typically cover a set period of time, like a month. But the date of the statement doesn't have to be during that period. For example, you might wait until the day after the period ends so you're sure to capture every transaction. In the Select Statement Options section, you can choose the statement date and the date range for the statement charges:

- **A/R Account.** If you've turned on the multiple currency preference (page 570), your company file has an Accounts Receivable account for each currency that you use. Before you generate statements, in the A/R Account drop-down menu, choose the correct currency Accounts Receivable account for the statements you want to create. (That's right—you have to repeat the statement generation steps for each currency you use.)

- **Statement Date.** Type the date that you want to appear on the statement. In Figure 11-2, the statement date is the last day of the statement period.

- **Statement Period From _ To _ .** This is the option you choose to create statements for a period of time. For example, if you produce monthly statements, in the From box, choose the first day of the month, and in the To box, choose the last day of the month.

- **All open transactions as of Statement Date.** Choosing this option adds every unpaid statement charge to the statement, regardless of when the original charges happened. This option is particularly helpful when you want to generate a list of all overdue charges so you can send a gentle reminder to woefully tardy customers. To filter the list of open transactions to only those overdue by a certain number of days, turn on the "Include only transactions over _ days past due date" checkbox, and type the number of days late.

Selecting customers

QuickBooks automatically selects the All Customers option because most companies send statements to every customer. But you can choose other options to limit the list of recipients. (The program remembers the option you chose the last time you opened the Create Statements window and selects it automatically.) Here are your customer options and reasons you might choose each one:

- **Multiple Customers.** To specify the exact set of customers to whom you want to send statements, choose the Multiple Customers option. For example, if most of your customers pay by check, you can choose this option to select the handful of customers that have charge accounts with you. This option also works for selecting customers that use the currency that goes with the Accounts Receivable account you selected.

  When you choose this option, a Choose button appears to the right of the Multiple Customers label. Click the Choose button. In the Print Statements dialog box that opens, QuickBooks automatically selects the Manual option. With this option selected, you can select each customer or job that you want to send a statement to by clicking individual customers or jobs or by dragging over several adjacent customers to turn on their checkmarks.

  The Automatic option isn't all that helpful—you must type a customer's name exactly as it appears in the Customer Name field in the customer's record to select that single customer. Unless you have gazillions of customers, scrolling through the list and clicking the name is probably faster.

- **One Customer.** To create a corrected statement for only one customer, choose this option. In the drop-down list that appears, click the down arrow, and then choose the customer or job.

- **Customers of Type.** If you categorize your customers by type and process their statements differently, choose this option. For example, you might spread your billing work out by sending statements to your corporate customers at the end of the month and to individuals on the 15th. In the drop-down list that appears, choose the customer type.

- **Preferred Send Method.** If you print some statements and email others, you'll have to create your statements in two runs. Choose this option and, in the drop-down list that appears, choose one of the send methods. For example, click the E-mail button to send statements to the customers who prefer to receive bills via email. (See page 315 for how to email documents.) Before you click Print or E-mail to produce statements, click View Selected Customers to make sure you've chosen the customers you want.

Tip: If you loathe stuffing envelopes and licking stamps, offer your customers a discount for receiving their statements via email. They're likely to say yes and you can shoot statements out from QuickBooks in a blink of an eye.

Setting printing options

In the Template box, QuickBooks automatically chooses the Intuit Standard Statement template, but you can choose your own customized template instead. In addition, you can control what QuickBooks adds to statements and which statements to skip:

- **Create One Statement.** In the Create One Statement drop-down list, choosing Per Customer can save some trees. QuickBooks generates one statement for each customer, no matter how many jobs you do for them. Charges are grouped by job. If you want to create separate statements for each job, choose Per Job.

- **Show invoice item details on statements.** Turning this checkbox on is usually unnecessary because your customers already have copies of the invoices you've sent, and extra details merely clutter your statement. Besides, if customers lose invoices or have questions, they're usually not shy about calling you.

- **Print statements by billing address zip code.** You'll want to turn on this checkbox if you have a bulk mail permit, which requires that you mail by Zip code.

- **Print due date on transactions.** QuickBooks turns on this checkbox because you'll typically want to show the due date for each entry on the statement.

- **Do not create statements.** Printing statements that you don't need is a waste of time and paper. QuickBooks includes several settings that you can choose to skip certain statements. For example, you can turn on the "with a zero balance" checkbox to skip statements for customers who don't owe you anything. If you want to send a statement to show that the last payment arrived and cleared the balance due, turn off this checkbox.

You might decide to skip customers unless their balance exceeds your typical cost of processing a statement. With a first-class stamp costing 44 cents and the added expense of letterhead, envelopes, and a label, you can skip statements unless the balance is at least $5 or so. Turn on the "with a balance less than" checkbox and, in the box to the right of the label, type the dollar value.

You can also skip customers with no activity during the period, which means *nothing* happened—no charges, no payments, no transactions whatsoever. QuickBooks automatically turns on the "for inactive customers" checkbox because there's no reason to send statements to customers who aren't actively doing business with you.

- **Assess Finance Charges.** If you haven't assessed finance charges already, click Assess Finance Charges to add finance charges due. (You can also assess finance charges before you start the statement process by clicking the Finance Charges icon on the Home page.) In the Assess Finance Charges dialog box, you still have an opportunity to turn off the checkmark for individual customers. For example, if a squirrel ate your customer's last statement, you can turn off the checkmark in that customer's entry to tell Quick-Books not to penalize them with a finance charge.

Previewing Statements

Before you print statements on expensive letterhead or send the statements to your customers, it's a good idea to preview them to make sure you've chosen the right customers and that the statements are correct. In the Create Statements window, click Preview. QuickBooks opens the Print Preview window (Figure 11-3), which works like its counterparts in other programs.

Here's how to preview statements before printing:

1. **Click "Prev page" or "Next page" to view statements.**

   If you left your reading glasses at home, click Zoom In to get a closer look. The Zoom In button switches to Zoom Out so you can return to a bird's-eye view.

2. **To return to the Create Statements window to print or email your statements, click Close.**

   The Print Preview window includes a Print button, but it's not the best way to print your statements. Clicking it begins printing your statements immediately so you have no chance to set your printer options like which printer to use or the number of copies. To set those print settings, as described on page 306, click Close, and then click Print in the Create Statements window.

Generating Statements

When you're absolutely sure the statements are correct, in the Create Statements window, click Print or E-mail to generate your statements. This section describes how to do both.

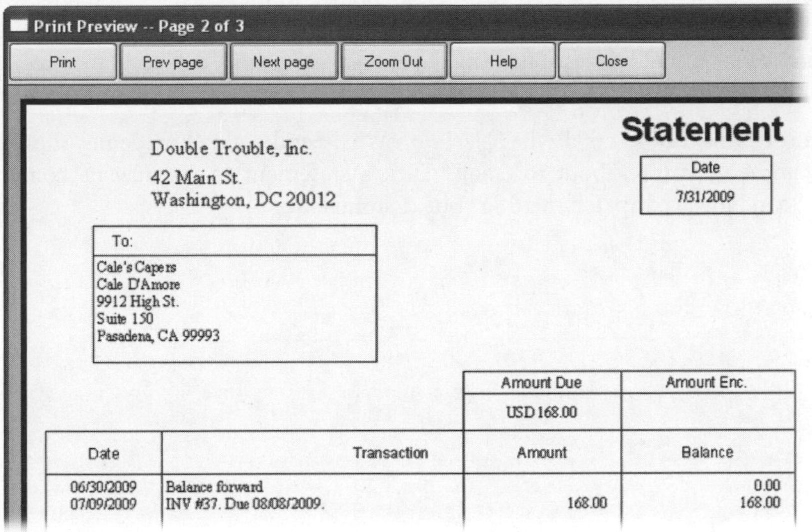

| Print | Prev page | Next page | Zoom Out | Help | Close |

Double Trouble, Inc.

42 Main St.
Washington, DC 20012

Statement

Date
7/31/2009

To:

Cale's Capers
Cale D'Amore
9912 High St.
Suite 150
Pasadena, CA 99993

Amount Due	Amount Enc.
USD 168.00	

Date	Transaction	Amount	Balance
06/30/2009	Balance forward		0.00
07/09/2009	INV #37. Due 08/08/2009.	168.00	168.00

Figure 11-3:
The first line in the body of a statement is "Balance forward", which is the amount due prior to the first transaction for the current statement. The value in the Amount Due field (not shown here) is the result of the Balance forward, plus all the transactions for that customer and job that happened during the statement date range, including payments.

To print your statements, do the following:

1. **In the Create Statements window, click Print.**

   QuickBooks opens the Print Statement(s) dialog box.

2. **Choose the printer you want to use.**

   For example, if you have one printer loaded with preprinted forms, select that printer in the "Printer name" drop-down list. See page 308 to learn how to designate a printer to use every time you print statements.

3. **Select one of the "Print on" options.**

   If you select the "Intuit Preprinted forms" option, QuickBooks doesn't print the name of the form or the lines around fields, because they're already on the pre-printed page. The "Blank paper" option tells the program to print the statement exactly the way you see it in print preview. The Letterhead option shrinks the form to leave a two-inch band at the top of the page for your company logo. If your letterhead is laid out in an unusual way (your logo down the left side of the page, for instance), create a custom statement template that leaves room for your letterhead elements, and then choose the "Blank paper" option.

4. **In the "Number of copies" box, type the number of copies you want to print.**

   For example, if you want one copy for the customer and a second one for your files, type 2.

5. **Click Print.**

To email your statement directly from QuickBooks, in the Create Statements window, click E-mail. If you use Microsoft Outlook, an Outlook window opens with the customer's email address filled in. The message contains the standard message you've set up for statements (page 580).

If you use QuickBooks email, the Select Forms To Send dialog box opens, showing the statements you're about to email. Click a statement to preview its content. Click Send Now to dispatch them to your customers.

CHAPTER 12

Transaction Timesavers

QuickBooks can zip you through the two basic ways you distribute your invoices and other sales forms: on paper and electronically. But within those two distribution camps, you can choose to send your forms as soon as you've completed them or place them in a queue to send in batches. For sporadic sales forms, it's easier to print or email them as you go. But when you generate dozens or even hundreds of sales orders, invoices, or statements, printing and emailing batches is a much better use of your time.

When you have workhorse transactions that you enter again and again, Quick-Books can memorize them and then fill in most, if not all, of the fields in future transactions for you. For transactions that happen on a regular schedule—like monthly customer invoices or vendor bills—the program can remind you when it's time to record a transaction, or add the transaction without any help from you. But you can also memorize transactions that you use occasionally, such as estimates, and call on them only when you need them.

QuickBooks' search features can also save you time, which you can appreciate if you've ever hunted frantically for a transaction. Whether you want to correct a billing problem on a customer invoice, check whether you paid a vendor's bill, or look for the item you want to add to an estimate, QuickBooks gives you several ways to search: You can look for different types of transactions within various date ranges in the Customer, Vendor, and Employee Centers. The Item List window sports a few search boxes for finding the items you want. On the other hand, the Find command is perfect for surgical searches. And Google search fans can install Google Desktop and use its magical powers to find anything in QuickBooks and the rest of your computer.

Printing Sales Forms

Before you start printing, you have some setup to do. But once QuickBooks' print settings are in place and there's paper in your printer, you can print forms with a click or two. For each type of form you print, QuickBooks wants to know the printer you want to use, the paper you print to (like preprinted forms or letterhead), and a few other details. The program remembers these settings, so you have to go through this process only once. From then on, QuickBooks fills the settings in automatically in the Print dialog box, but you can change them before you print if you want.

With these prep tasks behind you, you're ready to print. In QuickBooks, you can print a form right away or add it to a queue to print in batches. This section explains how to accomplish all these printing tasks.

Tip: If you want to make sure you don't forget to send your sales forms, you can create reminders (see page 573) for invoices, credit memos, sales receipts, and, if you use QuickBooks Premier or Enterprise, sales orders, that are queued up to print.

Setting Print Options

Many of the printer options in the "Printer setup" dialog box are the same as options you can set within your operating system, as you'll see in Figure 12-1. To assign and set up printers for forms in QuickBooks, choose File → Printer Setup. Then, choose the following settings:

- **Form Name.** You're free to print your invoices to your letterhead, timesheets in landscape orientation, and checks to a printer filled with preprinted checks. In QuickBooks, each form has its own print settings. In the Form Name dropdown list, choose the form you want to set up for printing.

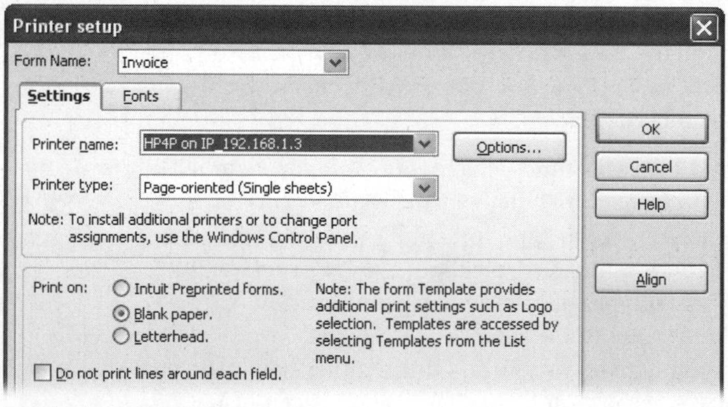

Figure 12-1:
The printers that you set up in your operating system are the ones that appear in QuickBooks' "Printer name" list. The program starts with the printing preferences you set up outside QuickBooks, but you can adjust those options by choosing a printer and then clicking Options.

- **Printer name.** Choose a printer to anoint as the standard for the form you selected (see the box on page 308). When you're printing forms, QuickBooks automatically selects this printer, but you can choose a different printer (page 311)—for instance, when you switch between printing paper documents and creating Adobe .pdf files that you can email.

GEM IN THE ROUGH

Managing Documents

The new document management feature in QuickBooks 2010 adds a whole new level of organizing power. It lets you attach documents to records in your company file, so for example, you can attach an electronic copy of a job contract to a customer record, a purchase order to a vendor record, a customer's complaint letter to a credit memo, or a photo to an item you sell. Just click the paperclip icon you see in the Customer Center, the Create Invoices window, and similar places. Sounds great, right? For a number of reasons, you may want to think twice about signing up for this new—and still evolving—service.

The biggest downside to QuickBooks' approach to document management is that it stores the attached documents *on the Internet.* When you launch document management, the program opens a browser window and asks you to log in. That means you might not be able to access your documents when you need them, for instance, if your Internet connection is slow as molasses or falters due to snow storms, sunspots, or bad network juju. Moreover, you might want your business documents to stay safe and sound on your own computer, rather than on an Intuit server. (Online storage does let you access your documents from any computer, but you can accomplish that by obtaining a static IP address for your computer or signing up for a service that lets you access your computer from anywhere. That way, you can access all your files, not just the ones in QuickBooks document management.)

Another disadvantage: this service isn't free. When this book was written, Intuit hadn't announced how much online document storage would cost. The first 100 MB of storage space is free, but you'll pay for more storage after that.

Document management has some annoying overhead as well. First, you have to sign up for the service separately for each company file you want to attach documents to. After that, when you open a company file, you have to log in using your Intuit account (page 29) to access document management. By comparison, other programs, including Microsoft Office, let you insert hyperlinks into your documents. These hyperlinks can point to a web page, a file on a shared drive, or a file on your computer, so you can link to your files regardless where they reside—at no extra charge and with no logins.

If you want to use the do-it-yourself approach to document management, set up a folder structure on your computer to organize your business documents. You can't click an icon in QuickBooks to access a related document, but you can give QuickBooks Search (page 320) a few keywords, like *invoice 915 spycam,* to find the files you need in no time.

On the other hand, you might like the convenience of opening related files by clicking the paperclip icon in QuickBooks, or scanning documents from within the program and immediately attaching them to records or storing them to attach later on. If you want to give QuickBooks document management a try, choose Company → Document Management → Learn About Document Management. (When you first open your company file in QuickBooks 2010, a window might pop up telling you about this new feature.)

UP TO SPEED

Setting a Default Printer for Forms

Before you print *any* documents in QuickBooks (not only invoices and other sales forms, but timesheets, pay stubs, reports, and so on), take a few minutes to set up the printer (or printers) you use. In QuickBooks, you can assign different printers for each type of document you generate. This feature can save a lot of time, wasted paper, and frustration, especially if you print invoices to multipart forms, paychecks to preprinted check forms, statements to your letterhead, and reports to plain paper. Keep each printer stocked with the right type of paper and you can print your documents with barely a glance at the print options.

Although you can assign a different printer to each of the 20 different QuickBooks forms, you probably have only one or two printers stocked with special paper. In addition, you can bypass printer setup for the forms you print using basic settings, such as printing to your workhorse printer on blank paper and using portrait orientation.

By first setting up printers in QuickBooks, the program fills in the print settings for you automatically when you print. Print dialog boxes still appear, so you can change any print options before committing your documents to paper.

QuickBooks keeps the options you choose within the program separate from the settings for the printer within the operating system. For example, if you use Windows printer options to set your most popular printer to portrait orientation, you can set that same printer to landscape in QuickBooks.

Here's how you assign printers and print options to QuickBooks forms:

1. Choose File → Printer Setup.

2. In the "Printer setup" dialog box, in the Form Name box, choose the form for which you want to assign a printer.

3. In the "Printer name" box, choose the printer you want to use.

4. Choose other print options, such as the type of paper.

5. Click OK.

- **Options.** If you want to adjust the properties for the printer you chose, click Options. Depending on the type of printer, in the printer Document Properties dialog box, you can change the document orientation, page order, pages per sheet, print quality, paper tray, color, and so on.

- **Printer type.** This setting and the others that follow in this list appear for most of the forms in the Form Name drop-down list, but not when you select Report or Graph. When you choose a printer name, QuickBooks fills in the "Printer type" box with its best guess of the type (and usually guesses right). If QuickBooks guesses wrong, simply choose the correct type in the drop-down list. If the printer feeds individual pages through, such as letterhead or blank paper, choose "Page-oriented (Single sheets)". If a printer feeds continuous sheets of paper with perforations on the edges, such as the green-striped paper so popular in the past, choose "Continuous (Perforated Edge)".

- **Intuit preprinted forms.** If you purchase preprinted forms, which typically include your company information, field labels, and lines that separate fields, choose this option. When you print your documents, QuickBooks sends only the data to fill in the form.

Note: When you use preprinted forms, a small misalignment can make your documents look sloppy and unprofessional. See the next page to learn how to align your documents to the paper in your printer.

- **Blank paper.** This option tells QuickBooks to print everything on your document template: company information, logo, labels, and data. This is also the easiest way to print because you don't have to worry about aligning the paper and the form. If you set up a template with your company logo and attractive fonts (page 621), you can produce a professional-looking form on blank paper.

- **Letterhead.** When you print to letterhead that already includes your company address and other information, you don't need to print that information on your documents. Choose this option to suppress the printing of your company information.

- **Do not print lines around each field.** Turning on this checkbox is a matter of personal preference. Lines around each field make it clear which information belongs to which label, but you might consider those lines unnecessary clutter. If your template separates fields to your satisfaction, turn off this checkbox to print only the labels and data, not borders around each field. Because preprinted forms include borders, QuickBooks automatically turns on this checkbox if you choose the "Intuit preprinted forms" option.

Aligning Forms and Paper

If you've ever gotten lost at your office supply store, you understand why printing includes so many options. You can print on different types of paper using different types of printers, and making the two line up properly can be a delicate process. Besides the invoices and other sales forms themselves, you might print ancillary documents like mailing labels and packing slips.

To save some trees and your sanity, make sure that the paper in your printer is aligned properly *before* you print, especially if you print to fancy letterhead or preprinted forms. When you use preprinted forms or continuous-feed paper with perforations for page breaks, the alignment of the paper is crucial. Otherwise, your data won't appear next to the correct labels or an invoice might print over the page break. It's a good idea to check the alignment of your forms and paper every time you print, but it's particularly important if you're printing a batch of documents. There's no faster way to waste time and paper than printing a big stack of invoices that don't line up with your expensive letterhead or preprinted forms. Here's how to save time, paper, and your mental health:

1. **Choose File → Print Forms, and then choose the type of form you want to print.**

   Select the forms you want to print and click OK to open the Print *<form>* dialog box, such as Print Invoices if you're printing invoices.

Note: You can align your form to printer paper in the "Printer setup" dialog box; click Align. As long as you don't move the paper in the printer, you won't have to align the paper each time you print. However, if someone else monkeys with the printer, you can align the form from the Print dialog box.

2. **To align your form to the paper, in the Print dialog box, click Align.**

   If you have more than one template to choose from, QuickBooks opens the Align Printer dialog box.

3. **Choose the template you want to use to align your paper, and then click OK.**

   If you're printing to a page-oriented printer, QuickBooks displays the Fine Alignment dialog box, described in step 4.

   If you're using a continuous-feed printer, your first step is a coarse alignment: Position the paper so the print head is just below a page break, click Coarse, and then click OK to print a sample form. Don't adjust the paper in your printer (QuickBooks warns you several times not to). The form that prints includes text indicating a pointer line. When the Coarse Alignment dialog box appears, in the Pointer Line Position box, type the number of the line preprinted in the paper margin. QuickBooks uses that line number to align the form and the paper. Click OK to print another sample. When the alignment is correct, click Close. You can then perform a fine alignment if necessary.

4. **In the Fine Alignment dialog box, shown in Figure 12-2, in the Vertical and Horizontal boxes, type numbers to represent the hundredths of an inch to move the form to line it up with the paper.**

   After you tweak the alignment, click Print Sample to check the printed form's appearance. When the form is aligned, click OK—and keep your mitts off the paper in the printer.

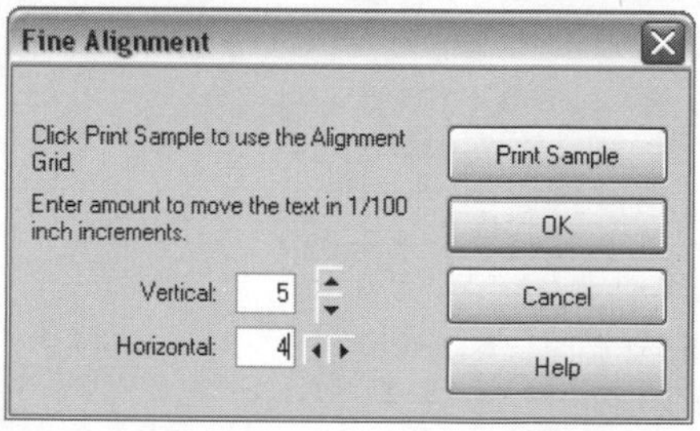

Figure 12-2:
A positive number in the Vertical box moves the form toward the top of the page. A positive number in the Horizontal box moves the form to the right on the page. Negative vertical and horizontal numbers move the form down and to the left, respectively.

Choosing a Print Method

Each type of sales form in QuickBooks gives you the same basic methods and options for printing documents on the Print drop-down menu, shown in the Create Invoices window in Figure 12-3.

Here's a guide to your choices for printing documents:

- **Print one form.** If you want to print the current form, in the form window's icon bar, click the Print icon. If you click the down arrow to the right of the Print icon, you can choose any of the print commands from the drop-down list. For instance, you can preview the form you're about to print, print the current form, print all the forms in your queue, or print special forms such as packing slips.

- **Printing in batches.** When you turn on the "To be printed" checkbox (below the line-item table in the window), QuickBooks adds the current form to a queue of forms that you'll print as a batch.

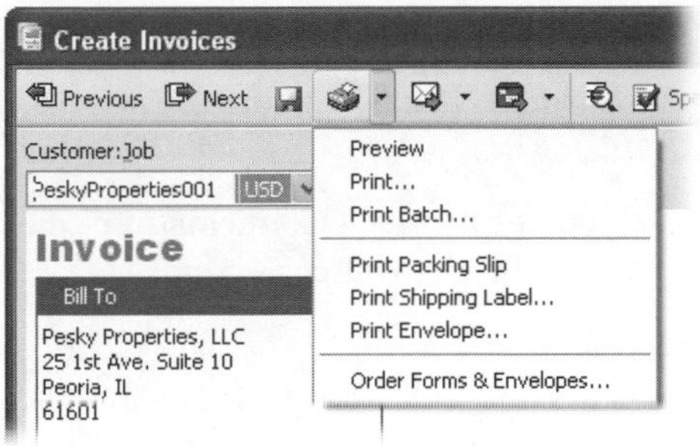

Figure 12-3:
*From a sales form window, you can print one document at a time or queue them up to print in batches. To process batches of several different types of documents, you can also choose File →
Print Forms.*

Printing One Form

When you display a form in its corresponding window, you can preview and print it right away. For example, in the Create Invoices window, to print the displayed invoice, click the Print icon or click the down arrow next to the Print icon and then choose Preview or Print. You'll see the Print One Invoice dialog box, where you can choose the printer and paper.

Note: To prevent embezzling, QuickBooks automatically saves a form when you print it. That way, if you change the form after you print, the audit trail shows a record of the change.

Printing in Batches

When you turn on the "To be printed" checkbox before you save a form, QuickBooks adds that form to a print queue. After you've checked that your printer contains the correct paper and that the paper is aligned properly, you can print all the forms in the queue in just a few steps:

1. **Choose File → Print Forms and then choose the type of forms you want to print. (Or, in the form window, like Create Invoices, for example, click the down arrow to the right of the Print icon and then choose Print Batch.)**

   QuickBooks opens the "Select *<type of form>* to Print" dialog box with all unprinted forms selected, as shown in Figure 12-4.

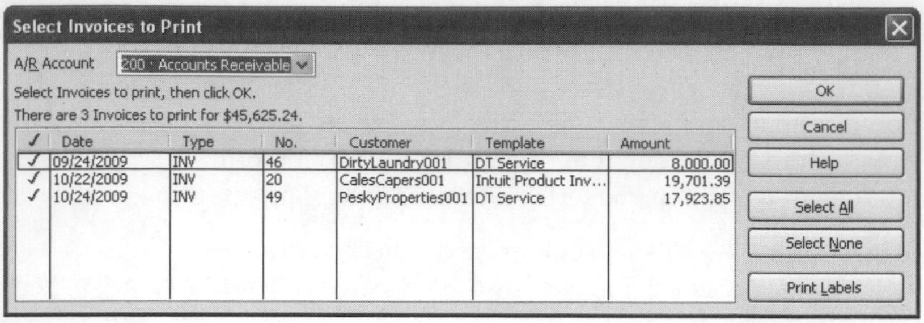

Select Invoices to Print

A/R Account 200 · Accounts Receivable ▾

Select Invoices to print, then click OK.
There are 3 Invoices to print for $45,625.24.

✓	Date	Type	No.	Customer	Template	Amount
✓	09/24/2009	INV	46	DirtyLaundry001	DT Service	8,000.00
✓	10/22/2009	INV	20	CalesCapers001	Intuit Product Inv...	19,701.39
✓	10/24/2009	INV	49	PeskyProperties001	DT Service	17,923.85

OK
Cancel
Help
Select All
Select None
Print Labels

Figure 12-4:
To remove any of the forms from the batch, click their checkmarks to turn them off. If you want to print labels, first click Print Labels. Then, after the labels have printed, click OK to print the forms.

2. **Click OK to print the selected forms in the queue.**

   QuickBooks anticipates the problems that can happen during printing (paper jams, low toner, or smears). After the program prints the forms, it opens the "Print *<type of form>* - Confirmation" dialog box.

3. **If a problem occurred, in the "Print <type of form> - Confirmation" dialog box, click the Reprint cell for each form that didn't print correctly.**

   If the whole batch is a loss, click Select All.

4. **Click OK to reprint the forms.**

Printing Mailing and Shipping Labels

QuickBooks can print mailing labels to go with the forms you print. Because the program prints labels for the customers selected in the "Select *<type of form>* to Print" dialog box, you have to print the labels *before* you print the forms. Here's how:

1. **Choose File → Print Forms, and then choose the type of forms for which you want labels.**

   QuickBooks opens the "Select *<type of form>* to Print" dialog box with all unprinted forms selected.

   If you want to print labels for a mailing without an associated sales form (like an open house announcement) choose File → Print Forms → Labels

2. **In the "Select *<type of form>* to Print" dialog box, click Print Labels.**

   QuickBooks opens the "Select Labels to Print" dialog box and automatically chooses the Name option, which prints labels for the customers or vendors associated with each form waiting to print.

3. **If you've created forms for a specific customer type or vendor type, choose the Customer Type or Vendor Type option and, in the drop-down list, choose the type you want to print labels for.**

   These options are better suited for printing labels *not* associated with your queued forms—for example, when you want to send a letter to your retail customers informing them of product rebates. Or you might use them if you process forms for retail and wholesale customers at different times of the month.

4. **To filter the printed labels by location, turn on the "with Zip Codes that start with" checkbox, and type the beginning of the Zip code area you want, as shown in Figure 12-5.**

   For example, if you're offering a seminar for people in the Denver area, you can type *801* in the box.

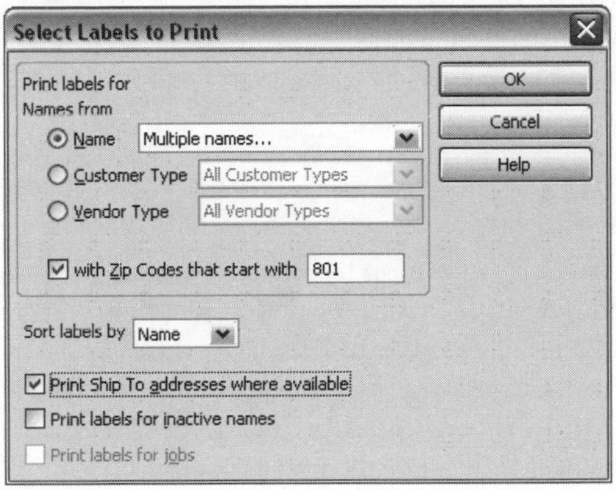

Figure 12-5:
If you want to print labels for a mailing that has nothing to do with money (like an announcement about your new office location) choose File → Print Forms → Labels. The "Select Labels to Print" dialog box opens, so you can jump right to selecting the recipients.

5. **In the "Sort labels by" box, choose Name or Zip Code.**

   If you use bulk mail, choose Zip Code so you can bundle your mail by Zip code as your bulk mail permit requires.

6. **If you want to print shipping labels rather than labels that use billing addresses, turn on the "Print Ship To addresses where available" checkbox.**

   The "Print labels for inactive names" checkbox might develop some cobwebs, but it can come in handy from time to time—for instance, if you need to send a letter to past and present customers to tell them about a product recall.

   When you send communication to different addresses for each job, even though the jobs are for the same customer, turn on the "Print labels for jobs" checkbox.

7. **After making sure that you've selected the labels you want, click OK.**

   QuickBooks opens the Print Labels dialog box.

8. **If you've already chosen the printer and settings for labels in Printer Setup, click Print and you're done.**

   However, if you want to print to different labels, in the Label Format drop-down list, choose the type of label you use. Find the vendor and label number (like Avery #5262) on the box of labels you have. The drop-down list includes popular Avery label formats along with several other options.

After you print your labels, QuickBooks closes the Print Labels dialog box, and returns to the "Print *<type of form>*" dialog box.

9. **Click OK to continue printing your queued forms.**

Note: For invoices and sales receipts, printing a shipping label for the current form is easy. In the Create Invoices or Enter Sales Receipt windows, click the down arrow next to the Print icon and then choose Print Shipping Label. The drop-down menu also includes the Print Envelope command. For envelopes, you'll have to specify the envelope size and whether you want to include the return address. (Turn off this checkbox if your envelopes have your return address on them.) You can even print a delivery barcode for addresses in the United States.

Printing Packing Slips

When you ship products to a customer, it's common to include a packing slip that tells the customer what they should have in their shipment. In QuickBooks, printing packing slips is a labor-intensive task because you have to print each packing slip individually from the Create Invoices window. The template that Intuit provides for packing slips is no more than an invoice without prices, no doubt assuming that warehouse workers don't care about the cost of the items they ship.

Here are the steps for printing the packing slip for an invoice:

1. **Open the Create Invoices window (press Ctrl+I).**

   Display the invoice for which you want to print a packing slip.

2. **Click the down arrow next to the Print icon, and then choose Print Packing Slip.**

   QuickBooks opens the Print Packing Slip dialog box, where you can choose print options if necessary.

3. **To print the packing slip, click Print.**

   QuickBooks closes the Print Packing Slip dialog box and prints the packing slip.

4. **Back in the Create Invoices window, click Save & Close.**

   QuickBooks changes the template in the Template box from the packing slip template back to the invoice template.

Tip: If you want QuickBooks to always choose a particular packing slip, change the packing slip template preference. Choose Edit → Preferences. Click the Sales & Customers icon, and click the Company Preferences tab. In the "Choose template for invoice packing slip" box, choose the packing slip template you want to use in most cases, and then click OK.

Emailing Sales Forms

If you've lost interest in paperwork, sending invoices and other sales forms electronically is much more satisfying. But to make your electronic sending as efficient as possible, make sure that all your customer records include the email addresses you want to use. Otherwise, you'll waste time typing email addresses one after another. The chance of a typo increases with each address you type.

If you use Outlook, Outlook Express, or Windows Mail, QuickBooks automatically uses your email program to send forms. QuickBooks opens new messages in your email program, which you can edit as you would any email. Then when you send the email, it shows up in your Sent Items folder or Sent Box.

If you use a different email program, you can still email sales forms using QuickBooks E-mail, which is a free service—you just have to register your email address. With QuickBooks E-mail, sending a form or a batch of forms opens a browser window to the QuickBooks E-mailing site. After the service sends your email, you'll see a message telling you that your messages were sent successfully.

Tip: Send yourself a test email to make sure QuickBooks emailing works.

Choosing a Send Method

QuickBooks has three ways to send sales forms. Similar to printing, you can email the current form or add forms to a queue to send in batches. Intuit also offers the QuickBooks' invoice mailing service (a subscription service described in the box on page 316).

- **Send one form.** If you want to email the current form, in the window's toolbar, click the Send icon, which looks like an envelope with an arrow, as shown in Figure 12-6.

- **Sending in batches.** When you turn on the "To be emailed" checkbox below the line-item table in a form window, QuickBooks adds the current form to the queue of forms that you'll email all at once. The Create Estimates window has a "To be emailed" checkbox, but for some reason, doesn't include a "To be printed" checkbox.

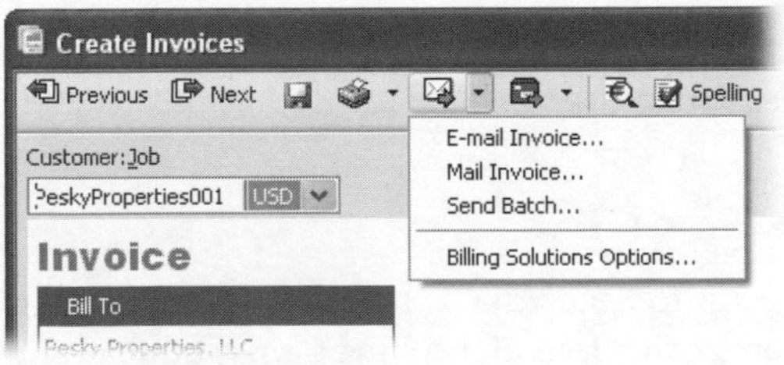

Figure 12-6:
If you click the down arrow to the right of the Send icon, you can choose any of the send commands from the drop-down list. For example, you can email the form you're about to print, send all the forms in your queue to be emailed, or send the invoice to the QuickBooks' invoice mailing service.

QuickBooks Mail Invoice Service

When you click the down arrow next to the Send icon, you'll see the Mail Invoice command. If you're perplexed by Intuit's decision to add a postal mailing option to the Send menu, the answer is in poor command naming. When you choose the Mail Invoice command, QuickBooks opens the Send Invoice dialog box, where you can send the invoice to QuickBooks' mailing service. The "Mail through Quick-Books" option is part of QuickBooks' Billing Solution service. This service costs money but it prints, folds, and mails your invoices to customers. The cost is $14.95 a month plus $.79 per invoice. If you're short of both time and office staff, it could be worth the money.

Invoices go to a centralized mail center that prints customized black and white invoices using your logo and invoice template, stuffs envelopes, and mails invoices with remittance tearoffs and return envelopes.

If you add the Merchant Services feature (another subscription service described on page 605), then your customers can pay via credit card. By subscribing to the invoice mailing service and Merchant services, your customers can pay you online with a credit card for any invoice—no matter how you sent it. This approach also means you can download payments into QuickBooks, reducing your transaction entry. And the Merchant service gets your payments into your bank account faster.

Emailing One Form

Here's how to email a form when you're looking at it in its corresponding window. These steps use the Create Invoices window as an example, but the steps work equally well for other sales forms.

1. **In the Create Invoices window, click the Send icon.**

    What happens when you click Send depends on the email program you use. If you use Outlook, Outlook Express, or Windows Mail, your email program opens and creates a new message with the fields from QuickBooks filled in, as shown in Figure 12-7.

2. **Modify the message in any way you want.**

    You can change the email addresses, subject, and email text that QuickBooks automatically adds.

3. **Click Send.**

Emailing in Batches

When you turn on the "To be e-mailed" checkbox for forms you create, Quick-Books adds them to an email queue. You can send all the forms that you've queued up in just a couple of steps:

1. **Choose File → Send Forms.**

    QuickBooks opens the "Select Forms to Send" dialog box, which lists all of your unsent forms of every type. The program selects all pending forms automatically.

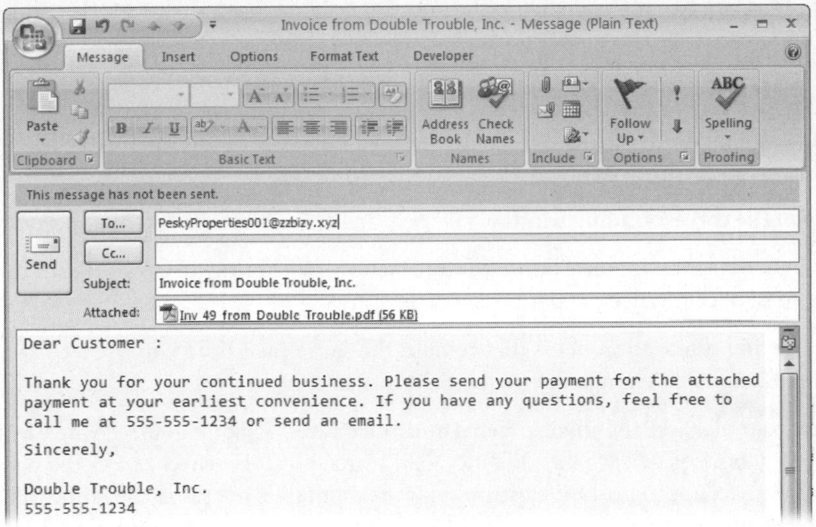

Figure 12-7:
Send the message as you would an email you created in your email program. For Outlook, click the Send button. When you email an invoice, QuickBooks attaches the form as an Adobe .pdf file. Customers who don't have Acrobat Reader installed on their computers can click the Acrobat Reader link to download the reader for free. Otherwise, the customer can just double-click the link to open the attachment.

2. **If you want to skip some of the forms, click their checkmarks to turn them off.**

   Click Select None to deselect all the forms. Click Select All to select all of the forms. You can also drag over several checkmarks to toggle their settings. When you select a form to send, a preview of the message appears below the table. If you notice a change that you want to make to the message, click Edit E-mail. In the Send <form name> dialog box, edit the message and then click OK to return to the "Select Forms to Send" dialog box.

3. **When you're ready, click Send Now.**

Note: You can also email forms from the window where you create those forms. For example, in the Create Invoices window, click the down arrow to the right of the Send icon, and choose Send Batch.

Memorized Transactions

When you enter the same transactions over and over, memorizing them for reuse saves time. QuickBooks can fill in most, if not all, of the fields for you. It can remind you to enter a transaction, such as a recurring client invoice for retainers, or even add the transaction without any help from you. For example, if your company's Internet service costs $259 each month and you pay it with an automatic credit card payment, you can memorize that credit card charge and tell Quick-Books to automatically enter the same credit card charge each month. Once you memorize a transaction, all you have to do is to choose the transaction you want to reuse and make sure that the values in the new transaction are correct before you save it.

Note: Memorizing bills you pay regularly is described in detail on page 211. The box on page 283 explains how you can memorize a boilerplate estimate to use on similar jobs in the future.

The Memorized Transactions List is an anomaly on the Lists menu because you don't create memorized transactions the way you do entries on other lists. Instead, you memorize existing transactions:

1. **Open the corresponding window for the transaction you want to memorize.**

   You can memorize any kind of transaction, including checks, credit card charges, bills, invoices, and journal entries.

2. **Fill in any transaction fields that remain the same each time you use a transaction. If the value changes, leave the field blank.**

   For example, add the invoice items and their rates. If your hours change from invoice to invoice, leave the Quantity field blank. Or, for a check, enter the payee and the account to post the expense to. If the amount is the same each time, fill in the amount. If the amount changes, leave the Payment or Deposit field blank. Later, when you use the memorized transaction, QuickBooks fills in all the fields except the ones you left blank, which you fill in with the value you want.

3. **In the transaction window (Create Invoices, for example), select the transaction and press Ctrl+M to open the Memorize Transaction dialog box, shown in Figure 12-8.**

   If you memorize a transaction in an account register, QuickBooks automatically fills in the Name box with the transaction's Payee name. If you memorize a form, the Name box remains blank until you fill it in.

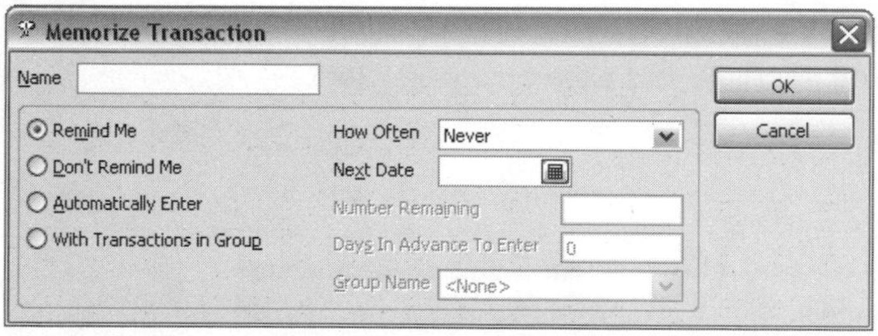

Figure 12-8:
You can also open this dialog box by right-clicking in a transaction window, such as the Create Invoices window, and then choosing Memorize Invoice (or Memorize Check, Memorize Credit Card Charge, and so on).

4. **In the Memorize Transaction dialog box, in the Name box, type a name that you'll recognize when you see it in the Memorized Transaction List.**

   You can use names like Monthly Telephone Bill or Health Insurance Premium for bills you pay, a customer name combined with a sales form, or the type of retainer, such as Full-time Programming Contract.

5. **Choose an option to specify whether you want QuickBooks to remind you when to enter transactions.**

Choosing the Remind Me option is the best of both worlds: QuickBooks adds the memorized transaction to the Reminders list and reminds you when it's time to enter the next transaction, but you can choose to skip the transaction. If you choose this option, specify how often you want to be reminded and pick the next date for a reminder. For example, if you pay your phone bill on the 10th of each month, in the How Often box, choose Monthly and in the Next Date box, pick the 10th of the next month.

If you don't use a transaction on a regular schedule, choose the Don't Remind Me option. QuickBooks won't add the memorized transaction to the Reminder List. When you want to use the transaction again, press Ctrl+T to open the Memorized Transaction List window. Select the transaction and click Enter Transaction.

If you want QuickBooks to enter the transaction on its next scheduled date without any action on your part, choose the Automatically Enter option. When you select this option, be sure to specify, in the Number Remaining box, the number of times QuickBooks should enter the transaction. Otherwise, your company might continue to make an installment payment long after the last payment was due. You can also specify how many days in advance you want QuickBooks to enter the transaction. Providing a few days of lead time helps you avoid late payments, as well as insufficient funds charges from your bank.

(Memorize sales forms with the "To be printed" or "To be e-mailed" checkbox turned on, so that the form appears when you go to print or email forms.)

6. **To memorize the transaction, click OK.**

If you want to use the transaction immediately, in the Memorized Transaction List window, simply click Enter Transaction. (If you create a memorized group [page 213], select the group, and then click Enter Transaction to record all the memorized transactions in the group.) If you created an invoice or other form simply to set up a memorized transaction, click Clear, and then click the Close button to close the window without saving the form.

Tip: See page 573 to learn how to convince QuickBooks to display reminders whenever you open your company file so you actually see them. That way, when you open the company file, the program displays a Start Up box that asks if you want to enter memorized transactions. Click Now to add them.

Using a Memorized Transaction

If you memorize a transaction that you use from time to time, you need a way to create a new transaction when you need it. You'll also use this technique if you set up a memorized transaction on a schedule, but want to create one right away. Here's how you use a memorized transaction:

1. **Choose Lists → Memorized Transaction List (or press Ctrl+T).**

   The Memorized Transaction List opens.

2. **Select the memorized transaction, and then click Enter Transaction.**

   The corresponding transaction window opens, such as Create Invoices, Write Checks, or Enter Credit Card Charges.

3. **Make any changes you want, and then click Save & Close.**

   That's all there is to it!

Editing a Memorized Transaction

Editing the information in a memorized transaction is technically editing and rememorizing it. Choose Lists → Memorized Transaction List to open the Memorized Transaction List window. Select the transaction and click Enter Transaction. Do your editing, and then press Ctrl+M to rememorize it with the changes you've made. When you click Replace, the edited transaction takes the place of the previous one in the Memorized Transaction List.

If the transaction *information* is correct but you want to change the recurrence schedule, select the memorized transaction in the Memorized Transaction List and press Ctrl+E to edit it. The Schedule Memorized Transaction dialog box appears with settings for reminders and the recurrence (page 318).

Finding Transactions

If you want to answer a customer's question about what they owe, it's easier when you have the invoice in front of you. The Create Invoices window shows only one invoice at a time, which can mean some furious clicking if you're trying to find one specific invoice out of the hundreds you've sent. QuickBooks has an all-encompassing search feature that uses Google Desktop to search not only transactions in your company file but files and emails on your entire computer. Whether you want to find overdue invoices, purchase orders, or paychecks, the Customer, Vendor, and Employee Centers make it easy to find transactions for a particular customer, vendor, or employee. The Item List window also has a few tools for finding the items you want. For more precise searches—to find all invoices that contain an item that's been recalled, say—the Find command is the way to go.

Searching with Google Desktop

If you use Google Desktop on your computer or the Google website, you already know how omniscient Google search can be. You can use the Google-powered QuickBooks Search to look for QuickBooks transactions, list items, even data outside your company file based on search criteria like names, amounts, dates, or text tucked away in bashful fields. Just like Google's regular search, you can search for multiple words or entries that don't contain the words you specify.

Tip: If you have Google Desktop (QuickBooks installs it the first time you use Search), you're ready to search. But if you're just getting on the Google Desktop bandwagon, click Edit → Search. If Google Desktop isn't installed, simply click OK to install it. In a few seconds, QuickBooks says you can use QuickBooks Search, which uses Google Desktop. If you listen closely, you'll hear your hard drive whirring. That's Google Desktop indexing your data so it can deliver results in nanoseconds.

Here's how to search using Google Desktop:

1. **Choose Edit → Search (or, on the QuickBooks icon bar, click the Search icon, which looks like a magnifying glass).**

   The QuickBooks Search browser window opens with a refreshingly simple search page reminiscent of the Google web page.

2. **In the search box, type the words or values you want to find, as shown in Figure 12-9.**

   You can type uppercase or lowercase letters and receive the same results. To search for an exact phrase, such as a customer or vendor name, type the phrase within quotes. To find results that *don't* contain the words or values you specify, type a hyphen (–) in front of the word, for example, "-audit" to throw out results that contain "audit".

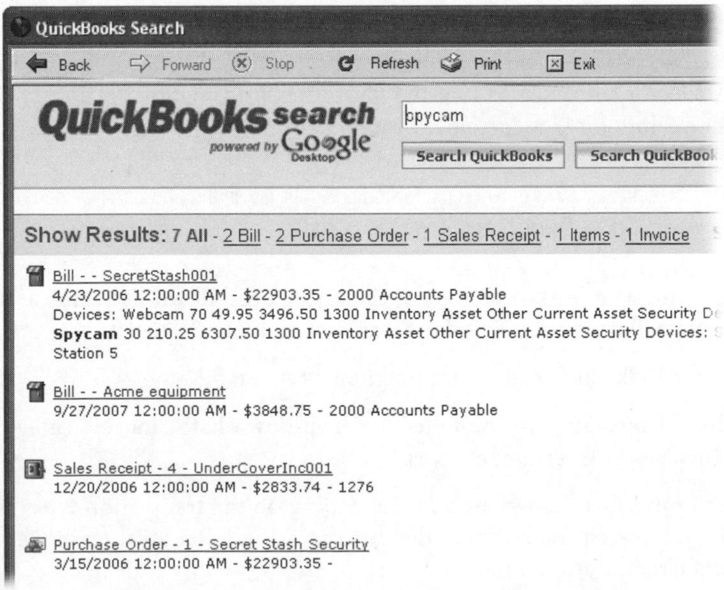

Figure 12-9:
Above the results, QuickBooks Search shows the different types of results it found and the number of each type. For example, the search in the figure found an item in 2 bills, 2 purchase orders, 1 sales receipt, 1 invoice, and 1 item.

3. **To search only in QuickBooks, click Search QuickBooks. To search Quick-Books and your computer, click "Search QuickBooks and Desktop".**

Searching your desktop along with QuickBooks finds files like Word documents, Excel spreadsheets, and emails. (The Search can peer inside files for the text you're looking for.)

4. **To narrow your search, type additional words in the search box.**

You can combine words that you want to include or exclude, such as "security audit -hack".

5. **To view a result, click its link.**

QuickBooks opens the corresponding window to the transaction or list item, such as Create Purchase Orders for a purchase order or the Edit Item List window for an item.

Searching with QuickBooks Centers

The Customer Center is a quick way to answer basic questions about your customers like "What sales orders are still open?" or "Has the customer paid all the invoices I've sent?" Likewise, you can track down bills, bill payments, and other vendor transactions in the Vendor Center. The Employee Center performs similar tasks for transactions like paychecks and nonpayroll transactions.

Here's how to use QuickBooks' centers to find transactions, using the Customer Center as an example:

1. **On the Home page, open the Customer Center by clicking Customers. On the Customer & Jobs tab, click the name of the customer or job.**

The list of active customers and jobs initially appears on the left side of the Center. When you select a customer or job, the Customer Information section at the top-right shows info for that customer or job record.

Tip: If you have trouble finding the customer on the Customer & Jobs tab, in the Find box, type part of the customer's name and then click the Search button, which has an icon that looks like a magnifying glass.

---

2. **To see a specific type of transaction, in the Show drop-down list, choose the transaction type like Invoices or Refunds, as shown in Figure 12-10.**

Initially, QuickBooks shows all the transactions of that type.

3. **To filter the list by status, in the Filter By drop-down list, choose a category like Open Invoices or Overdue Invoices.**

The choices in this drop-down list vary depending on the transaction type. For example, if you search for refunds, the choices are All Refunds, Cash/Check Refunds, and Credit Card Refunds.

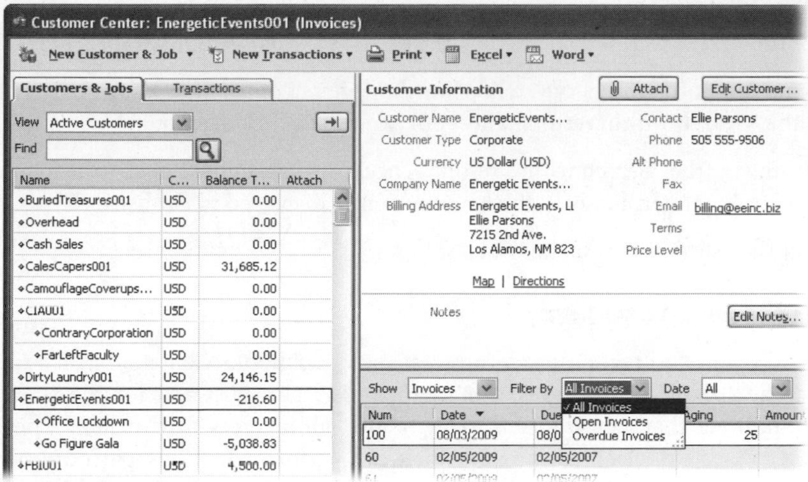

Figure 12-10:
As soon as you choose an entry in the Show, Filter By, or Date drop-down list, QuickBooks changes the transaction list to show only the transactions that meet all three criteria.

4. To find a transaction within a date range, in the Date drop-down list, choose the date range.

   The date range choices are the same as the ones you can choose for reports (page 508).

5. Double-click a transaction in the list to open the corresponding window to that transaction.

Finding Items

Since QuickBooks 2009, the Item List window has its own abbreviated search feature. You type what you're looking for, such as an item name or keyword, and the field you want to search, and QuickBooks filters the list for matching results.

Here's how you search for an item:

1. Choose Lists → Item List to open the Item List window.

   Or on the Home page, click Items & Services.

2. In the "Look for" box, type the text or value you're looking for.

   If you type more than one word, QuickBooks looks for items that contain the phrase you typed, for example, "fiber optic" to find all your fiber optic electronic devices.

3. In the "in" drop-down list, choose the field you want to search.

   QuickBooks automatically sets the "in" field to search all fields. If you want to narrow your search, choose Item Name/Number, Description, or another field. You can also choose "Custom fields" to search fields you've added to QuickBooks (page 155).

4. **Click Search.**

   The Item List window displays only the items that match your search criteria.

5. **To narrow your search, type a new word or phrase in the "Look for" box. Turn on the "Search within results" checkbox, and then click Search.**

   Turning on the "Search within results" checkbox tells QuickBooks to search for the new search term only in the items currently displayed in the list.

   To reset the list to display all items, click Reset.

Using the Find Command

The Find command takes more setup than the QuickBooks Centers, but it's ideal for finding specific transactions. For example, it lets you search for the specific invoice number that a customer is asking about, all invoices that include a product that's defective, or all the invoices for work performed by one partner (using classes). In fact, the Find command can mine every transaction field except Description (which is the perfect time to fall back on the Google Desktop–powered Search command (page 321).

The Find window has a Simple tab for straightforward searches and an Advanced tab to build searches as detailed as you want. QuickBooks remembers which one you used for your last search and displays that tab the next time you open the window.

Finding made simple

To use the simple version of the Find command, do the following:

1. **Choose Edit → Find (or press Ctrl+F), and then, in the Find window, click the Simple tab.**

   The Find window opens with the Transaction Type box set to Invoice and all the other fields blank.

2. **In the Transaction Type drop-down list, choose the transaction type (like Purchase Order or Bill).**

   The search fields are almost identical for each transaction type. From and To dates and the amount appear for every type, as shown in Figure 12-11.

3. **Fill in the fields with values you want to search by and then click Find.**

   You can fill in as many or as few fields as you want.

   When you click Find, the matching transactions appear in the table at the bottom of the window. Double-click a transaction to open it in its corresponding window, like Create Invoices for an invoice.

4. **To clear all the fields and start a new search, click Reset.**

   Click Close when you're done.

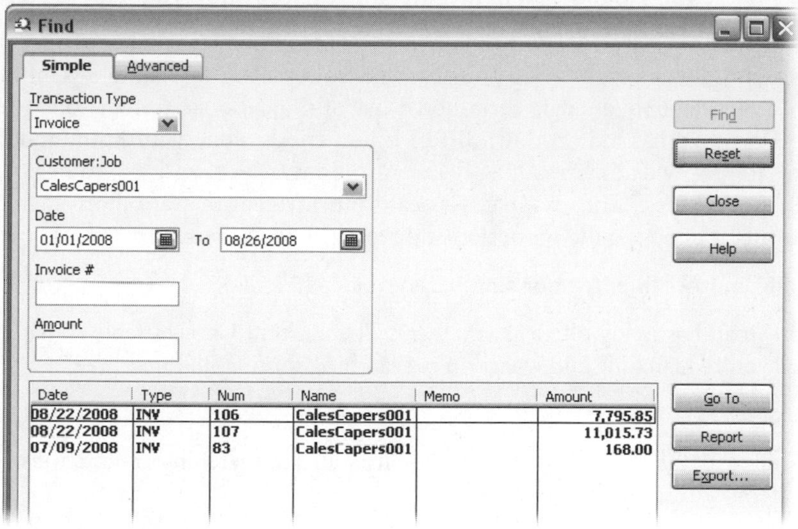

Figure 12-11:
The first field after Transaction type in the Find window is usually Customer:Job. However, it changes to Vendor when you search for purchase orders. The second-to-last field varies depending on the transaction type; for example, Invoice # for an invoice, Ref. No. for a bill, or P.O. No. for a purchase order.

Advanced find methods

The Advanced tab can search any transaction field. You can build up a set of filters to find exactly the transaction you want. Here's how:

1. **Choose Edit → Find (or press Ctrl+F), and then click the Advanced tab.**

   The Advanced tab starts with a clean slate every time you open the Find window.

2. **In the Filter list (Figure 12-12), choose the first field you want to search.**

   The Filter list starts with the most frequently used search fields like Account, Date, Item, and Transaction Type.

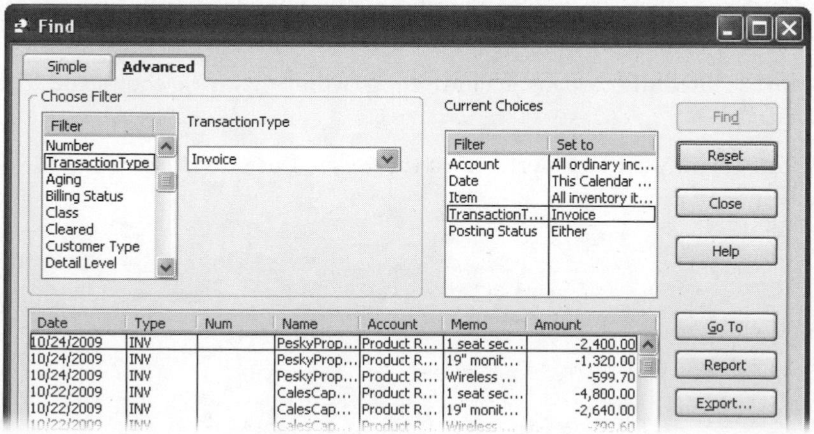

Figure 12-12:
After the most common search fields, other transaction fields appear alphabetically, starting with the Aging field. At the bottom of the Filter list, if you find other fields out of alphabetical order, they're custom fields you've defined (page 155).

3. **Select the settings to the right of the filter list to specify how you want to search the selected field.**

   The settings change depending on the field you select. For example, Transaction Type has only a single drop-down list of QuickBooks transaction types. The Date field has a drop-down list of time periods along with From and To boxes to specify dates. The Aging field has options (=, <=, and >=) to help you find late invoices. (For example, you can find invoices that are more than 30 days late by choosing the >= option and typing 30 in the box.)

4. **To add another filter to your search, repeat steps 2 and 3.**

   You can add as many filters as you want. The Current Choices table shows the fields you're searching and what you're searching for in each one.

5. **Click Find.**

   The table at the bottom of the window lists all the matching transactions (or line items within a transaction).

6. **If you get too many or too few results, repeat steps 2 and 3 to add or change filters, and then click Find again.**

   To edit a filter, select the field in the Filter list and change its settings. To remove a filter from the Current Choices list, select the filter, and then press Backspace.

7. **To clear all the filters, click Reset.**

   Click Close when you're done.

Using search results

After you find what you're looking for, you can inspect them more closely. Click one of the following buttons in the Find window:

- **Go To.** Select one of the results and then click this button to see the transaction in the corresponding transaction window (like Create Invoices) or account register.

- **Report.** This button opens a Find report window, which shows the listed transactions.

- **Export.** If you want to export your results, click this button. See page 596 for more info on exporting.

CHAPTER 13

Managing Accounts Receivable

In between performing work, invoicing customers, and collecting payments, you have to keep track of who owes you how much (known as *accounts receivable*) and when the money is due. Sure, you can tack on finance charges to light a fire under your customers' accounting departments, but finance charges are rarely enough to make up for the time and effort you spend collecting overdue payments. Far more preferable are customers who pay on time without reminders, gentle or otherwise.

On the other hand, sales receipts are the simplest and most immediate sales forms in QuickBooks. When your customers pay in full at the time of the sale—at your used music CD store, for example—you create a sales receipt so the customer has a record of the purchase and payment. At the same time, the QuickBooks sales receipt posts the money for the sale into your bank account (in QuickBooks) or the Undeposited Funds account. You can't use sales receipts for customers who don't pay in full, because sales receipts can't handle previous customer payments and balances.

Because companies need money to keep things running, you'll have to spend *some* time keeping track of your accounts receivable and the payments that come in. In this chapter, you'll learn the ins and outs of tracking what customers owe, receiving payments from them, and dinging them if they don't pay on time. You'll also learn how to create sales receipts for one sale at a time or to summarize a day's worth of merchandising.

The Aging of Receivables

You don't have to do anything special to *create* accounts receivable. They're the by-product of billing and invoicing your customers. But receivables that are growing long in the tooth are the first signs of potential collection problems. Some companies like to check the state of their accounts receivable every day, and with the Company Snapshot, Customer Center and built-in QuickBooks reports, you have three ways to do that in record time.

The Company Snapshot can show the balance each customer owes, as you can see in Figure 13-1. (If you don't see it, click Company Snapshot in the QuickBooks icon bar or choose Company → Company Snapshot.) When you want to see more detail about receivables, turn to QuickBooks built-in aging reports, described in the next section.

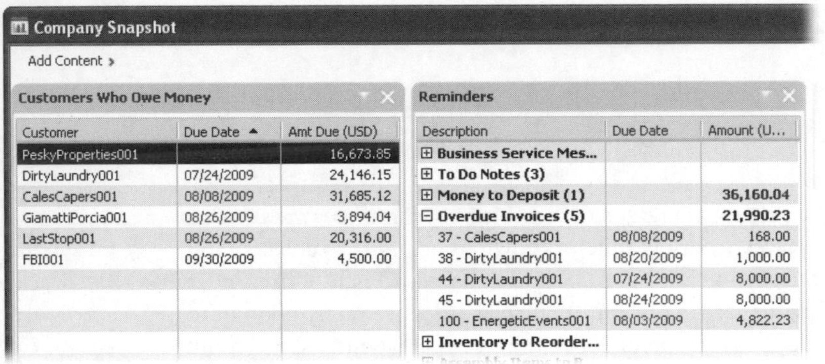

Figure 13-1:
The Customers Who Owe Money section shows who owes you money, how much they owe, and when it's due. (If this section doesn't appear in the window, click the Add Content link, click the green right arrow below the thumbnails until you see Customer Who Owe Money, and then click Add.) When balances are past due, the dates appear in red text for emphasis. If you display the Reminders section, you'll see overdue invoices, which are part of what make up your customers' balances.

When you open the Customer Center (in the Home page, click Customers, or choose Customers → Customer Center), QuickBooks automatically displays the Customers & Jobs tab, listing your customers and jobs and the balance owed by each one. If you select a customer or job name in the list, you can see the invoices or other sales transactions that generated the open balance on the right side of the window, as shown in Figure 13-2.

Accounts Receivable Aging Reports

Aging reports tell you how many days have passed since you sent each open invoice, and they're the first step to keeping your accounts receivable from growing overly ripe. It's a fact of business life that the longer a customer hasn't paid, the more likely it is that you'll never see that money. Taking action before an account lags too far behind limits bad debts and protects your profits.

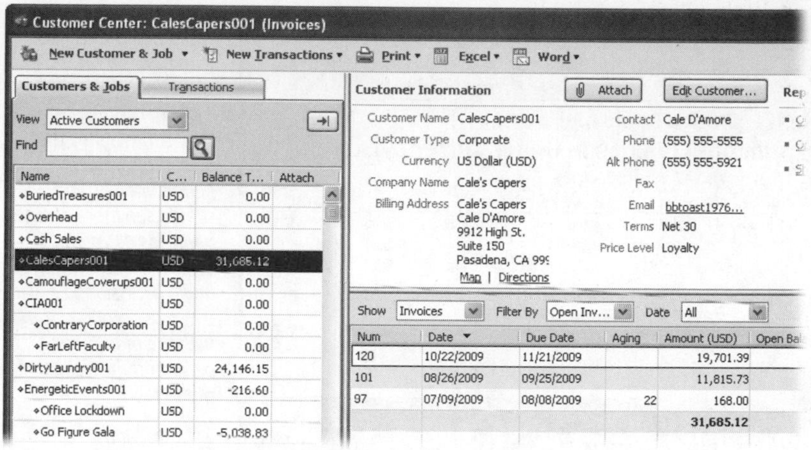

Figure 13-2:
To see the invoices that make up a customer's balance, select the customer in the Customers & Jobs tab. On the right side of the window, in the Show drop-down list, choose Invoices. Then, in the Filter By drop-down list, choose Open Invoices. If you want to focus on overdue invoices, in the Filter By drop-down list, choose Overdue Invoices.

QuickBooks includes two built-in aging reports: the A/R Aging Summary report and the A/R Aging Detail report. Aging reports show how much your customers owe for the current billing period (invoices that are less than 30 days old), as well as unpaid bills and invoices from previous periods (invoices that are between 1 and 30 days late, 31 to 60 days late, 61 to 90 days late, and more than 90 days late).

- **A/R Aging Summary.** For a fast look at how much money your customers owe you and how old your receivables are, choose Reports → Customers & Receivables → A/R Aging Summary, as shown in Figure 13-3 (top).

- **A/R Aging Detail.** To see each customer transaction categorized by age, as shown in Figure 13-3 (bottom), choose Reports → Customers & Receivables → A/R Aging Detail.

- **Accounts Receivable Graph.** The Accounts Receivable Graph doesn't show as much detail as either of the A/R Aging reports, but its visual nature makes aging problems stand out. To display this graph, choose Reports → Customers & Receivables → Accounts Receivable Graph. Ideally, you want to see the bars in the graph get smaller or disappear completely as the number of days overdue increases. To see more detail for a particular period, in the bar graph, double-click a bar. To see more detail for a customer, double-click the customer's name in the legend, or double-click the slice in the pie chart that corresponds with the customer.

Note: If you work with more than one currency, the Accounts Receivable Aging reports use your home currency to show all values. To see transactions in the currencies in which they were recorded, in the report window, click Modify Report. On the Display tab, below the "Display amounts in" label, select the "The transaction currency" option. Click OK.

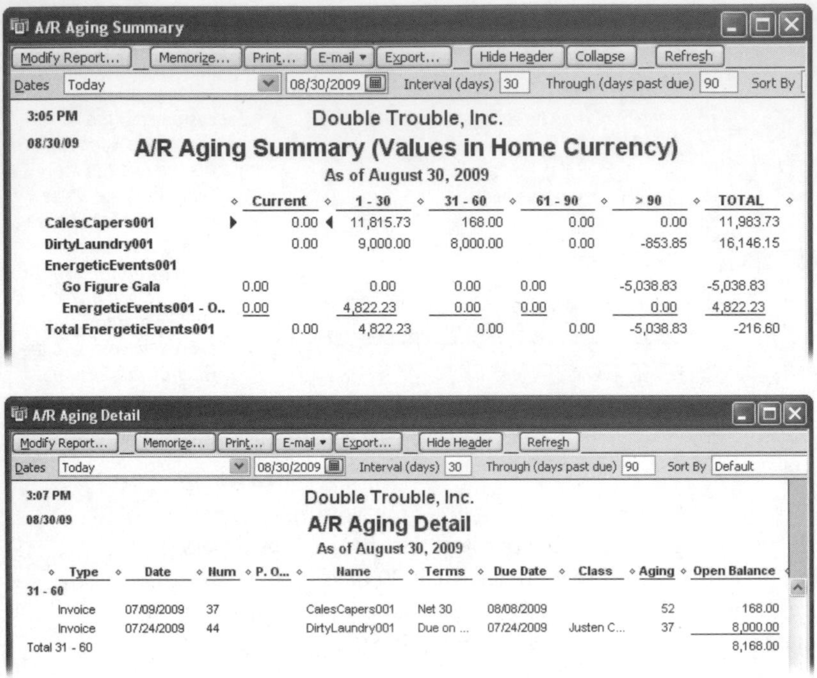

Figure 13-3:
Top: In the A/R Aging Summary report, QuickBooks lists customers and jobs and shows the money they owe in each aging period. Ideally, you should see more zero balances as you look at older periods. When you begin a mission to collect overdue accounts, start with the oldest aging period on the right side of the report.

Bottom: Many companies take at least 30 to 60 days to pay their bills, no matter how steep your finance charges. But when transactions age beyond what's typical for your customers, it's time to make phone calls or send reminder statements (page 299). If the built-in aging reports are too busy for your taste, feel free to remove columns that you don't use (page 624), like P.O. #.

Watching Receivables Trends

In the investment world, financial analysts study trends in accounts receivable. For example, if accounts receivable are increasing faster than sales, it means that customers aren't paying for everything they bought. Maybe the billing department is fond of long lunches, but it's more likely that customers aren't paying because they're on thin ice financially or they don't like the products or services they've received.

One way to measure how good a job your company does collecting receivables is with *days sales outstanding*, which is the number of days worth of sales it takes to match your accounts receivable. If accounts receivable grow faster than sales (meaning customers aren't paying), you'll see this measure get larger. Here's the formula for days sales outstanding:

```
Days sales outstanding = Accounts
receivable / (Sales/365)
```

Days sales outstanding below 60 (collecting accounts receivable with two months' worth of sales) is good. But if your company is in the retail business, you should aspire to the performance of high-volume giants such as Wal-Mart and Home Depot, who collect their receivables in less than a week.

Customer & Job Reports

Aging reports aren't the only goodies you can generate in QuickBooks. To see all the reports associated with customers and what they owe, choose Reports → Customers & Receivables. Here's an overview of when it makes sense to use these other reports:

- **Customer Balance Summary.** This report shows the same balance information you see automatically in the Customer Center, but here the job totals appear in one column and the customer totals are offset to the right. And unlike the Customers & Jobs tab, you can easily print this report.

- **Customer Balance Detail.** This report shows every transaction that makes up customers' balances, so it isn't short. It lists every transaction (such as invoices, payments, statement charges, and credit memos) for every customer and job, whether the customer is late or not. To inspect transaction details, double-click anywhere in the transaction's row to show the transaction in its corresponding window (Create Invoices for an invoice, for example). If you'd rather see the transactions for one customer, open the Customer Center (page 38), select the customer, and then, on the right side of the window, click the Open Balance link.

- **Open Invoices.** This includes unpaid invoices and statement charges, as well as payments and unapplied credits, so you can see if a payment or unapplied credit closes out a customer's balance. The report is sorted and subtotaled for each customer and job, so you can find an unpaid invoice quickly without repetitively clicking Previous in the Create Invoices window. When you find the invoice you want, double-click anywhere in that invoice's row to open it.

- **Collections Report.** When you're on a mission to collect the money that's owed you, the Collections report provides all the information you need. The report shows the past-due invoices and statement charges by customer and job with the due date and number of days that the transaction is past due. To make it easy to contact your customers, the report includes the customer contact name and phone number. Give the report to your most persistent employees and get ready to receive payments. If a customer has questions about a transaction, double-click the transaction's row to view the transaction in detail.

Tip: When customers have pushed their credit limits—and your patience—too far, you can easily create collection letters by merging information for overdue customers with mail merge collection letters in Word (see page 586).

- **Unbilled Costs by Job.** Another place you might leave money on the table is with job costs that you forgot to add to invoices. Run this report to see if there are expenses you haven't billed, the type of expense, when you incurred the cost, and other information. If you spot older expenses that you haven't yet billed, add them to the next invoice (page 270).

Receiving Payments for Invoiced Income

How you record an invoice payment depends on the *type* of payment. Most of the time, you'll click Receive Payments on the Home page, but you can also choose Customers → Receive Payments. Either way, you'll see the Receive Payments window, which handles full and partial payments, early payment discounts, credits, and downloaded online payments. The Receive Payments window works for most payments, but you record some types of payments in other places.

Here are the windows that can record payments and when you use them:

- **Receive Payments.** When your customers send you money, on the Home page, click Receive Payments to record them (page 38). This window is for full or partial payments that you receive *after* you've made a sale. Here you can apply early payment discounts, credits for returns, as well as downloaded online payments. (See page 335 for how you record the deposits for those payments.)

- **Create Invoices.** See the box on page 338 to learn how to record a partial payment that you receive before you prepare an invoice. These payments appear on the invoice you prepare and reduce its balance.

- **Create Credit Memos/Refunds.** If your customer makes a down payment or prepays an invoice, create credit memos to record these payments (page 342).

- **Enter Sales Receipts.** When your customers pay in full at the time of sale, record payments in this window (page 349), whether the customers pay with cash, check, or credit card.

For full or partial payments with or without discounts or credits, follow these steps to record payments you receive from your customers:

1. **On the Home page, click Receive Payments.**

   QuickBooks opens the Receive Payments window.

2. **In the Received From box, choose the customer or the job for which you received a payment, as shown in Figure 13-4.**

   If the customer sent a payment that covers more than one job, in the Received From box, choose the customer name—not any of the individual job names. QuickBooks adds the Job column to the Receive Payments table and fills in the rows with all the outstanding invoices for all of the customer's jobs. The job name appears in the table when an invoice applies to a specific job. When the cell in the Job column is blank, the invoice applies directly to the customer, not a job.

Note: If you select a customer set up to use a foreign currency, the A/R Account box automatically selects the Accounts Receivable account for the foreign currency. For euros, for example, you'll see Accounts Receivable - EUR.

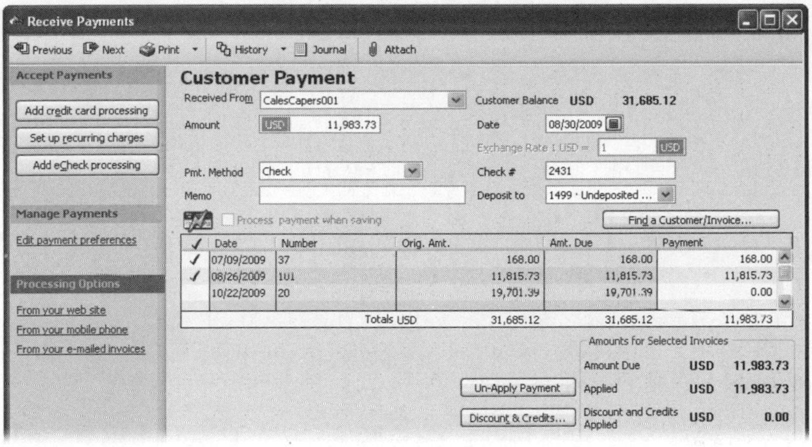

Figure 13-4:
When you choose a customer or job in the Received From box, the Customer Balance to its right shows the corresponding balance (including any credits available). The program also fills in the table with every unpaid invoice for that customer or job. If you choose a job and don't see the invoice you expect, in the Received From box, choose the customer (as shown here) to see all invoices for that customer and its jobs.

3. **In the Amount box, type the amount of the payment (if the customer uses a foreign currency, type the amount received in the foreign currency).**

   After you type the payment amount and either press Tab or click another box, QuickBooks automatically selects an invoice for you. If the payment amount exactly matches the amount of one or more unpaid invoices, QuickBooks is smart enough to select the invoices. If the customer sends some other amount of money, however, QuickBooks automatically selects the oldest unpaid invoices. Make sure that QuickBooks selects the correct invoices. Step 6 tells you how to select different invoices.

Tip: When you select a customer set up to use a foreign currency, the "Exchange Rate 1 <currency> =" box appears below the Date box, filled in with the current exchange rate set in QuickBooks. If you want to use a different exchange rate, type it in the "Exchange Rate 1 <currency> =" box. If the exchange rate you use when you receive the payment is different than the exchange rate you used on the invoice, Quick-Books automatically calculates the gain or loss (page 444) for the transaction.

---

4. **In the Pmt. Method box, choose the method that the customer used to make the payment.**

   If you choose Cash, QuickBooks displays the Reference # box where you can type a receipt number or other identifier. When you choose the Check payment method, QuickBooks displays the Check # box instead; type the number from the customer's check. For any type of credit card, in the Card No. box and Exp. Date boxes, type the card number and the month and year that the card expires. The Reference # box that appears is perfect for storing the credit card transaction number.

Note: If you want to sign up for Intuit payments services, such as accepting credit cards or electronic checks, click the "Add credit card processing" or "Add eCheck processing" buttons in the panel on the left side of the Receive Payments window. If you already subscribe to QuickBooks Merchant Services (page 605) and you want to process the payment on the customer's credit card, turn on the "Process payment when saving" checkbox above the table of invoices. You can download transactions for the payments you received online or via credit card. In the Receive Payments menu bar, simply click Get Online Pmts.

5. **In the Deposit To box, choose the account for the deposit, such as your checking or money market account.**

If you have only one account, you won't see this box at all. But if you have several accounts, such as checking, money market, and petty cash, then you can choose the account for the deposit.

QuickBooks chooses your Undeposited Funds account automatically, which means that the program holds payments in the Undeposited Funds account until you tell it to deposit those payments into a specific bank account. If you're the impatient type, or if your checking account balance is desperately low, you can deposit a payment directly to the bank account—as long as you follow that QuickBooks transaction with a real-world bank deposit.

Tip: To make reconciling your bank statement a bit easier (page 396), choose the Deposit To account based on the way your bank statement shows the deposits you make. If your bank statement shows a deposit total, regardless of how many checks were in the deposit, put payments in the Undeposited Funds account. But when your bank shows every check you deposit, choose your QuickBooks bank account so that each payment appears separately. Page 571 explains how to set a QuickBooks preference so that the program always chooses Undeposited Funds for payments.

6. **If QuickBooks selects the wrong invoices, or if you turned off the "Automatically apply payments" preference, in the first column in the unpaid invoice table (the checkmark column), click the cells for the invoices to which you want to apply the payment, as shown in Figure 13-5.**

When the payment doesn't match any unpaid invoices, QuickBooks selects the oldest invoices and adjusts the values in the Payment column to equal the payment total. If *you* select the invoices, you have to edit the values in the Payment column to match the total payment amount. Select a cell in the Payment column and type the new amount. When you press Tab or click elsewhere in the dialog box, you'll see the updated amount below the Payment column. When that value equals the value in the Amount box, you're done.

7. **If your customer reduced the payment by the available credit, click Discount & Credits. In the "Discount and Credits" dialog box, apply the credit to the payment.**

See page 335 for more detail about applying credits.

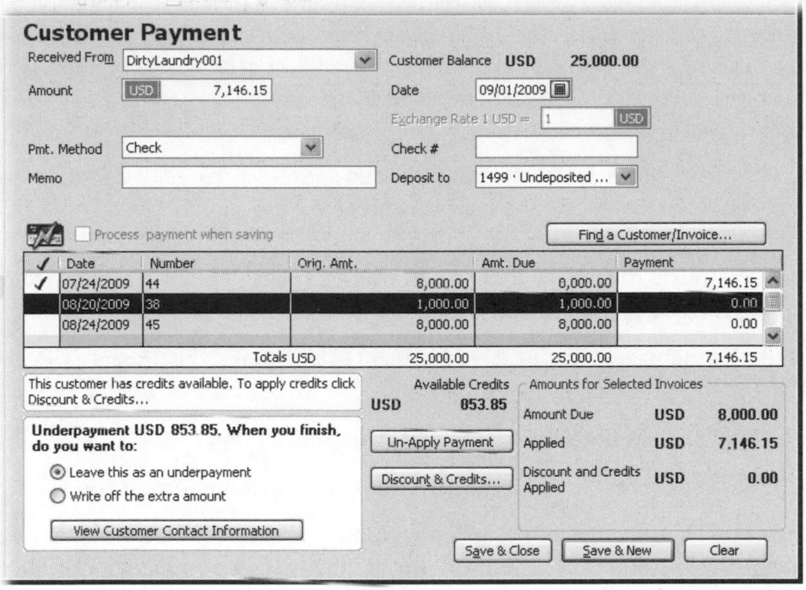

Figure 13-5:
Sometimes, the amount your customer sends doesn't match any combination of open invoices. If the customer paid too little or too much, you'll see an underpayment message (shown here) or an overpayment message. Before you edit values in the Payment column, see if the Available Credits value equals the Underpayment value. If it does, your customer reduced the payment by the available credit. See page 335 to learn how to apply credits.

8. If you want to print a payment receipt, in the Receive Payments window toolbar, click Print.

    QuickBooks opens the Print Lists dialog box. If necessary, change the print settings, and then click Print.

9. Click Save & Close to assign the payment to the selected invoices and close the window.

    If you want to apply another payment, click Save & New.

Tip: Say you realize that you've applied a payment to the wrong invoice. The easiest way to change a recent payment is to choose Customers → Receive Payments, and then click Previous until the correct payment transaction appears. In the invoice table, turn off the checkmark cell for the current selected invoice, turn on the checkmark cell for the correct invoice, and then click Save & Close.

Applying Credits to Invoices

When something goes awry with the services or products you sell, customers won't be bashful about asking for a refund or credit (page 288). And customers who buy from you regularly might *prefer* a credit against their next order rather than a refund, so that checks aren't flying back and forth in the mail. In a business sense, a credit is a lot like a customer payment that you can apply to invoices. In QuickBooks, you apply credits differently than actual customer payments, although you do both in the Receive Payments window.

Tip: For small credits, it's easier to wait until the customer sends a payment to apply the credit. Quick-Books keeps track of customer credit memos, so you don't have to remember that the credit is available. When the customer sends a payment and you choose that customer in the Receive Payments window, QuickBooks reminds you about the available credits. Then, you can apply the payment and the credit in the same transaction.

If a customer credit is sizable and the customer has unpaid invoices, you can apply the credit to those invoices whether the customer has sent an actual payment or not.

When you're ready to apply a credit to an invoice (page 288 tells you how to create a credit in the first place), here's what you do:

1. **On the Home page, click Receive Payments (or choose Customers → Receive Payments).**

   QuickBooks opens the Receive Payments window.

2. **In the Received From drop-down list, choose the customer or job you want.**

   When you choose a customer or job with an available credit, the Receive Payments window shows the amount of the credit, as shown in Figure 13-5. If you choose a customer, the Available Credits value represents all the credits available for all jobs for that customer.

3. **If your customer gave you instructions about which invoice should get the credit, click anywhere in the line for that invoice or statement except the checkmark column.**

   When you click a cell in the checkmark column, QuickBooks selects that invoice to receive a *real* payment.

4. **To apply the credit to the invoice or statement you selected, click Discount & Credits.**

   QuickBooks opens the "Discount and Credits" dialog box, shown in Figure 13-6.

5. **To apply a credit, click its checkmark cell to turn it on.**

   If the customer asked you not to apply a credit, turn off a credit's checkmark cell.

6. **Click Done.**

   When QuickBooks closes the "Discount and Credits" dialog box and returns to the Receive Payments window, you'll see the applied credit in two places, as shown in Figure 13-7.

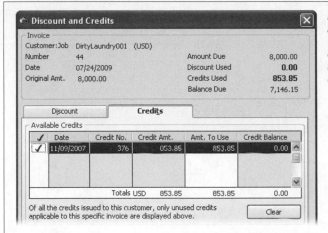

Figure 13-6:
If the credit doesn't appear in the "Discount and Credits" dialog box, it probably relates to a different job or to the customer only. If you want to apply a credit to a different job or to the customer account, see the box on page 341.

7. Click Save & Close to apply the credit to the invoice.

   If the customer's available credit is greater than the total for an invoice, you can still apply the credit to that invoice. QuickBooks reduces the invoice's balance to zero but keeps the remainder of the credit available to apply to another invoice. Simply repeat steps 1 through 6 to apply the leftover credit to another invoice.

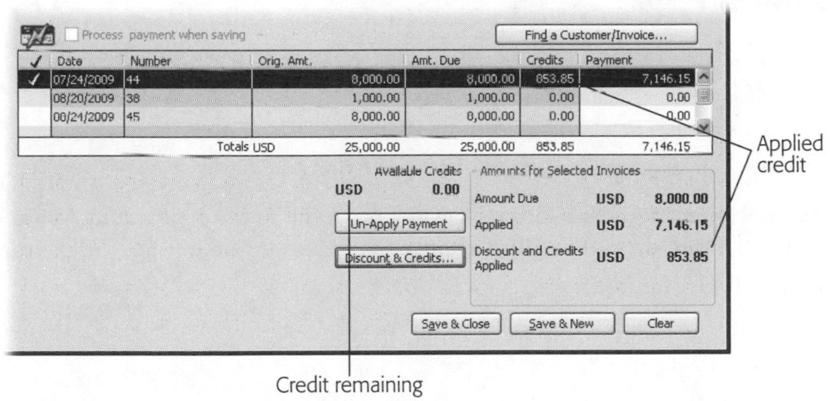

Figure 13-7:
When you apply a credit to an invoice, its amount appears in the Credits cell in the Receive Payments window. The credit also contributes to the "Discount and Credits Applied" value in the "Amounts for Selected Invoices" section. When you've applied all of a customer's credits, the Available Credits value equals 0.00.

Discounting for Early Payment

You don't know if customers are eligible for an early payment discount until they actually *pay early*, so it makes sense that you apply early payment discounts in the Receive Payments window. The procedure for applying an early payment discount is almost identical to applying a credit. In fact, if an invoice qualifies for both a credit and an early payment discount, you can apply them both while the "Discount and Credits" dialog box is open.

Different Ways to Apply Payments

Most of the time, customers send payments that bear some clear relationship to their unpaid invoices. For those payments, QuickBooks' preference to automatically select invoices (page 571) is a fabulous timesaver. You type the payment amount in the Amount box, and the program selects the most likely invoice for payment. When a payment matches an invoice amount exactly, this scheme works perfectly almost every time.

But every once in a while, you receive a payment that doesn't match up, and you have to tell QuickBooks how to apply the payment. For example, if the payment and the customer's available credit, taken together, match an open invoice, see page 334 to learn how to apply them to the invoice. If you have no idea what the customer had in mind, don't guess—contact the customer and ask how to apply the payment.

Regardless of the situation, in the Receive Payments window, you can adjust the values in the Payment column to match your customer's wishes.

Here's how to handle some common scenarios:

- **Customer includes the invoice number on the payment.** If QuickBooks selects an invoice other than the one the customer specifies, click the selected invoice's checkmark cell to turn it off. Turn on the checkmark for the desired invoice to make QuickBooks apply the payment to it.

- **Payment is less than any outstanding invoices.** In this case, QuickBooks applies the payment to the oldest invoice. Click Save & Close to apply the payment as is. Your customers will thank you for helping them avoid your finance charges.

- **Payment is greater than all of the customer's invoices.** If the payment is larger than all of the customer's unpaid invoices, also save the payment as is. You can then create a credit or write a refund check for the amount of the overpayment (page 288).

Note: If the discount is for something other than early payment, such as a product that's on sale, you add a Discount item to the invoice instead (page 265).

Here's how to take an early payment discount from a customer:

1. **On the Home page, click Receive Payments. In the Receive Payments window's Received From drop-down list, choose the customer or job for the payment you received.**

   In the table of open invoices, QuickBooks shows all the invoices or statements that aren't paid.

2. **Click the line (except the checkmark column) for the invoice or statement that the customer paid early.**

   QuickBooks applies the payment to the invoice. If the customer already deducted the early payment discount, the Receive Payments window shows an underpayment (page 335).

3. **To add an early payment discount to the invoice or statement you selected, click Discount & Credits.**

   QuickBooks opens the "Discount and Credits" dialog box. If the Credits tab is visible, click the Discount tab to display the Discount fields shown in Figure 13-8. If the date for the payment is earlier than the date shown as the Discount Date, QuickBooks uses the early payment percentage from the customer's payment terms to calculate the Suggested Discount. For example, if the customer gets a two percent discount for paying early, the suggested discount is two percent of the invoice total.

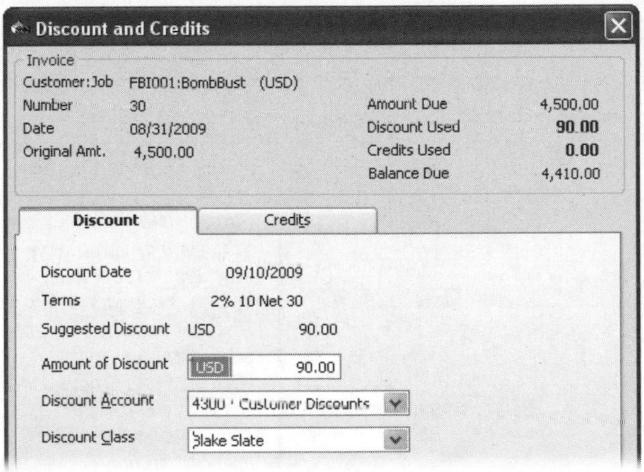

Figure 13-8:
In the "Amount of Discount" box, QuickBooks automatically fills in the suggested discount. You can type a different discount—if the customer paid only part of the invoice early, for instance. The Invoice section at the top of the dialog box shows the amount due on the invoice and the balance due after applying the early payment discount you chose. If the customer has already paid the invoice in full, the early payment discount becomes a credit for the next invoice.

Note: Customers often deduct their early payment discounts despite sending their payments after the early payment cutoff date. The typical reaction for most business owners is a resigned sigh. Although QuickBooks shows the suggested discount as zero when a customer doesn't actually pay early, you can show your customer goodwill and accept their payment. In the "Amount of Discount" box, simply type the discount that the customer took.

4. **In the Discount Account box, choose the income account you've set up to track customer discounts.**

   At first, you might consider posting customer discounts to one of your income accounts for products or services you sell. But customer discounts tend to fall off your radar when they're buried in your regular income. Keep track of the discounts you give by creating an income account specifically for discounts, called something imaginative like Customer Discounts.

   If you spot an *expense* account called Discounts, don't use that as your customer discount account either. An expense account for discounts is meant to track the discounts *you* receive from your vendors.

5. **If you use classes, in the Discount Class box, choose the class you want.**

   This class is typically the same one you used for the invoice in the first place.

6. **Click Done.**

   When QuickBooks closes the "Discount and Credits" dialog box and returns to the Receive Payments window, you'll see the discount in two or three places, as shown in Figure 13-9.

   The early payment discount appears both in the invoice table Discount column and in the value shown for "Discount and Credits Applied". If the customer paid the invoice in full, the early payment discount also becomes an overpayment.

Note: If a customer overpays, at the bottom left of the Receive Payments window, QuickBooks displays two options: create a credit for future use, or refund the amount to the customer. Unless your customer wants a refund, keep "Leave the credit to be used later" selected.

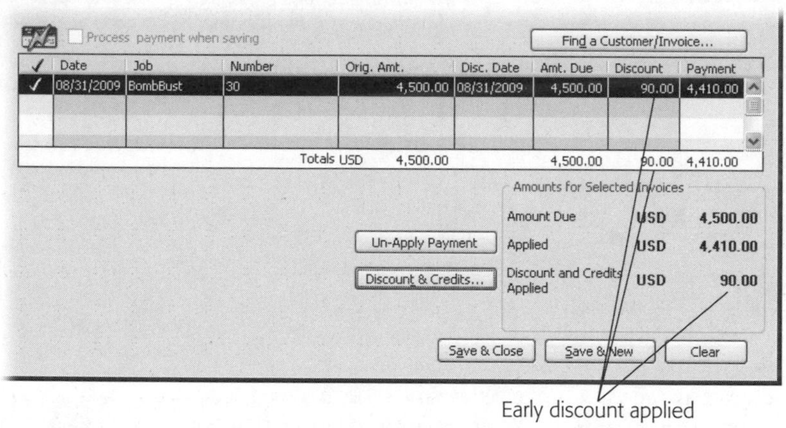

Figure 13-9:
When you apply an early payment discount to an invoice, it appears in the Discount cell. The discount also contributes to the "Discount and Credits Applied" value in the "Amounts for Selected Invoices" section.

Early discount applied

7. **Click Save & Close when you're done.**

   You've just processed the payment with the discount applied.

Deposits, Down Payments, and Retainers

Deposits, down payments, and retainers are all *prepayments*: money that a customer gives you that you haven't actually earned. For example, a customer might give you a down payment to reserve a spot in your busy schedule. Until you perform services or deliver products to earn that money, the down payment is more like a loan from the customer than income.

WORKAROUND WORKSHOP

Applying a Credit for One Job to a Different Job

If you work on several jobs for the same customer, your customer might ask you to apply a credit from one job to another. For example, perhaps the job with the credit is already complete and your customer wants to use that credit toward another job still in progress.

QuickBooks doesn't have a ready-made feature to transfer credits between jobs. The easy solution is to delete the credit memo for the first job and create a new one applying the credit to the job your customer specified. Your accountant probably won't approve, but the credit amount ends up applied to the job you want.

If you want to transfer the credit and satisfy your accountant, a couple of journal entries do the trick. But first you

have to create an account to hold these credit transfers. In your chart of accounts, create an account (page 53) using the Other Expense type and call it something like Credit Memo Transfers or Credit Memo Swap Account.

Because you're moving money in and out of Accounts Receivable and QuickBooks allows only one Accounts Receivable account per journal entry, you need *two* journal entries to complete the credit transfer. The first journal entry moves the credit from the first job into the transfer account, while the second journal entry completes the transfer from the transfer account to the new job. Figure 13-10 shows what the two journal entries look like.

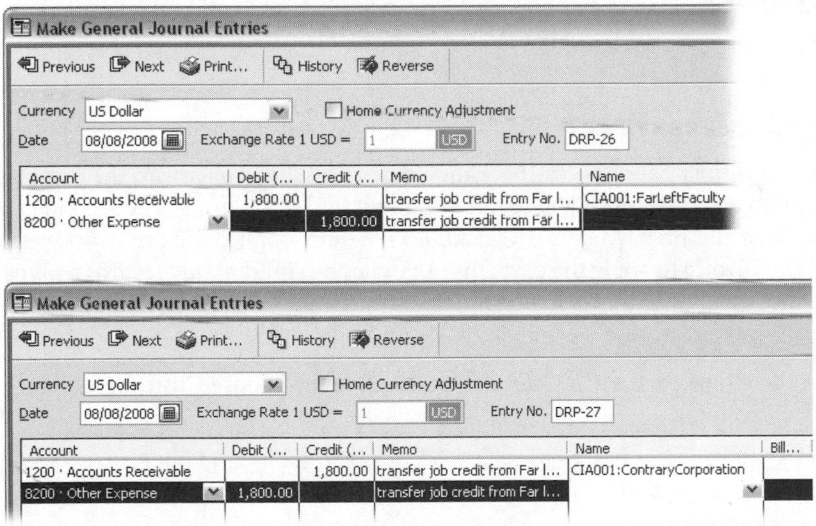

Figure 13-10:
The first journal entry transfers the amount of the job credit memo from the first job into the transfer account; you have to choose the customer and job in the Name cell. (Adding a memo helps you follow the money later.) The second journal entry transfers the amount of the job credit memo from the transfer account to the second job.

Receiving money for something you didn't do feels good, but don't make the mistake of considering that money yours. Prepayments belong to your customers until you earn them, and they require a bit more care than payments you receive for completed work and delivered products. This section explains how to manage all the intricacies of customer prepayments.

Setting Up QuickBooks for Prepayments

If you accept prepayments of any kind, you'll need an account in your chart of accounts to keep that money separate from your income. You'll also need an item that you can add to your invoices to deduct prepayments from what your customers owe:

- **Prepayment account.** If your customer gives you money and you never do anything to earn it, your customer is almost certain to ask for the money back. Because unearned money from a customer is like a loan, create an Other Current Liability account in your chart of accounts (see page 53) to hold prepayments. Call it something like Customer Prepayments.

- **Prepayment item.** If you accept prepayments for services, create prepayment items in your Item List. as shown in Figure 13-11.

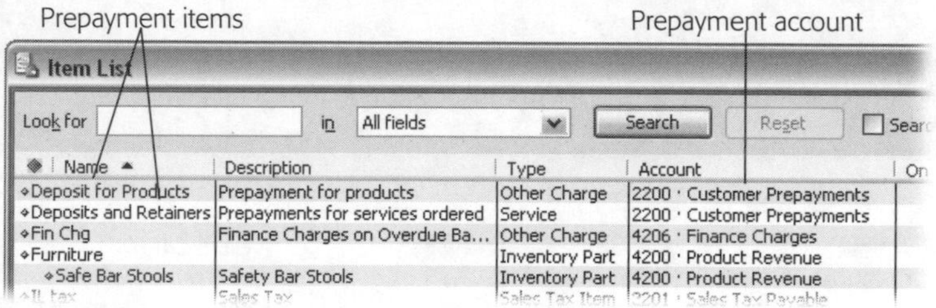

Prepayment items   Prepayment account

Figure 13-11:
If you accept deposits or retainers for services, create a Service item for them. For product deposits, create an Other Charge item. When you create items for prepayments, assign them to the prepayment account.

Recording Prepayments

When a customer hands you a check for a deposit or down payment, the first thing you should do is wait until you're out of earshot to yell "Yippee!" The second thing is to record the prepayment in QuickBooks. You haven't done any work yet, so there's no invoice to apply the payment to. A sales receipt not only records a prepayment in QuickBooks, but when printed, also acts as a receipt for your customer. Here's how to create one:

1. **On the Home page, click Create Sales Receipts (or choose Customers → Create Sales Receipts).**

   QuickBooks opens the Enter Sales Receipts window to a blank sales receipt. In the Customer:Job box, choose the customer or job for which you received a deposit or down payment.

Note: If the Create Sales Receipts icon doesn't appear on the Home page, choose Edit → Preferences and then click Desktop View. Click the Company Preferences tab and turn on the Sales Receipts checkbox.

---

2. Fill in the other header boxes as you would for a regular sales receipt or an invoice (page 258).

   If you use classes, in the Class box, choose a class to track the prepayment. If you have a customized template just for prepayments (page 620), in the Template drop-down list, choose that template. In the Date box, choose the date that you receive the prepayment. In the Payment Method box, pick the method the customer used to pay you. If the customer paid by check, in the Check No. box, type the check number for reference.

3. Here's the key to recording a prepayment to the correct account: In the Item table, click the first Item cell, and in the Item drop-down list, choose the prepayment item you want to use (for example, a Service item called something like Customer Prepayments or Deposits, as described on page 342).

   Depending on whether the deposit covers services or products, choose the Service item or Other Charge item you created for prepayments (page 342). Because your prepayment items are tied to an Other Current Liability account, QuickBooks doesn't post the payment as income, but rather as money owed to your customer.

4. In the Amount cell, type the amount of the deposit or down payment.

   You don't need to bother with entering values in the Qty or Rate cells. The sales receipt simply records the total that the customer gave you. You add the detail for services and products when you create invoices later.

5. Complete the sales receipt as you would for any other payment.

   For example, add a message to the customer. If you want to provide the customer with a receipt, turn on either the "To be printed" or "To be e-mailed" checkbox. In the Deposit To box at the bottom-left of the Enter Sales Receipt window, choose Undeposited Funds if you plan to hold the payment to deposit with others. If you're going to race to the bank as soon as your computer shuts down, choose your bank account.

6. Click Save & Close.

   QuickBooks posts the payment to your prepayment account and closes the Enter Sales Receipts window.

Applying a Deposit, Down Payment, or Retainer to an Invoice

When you finally start to deliver stuff to customers who've paid up front, you invoice them as usual. But the invoice you create has one additional line item that deducts the customer's prepayment from the invoice balance.

Create the invoice as you normally would with items for the services, products, charges, and discounts (Chapter 10). After you've added all those items, add the item to deduct the prepayment, as shown in Figure 13-12.

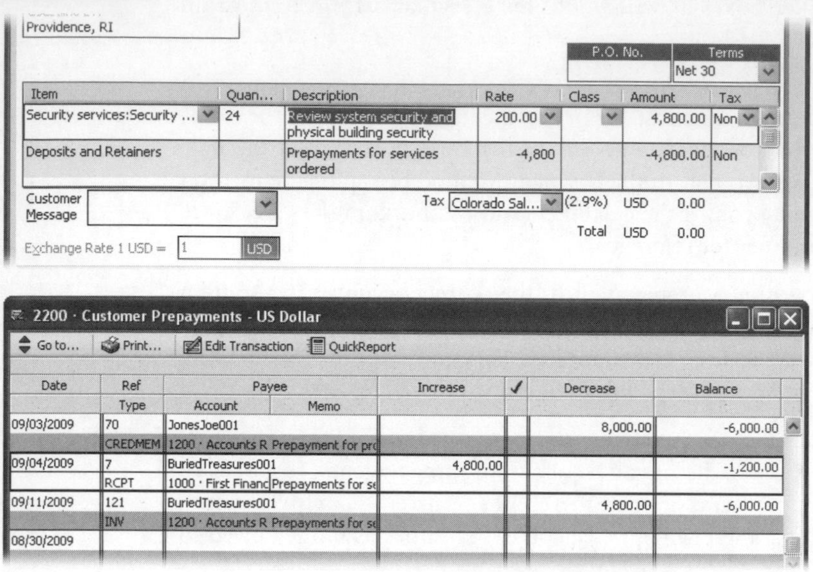

Figure 13-12:
Top: When you create an invoice for the customer, the prepayment offsets the customer's balance. To deduct the prepayment from the invoice balance, in the Amount cell, type the prepayment as a negative number.

Bottom: When you create a sales receipt for a deposit or down payment, QuickBooks adds the money to your prepayment Other Current Liability account. When you use the deposit to cover an invoice, QuickBooks transfers the money from the Other Current Liability account to reduce the customer's accounts receivable and add the money to the appropriate income account.

Note: If the charges on the invoice are less than the amount of the customer's deposit, deduct only as much of the deposit as you need. You can use the rest of the deposit on the next invoice.

Refunding Prepayments

Deposits and down payments don't guarantee that your customers follow through with their projects or orders. For example, a customer might make a deposit on décor for his bachelor pad. But when he meets his future wife at the monster truck rally, the plan for the bachelor pad is crushed as flat as the cars under the wheels of a truck. Of course, your customer wants his money back, which means you share some of his disappointment.

Your first step is to determine how much money your customer gets back. For example, if your customer cancels an order before you've purchased the products, you might refund the entire deposit. However, if the leopard-print wallpaper has already arrived, you might keep part of the deposit as a restocking fee.

After you decide how much of the deposit you're going to keep, you have to do two things. First, you need to move the portion of the deposit that you're keeping from the prepayment account to an income account. Second, you have to refund the rest of the deposit. Here's how to do both of these tasks:

1. **To turn the deposit you're keeping into income, create an invoice for the customer or job. Open the Create Invoices window (Ctrl+I), and in the Customer: Job box, choose the customer. Then, in the first Item cell, choose an item related to the cancelled job or order.**

   For example, if you're keeping a deposit for products you ordered, choose the "Non-inventory Part" item for those products. If the deposit was for services worked, choose the appropriate Service item.

2. **In the Amount cell, type the amount of the deposit that you're keeping.**

   Because items are connected to income accounts (see Chapter 5), this first line in the invoice gets the deposit that you're keeping to the correct income account for the products or services you sold.

3. **In the second line, add the prepayment item using a negative amount, as shown in Figure 13-13.**

   This item removes the prepayment from your liability account so you no longer owe the customer that money.

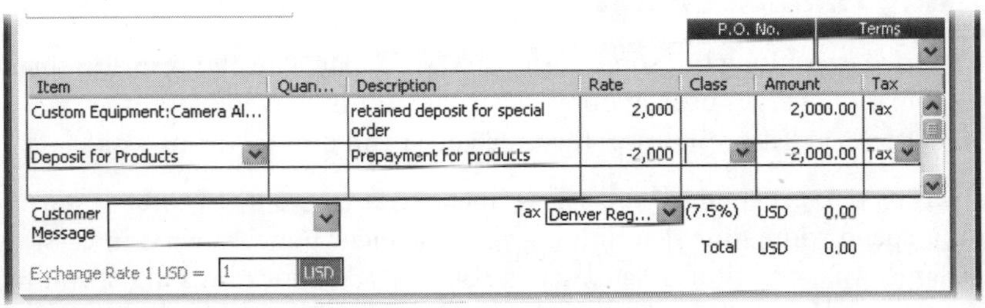

Figure 13-13:
In the Amount cell, type the amount of the deposit you're keeping as a positive number. Then, in the Amount cell for the prepayment, type a negative number, which makes the invoice balance zero. The prepayment item also deducts the deposit from the prepayment liability account, so you no longer "owe" your customer that money.

4. **Click Save & Close.**

   In saving the invoice, QuickBooks removes the deposit you're keeping from the prepayment liability account and posts that money to one of your income accounts. But if you aren't keeping the entire deposit, you have to refund the rest to the customer.

5. **To refund the rest of the deposit, create a credit memo for the remainder
   (page 288).**

   In the Create Credit Memos/Refunds window, in the Item cell, choose the same
   prepayment item you used in the invoice (a Service item for a deposit for services, an Other Charge item for deposits on products). In the Amount cell, type
   the amount that you're refunding.

6. **In the Create Credit Memos/Refunds window, click Save & Close.**

   QuickBooks removes the remaining deposit amount from your prepayment liability account. Because the credit memo has a credit balance, QuickBooks opens
   the Available Credit dialog box.

7. **In the Available Credit dialog box, choose the "Give a refund" option, and
   then click OK.**

   QuickBooks opens the "Issue a Refund" dialog box and fills in the customer or
   job, the account from which the refund is issued, and the refund amount. If you
   want to refund the deposit from a different account, choose a different refund
   payment method or account.

8. **Click OK to create the refund to your customer.**

   As soon as you mail the refund check, you're done.

Applying Finance Charges

If you've tried everything but some customers won't pay, you can resort to finance
charges. Finance charges usually don't cover the cost of keeping after the slackers,
but QuickBooks at least minimizes the time you spend on this vexing task.

Customers tend to get cranky if you spring finance charges on them without warning.
Up front, spend some time determining your payment policies: what interest rate
you'll charge, what constitutes "late," and so on. Include these terms in the contracts
your customers sign and on the sales forms you send. Then, after you configure
QuickBooks with your finance charge settings, a few clicks is all you'll need to add
those penalties to customer accounts.

Finance Charge Preferences

Before you apply finance charges, you need to tell QuickBooks how steep your
finance charges are, when they kick in, and a few other details. The Preferences
dialog box (choose Edit → Preferences) Finance Charge section is where all these
settings reside. Because your finance charge policies should apply to *all* your customers, these preferences appear on the Company Preferences tab, which means
only a QuickBooks administrator can change them. To learn how to set finance
charge preferences, see page 560.

Assessing Finance Charges on Overdue Balances

Make sure you apply payments and credits to invoices before you assess finance charges. Otherwise, you'll spend most of your time reversing finance charges and working to get back into your customers' good graces.

QuickBooks creates finance-charge invoices for the customers tardy enough to warrant late fees, but you don't have to print or send these invoices. Instead, assess finance charges just before you print customer statements (page 302) to have QuickBooks include the finance-charge invoices on statements, along with any outstanding invoices and unpaid charges for the customer.

Here's how you assess finance charges for slow-paying customers:

1. **On the Home page, click Finance Charges (or choose Customers → Assess Finance Charges).**

   The Assess Finance Charges window, shown in Figure 13-14, opens.

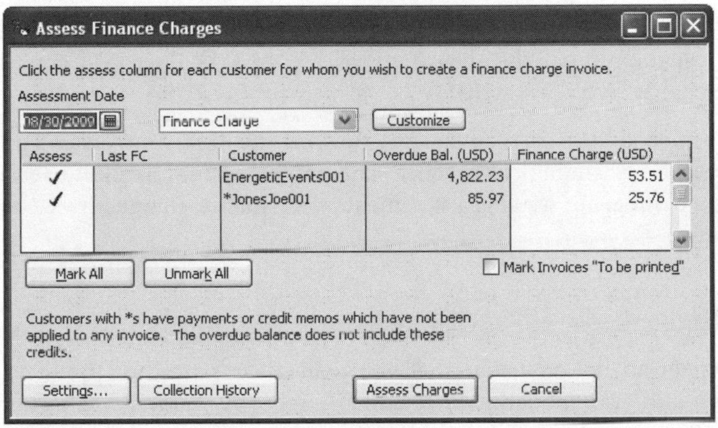

Figure 13-14:
In the Assess Finance Charges window, QuickBooks precedes a customer's name with an asterisk if the customer has payments or credits that you haven't yet applied. If you see any asterisks, click Cancel. After you've processed those payments (page 332) and credits (page 335), you're ready to start back at step 1. QuickBooks automatically chooses the current date as the date on which you want to assess finance charges, and selects all the customers with overdue balances.

2. **If you begin the process of preparing statements a few days before the end of the month, in the Assessment Date box, change the date to the last day of the month.**

   The last day of the month is a popular cutoff day for customer statements. When you change the date in the Assessment Date box and move to another field, QuickBooks recalculates the finance charges to reflect the charges through the new assessment date.

3. **Although QuickBooks automatically selects all customers with overdue balances, you can let some of your customers slide without penalty. In the Assess column, click the Assess cell for a customer to turn off the checkmark and skip her finance charges.**

   QuickBooks always displays every customer with an overdue balance, and there's no way to flag a customer as always exempt from finance charges. If you reserve finance charges for your most intractable customers, click Unmark All to turn off all the finance charges. Then, in the Assess column, click only the cells for the customers you want to penalize.

To view the invoices, payments, and credits for a customer, click the row for the customer and then click Collection History. QuickBooks displays a Collections Report with every transaction for that customer.

4. **If you want to change the finance charge amount, in the Finance Charge column, click the cell for the customer and type the new finance charge.**

   The only time you might want to do this is when you've created a credit memo (page 288) for a customer, but you don't want to apply it to an invoice. As long as the credit memo is out there, it's simpler to forego the finance charges until you've applied the credit.

5. **If you want to print and send the finance-charge invoices, turn on the "Mark Invoices 'To be printed'" checkbox. Then, to finalize the finance-charge invoices for the selected customers, click Assess Charges.**

   QuickBooks adds the finance-charge invoices to the queue of invoices to be printed. When you print all the queued invoices (page 311), the program prints the finance-charge invoices as well.

   If you plan to send customer statements, turn off the "Mark Invoices 'To be printed'" checkbox. Sending customers a statement to remind them of overdue balances is one thing, but sending a statement *and* a finance-charge invoice borders on nagging.

Cash Sales

Receiving payment at the same time that you deliver the service or products is known as a *cash sale*, even though your customer might pay you with cash, check, or credit card. For example, if you run a thriving massage therapy business, your customers probably pay for their stress relief before they leave your office—and no matter how they pay, QuickBooks considers the transaction a cash sale.

If your customers want records of their payments, you give them sales receipts. In QuickBooks, a Sales Receipt can do double-duty; it records your cash sale in the program *and* you can print it as a paper receipt for your customer. Although cash sales are a simultaneous exchange of money and goods (or services), you don't actually have to create a QuickBooks sales receipt at the time of the sale.

Here are the two most common ways of handling cash sales:

- **Recording individual sales.** If you want to keep track of which customers purchase which products, create a separate sales receipt for each cash sale. Individual sales receipts track both customers' purchases and the state of inventory.

Note: If you keep QuickBooks open on the computer in your store, you can print individual sales receipts for your customers. But keeping QuickBooks running on the store computer could be risky if the wrong people started snooping around in your records. And, unless you're completely proficient with sales receipts in the program, you might find paper sales receipts faster when your store is swamped. When there's a lull in your store traffic, you can enter individual receipts into your QuickBooks company file.

- **Recording batch sales.** If your shop gets lots of one-time customers, you don't care about tracking who purchases your products. But you still need to know how much inventory you have and how much money you've made. In this situation, you don't have to create a separate sales receipt for each sale. Instead, create a sales receipt for each business day, which shows how much money you brought in for the day and what you sold.

Creating Sales Receipts

Creating sales receipts in QuickBooks is identical to creating invoices (page 255), except for a few small differences. The Enter Sales Receipt window includes a Check No. box to track the customer's check number. For cash or credit cards, leave this box blank. In a cash sale, the customer pays immediately, so choose Cash from the Payment Method drop-down list. A cash sale also means you've got money to deposit; the account in the Deposit To box is where QuickBooks plops the money (page 334).

To create a sales receipt, on the Home page, click Create Sales Receipts (or choose Customers → Enter Sales Receipts). If you want to print the sales receipt for your customer after you've filled in all the fields, in the Enter Sales Receipts window's toolbar, click Print to have QuickBooks open the Print One Sales Receipt dialog box. To learn more about your printing options, see page 306.

Warning: Keeping track of customers who make one-time cash sales can clog your Customer:Job List with unnecessary information. Keep your customer list lean by creating a customer called Cash Sales (page 72).

Editing Sales Receipts

If you're still creating a sales receipt, you can jump to any field and change its value. Or, you can insert or delete lines in the sales receipt line-item table as your customer tosses another book on the pile or puts one back on the shelf. Although you can edit sales receipts after you've saved them, you won't do so very often. After all, the sale is complete, and your customer has left with her copy. However, you may want to edit the sales receipt after the sale to add more detailed descriptions to items, or to correct an error, for example. To do so, in the Enter Sales Receipts window, click Previous or Next until the receipt you want appears (or use the Find command described on page 324), and then make your changes.

Voiding and Deleting Sales Receipts

If you created a sales receipt by mistake and want to remove its values from your accounts, you might think about deleting the receipt. However, you should *always* void sales receipts that you don't want rather than deleting them.

Voiding a sales receipt resets the dollar values for the transaction to zero so that your account balances show no sign of the transaction. However, it also marks the transaction as void, so you have a record of it.

If you delete a sales receipt, it's gone for good. QuickBooks deletes the transaction, removing the dollar values and any sign of the transaction from your accounts. You'll see a hole in your numbering sequence of sales receipts and an entry in the audit trail that says you deleted the transaction (page 640).

To void a sales receipt, do the following:

1. **On the Home page, click Create Sales Receipts (or choose Customer → Enter Sales Receipts).**

   The Enter Sales Receipts window opens.

2. **Click Previous or Next until you see the sales receipt. Choose Edit → Void Sales Receipt or right-click the sales receipt and then choose Void Sales Receipt on the shortcut menu, as shown in Figure 13-15.**

   All the values in the form change to zero and QuickBooks adds the word "VOID:" to the Memo field. As a reminder of the reason that you voided the transaction, type the reason after "VOID:" in the Memo field.

3. **Click Save & Close.**

Figure 13-15:
Shortcut menus (available since QuickBooks 2009) make choosing commands easier. In earlier versions of the program, you had to choose the Edit menu to get to the Delete Sales Receipt and Void Sales Receipt commands. Now, a right-click in the Enter Sales Receipt window displays the shortcut menu shown here.

Memorizing a Batch Sales Transaction

If you want to reduce your paperwork by recording one batch sales receipt for each business day's sales, why not go one step further and *memorize* a batch sales receipt that you can reuse every day? Here's how:

1. **On the Home page, click Create Sales Receipts (or choose Customers → Enter Sales Receipts).**

   QuickBooks opens the Enter Sales Receipts window.

2. **In the Customer:Job box, choose the generic customer you created for cash sales.**

   If you haven't set up a cash sale customer, in the Customer:Job box, choose *<Add New>*. In the New Customer dialog box, fill in the Customer Name box with a name like Cash Sales. Then, click OK to save the customer and use it for the sales receipt.

3. **If you typically sell the same types of items every day, in Item cells, choose the items you sell regularly.**

   Leave the Qty cells blank because those values are almost guaranteed to change every day.

4. **Because a sales receipt is meant to handle cash, the total at the bottom of the form represents the bank deposit you make at the end of the day. If you want to split your daily sales among different types of payments (like Visa, Master-Card, and so on), add a payment item for each type of credit card and other payment type you accept, as shown in Figure 13-16.**

   Here's how: In the Item table, choose a payment type item, like Payment-Visa. (When you create a payment item [page 123], choose the "Group with other undeposited funds" option so you can control when you deposit the money.) In the Amount cell, type the amount of money that goes to Visa as a negative number. For example, if customers charged $100 on their Visas, type *−100*.

Tip: By splitting a sales receipt among different types of payments that group to Undeposited Funds, you can make a single deposit (page 354) to each merchant card account at the end of the day. To do so, choose Banking → Make Deposits. In the "Payments to Deposit" dialog box, choose the payment type in the "View payment method type" drop-down list. Select the deposits for that card, and then click OK to deposit them as they actually go to the bank or merchant card company. Repeat the Make Deposit command for each type of payment you accept. (This technique works as long as your merchant card company deducts their fees as a single amount, instead of a fee on every charge transaction.)

---

5. **When the sales receipt is set up the way you want, press Ctrl+M to open the Memorize Transaction dialog box.**

   In the Name box, type a name for the reusable sales receipt, such as Day's Cash Sales.

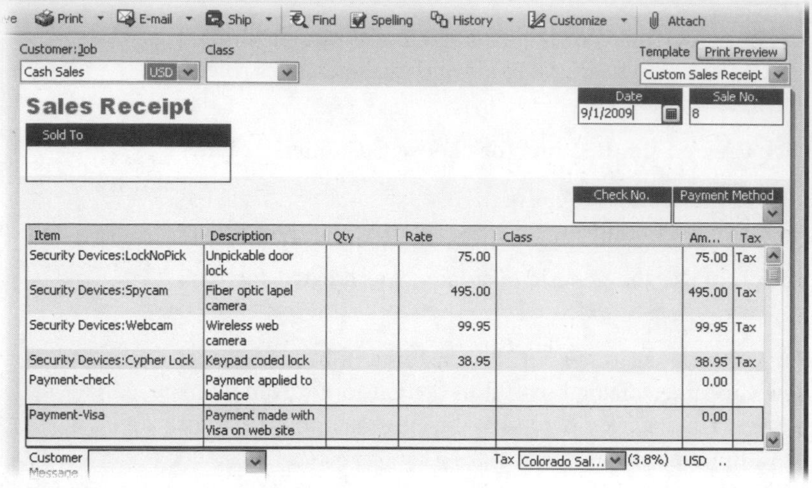

Figure 13-16:
Add a payment item line for every payment type you accept (American Express, Discover, debit cards, checks, and so on). Type a negative number for the amount charged to each type of payment. If the Total value doesn't match the amount of your cash deposit, add an item for excess or short cash to make your bank deposit balance. (The next section explains items for excess and short cash.)

6. **If you want to use this memorized sales receipt only on the days you have cash sales, choose the Don't Remind Me option.**

   If you receive cash sales every day, choose the Remind Me option and then, in the How Often box, choose Daily.

7. **To memorize the sales receipt, click OK.**

   QuickBooks closes the Memorize Transaction dialog box and adds the batch sales receipt to the Memorized Transaction List.

8. **In the Enter Sales Receipts window, click Clear to delete the information you used to set up the memorized sales receipt.**

   To create a new sales receipt for a day, press Ctrl+T to open the Memorized Transaction List window. In the Memorized Transaction List, click the memorized transaction for your batch sales receipt and then click Enter Transaction. QuickBooks open the Enter Sales Receipts window with a sales receipt based on the one you memorized. You can edit the items in the receipt, their quantities, and the prices to reflect your day's sales. When the sales receipt is complete, click Save & Close.

Reconciling Excess and Short Cash

When you take in paper money and make change, you're bound to make small mistakes. Unless you're lucky enough to have one of those automatic change machines, the cash in the cash register at the end of the day often disagrees with the sales you recorded. Over time, the amounts you're short or over tend to balance out, but that's no help when you have to record sales in QuickBooks that don't match your bank deposits.

The solution to this reality of cash sales is one final sales receipt at the end of the day that reconciles your cash register total with your bank deposit slip. But before you can create this reconciliation sales receipt, you need an account and a couple of items:

- **Over/Under account.** To keep track of your running total for excess and short cash, create an Income account, such as Over/Under. If you use account numbers, give the account a number so that it appears near the end of your Income accounts. For example, if Uncategorized Income is account number 4999, make the Over/Under account 4998.

- **Over item.** Create an Other Charge item to track the excess cash you collect, and assign it to the Over/Under account. Make sure that you set up this item as nontaxable.

- **Under item.** Create a second Other Charge item to track the amounts that you're short and assign it to the Over/Under account. This item should also be nontaxable.

At the end of each day, compare the income you recorded (run a Profit & Loss report and set the Date box to Today) to the amount of money in your cash register. Create a sales receipt to make up the difference. Here's how:

- If you have less cash than you should, create a Sales Receipt and, in the first line, add the Under item. In the Amount cell, type the amount that you're short as a negative number. When you save the sales receipt, QuickBooks adjusts your income record to match the money in the cash register.

- If you have too much cash, create a Sales Receipt and, in the first line, add the Over item. In the Amount cell, type the excess amount as a positive number. This sales receipt increases your recorded income to match the money you have on hand.

Note: If you notice that your cash count at the end of the day is always short, a fluke of probability could be at work. But the more likely answer is that someone is helping themselves to the cash in your till.

Making Deposits

Whether customers mail you checks or hand over wads of cash, taking those deposits to the bank isn't enough—you also have to record those deposits in QuickBooks. If you initially store payments in the Undeposited Funds account, you have to work your way through two dialog boxes to record deposits; otherwise, you have just one step. Both processes are described in this section.

Note: In the Receive Payments window, when you choose a bank account as the Deposit To account (page 334), there's nothing more to do after you save the payment—QuickBooks records the payment as a deposit to the bank account.

Choosing Payments to Deposit

When you store payments in the Undeposited Funds account, you end up with a collection of payments ready for deposit to go along with the paper checks you have to take to the bank. When you have payments queued up for deposit and choose Banking → Make Deposits (or on the Home page, in the Banking section, click Record Deposits), QuickBooks opens the "Payments to Deposit" dialog box. You can choose the payments you want to deposit in several ways, as shown in Figure 13-17.

Note: If you have other checks that you want to deposit, such as an insurance claim check or a vendor's refund, you'll have a chance to add those to your deposit in the Make Deposit dialog box.

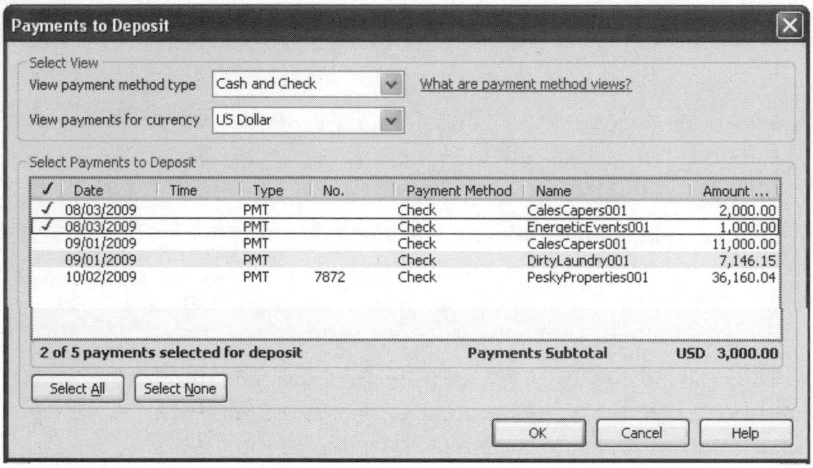

Figure 13-17:
If you have zillions of payments, you can filter the payments to deposit by payment method. In the "View payment method type" box, choose a payment method to display only those types of payments. If you want to record deposits for payments made in a foreign currency, in the "View Payments for currency" drop-down list, choose the currency. You enter your bank's exchange rate for the deposit in the Make Deposits window (page 355).

To choose specific payments to deposit, in the checkmark column, click each payment you want to deposit. To select every payment listed, click Select All. When you've selected the payments you want, click OK. QuickBooks closes the "Payments to Deposit" dialog box and opens the Make Deposits window, described next.

Recording Deposits

The Make Deposits window is like an electronic deposit slip, as you can see in Figure 13-18. The payments you choose to deposit are already filled in. If you have other checks to deposit besides customer payments, they won't show up automatically in the Make Deposits window, but you can add them to the table.

Note: If you're depositing a payment made in a foreign currency, in the "Exchange Rate 1 <currency>=" box, type the exchange rate that your bank used for the transaction (to find it, look at your bank statement or review the transaction on your bank's website). The table of deposits shows the deposit amount in the foreign currency. At the bottom of the window, you can see the deposit total in the foreign currency and your home currency.

After you make your foreign currency deposits, you can see how much you gained or lost due to changes in the exchange rate. Choose Reports → Company & Financials → Realized Gains & Losses. This report shows the payment amounts in your home currency, the exchange rate, and the resulting gain or loss.

Here's how you add these additional deposits:

1. **Click the first blank Received From cell and choose the vendor or name of the source of your deposit. Then, in the From Account, choose the account to which you're posting the money.**

   For example, if you're depositing a refund check for some supplies, choose the expense account for office supplies.

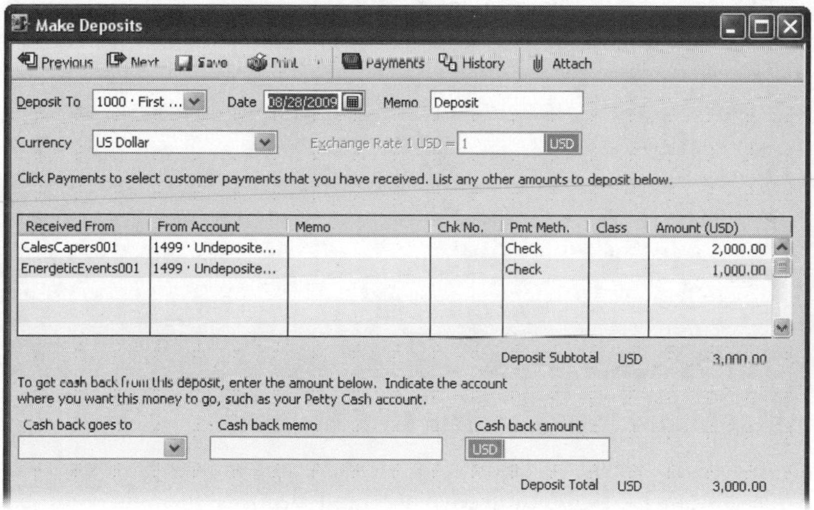

Figure 13-18:
In the Make Deposits window, you can specify the account into which you're depositing funds, the date, and each payment in the deposit. If you're in the habit of withdrawing some petty cash from your deposits, you can record that as well. To prevent yourself from bouncing checks, in the Date box, be sure to choose the date that you actually make the deposit.

2. **Fill in the rest of the cells (optional).**

   For customer payments, you can probably skip the Memo cell, but for refunds or checks from other sources, memos can help you remember why people sent you money. In case a question arises, typing the number of the check gives your customer or vendor a reference point.

Tip: If you want to withdraw some money for petty cash from your deposit, in the "Cash back goes to" box, choose your petty cash account. In the "Cash back amount" box, type the amount of cash you're deducting from the deposit.

If your company is a corporation, you can't just withdraw money for your personal use. By accounting for the cash in a petty cash account, you can record your cash expenditures in QuickBooks. If you own a sole proprietorship, you *can* withdraw cash for yourself. In that case, in the "Cash back goes to" box, choose your owner's draw account.

3. **When you've filled in all the fields, click Save & Close.**

   QuickBooks posts the deposits to your accounts.

UP TO SPEED

Putting Payment Deposit Types to Work

Choosing different types of payments before you get to the Make Deposits window takes extra work, but it's a good idea for several reasons. Here are a few reasons you might make multiple passes through the deposit process:

- **Different Deposit Types.** Many banks group different types of deposits, such as checks versus electronic transfers. To group your payments in QuickBooks the way your bank groups them on the monthly bank statement, in the "View payment method type" box, choose a payment method, and then click Select All to process those payments as a group.

- **Different Deposit Accounts.** If you deposit some payments in your checking account and other payments

to a savings account, select all the payments you want to deposit in the checking account. Then you can run through the deposit process a second time to deposit other checks to your savings account.

- **Reconciling Cash Deposits.** As you learned on page 352, counting cash is prone to error, so you're probably used to your bank coming up with a different cash deposit total than you did. Although QuickBooks groups cash and checks as one payment type, process your cash and check payments as two separate deposits. Then, if the bank changes the deposit amount, it's easy to edit your cash deposit.

Depositing Money from Merchant Card Accounts

When you accept payment via credit card, the merchant bank you work with collects your customers' credit card payments and deposits them in your bank account as a lump sum. Regardless of how credit card payments you receive appear on the merchant bank's statement, you record your deposits in QuickBooks the way they appear on your bank statement. For example, your merchant bank might show payments and merchant bank fees separately, whereas the amount deposited in your checking account is the net after the fees are deducted.

Here's how you deposit merchant credit card payments and fees into your bank account:

1. **On the Home page, click Record Deposits (or choose Banking → Make Deposits).**

   In the "Payments to Deposit" window, in the "View payment method type" drop-down list, choose the merchant card whose payments you want to deposit.

---

2. **Select the credit card payments you want to deposit, and then click OK.**

   QuickBooks opens the Make Deposits window, which lists the credit card payments in the deposit table.

   If the Deposit Subtotal doesn't match the deposit that appears on your bank statement, the merchant bank probably deducted its fees. You'll record those fees in the next step. To make merchant card deposits easier to track, ask your merchant card company to charge one lump sum for fees instead of charging for each transaction; they almost always say yes.

3. **In the first blank row in the Account cell, choose the account to which you post merchant card fees (such as Bank Service Charges). Then, in the Amount cell, type the merchant card fees as a negative number.**

   In the Make Deposits window, the Deposit Subtotal should equal the deposit that appears on your bank statement.

4. **Click Save & Close when you're done.**

Note: How soon you can enter your merchant card deposits in QuickBooks depends on how wired your company is. For example, the QuickBooks online banking service (page 605) downloads your merchant card deposits into your company file automatically. If you have online account access to your merchant card account, make the deposit in QuickBooks when you go online and see it in your transaction listing. But if you don't use any online services, enter the deposit in QuickBooks when the merchant card statement arrives in the mail.

UP TO SPEED

Following the Money Trail

If you use the windows in QuickBooks to create transactions, the program posts debits and credits to accounts without any action on your part. But if you're interested in how money weaves its way from account to account, here's what happens from the time you create an invoice to the time you deposit the customer payment into your bank account.

- **Create Invoices.** When you create an invoice, QuickBooks credits your income accounts because you've earned income, and debits the Accounts Receivable account because your customers owe you money.

- **Receive Payments.** When you receive payments into the Undeposited Funds account, QuickBooks credits the Accounts Receivable account because the customer balance is now paid off. The program debits the Undeposited Funds account because the money is now in that account waiting to be deposited.

- **Make Deposits.** When you deposit the payments queued in the Undeposited Funds account, QuickBooks credits the Undeposited Funds account to remove the money from that account, and debits your bank account to transfer the money into your bank account balance.

CHAPTER 14

Doing Payroll

If you decide to outsource the headaches of payroll to a payroll service company, as many businesses do, you can skip this chapter—except for the first section, which starts on page 360. With outsourced payroll, the only thing you have to do in QuickBooks payroll-wise is add a couple of transactions for each payroll, allocate salaries and wages, payroll taxes, and any other payroll expenses to the accounts in your chart of accounts. For a small payroll, outside services are a pretty good deal. The payroll service takes care of all the grunt work for the equivalent of the cost of a few hours of your time. Even with the highest level QuickBooks Payroll Service, you have to devote some time and brain power to payroll.

If you want to process payroll within QuickBooks, you first have to sign up for one of the payroll services that Intuit offers. To keep expenses low, you can choose a bare-bones service that provides only updated tax tables. At the other end of the spectrum, you can opt for QuickBooks' full-service payroll. Or you can compromise somewhere in the middle.

After you choose a level of QuickBooks payroll service, your next task is to set up everything the program needs to calculate payroll amounts. You can walk through each step on your own or use a wizard. Either way, the Payroll Setup wizard keeps track of what you've done and what you still have to do. This chapter takes you through every payroll step from the initial setup to running a payroll, printing checks, and remitting payroll taxes and reports to the appropriate government agencies.

Note: Payroll regulations are complex and vary depending on the size of your payroll and the states to which you remit payroll taxes. This chapter focuses on how to process payroll in QuickBooks. For more information on your company's payroll requirements, check with your accountant or the IRS and state tax agencies you work with.

Adding Payroll Transactions from an Outside Service

Lots of companies use outsourced payroll services, like ADP or Paychex, to avoid the brain strain of figuring out tax deductions and complying with payroll regulations. When you use one of these services, you send them your payroll data and receive reports about the payroll transactions that they processed. The payroll service takes care of remitting payroll taxes and other deductions to the appropriate agencies.

The problem is that none of these payroll transactions appear in your QuickBooks company file unless you add them. Fortunately, you don't have to enter every last detail into QuickBooks. You can create a journal entry debiting the payroll expense accounts and crediting your bank account (page 421). Or you can create a vendor in QuickBooks for payroll and then memorize a split transaction that distributes the money from your checking account into the appropriate expense accounts, as shown in Figure 14-1:

1. **Create a vendor for your payroll transactions.**

   On the QuickBooks Home page, click Vendors. In the Vendor Center toolbar, click New Vendor. You don't have to fill in all the fields in the New Vendor window; simply type a name like Payroll in the Vendor Name box and click OK.

2. **Open your payroll bank account's register window.**

   In the Chart of Accounts window, double-click the account name.

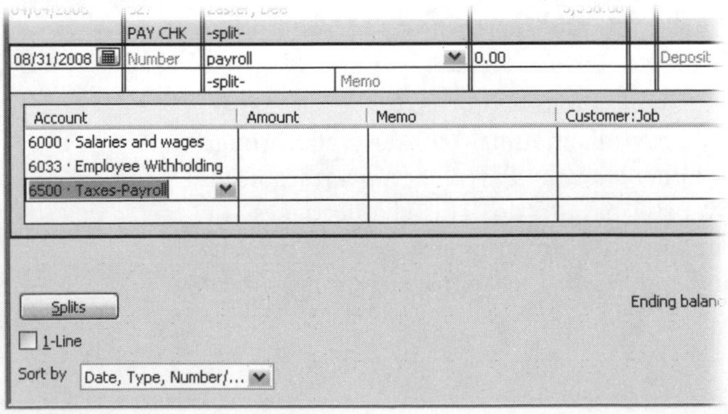

Figure 14-1: *In most cases, your payroll falls into three categories. Salaries and wages represent the net pay that employees receive from their paychecks. Employee withholdings are the taxes withheld from employees' paychecks like federal and state income taxes, social security and Medicare contributions, and local taxes. Payroll taxes are the taxes that your company pays, such as social security and Medicare. If you also pay officers' salaries, you can include a fourth expense account for them.*

3. **In the first blank transaction's Payee field, type the name of the payroll vendor you set up, and then click Splits.**

   The Splits pane opens below the transaction.

4. **Fill in the Account fields for each payroll expense.**

   You leave the Amount fields blank, because you're simply memorizing the transaction so you can record future payrolls, which usually have different amounts.

5. **To remember which accounts you allocate payroll to, memorize the payroll transaction by pressing Ctrl+M.**

   In the Memorize Transaction dialog box, type a name for the transaction. You can set up a reminder schedule that matches the frequency of your payroll (page 319). Click OK to memorize the transaction and close the Memorize Transaction dialog box.

6. **Back in the bank account register, click Restore to clear the values in the payroll transaction.**

   If you want to record a payroll, you can fill in the amount fields with the values from your payroll statement, and then click Record.

7. **To record a payroll, press Ctrl+T to open the Memorized Transactions list. Double-click the payroll transaction you memorized.**

   In the Write Checks window, in the Amount field, type the total amount that the payroll service withdrew from your payroll bank account. On the Expenses tab, fill in each Amount field with the values from your payroll services statement. Then, click Save & Close to record the transaction.

Note: To record the payroll service's fee, you can record a separate transaction in the payroll bank account using the vendor name for the payroll service. Assign the transaction to an expense account like Payroll Expenses.

Choosing a Payroll Service

If you don't use an outside payroll service, you'll probably choose one of Quick-Books' payroll services to process payroll in the program. These services help you calculate deductions, enter your results into your company file, print the paychecks, remit your payroll taxes, and generate the appropriate payroll tax reports. Without a payroll service, you have to perform all those tasks on your own. When you take the value of your time into account, even the most expensive payroll service might look like a good deal.

Intuit provides three payroll services, so you can choose between low-cost basic services, moderately priced and moderately featured services, and a more costly but comprehensive service. Choose Employees → Payroll Service Options → Learn About Payroll Options. QuickBooks opens a Web page (*http://payroll.intuit.com/ payroll_services*) that describes Intuit's offerings. QuickBooks' three payroll options fall into do-it-yourself or delegate-to-Intuit categories. Here's a quick overview to get you started:

- **Basic Payroll** is the first do-it-yourself option ($129 a year for up to three employees; $229 a year for four or more employees). You set everything up at the start, as you do for all the services. But then, for each payroll, you enter hours or payroll amounts, and QuickBooks uses the data in tax tables (downloaded so they're always up to date) to calculate the deductions and payroll taxes for you. Basic Payroll spits out reports with the info you need to fill out the federal and state tax forms you have to file. Your job is to print the paychecks from QuickBooks (or use direct deposit for an additional fee), fill out the government payroll tax forms, and send them in with your payment.

- **Enhanced Payroll** is a more robust version of do-it-yourself payroll. For starters, if you have to withhold state taxes, Enhanced Payroll can handle preparing federal and state payroll forms. You just print them, add your John Hancock, and mail them in. If the tax agencies you work with support e-file or e-pay services, Enhanced Payroll can file your tax forms and pay payroll taxes, too. This service also handles Workers' Compensation. It costs $249 per year for up to three employees, $349 a year for four or more employees.

- With **Assisted Payroll**, you don't have to make federal and state payroll tax deposits, file required tax reports during the year, or prepare W-2 and W-3 forms at the end of the year. The service handles all these tasks for you. In addition, Intuit guarantees that your payroll and payroll tax deposits and filings are accurate and on time. Of course, you have to send Intuit the correct data on time in the first place. But if Assisted Payroll then makes a mistake or misses a deadline, it pays the resulting payroll tax penalties. The price of the service varies depending on your payroll schedule and number of employees, but it's $60 per month plus $1 per employee per pay period. The one-time setup fee is $49, printing W-2s is $40 plus $4.25 for each W-2; and it costs another $10 per month for each additional state you have to work with.

Note: With any of these payroll services, direct deposit for employee paychecks costs $0.99 per paycheck.

Applying for a Payroll Service

Before you begin the mechanics of setting up your payroll, you have to select and sign up for one of the QuickBooks Payroll Services. To apply for one of Intuit's services, choose Employees → Payroll Service Options → Order Payroll Service.

QuickBooks opens a browser window to the QuickBooks Payroll Services website. Click Learn More to review Intuit's payroll options.

Before you click Buy Now to launch the online subscription process, gather the following info:

- The legal name of your company is on your Articles of Incorporation or other legal documents from when you formed your company.

- Your Federal Employer Identification Number (EIN) is a nine-digit number issued by the IRS.

- The legal names of each company principal, and the company's legal name and address.

Tip: If you aren't sure who the company principals are or what the company's legal name and address are, you can find them on your recent tax forms, incorporation documents, and so on.

- A mailing address (other than a post office box).

- If you're activating direct deposit, you also need the bank routing number and account number for the account from which you'll distribute payroll. You have to create this account in your company file before you activate direct deposit.

- A credit card number for the subscription fee.

After you submit the application, QuickBooks checks the company information and credit card number you provided. If it runs into any problems, a message tells you to contact Intuit (and conveniently lists the telephone number to call).

Note: When you install QuickBooks, the preference for payroll is turned on automatically. If you turned it off initially because you had no employees but now want to use payroll features, see page 571 to learn how to set payroll preferences based on the payroll service you choose.

Setting Up Payroll

The easiest way to begin setting up payroll is by choosing Employees → Payroll Setup, which launches the Payroll Setup wizard. Figure 14-2 shows how the wizard helps you see where you are in the payroll setup process. The following sections cover the payroll setup steps in detail.

You don't have to go through the entire payroll setup process in one shot. Click Finish Later if you want to take a break. The wizard remembers everything you've done when you return. Yes, you *have* to complete every bit of payroll setup before you can run a payroll.

Warning: Don't try to set up payroll the same day you want to run it for the first time. Intuit needs a few days to turn on your payroll service after you've completed your part of the setup process.

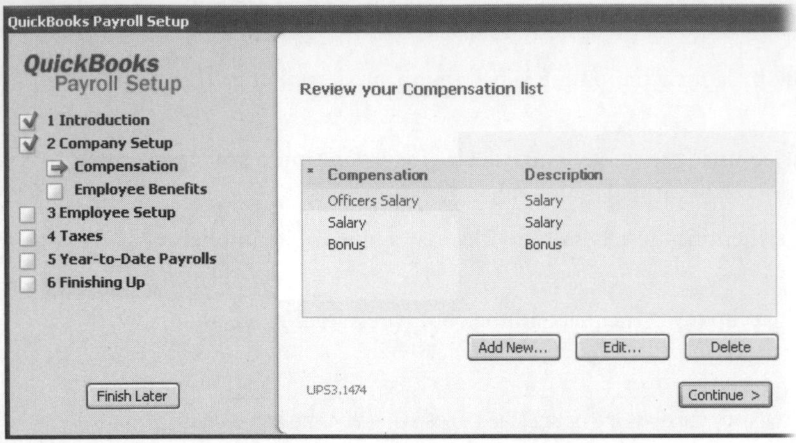

Figure 14-2:
A green arrow shows you which setup task you're working on (Compensation here). As you complete the steps for setting up payroll, the wizard adds a green checkmark to the completed tasks.

Setting Up Compensation and Benefits

The first payroll task is telling QuickBooks how you compensate your employees—whether you pay them a salary, hourly wages, or additional income such as bonuses or commissions. You also specify employee benefits like retirement contributions and insurance premiums—no matter whether the company or the employees pay for them. The QuickBooks Payroll Setup wizard takes the guesswork out of choosing items for payroll. All you have to do is turn on checkboxes for the items you use and answer a few simple questions. Here's how:

1. **Choose Employees → Payroll Setup.**

   The QuickBooks Payroll Setup wizard launches. Click Next to get past the introduction.

2. **Click Company Setup, and then click Compensation.**

   The wizard displays the payroll items you've selected. You can then add, edit, or delete items to reflect your payroll needs.

3. **To add another payroll item in the current category, click Add New (below the list of compensation items).**

   The Add New window includes checkboxes for the available items in that category, as shown in Figure 14-3.

4. **Turn on the checkboxes for the compensation items you use, answer any questions that the wizard asks, and then click Finish.**

   The selected items appear in the wizard's Compensation list, but behind the scenes they show up in the Payroll Item List (choose Lists → Payroll Item List). It also links those items to accounts in your chart of accounts, so you can track your payroll expenses. For example, a salary payroll item links to an Expense

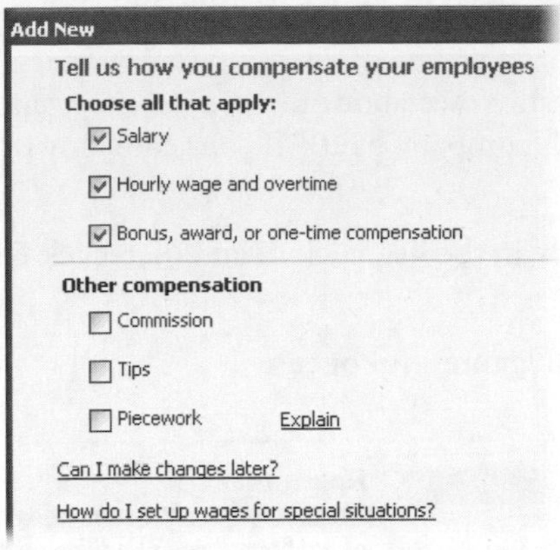

Figure 14-3:
You don't calculate each employee's pay per payroll cycle in the Payroll Setup wizard. Instead, you set up hourly or annual pay rates for each employee (even if they all get the same rate) as described on page 370. QuickBooks uses the employee pay rates to calculate the values for each paycheck.

Add New

Tell us how you compensate your employees

Choose all that apply:

☑ Salary

☑ Hourly wage and overtime

☑ Bonus, award, or one-time compensation

Other compensation

☐ Commission

☐ Tips

☐ Piecework   Explain

Can I make changes later?

How do I set up wages for special situations?

account, like Salaries & Wages. (To see these accounts, open the Payroll Item List, select the payroll item, and then press Ctrl+E. Click Next to see the expense account that goes with the item.) Likewise, if you deduct money from paychecks to pay taxes (page 370), the wizard connects the tax payroll item to a vendor (that is, the tax agency), so you're ready to send payroll taxes you owe. If QuickBooks adds items you don't need to the Payroll Item List, like extra pay for overtime, select an item, and then click Delete.

5. **To proceed to employee benefits, in the QuickBooks Payroll Setup wizard, click either Continue at the bottom-right of the window or Employee Benefits in the step navigation bar.**

   In the step navigation bar, you'll see several subcategories of employee benefits: Insurance Benefits, Retirement Benefits, Paid Time Off, and Miscellaneous.

6. **Click Insurance Benefits.**

   The Insurance Benefits list shows any insurance benefits you've already set up, like pre-tax health insurance premiums.

7. **Click Add New, and then turn on the checkboxes for items like "Dental insurance", "Vision insurance", Group Term Life, or Medical Care FSA (FSA stands for "flexible spending account").**

   If you don't know what a benefit represents, click the Explain link to the right of its name. If QuickBooks needs to know more about the benefit like who pays for it and whether it's tax-deductible, you'll see the Next button instead of the Finish button. For example, for dental insurance you pick whether you or the employee pays, or whether you split the cost. You can also set up a scheduled payment to pay the insurance premiums.

8. **When you're done answering questions, click Finish to close the Add New dialog box and return to the wizard.**

   The benefit(s) appear in the wizard's list. Notes about the benefit show up in parentheses after the benefit name, like "(company paid)" if your company pays the entire premium.

9. **If you want to edit an item that's already in the list, click it, and then click Edit (below the item list).**

   An Edit dialog box like the one shown in Figure 14-4 opens.

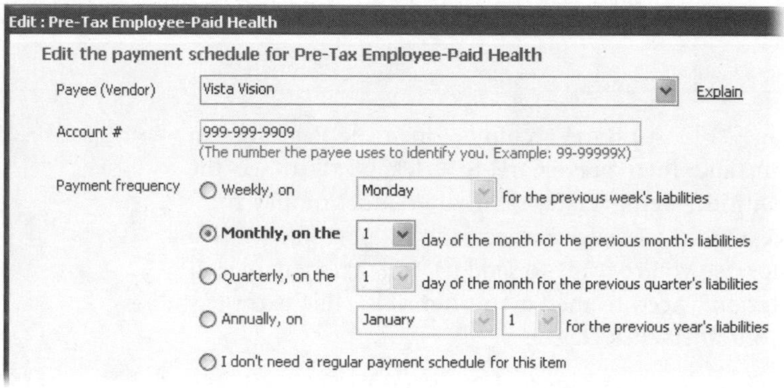

Figure 14-4:
The dialog box shows the name of the benefit you're editing, "Edit: Company-Paid Health," for example. Click Next or Previous to move through the screens of settings for the item.

10. **Repeat steps 6 through 9 for each category of employee benefits.**

    Retirement benefits include things like 401(k) contributions and company matching. Paid time off covers things like sick time and vacation. Miscellaneous cleans up with anything else that's added or deducted from paychecks, like cash advances, mileage reimbursements, or union dues. For additions or deductions that aren't covered by any of the Miscellaneous Item checkboxes, turn on either "Miscellaneous addition" or "Miscellaneous deduction".

    You aren't finished with the wizard just yet, but you're done setting up payroll items for compensation and benefits. See the next section to learn how to set up employees with the wizard.

Setting Up Employees

Before you dive into setting up employees with the Payroll Setup wizard, completing two prerequisites *first* can speed up your work. Besides, after defining all your payroll items, you could probably use a break. In the Payroll Setup wizard, click Finish Later and perform these two steps:

- **Gather employee information and records.** You need personal information, such as Social Security numbers and hire dates, along with signed W-4 and I-9 federal forms. For employees already on the payroll, you need their pay rates,

Choosing the Right Payroll Start Date

QuickBooks doesn't tell you this, but there's a right and wrong time to start using QuickBooks for payroll. You have to file 941 reports (Employer's Quarterly Federal Tax Returns) quarterly as their name implies. Therefore, Quick-Books won't let you summarize payroll data for the current quarter; you have to enter individual pay period totals from the beginning of the current quarter up to the date you start using QuickBooks payroll.

You can save yourself a lot of data entry by starting to use QuickBooks for payroll at the beginning of a quarter. You still have to enter summary values for each completed quarter in the current year, but you don't have to enter any individual payrolls.

the total pay they've received, and deductions taken, along with sick time and vacation balances.

- **Set up employee payroll defaults.** If you have more than a few employees, you can save time by setting up the payroll items that apply to *every* employee, like common deductions. That way, QuickBooks automatically fills in these payroll items for you when you create a new employee record. You then make only any necessary modifications for that individual. QuickBooks has a feature designed especially for this timesaving scheme, as described in the next section.

Setting employee defaults

Typically, you use a common set of payroll items for all your employees, such as salary, tax deductions, health insurance, and 401(k) contributions. Instead of assigning the same payroll items to each employee, you can save these standard items so that QuickBooks fills in most of the payroll fields for you. You can also specify the pay period you use and the class (page 138) to apply if you track performance by class.

To set up your standard payroll characteristics, on the QuickBooks Home page, click Employees. In the Employee Center window's toolbar, choose Manage Employee Information → Change New Employee Default Settings. In the Employee Defaults dialog box, you can set up standard items for every type of payroll item you use, as shown in Figure 14-5.

Note: If you track employee work hours in QuickBooks (page 188) and pay your employees by the hour, the program happily calculates their paycheck amounts. In the Employee Defaults dialog box, simply turn on the "Use time data to create paychecks" checkbox below the Earnings section. To determine the gross amount of paychecks, the program multiplies the hours on employee timesheets for the pay period by the employees' hourly rates.

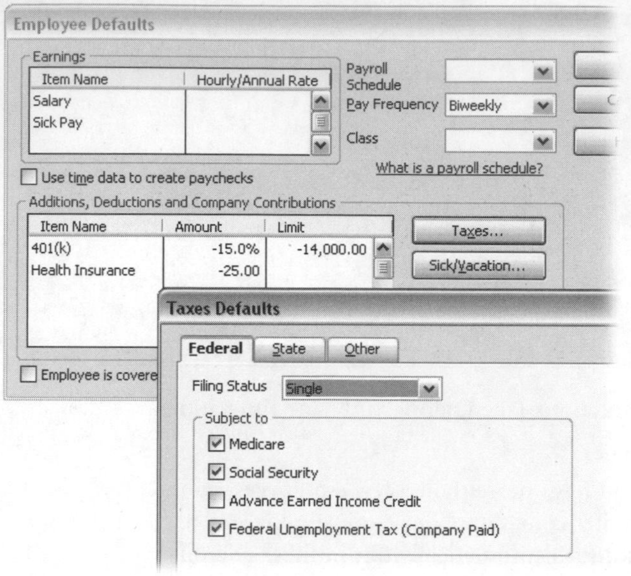

Figure 14-5:
Although your standard items for taxes don't appear in the "Additions, Deductions, and Company Contributions" list (background), when you click Taxes, you can see the payroll tax items assigned to each new employee (foreground). Similarly, by clicking Sick/Vacation, you can set how sick and vacation time accrue, the maximum accrued hours each year, and whether hours rollover from one year to the next. Sick and vacation time can accrue at the beginning of the year, so the employee receives the entire allotment as of January 1, or you can have some time accrue each pay period.

The Employee Defaults dialog box includes the same set of fields and checkboxes that you'll find in the Payroll Setup wizard and on the "Payroll and Compensation Info" tab in the New Employee window (in the Employee Center toolbar, click New Employee, and then, in the "Change tabs" drop-down list, choose "Payroll and Compensation Info"). When you edit an employee record, you can change any default payroll settings that don't apply to that employee.

Note: When you create a new employee, QuickBooks automatically fills in the fields you specified in Employee Defaults. For example, if you add a Salary item without an hourly or annual rate, QuickBooks adds the Salary item to each new employee's record but leaves the value field blank.

Creating employee records

You can create employee records in the Payroll Setup wizard (Employees → Payroll Setup) or by creating new employee records outside of the wizard (in the Employee Center, choose New Employee to open the New Employee window). The info you have to provide is the same, but the Payroll Setup wizard is easier to navigate.

Tip: You can run the Payroll Setup wizard any time you want. For example, if you hire a new employee, run the wizard and add the new employee's record right then and there.

With employee records in hand and payroll settings in place, you can add employees in no time with the Payroll Setup wizard. Choose Employees → Payroll Setup to open the wizard once again. In the wizard's navigation bar, click Employee List. The wizard prompts you to provide all the information it needs to process payroll, as Figure 14-6 shows.

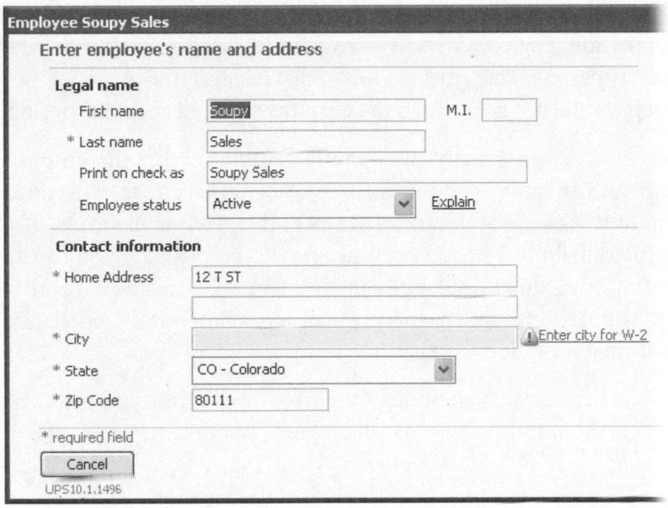

Figure 14-6:
The Payroll Setup wizard indicates required fields with an asterisk. If a required field isn't filled in, you'll see a warning explaining why QuickBooks needs the information (like the one to the right of the City box).

Here's how to fill out employee information in the Payroll Setup wizard:

- **Contact information.** For W-2 forms, you need the basic info about an employee (employee name and address). In the Payroll Setup wizard, if you add or edit an employee, the name and address screen collects the employee's contact information, including phone number and email. This screen also includes the "Employee status" drop-down list, where you choose Active or Inactive depending on whether the employee is working for you at the moment. If you want to add additional contact information, do so in the Edit Employee dialog box (in the Employee Center, right-click an employee's name and choose Edit on the shortcut menu).

- **Hiring information.** When you click Next on the "Enter employee's name and address" screen, this screen lets you fill in the basics about the person's employment: whether the employee is an officer, owner, or regular Joe; Social Security number; and hire date. You can also enter a release date, which is a diplomatic name for the last date the employee worked for you. (Although you enter hiring information in QuickBooks, you still need separate files outside of QuickBooks to keep track of employee information.)

Note: Corporations have to keep track of compensation to corporate officers separate from employee compensation, which you do by choosing Officer in the "Employee type" drop-down list. In addition, you'll need two separate expense accounts for compensation, such as Salaries & Wages for your employees and Officer Salaries for the officers.

- **Wages and compensation.** This screen is where you specify the compensation the employee receives, and payroll frequency. The wizard automatically displays the default payroll items for new employees. Turn on the checkboxes for the items that apply to the employee. The label doesn't tell you, but the Amount boxes expect the *annual* pay rate, not how much the employee is paid each pay period.

- **Benefits.** On this screen, you specify the benefit deductions for the employee, like 401(k) and health insurance. Besides turning benefits on or off, you can specify the deduction as a dollar amount or percentage. For example, if the employee wants to contribute 15 percent of her pay to her 401(k), you can type *15%* in the Amount box. QuickBooks fills in the Annual Limit box for 401(k) with the current annual limit set by the government. For other benefits, you have to type the annual limit, if one exists.

- **Sick time.** The sick time screen includes fields for specifying your sick time policies: how much the employee earns and when, maximum amounts, and current balances.

- **Vacation time.** The vacation time screen is almost identical to the sick time screen, except that it specifies the employee's vacation earnings.

- **Direct deposit.** If you offer direct deposit, you can turn on direct deposit for an employee and specify whether the deposit goes to only one bank account or to two (checking and savings, for example).

- **State tax.** The state tax screen has two drop-down lists for telling QuickBooks where the employee lives and works. The choices you make determine the state tax and unemployment tax that the employee pays. You'll have to answer more questions about state taxes after you tell the wizard about the federal taxes.

- **Federal tax.** On this screen, you tell the wizard about the employee's filing status, the number of allowances, extra withholding, and whether the employee is subject to deductions like Social Security and Medicare.

At long last, you'll see the Finish button in the bottom-right corner of the Employee dialog box. Click it to complete the setup. If you missed any info, an exclamation mark in a yellow triangle appears to the left of the employee's name.

An X in a red circle appears if there's a serious problem with something you entered. (The Summary column tells you what's missing.) Click Edit, and then fill in the missing information.

Setting Up Direct Deposit

Direct deposit makes everyone's life a little easier. You don't have to worry about guarding cashable checks until you deliver them to your employees. And your employees don't have to make a trip to the bank to deposit their earnings—the money transfers from your payroll account to the accounts that employees specify, such as checking and savings accounts.

Direct deposit is an add-on service (in other words, you have to pay extra for it) that you can sign up for no matter which QuickBooks payroll service you choose. Once you've activated the service (choose Help → Add QuickBooks Services and then, in the QuickBooks Products and Services Web page, click Payroll), you have to tell QuickBooks which bank and account gets the directly deposited money for each employee.

To make direct deposit work, you need the nine-digit routing number for the employee's bank and the employee's account number (or numbers) at that bank. Voided checks from employees are a great way to verify the routing and account numbers (and make sure it's their account). When you split direct deposits between two accounts, the money that goes to each has to add up to the total amount of the paycheck.

If you use a payroll service other than QuickBooks', don't sign up for QuickBooks direct deposit service. You work with your third-party payroll service to set up direct deposit.

You can then add more employees. Or, to move on to tax settings (in the Payroll Setup navigation bar, click Taxes), as described in the next section.

Setting Up Payroll Taxes

The next major step in setting up payroll is to tell QuickBooks your company's tax information: your tax identification numbers, the tax agencies you pay, and any local payroll taxes. In the Payroll Wizard navigation bar, click Taxes to see an overview of what you can expect. In the navigation bar, click "Federal taxes" to get down to work. The Federal tax screen simply lists the federal taxes for which you're responsible.

Note: You specify your federal tax ID number in the Company Information dialog box (choose Company → Company Information).

To add state taxes, in the navigation bar, click "State taxes". Then, below the list of state taxes, click Add New. When you choose a state, the wizard adds the typical taxes for that state like income tax, unemployment tax, and so on. You have to provide your account number with the state and enter the rate. (You have to wait until after January 1 to enter tax rates for the next year.) Select a tax and click Edit to change how the tax's name appears on paychecks or to change it to inactive (if you no longer employ people in a particular state, for instance).

Tip: If you use a QuickBooks payroll service, you can set up a schedule for your payroll tax payments. In the navigation bar, click "Schedule payments". Then in the Schedule Payments dialog box, you tell Quick-Books who to pay and when. QuickBooks keeps track of what you owe to each tax agency and reminds you when it's time to pay your taxes. (The reminders show up in the Payroll Center: choose Employees → Payroll Center.)

TROUBLESHOOTING MOMENT

Verifying Payroll Summaries

After you've typed in your historical payroll data, it's a good idea to generate payroll summary reports in QuickBooks to compare to the reports you received from your payroll service. From then on, these payroll summary reports let you review relevant payroll data before cutting payroll checks. They also tell you what your payroll liabilities are and when you have to pay them to the appropriate government agencies.

The Payroll Summary report shows what you've paid on each payroll item, such as employee wages, taxes and other withholdings, and employer payroll taxes. Choose Reports → Employees & Payroll → Payroll Summary. QuickBooks generates the report for the current calendar quarter to date, but you can change the date range to see how much you've paid for a month, quarter, or entire year (in the Payroll Summary report window, choose a date range in the Dates drop-down list, or type dates in the From and To boxes).

Compare the values in the QuickBooks report to the payroll service report for the same quarter. If the numbers are wildly disparate, you probably left out an employee or a payroll run when you entered payroll summaries. Check the summary report to make sure that each employee you paid appears and double-check the values.

Small discrepancies are probably data entry errors. Compare each amount in the summary report to the amounts on your payroll service reports. When you find the source of the problem, you can edit the payroll transactions to make the corrections.

The Payroll Detail Review report shows how QuickBooks calculates tax amounts on paychecks. For example, the percentage for Social Security remains the same, but Social Security deductions stop when the employee reaches the maximum Social Security wage.

Entering Historical Payroll

If you start using QuickBooks in the middle of a year, the best approach to record-keeping is entering all your financial transactions from the beginning of the year. At the end of the year, you and your accountant will be glad you did. But with payroll, it's *essential* to enter all the payrolls you've processed since the beginning of the year. That's the only way to produce W-2s at the end of the year that show the correct totals for the entire year. In addition, entering previous payroll data means that the payroll calculations take into account deduction limits. For example, for 2009, Social Security taxes apply to only the first $106,800 of income. Income that an employee earns beyond that is free of Social Security tax.

Tip: Toward the end of the year, the easiest solution is to wait until January 1 to switch to QuickBooks payroll.

If you use an outside service, you can add a single transaction with the year-to-date totals from the most recent statement the service sent you. For QuickBooks payroll services, you have two choices for getting this year's historical payroll information into your company file:

• **Run previous payrolls one by one.** This approach gives an added bonus: you can take practice runs through the payroll process and verify the values against existing payroll reports from your other system. If you take the dummy payroll approach, be sure to turn off the "To be printed" checkbox. Instead, fill in the check numbers from those past payrolls.

• **Use the Payroll Setup wizard to add payroll amounts for the payrolls you ran without QuickBooks payroll services.** Of course, you have to complete the first four wizard setup steps described on the previous pages. In the Payroll Setup wizard, when you see checkmarks in front of steps 1 (Introduction) through 4 (Taxes), you're ready to enter the year-to-date amounts. Gather your manual payroll records for the year so far and then, in the navigation bar, click Year-to-date Payrolls. You simply click through the screens and type in the values from each quarter's payrolls.

Running Payroll

Once your payroll setup is complete, generating payroll checks each pay period takes only a few minutes. Before you run payroll, you need up-to-date tax tables, as the box below explains. This section explains the steps for running a payroll, from selecting which employees you're going to pay to printing the checks.

WORD TO THE WISE

Updating Tax Tables

Make a habit of updating your tax tables every time before you run payroll. It's the best way to make sure you withhold the correct amounts. QuickBooks needs the most current tax tables to calculate your payroll taxes correctly and generate the correct payroll tax forms. No matter which QuickBooks payroll service you sign up for, updated tax tables are one of the benefits you receive with your subscription.

Before you run a payroll, download a tax update by choosing Employees → Get Payroll Updates. Click Update to start

the download. After the progress bar disappears, you'll see a confirmation message. Click OK to view the contents of the update.

If you sign up for the Assisted Payroll service, QuickBooks checks whether your tax information is the most current whenever you send payroll data, and downloads the update for you automatically if your tax tables are out-of-date.

Note: When you use direct deposit services, you have to run payroll at least two banking days before the actual pay date so the service can process the payroll and transfer money into your employees' accounts. The transmission date may change due to bank holidays, so be sure to check payroll messages from the bank to see if you need to transmit payroll data earlier than usual. If you pay employees by the hour, this processing period creates a lag in employees' pay. For example, if you pay employees for the hours they work between the 1st and the 15th of the month, direct deposits wouldn't appear in their accounts until the 17th at the earliest.

1. **Choose Employees → Pay Employees or on the Home page, click Pay Employees.**

   The Enter Payroll Information window (Figure 14-7) opens to the first screen where you set up the pay period and check date, and pick the employees to pay.

   The Bank Account box is automatically set to the account you choose for payroll in QuickBooks preferences as described on page 555.

2. **If the Pay Period Ends date isn't correct, choose the date you want.**

   Each time you run payroll, QuickBooks changes the date to the next payroll date based on the payroll frequency you set in Employee Defaults (page 367). In the Check Date box, choose the date you want on the paychecks you produce.

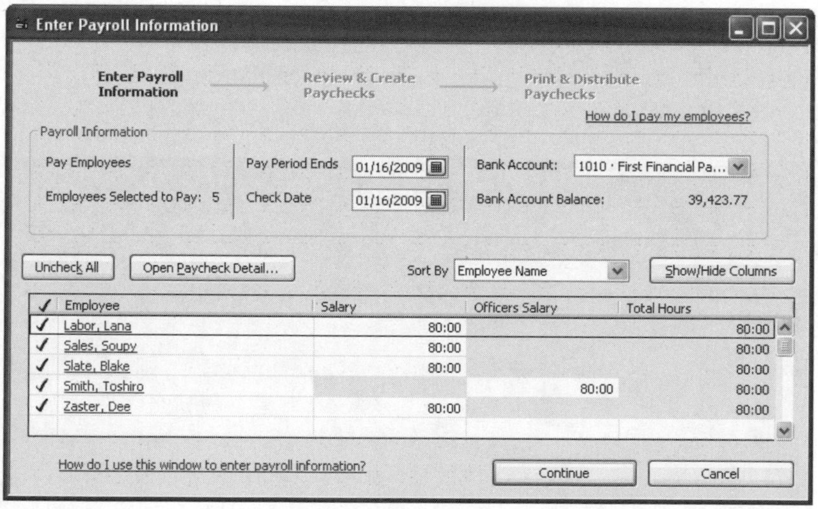

Figure 14-7:
Employees who are set to inactive status in the Employees List don't show up in the Enter Payroll Information window; neither do employees whose release dates (page 369) are prior to the date in the Pay Period Ends box.

3. **To select all your employees, which is the most common choice, click Check All above the employee table.**

   But if you pay employees by the hour, you might want to select only the employees who worked during the pay period. To select individual employees, click the employee's checkmark cell to turn it on.

4. **If you want to look at what QuickBooks calculated for employee paychecks, click Open Paycheck Detail above the employee table.**

   The Preview Paycheck dialog box (a real monster as Figure 14-8 shows) starts with the first selected employee's earnings and payroll items. You can change the values in white cells. Gray cells like the ones for year-to-date values aren't editable.

5. **Click Save & Next to view the next paycheck.**

   Or, click Save & Close to return to the Enter Payroll Information window without reviewing other employees' records.

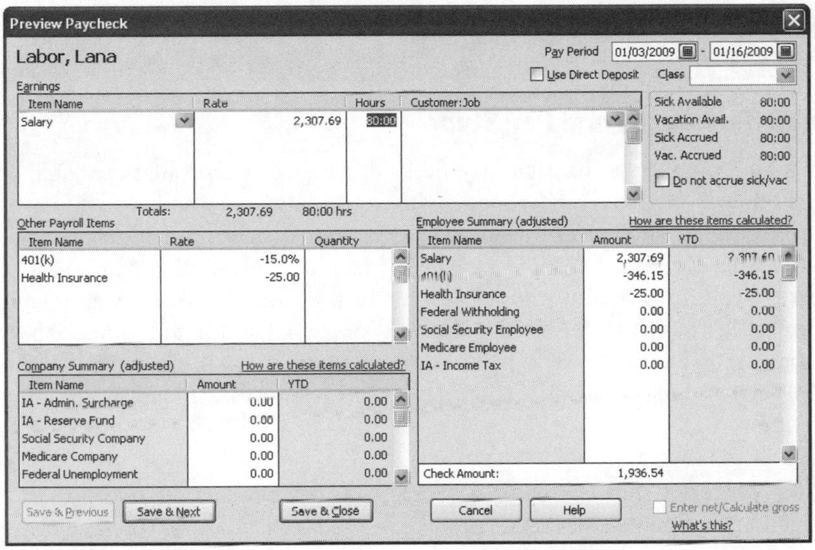

Figure 14-8:
In the Preview Paycheck dialog box, the Earnings section shows the gross amount of the employee's paycheck. For salaried employees, QuickBooks prorates the salary to the length of the pay period. In the Other Payroll Items section and Company Summary section, the program uses the tax tables and your payroll items to calculate paycheck deductions or additions. Below the Class box is available sick and vacation time. The Employee Summary section shows the entries you typically see on a pay stub.

6. **Back in the Enter Payroll Information window, click Continue to move on to creating paychecks.**

   The "Review and Create Paychecks" window opens, as shown in Figure 14-9. The employee table shows the values for each employee's paycheck and the total for each category. If you see any numbers that don't look right, click Open Paycheck Detail and repeat step 4 to correct the values.

7. **When everything looks good, you're ready to create the paychecks. In the "Review and Create Paychecks" window, click Create Paychecks.**

   QuickBooks creates the records for the paychecks, but you still have some printing to do, as the next section explains.

Deleting Duplicate Paychecks

If you get called away to handle a crisis before you print paychecks, you might forget where you were and create a second batch of paychecks for the same pay period. When you return to printing paychecks, you'll see the duplicates in the Select Paychecks to Print dialog box. What you *won't* see is a way to delete those paychecks. Getting rid of duplicate paychecks is one of the more obscure procedures in QuickBooks.

Here's what you need to do:

1. Choose Reports → Employees & Payroll → "Payroll Transactions by Payee" to run a report of paychecks for every employee.

2. In the report window, double-click a duplicate paycheck transaction to open the Paycheck window.

3. Press Ctrl+D (or right-click within the window and choose Delete Paycheck from the shortcut menu that appears) to delete the paycheck.

4. In the confirmation box that appears, click OK.

Printing Paychecks and Pay Stubs

When your employees want paper paychecks that they can deposit at the bank, you print the paychecks you just created (with accompanying pay *stubs*). But when employees use direct deposit (page 371) so the money goes directly to their bank accounts, you don't have to print paychecks. In fact, you shouldn't or you'll end up with two QuickBooks transactions deducting money from your payroll account. Still, your employees want a record of their pay for the period, so you print pay stubs instead. Printing paychecks and pay stubs is almost identical to printing expense checks. This section describes the process, including the minor differences.

Note: If you've signed up for QuickBooks' direct deposit, you still have to *create* paychecks, but you don't *print* them. After you create the direct deposit paychecks, you process them by choosing Employees → Send Payroll Data. (If you haven't signed up for direct deposit, you won't see this menu entry.) To send the paychecks, click Go Online, and when you're done, click Close.

---

1. **Before you print paychecks, load the printer with checks for the account you use for payroll, whether it's your regular checking account or a separate one.**

   If you clicked Create Paychecks in the "Review and Create Paychecks" window, you see the "Confirmation and Next Steps" dialog box. It shows how many paychecks are waiting to be printed, and how many are going to be deposited directly, as Figure 14-10 shows.

2. **To print paychecks, simply click Print Paychecks.**

   If you want to print pay stubs for direct deposits, click Print Pay Stubs. Instead of a check for an employee, a pay stub is like a report of the employees' payroll data that you can distribute. (If you forgot to load the printer with checks, click Close. You can print the checks or stubs later by choosing File → Print Forms → Paychecks or File → Print Forms → Pay Stubs.)

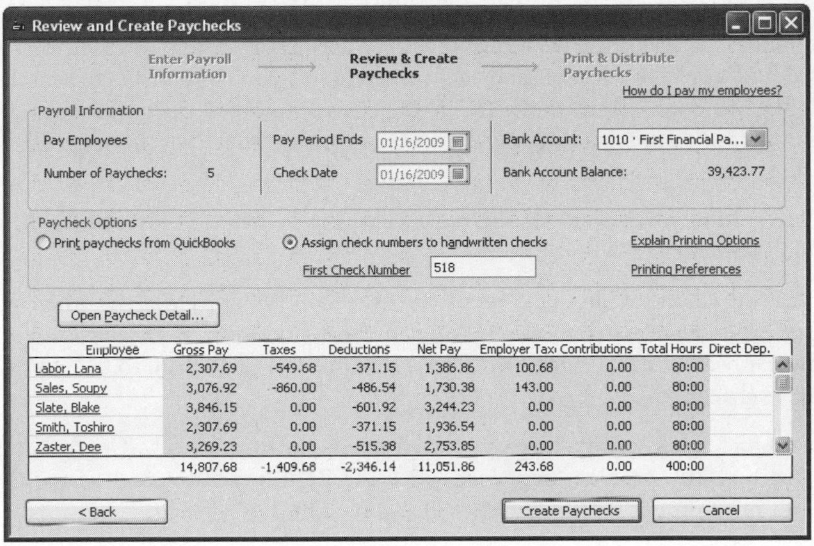

Figure 14-9:
If you're filling in payrolls you ran before using QuickBooks payroll services, select the "Assign check numbers to handwritten checks" option. In the First Check Number box, type the starting check number for that payroll run. For current payroll runs, select the option for how you produce paychecks. If you hand-write checks, type the first check number in the box. For employees who have their paychecks deposited directly (page 371), click the employee's Direct Deposit cell to turn on its checkmark.

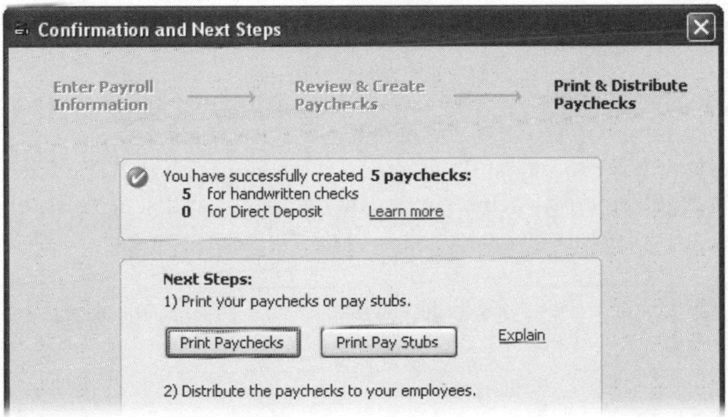

Figure 14-10:
Just above the Next Steps section is a status sentence that tells you how many paychecks you're printing and direct depositing. If you click Print Paychecks, the "Select Paychecks to Print" dialog box opens. Clicking "Print Paystubs" opens the "Select Paystubs to Print" dialog box.

3. In the "Select Paychecks to Print" dialog box (or "Select Paystubs to Print" dialog box), QuickBooks selects all the unprinted checks or pay stubs. Make sure that you're using the correct bank account and check number.

   If the account in the Bank Account box is wrong, choose the account you use for payroll from the drop-down list. In the First Check Number box, type the number on the first check in the printer.

   The "Select Paychecks to Print" dialog box automatically displays all paychecks, both direct deposit and paper. If you process paychecks and direct deposit paychecks in different ways, choose one of the Show options (Paychecks or Direct Deposit) to list only one type at a time.

4. **If you want to customize the data that appears on paychecks, click Preferences.**

   In the Payroll Printing Preferences dialog box, you can specify whether to print used and available vacation and sick time and—if you're security conscious—whether to omit all but the last four digits of employees' Social Security and bank account numbers. Click OK to return to the "Select Paychecks to Print" dialog box.

5. **When you're ready to print the paychecks, in the Select Paychecks to Print dialog box, click OK.**

   The Print Checks dialog box opens with the same options you see when you print expense checks (page 237). You can choose the style of check to use and how many checks are on the first sheet in the printer. Click Print to begin printing paychecks.

6. **After QuickBooks prints the paychecks, it opens the Print Checks-Confirmation dialog box. If a problem happened, click the Reprint cell for each check that didn't print properly, and then click OK to reprint those checks.**

   After the checks or stubs are printed, click Close and distribute the checks and pay stubs to your employees. If an employee loses a paycheck and wants you to print a new one, see the box on page 376.

Paying Payroll Taxes

In addition to paying your employees, you also have to remit payroll taxes and withholdings to a number of government agencies. There's no set answer for which payroll taxes you have to pay and when you need to pay them. The federal government has its requirements; each state has its own rules and schedules; and, in some areas, local governments tack on their own payroll taxes as well.

Note: QuickBooks Payroll services provide tables for federal *and* state payroll taxes. You have to calculate local taxes yourself.

Because the penalties for submitting payroll liabilities to the government are meant to hurt, you don't want to skip the reports that show how much you owe in payroll taxes and when the payments are due. The Payroll Liability Balances report shows how much you owe for each type of payroll tax for the current quarter. You'll find the information you need to fill in on state tax forms on the Employee State Taxes Detail report.

Government agencies send you letters telling you what your tax rates are and what payment schedule you have to follow. When you set up payroll in QuickBooks (page 371), you enter these details. The tax tables that QuickBooks' payroll services download update tax rates to what agencies are demanding at the moment. Because the specifics of remitting payroll taxes vary from company to company,

TROUBLESHOOTING MOMENT

Reissuing a Lost Paycheck

If an employee's paycheck gets lost, whether dropped by accident or by her bank, your employee is bound to want a new one. Because payroll checks affect tax returns and payroll liabilities, reissuing a paycheck while keeping payroll info straight requires a few steps. You need to keep your payroll expenses and payroll liabilities intact, and also eliminate the duplicate net pay from the original lost paycheck. Here's what you have to do:

1. First, verify that the paycheck hasn't cleared at your bank. If it hasn't, request a stop payment on the check.

2. Open your checking account register (in the Chart of Accounts window, double-click the account name) and find the lost paycheck. Jot down the original check number for later.

3. Double-click the paycheck to open the Paycheck window.

4. In the window's toolbar, click Print. In the Printed Check Number box, type a new check number (the next one in the sequence for your payroll checks). Click OK. You've reissued the paycheck with a new check number, but you still have to void the original lost check.

5. Press Ctrl+W to open the Write Checks window.

6. Make out the new check to the employee, but use the original check number for the lost check and type the *net* pay amount from the lost check in the amount field. In the account cell, choose Payroll Expenses.

7. Click Save & Close. This step removes the payroll taxes and liabilities from the original paycheck (because they're now part of the reissued paycheck). This newly created check represents only what you paid to the employee.

8. Void the check you just created: Select the check in the register and then choose Edit → Void Check. Voilà! You've just removed the amount you paid the employee on the lost check.

If you want to charge the employee for the stop payment fees, you can add a payroll deduction to the paycheck to reduce the employee's net pay. If the lost check was the bank's fault, it'll reimburse the employee for those fees.

you need to follow the instructions you receive from the tax agencies, your bank, and your accountant. Meanwhile, when it's time to remit payroll taxes, here's how you generate the payment checks:

1. Choose Employees → "Payroll Taxes and Liabilities" → Pay Payroll Liabilities (or on the Home page, click Pay Payroll Liabilities).

   QuickBooks opens the Select Date Range For Liabilities dialog box, where you specify the starting and ending dates for the payment period for a payroll tax. For example, the federal government determines payment frequency by the amount that you withhold from your employees' paychecks, and the most common frequency is monthly.

Note: If your deposit frequency changes—perhaps because you've hired a gaggle of new employees— you'll receive a letter from the IRS with your new deposit frequency.

2. **In the Dates drop-down list, choose the period for which you're paying payroll liabilities, such as Last Calendar Quarter or Last Month.**

   The Dates drop-down list includes the most typical date ranges you'll need. However, if you have a special date range to cover, in the From and To boxes, choose the starting and ending dates, respectively.

3. **Click OK.**

   The Pay Liabilities dialog box opens (Figure 14-11), listing all the payroll liabilities you have to remit and the agencies or organizations to whom you send the payments. QuickBooks automatically turns on the "To be printed" checkbox, which adds checks to the queue of checks to be printed. If you write the checks by hand, turn off this checkbox.

Tip: If you aren't changing the values on the checks, select the "Create liability check without reviewing" option. If you select the "Review liability check to enter expenses/penalties" option, you can make changes to the check before you print.

---

4. **In the Bank Account box, choose the bank account that you use for payroll.**

   QuickBooks fills in the account you specified in payroll preferences (page 555).

5. **In the Check Date box, choose the date you want on the checks.**

   Make sure that the check date meets the payment schedule requirements for the tax agency you're paying.

6. **Choose the payroll liabilities that you want to pay with one check by clicking the cell in the checkmark column for each payroll item.**

   The government isn't known for picking up on small details, such as two different payroll liabilities on the same check—unless the IRS is on an audit kick. So it's a good idea to create separate checks for each payroll liability to the same agency. To separate payments to the same vendor, select one payroll liability for a vendor during the first pass. After you've created the first batch of payroll liability checks, open the Pay Liabilities window once more and select another payment for the same vendor.

7. **When you've chosen the items you want to pay, click Create.**

   The window closes and QuickBooks creates checks for the payroll liabilities, but not as you might expect. Instead of creating one check for each payroll liability, the program creates a single check for each vendor (tax agency, insurance company, or other organization).

   If you turned on the "To be printed" checkbox, QuickBooks adds the checks to the queue of checks to be printed. If this checkbox is turned off, the program records the transactions in your company file, but you have to write the checks by hand.

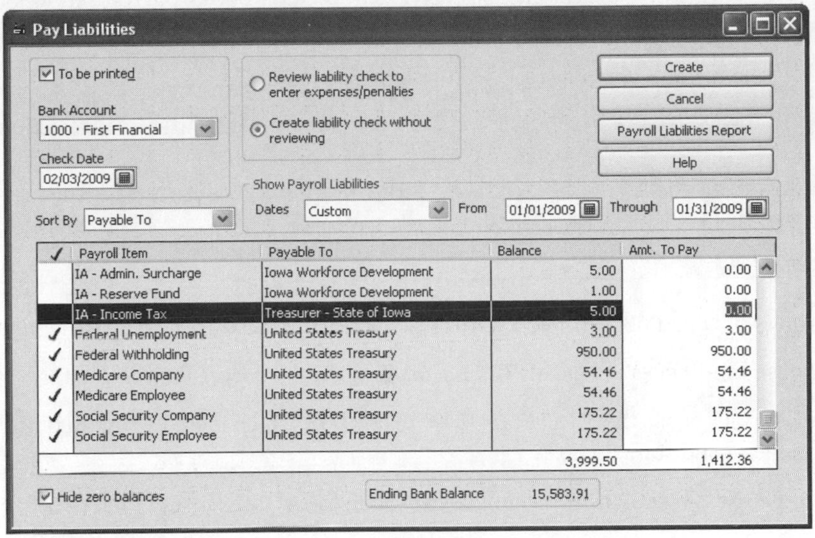

Figure 14-11:
To keep the list as concise as possible, turn on the "Hide zero balances" checkbox. QuickBooks displays only the liabilities that have a balance. But a payroll liability with a balance doesn't mean a payment is due. Select only the payroll items whose payment frequency requires a payment now. When you click one of the Medicare or Social Security payroll items, QuickBooks automatically selects the other, because both are due at the same time.

8. **To print the checks, choose File → Print Forms → Checks.**

   The "Select Checks to Print" dialog box opens.

9. **In the Bank Account drop-down list, choose the account you use for payroll.**

   If necessary, in the First Check Number box, type the first check number in your printer. QuickBooks automatically selects all the checks in the queue. If you want to prevent a check from printing in this run, uncheck it.

10. **Click OK to open the Print Checks dialog box.**

    The options for payroll liability checks are the same as paychecks and expense checks (page 236).

Note: If you use Assisted Payroll, the payroll service automatically makes your federal and state payroll tax liability payments. But you have to send the payroll data to the service so it knows how much to send to the appropriate tax agencies.

After you have checks in hand, fill in the coupons or forms that the tax agency sent you and send the payment and the payment coupon per the agency's instructions. For example, make federal payments at the bank where you keep your payroll account.

Preparing Payroll Tax Forms

Tax agencies require that you regularly submit forms documenting the payroll taxes and withholdings you're supposed to remit and how much you've already sent in. If you use Basic Payroll or a non-QuickBooks service, you can't produce payroll tax forms in QuickBooks. However, some QuickBooks payroll services let you print payroll tax forms and W-2s. If you subscribe to Enhanced Payroll, you can generate federal and state tax forms. Although the forms that QuickBooks produces aren't exact replicas of the preprinted forms you might receive from the government, they're close enough that you can send them in without fear of rejection.

Note: Many tax agencies are moving to phone and electronic filing. If you use one of these filing options, choose Reports → Employees & Payroll and then choose a report, like Employee State Taxes Detail, to get the values you need for your filing.

Regardless of which tax form you want to generate, the steps are basically the same:

1. **Choose Employees → Payroll Tax Forms & W-2s → Process Payroll Forms.**

   QuickBooks opens the Select Form Type dialog box, which includes option buttons for federal and state forms.

2. **Choose the "Federal form" option or the "State form" option, and then click OK.**

   The next dialog box that appears is the Select Payroll Form dialog box, which lists the federal and state forms that QuickBooks can generate. Depending on the form you choose, you specify the filing period.

   How you specify the filing period varies by form. If you choose the Quarterly Form 941, in the Quarter drop-down list, choose the quarter for which you want to generate a report. QuickBooks changes the date in the Quarter Ending box to match the quarter you choose. Form 940 requires only the filing year, and W-2s don't need anything.

3. **To export your payroll data to the form and display the filled-in form, click OK.**

   The form appears in the Payroll Tax Form window. Although QuickBooks formats the form so it's easy for you to read and review, when you print the form, it looks like the preprinted forms you receive from the tax agency. To print the form, in the Payroll Tax Form window, click Print. Now you're ready to mail the report in.

CHAPTER 15

Bank Accounts, Credit Cards, and Petty Cash

You've opened your mail, plucked out your customers' payments, and deposited them in your bank account (Chapter 13); in addition to that, your bills are paid (Chapter 9). Now you can sit back and relax knowing that *most* of the transactions in your bank and credit card accounts are accounted for. What's left?

Some stray transactions might pop up—an insurance claim check to deposit, restocking your petty cash drawer, or a fee from your bank for a customer's bounced check, to name a few. Plus, running a business typically means that money moves between accounts—from interest-bearing accounts to checking accounts or from merchant credit card accounts to savings. If you come across a financial transaction, you can enter it in QuickBooks, whether you prefer the guidance of dialog boxes or the speed of an account register window.

Reconciling your accounts to your bank statements is another key process you don't want to skip. You and your bank can both make mistakes, and *reconciling* your accounts is the best way to catch these discrepancies. Once the bane of book-keepers everywhere, reconciling is practically automatic now that you can download transactions electronically and let QuickBooks handle the math.

In this chapter, the section on reconciling is the only must-read. If you want to learn the fastest way to enter any type of bank account transaction, don't skip the first section, "Entering Transactions in an Account Register" on page 384. You can read about transferring funds, loans, bounced checks, and other financial arcana covered in this chapter as the need arises.

Entering Transactions in an Account Register

QuickBooks includes windows and dialog boxes for making deposits, writing checks, and transferring funds, but you can also construct these transactions right in a bank account's register window. Working in a register window has two advantages over the dialog boxes:

- **Speed.** Entering a transaction in a register window is fast, particularly when keyboard shortcuts, like pressing Tab to move between fields, are second nature.

- **Visibility.** Windows, such as Write Checks, keep you focused on the transaction at hand. You can't see other transactions unless you align the transaction window and the register window side by side. In a register window, you can look at previous transactions for reference and avoid entering duplicate transactions.

Opening a Register Window

You have to open a register window before you can enter transactions in it. Opening a register window couldn't be easier. If you want to open a bank account or credit card register, at the top-right of the Home page, under Account Balances, double-click the account you want to see. Here's how you can open any kind of account:

1. **If the Chart of Accounts window isn't open, press Ctrl+A (or, on the Home page, click Chart of Accounts).**

   The window pops open, listing all accounts you've set up in QuickBooks.

2. **In the Chart of Accounts window, double-click the bank account whose register window you want to open.**

   As you can see in Figure 15-1, this method can open register windows for more than just bank accounts. See the box on the next page to learn about different ways to handle credit card accounts.

Note: Income and expense accounts don't have registers in QuickBooks. When you double-click an income or expense account, QuickBooks generates a QuickReport of the transactions for that account. From the report window, you can take a closer look at a transaction by double-clicking it.

Creating a Transaction in an Account Register

The steps for creating a check in your checking account register (page 240) work for deposits and transfers, too, with only a few minor adjustments. Here's how to fill in the cells in the register window to create any kind of bank transaction:

- **Date.** When you first open a bank account register window, QuickBooks automatically puts the current date in the Date cell of the first blank transaction. Tweaking the date by a few days is as easy as pressing + or - until the date is the one you want. To become a master of keyboard shortcuts for dates, read the box on page 387.

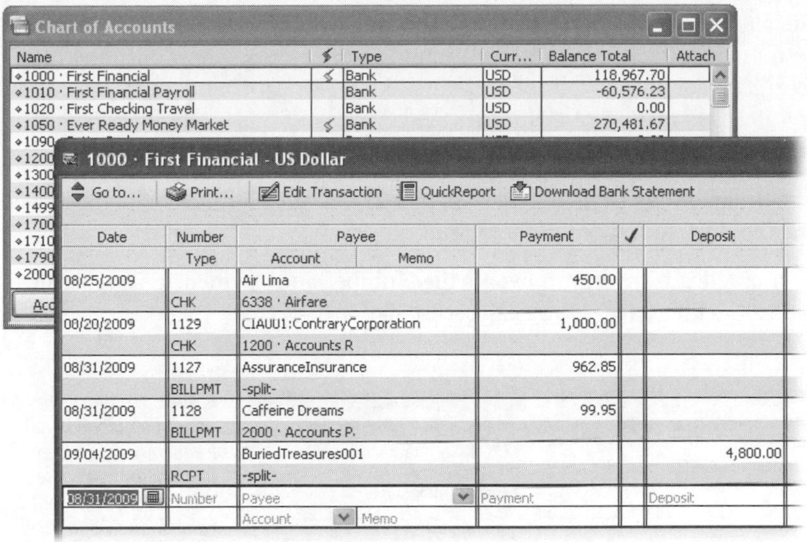

Figure 15-1:
You can open a register window by double-clicking any type of account with a balance, including checking, savings, money market, and petty cash accounts. In fact, double-clicking opens the register for any account on your balance sheet (Accounts Receivable, Accounts Payable, Credit Card, Asset, Liability, and Equity accounts).

FREQUENTLY ASKED QUESTION

Managing Credit Card Accounts

Are credit cards accounts or vendors?

In QuickBooks, credit cards can be accounts or vendors, depending on how you prefer to record your credit card transactions. Here's the deal:

- **Credit card account.** If you prefer to keep your expenditures up-to-date in your company file, create an account for your credit card and enter the charges as they happen (which takes no time at all if you download credit card transactions; page 529 tells you how). Then, you reconcile a credit card account as you would a checking account (page 399), but QuickBooks makes that easy. To prevent credit card charge payee names from filling your Vendor List with entries you don't need, store names in the Memo cell or create more general vendors like Gas, Restaurant, and Office Supplies.

- **Credit card vendor.** Setting up a credit card as a vendor has a few advantages: You don't have to reconcile a credit card account when you receive your credit card statement. The name of every emporium and establishment you bless with credit card purchases won't fill up your Vendor List. And instead of entering credit card charges as they happen, you can wait until you receive your credit card statement. The drawback is that you still have to allocate the money you spent to the appropriate accounts, and you can't download that split transaction from your credit card company. With statement in hand, in the Enter Bills window, enter a bill (page 238) for the total amount on your credit card statement. Then, on the Expenses and Items tabs, add entries to allocate charges to the appropriate expense accounts.

- **Number.** When you jump to the Number cell (press Tab), QuickBooks automatically fills in the next check number for the bank account. If the number doesn't match the paper check you want to write, press + or – until the number is correct. (For some types of accounts like credit cards and assets, the register has a Ref field instead of a Number field. You can fill in a reference number for the transaction or leave it blank.)

To make an online payment (see Chapter 22), in the Number cell, type S, which QuickBooks promptly changes to *Send*.

To enter a deposit, you can bypass the Number and Payment cells regardless of what values they have, as you can see in Figure 15-2.

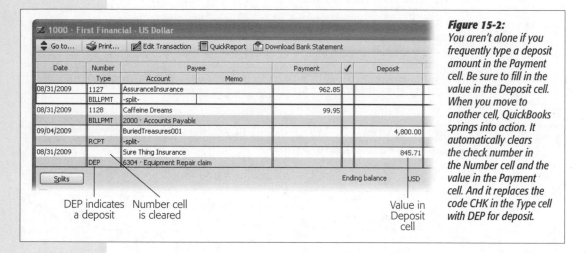

Figure 15-2:
You aren't alone if you frequently type a deposit amount in the Payment cell. Be sure to fill in the value in the Deposit cell. When you move to another cell, QuickBooks springs into action. It automatically clears the check number in the Number cell and the value in the Payment cell. And it replaces the code CHK in the Type cell with DEP for deposit.

DEP indicates a deposit   Number cell is cleared   Value in Deposit cell

Note: QuickBooks keeps track of handwritten and printed checks separately. When you use the register window to create a check, QuickBooks fills in the Number cell by incrementing the last *handwritten* check number. When you choose File → Print Forms → Checks, the program fills in the First Check Number box by incrementing the last *printed* check number.

- **Payee.** QuickBooks doesn't require a value in the Payee cell. In fact, for the occasional payee, it's better to leave that payee name out of the Payee cell for deposits, transfers, or petty cash transactions, so your Vendors list doesn't fill up with names you rarely use. Instead, type a Payee name like *Deposit* or *Petty Cash* and then fill in the Memo cell with a description of the transaction, like *Insurance Claim*.

Tip: If you want to fill in the Payee cell without filling up the Vendors list, create more general names, like Deposit, Transfer, Petty Cash, and Gasoline. Then you can fill in the Payee cell for every fuel purchase with *Gasoline* and type the name of the service station in the Memo cell.

Keyboard Shortcuts for Dates

If pressing + or – to increment dates seems rudimentary to you, add some of the following keyboard shortcuts to your date-selection arsenal. When the cursor is in the Date field, jump directly to favorite dates:

- **T (for Today).** Press T to change the date to today's date.

- **M (for Month).** Press M to select the first day of the current month. Pressing M additional times jumps to the first day of previous months.

- **H (for montH).** Press H to select the last day of the current month. Pressing H additional times jumps to the last day of months in the future.

- **W (for Week).** Press W to choose the first day of the current week. Pressing W additional times jumps to the first day of previous weeks.

- **K (for weeK).** Press K to choose the last day of the current week. Pressing K additional times jumps to the last day of future weeks.

- **Y (for Year).** Press Y to choose the first day of the current year. Pressing Y additional times jumps to the first day of previous years.

- **R (for yeaR).** Press R to choose the last day of the current year. Pressing R additional times jumps to the last day of future years.

You can press these letters multiple times to pick dates further in the past or the future and combine them with pressing + and – to reach any date you want. But face it: After half a dozen keystrokes, it might be easier to type a numeric date, such as 12/14/09, or to click the Calendar icon and choose the date.

As you start typing the name of the payee, QuickBooks scans the names in the various lists in your company file (Vendors, Customers, Other Names, and so on) and selects the first name it finds that matches all the letters you've typed so far. As soon as QuickBooks selects the one you want, press Tab to move to the Payment cell.

- **Payment or Charge.** For checks you write, fees that the bank deducts from your account, or petty cash withdrawals, type the amount in the Payment cell. In a credit card register, this field is named Charge for the credit card charges you make.

- **Deposit.** For deposits you make to checking or petty cash, or interest you earned, type the amount in the Deposit cell. In a credit card register, this field is called Payment, because you make payments *to* a credit card account (instead of making a payment *from* a checking account).

Note: In QuickBooks transactions, money either goes out or comes in—there's no in-between. When you enter a value in the Payment cell, QuickBooks clears the Deposit cell value, and vice versa.

- **Account.** The Account cell can play many roles. For instance, when you're creating a check, choose the account for the expense it represents. If you're making a deposit, choose the income or expense account to which you want to post the deposit. (Depositing an insurance claim check that pays for equipment repair reduces the balance of the expense account for equipment maintenance and repair.) If you're transferring money from another bank account, choose that account instead.

FREQUENTLY ASKED QUESTION

Contributing Money to Your Company

How do I record the money I contribute to my company?

If you're incorporating a company, most attorneys suggest that you contribute some cash to get the company off the ground. This money is called *owners' equity*.

The QuickBooks EasyStep Interview (page 21) usually creates an equity account called Owners' Contribution or something similar. If you don't have an owners' equity account, create one in the Chart of Accounts window (page 53).

In the New Account dialog box, be sure to choose the Equity account type.

The transaction for your deposit adds the money to your bank account, but you want the money to appear in your owner's equity account on the balance sheet. To accomplish this feat, in the deposit transaction's Deposit cell, enter the amount of your check, and then in the Account cell, choose the owner's equity account you've created.

Tip: If you want to assign a transaction to several accounts, click Splits. Figure 9-2 (page 209) shows how to distribute dollars to different accounts.

• **Memo.** Filling in the Memo cell can jog your memory no matter what type of transaction you create. Enter the bank branch for a deposit (in case your deposit ends up in someone else's account), the restaurant for a credit card charge, or the items you purchased with petty cash. The transaction reminders just keep coming—the contents of the Memo cell appear in the reports you create.

Note: Remember your accountant's insistence on an audit trail? If you create a transaction by mistake, don't delete it. Although QuickBooks' audit trail keeps track of transactions that you delete, the omission can be confusing to others—or to you after some time has passed.

If you void a transaction instead, the amount (payment or deposit) changes to zero. The voided transaction still appears in your company file, so you know that it happened, but it doesn't affect any account balances or financial reports. Before you void a transaction, add a note in the Memo field that explains why you're voiding it. In a register window, right-click a transaction and choose the appropriate Void command (Void Check, Void Deposit, and so on) on the shortcut menu.

Handling Bounced Checks

Bouncing one of your own checks is annoying and embarrassing. And banks charge for each check you bounce (and, often, they craftily pay your larger checks before the smaller ones to rack up as many bounced check charges as possible). Besides depositing more money to cover the shortfall and paying those bank fees, you have to tell people to re-deposit the checks that bounced or write new ones.

When someone pays *your* company with a rubber check, it's just as annoying. In addition to the charges your bank might charge for re-depositing a bounced check, you have to do a few things to straighten out your records in QuickBooks when a customer's check bounces, such as:

- Record a new transaction that removes the amount of the bounced check from your checking account, because the money never made it that far.

- Record any charges that your bank levies on your account for your customer's bounced check.

- Invoice the customer to recover the original payment, your bounced check charges, and any additional charges you add for your trouble.

Setting Up QuickBooks to Handle Bounced Checks

Before you can re-invoice your customers, you first need to create items for bounced checks and their associated charges.

Bounced check reimbursement item

When a check you deposit bounces, you'll see two transactions on your next bank statement: the original deposit and a second transaction that removes the amount when the check bounces. You have to do the same thing in your company file, so you don't overestimate your bank balance and write bad checks of your own. Because the customer hasn't really paid you, the amount of the check should go back into your Accounts Receivable account.

To create an item that removes the amount of the bounced check from your bank account, create an Other Charge item, such as BadCheck. Here's how:

1. **Choose Lists → Item List to open the Item List window, and then press Ctrl+N.**

   The New Item window opens.

2. **In the Type drop-down list, choose Other Charge.**

   The Other Charge item type is perfect for miscellaneous charges that don't fit any other category.

3. **In the Item Name/Number box, type the item name, BadCheck in this example. In the Account drop-down list, choose your bank account. Click OK.**

   The new item appears in the Item List.

Service charges for bounced checks

Companies typically request reimbursement for bounced check charges, but many companies tack on *additional* service charges for the inconvenience of processing a bounced check. Depending on how you account for these charges, you'll use one or two Other Charge type items:

- **Bounced check charge reimbursement.** To request reimbursement from a customer for your bank's bounced check charges, you need an Other Charge item that you can add to an invoice, called something like *BadCheck Charge*. Be sure to choose a nontaxable code for the item so that QuickBooks doesn't calculate sales tax.

QuickBooks doesn't care whether you post this item to an income account or an expense account. For example, you can post reimbursed bounced check charges to the same income account you use for other types of service charges. Although the customer's reimbursement appears as income, the bank charge you paid is an expense. The effect on your net profit (income minus expenses) is zero.

You can also post bounced check reimbursements directly to the same expense account you use for bank service charges. Then when you pay your bank's bounced check charge, QuickBooks debits the bank service charge account. When the customer pays you back, QuickBooks credits the bank service charge account. The effect on net profit is still zero.

- **Bounced check service charge.** If you post your bank's bounced check charges to an income account (such as a Service Charge income account), you can use the same item for any *extra* service charge you apply for the hassle of handling bounced checks. However, if you post customers' bounced check charge reimbursements to your bank service charge *expense* account, you need a separate item for your additional service charge. Create an Other Charge type item for the additional service charge. For the item's Account, choose your service charge income account. Like the bounced check charge reimbursement item, make this charge nontaxable.

Recording Bank Charges

The easiest place to record a bounced check charge is in the bank account register window. This technique works for any bank charge your bank drops on your account or for service charges and interest your credit card company levies:

1. **Press Ctrl+A to open the Chart of Accounts window.**

   In the Chart of Accounts window, double-click your bank account to open its register window.

2. **In the Date cell in the first blank transaction, choose the date when the bank assessed the charge.**

   QuickBooks automatically fills in the Number cell with the next check number. Be sure to delete that number before saving the transaction to keep your QuickBooks check numbers synchronized with your paper checks.

3. **In the Payee cell, type the name of your bank or credit card company.**

   You can also type a generic payee name like *Bank Charge*.

4. **Type the details of the bank charge in the Memo cell, as shown in Figure 15-3.**

   For a bounced check charge, add the name of the customer, a note that a check bounced, and the number of the check that bounced.

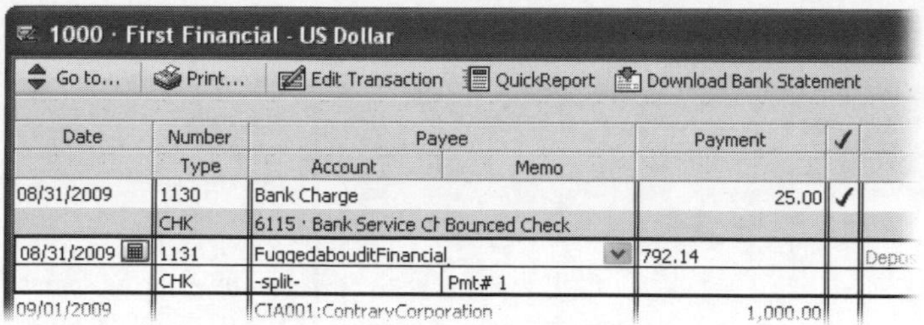

Figure 15-3:
In the Memo cell, type a description of the bank charge, such as "bounced check charge," "minimum balance charge," the bounced check number, and so on.

5. **In the Payment cell, type the amount of the bank charge. In the Account cell, choose the account you use to track bank charges or bounced check charges (see previous page).**

If you're recording a bank charge other than a bounced check, choose your expense account for bank service charges in the Account cell. Likewise, choose the service charge expense account if you don't use statements.

You have to include a bounced check charge item on a new invoice in order to recoup this cost, as described next.

Tip: The Customer:Job cell provides a shortcut to invoicing a customer for bounced check charges. While the transaction is still selected, click Splits to open the Splits table. The Account, Amount, and Memo fields are already filled in with the values you've provided so far. To make the bank charge billable to the customer who bounced the check, in the Customer:Job cell, choose the customer. In the Billable? Cell, turn on the checkbox. Then, you can add this billable charge along with any others to the customer's next invoice (as described in step 5 above).

---

6. **Click Record.**

QuickBooks saves the bank charge in your account.

Re-invoicing for Bounced Checks

With the bounced check items described on page 389, you can update all the necessary account balances just by re-invoicing the customer for the bounced check. Here's the short-and-sweet approach:

1. **On the Home page, click Invoices (or press Ctrl+I).**

The program opens the Create Invoices window.

2. **In the Customer:Job box, choose the customer who wrote you a bad check.**

You don't have to bother filling in fields like P.O. Number or shipping.

3. **In the item table, add an item for the bounced check itself ("BadCheck" in Figure 15-4).**

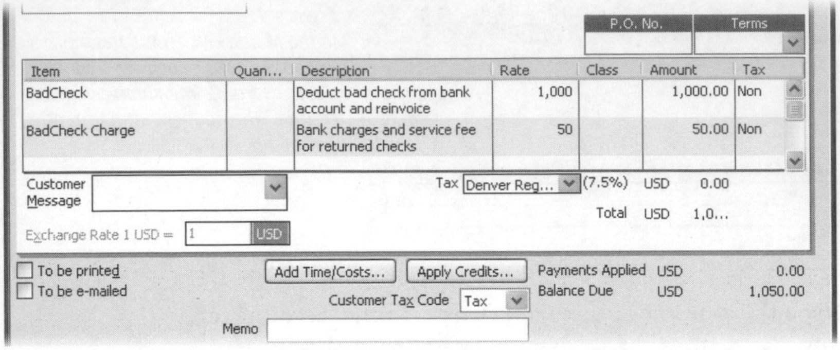

Figure 15-4:
To re-invoice the customer for the amount of the check that bounced, in the first Item cell, choose the item for a bounced check ("BadCheck" in this example). In the Amount cell, type the amount of the bounced check. In the second item cell, choose the item for bounced check charges. The amount covers the bank's charge for a bounced check and includes any additional service fee you charge.

4. **In the Amount cell for the bounced check item, type the amount of the returned check itself.**

   QuickBooks added any sales tax owed to the original invoice, so include the full amount of the bounced check.

5. **Add a second item to recoup the bounced check fees that your bank charged you. In the Amount cell for the bad check charge item, type the amount you're charging.**

   If you really want to deter customers from writing bad checks, in addition to making them pay your bank fees, you can add on a fee for your own trouble. In Figure 15-4, BadCheck Charge covers the bank's $25 charge plus an additional $25 fee the company collects for itself.

   If you recorded the bounced check charge in your bank account as a billable cost to your customer (page 391), the Billable Time/Costs dialog box opens. Keep the "Select the outstanding billable time and costs to add to this invoice" option selected and click OK. In the "Choose Billable Time and Costs" dialog box, click the Expenses tab and select the bank charge. Click OK to add the bank charge to the invoice.

6. **When you save the invoice, QuickBooks updates your bank account and Accounts Receivable account balances, as shown in Figure 15-5.**

   When you first invoice a customer, the invoice amount gets added on to your Accounts Receivable balance. The customer's original payment reduced the Accounts Receivable balance, but the bounced check means you have to remove the original payment amount from your records. By re-invoicing the customer, you re-establish the balance as outstanding and add the invoice amount back into Accounts Receivable.

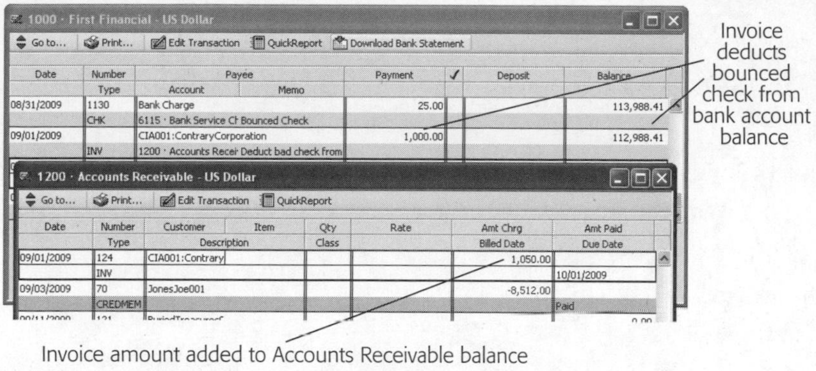

Invoice deducts bounced check from bank account balance

Invoice amount added to Accounts Receivable balance

Figure 15-5:
The item for a bounced check is linked to your bank account, so adding it to an invoice deducts the value of the bad check from your bank account balance (background). The new invoice adds the amount of the bounced check and service charges back into Accounts Receivable (foreground).

7. **When the customer sends you a check for this new invoice, simply choose Receive Payments to apply that check as a payment for the invoice.**

    QuickBooks reduces the Accounts Receivable balance by the amount of the payment. If your customer and the money they owe you are gone for good, see the box on page 394 to learn what to do next.

Transferring Funds

With the advent of electronic banking services, transferring funds between accounts has become a staple of account maintenance. Companies stash cash in savings and money market accounts to earn interest and then transfer money into checking right before they pay bills.

Fund transfers have nothing to do with income or expenses—they merely move money from one balance sheet account to another. For example, if you keep money in savings until you pay bills, the money moves from your savings bank account (an asset account in your chart of accounts) to your checking bank account (another asset account). Your income, expenses, and, for that matter, your total assets, remain the same before and after the transaction.

Transferring funds in QuickBooks is easy, whether you use the Transfer Funds dialog box or enter the transaction directly in an account register. The steps for creating a transaction in an account register appear on page 384. If you create a transfer in a bank account register (a savings account, for example), in the Account field, choose the bank account to which you're transferring funds (checking, say). Here's how to use the Transfer Funds Between Accounts window:

1. **Choose Banking → Transfer Funds.**

    QuickBooks opens the Transfer Funds Between Accounts window, shown in Figure 15-6.

TROUBLESHOOTING MOMENT

Writing Off Bad Debt

If you try contacting your customer for payment only to find that the telephone is disconnected, the forwarding address has expired, and an eviction notice is stapled to the office door, you probably aren't going to get your money. In accounting, admitting that the money is gone for good is called *writing off bad debt*.

The invoice you create for a customer represents income *only if* the customer pays it. So, to write off bad debt, you have to remove the income for the unpaid invoice from your financial records. You do that by offsetting the income with an equal amount of expense—you guessed it: the bad debt.

Suppose you invoiced your customer for $5,000, but you realize that you'll never see the money. The $5,000 is sitting in your Accounts Receivable account as an asset. Here's how to remove that money from the Accounts Receivable account by means of a bad debt expense:

1. If you don't have an account for bad debt, create an Other Expense type account and name it Bad Debt.

2. Create an Other Charge item and name it Bad Debt. Point it to the Bad Debt account you created (page 53). Be sure to make the item nontaxable.

3. On the Home page, click Refunds & Credits.

4. In the Create Credit Memos/Refunds window's Customer:Job box, choose the customer.

5. In the first item cell, choose the Bad Debt item. When the warning about the item being associated with an expense account appears, simply click OK.

6. In the Amount cell, type the amount that you're writing off as bad debt.

7. Click Save & Close.

8. The Available Credit dialog box opens and asks you what you want to do with the credit. Select the "Apply to an invoice" option and click OK.

9. In the "Apply Credit to Invoices" dialog box, turn on the checkmark for the invoice that the customer isn't going to pay.

10. Click Done.

When you apply the write-off as a credit against an invoice, QuickBooks removes the money from the Accounts Receivable account, so the program no longer thinks your customer owes the money. And it adds the money to the appropriate income account and to the Bad Debt expense account, so your net profit shows no sign of the income. In addition, if you run a Job Profitability Detail report for the customer, the bad debt appears as a negative number in the Actual Revenue column, that is, a cost that reduces the profitability of the job.

2. **After you choose the accounts for the transfer, in the Date box, choose the date of the transfer and, on the Transfer Amount line, type the amount you're transferring from one account to the other.**

   Typically, you transfer money because you don't have enough cash in one of your accounts to pay bills. But if you want to record the reason for the transfer, in the Memo box, replace Funds Transfer (which QuickBooks adds automatically) with your reason.

3. **Click Save & Close.**

   That's it. Or, if you've got more transfers to make, click Save & New. In the account register window for either account in the transfer, QuickBooks identifies the transaction with the code TRANSFR in the Type cell.

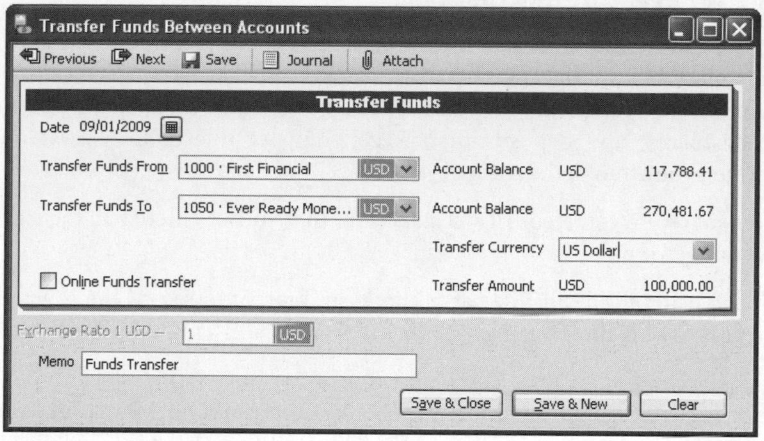

Figure 15-6:
QuickBooks' Transfer Funds Between Accounts window has one advantage over entering transfers in a bank account register: You can't create a payment or deposit by mistake. That's because you can't save a transfer in the window until you specify both the account that contains the money and the account into which you want to transfer the funds. In addition, the Transfer Funds From and Transfer Funds To drop-down menus show only balance sheet accounts (bank, credit card, asset, liability, and equity accounts).

Reconciling Accounts

Reconciling a bank statement with a paper check register is tedious and error-prone. Besides checking off items on two different paper documents, the check register and the bank statement never seem to agree—primarily due to arithmetic mistakes you make. With QuickBooks, you can leave your pencils unsharpened and stow your calculator in a drawer.

When all goes well, you can reconcile your account in QuickBooks with a few mouse clicks. Discrepancies crop up less often because QuickBooks does math without mistakes. But problems occasionally happen—transactions might be missing or numbers won't match. When your bank statement and QuickBooks account don't agree, QuickBooks helps you find the problems.

Preparing for the First Reconciliation

If you didn't set the beginning balance for the QuickBooks account to the beginning balance on a bank statement, you might wonder how you can reconcile the bank account the first time around. The best way to resolve this issue is to enter the transactions that happened between your last statement's end date and the day you started using QuickBooks. Or you can create a journal entry (page 420) to record the beginning balance. (You'll select these items as part of the first reconciliation as described on page 397.)

Warning: Alternatively, the program can align your statement and account the first time you reconcile, as described in the box on page 398. The program generates a transaction that adjusts your account's opening balance to match the balance on your bank statement. Account opening balances post to your Opening Bal Equity account, so these adjustments affect your Balance Sheet. If you enter an adjustment, let your accountant know that you changed the opening balance so she can address that change while closing your books at the end of the year.

Preparing for Every Reconciliation

QuickBooks lets you create and edit transactions in the middle of a reconciliation, but that doesn't mean it's the right way to work. Because bookkeeping in QuickBooks creates an electronic paper trail of forms, you're better off recording transactions like bills, payments, and deposits first. Reconciling your account flows more smoothly when your transactions are up-to-date.

Take a moment *before* you reconcile to make sure that you've entered all the transactions in your account:

- **Bills.** If you paid bills by writing paper checks and forgot to record the payments in QuickBooks, on the Home page, click Pay Bills and enter those payments (page 226).

- **Checks.** Checks missing from your checkbook but not in QuickBooks are a big hint that you wrote a paper check and didn't record that check in QuickBooks. Create any missing check transactions in the account register (page 240) or choose Banking → Write Checks.

- **Transfers.** Create missing transfers in the account register (page 393) or choose Banking → Transfer Funds.

- **Deposits.** If you forgot to deposit customer payments in QuickBooks, on the Home page, click Record Deposits to add those deposits to your bank account (page 354). If a deposit appears on your bank statement but doesn't show up in the "Payments to Deposit" dialog box, you might have forgotten to receive the payment in QuickBooks. For deposits unrelated to customer payments, create the deposit directly in the account register (page 384).

Tip: The easiest way to spot payments you haven't deposited in QuickBooks is to open the register window for the Undeposited Funds account (double-click it in the Chart of Accounts window). If the balance is greater than zero, you haven't deposited all the payments you received.

- **Online transactions.** If you use Online Payment or Online Account Access, download online transactions (page 533) before you start to reconcile your account.

Starting a Reconciliation

Reconciling an account is a two-part process, and QuickBooks has separate dialog boxes for each part. The first part includes choosing the account you want to reconcile, entering the ending balance from your bank statement, and entering service charges and interest earned during the statement period. Here's how to kick off account reconciliation:

Tip: If your workload gets ahead of you, several months could go by before you have time to reconcile your account. Don't try to reconcile multiple months at once. Discrepancies are harder to spot, and locating the source of problems will tax your already overworked brain. Put your bank statements in chronological order and then walk through the reconciliation process for each statement.

1. **On the Home page, click Reconcile or choose Banking → Reconcile. In the Begin Reconciliation dialog box's Account drop-down list, choose the account you want to reconcile.**

   The Begin Reconciliation dialog box displays information about the previous reconciliation, as shown in Figure 15-7.

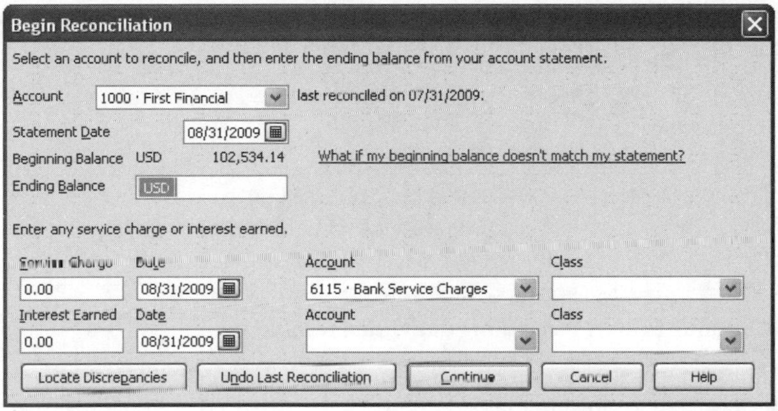

Figure 15-7:
QuickBooks uses the ending balance from the previous reconciliation to fill in the beginning balance for this reconciliation. If the beginning balance in the Begin Reconciliation dialog box doesn't match the beginning balance on your bank statement, click Cancel and turn to page 402 to learn how to correct the problem.

Tip: If the bank account register window is already open, it's easier to start reconciling by choosing Banking → Reconcile (or right-clicking the register window and choosing Reconcile on the shortcut menu that appears). With this approach, QuickBooks opens the Begin Reconciliation dialog box and automatically selects the active bank account.

The date of the previous reconciliation appears to the right of the Account box. (No date appears if you're reconciling the account for the first time.) Quick-Books fills in the Statement Date box with a date one month after the previous reconciliation date. If that date doesn't match your bank statement's ending date, type the date from you bank statement in the Statement Date box.

2. **In the Ending Balance box, type the ending balance from your bank statement.**

   If you turned on multiple currencies, the account currency appears to the right of the Beginning Balance and Ending Balance labels. For a foreign currency account, enter the ending balance in the foreign currency, which is the ending balance that appears on your bank statement.

3. **If your bank levies a service charge on your account, in the Service Charge box, type the service charge amount. If you download transactions from your bank, leave this box blank.**

   In the Date box to the left of the Service Charge box, choose the date that the service charge was assessed. In the Account box, choose the account to which you want to post the charge (usually Bank Service Charges or something similar). QuickBooks creates a transaction for you.

Tip: If you use online banking, chances are you've already downloaded your service charge and interest transactions. If this is the case, don't enter them in the Begin Reconciliation dialog box or you'll end up with duplicate transactions.

---

4. **If you're reconciling an account that pays interest, in the Interest Earned box, type the interest you earned from the bank statement.**

   As you did for service fees, specify the date and the account that you use to track interest you earn.

Note: If you track service fees and interest earned by class, in the Class boxes, choose the appropriate class. For example, classes might apply if you use them to track performance by region. However, if you use classes to track sales by partner, you don't have to specify a class for interest earned.

---

5. **Click Continue to start reconciling individual transactions.**

   QuickBooks opens the Reconcile window, where you reconcile the individual transactions, as described in the next section.

WORKAROUND WORKSHOP

Adjusting an Account That Won't Reconcile

When the Difference value in the Reconcile dialog box obstinately refuses to change to 0.00, reconciling without finding the problem *is* an option. For example, if you're one penny off and you can't solve the problem with a quick review, that one cent isn't worth any more of your time. As you complete the reconciliation, QuickBooks can add an adjustment transaction to make up the difference.

In the Reconcile window, if you click Reconcile Now without zeroing the Difference value, QuickBooks automatically opens the Reconcile Adjustment dialog box. The program tells you what you already know: There's an unresolved difference between the Ending Balance from your bank statement

and the Cleared Balance in QuickBooks. If you decide to try to fix the problem, click Return to Reconcile. Or, click Leave Reconcile if you want to research the problem. When you restart the reconciliation, all the work you've done so far is still there.

To create an adjustment transaction, click Enter Adjustment. QuickBooks creates a general journal entry to adjust the balance. If you stumble across the source of the discrepancy later, you can delete the adjustment journal entry or create a reversing entry (page 421).

Reconciling Transactions

The Reconcile window groups payments and charges (items that reduce your balance) on the left side and deposits and other credits on the right side. Marking transactions as cleared is a matter of toggling transaction checkmarks on and off, as you can see in Figure 15-8.

Note: Initially, QuickBooks sorts transactions by date with the earliest transactions first. If you want to sort the transactions by another field (for example, Chk # if you're trying to find the check that's preventing you from reconciling successfully), click the column heading for that field. An up arrow indicates that the column is sorted in ascending order (smallest to largest values). Click the column heading again to reverse the order (largest to smallest).

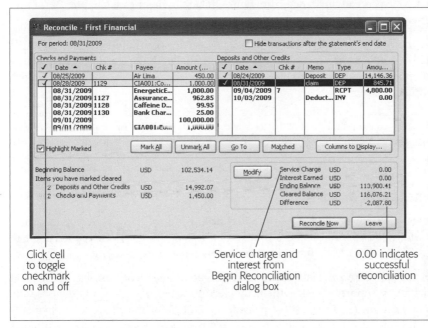

Click cell to toggle checkmark on and off

Service charge and interest from Begin Reconciliation dialog box

0.00 indicates successful reconciliation

Figure 15-8:
For each transaction that appears on your bank statement, in the Reconcile window, turn on the checkmark for the matching QuickBooks transaction. If you turn on a checkmark by mistake, just click it again to turn it off. When you mark transactions as cleared, QuickBooks updates the Cleared Balance and Difference values below the table. The program also shows the service charge and interest you entered in the Begin Reconciliation dialog box as a reminder that the program created those transactions for you.

Tip: Initially, the Reconcile window lists all uncleared transactions in the account regardless of when they happened. If transactions after the statement ending date are mixed in, you could select unnecessary transactions by mistake. To filter the list to likely candidates for clearing, turn on the "Hide transactions after the statement's end date" checkbox (at the top-right corner of the window). If you don't see transactions that appear on your bank statement, turn the checkbox off. You might have created a transaction with the wrong date.

QuickBooks includes several shortcuts for marking a transaction as cleared. See whether any of these techniques simplify your work:

- **Mark All.** If you usually end up clearing most of the transactions in the list, click Mark All to select all the transactions. Then turn off the checkmarks for the transactions that don't appear on your bank statement. If you were distracted and selected several transactions by mistake, click Unmark All to start over.

- **Selecting contiguous transactions.** Dragging down the checkmark column selects every transaction you pass. This approach isn't that helpful if you compare one transaction at a time or if your transactions don't appear in the same order as those on your bank statement.

- **Online account access.** Click Matched to automatically clear the transactions that you've already matched from your QuickStatement (see Chapter 22). Enter the ending date from the printed statement, and then click OK.

When the Difference value changes to 0.00, your reconciliation is a success. To officially complete the reconciliation, click Reconcile Now. The Select Reconciliation Report dialog box opens. If you don't want to print a reconciliation report, simply click Close.

Note: When you reconcile a credit card account and click Reconcile Now, QuickBooks opens the Make Payments window. You can choose to write a check or enter a bill to make a payment for your credit card account.

Reconciliation Reports

After you click Reconcile Now in the Reconcile window, you might notice a short delay while QuickBooks generates your reconciliation reports. These reports come in handy as a benchmark when you try to locate discrepancies in a future reconciliation.

When the Select Reconciliation Report dialog box opens, you can display or print reconciliation reports (or skip them by clicking Close, if you want). Choose the Summary option for a report that provides the totals for the checks and payments you made and also for the deposits and credits you received. To save the reports for future reference, click Print. Click Cancel to close the dialog box without printing or viewing the reports. You can look at them later by choosing Reports → Banking → Previous Reconciliation. Figure 15-9 shows you what a detailed reconciliation report looks like.

Modifying Transactions During Reconciliation

QuickBooks immediately updates the Reconcile window with changes you make in the account register window, so it's easy to complete a reconciliation. Missing transactions? Incorrect amounts? Other discrepancies? No problem. You can jump to the register window and make your changes. When you click the Reconcile window, the changes are there.

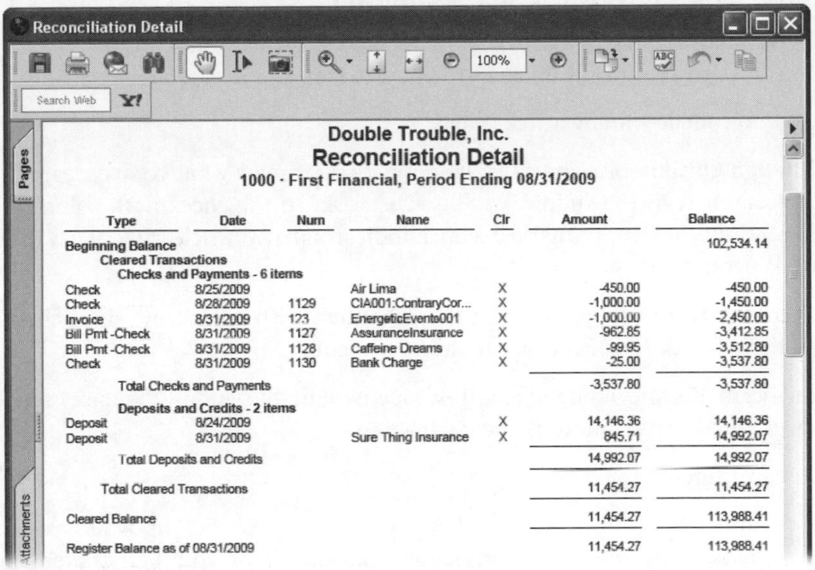

Double Trouble, Inc.
Reconciliation Detail
1000 · First Financial, Period Ending 08/31/2009

Type	Date	Num	Name	Clr	Amount	Balance
Beginning Balance						102,534.14
Cleared Transactions						
Checks and Payments - 6 items						
Check	8/25/2009		Air Lima	X	-450.00	-450.00
Check	8/28/2009	1129	CIA001:ContraryCor...	X	-1,000.00	-1,450.00
Invoice	8/31/2009	123	EnergeticEvents001	X	-1,000.00	-2,450.00
Bill Pmt -Check	8/31/2009	1127	AssuranceInsurance	X	-962.85	-3,412.85
Bill Pmt -Check	8/31/2009	1128	Caffeine Dreams	X	-99.95	-3,512.80
Check	8/31/2009	1130	Bank Charge	X	-25.00	-3,537.80
Total Checks and Payments					-3,537.80	-3,537.80
Deposits and Credits - 2 items						
Deposit	8/24/2009			X	14,146.36	14,146.36
Deposit	8/31/2009		Sure Thing Insurance	X	845.71	14,992.07
Total Deposits and Credits					14,992.07	14,992.07
Total Cleared Transactions					11,454.27	11,454.27
Cleared Balance					11,454.27	113,988.41
Register Balance as of 08/31/2009					11,454.27	113,988.41

Figure 15-9: *When you choose the Detail option and click Display, the report shows your beginning and ending balances and every transaction you cleared. View a reconciliation report at any time by choosing Reports → Banking → Previous Reconciliation.*

Tip: If you can see the register window and the reconciliation window at the same time, click the one you want to work on. If the Open Windows list appears in the navigation bar on the left side of the QuickBooks window (choose View → Open Window List), you can click names there to change the active window or dialog box.

Here's how to make changes while reconciling:

- **Adding transactions.** If a transaction appears on your bank statement but isn't in QuickBooks, switch to the account register window and add the transaction (page 384).
- **Deleting transactions.** If you find duplicate transactions, in the account register window, select the transaction and press Ctrl+D. You have to confirm your decision before the program deletes the transaction. The Reconcile window removes the transaction if you delete it.
- **Editing transactions.** If you notice an error in a transaction, in the Reconcile window, double-click the transaction to open the corresponding window (Write Checks for checks, Make Deposits for deposits, Transfer Funds Between Accounts for transfers, and so on). Correct the mistake and save the transaction by clicking Record or Save, depending on the window.

Stopping and Restarting a Reconciliation

If your head hurts and you want to take a break, don't worry about losing the reconciliation work you've already done. Here's how to stop and restart a reconciliation:

1. **In the Reconcile window, click Leave.**

   Although QuickBooks closes the window, it remembers what you've cleared. In the account register window, you'll see asterisks in the checkmark column for transactions that you've marked, which indicates that your clearing of a transaction is pending.

2. **When you're re-energized, open the account register window, right-click it, and then choose Reconcile on the shortcut menu.**

   The Begin Reconciliation dialog box opens with the ending balance, service charge, and interest amounts already filled in.

3. **Click Continue.**

   The transactions you marked are, happily, still marked. Pick up where you left off by marking the rest of the transactions that cleared on your bank statement.

Correcting Discrepancies

If you modify a transaction that you've already reconciled, QuickBooks *should* freak out and wave a clutch of red flags at you. After all, if you cleared a transaction because it appeared on your bank statement, the transaction is complete, and changing it in QuickBooks doesn't change it in your bank account. Yet QuickBooks lets you change or delete cleared transactions.

But make no mistake: changing previously cleared transactions is the quickest way to create mayhem when reconciling your accounts. For example, in the account register window, clicking a checkmark cell resets the status of that transaction from reconciled (a checkmark) to cleared (an asterisk), which then removes that transaction's amount from the Beginning Balance when you try to reconcile the account. And *that* means that the Beginning Balance won't match the beginning balance on your bank statement, which is one reason you might be reading this section.

The Discrepancy Report

To correct discrepancies created by transaction editing, you have to restore each modified transaction to its original state, and the Discrepancy Report provides the information you need to know to do that. The Discrepancy Report (Figure 15-10) shows you changes that were made to cleared transactions. To create the Discrepancy Report, in the Reconcile window, click Locate Discrepancies, and then, in the Locate Discrepancies window, click Discrepancy Report. You can also choose Reports → Banking → Reconciliation Discrepancy.

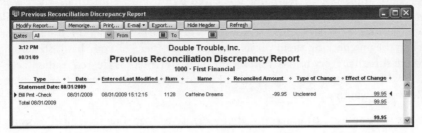

Figure 15-10:
To edit a transaction, in the Discrepancy Report, double-click the transaction to open its corresponding window or dialog box.

Seeing transactions on the Discrepancy Report is a big step toward correcting reconciliation problems. Here's how you interpret the crucial columns in the report:

- **Entered/Last Modified.** This is the date that the transaction was created or modified, which doesn't help you restore the transaction, but might help you find the person who's changing reconciled transactions.

- **Reconciled Amount.** This is the transaction amount when you cleared it during reconciliation. If the transaction amount changed, use this value to restore the transaction amount to its original value. For example, in Figure 15-10, –99.95 represents a check or charge for $99.95.

- **Type of Change.** This indicates the transaction change. For example, "Amount" means that the transaction amount changed. "Deleted" indicates that the transaction was deleted. (The only way to restore a deleted transaction is to recreate it from scratch.) "Uncleared" indicates that someone removed the reconciled checkmark in the account register.

- **Effect of Change.** This value indicates how the change affected the beginning balance for your reconciliation. For example, the $99.95 check that was reset added $99.95 to your bank account. When the Beginning Balance is off and the amount in the "Effect of Change" column matches that discrepancy, you can be sure that restoring these transactions to their original state will fix your problems.

Other ways to find discrepancies

Sometimes, your reconciliation doesn't match because of subtle errors in transactions or because you've missed something in the current reconciliation. Try the following techniques to help spot problems:

- **Search for a transaction equal to the amount of the discrepancy.** Press Ctrl+F to open the Find window. In the Choose Filter list, choose Amount. Select the = option and type the amount in the box, and then click Find to run the search.

***

Note: Using Find in this way works only if the discrepancy is caused by *one* transaction that you cleared or uncleared by mistake. If more than one transaction is to blame for the discrepancy, the amount you're trying to find is the total of all the erroneously cleared transactions, so Find won't see a matching value.

***

- **Look for transactions cleared or uncleared by mistake.** Sometimes, the easiest way to find a discrepancy is to start the reconciliation over. In the Reconcile window, click Unmark All to remove the checkmarks from all the transactions. Then, begin checking them off as you compare them to your bank statement. Make sure that every transaction on the bank statement is cleared in the Reconcile window. Also, check that no additional transactions are cleared in the Reconcile window.

- **Look for duplicate transactions.** If you create transactions in QuickBooks and download transactions, it's easy to end up with duplicates. And when you clear both of the duplicates, the mistake is hard to spot. If that's the case, you have to scroll through the register window looking for multiple transactions with the same date, payee, and amount.

***

Tip: Count the number of transactions on your bank statement. Compare that number to the number of cleared transactions displayed on the left side of the Reconcile window, shown in Figure 15-8. Of course, this transaction count won't help if you enter transactions in QuickBooks differently than they appear on your bank statement. For example, if you deposit every payment individually but your bank shows one deposit for every business day, your transaction counts won't match.

***

- **Look for a deposit entered as a payment or vice versa.** To find an error like this, look for transactions whose amounts are half the discrepancy. For example, if a $500 check becomes a $500 deposit by mistake, your reconciliation will be off by $1000 ($500 because a check is missing and another $500 because you have an extra deposit).

- **Look at each cleared transaction for transposed numbers or other differences between your statement and QuickBooks.** It's easy to type $95.40 when you meant $59.40.

***

Note: If these techniques don't uncover the problem, your bank might have made a mistake (page 405).

***

Undoing the Last Reconciliation

If you're having problems with this month's reconciliation but suspect that the guilty party is hiding in *last* month's reconciliation, you can undo the last reconciliation and start over. When you undo a reconciliation, QuickBooks returns the transactions to an uncleared state.

In the Begin Reconciliation dialog box (choose Banking → Reconcile), click Undo Last Reconciliation. The Undo Previous Reconciliation dialog box opens. Although the button label and the dialog box title don't match, they both represent the same process. In the Undo Previous Reconciliation dialog box, click Continue. When the Undo Previous Reconciliation message box appears telling you that the previous reconciliation was successfully undone, click OK.

QuickBooks unclears all the transactions back to the beginning of the previous reconciliation and returns to the Begin Reconciliation dialog box. Change the values in the Begin Reconciliation dialog box, and then click Continue to try another reconciliation.

Note: Although QuickBooks removes the cleared status on all the transactions including service charges and interest, it doesn't remove the service charge and interest transactions that it added. When you restart the reconciliation, in the Begin Reconciliation dialog box, don't re-enter the service charges or interest.

When Your Bank Makes a Mistake

Banks do make mistakes. Digits get transposed, or amounts are flat wrong. When this happens, you can't ignore the difference. In QuickBooks, add an adjustment transaction (page 398) to make up the difference, but be sure to tell your bank about the mistake. It's always a good idea to be polite in case the error turns out to be yours.

When you receive your *next* statement, check that the bank made an adjustment to correct its mistake. You can delete your adjustment transaction or add a reversing journal entry to remove your adjustment and reconcile as you normally would.

Tip: For a reminder to check your next statement, create a To Do Note (Company → To Do List and press Ctrl+N).

Managing Loans

Unless your business generates cash at an astonishing rate, you'll probably have to borrow money to purchase big ticket items that you can't afford to do without, such as a deluxe cat-herder machine. The asset you purchase and the loan you assume are intimately linked—you can't get the equipment without borrowing the money.

But in QuickBooks, loans and the assets they help purchase aren't connected in any way. You create an asset account (page 53) to track the value of an asset that you buy. If you take out a loan to pay for that asset, you create a liability account to track the balance of what you owe on the loan. With each payment that you make on your loan, you pay off a little bit of the loan's principal as well as a chunk of interest.

Note: On your company's balance sheet, the value of your assets appears in the Assets section, and the balance owed on loans shows up in the Liabilities section. The difference between the asset value and your loan balance is your *equity* in the asset. Suppose your cat-herder machine is in primo condition and is worth $70,000 on the open market. If you owe $50,000 on the loan, your company has $20,000 in equity for that machine.

Most loans *amortize* your payoff, which means that each payment represents a different amount of interest and principal. In the beginning of a loan, amortized loan payments are mostly interest and very little principal, which is great for tax deductions. By the end, the payments are almost entirely principal. Making loan payments in which the values change each month would be a nightmare if not for QuickBooks' Loan Manager, which is a separate program that comes with QuickBooks and can gather information from your company file. This program calculates your loan amortization schedule, posts the principal and interest for each payment to the appropriate accounts, and handles escrow payments and fees associated with your loans.

Note: Loan Manager doesn't handle loans in which the payment covers only the accrued interest (called *interest-only loans*). For loans like these, you have to set up payments yourself (page 206) and allocate the payment to principal and interest using the values on your monthly loan statement.

Setting Up a Loan

Whether you use Loan Manager or not, you have to create accounts to keep track of your loan. You probably already know that you need a liability account for the amount of money you owe. But you also need accounts for the interest you pay on the loan and escrow payments (such as insurance or property tax) that you make:

- **Liability account.** Create a liability account (page 53) to track the money you've borrowed. For mortgages and other loans whose terms are longer than a year, use the Long Term Liability type. For short-term loans (terms of one year or less), use the Other Current Liability type.

  When you create the liability account, add the account number but forego the opening balance. The best way to record money you borrow is with a journal entry (page 421), which credits the liability account for the loan and debits the bank account where you deposited the money.

Note: If you've just started using QuickBooks and have a loan that you've partially paid off, fill in the journal entry with what you owed on the loan statement that's dated just before your QuickBooks company start date. Then, enter any loan payments you've made since that statement's ending date.

- **Loan interest account.** The interest that you pay on loans is an expense, so create an Expense account (or an Other Expense account type if that's the type of account your company uses for interest paid) called something like Interest Paid. Loan Manager shows Other Expense account types in its account drop-down lists, although the accounts are listed in alphabetical order, not by type.

- **Escrow account.** If you make escrow payments, such as for property taxes and insurance, create an account to track the escrow you've paid. Because escrow represents money you've paid in advance, use a Current Asset account type.

- **Fees and finance charge expense account.** Chances are you'll pay some sort of fee or finance charge at some point before you pay off a loan. If you don't have an account for finance charges yet, set up an Expense account for these fees.

There's one last QuickBooks setup task to complete *before* you start Loan Manager: You have to create the lender in your Vendor List (page 135). The box below tells you what to do if you forgot any of these steps before you started Loan Manager.

WORKAROUND WORKSHOP

Where Are My Accounts and Vendors?

Loan Manager looks like a command on the Banking menu in QuickBooks, but it's actually a separate small program. When you start Loan Manager, it gleans information from your company file, such as the liability account you created for the loan and the vendor entry you set up for your lender.

If you forgot to create accounts or your lender in Quick-Books, you'll probably jump to your Chart of Accounts window or Vendor List and create them. The problem is you *still* won't see those new elements in Loan Manager's drop-down lists. You have to close Loan Manager (losing all the data you've already entered) and create those entries in QuickBooks. After you've created the vendor and all the accounts you need, choose Banking → Loan Manager to restart the Loan Manager program, which now includes your lender and loan accounts in its drop-down lists.

Adding a Loan to Loan Manager

Loan Manager makes it so easy to track and make payments on amortized loans, it's well worth the steps required to set it up. Before you begin, gather your loan documents like chicks to a mother hen, because Loan Manager wants to know every detail of your loan, as you'll soon see.

Basic setup

With your account and vendor entries complete (see page 406 and the box above), follow these steps to describe your loan:

1. **Choose Banking → Loan Manager.**

   QuickBooks opens the Loan Manager window.

2. **In the Loan Manager window, click "Add a Loan".**

   QuickBooks opens the Add Loan dialog box, which has several screens for all the details of your loan. After you fill in a screen, click Next to move to the next one.

3. **In the Account Name drop-down list, choose the liability account you created for the loan.**

   QuickBooks lists only Current Liability and Long Term Liability accounts.

4. **In the Lender drop-down list, choose the vendor you created for the company you're borrowing money from.**

   If you haven't set up the lender as a vendor in QuickBooks, you have to close Loan Manager. After you've created the vendor in QuickBooks, choose Banking → Loan Manager to restart the Loan Manager program, which now shows the lender in the Lender drop-down list.

5. **In the Origination Date box, choose the date that matches the origination date on your loan documents.**

   Loan Manager uses the loan origination date to calculate the number of remaining payments, the interest you owe, and when you'll pay off the loan.

6. **In the Original Amount box, type the total amount you borrowed when you first took out the loan.**

   The Original Amount box is aptly named because it's *always* the amount that you originally borrowed. For new loans, the current balance on the loan and the Original Amount are the same. If you've paid off a portion of a loan, your current balance (below the Account Name box in Figure 15-11) is lower than the Original Amount.

7. **In the Term boxes, specify the length of the loan. Click Next to advance to the screen for payment information.**

   The next section tells you how to deal with payment info.

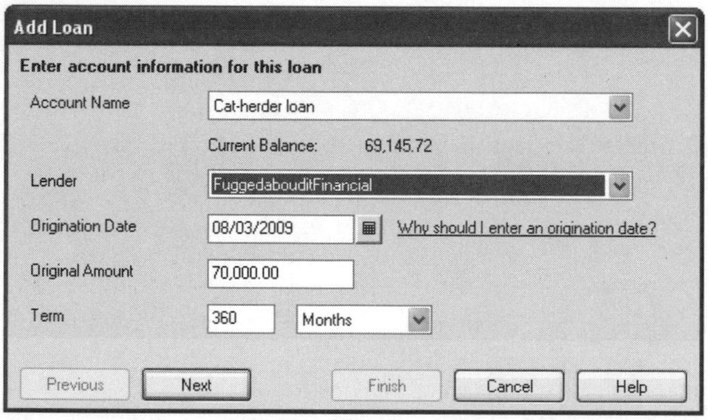

Figure 15-11:
Loan Manager automatically selects Months in the Term drop-down list. Specifying the number of months for a 30-year loan is a great refresher for your multiplication tables, but you don't want to confuse Loan Manager by making an arithmetic error. In the Term drop-down list, choose the period (such as Years). Then, you can fill in the first Term box with the number of periods shown on your loan documents.

Payment information

When you specify a few details about your loan payments, Loan Manager can calculate a schedule of payments for you. To make sure you don't forget a loan payment (and incur outrageous late charges), you can tell Loan Manager to create a QuickBooks reminder for your payments. Here's how:

1. **In the "Due Date of Next Payment" box, choose the next payment date.**

   For a new loan, choose the date for the first payment you'll make. For an existing loan, choose the date for your next payment, which usually appears on your last loan statement.

2. **In the Payment Amount box, type the total payment for principal and interest.**

   If you don't know what your payment is, you can find it in your loan documents. Loan Manager automatically fills in the Next Payment Number box with the number 1. For loans that you've made payments on already, type the number for the next payment (this, too, should appear on your last loan statement).

3. **In the Payment Period drop-down list, choose the frequency of your payments.**

   Loans typically require monthly payments, even when their terms are in years. Regardless of which period you chose on the first Add Loan screen in the Term drop-down list, in the Payment Period drop-down list, choose how often you make loan payments.

4. **If your loan includes an escrow payment, choose the Yes option.**

   Then specify the amount of escrow you pay each time and the account to which you want to post the escrow, as shown in Figure 15-12.

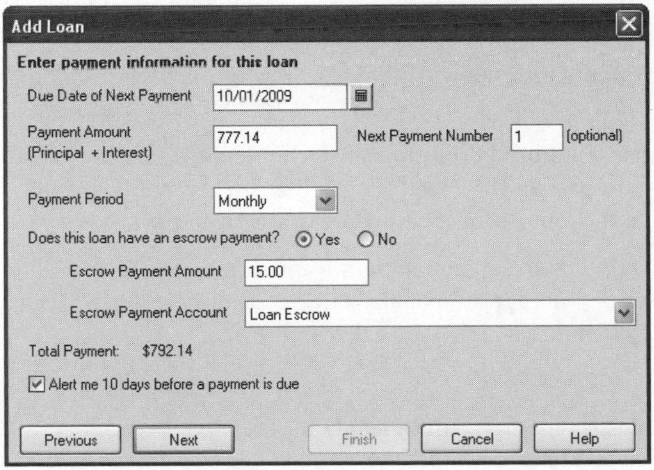

Figure 15-12:
Most mortgages include an escrow payment for property taxes and property insurance. Escrow accounts are asset accounts, because you're setting aside some money to pay expenses later. When you add an escrow payment, Loan Manager updates the value of the Total Payment to include principal, interest, and escrow.

5. If you want a reminder 10 days before a loan payment is due, turn on the "Alert me 10 days before a payment is due" checkbox.

   Loan Manager tells QuickBooks how often and when payments are due, so Quick-Books can create a loan payment reminder in the Reminders List (page 573).

6. Click Next to advance to the screen for entering interest rate information.

   The next section tells you how to deal with interest rate info.

Interest rate information

For Loan Manager to calculate your amortization schedule (the amount of principal and interest paid with each payment) you have to specify the interest rate. Here's how:

1. In the Interest Rate box, type the interest rate for the loan.

   Use the interest rate that appears on your loan documents. For example, although you probably make monthly payments, the loan document usually shows the interest rate as an annual rate.

2. In the Compounding Period box, choose either Monthly or Exact Days, depending on how the lender calculates compounding interest.

   If the lender calculates the interest on your loan once a month, choose Monthly. The other option, Exact Days, calculates interest using the annual interest rate divided over a fixed number of days in a year. In the past, many lenders simplified calculations by assuming that a year had 12 months of 30 days each, resulting in the Compute Period choice 365/360. Today, lenders often use the number of days in a year, which is the Compute Period 365/365.

3. In the Payment Account drop-down list, choose the account from which you make your payments, whether you write checks or pay electronically.

   In the Payment Account drop-down list, Loan Manager displays your bank accounts.

4. In the Interest Expense Account drop-down list, choose the account you use to track the interest you pay. In the Fees/Charges Expense Accounts drop-down list, choose the account you use for fees and late charges you pay.

   Expense accounts and Other Expense accounts are co-mingled in these drop-down lists, because accounts appear in alphabetical order, not sorted by account type.

5. Click Finish.

   Loan Manager calculates the payment schedule for the loan and adds it to the list of loans in the Loan Manager window, shown in Figure 15-13.

Note: If Loan Manager shows the loan balance as zero, you aren't off the hook for paying back the loan. Loan Manager grabs the loan balance from the QuickBooks liability account you created for the loan. The loan balance in Loan Manager is zero if you forgot to create the journal entry to set the liability account's opening balance.

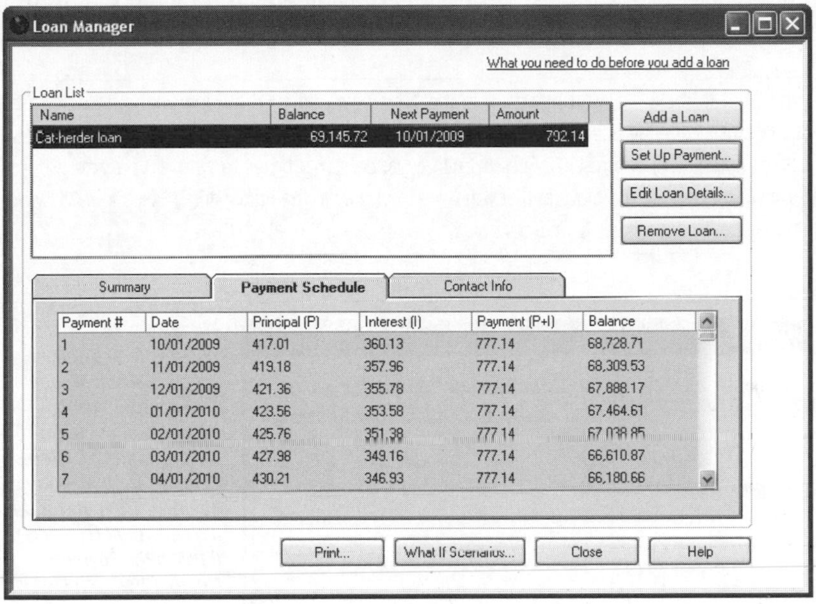

Figure 15-13:
When you select a loan in the Loan List table, Loan Manager displays information about that loan in the tabs at the bottom of the window. Most of the information on the Summary tab is information you entered, although Loan Manager does calculate the maturity date (the date when you pay off the loan). Loan Manager pulls the information on the Contact Info tab directly from the lender's Vendor record in QuickBooks. The Payment Schedule tab (shown here) lists every payment with the amount of principal and interest they represent.

Modifying Loan Terms

Some loan characteristics change from time to time. For example, if you have an adjustable-rate mortgage, the interest rate changes every so often. And your escrow payment usually increases as your property taxes and insurance go up. To make changes like these, in the Loan Manager window (choose Banking → Loan Manager), select the loan, and then click Edit Loan Details.

Loan Manager takes you through the same screens you saw when you first added the loan. If you change the interest rate, the program recalculates your payment schedule. For a change in escrow, the program updates your payment to include the new escrow amount.

Setting Up Payments

You can set up a loan payment check or bill in Loan Manager, which hands off the payment info to QuickBooks to record in your company file. Although Loan Manager can handle this task one payment at a time, it can't create recurring payments to send the payment that's due each month. When you see the QuickBooks reminder for your loan payment, you have to run Loan Manager to generate the payment:

1. **In the Loan Manager window, select the loan you want to pay, and then click Set Up Payment.**

   Loan Manager opens the Set Up Payment dialog box and fills in the information for the next payment, as you can see in Figure 15-14.

Tip: If you want to make an extra payment, in the "This payment is" drop-down list, choose "An extra payment". Because extra payments aren't a part of the loan payment schedule, Loan Manager changes the values in the Principal (P), Interest (I), Fees & Charges, and Escrow boxes to zero. If you want to prepay principal on your loan, type the amount that you want to prepay in the Principal (P) box. Or, if you want to pay an annual fee, fill in the Fees & Charges box.

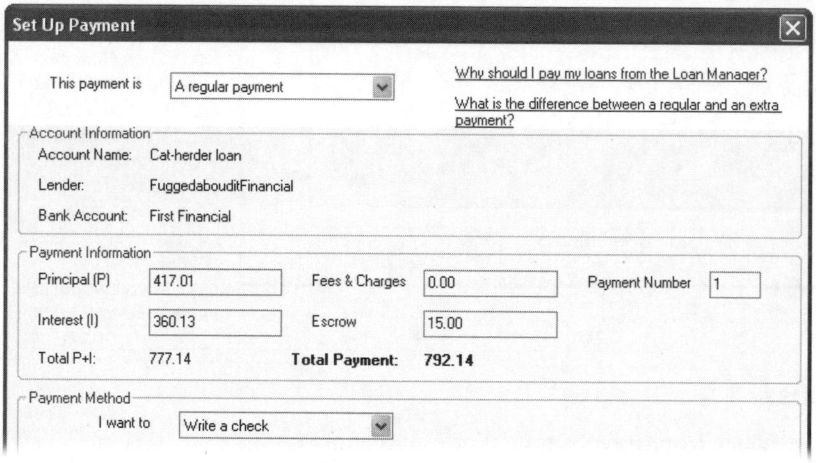

Figure 15-14:
When you click Set Up Payment, Loan Manager fills in the Payment Information section with the principal and interest amounts from the loan payment schedule for the next payment that's due. It fills in the Payment Number box with the number of the next payment due.

2. **In the Payment Method drop-down list at the bottom of the window, choose "Write a check" or "Enter a bill", and then click OK.**

   Loan Manager opens the QuickBooks Write Checks or Enter Bills window, respectively, and fills in the boxes with the payment information. You can change the payment date or other values if you want.

Note: Because Loan Manager and QuickBooks are separate programs, you might notice a delay as the programs communicate.

---

3. **In the QuickBooks Write Checks or Enter Bills window, click Save & Close.**

   The window in QuickBooks closes and you're back in the Loan Manager window. You'll see the value in the loan's Balance cell reduced by the amount of principal that the payment paid off. Click Close.

If you want to print the payment schedule for your loan, in the Loan Manager window, click Print. Or, if you pay off a loan and want to remove it from Loan Manager, select the loan, and then click Remove Loan. Removing a loan from Loan Manager doesn't delete any loan transactions or loan accounts in QuickBooks.

Note: If your loan payments include escrow, each payment deposits the escrow amount into your QuickBooks escrow asset account. When your loan statement shows that the lender paid expenses from escrow—like insurance or property taxes—you can record the corresponding payment in QuickBooks. Open the escrow account register window (page 384). In the first blank transaction, choose the date and the payee, such as the insurance company or the tax agency. In the Decrease field, type the payment amount (because the payment reduces the balance in the escrow account). Click Record.

What-If Scenarios

Because economic conditions and interest rates change, loans aren't necessarily stable things. For example, if you have an adjustable-rate loan, you might want to know what your new payment is. Or, you might want to find out whether it makes sense to refinance an existing loan when interest rates drop. The What-If Scenarios button is your dry-erase board for trying out loan changes before you make up your mind.

When you click What-If Scenarios, Loan Manager opens the What-If Scenarios dialog box. Take your pick from these five scenarios:

Note: The changes you make in the What-If Scenarios dialog box don't change your existing loans. If you switch to a different scenario or close the dialog box, Loan Manager doesn't save the information. If you want a record of different scenarios, click the Print button.

- **What if I change my payment amount?** Paying extra principal can shorten the length of your loan and reduce the total interest you pay. Choose this scenario and then, in the Payment Amount box on the right side of the dialog box, type the new amount you plan to pay each month. When you click Calculate, Loan Manager calculates your new maturity date, shows how much you'll pay overall, and how much you'll pay in interest.

- **What if I change my interest rate?** If you have an adjustable-rate loan, choose this scenario to preview the changes in payment, interest, and balloon payment for a different rate, higher or lower.

- **How much will I pay with a new loan?** You don't have to go through the third degree to see what a loan will cost. Choose this scenario to quickly enter the key information for a loan and evaluate the payment, total payments, total interest, and final balloon payment.

- **What if I refinance my loan?** When interest rates drop, companies and individuals alike consider refinancing their debt to save money on interest. With this scenario, type in a new term, payment, interest rate, and payment date to see whether it's worth refinancing, as shown in Figure 15-15.

- **Evaluate two new loans.** Type in the details for two loans to see which one is better.

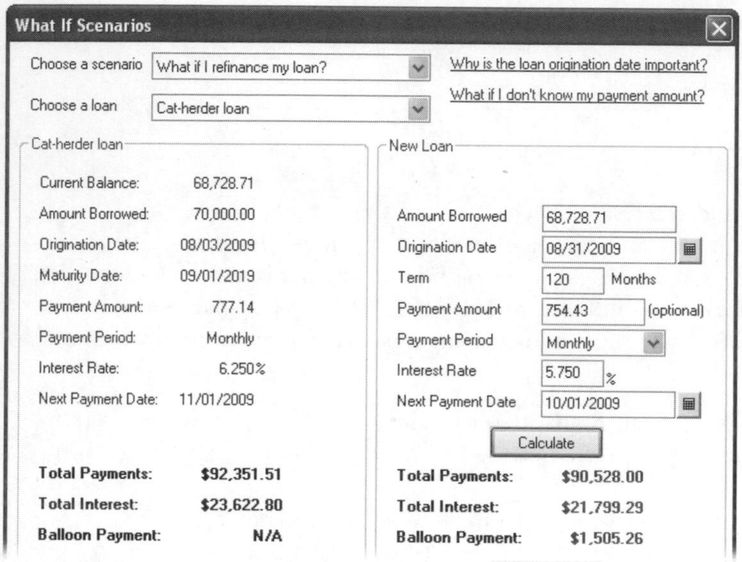

Figure 15-15:
The refinance calculator in Loan Manager doesn't provide everything you need to decide whether to refinance. Many loans come with closing costs that you should take into account. In this example, the new loan costs $90,528.00 over the life of the loan, and the current loan costs $92,351.51. If closing costs are $2,500, you won't save any money with the new loan.

Tracking Petty Cash

Dashing out to buy an extension cord so you can present a pitch to a potential client? Chances are you'll get money from the petty cash drawer at your office. *Petty cash* is the familiar term for money spent on small purchases, typically less than $20.

Many companies keep a cash drawer at the office and dole out dollars for small, company-related purchases that employees make. But for the small business owner with a bank card, getting petty cash is as easy as withdrawing money from an ATM. Either way, petty cash is still company money. And that means you have to keep track of it and how it's spent.

Recording ATM Withdrawals and Deposits to Petty Cash

In QuickBooks, adding money to your petty cash account mirrors the real world transaction. You either write a check made out to Cash (or the trustworthy employee who's cashing the check), or you withdraw money from an ATM. To write a check for your petty cash account, you can simply open the Write Checks window (choose Banking → Write Checks or, on the Home page, click Write Checks). Withdrawing cash from an ATM requires the Transfer Funds window (choose Banking → Transfer Funds).

If creating transactions in the account register window (page 384) is OK with you, you can use the same steps whether you replenish your petty cash with a check or ATM withdrawal:

1. **In the Chart of Accounts window (press Ctrl+A to open it), double-click your checking account to open the register window.**

   If the current date (which QuickBooks fills in automatically) isn't the day you added money to petty cash, choose the correct date.

2. **If you're withdrawing money from an ATM, clear the value in the Number cell.**

   If you're writing a check to get petty cash and QuickBooks fills in the Number cell with the correct check number, continue to the Payee cell. Otherwise, type the correct check number in the cell.

3. **Whether you're writing a check or using an ATM, in the Payee cell, type a name such as Cash or Petty Cash.**

   If you made a check out to one of your employees, in the Payee cell drop-down list, choose the employee's name.

4. **In the Payment cell, type the amount that you're moving from the checking account to petty cash.**

   If you track classes in QuickBooks, this is one time to ignore the Class cell. You assign classes only when you record purchases made with petty cash.

5. **In the Account cell, choose your petty cash account.**

   If you don't have a petty cash account in your chart of accounts, be sure to choose the Bank type when you create the account. When you do so, your petty cash account appears at the top of your balance sheet with your other savings and checking accounts.

6. **Click Record to save the transaction.**

   That's it!

Recording Purchases Made with Petty Cash

As long as company cash sits in the petty cash drawer or your wallet, the petty cash account in QuickBooks holds the cash. But when you spend some of the petty cash in your wallet or an employee brings in a sales receipt for purchases, you have to record what that petty cash purchased.

The petty cash account register is as good a place as any to record these purchases. In the Chart of Accounts window, double-click the petty cash account to open its register window. Then, in a blank transaction, follow these guidelines to record your petty cash expenditures:

- **Number cell.** Although petty cash expenditures don't use check numbers, QuickBooks automatically fills in the Number cell with the next check number anyway. The easiest thing to do is ignore the number and move on to the Payee or Payment cell.

- **Payee cell.** QuickBooks doesn't require a value in the Payee cell, and for many petty cash transactions, entering a Payee would just clog your lists of names, so leave the Payee cell blank. You can type the vendor name or details of the purchase in the Memo cell if you want a record of it.

- **Payment cell.** In the Payment cell, type the amount that was spent.

- **Account cell.** Choose an account to track the expense.

Note: To distribute the petty cash spent to several accounts, click Splits. In the table that appears, you can specify the account, amount, customer or job, class, and a memo for each split (page 209).

WORKAROUND WORKSHOP

Petty Cash Advances

Good management practices warn against dishing out petty cash without a receipt. But suppose an employee asks for cash in advance to purchase a new lava lamp for the conference room? There's no receipt, but you really want the lava lamp to impress the CEO of a tie-dye company.

The solution in the real world is to write a paper IOU and place it in the petty cash drawer until the employee coughs up a receipt. In QuickBooks, record the advance as if the purchase were already complete. For the lava lamp, create the transaction using entries like these:

- In the Amount cell, type the amount of money you advanced to the employee.

- In the Account cell, choose the account for the expenditure.

- In the Memo cell, include a note about the employee who received the advance, the IOU in the petty cash drawer, and what the advance is for.

When the employee comes back with a receipt, you can update the transaction's Memo cell to show that the IOU has been repaid. If the employee brings change back, create a deposit to replace that money in the petty cash account.

CHAPTER 16

Making Journal Entries

Intuit claims that you don't need to know double entry accounting (page 7) to use QuickBooks. Most of the time, that's true. When you write checks, receive payments, and perform many other tasks in QuickBooks, the program unobtrusively handles the double-entry accounting for you. But every once in a while, Quick-Books transactions can't help, and your only choice is moving money around directly between accounts.

In the accounting world, these direct manipulations are known as *journal entries*. For example, if you posted income to your only income account but have since decided that you need several income accounts to track the money you make, journal entries are the mechanism for transporting money from that original income account to the new ones.

The steps for creating a journal entry are deceptively easy; it's assigning money to accounts in the correct way that's maddeningly difficult for weekend accountants. And unfortunately, QuickBooks doesn't have any magic looking glass that makes those assignments crystal clear. This chapter gets you started by showing you how to create journal entries and providing examples of journal entries you're likely to need.

Note: In the accounting world, you'll hear the term "journal entry," and see it abbreviated JE. Although QuickBooks uses the term "general journal entry" and the corresponding abbreviation GJE, both terms and abbreviations refer to the same account register changes.

Balancing Debit and Credit Amounts

In double-entry accounting, both sides of any transaction have to balance, as the transaction in Figure 16-1 shows. When you move money between accounts, you increase the balance in one account as you decrease the balance in the other—just as shaking some money out of your piggy bank decreases your savings balance and increases the money in your pocket. These changes in value are called *debits* and *credits*. If you commit anything about accounting to memory, it should be the definitions of debit and credit, because these are the key to successful journal entries, accurate financial reports, and understanding what your accountant is talking about.

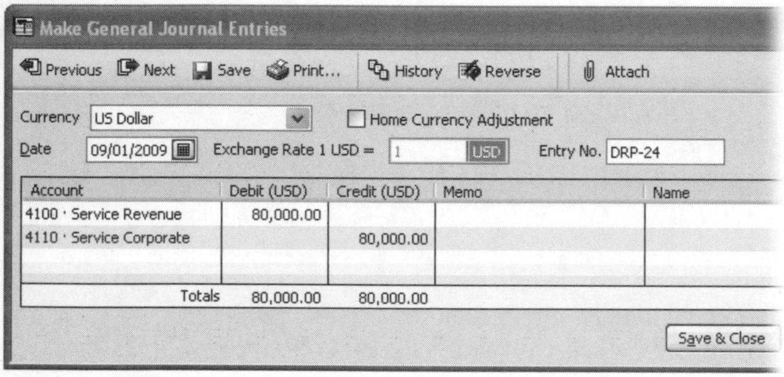

Figure 16-1:
For each transaction, the total in the Debit column has to equal the total in the Credit column. To transfer money from one income account to another, you debit the original account (decrease its income) and credit the new account (increase its income).

Table 16-1 shows what debits and credits do for different types of accounts and can take some of the pain out of creating journal entries. For example, buying a machine is a debit to the equipment asset account because it increases the value of the equipment you retain. A loan payment is a debit to your loan account because it decreases your loan balance. And (here's a real mind-bender) a credit card charge is a credit to your credit card liability account because purchases on credit increase the amount you owe.

Note: One reason that debits and credits are confusing is that the words have the exact opposite meanings when your bank uses them. In your personal banking, a debit to your bank account decreases the balance and a credit to that account increases the balance.

As you'll see in examples in this chapter, you can have more than one debit or credit entry in one journal entry. For example, when you depreciate equipment, you can include one debit for depreciation expense and a separate credit for the depreciation on each piece of equipment.

Table 16-1. How debits and credits change the values in accounts

Account type	Debit	Credit
Asset	Increases balance	Decreases balance
Liability	Decreases balance	Increases balance
Equity	Decreases balance	Increases balance
Income	Decreases balance	Increases balance
Expense	Increases balance	Decreases balance

Some Reasons to Use Journal Entries

Here are a few of the more common reasons that businesses use journal entries:

- **Reassigning accounts.** As you work with QuickBooks, you might find that the accounts you originally created don't track your business the way you want. For example, suppose you started with one income account for all the consulting services you provide. Now you have three income accounts: one for income from designing consumer surveys, a second for income for conducting surveys, and a third for the money you make working the statistics to deliver the right results. To move income from your original account to the correct new account, you debit the income from the original account and credit it to the new account, as described on page 425.

- **Correcting account assignments.** If you assigned an expense to the wrong expense account, you or your accountant can create a journal entry to reassign the expense to the correct account. If you've developed a reputation for mis-assigning income and expenses, your accountant might ask you to assign any questionable transactions to uncategorized income or expense accounts. Then, when she gets the file at the end of the year, she can create journal entries to assign those transactions correctly. You can verify that the assignments and account balances are correct by running a trial balance (page 446).

Note: If you enter a transaction in QuickBooks by mistake, you can delete it. However, since most accountants prefer to keep records of *all* transactions, even erroneous ones, the most common approach to correcting mistakes is to create a journal entry that moves money to the correct accounts.

- **Reassigning jobs.** If a customer hires you for several jobs, your customer might ask you to apply a payment, credit, or expense from one job to another. For example, if expenses come after one job is complete, your customer might want to apply them to the job still in progress. QuickBooks doesn't have a command to transfer money between jobs, but a general journal entry does the trick as page 425 explains.

- **Reassigning classes.** Journal entries can transfer income or expenses from one class to another. For example, nonprofits often use classes to assign income to programs. If you need to transfer money to a program, create a journal entry that has debit and credit entries for the same income account, but changes the class (see page 423).

- **Depreciating assets.** Each year that you own a depreciable asset, you decrease its value in the appropriate asset account in your chart of accounts (page 45). Because no cash changes hands, QuickBooks doesn't have a command to handle depreciation of assets as it does for transactions like bills, invoices, and checks. As you'll learn on page 427, a journal entry for depreciation debits the depreciation expense account (increases its value) and credits the asset account (decreases its value).

- **Recording transactions for a payroll service.** If you use a third-party payroll service like Paychex or ADP, the payroll company sends you a report. To get the numbers from the report into your company file where you need them, you can use journal entries. For example, you can move money to your payroll account, record paychecks, and record the additional expenses that employers incur.

- **Recording year-end transactions.** The end of the year is a popular time for journal entries, whether your accountant is fixing your more creative transactions or you're creating journal entries for non-cash transactions before you prepare your taxes. For example, if you run a small business out of your home, you might want to show a portion of your utility bills as expenses for your home office. When you create a journal entry for this transaction, you debit the office utilities account and credit an equity account for your owner's contributions to the company.

WORKAROUND WORKSHOP

Creating Opening Balances with Journal Entries

QuickBooks has some arbitrary, but unyielding, rules about Accounts Payable (AP) and Accounts Receivable (AR) accounts in general journal entries. Each general journal entry can have only one Accounts Payable or Accounts Receivable account, and that account can appear on only one line of the journal entry. And if you do add an Accounts Payable account, you also need to choose a vendor in the Name field. For Accounts Receivable accounts, you have to choose a customer name in the Name field.

These rules are a problem only when you want to use general journal entries to set the opening balances for customers or vendors. The hardship, therefore, is minute, because the preferred approach for building opening balances for vendors and customers is to enter bills and customer invoices. These transactions provide the detail you need to resolve disputes, determine account status, and track income and expenses.

You can get around QuickBooks' AP and AR limitations by setting up the opening balances in all your accounts with a journal entry based on your trial balance. Simply create the journal entry without the amounts for Accounts Payable and Accounts Receivable, as shown in Figure 16-2.

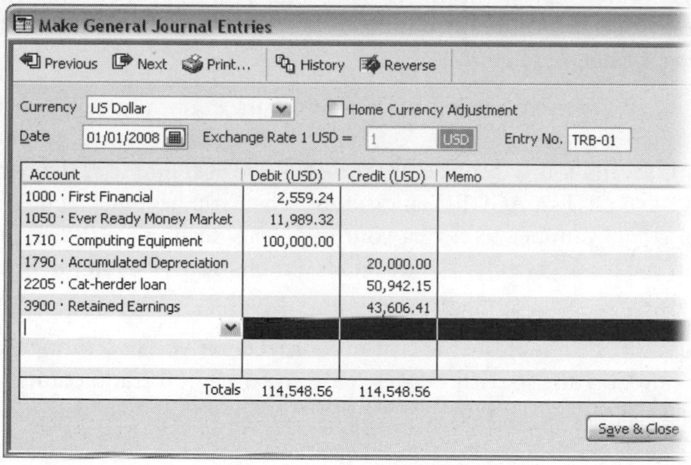

Figure 16-2:
When you use journal entries to create opening balances, you have to adjust the values in your equity account (like Retained Earnings) to reflect the omission of AP and AR. Now you can create your open customer invoices and unpaid vendor bills to build the values for Accounts Receivable and Accounts Payable. When your AP and AR account balances match the values on the trial balance, the equity account will also match its trial balance value.

Creating General Journal Entries

In essence, every transaction you create in QuickBooks is a journal entry. When you write checks, the program balances the debits and credits behind the scenes.

To explicitly create QuickBooks general journal entries, you first need to open the Make General Journal Entries window using any of the following methods:

- Choose Company → Make General Journal Entries.

- If the Chart of Accounts window is open, right-click anywhere and then choose Make General Journal Entries on the shortcut menu.

- If the Chart of Accounts window is open, click Activities and then choose Make General Journal Entries.

Here are the basic steps for creating a general journal entry in QuickBooks:

1. **In the Make General Journal Entries window, choose the date on which you want the general journal entry to happen.**

   If you're creating a general journal entry to reassign income or an expense to the correct account, you should use the date that you make the correction. However, when you or your accountant make end-of-year journal entries—to add the current year's depreciation, say—it's common to use the last day of the fiscal year as the date.

Note: If you turn on the multiple currency preference (page 570), the Make General Journal Entries dialog box includes boxes for the currency and the exchange rate. If you select an account that uses a foreign currency in a journal entry line, QuickBooks fills in the exchange rate and asks you to confirm that the exchange rate is correct. If it isn't, open the Currency List (choose Lists → Currency List) and update the exchange rate for the currency (page 444).

---

2. Although QuickBooks automatically assigns numbers to general journal entries, you can specify a different number. In the Entry No. box, type the entry number you want.

   When you type an entry number, QuickBooks fills in the entry number for your *next* entry by incrementing the one you typed. For example, suppose your accountant adds several journal entries at the end of the year and uses the entry numbers ACCT-1, ACCT-2, ACCT-3, and so on. When you begin using the file again, you can type a number to restart your sequence, such as DRP-8. When you create your next journal entry, QuickBooks automatically fills in the Entry No. box with DRP-9.

   You can also use words to indicate the type of journal entry you're creating. For example, you can label the journal entries that record payroll transactions for your outside payroll service with PAY.

Note: If you don't want QuickBooks to number general journal entries automatically, you can turn off the automatic numbering preference in the Accounting preferences section (page 551).

---

3. Fill in the first line of your general journal entry, which can be either a debit or a credit. For details about filling in each field in a general journal entry line, see the next section.

   When you click the Account cell in the next line, QuickBooks automatically enters the offsetting balance, as shown in Figure 16-3.

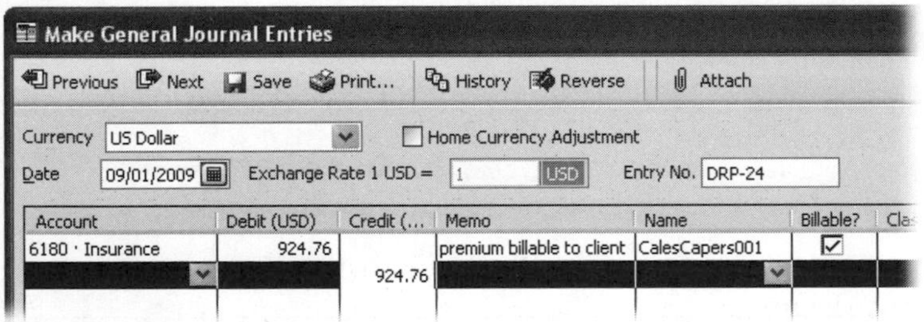

Figure 16-3:
If the first line you enter is in the Debit column, QuickBooks helpfully enters the same amount in the Credit column in the second line. If your first line is a credit, QuickBooks fills in the second line with the same amount in the Debit column.

4. Fill in the second line of the general journal entry.

   If your second line doesn't balance the debit and credit columns, continue adding additional lines until you've added debit and credit amounts that balance.

   If the offsetting value that QuickBooks adds to the second line is what you want, all you have to do is choose the account for that line, and then click Save & Close.

5. **When the debit and credit columns are the same, click Save & Close to save the general journal entry and close the Make General Journal Entries window.**

   If you want to create another general journal entry, click Save & New.

Filling in General Journal Entry Fields

Each line of a general journal entry includes a number of fields, although for most general journal entries, the key fields are the Account field, either the Debit or Credit field, and the Memo field. But every field comes in handy at some point, so they're all worth knowing about. Here's what each field does and when you might fill them in:

- **Account.** Choose the account that you want to debit or credit. Every line of every general journal entry has to have an assigned account.

- **Debit.** If you want to debit the account on the line, type the amount of the debit in this field.

- **Credit.** If you want to credit the account on the line, type the amount of the credit in this field.

- **Memo.** Entering a memo is a huge help when you go back to review your journal entries. For example, if you're reclassifying an uncategorized expense, type something like "Reclassify expense to correct account." For depreciation or insurance, you can include the dates covered by the journal entry.

Note: In QuickBooks Premier and Enterprise editions, the Autofill preference (Accounting, My Preferences tab) tells the program to fill each subsequent Memo field with the text from the first one.

- **Name.** If you're debiting or crediting an Accounts Receivable or Accounts Payable account, you have to choose a name, as explained in the box on page 420. However, you might also fill in the Name field if you're creating a journal entry for billable expenses and want to assign the expenses to a customer.

- **Billable?.** The Billable? column lets you designate part of your journal entry as billable expenses. When you choose a name in the Name field, QuickBooks automatically adds a checkmark in the Billable field, as shown in Figure 16-3. If you don't want to make the value billable to the customer, turn off the checkmark in the Billable? field. Leave this field alone when you create general journal entries to reassign some of your existing expenses to be billable to a customer.

- **Class.** General journal entries are transactions just like checks and invoices, which means you should choose a class for each line to keep your class reports accurate. If you create a general journal entry to reassign income or expense to a different class, the Account on each line stays the same, but the class you choose is different.

Tip: You can use the Find feature to track down a journal entry. Choose Edit → Find to open the Find window. In the Filter list, choose Transaction Type. Next, in the Transaction Type drop-down list, choose Journal. Click Find to display the journal entries you've created.

Checking General Journal Entries

If you stare off into space and start mumbling "Debit entries increase asset accounts" every time you create a general journal entry, it's wise to check that the general journal entry did what you wanted. Those savvy in the ways of accounting can visualize debits and offsetting credits in their heads, but for novices, thinking about the changes you expect in your profit and loss report or balance sheet is easier.

For example, if you plan to create a journal entry to reassign expenses in the Uncategorized Expenses account to their proper expense account homes, you'd expect to see the value in the Uncategorized Expenses account drop to zero while the values in the correct expense accounts increase. Figure 16-4 shows how you use a profit and loss report (see page 430) to check your general journal entries.

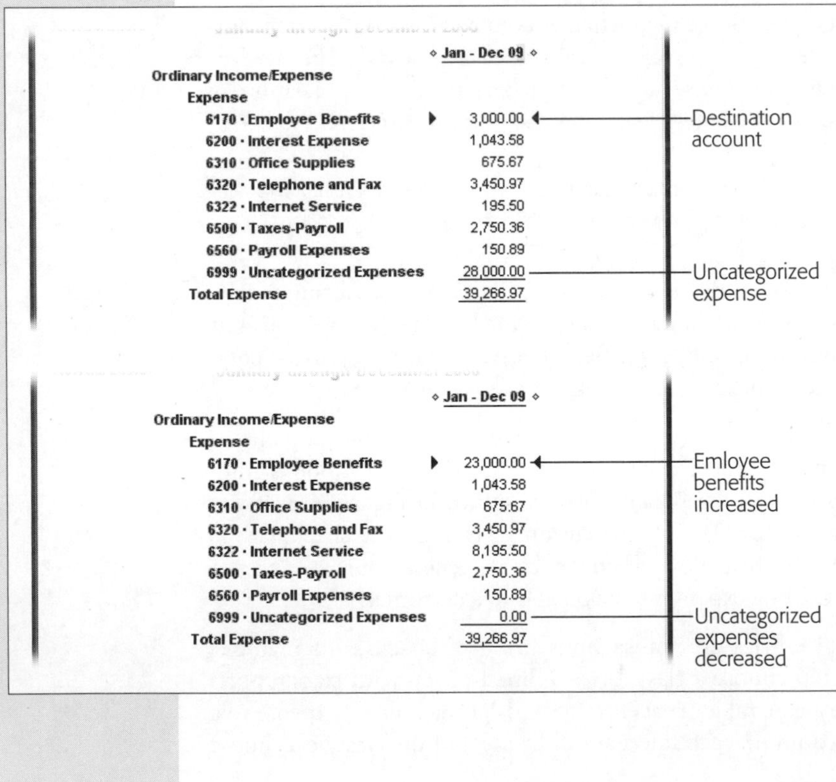

Figure 16-4:
Top: Before you create your general journal entry, review your Profit & Loss report to look at the accounts that you expect to change. Here, the Uncategorized Expenses account has $28,000 in it. The Employee Benefits account, which is one of the destinations for your uncategorized expenses, has $3,000.

Bottom: After the general journal entry reassigns the expenses, the Uncategorized Expenses account decreases, as you'd expect, and the Employee Benefits account increases.

Note: Some general journal entries affect both Balance Sheets and Profit & Loss reports. For example, as you'll see on page 427, a depreciation journal entry uses an asset account, which appears only in the Balance Sheet, and an expense account, which appears only in the Profit & Loss report. In situations like this, you'll have to review both reports to verify your numbers.

Reclassifications and Corrections

As you work with your QuickBooks file, you might realize that you want to use different accounts. For example, as you expand the services you provide, you might switch from one top-level income account to several specific income accounts. Expense accounts are also prone to change—when the Telephone account splits into separate accounts for landline service, wireless service, and Internet service, for example. For that matter, any type of account is a candidate for restructuring, as one building grows into a stable of commercial properties or you move from a single mortgage to a bevy of mortgages, notes, and loans.

Reclassifying Accounts

Whether you want to shift funds between accounts because you decide to categorize your finances differently or you simply made a mistake, you're moving money between accounts of the same type. The benefit to this type of general journal entry is that you only have to think hard about one side of the transaction. As long as you pick the debit or credit correctly, QuickBooks handles the other side for you.

Debits and credits work differently for income and expense accounts, and Figure 16-5 shows you how to set them up for different types of adjustments.

Accountants sometimes create what are known as *reversing journal entries*. These are general journal entries that move money in one direction on one date and then move the money back to where it came from on another date. Reversing journal entries are common at the end of the year, when you need your books configured one way to prepare your taxes and another way for your day-to-day bookkeeping.

Note: It's easy enough to create two general journal entries, each using the same accounts, but with opposite assignments for debits and credits. In QuickBooks Premier Edition, the Make General Journal Entries dialog box includes a Reverse command, which automatically creates a reversing journal entry for you.

Reassigning Jobs

If you need to transfer money between different jobs for the same customer, general journal entries are the answer. For example, your customer might ask you to apply a credit from one job to another, because the job with the credit is already complete, so your customer wants to apply that credit toward a job that's still in progress.

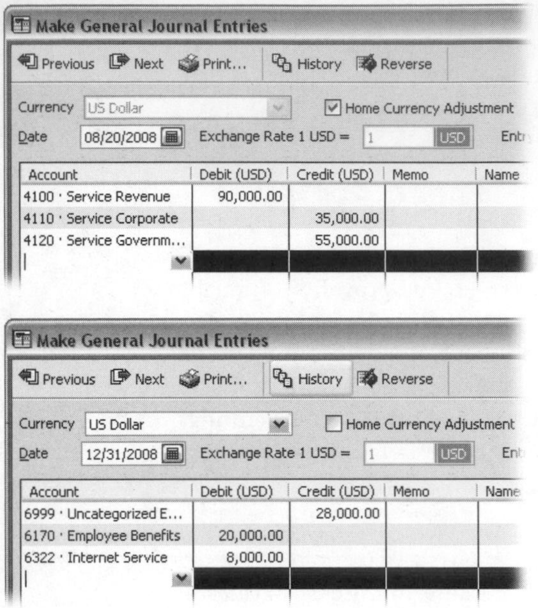

Figure 16-5:
Top: When you transfer money between income accounts, you debit the original income account to decrease its value and credit the new income accounts to increase their value.

Bottom: Expense accounts are the opposite. You credit the original expense account to decrease its value and debit new expense accounts to increase their value.

When you move money between jobs, you're transferring that money in and out of Accounts Receivable. Because QuickBooks allows only one Accounts Receivable account per journal entry, you need *two* journal entries to transfer the credit completely. (Figure 13-10 on page 341 shows what these journal entries look like.) You also need a special account to hold the credit transfers. An Other Expense account called something like Credit Transfers will do. After you have the transfer account in place, here's how the two journal entries work:

- **Transfer the credit from the first job to the transfer account.** In the first journal entry, you debit Accounts Receivable for the amount of the credit. Be sure to choose the customer and job in the Name field. This half of the journal entry removes the credit from the job's balance. In the second line of the journal entry, choose the transfer account. The amount is already in the Credit cell, which is where you want it for moving the amount into the transfer account.

- **Transfer the money from the transfer account to the second job.** In this journal entry, debit the transfer account for the money you're moving. Then, the Accounts Receivable account receives the amount in its Credit cell. In the Name cell, choose the customer and the second job. This journal entry transfers the money from the transfer account to the second job's balance.

Recording Depreciation with Journal Entries

When you own an asset, such as the deluxe Cat-o-matic cat herder, the machine loses value as it ages and clogs with furballs. *Depreciation* is an accounting concept, intimately tied to IRS rules, that reduces the value of the machine and lets your financial reports show a more accurate picture of how the money you spend on assets links to the income your company earns. Typically, you'll calculate depreciation in a spreadsheet so you can also see the asset's current depreciated value and how much more it will depreciate.

But depreciation doesn't deal with hard cash, which is why you need to create a general journal entry to enter it. Unlike some other general journal entries with a wide choice of accounts, depreciation journal entries are easy to create, because the accounts you can choose are limited. The debit account is an expense account, usually called Depreciation Expense. (If you don't have a Depreciation Expense account, see page 53 to learn how to create one.) The offsetting account is the account for the fixed asset that you're depreciating.

Tip: If you depreciate the same amount each year, memorize the first depreciation transaction you create (page 317). The following year, when it's time to enter depreciation, press Ctrl+T to open the Memorized Transaction List window. Select the depreciation transaction, and then click Enter Transaction. Another way to copy a journal entry is to click Previous until you see the journal entry you want. Then, right-click the Make General Journal Entries window and choose Duplicate Journal Entry from the shortcut menu. Make the changes you want and click Save & Close.

For a depreciation general journal entry, you want to reduce the value of the fixed asset account and add value to the Depreciation Expense account. If you remember that debit entries increase the value of expense accounts, you can figure out that the debit goes with the expense account and the credit goes to the fixed asset account. Figure 16-6 shows how depreciation debits and credits work.

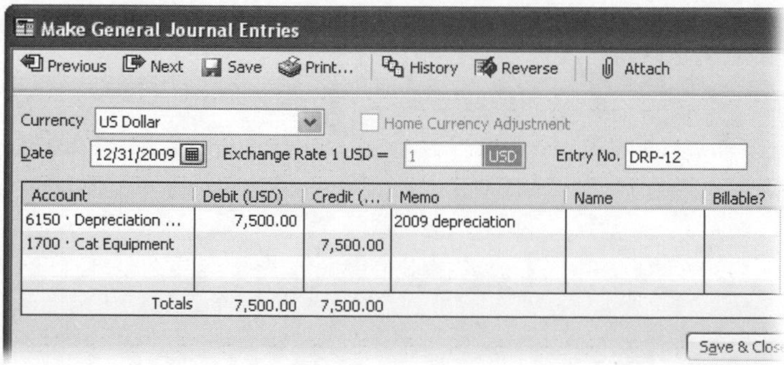

Figure 16-6:
If you have several assets to depreciate, you can add a credit line for each asset. In this case, the Depreciation Expense debit is the total of all the depreciation credits.

Recording Owners' Contributions

If you run your business from your home, you may want to allocate a portion of your utility bills, homeowners' insurance premiums, repairs to your home, and other home-related expenses to your company. The money you spent on home office expenses is already out the door, but those expenditures are equivalent to personal funds you contribute to your business. To show this contribution in QuickBooks, you credit the total expenses for your home office to an equity account for your owner's contributions to the company. Then, you debit expense accounts for each type of home office expense, as shown in Figure 16-7.

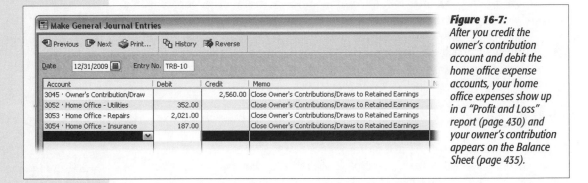

Figure 16-7:
After you credit the owner's contribution account and debit the home office expense accounts, your home office expenses show up in a "Profit and Loss" report (page 430) and your owner's contribution appears on the Balance Sheet (page 435).

Generating Financial Statements

When you keep your company's books day after day, all those invoices, checks, and other transactions blur together. But hidden within that maelstrom of figures is important information for you, your accountant, your investors, and the IRS. When consolidated and presented the right way, your books can tell you a lot about what your company does right, does wrong, could do better, and has to pay in taxes.

Over the years, the Financial Accounting Standards Board (FASB) has nurtured a standard of accounting known as GAAP (Generally Accepted Accounting Principles). GAAP includes a trio of financial statements that together paint a portrait of company performance: the income statement (also known as the Profit & Loss report), the balance sheet, and the statement of cash flows.

Generating financial statements in QuickBooks is easy. But unless you understand what financial statements tell you and you can spot suspect numbers, you may end up generating fodder for your paper shredder. If you're new to business, get started by reading about what the income statement, balance sheet, and statement of cash flows do. If you're already an expert, you can jump to the section on generating these reports in QuickBooks (page 433).

Note: When you close out a year on your company books, these three special financial reports are a must. You'll learn how financial statements fit into your year-end procedures in Chapter 18. If you're a business maven and need a bunch of additional reports to manage your business, Chapter 21 has instructions for finding the reports you need and customizing them to your demanding specifications.

The Profit & Loss Report

The Profit & Loss report is more like a video than a snapshot. It covers a period of time, usually a month, quarter, or a full year, and it shows whether your company is making money—or hemorrhaging it.

Understanding the Profit & Loss Report

The money you make in sales (income) sits at the top of the Profit & Loss report. Beneath it, your expenses gradually whittle away at that income until you're left with a profit or loss at the bottom. The Profit & Loss report (Reports → Company & Financial → Profit & Loss Standard) and the bullet points that follow explain the progression from sales to the net income your company earned after paying the bills.

- **Income.** The first category in a Profit & Loss report is income, which is simply the revenue your company generates by selling products and services to your customers. Regardless of how you earn revenue (selling services, products, or even charging fees), the Profit & Loss report shows all the income accounts in your chart of accounts and how much you brought into each, as shown in Figure 17-1.

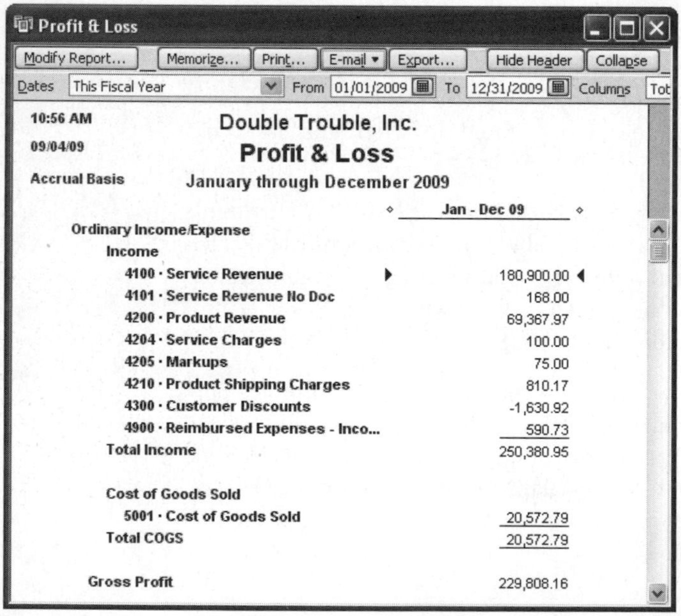

Figure 17-1:
The Income section at the top of the Profit & Loss report lists the accounts that represent the money you make when you sell to customers. Frustratingly, most companies have to subtract the cost of goods sold from income to figure out how much they really brought in. Cost of goods sold usually includes the cost of materials and labor to build products, or the cost of the products you purchase for resale.

Tip: The Profit & Loss report lists accounts in the order they appear in the Chart of Accounts. If you want to report your income and expenses in a specific order, you can rearrange the accounts in the Chart of Accounts window (press Ctrl+A to open it). Hover the pointer over the diamond to the left of the account name. When the pointer changes to a four-headed arrow, drag it to where you want to move the account.

- **Cost of Goods Sold.** Unless you gather rocks from your yard and then sell them as alien amulets, the products you sell carry some initial cost. For example, with products you purchase for resale, the cost is the original price you paid for them, the shipping costs you incurred to get them, and so on. In the Profit & Loss report, Cost of Goods Sold adds up the underlying costs associated with your product sales.

  By the way, if you don't sell inventory items, you might not have a Cost of Goods Sold section. Most of the time, Cost of Goods Sold relates to the costs of buying materials and building the products you sell. But depending on the type of business, Cost of Goods Sold can include labor costs, product shipping, an agent's percentage, and so on.

- **Gross Profit.** Gross profit is the profit you make after subtracting the Cost of Goods Sold. For example, if you sell equipment for $100,000 and you paid $60,000 to purchase that equipment, your gross profit is $40,000. The box below explains how to see whether your gross profit is in line with your industry.

UP TO SPEED

Profit Percentage

There's no question that sales are important. But the *percentage gross profit* you achieve is your first test of whether you're keeping up with your competitors. Compare the ratio of gross profit to sales to see if your company is in line with the industry. For example, in construction, gross profit between 40 and 60 percent is typical. QuickBooks is happy to calculate percentage gross profit for you. Here's what you do:

1. In the Profit & Loss report window's menu bar, click Modify Report.

2. In the Modify Report: Profit & Loss dialog box, click the Display tab (if it isn't already visible).

3. Turn on the "% of Income" checkbox and click OK.

QuickBooks adds another column showing the percentage of income that each row in the report represents, as you can see in Figure 17-2.

- **Expenses.** The next and longest section is for expenses—all the things you spend money on running your business, sometimes called *overhead*. For example, office rent, telephone service, and bank fees all fall into the overhead expense bucket. The name of the game is to keep these expenses as low as possible without hindering your ability to make money.

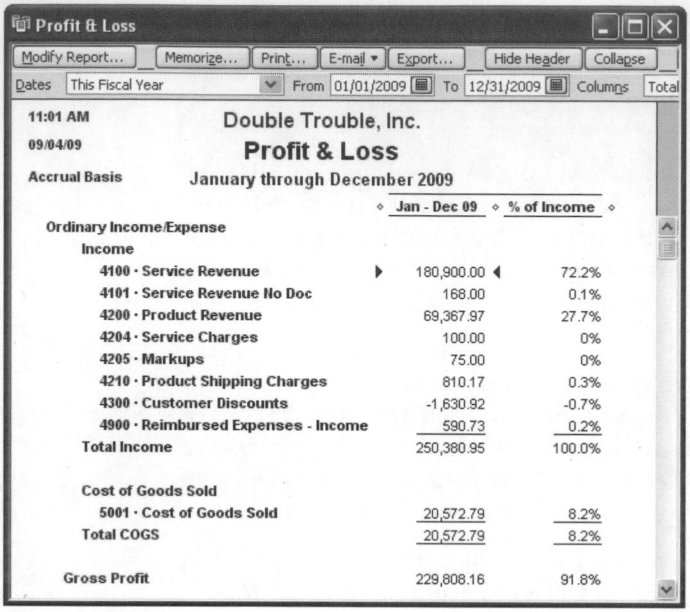

Profit & Loss

Modify Report... | Memorize... | Print... | E-mail ▾ | Export... | Hide Header | Collapse

Dates: This Fiscal Year | From 01/01/2009 | To 12/31/2009 | Columns: Total

11:01 AM
09/04/09
Accrual Basis

Double Trouble, Inc.
Profit & Loss
January through December 2009

	Jan - Dec 09	% of Income
Ordinary Income/Expense		
Income		
4100 · Service Revenue	180,900.00	72.2%
4101 · Service Revenue No Doc	168.00	0.1%
4200 · Product Revenue	69,367.97	27.7%
4204 · Service Charges	100.00	0%
4205 · Markups	75.00	0%
4210 · Product Shipping Charges	810.17	0.3%
4300 · Customer Discounts	-1,630.92	-0.7%
4900 · Reimbursed Expenses - Income	590.73	0.2%
Total Income	250,380.95	100.0%
Cost of Goods Sold		
5001 · Cost of Goods Sold	20,572.79	8.2%
Total COGS	20,572.79	8.2%
Gross Profit	229,808.16	91.8%

Figure 17-2: *You can use the percentages in the "% of Income" columns to analyze company performance in other ways. For example, when you're trying to find places to cut costs, look for expense accounts that take up a large percentage of your income. Or compare the percentage of net profit to the average for your industry.*

- **Net Ordinary Income.** QuickBooks uses the term Net Ordinary Income to describe the money that's left over after you pay the bills. You've probably also run across this measure referred to as *net profit* or *net earnings*. Figure 17-3 shows the expenses and net ordinary income portion of a Profit & Loss report.

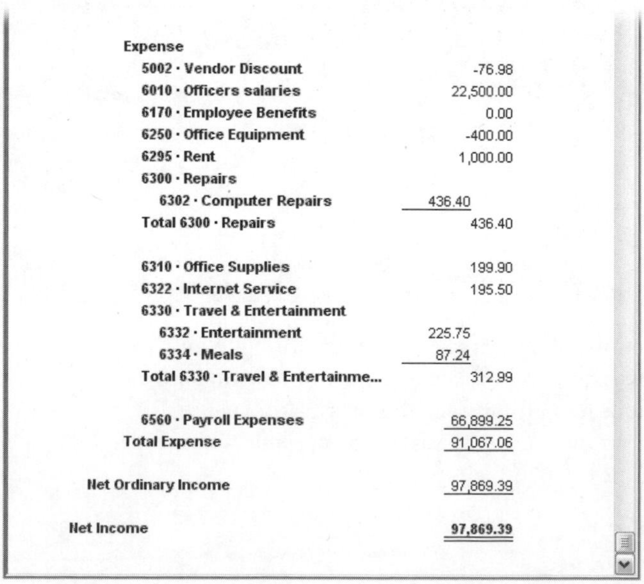

Expense		
5002 · Vendor Discount		-76.98
6010 · Officers salaries		22,500.00
6170 · Employee Benefits		0.00
6250 · Office Equipment		-400.00
6295 · Rent		1,000.00
6300 · Repairs		
6302 · Computer Repairs	436.40	
Total 6300 · Repairs		436.40
6310 · Office Supplies		199.90
6322 · Internet Service		195.50
6330 · Travel & Entertainment		
6332 · Entertainment	225.75	
6334 · Meals	87.24	
Total 6330 · Travel & Entertainme...		312.99
6560 · Payroll Expenses		66,899.25
Total Expense		91,067.06
Net Ordinary Income		97,869.39
Net Income		97,869.39

Figure 17-3: *If your company makes more money than it spends, your net income (also called net profit) is a positive number. Despite the report's name, QuickBooks doesn't label your result a loss when your company spends more than it makes. Instead, a loss shows up as a negative number for net income.*

• **Other Income/Expense.** Income and expenses that don't relate to your primary business fall into the Other Income/Expenses category. The most common entrants are the interest income you earn from your savings at the bank, the interest you pay on your loans, or bad debt. In this category, income and expense are bundled together and offset each other. The result is called Net Other Income. For example, if you have only a smidgeon of cash in savings but a honking big mortgage, Net Other Income will be a negative number.

• **Net Income.** At long last, you reach the end of the report. Net Income is the money that's left after subtracting all the costs and expenses you incur. If Net Income is positive, congratulations—your company made money! When Net Income is negative, your expenses were more than your income, and something's gotta give.

Generating a Profit & Loss Report

If you choose Reports → Company & Financial, QuickBooks gives you several built-in Profit & Loss reports to choose from. Choose Profit & Loss Standard to see a month-to-date report, which, if you've built your mom-and-pop shop into a merchandising monster, might be just the one you want.

Note: Before you generate your first financial statements, be sure that QuickBooks reports your numbers using your company's own accounting method. The Summary Reports Basis preference (page 577) sets your reports to use either accrual or cash accounting. When you choose the Cash option, your Profit & Loss reports show income only after you receive customer payments, and show expenses only after you pay bills. With the Accrual option, income appears in Profit & Loss reports as soon as you record an invoice or other type of sale, and expenses show up as soon as you enter bills.

But for many small companies, month-to-date numbers can be rather sparse. You can change the month-to-date report that QuickBooks produces into a year-to-date Profit & Loss report, as described in Figure 17-4. (The box on page 437 tells you how to save a Profit & Loss report after you tweak it to look the way you want.)

Tip: In accounting, *pro forma* reports are financial statements that show financial results *excluding* unusual or one-of-a-kind transactions. In business lingo, pro forma means projected results. QuickBooks doesn't produce pro forma reports out of the box, but you can trick it into doing so. Create a new company file (page 21) using the same accounts as your real company file and create a journal entry (page 421) to set the values for all your accounts. Anytime you want to create a pro forma report, edit the account debits and credits in the journal entry to the values you want, and then run whichever report you want.

Other Profit & Loss Reports

If the Profit & Loss Standard report in the previous section isn't what you want, take a few minutes to see if any of the other built-in Profit & Loss reports fit the

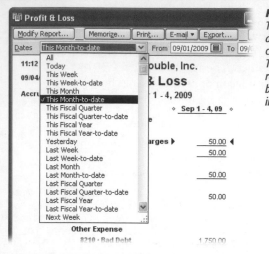

Figure 17-4:
The Dates drop-down list includes dozens of commonly-used date ranges for the current and previous fiscal year. If you choose "This Fiscal Year-to-date", the dates in the From and To box change to the first of the year and today's date, respectively. To select exactly the dates you want, scroll to the bottom of the Dates drop-down list, choose Custom, and then, in the From and To boxes, type or choose the dates you want.

bill. Here's a guide to the other Profit & Loss reports on the Reports → Company & Financials menu and when you might use them:

- **Profit & Loss Detail.** Only the tiniest of companies—or the most persnickety of bookkeepers—uses this report regularly. The Profit & Loss Detail report is a year-to-date report that includes a separate line for every service and product you sold, every other charge that produced revenue, and every item on every bill you paid. It comes in handy when the numbers on your standard report seem a bit off and you want to find the culprit.

Tip: If you spot questionable numbers in a Profit & Loss report, just double-click the number for a closer inspection. When you hover the pointer over a number, an icon that looks like a Z inside a magnifying glass appears; that's your clue that double-clicking the number will drill down into the details. For example, if you double-click a number in a Profit & Loss Standard report, QuickBooks displays a Transaction Detail By Account report with each transaction that contributed to the total. In a Profit & Loss Detail report, double-clicking a transaction opens the Create Invoices window (or corresponding window) to view that transaction.

- **Profit & Loss YTD Comparison.** This report pits the Profit & Loss results for two periods side by side: the current month to date and the year to date. You might find a reason to run this report, but comparing a period to its predecessor from the previous year usually shows business trends more clearly (see the next report), especially for seasonal businesses such as retail or landscaping.

- **Profit & Loss Prev Year Comparison.** If you own a gift shop, you know that sales are highest around the holidays. If you compare the last quarter of one year to the first quarter of the next, the Profit & Loss report would look pretty grim. Sales would be down and possibly exacerbated by returns from holiday purchases. To see whether your business is growing, compare your previous year to the current year with the report shown in Figure 17-5.

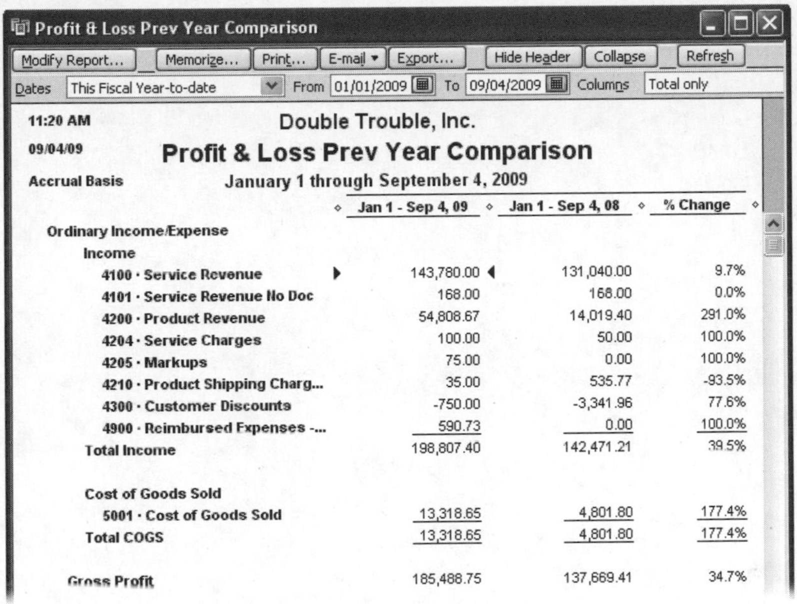

	Jan 1 - Sep 4, 09	Jan 1 - Sep 4, 08	% Change
Ordinary Income/Expense			
Income			
4100 · Service Revenue	143,780.00	131,040.00	9.7%
4101 · Service Revenue No Doc	168.00	168.00	0.0%
4200 · Product Revenue	54,808.67	14,019.40	291.0%
4204 · Service Charges	100.00	50.00	100.0%
4205 · Markups	75.00	0.00	100.0%
4210 · Product Shipping Charg...	35.00	535.77	-93.5%
4300 · Customer Discounts	-750.00	-3,341.96	77.6%
4900 · Reimbursed Expenses -...	590.73	0.00	100.0%
Total Income	198,807.40	142,471.21	39.5%
Cost of Goods Sold			
5001 · Cost of Goods Sold	13,318.65	4,801.80	177.4%
Total COGS	13,318.65	4,801.80	177.4%
Gross Profit	185,488.75	137,669.41	34.7%

Figure 17-5: *The Profit & Loss Prev Year Comparison report sets the Dates box to "This Fiscal Year-to-date" and shows your results for the current year in the first column and those from the previous year in the second column. If you want to see where growth is strong or stagnant, include the columns that show the change in dollars or percents (page 436). Right after your fiscal year ends, you can change the Dates box to "Last Fiscal Year" to compare the year you just finished to the one before.*

- **Profit & Loss by Job.** If you suspect that some of your customers and jobs are less profitable than others—and you want to learn from your mistakes—choose the Profit & Loss by Job report. In this report, each of your customers and jobs appears in its own column so you can compare how much profit you made for each. The box on page 436 tells you how to compare apples to apples.

- **Profit & Loss by Class.** When you use classes to track performance for different business units or locations, use this report to produce a Profit & Loss report for each business entity. Each class has its own column. If you'd rather generate a Profit & Loss report that shows only one class, modify the report to filter for that one class (see page 514). Unclassified is the label for last column in this report, which represents all the transactions that don't have a class assignment.

- **Profit & Loss Unclassified.** Before you pretty up and print your class-based Profit & Loss reports, run this one to see the numbers for transactions without class assignments. Depending on how you use classes, unclassified transactions might be perfectly acceptable. For example, if you track income by partner, overhead expenses aren't related to individual partners. You shouldn't see any non-zero values for income accounts, but you might see expense accounts with non-zero values.

The Balance Sheet

If a Profit & Loss report is like a video, a balance sheet is more like a portrait. This report shows how much your company owns (assets), how much it owes (liabilities),

UP TO SPEED

Comparing Profitability

Because jobs vary in size, it's hard to compare profitability by looking at the straight numbers. For example, one job may produce $50,000 in total income with $10,000 in net income. Another job also produces $50,000 in total income, but only $5,000 in net income. To see which customers and jobs are truly profitable, percentages are the answer. Suppose each job's total income represents 10 percent of your total income for the year. The job with $10,000 in net income may represent 15 percent of your net income, while the other job, at $5,000 net income, is only 7.5 percent.

To add columns that show the percentage that a job contributes to your overall income and profit, do the following:

1. In the "Profit & Loss by Job" report's menu bar, click Modify Report.

2. In the Display tab that opens in the dialog box, turn on the "% of Row" checkbox (at the bottom-right), and then click OK.

3. In the report, look at a customer's percentage in the "% of Row" column for Total Income. That's the percentage of your company's income that comes from that customer.

4. Then, look at a customer's percentage in the "% of Row" column for Net Income. If that percentage is lower than the percentage for total income, the customer is less profitable than average. When the Net Income percentage is higher than the Total Income percentage, the customer is more profitable than average.

and the equity in the company at a given point in time. While a Profit & Loss report tells you whether you're making money, the balance sheet (Reports → Company & Financial → Balance Sheet Standard) measures your company's financial strength.

Understanding the Balance Sheet

One thing you can count on with a balance sheet is that the total assets in the report always exactly balance the total of the liabilities and equity, as you can see in Figure 17-6. The key to a good-looking balance sheet is not having too much debt. How much is too much? It depends on the industry you're in, but the acid test is if you closed up shop today and sold all your assets, would you have enough money to pay off your liabilities? If the answer is no, you'll have a hard time finding a bank to loan you more money. A balance sheet is strong when it shows a lot of assets but not many liabilities.

Here's what to look for in each section of a balance sheet:

- **Assets.** Assets are things of value that a company owns, such as equipment, land, product inventory, accounts receivable, cash, and even brand names. On a balance sheet, you want to see significantly more money in the asset section than in the liabilities section.

WORKAROUND WORKSHOP

Making Year-to-Date Your Profit & Loss Standard

If you snort with displeasure every time QuickBooks displays a month-to-date Profit & Loss report, you *can* do something about it. Memorizing reports is easy and saves you time and irritation. After you've memorized your ideal Profit & Loss report, you can choose it from one of the Reports submenus or the Report Center as easily as choosing the program's built-in reports. Here's how:

1. In the Profit & Loss report window, find the Dates drop-down list, and then choose the date range (This Fiscal Year-to-date, for example).

2. Make any other changes you want (see Chapter 21).

3. When you like the way the report looks, in the Profit & Loss window's menu bar, click Memorize. QuickBooks opens the Memorize Report dialog box.

4. In the Memorize Report dialog box, type the name of the report. For example, for the year-to-date report, type something like "P&L Year-to-date."

5. If you want to add the report to a group of reports, turn on the "Save in Memorized Report Group" checkbox, and then choose the group in the drop-down list. (See page 502 to learn how to create your own report groups.)

6. To memorize the report, click OK.

7. To view the report, choose Reports → Memorized Reports → "P&L Year-to-date". If you added the report to a group, choose Reports → Memorized Report → <group name> → "P&L Year-to-date". Or in the Report Center, click the Memorized tab.

TOTAL ASSETS	**504,477.29**
LIABILITIES & EQUITY	
Liabilities	
Current Liabilities	
Accounts Payable	
2000 · Accounts Payable	5,319.70
20000 · Accounts Payable - CNY	731.90
Total Accounts Payable	6,051.60
Other Current Liabilities	
2100 · Payroll Liabilities	12,293.46
2200 · Customer Prepayments	-1,200.00
2201 · Sales Tax Payable	2,645.22
Total Other Current Liabilities	-10,848.24
Total Current Liabilities	-4,796.64
Long Term Liabilities	
2205 · Cat-herder loan	68,728.71
Total Long Term Liabilities	68,728.71
Total Liabilities	63,932.07
Equity	
3000 · Opening Bal Equity	7,024.75
3900 · Retained Earnings	317,356.65
Net Income	116,163.82
Total Equity	440,545.22
TOTAL LIABILITIES & EQUITY	**504,477.29**

— Liabilities much less than assets

— Equity in company

Figure 17-6:
The Balance Sheet report earns its name because of math, not magic, and this is the formula that puts the balance into a balance sheet: Equity = Assets–Liabilities. As you buy more or borrow more, the value of your equity changes to make up the difference.

Note: Even with assets, you can have too much of a good thing. Assets aren't corporate collectors' items. Companies should use assets to make money. A measure called *return on assets* (the ratio of net income to total assets) shows whether a company is using assets effectively to produce income. Return on assets varies from industry to industry, but, typically, less than five percent is poor.

- **Liabilities.** Liabilities include accounts payable (bills you haven't yet paid), unpaid expenses, loans, mortgages, and even future expenses, such as pensions. Debt on its own isn't bad. It's *too much* debt that can drag a company down, particularly when business is slow. Debt payments are due every month whether your business produced revenue or not.

- **Equity.** Equity on a balance sheet is the corporate counterpart of the equity you have in your house. When you buy a house, your initial equity is the down payment you make. But both the increasing value of your house and the decreasing balance on your mortgage contribute to an increase in your equity. Equity in a company is the dollar value that remains after you subtract liabilities from assets.

Generating a Balance Sheet Report

A balance sheet is a snapshot of accounts on a given date. The difference between the built-in balance sheet reports that QuickBooks offers is whether you see only account balances or all the transactions that make up those balances. Choose Reports → Company & Financial and you can choose any of the following reports on the menu:

- **Balance Sheet Standard.** This report includes every asset, liability, and asset account in your chart of accounts—unless the account has a zero balance. QuickBooks automatically sets the Dates box to "This Fiscal Year-to-date", so the report opens showing your balance sheet for the current date. If you want to see the balance sheet at the end of a quarter or end of the year, in the Dates box, choose This Fiscal Quarter, This Fiscal Year, or Last Fiscal Year.

- **Balance Sheet Detail.** Printing the Balance Sheet Detail report is a good way to use up the last of your old printer paper, but it isn't that useful for managing your business. This report shows the transactions over a period in each of your asset, liability, and equity accounts. Should a number on your regular balance sheet report look odd, use this report to verify your transactions. Double-click the value for transactions to open the corresponding window, such as Enter Bills.

- **Balance Sheet Summary.** If you want to see the key numbers in your balance sheet without scanning past the individual accounts in each section, this report shows subtotals for each category of a balance sheet, as shown in Figure 17-7.

- **Balance Sheet Prev Year Comparison.** If you want to compare your financial strength from year to year, this report has four columns at your service: one each for the current and previous year, one for the dollar change, and the fourth for the percentage change.

Accrual Basis	As of September 4, 2009	
	◇ Sep 4, 09 ◇	
ASSETS		
Current Assets		
Checking/Savings	▶ 315,637.85 ◀	
Accounts Receivable	83,798.19	
Other Current Assets	45,042.15	
Total Current Assets	444,478.19	
Fixed Assets	59,999.10	
TOTAL ASSETS	504,477.29	
LIABILITIES & EQUITY		
Liabilities		
Current Liabilities		
Accounts Payable	6,051.60	
Other Current Liabilities	-10,848.24	
Total Current Liabilities	-4,796.64	
Long Term Liabilities	68,728.71	
Total Liabilities	63,932.07	
Equity	440,545.22	
TOTAL LIABILITIES & EQUITY	504,477.29	

Figure 17-7:
For assets and liabilities, the summary report separates current assets from other assets. Current assets are those you can convert into quick cash to keep things going when business is slow. Similarly, liabilities can be either current or long-term. Credit cards are current liabilities, since you have to pay the bill each month. With long-term loans, the next twelve months of payments are current liabilities and the rest of the balance is long-term liability.

Note: When you review your Balance Sheet Prev Year Comparison report, you typically want to see decreasing liabilities. If liabilities have *increased*, then assets should have increased as well. You don't want to see more debt without more assets to show for the trouble. Equity is the value of your—and your shareholders'—ownership in the company, so it should increase each year. (If you use QuickBooks to keep the books for your one-person consulting company, the equity may not increase each year if, for example, you use the same assets like your laptop and printer, and withdraw most of the profit you make as your salary.)

The Statement of Cash Flows

Thanks to non-cash accounting anomalies like accrual reporting and depreciation, profit and loss reports don't tell you how much cash you have on hand. Cash flow helps you figure out whether your company generates enough cash to keep the doors open. Your balance sheet might look great—$10 million in assets and only $500,000 in liabilities. But if a $50,000 payment is due and you only have $3,000 in the bank, you have cash flow problems.

Understanding the Statement of Cash Flows

The concept of cash flow is easy to understand. In the words of every film-noir detective, follow the money. Cash flow is nothing more than the real money that flows in and out of your company—not the non-cash transactions, such as depreciation, that you see on a Profit & Loss report.

Figure 17-8 shows sources of cash in a sample statement of cash flows.

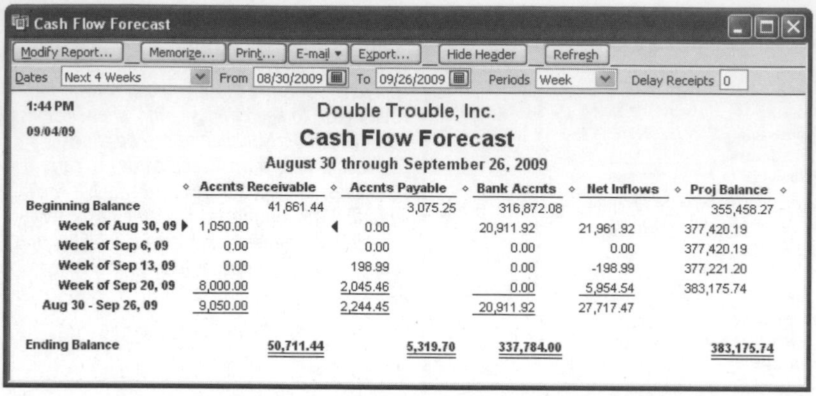

	Accnts Receivable	Accnts Payable	Bank Accnts	Net Inflows	Proj Balance
Beginning Balance	41,661.44	3,075.25	316,872.08		355,458.27
Week of Aug 30, 09	1,050.00	0.00	20,911.92	21,961.92	377,420.19
Week of Sep 6, 09	0.00	0.00	0.00	0.00	377,420.19
Week of Sep 13, 09	0.00	198.99	0.00	-198.99	377,221.20
Week of Sep 20, 09	8,000.00	2,045.46	0.00	5,954.54	383,175.74
Aug 30 - Sep 26, 09	9,050.00	2,244.45	20,911.92	27,717.47	
Ending Balance	50,711.44	5,319.70	337,784.00		383,175.74

Figure 17-8: *Cash from operating activities is the most desirable. When a company's ongoing operations generate cash, the business can sustain itself without cash coming from other sources. Buying and selling buildings or making money in the stock market using company money are investing activities (not shown here). Borrowing money or selling stock in your company brings in cash from outside sources, called financing activities. (New companies often have no other source of cash.)*

Warning: When you sell an asset, which is an investing activity, it shows up as a gain or loss on the Profit & Loss report, which *temporarily* increases or reduces net income. Beware: the effect of investing activities on the Profit & Loss report can hide problems brewing in your operations, which is why you should examine the "Statement of Cash Flows" report. If your income derives mainly from investing and financing activities, instead of operating activities, you've got a problem.

Generating a Statement of Cash Flows

To create a "Statement of Cash Flows", QuickBooks automatically deals the accounts that appear in your company's balance sheet into one of the three cash flow categories: Operating, Investing, and Financing. And the program almost always gets those assignments right. For example, Accounts Receivable and Inventory appear as operating accounts, fixed asset accounts show up as investing, and accounts for loans fall under financing. Unless you're a financial expert or your accountant gives you explicit instructions about a change, you're better off leaving the QuickBooks account classifications alone. If you need to reassign accounts for your "Statement of Cash Flows" report, this section tells you how.

Generating a "Statement of Cash Flows" is easy, because you have only one report to choose from. Simply choose Reports → Company & Financial → "Statement of Cash Flows". QuickBooks creates the report (see Figure 17-8) with your cash flow for your fiscal year to date. To view the "Statement of Cash Flows" for a quarter or a year, in the Dates box, choose This Fiscal Quarter or This Fiscal Year.

Note: The Operating Activities section of the report includes the unfortunate label: "Adjustments to reconcile Net Income to net cash provided by operations". QuickBooks calculates the net income at the top of the "Statement of Cash Flows" on an accrual basis (income appears as of the invoice date, not the day the customer pays). But the "Statement of Cash Flows" is by nature a cash-based report. So the program has to add and subtract transactions to get net income on a cash basis.

Expert Cash Flow Analysis

Thanks to today's accounting rules, cash isn't always connected to revenues and expenses. And a dollar in sales isn't necessarily a dollar of cash. Here's what financial analysts look for when they evaluate a company's health based on its "Statement of Cash Flows":

- Net income on the Profit & Loss report that's close to the cash from operating activities means net income is mostly from business operations and the company can support itself.

- Cash from operations that's growing at the same rate or faster than the growth of net income indicates that the company is maintaining or even improving its ability to sustain business.

- Cash that's increasing means the company won't have to resort to financing to keep the business going.

- Negative cash flow is often the sign of a rapidly growing company—without financing, the company grows only as fast as it can generate cash from operations. If a company isn't growing quickly and still can't generate cash, something's wrong.

- If an increase in cash comes primarily from selling assets, the company future looks grim. Selling assets to raise cash sometimes means the company can't borrow any more, because banks don't like what they see. Because assets often produce sales, selling assets means less cash generated in the future—and you can see where that leads.

The account assignments for the "Statement of Cash Flows" report are a collection of preferences you can find in the Preferences dialog box. Here's how to view the account assignments or change them:

1. **Choose Edit → Preferences to open the Preferences dialog box.**

   In the Preferences icon bar, click Reports & Graphs, and then click the Company Preferences tab.

2. **Click Classify Cash.**

   QuickBooks opens the Classify Cash dialog box. As described in Figure 17-9, here's where you change your account categories.

3. **When the assignments are the way you want, click OK to close the dialog box.**

   That's it—you've reassigned the accounts.

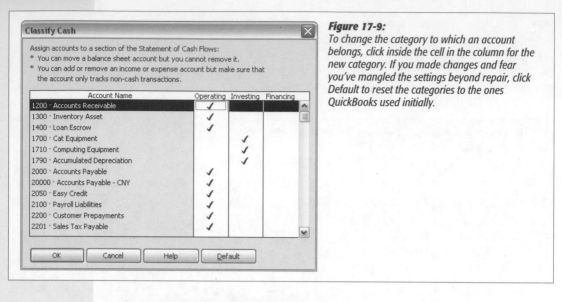

Figure 17-9:
To change the category to which an account belongs, click inside the cell in the column for the new category. If you made changes and fear you've mangled the settings beyond repair, click Default to reset the categories to the ones QuickBooks used initially.

Other Helpful Financial Reports

Although financial statements are the ones that other people like shareholders and the IRS want to see, other financial reports help you, the business owner, keep tabs on how your enterprise is doing. This section introduces a few other QuickBooks reports that help you evaluate your business performance.

Note: Reports that apply to specific bookkeeping and accounting tasks are explained in the chapters for those tasks, such as accounts receivable reports in Chapter 13, "Managing Accounts Receivable".

- **Reviewing income and sales.** If you're introducing enhanced services to keep your best customers—or you're looking for the customers you *want* your competition to steal—use the "Income by Customer Summary" report. Choose Reports → Company & Financial → "Income by Customer Summary" to see total income for each of your customers; that is, the total dollar amount from all of a customer's invoices and statement charges. Customers with low income totals might be good targets for more energetic sales pitches. High income values could indicate customers ripe to purchase more of your goods and services. If you find that most of your income comes from only a few customers, you may want to protect your income stream by lining up more customers. (One thing this report doesn't show is how profitable your sales to customers are. Page 431 explains how to see that.)

Note: If you want to produce a report that shows performance trends over several years, you have to export report data to Excel or a report program like Crystal Reports.

- **Reviewing expenses.** On the expense side, the "Expenses by Vendor Summary" report shows how much you spend with each vendor. If you spend tons with certain vendors, maybe it's time to negotiate volume discounts, find additional vendors as backups, or set up electronic ordering to speed up deliveries.

- **Comparing income and expenses.** The Income & Expense Graph (on the same submenu) includes a bar graph that shows income and expenses by month and a pie chart that breaks down either income or expenses. You can't change the time periods for each set of bars on the graph, so it's not much help with spotting trends. You can click Income or Expense at the bottom of the window to see the breakdown of income or expense. To specify how income or expense is broken down, click By Account, By Customer, or By Class in the window icon bar.

- **What you've sold.** Most companies analyze their sales to find ways to improve. Maybe you want to beef up sales to customers who haven't bought from you in a while, turn good customers into great ones, or check on how well your stuff is selling. The Sales By Customer Summary is a terse listing of customers and how much you've sold to each one during the timeframe you specify (it shows "This Month-to-date" initially). Choose Reports → Sales → Sales By Customer Summary to run it.

    The Sales Graph presents sales data in a cheery rainbow of colors, but you can quickly switch the graph to show the breakdown of sales by customer, item, and sales rep. Choose Reports → Sales → Sales Graph to generate it. The bar graph shows sales by month for the year to date. If you want to change the duration covered by the graph, click Dates and specify the date range you want. The pie chart shows sales slices based on the category you choose. In the window's button bar, click By Item, By Customer, or By Rep to switch between seeing pie slices for items, customers, and sales reps, respectively.

    The Sales By Item Summary shows how much you sell of each item in your Item List, starting with inventory items, then non-inventory parts, and finally service items. This report includes a column for average cost of goods sold (COGS) and gross margin, which apply only to inventory items you sell.

- **Forecasting cash flow.** You may be wondering whether you have any invoices due that will cover a big credit card bill that's coming up or whether income over the next few weeks is enough to meet payroll. Use the Cash Flow Forecast report to see how much cash you should have over the next four weeks, as shown in Figure 17-10. The Beginning Balance line shows the current balance for your Accounts Receivable, Accounts Payable, and bank accounts. The Proj Balance column shows how much money you should have in your bank accounts at the end of each week (or longer if you choose a different period in the Periods drop-down list). If a number in the column starts flirting with zero, you're about to run out of cash. You'll have to speed up some customer payments, transfer cash from another account, or look into a short-term loan.

POWER USERS' CLINIC

Realized Gains and Losses

If you work with more than one currency, changes in exchange rates can lead to gains or losses on your transactions. Say you send a customer an invoice for €1,000 when the euro to dollar exchange rate is 1.459. The invoice total in your home currency (dollars, in this example) is $1,459. The customer mails you a check for €1,000. However, by the time you deposit the customer's payment, the going euro to dollar exchange rate is 1.325, which means each euro is worth fewer dollars. At that exchange rate, your bank records a deposit of $1,325 in your account. Thanks to the inevitable fluctuations in exchange rates, you've lost $134 on the transaction.

To see how much you've gained or lost on foreign currency transactions, choose Reports → Company & Financial → Realized Gains & Losses.

To see *potential* gains or losses based on the latest exchange rate, choose Reports → Company & Financial → Unrealized Gains & Losses. In the Enter Exchange Rates dialog box, enter the exchange rates you want to apply. When you click Continue, the Unrealized Gains & Losses report shows gains and losses for the balances in your Accounts Receivable and Accounts Payable accounts.

To report your financial results accurately, you must adjust the value of accounts set up in foreign currencies (page 55) based on the exchange rate as of the end date for the report. In QuickBooks, you can download the most recent exchange rates by choosing Company → Manage Currency → Download Latest Exchange Rates. Or, to find exchange rates for a given date, go to *www.xe.com/ict*. Then you can choose Lists → Currency List and edit the currencies to enter the exchange rates you got online.

To adjust account values, choose Company → Manage Currency → Home Currency Adjustment. In the Home Currency Adjustment dialog box, choose the date for the adjustment. Then, choose the currency and the exchange rate you want to use. Click Calculate Adjustment, and customers and vendors who use that currency appear in the dialog box's table. Select the ones you want to adjust, and then click Save & Close.

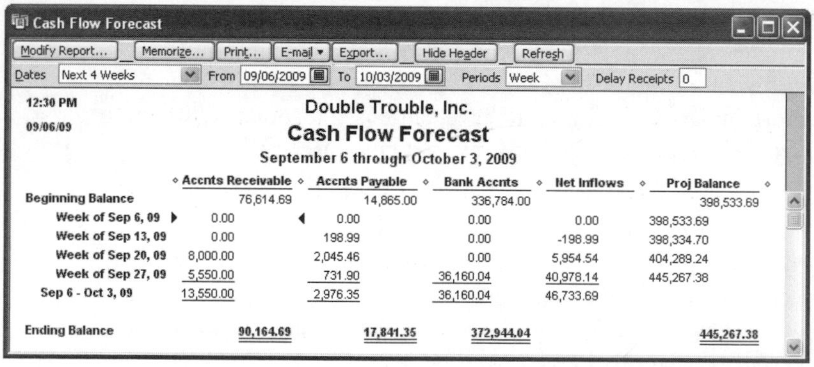

	Accnts Receivable	Accnts Payable	Bank Accnts	Net Inflows	Proj Balance
Beginning Balance	76,614.69	14,865.00	336,784.00		398,533.69
Week of Sep 6, 09	0.00	0.00	0.00	0.00	398,533.69
Week of Sep 13, 09	0.00	198.99	0.00	-198.99	398,334.70
Week of Sep 20, 09	8,000.00	2,045.46	0.00	5,954.54	404,289.24
Week of Sep 27, 09	5,550.00	731.90	36,160.04	40,978.14	445,267.38
Sep 6 - Oct 3, 09	13,550.00	2,976.35	36,160.04	46,733.69	
Ending Balance	90,164.69	17,841.35	372,944.04		445,267.38

Figure 17-10: *QuickBooks sets up the report initially to show cash flow over the next four weeks. To view additional weeks, in the From and To boxes, type the date range you want. If you want to review cash flow for a longer period, in the Dates drop-down list, choose Next Fiscal Quarter or Next Fiscal Year. To change the length of each period in the report, in the Periods drop-down list, choose from Week, Two Weeks, Month, and so on.*

CHAPTER 18

Performing End-of-Year Tasks

As if your typical workday isn't hectic enough, the end of the year brings an assortment of additional bookkeeping and accounting tasks. As long as you've kept on top of your bookkeeping during the year, you can delegate most of the year-end tasks to QuickBooks with a few mouse clicks. (If you shrugged off your data entry during the year, even the mighty QuickBooks can't help.) This chapter describes the tasks you have to perform at the end of each fiscal year (or other fiscal period, for that matter) and how to delegate them to QuickBooks.

Checking for Problems

If you work with an accountant, you may never run a report from the Accountant & Taxes submenu unless your accountant asks you to. But if you prepare your own tax returns, running the following reports at the end of each year will help sniff out any problems:

- Run the **Audit Trail** report frequently, especially if several people work on your company file, to watch for suspicious transactions—deleted invoices or modifications to transactions after they've been reconciled. People make mistakes, and the Audit Trail is also good for spotting inadvertent changes to transactions. QuickBooks initially includes transactions entered or modified today, but you can choose a different date range to review changes since your last review (in the Audit Trail report window, choose a date range in the Date Entered/Last Modified drop-down list, or type dates in the From and To boxes).

- The **Voided/Deleted Transactions** report focuses on transactions that—not surprisingly—have been voided or deleted.

Viewing the Trial Balance

The *Trial Balance* report is a holdover from the quaint days of paper-based accounting. The name refers to the report's original purpose: totaling the balances of every account in debit and credit columns to see whether pluses and minuses balanced. If they didn't, the bookkeeper had to track down the mistakes and try again.

QuickBooks doesn't make arithmetic mistakes, so you don't need a trial balance to make sure that debits and credits match. Nonetheless, the Trial Balance report is still handy. Accountants like to examine it for errant account assignments before diving into tax preparation or giving financial advice—and for good reason. The Trial Balance report is the only place in QuickBooks where you can see all your accounts *and* their balances in the same place, as shown in Figure 18-1.

To display the Trial Balance report, choose Reports → Accountant & Taxes → Trial Balance. QuickBooks then generates a Trial Balance report for the previous month. If you want to see the trial balance for your entire fiscal year, choose This Fiscal Year in the Dates box. The accounts appear in the same order that you see in the Chart of Accounts window (page 53).

Generating Year-End Financial Reports

At the end of every year, tax preparation stimulates a frenzy of financial reporting as companies submit fiscal year Profit & Loss reports (page 430) and balance sheets (page 435) as part of their tax returns. But tax forms aren't the only reason for year-end reports. Before you hand over your company file to your accountant or prepare final reports for your tax return, run year-end reports for these reasons, too:

- If you work with more than one currency, adjust account balances to reflect the current value based on currency exchange rates. See page 444 to learn how to do this.

- Inspect year-end reports for funny numbers. They might mean that you posted a transaction to the wrong account or created a journal entry incorrectly.

- Analyze your annual results to spot problems with your operations or look for ways to improve.

After you complete your initial review of the year-end reports and make any corrections to transactions, you'll generate another set of year-end reports *after* you've inspected your results and corrected any mistakes. Then, your accountant (if you work with one) is next in line to see your company file (page 451).

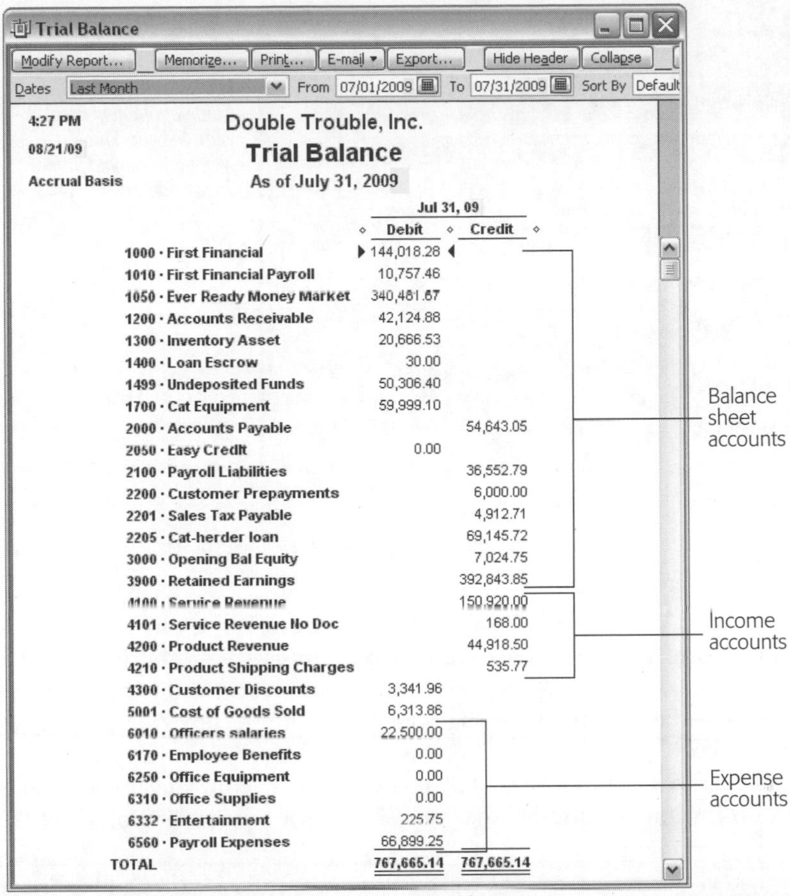

4:27 PM
08/21/09
Accrual Basis

Double Trouble, Inc.
Trial Balance
As of July 31, 2009

	Jul 31, 09 Debit	Jul 31, 09 Credit
1000 · First Financial	144,018.28	
1010 · First Financial Payroll	10,757.46	
1050 · Ever Ready Money Market	340,481.67	
1200 · Accounts Receivable	42,124.88	
1300 · Inventory Asset	20,666.53	
1400 · Loan Escrow	30.00	
1499 · Undeposited Funds	50,306.40	
1700 · Cat Equipment	59,999.10	
2000 · Accounts Payable		54,643.05
2050 · Easy Credit	0.00	
2100 · Payroll Liabilities		36,552.79
2200 · Customer Prepayments		6,000.00
2201 · Sales Tax Payable		4,912.71
2205 · Cat-herder loan		69,145.72
3000 · Opening Bal Equity		7,024.75
3900 · Retained Earnings		392,843.85
4100 · Service Revenue		150,920.00
4101 · Service Revenue No Doc		168.00
4200 · Product Revenue		44,918.50
4210 · Product Shipping Charges		535.77
4300 · Customer Discounts	3,341.96	
5001 · Cost of Goods Sold	6,313.86	
6010 · Officers salaries	22,500.00	
6170 · Employee Benefits	0.00	
6250 · Office Equipment	0.00	
6310 · Office Supplies	0.00	
6332 · Entertainment	225.75	
6560 · Payroll Expenses	66,899.25	
TOTAL	767,665.14	767,665.14

Figure 18-1: *If the account balances in your Trial Balance report look a little off, check the heading at top-left. If you see the words "Accrual Basis" in the heading, but you use cash accounting for your business (see page 577 to learn how to set this preference), you've found the culprit. The same goes if the heading says "Cash Basis" but use accrual accounting. To set things right, click Modify Report in the menu bar. Then, in the Modify Report dialog box, choose the Accrual option or the Cash option, and then click OK.*

GEM IN THE ROUGH

The QuickBooks Year-End Guide

QuickBooks Help contains a handy guide to typical year-end tasks, especially if you aren't familiar with what you have to do to wrap up a year for your business. But you can easily miss seeing it on the Help menu. When you choose Help → Year-End Guide, the program opens a special browser window displaying the QuickBooks Year-End Guide (Figure 18-2). You see a list of activities related to general tax preparation and end-of-year dealings with sub-contractors or employees. You may find some end-of-year tasks you didn't know you had!

The first time you view the guide, turn on the checkmarks for each issue that pertains to your organization. Since the guide's an HTML document, it works just like a web page. If you need help with the steps for an activity, click its link to open the corresponding QuickBooks Help topic. Clicking Save Checkmarks stores your choices—a handy reminder of your to-do list for the next fiscal year.

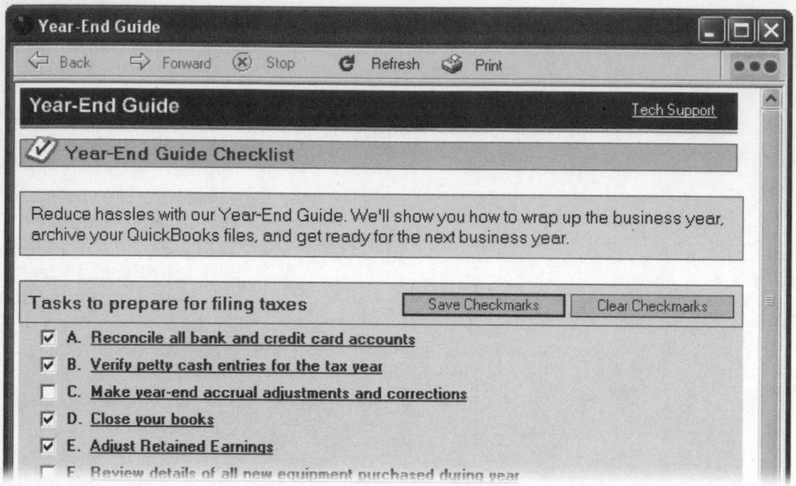

Figure 18-2:
Click Save Checkmarks to store your choices. When you open the Year-End Guide again next fiscal year, the checkmarks are waiting to remind you of your to-do list.

Chapter 17 has the full scoop on generating financial statements. Here's a quick review of how to generate year-end reports:

- **Profit & Loss.** You'll need a Profit & Loss report for the entire fiscal year for your tax return. While individuals receive W-2s to show how much money they made in a year, for companies, the Profit & Loss report shows the year's net income. Whether you're inspecting your report for accuracy or producing a report for taxes, generate a Profit & Loss report by choosing Reports → Company & Financial → Profit & Loss Standard. If the date on which you generate the report is within the fiscal year, choose This Fiscal Year in the Dates box.

Tip: If you want to make a year-end Profit & Loss report as easy to access as the Profit & Loss Standard report, memorize your year-end report as described on page 437.

Even the most meticulous bookkeeper isn't likely to notice a few dollars missing from an account. But checking a report for glaring mistakes is worth the few minutes it takes. If you pay your taxes based on erroneous numbers and end up being audited, the ensuing tax penalties and interest are sure to cost more than the time you saved.

- **Balance Sheet.** A Balance Sheet report for the entire fiscal year also accompanies your tax return. Choose Reports → Company & Financial → Balance Sheet Standard. If the date on which you create the report is within the fiscal year for the report, choose This Fiscal Year in the Dates box. If you generate the Balance Sheet after the end of the fiscal year, choose Last Fiscal Year. See the box on page 449 to learn how the Retained Earnings account value changes from one fiscal year to the next.

- **Statement of Cash Flow.** Although a "Statement of Cash Flows" report (see page 439) isn't required for your corporate tax return, looking at cash flow can highlight financial problems before they snowball.

Net Income and Retained Earnings

I just changed the date on my Balance Sheet report from December 31 of last year to January 1 of this year and the Net Income and Retained Earnings numbers are different. What's the deal?

At the end of a fiscal year, account balances go through some changes to get your books ready for another year of commerce. For example, at the end of one fiscal year, your income and expense accounts show how much you earned and spent during the year. But come January 1 (or whatever day your fiscal year starts), all those accounts have to be zero so you can start your new fiscal year fresh. QuickBooks makes this happen by adjusting your net income behind the scenes.

Suppose your Net Income in the Profit & Loss report is $102,000 on December 31, 2009. That number appears at the bottom of the Balance Sheet report as the value of the Net Income account (in the Equity section). At the beginning of the new fiscal year, QuickBooks automatically moves the previous year's net income into the Retained Earnings equity account, which resets the Net Income account to zero.

Some companies like to keep equity for the current year separate from the equity for all previous years. To do this, you need one additional equity account and one simple journal entry. Create an equity account (page 53) called something like Past Equity with an account number greater than the one you use for Retained Earnings. For example, if Retained Earnings is 3900, set Past Equity to 3950.

When you close your books at the end of the year, create a journal entry to move the current value from the Retained Earnings account and add it to the equity in the Past Equity account. Then, when QuickBooks moves the current year's net income into the Retained Earnings equity account, you can see both equity values, as shown in Figure 18-3.

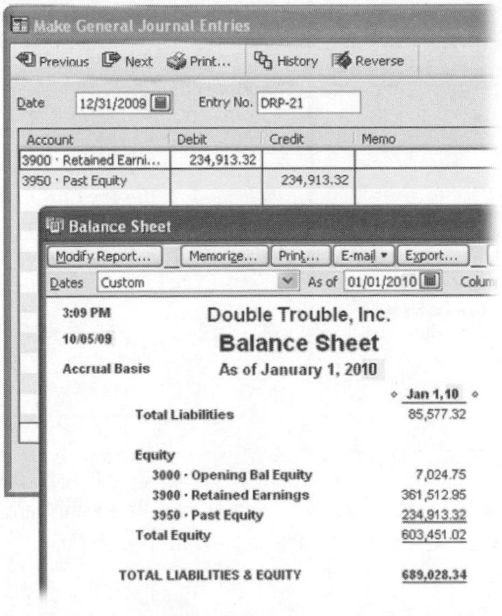

Figure 18-3:
When you close your books at the end of a fiscal year, you can create a journal entry to transfer the previous year's retained earnings from the Retained Earnings account to the equity in the Past Equity account. Date the journal entry the last day of the fiscal year (12/31/2009, as shown in the background). In effect, you debit the Retained Earnings account and credit the Past Equity account. The Balance Sheet for the first day of the next fiscal year (1/1/2010, in the foreground) has the previous year's retained earnings added to the Past Equity account and the previous year's net income in the Retained Earnings account.

Generating Tax Reports

Whether your accountant has the honor of preparing your taxes or you keep that excitement for yourself, you can save accountant's fees and your own sanity by making sure your company file is ready for tax season. The key to a smooth transition from QuickBooks to tax preparation is linking each account in your chart of accounts to the correct tax line and tax form.

Whether you prepare your own taxes or let your accountant do the honors, a review of the Income Tax Preparation report (choose Reports → Accountant & Taxes → Income Tax Preparation) can save you money on accountant's fees and IRS penalties (as well as keep more of your hair attached to your scalp). This report lists the accounts in your chart of accounts and shows the tax line to which you assigned it (Figure 18-4). If an account isn't linked to the correct tax line—or worse, not assigned to *any* tax line, the Income Tax Summary report, which lists each line on your tax return with the amount you have to report, won't give you the correct values. See page 56 to learn how to connect an account to a tax line.

When all the accounts in your chart of accounts are assigned to tax lines, you can generate a report with all the values you need for your company's tax return. Choose Reports → Accountant & Taxes → Income Tax Summary. Because you usually run this report after the fiscal year ends and all the numbers are in, Quick-Books automatically fills in the Dates box with Last Tax Year.

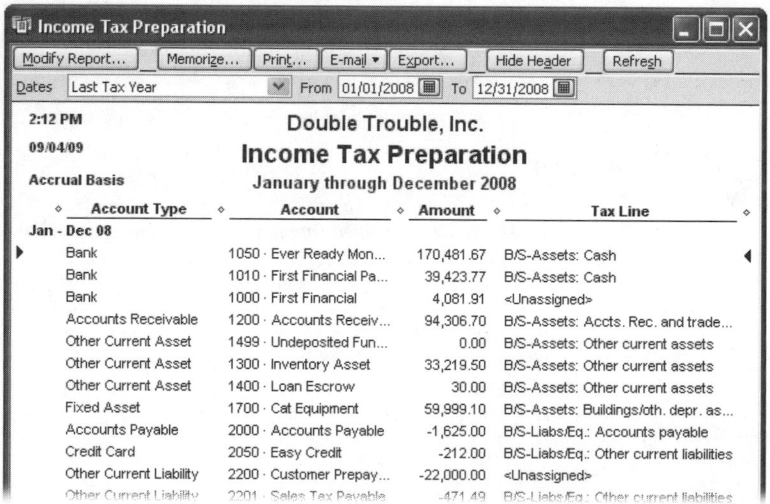

Figure 18-4:
If you see "Unassigned" in the Tax Line column, you'll have to assign a tax line to that account. (The easiest way to identify the correct tax line is to ask your accountant.) To edit an account, press Ctrl+A to display the Chart of Accounts window. Select the account, and then press Ctrl+E to open the Edit Account dialog box. In the Tax Line entry drop-down list, choose the tax form for that account.

Note: As one last reminder of unassigned accounts, the last two lines of the Income Tax Summary report are "Tax Line Unassigned (balance sheet)" and "Tax Line Unassigned (income/expense)". To see the transactions that make up one of these unassigned values, double-click the number in the corresponding line.

Year-End Journal Entries

Journal entries run rampant at the end of the year. If your accountant makes journal entries for you or gives you instructions, you might be perfectly happy not knowing what these journal entries do. But if you go it alone, you need to know which journal entries to make.

For example, if you purchase fixed assets, you need to create a general journal entry to handle depreciation. You might also create journal entries so you can produce accrual-based reports from your cash-based books.

If this book explained all the possible end-of-year journal entries, its weight would crush your desk. If you aren't an accounting expert, don't waste precious time trying to figure out your journal entry needs; the cost of an accountant's services is piddling in comparison. Once you know what journal entries you need, Chapter 16 explains how to create them.

Sharing the Company File with Your Accountant

If you work with an accountant who uses QuickBooks, there are times when a tug of war over your company file is inevitable. You want to perform your day-to-day bookkeeping, but your accountant wants to review your books, correct mistakes you've made, enter journal entries to prepare your books for end-of-quarter or end-of-year reports, and so on. QuickBooks has two ways for you and your accountant to share:

- With a QuickBooks **accountant's review copy**, you and your accountant can stop squabbling because you can each have your own copy of the company file. You work on everyday bookkeeping tasks while your accountant tackles cleaning up earlier periods.

- The **external accountant user** is a super-powered user (in QuickBooks 2009 and later) who can look at anything in your company file—except sensitive customer information like credit card numbers. You set up an external accountant user in your company file for your accountant so he can log into your file, review every nook and cranny of your company's data (with a new Client Data Review tool especially designed for accountants), make changes, and keep track of which changes are his and which are yours.

This section explains how to use both these approaches.

Creating an Accountant's Review Copy

The secret to an accountant's review copy is a cutoff date that QuickBooks calls the *dividing date*; transactions before the dividing date are fair game for your accountant who can work in the comfort of his own office. Transactions after that date are under your command in your original company file. When your accountant sends a file with changes back to you, the program makes short work of merging your accountant's changes into the company file. The box below describes other ways you can collaborate with your accountant.

Ways to Work with an Accountant

For most companies, QuickBooks is no substitute for an accountant. As financial professionals, accountants have the inside track on how best to monitor your business and keep you out of financial trouble. You can integrate your accountant's advice into your company file in several ways:

- **The accountant's review copy.** An accountant's review copy (described below) makes everyone more efficient. Both you and your accountant can work on your own copies of the company file. The one drawback is that both of you have to live with a few restrictions on what you can do in your copies (see page 454).

- **A backup or portable copy.** You can give your accountant *exclusive* access to your company file by sending her a backup or portable copy (page 176) of the file. When your accountant finishes evaluating your books and making the changes she wants, you can either begin using the copy she sends back to you or make corrections or adjustments in your company file based on her recommendations. For example, your accountant can send you a document listing the journal entries you need to create to adjust your accounts. After you create those journal entries, your company file contains all of your transactions and the adjustments your accountant requested.

- **Working onsite.** An accountant can work on the company file right in your office with a login password from you (in QuickBooks 2009 or later, the external accountant user gives your accountant special tools for working with your data). However, accountants are prone to doing things that require the company file to be in single-user mode, which might disrupt your day-to-day bookkeeping process.

- **The paper method.** If your accountant prefers to work with his own accounting system, you'll have to print the lists and reports that she requires. Then, when she gives you a list of changes and journal entries, you'll have to make those changes in your company file.

In addition to these options, QuickBooks Premier and Enterprise Editions include a remote access service, which lets your accountant access your QuickBooks company file over the Internet. Or you can use a remote access service like those offered at *http://www.mypc.com* or *http://www. logmein.com*.

You can't create an accountant's copy in multi-user mode. To switch to single-user mode, first make sure that everyone else logs out of the company file, and then choose File → "Switch to Single-user Mode". After that, creating an accountant's review copy is a lot like creating other kinds of copies of your company file:

1. **Choose File → Accountant's Copy → Save File. Because the Save As Accountant's Copy dialog box automatically selects the Accountant's Copy option, click Next.**

   If your accountant has to have unrestricted access to the file, select the Portable or Backup File option instead and see page 163 to learn how to create those types of files.

2. In the "Set the dividing date" screen shown in Figure 18-5, choose the date when control over transactions changes hands. Click Next. In the message box about closing windows, click OK.

Tell the "Set the dividing date" screen what date you want as the dividing line between your work and your accountant's work. Most of the screen explains what each of you can do before and after the dividing date.

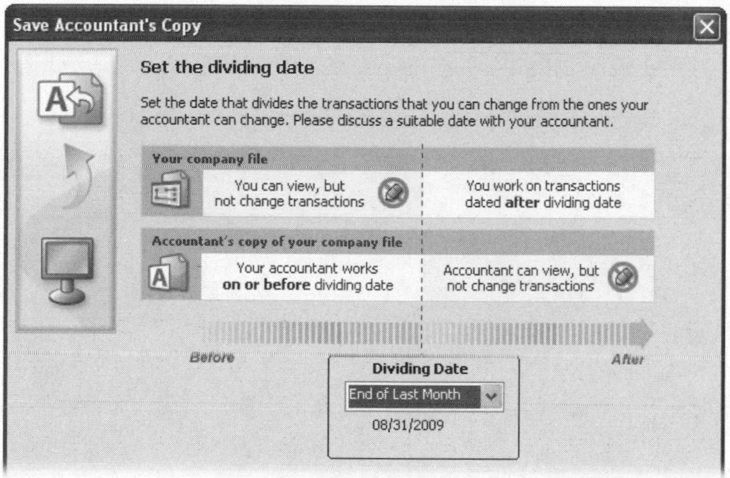

Figure 18-5:
The date you use is often the end of a fiscal period. The Dividing Date drop-down list gives you only a brief list of choices, one of which, fortunately, is Custom. If you want to specify a date, choose Custom and then type or choose the date in the date box that pops onto the screen. The other choices include End of Last Month, 2 Weeks Ago, and 4 Weeks Ago.

Tip: If you have a few dozen windows open and laid out just the way you want, there's no need to wail or gnash your teeth as QuickBooks closes all your windows to create the accountant's copy. Before you create the accountant's copy, save the current window arrangement so the program can reopen all those windows for you (page 558). Simply choose Edit → Preferences and, in the Preferences icon bar, click Desktop View. On the My Preferences tab, choose the "Save current desktop" option.

3. **Choose the folder or media where you want to save the copy.**

In the Save Accountant's Copy dialog box, you can choose any drive or folder as the destination for your accountant's file. QuickBooks sets the "Save as type" box to QuickBooks Accountant's Copy Transfer Files (*.qbx), and automatically names the accountant's review copy using the company file name followed by "Acct Transfer" and the date you create the file. The extension .qbx stands for QuickBooks Accountant Transfer File. As usual, you're free to edit the filename. Accountant's review copies use the QuickBooks portable file format, so they're usually small enough to email or save to a USB thumb drive. For example, a 10-megabyte company file may shrink to an accountant's review copy that's less than 1 MB.

4. **To create the accountant's review copy, click Save.**

   Once you create an accountant's copy, QuickBooks reminds you that it exists. In the QuickBooks program window's title bar, you'll see the words Accountant's Changes Pending immediately after the company name.

5. **Send the file to your accountant.**

   Email the file to your accountant, or copy it to a CD or a USB thumb drive and send it.

Note: If you use a password on your company file (and it's an excellent idea, no matter how tiny your company is), don't forget to tell your accountant the password for account you've set up for him.

FREQUENTLY ASKED QUESTION

Bookkeeping During Accountant's Review

Are there any limitations I should know about before I create an accountant's review copy?

QuickBooks locks parts of your company file when an accountant's review copy exists, so both you and your accountant have to live with a few minor restrictions. Most of the taboo tasks can wait during the few weeks that your accountant has a copy of your file.

While you're sharing the company file, you can work on transactions after the dividing date, so your bookkeeping duties are unaffected. You can also add entries to lists or edit the information in list entries, but you *can't* merge or delete list entries until you import your accountant's changes. Similarly, you can add accounts, but you can't edit, merge, or deactivate accounts. Adding subaccounts is a no-no, too.

With a few restrictions, your accountant can work on transactions dated on or before the dividing date, whether it's

adding, editing, voiding, or deleting transactions. For example, payroll, non-posting transactions (like estimates), transfers, sales tax payments, and inventory assemblies are completely off limits. Because the limitations vary depending on what your accountant is trying to do, QuickBooks highlights fields in an accountant's copy to show the changes your accountant can make that go back to you. Fields that aren't sent back to you aren't highlighted.

Your accountant can reconcile periods that end before the dividing date or change the cleared status of these earlier transactions. However, lists aren't very accommodating. Your accountant typically can only view lists, because you may be using them. Your accountant can add accounts to the chart of accounts and add items to some lists. For example, she can add customers, vendors, items, classes, fixed assets, sales tax codes, employees, and other names. Editing, inactivating, merging, and deleting depend on the list.

Sending a Copy Directly to Your Accountant

Intuit is happy to act as a go-between for accountant's review copies. In QuickBooks, you can tell the program to create an accountant's review copy *and* send it to your accountant. Actually, the copy goes up on an Intuit server and your accountant gets an email that the file is waiting. As long as you don't mind your company file sitting on an Intuit server somewhere, this method may be faster than creating and shipping the accountant's copy yourself. Here's what you do to start the ball rolling:

1. **Choose File → Accountant's Copy → "Send to Accountant".**

   The Send Accountant's Copy dialog box opens and tells you about Intuit's Accountant's Copy File Transfer service. Click Next.

2. **In the "Set the dividing date" screen, choose the date that marks when you or your accountant is in charge. Click Next.**

   The Dividing Date drop-down list has the same options as if you were creating a copy without sending it.

3. **In the "Information for sending the file (1 of 2)" screen, type your accountant's email address twice.**

   Make sure the email address is correct—you don't want to accidentally send your financial information to the wrong person.

4. **Then, type your name and email address in the other boxes, so your accountant knows who the copy came from. Click Next.**

5. **In the "Information for sending the file (2 of 2)" screen, type a password to protect your file.**

   Type the password in the "Reenter password" box to prevent typos from sneaking in. The password has to be a strong password: at least seven characters, at least one number, and at least one uppercase letter. In the Note box, type any instructions for your accountant. Don't include the password in the Note box; instead, tell your accountant what the password is over the phone or in a separate email.

6. **Click Send.**

   QuickBooks closes all its windows and tells you that it's creating and sending an accountant's copy. You'll see a confirmation dialog box in QuickBooks (click OK to close it) and a confirmation email in your inbox when the copy has settled successfully onto Intuit's server.

   Your accountant receives an email that the file is waiting with a link to the download page. (The link is good for 14 days; then Intuit deletes your file from the server.) All you have to do is wait for your accountant to send you a file with changes. Then, you import those changes as described in the next section.

Merging Accountant Changes into Your Company File

When your accountant sends back your company file, the file extension changes from .qbx to .qby—the file extension for an accountant's review copy import file.

(Y follows X in the alphabet. Get it?) If you've imported data (like customer records) into QuickBooks (page 602), the following steps should be familiar:

1. **If your accountant sent you a CD or disk, insert it into the appropriate drive on your computer. If your accountant sent the file as an email attachment, make sure to jot down the folder on your computer where you saved the attachment.**

    If your company file isn't open, open it. Back up your company file (page 163) *before* you import your accountant's changes.

2. **Choose File → Accountant's Copy → Import Accountant's Changes. In the Import Changes From Accountant's Copy dialog box, navigate to the disk or folder that contains the accountant's file and then double-click the file name.**

    QuickBooks displays the changes your accountant made, as you can see in Figure 18-6. Click Expand All to see the entire list. Review the changes to see if any changes conflict with work that you've done while your accountant worked on the copy. Each change comes with an explanation of how to deal with these conflicts.

3. **To make the changes in your company file, click Incorporate Accountant's Changes. (If you decide not to import the changes, click Close instead.)**

    QuickBooks backs up your company file and then imports your accountant's changes. After you review the changes, click Close.

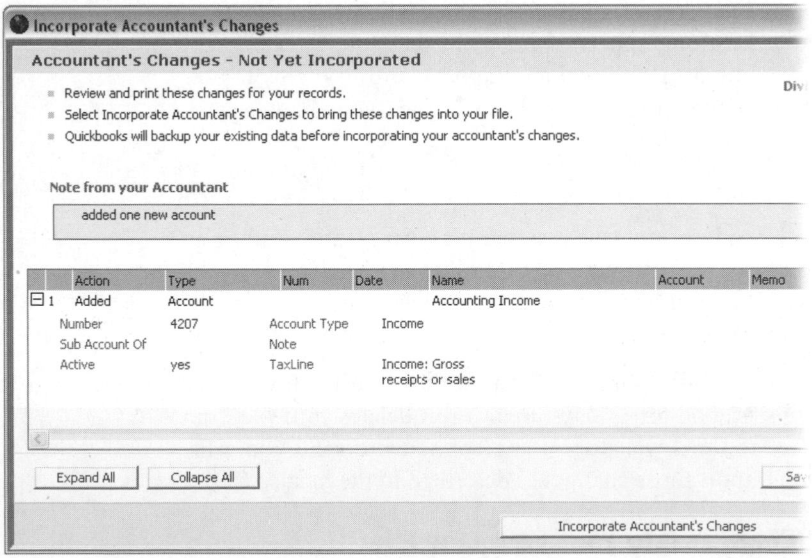

Figure 18-6:
If you want a record of your accountant's changes, click Print. Or to save a copy to a PDF format file, click "Save as PDF".

Tip: If your accountant has to correct some of your work, make a point of studying those corrections. Learning from your mistakes can translate into lower accountant's fees.

Canceling an Accountant's Review Copy

From time to time, you might want to get rid of the accountant's review copy without importing any of the changes. For instance, you created an accountant's review copy by mistake or your accountant had so few changes that she told you the changes to make. Unlocking your company file so you can get back to performing any type of task requires nothing more than choosing File → Accountant's Copy → Remove Restrictions. The Remove Restrictions dialog box warns you that you won't be able to import changes from the accountant's review copy if you remove restrictions. To show that you know what you're doing, turn on the "Yes, I want to remove the Accountant's Copy restrictions" checkbox, and then click OK. The words Accountant's Change Pending disappears from the QuickBooks window's title bar.

Setting Up an External Accountant User

Starting with QuickBooks 2009, the *external accountant user* lets your accountant peruse your bookkeeping data and make changes while protecting your customers' sensitive financial info. When your accountant logs in as an external accountant user, she can use the Client Data Review to look for problems and clean up any she finds. For example, your accountant can look at the changes you've made to lists like the chart of accounts and Items List, scan your company file for payments or credits you haven't applied, or find sales taxes or payroll liabilities that you didn't record correctly.

Note: An external accountant user lets an accountant use Client Data Review from within clients' editions of QuickBooks. When someone logs in as an external accountant user, the Client Data Review command appears on the Company menu in any QuickBooks edition including Pro and Premier.

Here's how you set up an external accountant user:

1. **Log in to your company file as the administrator (page 630).**

   Only an administrator can create an external accountant user (who can perform tasks that even someone with administrator privileges can't, like run the Client Data Review tool).

2. **Choose Company → "Set Up Users and Passwords" → Set Up Users.**

   The User List dialog box opens.

3. **Click Add User.**

   The "Set up user password and access" dialog box opens.

4. **In the User Name box, type the name for the external accountant user. In the Password and Confirm Password boxes, type the external accountant user's password. Click Next.**

   The "Access for user" screen appears.

---

5. **Select the External Accountant option, and then click Next.**

Because the external accountant user is so powerful, QuickBooks asks if you want to give that level of access to the person. Click Yes.

6. **Click Finish.**

Note: You can also change an existing user to an external accountant user. Log in to your company file as an administrator, and choose Company → "Set Up Users and Passwords" → Set Up Users. In the User List window, select the person you want to change and click Edit User. Change the name and password if you want, and then click Next. On the "Access for user" screen, select the External Accountant option, click Next, and then click Finish.

1099s

In QuickBooks, paying independent contractors is no different than paying other vendors. You enter bills from your contractors and then you pay those bills. No messy payroll transactions; no fuss with benefits or other regulatory requirements. But at the end of the year, you have to generate 1099s for your independent workers.

If you set up QuickBooks to track 1099 payments (page 583) and your contractors as 1099 vendors (page 136), generating 1099s is a piece of cake. But before you push a stack of 1099 forms through your printer, it's a good idea to make sure your records are up-to-date and accurate.

Note: If you use one of QuickBooks' payroll services, you can print W-2s for your employees. Choose Employees → Payroll Tax Forms & W-2s → Process Payroll Forms. See page 382.

Generating 1099 Reports

To review the amounts you've paid to 1099 vendors, choose Reports → Vendors & Payables, and then choose either of the following reports:

- **1099 Summary.** This report includes each vendor you've set up as a 1099 vendor and the total amount you've paid the vendor. If any amount looks questionable, just double-click it to display the transactions for the vendor. Although the report lists only the vendors you set up as eligible for 1099 status, as shown in Figure 18-7, you can modify it to make sure you haven't left any 1099 vendors out. In the first 1099 Options drop-down list, choose "All vendors".

  If the 1099 Summary report is empty, your 1099 account mappings may be missing. In the 1099 Summary report toolbar, in the middle drop-down list, choose "All allowed accounts" to see payments you made to 1099 vendors regardless of the account. If your vendors leap into view, you need to map your accounts to 1099 boxes, as described on page 461.

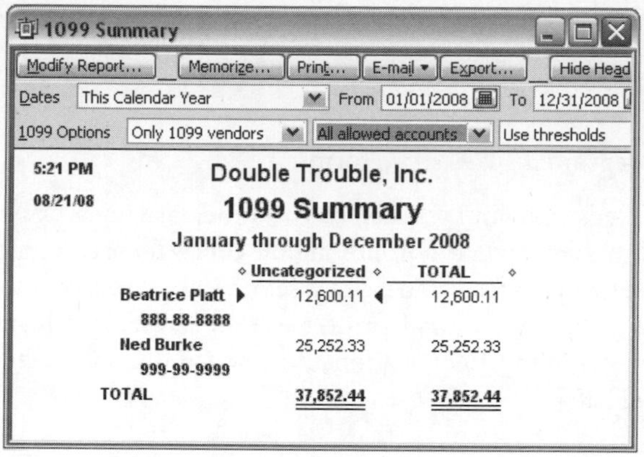

Figure 18-7:
Regardless of the fiscal year you use for your company, payroll and 1099 tasks run on a calendar year, because your employees and subcontractors pay taxes for each calendar year. That's why the Dates drop-down list for the 1099 Summary report includes calendar year date ranges.

Note: The federal government gives you the tiniest of breaks by setting thresholds for total payments to 1099 vendors. If you pay vendors less than the threshold, you don't have to generate 1099s for them. (For nonemployee compensation, the threshold is currently $600.)

In the 1099 Summary report window, QuickBooks sets the last box for 1099 options to "Use thresholds". This choice filters the vendors in the report to those that exceed the government's threshold. If you want to see all of your 1099 vendors, regardless of what you paid them, in the third box, choose "Ignore thresholds".

- **1099 Detail.** If you pay your independent contractors on a regular schedule, this report can pinpoint errors because it shows the transactions that produce the vendor's 1099 amount. If you see a gap in the payment schedule or two transactions in the same month, double-click a transaction amount to open the corresponding window, such as Write Checks.

Printing 1099-MISC Forms

The steps to start printing 1099 forms are simple, but as with any printing task, fraught with nagging details:

1. **Order printable 1099-MISC and 1096 forms.**

   1099-MISC and 1096 forms use special ink so that government agencies can scan the forms. Intuit sells kits with preprinted 1099 forms. In your browser, navigate to *http://intuitmarket.intuit.com*. In the horizontal navigation bar, click Tax Products, and then choose 1099 Kits.

   You can also order 1099 forms directly from the IRS. Navigate to *www.irs.gov*, and click the "Forms and Publications" link. On the Forms and Publications page, under the Order heading, click the "Employer forms and instructions" link. In the value box for the 1099 MISC form (about halfway down the list), type the quantity of forms you need, scroll to the bottom of the page, and then click "Add to Cart".

Note: You can print 1099-MISC forms for up to 249 vendors. If you've got oodles more 1099 vendors—or even 250—the IRS requires you to file 1099 forms electronically. Bypass printing the forms in QuickBooks and use the government's hopefully easy-to-use system.

2. **Load your printer with preprinted 1099-MISC forms.**

   If you use a printer that feeds individual sheets, don't bother placing a Copy 2 form after each Copy 1 form so that you can print multiple copies for each vendor. It's a lot easier to load the Copy 1 sheets and print a set of 1099 forms on those sheets and then load the Copy 2 forms and print a second set of 1099 forms. You'll send the Copy 1 sheets to the 1099 vendors, but the Copy 2 sheets go to the government in one big batch.

Note: If you use a dot matrix printer, you might have to adjust the printer to handle the thickness of the multiple-copy forms.

3. **Choose Vendors → Print 1099s/1096.**

   QuickBooks opens the 1099 and 1096 wizard, which makes it easy to verify your 1099 information before you begin printing.

4. **In the 1099 and 1096 wizard, click Run Report to look at a Vendor 1099 Review report.**

   After QuickBooks runs the report, if you see vendors whose 1099 eligibility is incorrect, double-click their names to open the Edit Vendor dialog box and make changes. For example, if a vendor's record doesn't have a tax ID or address, in the Edit Vendor dialog box, add the missing information (see page 135). When you're done, close the Vendor 1099 Review report window.

5. **In step 2 of the 1099 and 1096 wizard, click Map Accounts to review or modify your preferences for 1099 accounts. Click OK when you're done.**

   QuickBooks opens the Preferences dialog box to the Tax: 1099 section, as shown in Figure 18-8.

6. **In step 3 of the 1099 and 1096 wizard, click Run Report to look at the 1099 Summary report.**

   This is your chance to make sure you're printing 1099s for the right vendors and for the correct amounts.

7. **In step 4 of the 1099 and 1096 wizard, click Print 1099s.**

   QuickBooks opens the "Printing 1099-MISC and 1096 Forms" dialog box with the date range set to the previous calendar year. If you're generating the forms during the calendar year, in the drop-down list for the top box, choose This Calendar Year.

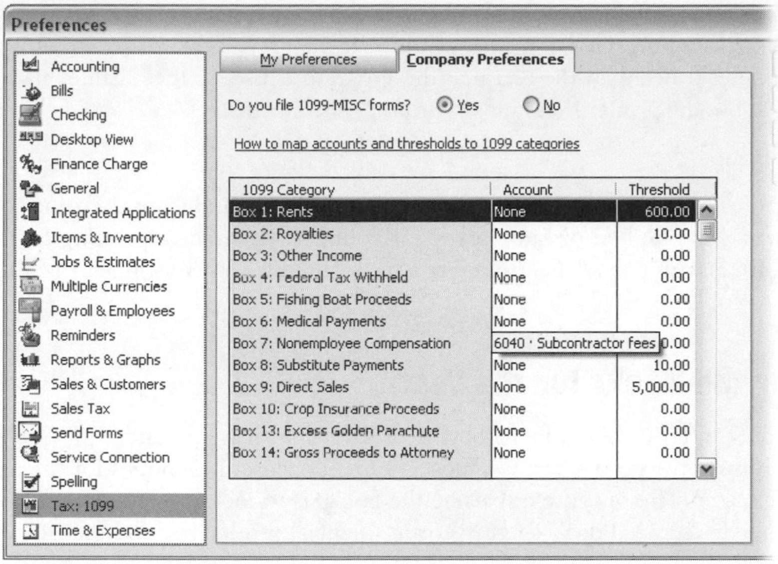

Figure 18-8:
On the Company Preferences tab, assign an account to each 1099 category that you issue 1099s for. For example, if you pay subcontractors for work, you can assign the account for subcontractors' fees to the Box 7: Nonemployee Compensation 1099 category.

8. Click OK.

   QuickBooks opens the "Select 1099s to Print" dialog box shown in Figure 18-9, and automatically selects every vendor whose pay exceeds the government threshold.

9. **When the Valid ID and Valid Address columns are replete with the word Yes, click Preview 1099 to see the final forms before they print.**

   In the Print Preview window, click Zoom In (if necessary) to verify the information. When you've reviewed the forms, click Close.

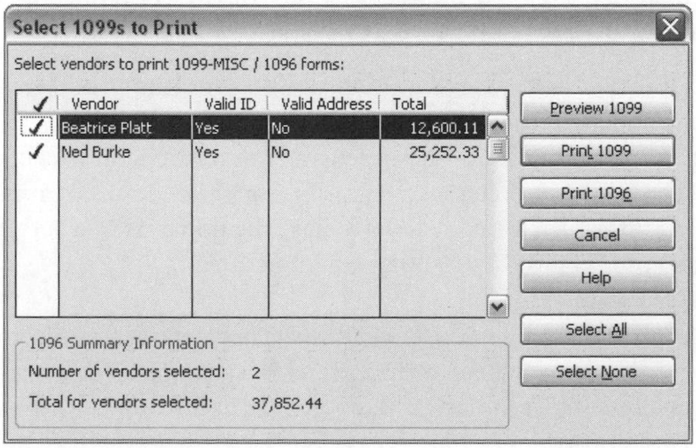

Figure 18-9:
Besides columns for vendor name and total pay, the table in the dialog box includes the Valid ID and Valid Address columns. If you tend to create vendors on the fly without bothering to enter pesky details like their tax ID numbers or street address, scan these columns for the word No. If you see it in any cell, click Cancel and edit your vendors to add this essential information. Then, repeat steps 7 and 8 and verify that all the Valid ID and Valid Address cells say Yes.

10. **Click Print 1099.**

    QuickBooks opens the Print 1099 window. If the preprinted forms are waiting in a printer other than the one that the program chose, in the "Printer name" box, choose the printer that holds your preprinted forms.

11. **Click Print.**

    Preprinted forms usually include Copy 1 for the vendor and Copy 2 for the government. But you'll also want a copy for your files. Instead of printing a third set of 1099s, run one of the printed sets through your copy machine or printer/scanner/copier.

Closing the Books for the Year

A few months after the end of a fiscal year, when tax returns rest under the gimlet-eyed scrutiny of the tax authorities, most companies close their books for the previous fiscal year. The purpose of closing the books is to lock the transactions that you've already reported on tax returns or in financial results, because the IRS and shareholders alike don't look kindly on changes to the reports they've received.

QuickBooks, on the other hand, doesn't care if you close the books in your company file. The closing task is mainly to protect you from the consequences of changing the numbers in previous years (like altering the company file so that it no longer matches what you reported to the IRS). Once you've set a closing date for your company file (described next), changes to transactions on or before the closing date show up on the Closing Date Exception report (choose Reports → Account & Taxes → Closing Date Exception Report). But you're free to keep your books open if you're not worried about editing older transactions by mistake. If you *do* close your books in QuickBooks, the program *still* gives you a way to edit transactions prior to the closing date. Unlike other bookkeeping programs in which closed means closed, in QuickBooks, folks who know the closing date password can still change and delete closed transactions, say to correct an egregious error before you regenerate all of your end-of-year reports.

Closing the books in QuickBooks takes place in an unlikely location: the Preferences dialog box. Switch to single-user mode before you close your books. When everyone else has logged off, choose Edit → Preferences and, in the icon bar, click Accounting and then the Company Preferences tab. (Only a QuickBooks administrator can set the password for the closing date.) To close the books as of a specific date, click Set Date/Password. Figure 18-10 shows what to do next.

Tip: Don't cut and paste the password from the Closing Date Password box to the Confirm Password box. These boxes display filled circles instead of the actual characters, which means you can't see typos. If you set a password with a typo in it, you'll be unlikely to stumble on the correct password, and your closed books will remain shut as tight as a clam.

After you've set a password for the closing date, you'll have to enter that password whenever you want to modify transactions prior to that date. For example, if you try to edit a check that you wrote before the closing date, QuickBooks opens a message box with a Password box in it. Type the closing date password, and then click OK to complete your edit.

Tip: After you've completed all your QuickBooks year-end activities, create a backup of your company file (page 163). With all the data that contributed to your financial reports and tax forms in this backup, you're not going overboard by creating two copies of the backup: one to keep close by in your office and one stored safely offsite in case of emergency.

CHAPTER 19

Managing Inventory

As you record inventory purchases and sales in QuickBooks, the program keeps track of your inventory behind the scenes, just as the point-of-service systems at the grocery stores do when a cashier scans the items you buy. The seemingly automatic tracking in QuickBooks isn't truly automatic. This chapter begins by reviewing the setup tasks that make the program work its magic.

Good inventory management means more than updating the number of items that QuickBooks thinks you have on hand. To keep the right number of items in stock, you also need to know how many you've sold and how many are on order. To make decisions like how much to charge or which vendor to use, you have to evaluate your purchases and the prices you pay for your inventory. In this chapter, you'll learn how to make the most of the inventory reports that QuickBooks provides.

Another important yet challenging aspect of inventory is keeping your Quick-Books records in sync with what's sitting on the shelves in your warehouse. Inventory can go missing due to theft and damage of all kinds, so you might not have as many products in stock as you think you do. QuickBooks can't help much with the dusty business of rifling through boxes and counting carafes, coffee mugs, and the occasional centipede. But after the counting is complete, QuickBooks *can* help you adjust its records to match the reality in your warehouse. Adjusting inventory works for more than inventory counts. You can use this process to write off inventory that you have in your warehouse but can't sell because it's dented, dirty, or too darned ugly.

The QuickBooks Inventory Process

Before you look at the tools that QuickBooks has to manage your inventory, here's a quick review of how QuickBooks tracks inventory as you buy and sell products.

Setting Up Inventory Items

As you learned in Chapter 4, you set the stage for tracking when you create inventory items in QuickBooks. Inventory items in your Item List include purchase costs, sales prices, and accounts, all of which direct the right amount of money into the right income and expense accounts as you buy and sell inventory.

Here are the fields in an item record that QuickBooks uses to track your inventory:

- **Cost.** What you pay for one unit of the item.

- **Sales Price.** The price you typically charge for the item (for the same unit size you used in the Cost field).

- **Asset Account.** The asset account that holds the value of the inventory you buy.

- **Income Account.** The account for the income you receive when you sell this item.

- **COGS Account.** The account to which you post the item's cost when you sell it (known as cost of goods sold).

Note: As you sell inventory, QuickBooks deducts dollars from the inventory asset account and adds them to the cost of goods sold account. For a refresher on how inventory postings work, see the box on page 113.

When you sell your time, you can always try to squeeze another work hour into your day. But when you run low on inventory, the only solution is to buy more. For products that you keep in stock, knowing how many you have on hand is essential. QuickBooks keeps a running total of how many units you've purchased and how many you've sold. The difference between these two numbers conveniently tells you how many should be in your warehouse. The running total of inventory on hand stays with the item in your Item List, as Figure 19-1 shows.

Figure 19-1:
The On Hand value in the Item List shows you how many you have in stock. As you purchase inventory or sell it to your customers, QuickBooks updates the On Hand value with the number you bought or sold.

Purchasing and Selling Inventory

Unless you practice just-in-time inventory management, you need inventory in your warehouse to fill customer orders. Here's a quick review:

- **Ordering inventory.** Companies typically create purchase orders for inventory products they buy (page 215). These business forms don't change anything in your QuickBooks company file (that's why they're called *non-posting transactions*). But they're useful for verifying that the shipments you receive match what you ordered—not unlike opening a pizza box before you leave the parlor to make sure you didn't get an anchovy and garlic pizza by mistake. Chapter 9 explains how to order inventory and then pay for the inventory you receive.

- **Purchasing inventory.** When you receive a shipment, you record it in Quick-Books so you know you have products to sell. The program increases the number of products on hand by the number in the shipment and adds the value of the shipment to the inventory asset account.

- **Selling Inventory.** Finally, when you sell some of your inventory, the income makes all your bookkeeping seem worthwhile. When you create invoices (Chapter 10), sales receipts, or other sales forms (Chapter 11), QuickBooks deducts the units you sold from the item's On Hand value. The income from the sale posts to an income account, while the cost of the units you sold moves from the inventory asset account to a cost of goods sold account.

  When you sell inventory, the program also compares the new On Hand value to your Reorder Point (page 117). When the inventory on hand drops below your reorder point, QuickBooks reminds you that it's time to order more. The box below tells you how to shut off reminders for items you aren't selling at the moment.

TROUBLESHOOTING MOMENT

Working with Seasonal Items

The Item List is home to items for every service and product you sell, and it can get really long really fast, especially if you sell different items at different times of the year. For example, if you stock your store with lawn chairs in the spring, you don't want to scroll past dozens of outdoor items the other 9 months of the year. And QuickBooks' reminders about reordering out-of-season items get old fast.

Fortunately, you can make seasonal items inactive, which temporarily removes them from the Item List and silences the reminders. In the Item List window (choose Lists →

Item List to open it), right-click the item and choose Make Item Inactive from the shortcut menu.

When you want to reactivate the item, at the bottom of the Item List window, turn on the "Include inactive" checkbox. QuickBooks displays a column with an X as its heading and each inactive item sports an X in that column. To reactivate the item, click the X next to its name. If the item includes subitems, in the Activate Group dialog box, click Yes to reactivate the item and all its subitems.

Running Inventory Reports

Checking the vital signs of your inventory is the best way to keep it healthy. When products are hot, you have to keep them in stock or you'll lose sales. And, if products grow cold, you don't want to get stuck holding the bag (or the lime-green luggage). For all other temperatures, most companies keep tabs on inventory trends and compare them to what's going on in sales. For example, when the value of your inventory is increasing faster than sales, sales could be poor because your prices are too high, competition is encroaching on your market, or the Salvador Dali Chia Pets simply didn't catch on.

Good inventory management means keeping enough items in stock to meet your sales, but not so many that your inventory grows obsolete before you can sell it. The inventory reports in QuickBooks aren't fancy, but they tell you most of what you need to know. You can run any of the inventory reports by choosing Reports → Inventory and then picking the report you want.

Note: The QuickBooks inventory reports show only the active inventory items in your Item List. If you run inventory reports without reactivating all your inventory items (page 130), the inventory values in the reports won't be correct. By contrast, financial statements such as the Balance Sheet include your total inventory value for active and inactive inventory items alike.

Inventory Valuation: How Much Is Inventory Worth?

QuickBooks includes two reports that tell you how much your inventory is worth: the Inventory Valuation Summary and Inventory Valuation Detail. Here's what each one does.

Inventory Valuation Summary report

The Inventory Valuation Summary report, shown in Figure 19-2, is a tidy overview of the inventory you have on hand, what it's worth as an asset, and what it's worth when you sell it. (See the box on the next page if your inventory isn't worth as much as it used to be.) The first column in these reports shows the names of the inventory items from your Item List. Subitems appear indented beneath their parent items. QuickBooks initially uses the current month-to-date for the date range for this report.

Here are the other columns in the report and why they are (or aren't) important to inventory health:

- **Item Description.** This text is the description you entered in the item record in the "Description on Purchase Transactions" box. A description doesn't help manage your inventory, but it does identify which inventory item you're looking at, particularly when you use part numbers or abbreviations for item names.

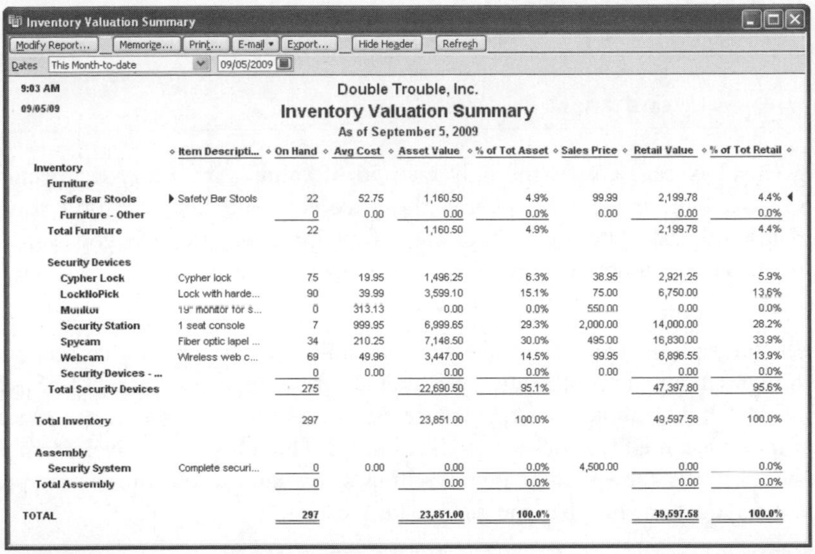
Inventory Valuation Summary

Modify Report... Memorize... Print... E-mail Export... Hide Header Refresh

Dates This Month-to-date 09/05/2009

9:03 AM

09/05/09

Double Trouble, Inc.

Inventory Valuation Summary

As of September 5, 2009

	Item Descripti...	On Hand	Avg Cost	Asset Value	% of Tot Asset	Sales Price	Retail Value	% of Tot Retail
Inventory								
Furniture								
Safe Bar Stools	Safety Bar Stools	22	52.75	1,160.50	4.9%	99.99	2,199.78	4.4%
Furniture - Other		0	0.00	0.00	0.0%	0.00	0.00	0.0%
Total Furniture		22		1,160.50	4.9%		2,199.78	4.4%
Security Devices								
Cypher Lock	Cypher lock	75	19.95	1,496.25	6.3%	38.95	2,921.25	5.9%
LockNoPick	Lock with harde...	90	39.99	3,599.10	15.1%	75.00	6,750.00	13.6%
Monitor	19" monitor for s...	0	313.13	0.00	0.0%	550.00	0.00	0.0%
Security Station	1 seat console	7	999.95	6,999.65	29.3%	2,000.00	14,000.00	28.2%
Spycam	Fiber optic lapel ...	34	210.25	7,148.50	30.0%	495.00	16,830.00	33.9%
Webcam	Wireless web c...	69	49.96	3,447.00	14.5%	99.95	6,896.55	13.9%
Security Devices - ...		0	0.00	0.00	0.0%	0.00	0.00	0.0%
Total Security Devices		275		22,690.50	95.1%		47,397.80	95.6%
Total Inventory		297		23,851.00	100.0%		49,597.58	100.0%
Assembly								
Security System	Complete securi...	0	0.00	0.00	0.0%	4,500.00	0.00	0.0%
Total Assembly		0		0.00	0.0%		0.00	0.0%
TOTAL		297		23,851.00	100.0%		49,597.58	100.0%

Figure 19-2: *Because the report is a snapshot of inventory value, Month-to-date, Quarter-to-date, and Year-to-date ranges all produce the same results. But if you want to see the inventory value as of a different date, in the date box, choose the date you want.*

TROUBLESHOOTING MOMENT

When Inventory Loses Value

Inventory valuation reports show the value of your inventory based on the average cost that you paid for your items. But that inventory value doesn't always tell the whole story.

If you have several cartons of oh-so-passé women's stirrup pants, the *true* value of that inventory is worthless. Although admitting that you made a mistake is painful, writing off that inventory as unsellable turns the inventory into a business expense, which reduces your net profit and, therefore, the taxes you pay.

In QuickBooks, you can write off obsolete inventory with an inventory adjustment (page 476). To remove the inventory from your QuickBooks item record, you change both the quantity on hand and the asset value to zero. Here's what to do.

1. Choose Vendors → Inventory Activities → "Adjust Quantity/Value on Hand".
2. In the "Adjust Quantity/Value on Hand" dialog box, in the Adjustment Account drop-down list, choose an expense account, such as Unsalable Inventory. You're moving the value of the inventory from the inventory asset account into an expense account.
3. Click the item's New Qty cell, and then type 0.
4. Click Save & Close.

- **On Hand.** To calculate the On Hand value, QuickBooks subtracts the number of products you sold and adds the number of products you received. You can quickly check for items that are close to being out of stock. However, items sell at different rates, so the reorder point reminder (page 117) is a better indication that something is perilously close to selling out.

Note: When you add an out-of-stock item to an invoice, QuickBooks warns you but doesn't prevent you from selling products you don't have. When the On Hand value is negative, you know it's time to order more—and to ask for express shipping. Negative numbers can also remind you to record in QuickBooks inventory items you received at the warehouse (page 220).

- **Avg Cost.** Average cost is the only method of valuing inventory that Quick-Books can handle. QuickBooks uses the price you paid for every unit you've purchased to calculate the average cost of an inventory item. If you want to watch price trends so you can adjust your sales prices accordingly, review your most recent bills for inventory purchases.

- **Asset Value.** Asset Value is the average cost multiplied by the number on hand. Although changes in asset value over time are more telling, a snapshot of asset value can show trouble brewing. An excessive asset value for one item is a sign that inventory might be obsolete—the item hasn't sold, so you have too many on hand. If you know that the item *is* selling, streamlining your purchasing process can reduce the number you need to keep on hand.

- **% of Tot Asset.** This column shows the percentage of an item's asset value compared to the total asset value of all inventory items. Higher percentages might mean that a product isn't selling well and you have too much in stock, but higher percentages can also mean a product is a significant part of your sales strategy. This measurement has meaning only in light of your business strategy and performance.

- **Sales Price.** You set this price in the item record, but it's meaningless if you regularly change the item's price or charge different prices to different customers. If you didn't set a sales price for an item, you'll see 0.00 in the report.

- **Retail Value.** Because the retail value is the sales price multiplied by the number on hand, this value is useful only if the value in the Sales Price column is the typical sales price for the item.

- **% of Tot Retail.** This percentage is what the item's retail value represents of your total inventory's retail value. Different products sell at different profit margins, which you can see when the retail percentage differs from the asset value percentage.

Inventory Valuation Detail report

The Inventory Valuation Detail report lists every transaction that increases or decreases the number of items you have on hand. Although it can grow lengthy, this report can help you figure out where your inventory went (and perhaps jog your memory about inventory transactions that you forgot to add in Quick-Books). As in other reports, you can double-click a transaction to see its details.

Inventory Stock Status

As you might expect, Inventory Stock Status reports tell you where your inventory stands today and how that will change based on your outstanding purchase orders. The "Inventory Stock Status by Item" report is a great place to see which inventory items you need to reorder, as Figure 19-3 shows.

Tip: If you want to use a bar code reader to scan your inventory, go to Intuit's marketplace (*http://marketplace.intuit.com*). In the Find Apps search box, type *bar code* to find third-party bar code reader solutions.

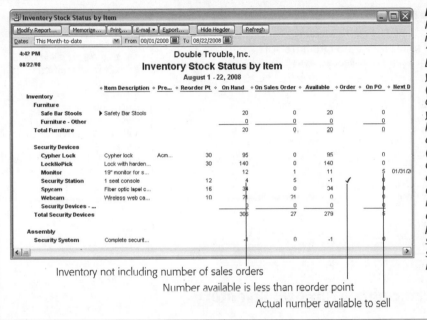

Inventory not including number of sales orders

Number available is less than reorder point

Actual number available to sell

Figure 19-3:
For every active inventory item, the "Inventory Stock Status by Item" report shows you the reorder points (in the Reorder Pt column), the number you have on hand (On Hand), and how many are available to sell (Available). However, a checkmark in the Order column is the most obvious signal that you need to reorder. If you added an item to a purchase order, you can see whether that shipment is enough to restock your warehouse.

Note: If you upgrade to QuickBooks Premier or Enterprise, the Inventory Stock Status reports also show how many items you've added to sales orders for future delivery.

The "Inventory Stock Status by Vendor" report shows the same information, but groups and subtotals items by vendor. If you seem to run low on products from a particular vendor, you might want to increase the reorder point for those products to fine-tune your lead time.

Viewing One Inventory Item

The Inventory Item QuickReport is a fast yet thorough way to see what's going on with a particular item. In the Item List window, select the item you want to review and press Ctrl+Q.

The Inventory Item QuickReport includes purchase and sales transactions for the item (Figure 19-4). In the On Hand As Of section, invoice transactions represent the sales you've made to customers, so the numbers are negative. Bills or Item Receipts are your purchases from vendors, which increase the number on hand. The On Purchase Order As Of section includes the number of products you've ordered but haven't yet received. At the bottom of the report, the TOTAL As Of tells you how many products you'll have in stock when all your purchase orders are filled.

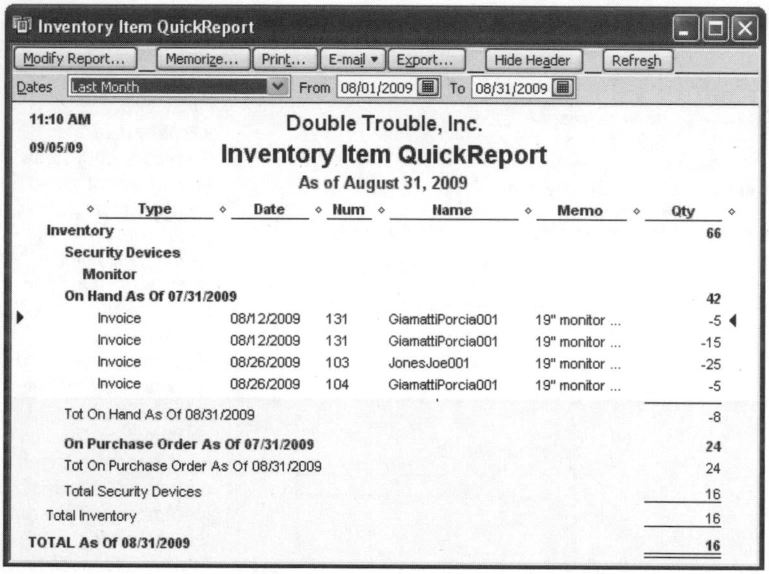

Figure 19-4:
The Inventory Item QuickReport report summarizes the number you have on hand as well as the number that are on order. You can generate the report in the Item List window by first selecting the item. Then, either press Ctrl+Q or click Reports and choose "QuickReport: <item name>" from the drop-down menu (where <item name> is the name of the item you selected).

Performing a Physical Inventory

Although QuickBooks can calculate how many products you have on hand based on your purchases and sales, it has no way of knowing what's happening in your warehouse. Employees help themselves to products; fire consumes some of your inventory; or a burst pipe turns your India ink sketches into Rorschach tests. Only a physical count of the items you keep in stock tells you how many units you *really* have to sell.

QuickBooks does the only thing it can to help you count your inventory: It provides the Physical Inventory Worksheet report, which lists each inventory item in your Item List and how many units should be on hand. To see it, choose Reports → Inventory → Physical Inventory Worksheet. The Physical Count column has blank lines, so you can write in how many you find, as you can see in Figure 19-5. (See the box on page 473 to learn how to count inventory while business continues to chug along.)

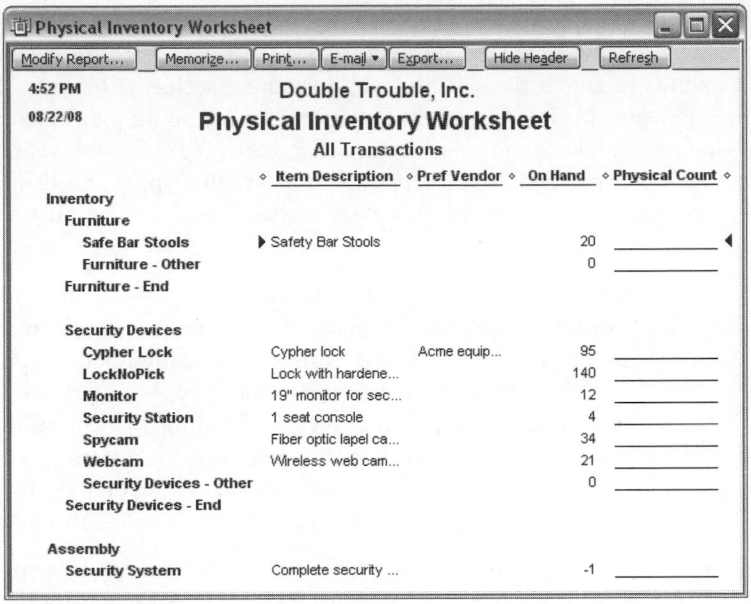

Figure 19-5:
Your preferred vendor has nothing to do with counting inventory, yet the column appears on the Physical Inventory Worksheet. If you click Modify Report in the report window toolbar, you'll see no way to modify the columns that appear. However, you can hide the Pref Vendor column by hovering the pointer over the diamond to the right of the Pref Vendor heading and then dragging to the diamond to the left of the heading.

The Physical Inventory Worksheet doesn't offer any customizable settings. For example, you can't sort the inventory items, say to list them by the warehouse aisles where they're kept. To build a worksheet with only the columns you want and with inventory items listed in the order you want, in the toolbar, click Export. Then, in Excel or another program, you can modify the report to your liking. (See page 599 to learn the ins and outs of exporting a QuickBooks report.)

TROUBLESHOOTING MOMENT

Freezing Inventory While You Count

It's sheer madness to ship customer orders out and receive inventory shipments while you're trying to count the products you have on hand. QuickBooks doesn't have a feature for freezing your inventory while you perform the physical count, but you can follow procedures that do the same thing.

Because a physical inventory count disrupts business operations, most companies schedule it during slow periods and off hours. To keep the disruption to a minimum, print the Physical Inventory Worksheet just before you start the count. Then, until the count is complete, do the following to keep the inventory stable:

- **Sales.** In QuickBooks, create invoices for inventory sales as you would normally. After you save an invoice, edit it and mark it as pending (page 276). When the count is complete, edit pending invoices again to mark them as final, fill the orders, and send the invoices.

- **Purchases.** If you receive inventory shipments during the count, don't unpack the boxes until you've completed the physical count. In QuickBooks, don't use any of the commands for receiving inventory (page 218).

Adjusting Inventory in QuickBooks

As you probably know, inventory can succumb to breakage, theft, and the damage caused by a paintball fight in the warehouse. When these accidents happen, the first response is to report the loss to your insurance company. Adjusting the quantity of inventory in QuickBooks follows close behind. Similarly, if you have inventory that you can't sell—like personal computers with 10 MB of disk space and 11-inch monitors—adjust the inventory in QuickBooks when you take the computers to the recycling center.

An inventory adjustment is also in order after almost every physical inventory count you perform, because the quantities for inventory in the real world rarely match the quantities in QuickBooks. *Shrinkage* is the polite name for the typical cause of these discrepancies. To be blunt, employees, repair people, and passersby attracted by an unlocked door may help themselves to a five-finger discount. And you not only take the hit to your bottom line, but you're stuck adjusting your QuickBooks records to account for the theft. On the other hand, if you have more inventory than you expect, you may have forgotten to ship products to customers.

It's no surprise, then, that QuickBooks has a command for this multipurpose accounting task. Adjusting both the quantity of inventory and its value takes place in the aptly named "Adjust Quantity/Value on Hand" window.

Fiddling with inventory that you already own might not seem like a vendor-related task, but QuickBooks keeps all inventory commands in the same place—the Vendors menu. To open the "Adjust Quantity/Value on Hand" window, choose Vendors → Inventory Activities → "Adjust Quantity/Value on Hand" or on the Home page, click Adjust Quantity On Hand.

When QuickBooks opens the "Adjust Quantity/Value on Hand" window, all you have to enter are the quantities for your inventory items to match what's in your warehouse or to reflect inventory you're writing off, as shown in Figure 19-6. QuickBooks uses the average cost of each inventory item to calculate the dollar value that the new quantities represent. By turning on the Value Adjustment checkbox (below the left side of the table), you can enter actual values to mimic "last in/first out" or "first in/first out" costing, which is described on page 476.

Adjusting Quantities

When you adjust inventory quantities, QuickBooks fills in or calculates some of the fields for you. Here are guidelines for filling in the remaining fields of the Adjust Quantity/Value on Hand window:

• **Adjustment Date.** QuickBooks fills in this box with the current date. If you like to keep your journal entries and other bookkeeping adjustments together at the end of a quarter or year, type the date when you want to record the adjustment.

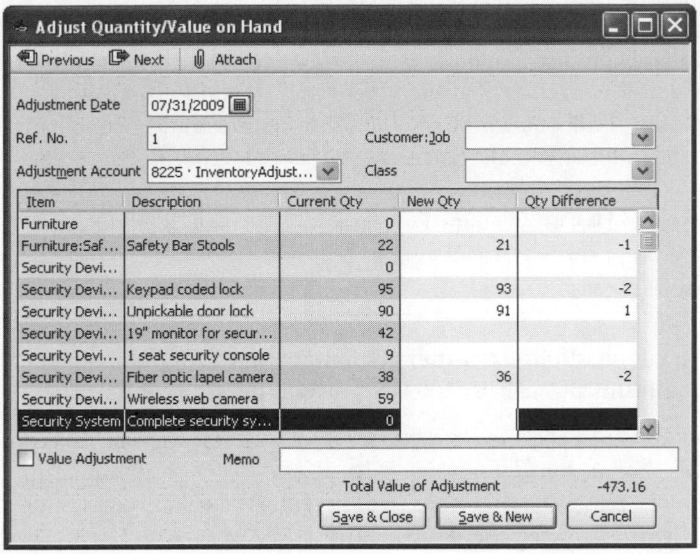

Figure 19-6:
QuickBooks shades the columns you can't change. When the Value Adjustment checkbox is turned off, the New Qty and Qty Difference columns are the only ones that you can edit.

- **Ref. No.** QuickBooks doesn't require a reference number, but they come in handy when discussing your books with your accountant. QuickBooks increments the number in this box by one each time you adjust inventory.

- **Adjustment Account.** Choose an expense account to which you want to post the cost of the inventory adjustment. For example, if you adjust the quantity of an item to match the physical count, choose an account such as Inventory Adjustment. If you're writing off obsolete or damaged inventory, choose an expense account, such as Unsalable Inventory. Because you can assign only one account to each inventory adjustment, create one adjustment for physical count changes, and then click Save & New to start an adjustment for write-offs.

Note: If the expense account you want to use doesn't exist, at the top of the drop-down list, choose *<Add New>*. In the New Account dialog box, fill in the boxes. When you click OK, QuickBooks fills in the Adjustment Account box with the account you just created.

- **Customer:Job.** If you want to send products to a customer or job without adding the items to an invoice, choose the customer or job in this drop-down list. QuickBooks assigns the cost of the adjustment to the customer or job.

Tip: A better way to give products to a customer or job is to add them to an invoice with a price of $0.00. Your generosity remains on the record lest your customer forgets.

- **Class.** If you use classes to track sales, choose the appropriate one. For example, if one partner handles sales for the item you're adjusting, choose the class for that partner so the expense applies to that class.

- **New Qty.** When the Value Adjustment checkbox is turned off, you can type a number in either the New Qty or the Qty Difference cell. If you're making an adjustment due to a physical count, in the New Qty cell, type the quantity from your physical count worksheet. On the other hand, if you know you lost four cartons of *Chivalry Today* magazine in a feminist demonstration gone bad, it's easier to type the number you lost (such as *–400*) in the Qty Difference cell.

Note: If you're ready to admit that the pet rock fad isn't coming back, you can write off your entire inventory by filling in the New Qty cell with *0*. In the Adjustment Account drop-down list, choose an expense account, such as Unsalable Inventory.

- **Memo.** To prevent questions from your accountant, in the Memo cell, type the reason for the adjustment, such as "2009 end-of-year physical count."

After you fill in all the boxes, click Save & Close (or Save & New if you want to create a second adjustment, for instance, for write-offs). If you decrease the quantity on hand, QuickBooks decreases the balance in your inventory asset account (using the average cost per item). To keep the double-entry bookkeeping principles intact, the decrease in the inventory asset account shows up as an increase in the expense account you chose. If the adjustment increases the quantity or value of your inventory, your inventory asset account balance increases and the balance in the expense account decreases.

UP TO SPEED

LIFO and FIFO Inventory Costing

"First in/first out" costing means that a company values its inventory as if the first products it receives are the first ones it sells. (Your grocery store always puts the milk closest to expiration at the front of the refrigerator, doesn't it?)

"Last in/first out" costing assumes that the last products in are the first ones sold. This method is like unpacking a moving van: The last valuables you packed are the first ones that come out.

The costing method that a business uses doesn't have to match the order in which it sells products. When you start your business, you can choose a costing method—but you have to stick with it. For example, when prices are on the

rise (as they almost always are), "last in/first out" costing reduces your profit and taxes owed because you're selling the products that cost the most first. However, with the steady decrease in electronics prices, "first in/first out" probably produces the least profit. Unless you're sure which method you want to use, you're better off asking your accountant for advice.

Unfortunately, even with the "Adjust Quantity/Value on Hand" dialog box, you can't achieve true LIFO or FIFO costing in QuickBooks. The program still uses average cost to move money from your inventory asset account to your cost of goods sold account when you add products to an invoice or sales receipt.

Adjusting Quantities and Values

Calculating inventory value using the average cost for your items is convenient—and in QuickBooks, it's the only reasonable choice. Using other methods for calculating inventory, like "first in/first out" and "last in/first out" (see the box above) quickly turn into a full-time job. But if that's what you want, you can make the program do it. Because QuickBooks can handle only average cost for inventory, your sole workaround for achieving LIFO or FIFO costing is to adjust dollar values in the "Adjust Quantity/Value on Hand" window.

When you turn on the Value Adjustment checkbox, QuickBooks displays the Current Value and New Value columns. To adjust the value of an item in inventory, in the New Value column, type the dollar value of the inventory. For example, to write off your entire inventory of pet rocks, in the New Value cell, type *0.00*.

Mimicking LIFO or FIFO costing takes some effort because you have to review the bills for all your purchases of the inventory item. Here's what you have to do to value your inventory using LIFO:

1. **Choose Reports → Purchases → "Purchases by Item Detail".**

   QuickBooks generates a report that shows your purchase transactions grouped by inventory item.

2. **For the quantity of the item that you have on hand, add up the prices you paid for your earliest purchases, as shown in Figure 19-7.**

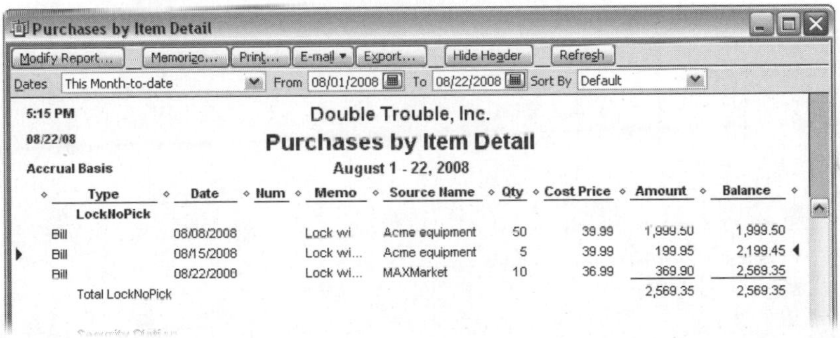

Figure 19-7:
In the "Purchases by Item Detail" report, the Cost Price column shows your price for an item with each purchase. For example, the first 55 locks cost $39.99 each and the last 10 cost $36.99 each. The LIFO value for 20 locks would be 10 multiplied by $36.99 and 10 multiplied by $39.99, or $769.80. To value the inventory using FIFO, start with the costs for the items purchased first: 20 locks at $39.99, or $799.80.

3. **In the "Adjust Quantity/Value on Hand" dialog box in the New Value cell, type the amount you just calculated.**

   When you click Save & Close, QuickBooks decreases the balance in your inventory asset account using the value in the New Value cell instead of the average cost per item.

CHAPTER 20

Budgeting and Planning

As you've no doubt noticed in business and in life, the activities that cost money almost always seem to outnumber those that bring money in. If you run your own business for a hobby, you may not need to plan ahead or use a budget. But most companies want to make money and most nonprofits want to do the most with the funds they have, so budgeting and planning are essential business activities.

Like any kind of plan, a budget is an estimate of what's going to happen. You'll never produce exactly the numbers you estimate in your budget. (If you do, someone's playing games with your books.) But comparing your actual performance to your budget can tell you that it's time to crack the whip on the sales team, rein in your spending, or both.

Budgeting in QuickBooks is both simple and simplistic. QuickBooks handles basic budgets and even provides some handy shortcuts for entering numbers quickly. On the other hand, you can't see whether your budget is working as you build it, and playing what-if games with budgets requires some fancy footwork.

QuickBooks also lets you create forecasts of future performance, although forecasts look just like budgets and have all the same data entry tools—and the same limitations. The bottom line: if you gather budget numbers from dozens of divisions and perform statistical analysis on the results to build your final budget or you chafe at QuickBooks' limited budgeting features, you'll need a program other than Quick-Books (like Excel) to massage the numbers. Then you can import your budgetary masterpiece into QuickBooks to compare your performance to the budget.

QuickBooks also includes a couple of planning tools, the Cash Flow Projector (Company → Planning & Budgeting → Cash Flow Projector) and the Business Plan Tool (Company → Planning & Budgeting → Use Business Plan Tool). These wizards ask a bunch of questions, but are often short on the in-depth answers that businesses need.

GEM IN THE ROUGH

Budgets and Forecasts

The Set Up Budgets and Set Up Forecast commands on the Company → Planning & Budgeting submenu open dialog boxes that look strikingly similar. In fact, other than replacing the word "Budgets" with "Forecast," they're identical. So how do you decide whether to use a budget or a forecast?

In QuickBooks, you can have only one budget for a period. For example, your budget for 2010 might be a profit and loss budget. The main thing a forecast does is let you have two versions of planning numbers for the same timeframe. So, you can create a profit and loss budget and a separate forecast for the same fiscal year, using the budget to reflect your most likely results and the forecast to show the numbers under more optimistic (or pessimistic) conditions.

QuickBooks has reports (Reports → Budgets & Forecasts) that compare your actual performance to budgets and forecasts, so you can see the same information for both.

As you'll learn in this chapter, you can create several budgets for the same period, but you can have only one of them loaded in QuickBooks at a time. The same is true for forecasts. If you want to turn a forecast into a budget, you have to go through the export-import procedure you'll learn on page 489.

The bottom line: Use budgets unless you want a second set of planning numbers readily available. If you decide to create forecasts, the instructions in this chapter apply to them, too.

Types of Budgets

To most people, the word "budget" means a profit and loss budget—one that estimates what your income and expenses will be over a period of time. QuickBooks provides profit and loss budgets that are based on the income and expense accounts in your chart of accounts (see Chapter 3) and typically span the fiscal year for your company. See the box above to learn how forecasts differ from budgets.

Balance sheet budgets aren't as common, but you can create them in QuickBooks as well. Balance sheets are snapshots of your assets and liabilities, and balance sheet budgets follow the same format by showing the ending balance for your asset, liability, and other balance sheet accounts.

Note: Most companies plan for major purchases and their accompanying loans outside of the budgeting process. If a company needs an asset to operate, executives usually analyze costs, benefits, payback periods, internal rates of return, and so on before making purchase decisions. They evaluate cash flow to decide whether to borrow money or to use cash generated by operations. But after that, the additional income generated by the assets and the additional interest expense for the loans show up in the profit and loss budget.

QuickBooks' profit and loss reports come in three flavors, each helpful in its own way:

- **Company profit and loss.** The most common type of budget includes all the income and expenses for your entire company. This is the budget that management struggles to meet or strives to exceed—whether that's to produce the net profit that keeps shareholders happy or to generate the cash needed to run the company. With a QuickBooks "Budget vs. Actual" report (page 493), you can compare your actual results to your budget.

- **Customer or job budget.** A customer or job-based profit and loss budget forecasts the income and expenses for a single customer or job. Projects that come with a lot of risk have to offer the potential for lots of profit to be worthwhile. By generating a profit and loss budget for a customer or job, you can make sure that the profitability meets your needs.

- **Class budget.** If you use classes to track income and expenses—for different regions of the country, say—you can create profit and loss budgets for each class. Class budgets work particularly well when you track income and expenses for independent sections of your company: regions, business units, branches, and so on. If most of the company expenses are pooled and classes track only income and reimbursable expenses, you can still create class-based budgets. In those budgets, you just ignore all the accounts that don't apply to your class-tracking scheme.

Ways to Build Budgets

If you've just started your business, you may have a business plan that includes estimates of your income and expenses. But you don't have any existing financial data to use as a basis for a budget. Either way, there's a method for building a QuickBooks budget. And, if you're willing to import and export data, QuickBooks gives you two additional ways to build budgets. Here are your options and what each has to offer:

- **From scratch.** This method is the most tedious, but it's your only option when you don't have budget numbers or existing data to use. You have to type all the numbers, but fortunately you only have to use this approach for your first budget.

- **From previous year's budget.** If you created a budget for the previous year, you can use it as the basis for next year's budget. Although playing with multiple budgets might seem like Business 101 to you, copying budgets requires some exporting and importing games in QuickBooks (page 489).

- **From previous year's actual results.** Building a new budget from a previous budget usually requires less editing than building one from actual results. However, if this is your first budget and you have at least a year's worth of data in QuickBooks, it's much easier to use existing data as a starting point and edit only the values that change.

- **From data in another program.** If you're a wiz at building budgets in another program or export QuickBooks budgets to work out what-if scenarios, you can import budget data into QuickBooks.

Creating Budgets in QuickBooks

If you want to build a budget directly in QuickBooks, the Set Up Budgets wizard is all you need. Profit and loss budgets; balance sheet budgets; budgets for customers, jobs, and classes; and budgets built from scratch or from previous year's data—the Set Up Budgets wizard does it all.

Before you dive into building a budget, you have to perform two setup steps outside of budgeting if you want your budgets to work properly:

- **Fiscal year.** QuickBooks uses the first month of your fiscal year as the first month in the budget. To check that you defined your fiscal year correctly, choose Company → Company Information. In the Company Information dialog box, head to the Report Information section and make sure that the month in the "First month in your Fiscal Year" box is indeed the first month of your fiscal year.

- **Active accounts.** QuickBooks budgets cover only the accounts that are active in your chart of accounts. To activate any accounts you want to budget, press Ctrl+A to open the Chart of Accounts window. Then, turn on the "Include inactive" checkbox. (If no accounts are inactive, the "Include inactive" checkbox is grayed out.) For any inactive account that you want in your budget, click the X to the left of the account name to reactivate the account.

To start the budget wizard, choose Company → Planning & Budgeting → Set Up Budgets. Depending on whether you already have a budget in QuickBooks, the program displays one of two different wizards. The Create New Budget wizard, shown in Figure 20-1, appears if this is your first budget in this company file.

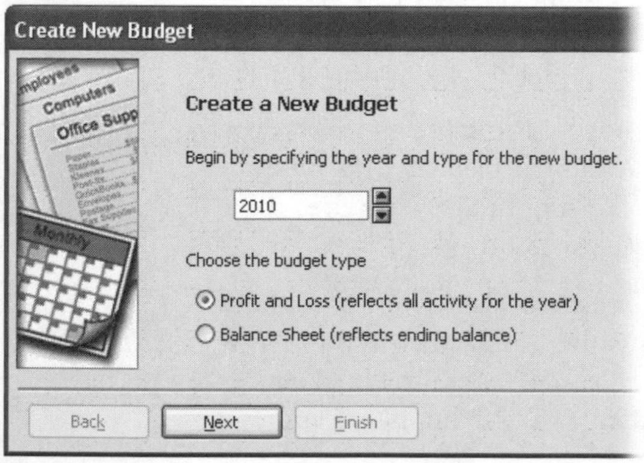

Figure 20-1:
In the Create New Budget wizard, you tell QuickBooks about the budget you want to create: the year, the type, and whether it works with customers, jobs, or classes. If you already have at least one budget in the company file, QuickBooks opens the Set Up Budgets wizard (page 484) to the most recent budget you created. To create another budget in that wizard, click the Create New Budget button to launch the wizard shown here.

The steps for setting up a new budget are the same whether QuickBooks displays the Create New Budget wizard automatically or you click the Create New Budget button:

1. **In the first "Create a New Budget" screen (Figure 20-1), choose the fiscal year for the budget, and then click Next.**

   QuickBooks automatically fills in the next calendar year (perhaps assuming that you're done budgeting for the current year). Click the up and down arrows to the right of the year box to choose the fiscal year you're budgeting for.

   The program automatically selects the Profit and Loss option, because most budgets cover income and expenses for a year. If you want to create a balance sheet budget, select the Balance Sheet option instead.

Tip: If you create a balance sheet budget, there are no additional criteria to set before you build the budget for your balance sheet accounts. In the Create New Budget wizard, clicking Next displays a screen that tells you to click Finish. When you do, a table containing your balance sheet accounts appears in the Set Up Budgets window, and you can begin to type ending balances.

---

2. **In the "Additional Profit and Loss Budget Criteria" screen, select the option for the flavor of profit and loss budget you want, and then click Next.**

   QuickBooks automatically selects the "No additional criteria" option, which creates the most common type of budget: a profit and loss budget for the entire company. Choose the Customer:Job option to build a budget for a specific customer or job. If you have QuickBooks classes turned on (page 551), you can also choose the Class option to build a class-based budget.

3. **In the "Choose how you want to create a budget" screen, select the "Create budget from previous year's actual data" if you have actual data and want to use it for your budget.**

   This option transfers the monthly income and expense account totals from the previous year into the budget. Although QuickBooks selects the "Create budget from scratch" option initially, the data entry it requires is necessary only when you don't have any other numbers to use.

Tip: You're probably looking for the one option that the "Choose how you want to create a budget" screen doesn't have—one that creates a new budget based on an existing budget. See page 489 to learn how to create a budget in this way.

---

4. **Click Finish.**

   QuickBooks opens the Set Up Budgets wizard, which shows a monstrous table. The rows represent each active account in your chart of accounts. Each column is one month of the fiscal year. If you opted to create a budget for a customer,

---

job, or class, the Set Up Budgets window includes either the Current Customer: Job drop-down list containing all your active customer and jobs, or the Class drop-down list containing all your active classes. Before you start entering values for a customer, job, or class budget, choose the customer, job, or class.

> **Note:** If your screen resolution is less than 1024 x 768, the Set Up Budgets window also includes the Show Next 6 Months button, because the screen can't display the entire year. QuickBooks initially displays January through June. Click Show Next 6 Months to display July through December, which also changes the button's label to Show Previous 6 Months.

Filling in Budget Values

Regardless of which type of budget you create, filling in and editing values is the same. To add budget values to an account, in the Account column, click the account. QuickBooks automatically selects the cell in the first month column in that row. If you're filling in the entire year's worth of numbers, type the value for the first month, press Tab to move to the next month, and continue until you've entered values in all 12 months. As you add values to each month, the Annual Total column displays the total for all months, as shown in Figure 20-2.

Filling in a few budget cells is usually enough to convince you that data entry shortcuts are in order. Because budgets are estimates, you don't need extraordinarily detailed or precise values. QuickBooks gives you two ways to enter values faster, described next.

Copy Across Columns

In the Set Up Budgets window (Company → Planning & Budgeting → Set Up Budgets), you can copy a number from one cell in a row to all the cells to the right in the same row, as demonstrated in Figure 20-3.

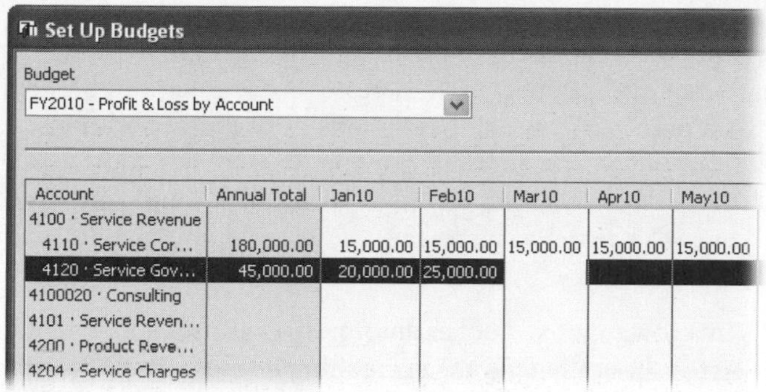

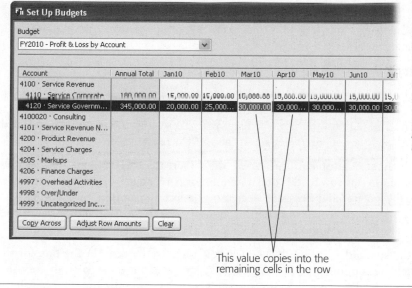

Figure 20-2:
If the account names and budget values are hopelessly truncated and you have screen real estate to spare, widen the Set Up Budgets window by dragging a corner. The columns show more of the cell contents as you widen the dialog box. To resize an individual column, hover the pointer over the vertical line to the right of the column header. When the pointer turns into a two-headed arrow, drag to the right or left.

Figure 20-3:
To copy a value into the remaining cells in a row, type the value in the cell for the first month of the new value. For example, in the cell for Service Government for March 2010, type 30000. When you click Copy Across, QuickBooks copies 30,000 into the cells for April through December.

This value copies into the remaining cells in the row

This shortcut is fabulous when a monthly expense remains the same throughout the year, like office rent, for example. But it also works if a price changes mid-year. For example, suppose the corporate concierge you've hired to run errands for your employees announces that his rates are going up in May. If your budget contains the old rate in every month, click the cell for May and type the new rate. Then, when you click Copy Across, the new rate appears from May through December.

Tip: If you mistakenly added values to cells that should be blank, Copy Across is the fastest way to empty a row. Clear the first month's cell by selecting the value and then pressing Backspace. Immediately click Copy Across to have QuickBooks clear all the other cells in the row.

Adjust Row Amounts

In the Set Up Budgets window (Company → Planning & Budgeting → Set Up Budgets), the Adjust Row Amounts button lets you increase or decrease monthly values by a dollar amount or a percentage, which has zillions of useful applications. Say you created a budget from previous year's data, but you want to increase this year's values by 10 percent. Or maybe your company is growing quickly and you want to apply some heat to your sales force by increasing the income you aim to pull in each month.

Changing all the cells in a row by a fixed dollar amount isn't as useful as you might think, because Copy Across basically does the same thing in most cases. But when you change budget amounts by percentages, QuickBooks takes care of the percentage calculations for you. Here's what you do:

1. **Click the row you want to adjust.**

   If you want to start the adjustment with a specific month, click the cell for the starting month.

2. **Click Adjust Row Amounts.**

   QuickBooks opens the Adjust Row Amounts dialog box and automatically selects your previous choice in the "Start at" box. "1st month" starts adjustments in the first month of the fiscal year. To start at the month you selected, from the "Start at" drop-down list, choose "Currently selected month".

3. **QuickBooks automatically selects the "Increase each remaining monthly amount in this row by this dollar amount or percentage" option because prices usually go up. If prices are decreasing, select the option that begins with "Decrease each remaining monthly amount". In the corresponding value box, type the dollar amount or the percentage, and then click OK.**

   If the landlord tells you that rent is going up five percent, in the box for the "Increase" option, type 5%. QuickBooks increases the value in all the remaining cells by five percent. So if your rent was $5,000 a month, the values in all the remaining months change to $5,250.

   To add a dollar amount to the remaining cells, type that dollar value. For example, to add $1,000 a month to the Rent cells, in the box for this option, type *1000*. Each subsequent cell in the Rent row increases by 1,000. Of course, you can do the same thing by typing the new rent amount in the cell for the first month to which it applies, and then clicking Copy Across.

Note: The Adjust Row Amounts command is for adjusting existing budget values, not filling in blank cells. For example, when you select the "Increase each remaining monthly amount in this row by this dollar amount or percentage" option and type 100 in the text box, QuickBooks adds 100 to the values in the month cells. If the January cell is set to 1,000, it increases to 1,100. However, if the remaining months' cells are zero (0), they increase to 100.

4. If you set the "Start at" box to "Currently selected month", the "Enable compounding" checkbox appears. If you want to adjust each month's value based on the previous month's value, turn on this checkbox.

When you compound dollar amounts, QuickBooks adds the dollar amount you specify to the next month's value. If January's value is 25,000 and you change the value by 1,000, February's value is 26,000, as shown in Figure 20-4. Then, March's value increases by another 1,000 to 27,000.

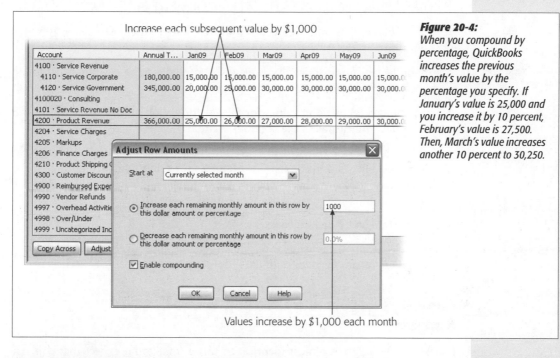

Increase each subsequent value by $1,000

Values increase by $1,000 each month

Figure 20-4:
When you compound by percentage, QuickBooks increases the previous month's value by the percentage you specify. If January's value is 25,000 and you increase it by 10 percent, February's value is 27,500. Then, March's value increases another 10 percent to 30,250.

Creating Additional Customer:Job or Class Budgets

In QuickBooks, there's no way to store several versions of a fiscal year budget that covers your entire operation. But you can create additional budgets for the same fiscal year, for different customers, jobs, or classes.

After you create your first budget, the Set Up Budgets dialog box opens with the most recent fiscal year budget in the budget table. But if you've created at least one budget for a customer or job, the Budget drop-down list includes an entry like "FY2010-Profit & Loss By Account and Customer:Job". Class budgets show up in the Budget drop-down list looking something like "FY2010-Profit & Loss By Account and Class".

Class budgets work the way Customer:Job budgets do. In fact, if you replace every instance of "Customer:Job" in the following procedure with "Class", you'll have the instructions for creating Class budgets. Here's how you create and save additional Customer:Job or Class budgets:

1. **In the Budget drop-down list, choose the customer and job budget for the fiscal year you want to budget.**

   QuickBooks adds the Current Customer:Job box to the Set Up Budgets window in between the Budget box and the table of budget values.

2. **In the Current Customer:Job drop-down list, choose the customer or job that you want to budget.**

   Any budgetary numbers you've previously entered for the customer or job for the selected fiscal year appear in the budget table.

3. **In the budget table, fill in values for the Customer:Job budget using any of the techniques you learned in the previous section.**

   Unlike a budget for your entire operation, customer or job budgets may have values for only a few accounts. For example, for a job that includes products, services, and reimbursable expenses, your budget may have values only for income accounts and the expense accounts for reimbursable expenses.

4. **Save the budget by clicking Save.**

   If you choose another customer or job without clicking Save, QuickBooks asks if you want to record the budget. In the Recording Budget message box, click Yes.

Copying Budgets and Creating What-if Budgets

If next year's budget is almost identical to this year's, you'd expect that copying your current budget and changing a few numbers would be quick and easy. But QuickBooks lacks a built-in mechanism for copying an existing budget to a new budget! Similarly, because QuickBooks allows only one budget of each type for the same fiscal year, you can't create what-if budgets within the program to see which one is the best.

To do *any* kind of budget modification beyond typing in values or using Copy Across and Adjust Row Amounts, you have to export your budgets to a spreadsheet program and make modifications or what-if copies there. Then, when you've got the budget you want, you can import the file back into QuickBooks to use the new budget. For example, you can export your QuickBooks budget into Microsoft Excel and copy the budget into several worksheets. One worksheet could be a bare-bones budget in case a client with shaky finances disappears. A second worksheet could represent your happy-dance budget if you snag that big new client. And a third worksheet could be your most likely results, somewhere between the two extremes.

A command that copies a budget would be convenient—even Quicken, Intuit's software for personal finances, has one. Exported budget files list entries for fiscal years and accounts in no particular order. For that reason, the easiest way to create budgets or play budget what-if games is in Excel and then import the final budget into QuickBooks.

Note: You can't export only the budget you want to copy or play with. When you export the Budgets list in QuickBooks, the export file includes entries for every budget for every fiscal year. If you created budgets for customers, jobs, and classes, you'll get entries for those, too. When you work on the budgets in a spreadsheet, you can ignore the entries for those other budgets—or you can delete those rows in the spreadsheet to prevent inadvertent changes to budgets you're happy with.

Here's how you export QuickBooks budgets and import your changes:

1. **Choose File → Utilities → Export → "Lists to IIF Files".**

   QuickBooks opens an Export dialog box with checkboxes for each type of list you can export.

2. **In this first Export dialog box, turn on the Budgets checkbox, and then click OK.**

   QuickBooks opens a second Export dialog box, which looks like a Save As dialog box. However, the "Save as type" box is automatically filled in with IIF Files (*.IIF).

3. **In the second Export dialog box, navigate to the folder where you want to save the export file and in the "File name" box, replace *.IIF with the name for your export file.**

   To keep your files organized, save all your export files in the same folder, called something like QBExport_Files. Name the export file something like *QBBudgets.iif*.

4. **Click Save to export the budgets from QuickBooks.**

   When a QuickBooks Information box appears telling you that the export was successful, click OK to dismiss it.

5. **In a spreadsheet program like Excel, open the budget export file.**

   IIF files are tab-delimited text files (see page 597). To open one in Excel 2007, click the Office button and then choose Open (in Excel 2003, choose File → Open). In the Open dialog box, head to the "Files of type" box, and then choose All Files so you can see every file in your folders. Navigate to the folder that contains the IIF export file and double-click its filename. The Excel Text Import Wizard appears. You don't have to specify any special formats to tell Excel how to read the file; you can just click Finish to import the file into Excel.

6. At first, rows for different year's budgets and account names are in no particular order. To change the order of the budget rows, select all the rows below the one that begins with !BUD (Figure 20-5). Then choose Data → Sort and sort the workbook first by start date (STARTDATE) and then by account (ACCNT).

This sorting method intersperses income and expense accounts, but the good thing is it groups all the entries for each fiscal year together. Because companies typically have fewer income accounts, it's quicker to move the rows for income accounts above the expense accounts.

Tip: If you plan to do all your budgeting work in Excel, take the time to delete the rows for older budgets. Then rearrange the rows for income and expense accounts the way you want. Save the Excel workbook as a template for building all your budgets.

---

7. While you're still in Excel, if you want to use an existing budget to create next year's budget, all you do is change the year in the STARTDATE column.

The Excel worksheet includes a column labeled STARTDATE, which contains the date that the fiscal year for the budget begins. Use Excel's Replace command (press Ctrl+H) to change the year to the new budget (Figure 20-5). In Excel 2007, you can also choose the Home tab and then click Find & Select → Replace (at the right end of the ribbon); in Excel 2003, choose Edit → Replace. Ctrl+H opens the "Find and Replace" dialog box in both Excel 2003 and 2007.

To modify budget numbers, edit the budget values in the Excel worksheet.

Note: If you create several what-if budgets in Excel, be sure to copy the data for only your final budget into a file for importing into QuickBooks. Compare the keywords and column headings in the Budget list export file to those in the file you plan to import to make sure that the data imports the way you want. For example, a row that begins with !BUD lists the keywords that identify columns, such as ACCNT for your accounts and AMOUNT for your budget values. (Rows for budget entries have to begin with a cell containing the keyword BUD. For more information on importing and exporting data, see Chapter 24.)

---

8. In Excel 2007, click the Office button and then choose Save As → Other Formats. (In Excel 2003, choose File → Save As.) In the Save As dialog box, save the modified file with a new file name.

In the Save As dialog box, Excel chooses Text (tab delimited) as the file type.

9. To import the modified IIF file, back in QuickBooks, choose File → Utilities → Import → IIF Files.

QuickBooks opens the Import dialog box and automatically chooses IIF Files (*.IIF) in the "Files of type" box. If you don't see your file, in the "Files of type" box, choose All Files (*.*).

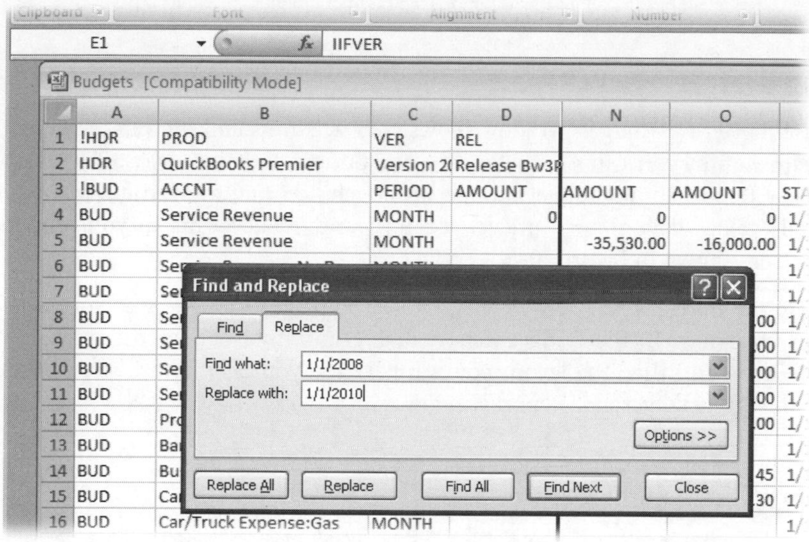

Figure 20-5:
The budget entries for 2009 budgets include "1/1/2009" in the STARTDATE column. To create a budget for 2010, change the contents of these cells to "1/1/2010". Budget entries for customer, job, or class budgets include the customer and job name in the CUSTOMER column or the class name in the CLASS column. If you leave all the rows for budgets that you aren't changing in the spreadsheet, QuickBooks imports those budgets, too. However, if you didn't change any values, the newly imported budgets look the same in QuickBooks as they did before the import.

10. **Double-click the name of the IIF file that contains your edited budget.**

When a QuickBooks Information box appears telling you that the import was successful, click OK to dismiss it.

11. **Choose Company → Planning & Budgeting → Set Up Budgets.**

If you created a budget for a new fiscal year, in the Set Up Budgets window, the Budget drop-down list now contains an entry for the budget for the new year. If you used a spreadsheet to edit an existing budget, in the Budget drop-down list, choose the entry for that budget to see your updated values in the budget table.

Running Budget Reports

A budget gives you a target to aim for. The Set Up Budgets window lets you type values for income and expense accounts, but it doesn't show you whether your budget results in a net profit or loss. For that, you need a budget report (or your budget exported to a spreadsheet, as described on page 489). And to see how your business is doing compared to your budget, you need a budget report that shows budget and actual numbers side by side. QuickBooks provides four types of budget reports, one to review budgets you've created and the other three to compare your performance to your plan. This section describes the types of budget reports, what they're useful for, and how to create and format them.

Note: To learn about *all* the options for customizing any kind of report, see Chapter 21.

The Budget Overview Report

Because the Set Up Budgets window shows your accounts and the values you enter for each month, you can't see whether your budget actually works. The Budget Overview Report shows budget numbers for each account and month, but it also subtotals values if you use top-level accounts and subaccounts in your chart of accounts, as shown in Figure 20-6.

To view the Budget Overview Report, choose Reports → Budgets & Forecasts → Budget Overview. In the Budget Report dialog box, first choose the budget you want to view and then the layout you want. When you click Finish, QuickBooks opens the Budget Overview Report window.

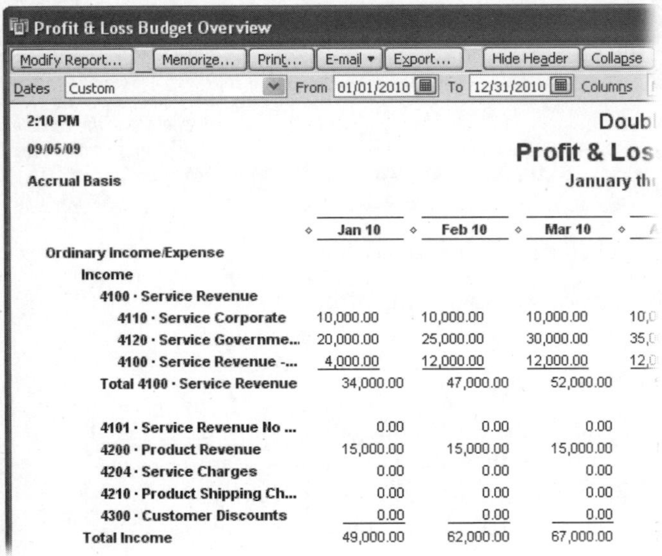

Figure 20-6:
Although you build budgets month by month, many businesses (particularly ones with shareholders) focus on quarterly performance. To view your budget by quarter instead of by month, in the Columns drop-down list, choose Quarter. To see whether you earn enough income to cover expenses, at the bottom of the report, look for net income (income minus expenses) for each month and for the entire year.

Note: The Budget Overview Report includes only accounts that have budget values; accounts without budget values stay out of view.

Report layouts

If you create a report for a profit and loss budget for your entire company, the only layout option in the Budget Report dialog box is Account By Month, which lists the accounts in the first column with each subsequent column showing one month of the fiscal year. You can change the columns to different durations in the Budget Overview window (Figure 20-6).

Memorizing Budget Reports

When you generate budget reports, you have to specify which budget you want to see and the layout of rows and columns. In addition, in the report window, you might click Modify Report to change the date range, the columns that appear, and so on. All in all, to get the budget report you really want might require a dozen or more small customizations.

Rather than reapply all these tweaks each time you generate the report, memorize the customized report so you can regenerate it with one click. Here's how:

1. In any report window, click Memorize. QuickBooks opens the Memorize Report dialog box.

2. In the Name box, type a name for the customized report, such as "P&L Budget vs. Actual 2010".

3. If you want to save the report in a special group, turn on the Save in Memorized Report Group checkbox. In the drop-down list, choose the group. For example, for budget reports, you might store the report in the Company group. If you don't save the report to a special group, QuickBooks adds the memorized report to the Memorized Report submenu.

4. Click OK.

To run the report, choose Reports → Memorized Reports. If you didn't save the report to a memorized group, choose the report name on the Memorized Reports submenu. If you did save the report in a memorized group, on the Memorized Reports submenu, choose that group, and then choose the report's name.

If you choose a Customer:Job budget in the Budget Report dialog box and then click Next, the Budget Overview Report includes these layout options:

- **Account By Month.** This layout lists accounts in the first column with months of the fiscal year in the subsequent columns. The values in the monthly columns represent the totals for *all* the Customer:Job budgets you've created.

- **Account By Customer:Job.** This layout lists accounts in the first column and includes additional columns for each customer or job you've budgeted. Each customer and job column shows its annual totals.

- **Customer:Job by Month.** This layout adds a row for each customer and additional rows for each job that customer has. The columns are for each month of the fiscal year. The value for a job and month represents the total budgeted value for all accounts.

Budget vs. Actual Report

The "Budget vs. Actual" report compares the budget you created to the actual income and expenses your business achieved. Run this report monthly for early warnings should your performance veer off track. For example, if your income is short of your target, the "% of Budget" column shows percentages less than 100 percent, as is painfully apparent in Figure 20-7. Income percentages greater than 100 percent mean you're making more than you planned. On the other hand, costs greater than 100 percent indicate that expenses are ballooning beyond your budget.

Income less than 100% is below budget

Figure 20-7:
The column with the heading for a month and year (or quarter like "Jan - Mar 09" as shown here) is your actual performance. The Budget column includes the budgeted values for the same month and year. You can also show the difference between the two in dollars (the Over Budget column) and percentage (% of Budget column).

🔲 Profit & Loss Budget vs. Actual

[Modify Report...] [Memorize...] [Print...] [E-mail ▾] [Export...] [Hide Header] [Collapse] [Refresh]

Dates [This Fiscal Year-to-date ▾] From [01/01/2009 🔳] To [08/24/2009 🔳] Columns [Quarter ▾] Sort By [Default]

12:14 PM
08/24/09
Accrual Basis

Double Trouble, Inc.
Profit & Loss Budget vs. Actual
January 1 through August 24, 2009

	Jan - Mar 09	Budget	Over Budget	% of Budget	Apr - Jun 09
Ordinary Income/Expense					
Income					
4100 · Service Revenue					
4110 · Service Corporate	0.00	45,000.00	-45,000.00	0.0%	0.00
4120 · Service Government	0.00	78,000.00	-78,000.00	0.0%	0.00
4100 · Service Revenue - Ot...	47,880.00	91,257.50	-43,377.50	52.5%	36,000.00
Total 4100 · Service Revenue	47,880.00	214,257.50	-166,377.50	22.3%	36,000.00
4100020 · Consulting	0.00				0.00
4101 · Service Revenue No Doc	0.00				0.00
4200 · Product Revenue	32,899.10	3,899.60	28,999.50	843.7%	0.00
4204 · Service Charges	0.00				0.00
4205 · Markups	0.00				0.00
4206 · Finance Charges	0.00				0.00
4210 · Product Shipping Charg...	0.00				0.00
4300 · Customer Discounts	0.00				0.00
4900 · Reimbursed Expenses...	0.00				0.00
4990 · Vendor Refunds	0.00				0.00
4997 · Overhead Activities	0.00				0.00
4998 · Over/Under	0.00				0.00
4999 · Uncategorized Income	0.00				0.00
Total Income	80,779.10	218,157.10	-137,378.00	37%	36,000.00

Income greater than 100% is ahead of budget

To view the "Budget vs. Actual" report, choose Reports → Budgets & Forecasts → "Budget vs. Actual". Choose the budget you want to view and the layout you want. When you click Finish, QuickBooks opens the "Budget vs. Actual" report window.

Tip: If the numbers in your report don't seem right, the culprit could be the wrong choice of Accrual or Cash reporting. Click Modify Report and click the Accrual or Cash option to match your reporting style. Page 7 explains the difference between cash basis and accrual reporting.

Profit & Loss Budget Performance Report

The Profit & Loss Budget Performance report also compares budgeted versus actual values, but initially shows the actual values for the current month with the budgeted values for the entire month in the Budget column. Two additional columns show the actual and budgeted values for the year to date.

Use this report to check your performance before the end of the month. Because the budget numbers represent the entire month, you shouldn't expect a perfect match between actual and budgeted values. But if your income or expenses are way off the mark, you can take corrective action.

Budget vs. Actual Graph

To have QuickBooks automatically generate a graph comparing your budget to actual performance, choose Reports → Budgets & Forecasts → "Budget vs. Actual Graph". This graph displays the differences between your budgeted and actual values in two ways:

• The upper bar graph shows the difference between your actual net income and budgeted net income for each month. When your actual net income exceeds the budgeted value, you've made more money than you planned. The bar is blue and appears above the horizontal axis. If the actual net income is less than the budget, the bar is red and drops below the horizontal axis.

• The lower bar graph sorts accounts, customers, or classes (depending on the report you chose) that are the furthest from your budgeted values (either above or below). For example, if you display a "P&L by Accounts and Jobs" graph, you can see the customers and jobs that exceeded your budget by the largest amount or fell the furthest short.

CHAPTER 21

Working with QuickBooks Reports

QuickBooks comes with loads of built-in reports that show what's going on with your company's finances. But a dozen report categories with several reports tucked in each category can make for a frustrating search, particularly if you're new to both business *and* QuickBooks. The first challenge is knowing what type of report tells you what you need to know. For example, a profit and loss (P&L) tells you how much income and expenses you had, but a balance sheet shows how much your company is worth.

The second challenge is finding the report you want in QuickBooks. After you decide you want to compare the profit of the items you sell, do you look for the corresponding QuickBooks report in the Sales category, Inventory category, or Jobs, Time & Mileage? (If you guessed Jobs, Time & Mileage despite that category's project-oriented name, you're right.) On the other hand, the Profit & Loss by Job report appears in both the Company & Finance category and the Jobs, Time, and Mileage category.

The Report Center is a handy way to find the reports you want. In QuickBooks 2010, it has a sleek new look and some cool new timesaving features. Flipping through this book can be even faster, which is why each chapter in this book describes the built-in reports that correspond to the bookkeeping tasks the chapter covers, what they're good for, and where you can find them.

A third challenge—for even the most knowledgeable QuickBooks aficionado—is that the built-in reports might not do exactly what you want. A date range is off, information that you don't want shows up, or the data is grouped in ways that don't make sense for your business. After using QuickBooks for a while, most businesses tweak the program's built-in reports. This chapter also explains how to customize reports to get what you want.

There's no point in letting good customization go to waste, so you'll also learn how to memorize your customized reports, add them to QuickBooks menus for fast access, and even how to exchange particularly handy customized reports between company files.

Finding the Right Reports

If you know what kind of report answers your burning business question, finding the right report can be as simple as dragging your mouse through the Reports menu to a likely category, and then, on the category submenu, clicking the name of the report you want. But if you need help figuring out what a report does and what one looks like, the Report Center could be your new best friend.

On the QuickBooks icon bar, click Report Center (or choose Reports → Report Center). This window shows a clickable list of the same report categories and reports as on the Reports menu. But unlike the menu, the Report Center gives you all sorts of hints for finding the right report. In QuickBooks 2010, the Report Center also offers several new shortcuts for getting to the right report fast, as you can see in Figure 21-1.

On the left side of the Report Center, you'll initially see built-in report categories. To see the reports in a category, click the category name, like Company & Financial, Sales, or Banking. These categories are the same ones you see on the Reports menu (page 502).

Reviewing Reports in the Report Center

In QuickBooks 2010, the Report Center has three ways to view the reports in a category. You can choose the one you want to use, depending on your preference and your computer's horsepower:

• **Carousel View**, which QuickBooks selects out of the box, is eye candy more than a useful search tool. When you pick a report category with this view, a sample report (one that doesn't use your company data) appears in the center of the window. In addition to the report title, the question that the report answers appears above the sample, such as "What are my company's total expenses for each vendor?" for the "Expenses by Vendor Summary" report. Other reports in the category wait in the wings to the left and right of the selected report. Click one of these angled reports to bring it front and center.

Below the report, you can change the date range by clicking the down arrow to the right of the current date range and choosing the new date range. To run the report, double-click the report thumbnail or click the "Display report" icon (a dog-eared piece of paper). To use this view, click the Carousel View icon (which looks like a slide projector if you use you're imagination) in the upper-right corner of the Report Center toolbar.

Note: Carousel View takes a lot of horsepower, so you might see a message about it running slow on your computer. Choose List View or Grid View to navigate reports more quickly and effectively.

- **List View** is your best bet when you want hints about the right reports and also want to get to those reports quickly. Select a category, and the titles of the category's reports and the questions they answer appear in a space-saving list. When you select a report, the date range and report-related icons appear below the title, which you'll learn about shortly. To use this view, click the List View icon, which looks like three horizontal bars.

- **Grid View**, shown in Figure 21-1, displays small thumbnails of each type of report in the selected category. To see more reports in the category, scroll down. When you select a report, the date range and report-related icons appear below the title. Click the Grid View icon, which looks like four small boxes in a grid, to display this view.

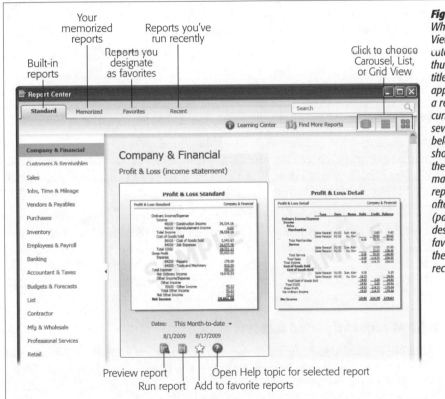

Figure 21-1:
When you use the Grid View and click a report category, small thumbnails and report titles for that category appear. When you click a report thumbnail, the current date range and several icons appear below the report as shown here. The tabs at the top of the window make it easy to get to the reports you use most often: memorized reports (page 518), reports you designate as your favorites (page 501), and the ones you've run recently.

Tip: If you don't see the kind of report you want, you may not have to customize a report yourself. The Reports Library within the online Intuit Community has dozens of reports and spreadsheets that you can download. In the Report Center to the left of the view icons, click the Find More Reports link, which opens a browser window to the Reports library. Click the category of report you want, such as Banking, Customers, or Vendors. To download reports, simply click the link in the Download column. If the link says something like Download Banking Reports, you'll download several banking reports. A link like Accounts With No Tax Line Assignments.QBR downloads a single report (in this example, one for identifying accounts not assigned to tax lines). See page 521 for how to import reports into your company file.

Working with Reports in the Report Center

When you select a report in the Report Center, you'll see the date range for the report and icons for performing report-related tasks:

- **Date range.** QuickBooks displays the current date range for the report and the dates the range represents, for example, This Fiscal Year and "1/1/2010 12/31/2010". To change the date range before you run the report, click the date range (This Fiscal Year, in this example) and then choose the new range from the drop-down list. (See page 508 to learn about the date ranges you can choose from.)

- **Preview a report.** Click the icon that looks like a dog-eared piece of paper with a magnifying glass to see a sample of the report you've selected. These samples are only helpful for built-in reports that QuickBooks provides. On the Memorized tab of the Report Center, the report icons and the samples say nothing more than "Memorized Report". You have to run the report to see what it looks like.

- **Run a report.** The icon that looks like a dog-eared piece of paper has a tool tip that says "Display report". If you click this icon, QuickBooks runs the report and displays it in a report window. When the report is open in a report window, click Modify Report in the window tool bar to make changes to the report (page 507).

- **Learn more.** If you want to know more about a report and how you can customize it, in the Report Center, select the report and then click the "Learn more about this report" icon (a blue circle containing a white question mark). Quick-Books opens the Help topic for the report, which gives hints about how to use the report and how to customize it. If you click this icon for a memorized report, QuickBooks opens the "Work with memorized reports" Help topic.

Finding Frequently-used Reports

In QuickBooks 2010, the Report Center initially displays its built-in reports and the categories to which they belong. However, the Center also offers quick access to reports that you run often:

- **Memorized reports.** If you modify reports to suit your needs, you can memorize them (page 518) and run them again and again with all your customized settings already in place. In the Report Center, click the Memorized tab to see your memorized report groups (page 502). When you select a group, the window displays the reports within that group.

Note: The Grid View and Carousel View aren't very helpful for memorized reports. The thumbnails that appear simply say Memorized Report because QuickBooks doesn't have any samples of the reports you've memorized.

- **Favorite reports.** QuickBooks 2010 lets you vote for your favorite reports so you can get to them in a jiffy. In the Report Center, the Favorites tab displays all the reports that you designate as your favorites. Whenever you select a report in the Report Center, a "Mark as Favorite" icon (a white star with a yellow border) appears. If the report is one that you run more often than you check email, simply click the icon, and QuickBooks adds the report to the Favorites tab and turns the star yellow to indicate a favorite report.

- **Recent reports.** You can quickly rerun a report you used recently by clicking the Recent tab and then choosing the report you want. For example, if you produced a "Sales by Customer" report a few days ago and need to run it again, on the Recent tab, look below the Last 1-7 days heading, click the report name, and then click the "Display report" icon.

- **Search.** If you don't know which built-in report you want, you can use keywords to narrow down your choices. For example, if you know you want to see how much equity you have in your company, in the Search box at the upper right of the Report Center, type *equity*. A Search Results tab appears with a list of reports that include equity, such as Balance Sheet Standard, Net Worth Graph, and Balance Sheet Prev Year Comparison.

Tip: If you type more than one keyword, your search results are likely to grow longer, not shorter, because QuickBooks looks for reports that contain *any* of the keywords you provide.

Running Reports

QuickBooks tries to atone for any difficulties you might have finding the right reports by scattering commands to run reports throughout the program in windows, menus, and centers. While you're learning and want to choose from every built-in report that QuickBooks has, stick with the Report Center (described in detail on page 498). When you're more familiar with what QuickBooks reports do, the Reports menu is the quickest route to running reports, as shown in Figure 21-2. The box on page 502 gives you a shortcut for when you want to run several reports at the same time.

You can run reports from many location in QuickBooks. Here's how you run reports depending on where you find them in the program:

- **The Report Center.** Select the report you want to run. If you want to change the date range before you run the report, click the current date range, and then choose the new range on the drop-down list. To run the report, click the icon that looks like a dog-eared piece of paper, as shown in Figure 21-1.

Running Multiple Reports

Perhaps you perform the same tasks every month—calling customers with overdue invoices, checking inventory, and reviewing sales by item, for example—and you need reports to complete each task. If you run reports one at a time, you might sit for hours in front of the computer with nothing but the occasional click to break the monotony, while Quick-Books slowly transforms your data into report hard copies.

But you don't have to do it that way. Tucked away on the Reports menu is the Process Multiple Reports command, which runs all the reports you choose one after the other. Stock the printer with paper, make sure the toner cartridge isn't running low, and then use Process Multiple Reports to run dozens of reports while you do something else, or even better, head home (as long as the printer is located in a secure location).

Process Multiple Reports works only with memorized reports, because you have no opportunity to customize the reports it runs. So customize each report you run regularly to include the correct information, apply the formatting you want, and then memorize each one (page 508).

When you choose Reports → Process Multiple Reports, QuickBooks opens the Process Multiple Reports window. It lists all of your memorized reports in the order that they appear on the Memorized Reports submenu—but doesn't automatically select them, as shown in Figure 21-4.

To include or remove a report to process, click its check-mark cell to toggle the checkmark on or off. When all the reports you want to print have checkmarks, click Print. QuickBooks opens the Print Reports dialog box. All you have to do is choose the Printer name and the "Number of copies" and click Print to start pushing reports through the printer.

Another way to run multiple reports is to create a report group with all the reports you want to run (see the box on page 518). Call it something like MonthlyReports or Quar-terlyReports. Then, you can run the reports by opening the Memorized Reports window (Reports → Memorized Reports → Memorized Reports List). Right-click the report group you want to run and then choose Process Group from the shortcut menu that appears.

- **Reports menu.** This menu patiently waits in the QuickBooks menu bar. To run a report, choose Reports, and then choose the report category you want (such as Memorized, Company & Financial, or Vendors & Payables). On the submenu that appears (Figure 21-2), choose the report you want to run. (If another sub-menu appears, drag until you can choose the report you want.) A report window opens to the report you chose.

- **Favorites menu.** In QuickBooks 2010, the Favorites menu is the new kid on the program's menu bar (page 609). If you add a report to the Favorites menu, run the report by choosing Favorites → <report name>.

- **Icon bar.** You can customize the icon bar (page 609) to include your all-time favorite reports or a category of reports. To run a report from the icon bar, click the report's icon.

- **List windows.** In a list window, such as the Chart of Accounts window, Item List window, or Payroll Item List window, click the Reports button at the bottom of the window and then choose the report you want to run on the drop-down list that appears.

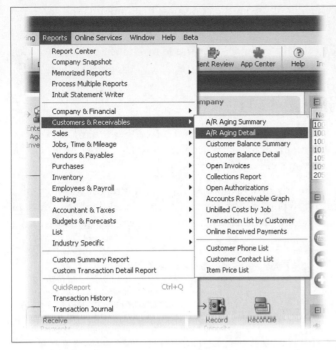

Figure 21-2:
The Reports menu not only includes built-in QuickBooks reports and reports you memorize; it also launches the Report Center, the Company Snapshot, and contains the Process Multiple Reports command, described in the box on page 502.

- **Vendor, Customer, and Employee Centers.** In a center toolbar, choose Print or Excel to create a hard copy (page 504) or to export an Excel file (page 599) of a Vendor List, Customer List, or Employee List report. To run reports about a specific customer or vendor, open the Customer Center or Vendor Center. Select the customer, job, or vendor to display the information on the right side of the Center's window. Then, click one of the report links like QuickReport or Open Balance.

Note: Some features on reports should remain consistent for every report that a company generates, such as whether you use cash or accrual accounting. (Page 7 describes the difference between cash and accrual accounting and why you might choose one or the other.) A QuickBooks administrator can set company-wide report preferences to ensure that reports show financial information correctly and consistently. But even without administrator powers, you can still specify a few settings for the reports and graphs you run. See page 577 to learn how to set report and graph preferences.

Some reports take a long time to generate, because they pull data from every corner of the company file. And running your company file in multi-user mode exacerbates the problem. If you're hunkering down to a report-running session of epic proportions, here are some tips for speeding up your work:

- Wait until everyone else has logged out of the company file.

- If possible, log into QuickBooks from the computer that contains the company file. Otherwise, log into the fastest computer on your network.

- In QuickBooks, switch the file to single-user mode by choosing File → "Switch to Single-user Mode".

Printing and Saving Reports

In QuickBooks, you can turn any report you create into either a hard copy or an electronic file. If you save a report as a file, you can use it to feed other programs or edit the report in ways that you can't do in QuickBooks.

Printing a report doesn't take any imagination. At the top of a report window, click the Print button. In the Print Reports dialog box that opens, QuickBooks has most of the same printing options you find in other programs, as you can see in Figure 21-3.

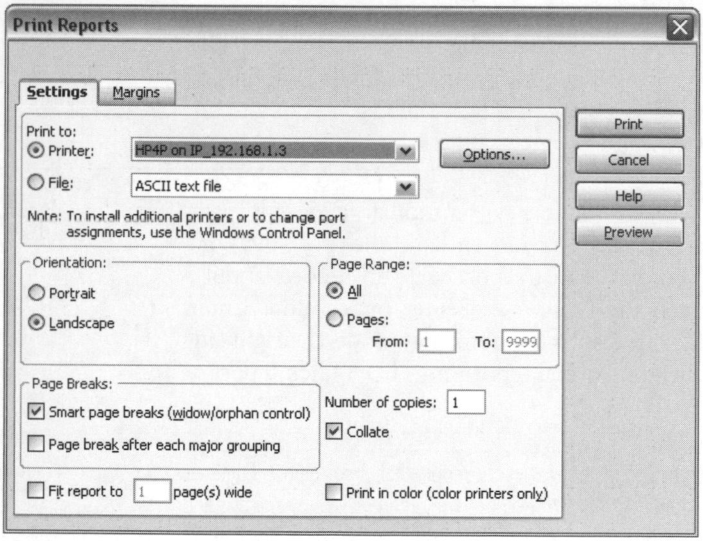

Figure 21-3:
Select the Printer option and then, in the Printer drop-down list, choose the printer to which you want to send the report. You can print reports in portrait or landscape orientation. You can also specify the pages you want to print, how many copies to print, where you want page breaks, and whether to print in color. If a report is a bit too wide to fit on one page, turn on the "Fit report to" checkbox, which lets you force the report onto one (or more) pages.

In the Print Reports dialog box, the Page Breaks section has two checkboxes that control where page breaks are placed in a report:

- To add a page break after major sections of the reports like Income and Expenses in a Profit & Loss report, turn on the "Page break after each major grouping" checkbox. When this checkbox is turned off (as it is initially), the report starts a new section on the same page.

- To stuff as much report as possible onto the fewest pages, turn off the "Smart page breaks" (widow/orphan control) checkbox. When you do so, QuickBooks prints to the very last line of a page, even if it means that a single row of a section appears on one page with the rest of the section on another. The box on page 513 describes another way to squeeze more report onto a page.

Saving Reports to Files

Intuit gives you three places to transform reports into files. The Print Reports dialog box has an option to create ASCII text files, tab-delimited files, and comma-delimited files. But you can also create comma-delimited files and Excel workbooks by choosing Export in any report window. (The comma-delimited files that you create in both dialog boxes are identical, so you can generate them whichever way you prefer.) Your third option is to print forms or reports as .pdf files.

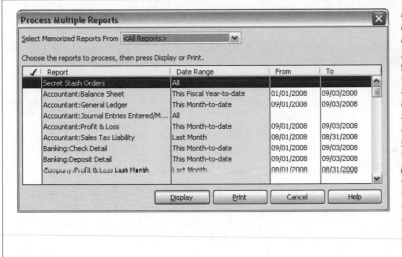

Figure 21-4:
In the Select Memorized Reports From drop-down list, you can choose a memorized group of reports to have QuickBooks automatically select all the reports in that memorized group. To streamline Process Multiple Reports, create a memorized group (page 502) for each collection of reports you process and call it something like EndofMonth or EndofQuarter. Then, in the Process Multiple Reports dialog box, you can select the entry for the memorized group of reports and print them all at once.

Here are the three ways you can create files for reports and the differences between them:

- **Print to file.** In a report window, click Print to open the Print Reports dialog box. Just below the Printer option are the File option and a drop-down list, which includes "ASCII text file", "Comma delimited file", and "Tab delimited file". After you choose the type of file and then click Print, QuickBooks opens the Create Disk File dialog box, where you can specify the filename and where you want to save the file.

   The ASCII text file format produces a text file that *looks* like the report, but it uses different fonts and uses space characters to position values in columns. This type of file isn't suitable for importing into spreadsheets or other programs, but you can use it to store an electronic version of your report.

Note: If you plan to import the information into another program, use a tab- or comma-delimited file, which use tab characters or commas, respectively, to separate each value. Many programs can read files in these formats.

- **Export to spreadsheet file.** In a report window, click Export to open the Export Report dialog box. In the Export Report dialog box, if you choose to export the report to a new workbook or a worksheet in an existing Excel workbook, click Export to open the report in Excel. If you want to tell QuickBooks how you want to set up the Excel spreadsheet, click the Advanced tab, and choose settings, as shown in Figure 21-5, before you click Export.

If you choose the "a comma separated values (.csv) file" option on the Basic tab and click Export, QuickBooks opens the Create Disk File dialog box, where you can type a file name and choose a location to save the file.

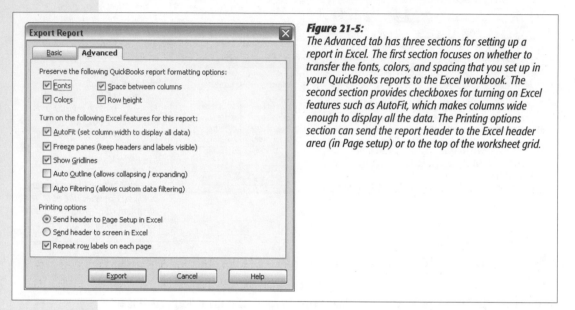

Figure 21-5:
The Advanced tab has three sections for setting up a report in Excel. The first section focuses on whether to transfer the fonts, colors, and spacing that you set up in your QuickBooks reports to the Excel workbook. The second section provides checkboxes for turning on Excel features such as AutoFit, which makes columns wide enough to display all the data. The Printing options section can send the report header to the Excel header area (in Page setup) or to the top of the worksheet grid.

- **Save as a .pdf file.** To save a report as a PDF (Acrobat) file, run the report. When the report's open, choose File → Save As PDF. In the "Save document as PDF" dialog box, navigate to the folder where you want to save the file, type the filename in the "File name" box, and then click Save. (File → Save As PDF also works for saving forms like invoices and sales receipts as PDF files. When you tell QuickBooks to email forms, the program automatically creates a .pdf file of the form and attaches it to the email message.)

- **Email an Excel file or .pdf file.** To email a report, in a report window, click Email and then choose "Send report as Excel" or "Send report as PDF".

Customizing Reports

The report window is teeming with ways to customize reports. Some tools are easy to spot like the buttons and drop-down lists at the top of a report window. But you can also drag and right-click elements in a report to make smaller changes. Here's where you go to customize a report:

- **Run custom reports from the Reports menu.** If you make it all the way through the QuickBooks report categories without finding the report you want, don't give up hope. The Reports menu includes two entries for building custom reports from scratch. Choose Custom Summary Report to build a report that displays subtotals by some kind of category. For instance, you could customize a summary report to create an income statement for all customers of a particular type. The Custom Transaction Detail Report lets you customize transaction reports to show exactly the fields you want to see.

As soon as you choose one of these custom reports, QuickBooks opens both the report window and the Modify Report dialog box—because a custom report needs *some* kind of customization. You can set up the contents and appearance of the report any way you want, as shown in Figure 21-6. For a custom transaction report, the Modify Report dialog box includes a list of fields that you can turn on and off, as well as checkboxes for specifying how you want to sort and total the results.

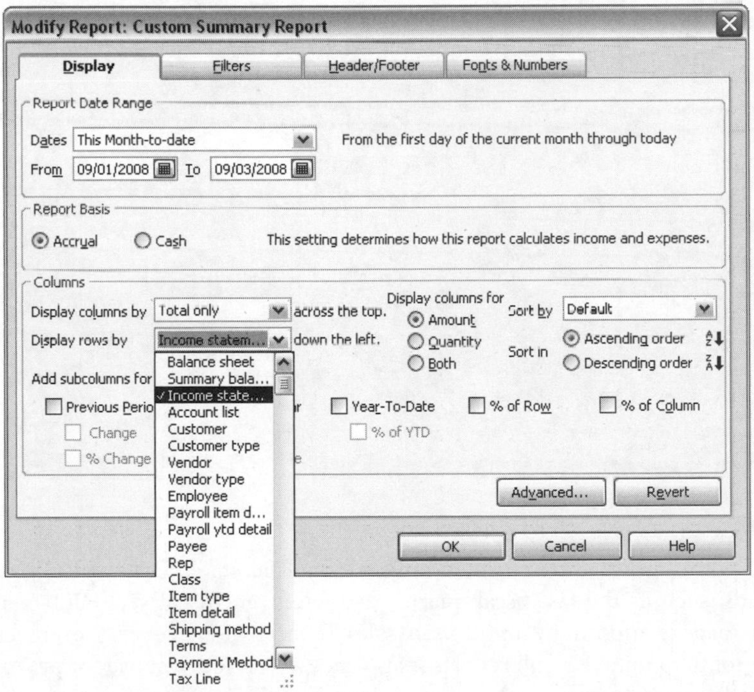

Figure 21-6:
In addition to date ranges, filters, and other customizations (page 508), you can control what QuickBooks displays in the rows and columns of a custom report. The entries in the "Display columns by" and "Display rows by" drop-down lists are the same, so you can set up a report to show your data across or down. A report that uses the same category for both columns and rows doesn't make any sense, so be sure to choose different entries for columns and rows. The Modify Report dialog box for custom reports also includes checkboxes for comparing values to previous periods as well as showing dollar and percentage differences, like budget versus actual reports do.

- **Report window button bar.** Across the top of the report window, the button bar includes the Modify Report button, which opens the all-powerful customization tool—the Modify Report dialog box. The button bar includes other handy customization buttons like Hide Header and Collapse, discussed in the box below.

- **Report window tool bar.** Below the button bar is a customization toolbar, where you can choose the date range, the columns to display, and which column to use for sorting the report's contents.

- **Report window.** Hidden within the report itself are a few customization features. For example, by right-clicking text in a report, you can format its appearance. Dragging the small diamonds between columns changes the column width and, for detailed reports, you can drag columns to new locations.

Read on to learn about all the techniques available for making a report exactly what you want.

FREQUENTLY ASKED QUESTION

Viewing More Report on Your Screen

How can I see more of a report on my screen?

If your computer monitor is a closer relative to your mobile phone than to your widescreen TV, you can use several techniques to stuff more of the report onto your monitor:

- **Hide Header.** While you're working on a report, you don't need the report header to tell you which type of report you're using, your company's name, or the date range. In the report window button bar, click Hide Header to hide the report header and display more report content. The printed report that you send to others still includes the header. To redisplay the hidden header, in the button bar, click Show Header.

- **Collapse.** If the report window button bar has a Collapse button, you can get a high-level view of a report by hiding subaccounts, the individual jobs for your customers, and subclasses. QuickBooks totals the results for the subaccounts, jobs, or subclasses under the main account, customer, or class, respectively. Unlike the Hide Header button, Collapse affects the onscreen view *and* your printed report. To redisplay the collapsed entries, click Expand.

Date Ranges

Different reports call for different date ranges. Financial statements typically use fiscal periods, such as the last fiscal quarter or the current fiscal year. But many companies manage month by month, so sales reports often cover the current month or month to date. Payroll reports span whatever period you use for payroll, whether that's one week, two weeks, or a calendar month. And tax reports depend on the tax periods required by the tax agencies you answer to.

The best place to choose the date range depends how much report modification you have in mind:

- **If the date range is the only thing you want to change**, the report window toolbar is the way to go. In the Dates drop-down list, choose the preset date range you want, or, in the From and To boxes, pick the starting date and ending date for the report, respectively.

- **If you plan to change more than the date**, click Modify Report instead. In the Modify Reports dialog box, the Report Date Range section includes the same date-setting features as the report window toolbar—as well as several additional tabs and sections for every other type of customization.

QuickBooks has two dozen preset date ranges that work based on today's date. For example, if it's June 15, 2010 and your company uses the calendar year as its fiscal year, This Fiscal Year represents January 1 through December 31, 2010, but Today is simply 6/15/2010. And, if none of these date ranges do what you want, in the report window toolbar, you can set specific start and end dates in the From and To boxes.

The preset date ranges are numerous because they mix and match several types of date ranges.

- **Durations.** Some preset periods represent durations, such as Week, Month, Fiscal Quarter, Fiscal Year, Tax Quarter, and Tax Year. At the extremes, you can pick All to encompass every date in your company file, or Today, which includes only today.

- **This, Last, and Next.** For each duration, you can choose the current period (such as This Fiscal Quarter), the previous period (Last Fiscal Quarter), or the next period in the future (Next Fiscal Quarter).

- **Full and to-date.** You can also pick between a full period and the period up to today's date. For example, on June 15, "This Month" covers June 1 through June 30. "This Month-to-date" represents June 1 through June 15.

Note: QuickBooks includes one additional choice, Next Four Weeks, which many businesses use when checking cash flow.

Subtotals

Many of QuickBooks' built-in reports calculate subtotals. For instance, Profit & Loss summary reports include subtotals by income, cost of goods sold, expenses, and so on. Sales reports by customer subtotal the sales for all the jobs you do for a customer.

When you create a detailed report, such as "Sales by Customer Detail", the report shows every transaction for that report, and you can subtotal the results in any way that makes sense for that type of report, as shown in Figure 21-7.

Depending on the report you pick, some choices in the "Total by" drop-down list are more appropriate than others. For example, you might decide to subtotal a sales report by Customer Type, Rep, or the Account list to see which types of customer provide the most business, which sales rep makes the most sales, or which income account pulls in the most money. Subtotaling a sales report by Workman's Comp Code doesn't make any sense—and QuickBooks isn't subtle about saying so: The report displays a zero balance and no rows of data.

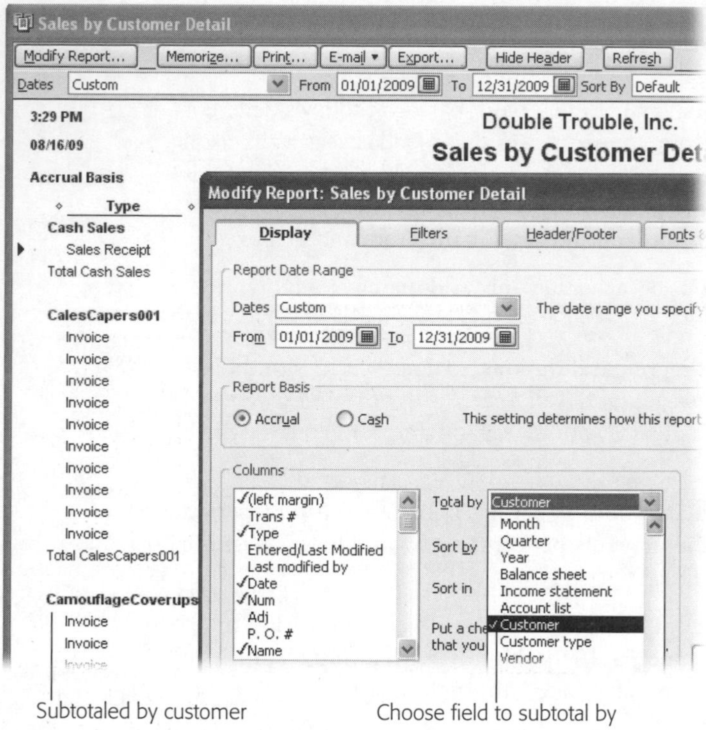

Figure 21-7:
When you run a report with transaction details, QuickBooks picks a category for subtotals. For example, the "Sales by Customer Detail" report starts with sales subtotaled by customer. To change the subtotal category, in the report window, click Modify Report, and in the "Total by" box, choose another field, like Class or "Customer type".

Subtotaled by customer   Choose field to subtotal by

Tip: When a selection in the "Total by" drop-down list empties your report, choosing a different field might *not* bring back your report's contents. Close the report by clicking the report window's Close button (the X button on the right side of the window title bar). In the Memorize Report box that QuickBooks displays, be sure to click No or you'll memorize an empty report. Then run the report anew by choosing it from the appropriate category within the Reports menu.

Customizing the Columns in Reports

Some reports start with only one column, but they don't have to stay that way. Depending on the type of report, you can change the columns that appear in several ways like showing columns for each time period or choosing fields to display in separate columns. Then, if you find that your appetite for columns is larger than your computer screen, you can remove, resize, and reorder the columns.

Adding and removing columns in summary reports

As you manage your business, you'll want to see results for different date ranges in the reports you generate. For example, during a year, you might create a Profit & Loss report to show your financial status by month, for each fiscal quarter, and for the entire year. If the report window toolbar includes a Columns drop-down list (which it does for summary-type reports), choosing an entry there is the quickest way to change the categories that columns represent (see Figure 21-8). You can make the same choices in the Modify Report dialog box using the "Display columns by" drop-down list.

The Modify Report dialog box provides different comparison checkboxes for each type of report. For example, when you click Modify Report for a Profit & Loss report, you'll find additional checkboxes to compare results to the previous period, previous year, or the year to date, *and* to show dollar and percentage comparisons. If you want to focus on the percentage difference between budget and actual values, then turn off the "$ Difference" checkbox.

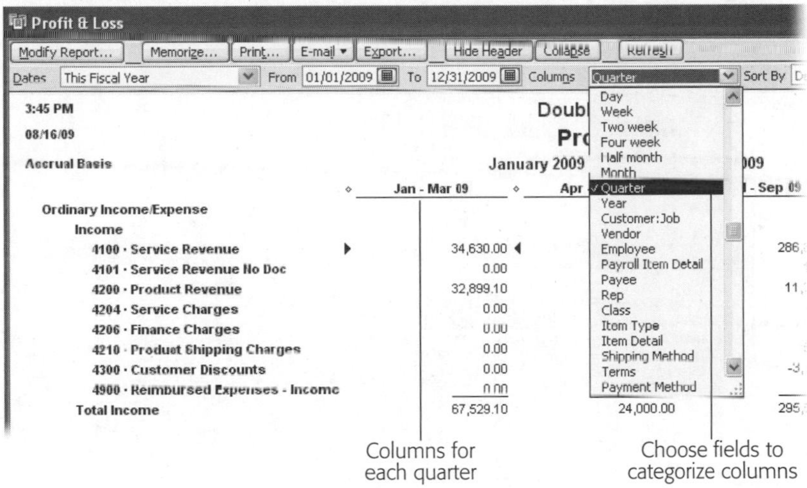

Figure 21-8:
In the report window toolbar, the Columns drop-down list sets the categories for the columns in your report—basically, subtotaling by column. When you choose Quarter, the report changes from a single year-long total to columns that subtotal each fiscal quarter (as shown here). In the Columns drop-down list, choose another type of category like Class or Customer:Job to slice results up differently. Choosing Class makes QuickBooks include a column for each class you use.

The Profit & Loss Modify Report dialog box even includes checkboxes for "% of Column", "% of Row", "% of Income", and "% of Expense". If you generate a Profit & Loss report by quarter and turn on the "% of Row" checkbox, the report shows each quarter's performance as a percentage of the full year's results.

Adding or removing columns in detail reports

Reports that show transaction details, such as Profit & Loss Detail or Inventory Valuation Detail, use columns for data fields like Name or Memo. To change the columns that appear in a detail report, in the report window, click Modify Report, and then choose the columns you want to add or remove, as shown in Figure 21-9.

Resizing and moving columns

Some columns seem to use more room than they need, while others truncate their contents. Figure 21-10 shows you how to resize columns or rearrange the order in which they appear.

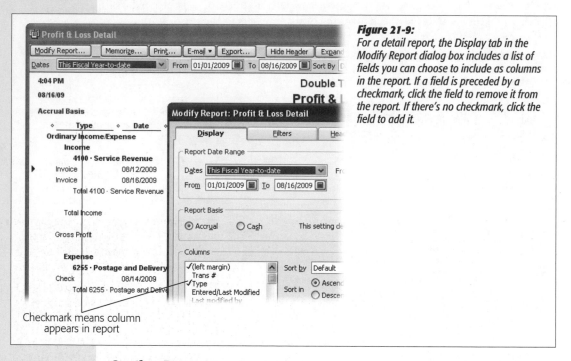

Checkmark means column appears in report

Figure 21-9:
For a detail report, the Display tab in the Modify Report dialog box includes a list of fields you can choose to include as columns in the report. If a field is preceded by a checkmark, click the field to remove it from the report. If there's no checkmark, click the field to add it.

Sorting Reports

QuickBooks' built-in reports come pre-sorted, but the order is rarely obvious. When you first generate a report, the Sort By box is set to Default, which means different things for different reports. For example, if you create a "Sales by Customer Detail" report, QuickBooks groups the transactions by customer, but it sorts the transactions for each customer from earliest to most recent. (Unlike Excel, QuickBooks sorts by only one field at a time.)

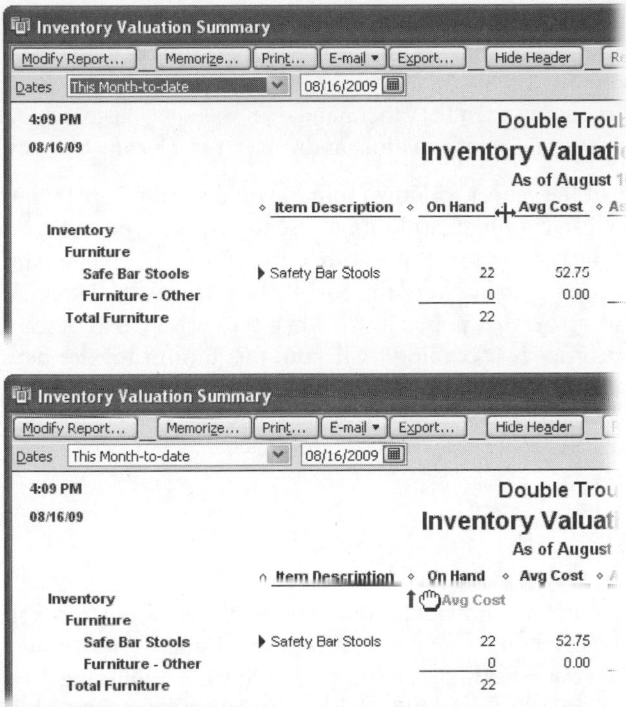

Figure 21-10:
Top: Any report that has more than one column also has a small diamond between each column heading. If you mouse over the diamond, it turns into a two-headed arrow. Drag to the right to make the column wider, or to the left to make the column narrower. A Resize Columns dialog box asks if you want to set all the columns to the same size. Click Yes to resize all the columns. Click No to resize only the one.

Bottom: In detail and list reports, when you position the mouse pointer over a column heading, it turns into a hand icon to indicate that you can move the column to another location. As you drag, the pointer shows both the hand icon and the name of the column. And, when you get close to the left side of a column, a red arrow appears to show where the program will move the column if you release the mouse button (shown here). Drag the diamond out of the window to remove the column from the report.

Fitting More Report onto Each Page

When a report is rife with columns, it's hard to fit everything onto a single piece of paper. QuickBooks automatically prints the columns that don't fit on additional pages, but reports that span multiple pages cause paper rustling and lots of grumbling. Try these approaches for keeping your report to one page:

- Before you click Print, reduce the width of the columns. In the report window, drag the diamond to the right of a column heading to make the column narrower (or wider), as shown in Figure 21-10.

- In the Print Reports dialog box (in a report window, click Print), turn on the "Fit report to page(s) wide" checkbox and, in the number box, type *1*.

- In the Print Reports dialog box, choose the Landscape option for page orientation. When a report almost fits on an 8 1/2"×11" sheet of paper, switching to landscape orientation should do the trick.

- Use legal-size paper (8 1/2"×14") if your printer can handle it.

The fields you can use to sort depend on the report. For the "Sales by Customer Summary" report, you can choose from only two columns to sort by. The Sort By box includes Default and Total. Default sorts the report by customer name in alphabetical order. Total sorts the report by the total sales for each customer, from the smallest to largest dollar amount. On the other hand, the "Sales by Customer Detail" report includes several columns of information, and you can sort by any of them.

If a report is sortable, in the report window toolbar, you'll see the Sort By box. In the Sort By drop-down list, choose the column to use to sort the report. As soon as you change the Sort By box to something other than Default, the Ascending/Descending button appears to the right of the Sort By box. (It has the letters A and Z on the left and a blue arrow that points down when the sort order is descending and up when the sort order is ascending.) Clicking this button toggles between sorting in ascending and descending order.

Note: The Modify Report dialog box also includes a Sort By drop-down list, but option buttons differentiate between Ascending and Descending order.

Filtering Reports

Detail reports (the ones that list individual transactions) usually show more information than you want. For example, a "Purchases by Item Detail" report could run page after page, listing your weekly purchases of Turtle Chow. Filtering a report removes transactions that don't meet your criteria, so you can home in on just the Turtle Chow purchases from Myrtle's Turtle Mart.

In QuickBooks, you can apply as many filters as you want at the same time. Each filter adds one more test that a transaction has to pass to appear in your report. For example, when you set the date range for a report, what you're really doing is adding a filter that restricts transactions to the ones that happened between the starting and ending dates. Then, if you want to find the sales for only your corporate customers, you can add a filter based on the Customer Type field.

QuickBooks provides dozens of filters, from the most common, such as dates, items, and transaction types, to the less useful, such as Workmen's Comp Codes and FOB (that's "free on board," discussed on page 579).

Built-in reports already have filters, but you can customize a built-in report by adding extra filters or editing or removing the existing filters. Here are the steps:

1. **In the report window, click Modify Report and then, in the Modify Report dialog box, click the Filters tab. In the Choose Filter list, choose the field you want to filter by.**

   Depending on the field you choose as a filter, QuickBooks provides different criteria, one example of which is shown in Figure 21-11.

2. **Using the drop-down lists or options that appear, specify the filter criteria you want to apply.**

   For instance, if you filter by account, in the Account drop-down list, you can choose a category such as "All bank accounts", or you can choose "Selected accounts", and then click each one you want to include. Or you can click a single account. QuickBooks adds the filter to the list of Current Filter Choices.

3. **To remove a filter, in the Current Filter Choices list, select the filter, and then click Remove Selected Filter.**

   QuickBooks removes the filter from the list.

4. **To edit a filter, in the Current Filter Choices box, select the filter you want to change. In the Choose Filter section, make the changes you want.**

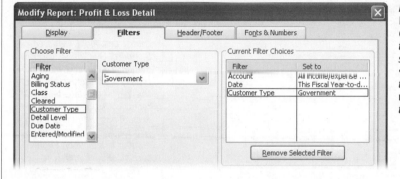

Figure 21-11:
When you choose a field in the Choose Filter list, the criteria for that field appear. If you're not sure what a field and its criteria settings do, click "Tell me more" to open the QuickBooks Help window to the topic about that filter.

Report Headers and Footers

You don't have complete control over what appears in report headers and footers, but you can choose from several fields common to all of them. For example, fields like Company Name, Report Title, and Date Prepared are options for a header, and page number is one option for footers. To change the header and footer contents for the report you're working on, in the Modify Report dialog box, click the Header/Footer tab.

Note: To set standards for all report headers and footers, open Report preferences (page 576) and then set the fields you want.

QuickBooks pulls data from your company file to automatically fill in the header and footer text boxes. For example, if you use a built-in "Sales by Customer Detail" report, the program fills in the Report Title box with—you guessed it— "Sales by Customer Detail". If you have a more eloquent title for the report, type it in the box.

The Show Footer Information section provides the Extra Footer Line box for typing whatever you want. The text appears in the bottom-left corner of the report page. This text isn't associated with any field in QuickBooks, so it's blank unless you type something.

The last checkbox in both the Show Header Information and Show Footer Information sections controls the pages on which the headers and footers appear. To conserve paper, turn off the "Print header on pages after first page" checkbox so QuickBooks includes the header on the first page only. If you want to omit the page number on the first page, turn off the "Print footer on first page" checkbox.

The right side of the Header/Footer tab is the Page Layout section, which lets you position header and footer fields to a very limited extent, as shown in Figure 21-12.

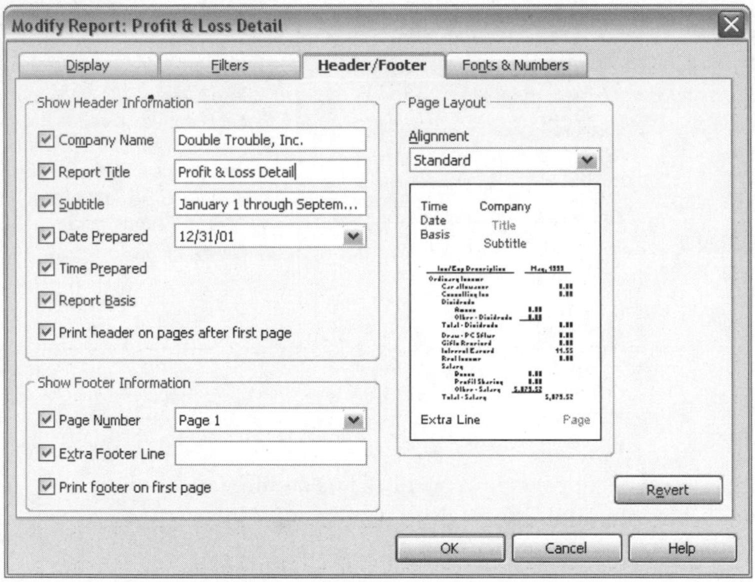

Figure 21-12:
If you want to realign the header and footer contents, in the Alignment drop-down list, choose Left, Right, Centered, or Standard. QuickBooks chooses Standard automatically, which centers the Company name and title; places the date, time, and report basis (Cash basis or Accrual basis) on the left; and puts the extra line and page number in the left and right corners of the footer.

Fonts and Numbers

The fonts you use or the way you display numbers doesn't change the underlying financial message, but an attractive and easy-to-read report can make a good impression. Just like the fields that appear in the header and footer, you can set QuickBooks' preferences to assign the same font and number formats for all your reports.

On the other hand, changing fonts directly in a report is quick, and has the added advantage of letting you see exactly what the report looks like with the new formatting, as Figure 21-13 shows.

Right-click text to format that type of text

If you already have the Modify Report dialog box open, click the Fonts & Numbers tab. The Fonts section on the left side of the tab lists the different text elements in your report, such as Column Labels, Company Name, and Transactions. To change a font, select a text element and click Change Font, which opens the same dialog box you get when you right-click the element in the report.

The right side of the Fonts & Numbers tab has options for changing the appearance of numbers. Negative numbers are usually a curse in the financial world, so accountants use several methods to make them stand out. If you're not sure which style of negative number you like, choose an option and check the number in the Example area. In QuickBooks, you can choose among three ways to show negative numbers:

- **Normally.** This option shows negative numbers preceded by a minus sign, like −1200.00.

- **In Parentheses.** This option places negative numbers within parentheses without a minus sign, for example, (1200).

- **With a Trailing Minus.** This option places the minus sign after the number: 1200−.

Tip: If you use a color printer or display reports on your computer screen, make negative numbers even harder to ignore by turning on the In Bright Red checkbox.

To make big numbers easier to read, in the Show All Numbers section, turn on the "Divided by 1000" checkbox. This removes one trio of zeros from numbers, so that $350,000,000 shows up as $350,000 in a report. And, if a report tends to contain mostly zero values, you can keep the report lean by turning on the "Except zero amounts" checkbox. Turn on the Without Cents checkbox to show only whole dollars.

Memorizing Reports

If you take the time to customize a report to look just the way you want, it'd be silly to jump through those same hoops every time you run the report. By memorizing your modified reports, you can run them again and again with all your customizations just by choosing Reports → Memorized Reports, and then picking the report's name on the appropriate submenu.

When you memorize a report, QuickBooks remembers the settings—like date range and filter criteria—but not the data itself. So if you memorize a report whose date range is set to This Month, the report shows the results for June when you run the report in June, but shows results for December when you run the report in December.

Here's how you memorize a report you've customized:

1. **Review the report to make sure it has the information and formatting you want.**

   If you notice later that you missed a setting, you can make that change and memorize the report again.

2. **In the report window, click Memorize.**

   QuickBooks opens the Memorize Report dialog box, which is small and to the point. If you're memorizing a standard report, the dialog box contains a Name box and a checkbox for choosing a memorized report group. If you're rememorizing an existing memorized report, the dialog box contains Replace, New, and Cancel buttons. Click Replace to rememorize the existing report with the new settings. Click New to create a new memorized report from the current one.

3. **In the Name box, type a name that indicates what the report shows, like *Deadbeat Payees*.**

4. **If you want to save the report in a special group, turn on the "Save in Memorized Report Group" checkbox.**

   You can then choose the group. QuickBooks comes with several built-in groups like Accountant, Company, and Customers, which appear on the Memorized Reports submenu, and shown in Figure 21-14. But you can create your own groups as the box on page 502 explains.

5. **Click OK to memorize the report.**

Voilà—you're done. If you're going to use the report over and over, consider adding it to the Favorites menu or to the QuickBooks icon bar (page 609), you can run the report by choosing it from the Favorites menu or clicking its icon, respectively.

Tip: The Memorized Report List window comes in handy if you want to edit or delete reports. Choose Reports → Memorized Reports → Memorized Reports List. In the window, select the report you want to work on and then click Memorized Report at the bottom of the window. On the drop-down menu, choose Edit to change the report name or the group where it's memorized. Choose Delete Memorized Report to obliterate it from the list.

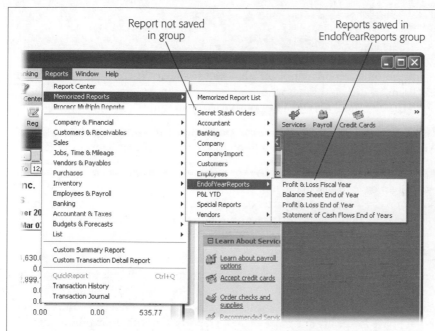

Figure 21-14:
The Memorized Reports submenu displays QuickBooks' built-in report groups and any report groups that you create. To choose a report from a group, hove the pointer over the group, and then choose the report you want to run. If you don't memorize a report to a group, the report appears above the groups on the submenu, like the Secret Stash Orders report, shown here.

Swapping Reports Between Company Files

Suppose you're one of several business owners who meet to share ideas. Some of your colleagues rave about the QuickBooks reports they've customized, and you'd like to use the reports they've created. If they're willing to share their ideas, you can swap reports by trading report template files.

Report templates contain the layouts, filters, and formatting for memorized reports. Someone can export a memorized report as a report template, and someone else can import that file to save the report in a different company file. For example, if your accountant likes to see information in very specific ways, she can give you a report template file so you can produce the reports she wants to see.

The Memorized Group Doesn't Exist

In the Memorize Report dialog box, search all you want, but you won't find a way to create a new memorized group. In fact, you have to create a memorized group *before* you can add a memorized report to that group.

Unfortunately, QuickBooks doesn't make it easy to find the command for creating a memorized group. Here's the secret:

1. Choose Reports → Memorized Reports → Memorized Report List. QuickBooks opens the Memorized Report List window, which lists memorized groups and the reports they contain.

2. At the bottom of the window, click Memorized Report and then choose New Group.

3. In the New Memorized Report Group dialog box, find the Name box, and then type the group name. Click OK.

Now, when you memorize a report, the new group appears in the "Save in Memorized Report Group" drop-down list.

Most of the time, report templates play well between different QuickBooks editions (Premier, Pro, and Enterprise) and from version to version (2008, 2009, and so on). However, here are a couple points to keep in mind:

• If you use QuickBooks Pro, you can only import templates that others create. You need QuickBooks Premier edition to *export* report templates.

• QuickBooks patches can affect the compatibility between versions. In that case, you might have to install the most recent QuickBooks update if you want to use someone else's report templates. (QuickBooks displays a warning if an update or version incompatibility exists with a report template you try to import.)

Exporting a Report

Whether you export one report or an entire group, QuickBooks stores the report settings in a single file with a .qbr file extension (for "QuickBooks report"). Because report templates are meant to move between QuickBooks company files, you don't have to specify any more than the reports you want to export and the file to which you want to export them:

1. **Choose Reports → Memorized Reports → Memorized Report List.**

   QuickBooks opens the Memorized Report List window.

2. **Select the report or memorized group that you want to export.**

   For example, if your customized reports are all memorized in the Special Reports memorized group, select Special Reports.

Note: In the Memorized Report List, you can select only a single report or a single group. Ctrl+clicking and Shift+clicking don't select several individual reports.

3. **Click Memorized Report, and then choose Export Template.**

QuickBooks opens the "Specify Filename for Export" dialog box, which is nothing more than a Save As dialog box that automatically sets the file type to QuickBooks Report Files (*.QBR). The program also automatically applies the report or group name as the name in the "File name" box. If you want to use a different name, say to add the date you exported the reports, in the "File name" box, type the new name.

4. **Navigate to the folder where you want to save the template.**

For example, your folder for QuickBooks export files.

5. **Click Save.**

QuickBooks saves the settings for the report or reports to the file. The next section tells you how to *import* a report template.

Note: QuickBooks won't export memorized reports with filters that reference an account, customer, or other entry specific to your company file, because those report filters won't work in a company file that doesn't contain that account, customer, or entry.

Importing Report Templates

Importing reports from a template file is even easier than exporting reports. In the Memorized Report List window (choose Reports → Memorized Reports → Memorized Report List), click Memorized Report, and then choose Import Template. QuickBooks opens the Select File to Import dialog box with the "Files of type" box set to "QuickBooks Reports Files (*.QBR)". All you have to do is navigate to the folder that contains the report template file and double-click the filename (or select the filename and then click Open).

Note: If you try to import a report or group with the same name as a report or group already in your company file, QuickBooks displays a warning and recommends that you change the name of the report or group that you're importing. Click OK and remember to change that name before you save the imported report or group.

Depending on whether you're importing one report or a group, QuickBooks opens a different dialog box:

- **Single report.** QuickBooks opens the Memorize Report dialog box. As you would if you were memorizing a custom report of your own design, in the Name box, type the name you want for the report, and if you wish, choose a Memorized Report Group.

- **Report group.** When you import a report group, the program opens the Import Memorized Reports Group With Name dialog box. QuickBooks fills in the Name box with the group name from the original company file, but you can type a different name. When you click OK, the program memorizes all the imported reports with their original names in the new group in your company file.

Online Banking Services

In the 20th century, you had to wait until your bank statement arrived (by snail mail) to find out what your account balances were and which transactions had cleared. But in the brave new world of online banking, you can view those balances and transactions any time, and even download them into your company file.

By synchronizing your real bank accounts with the bank accounts in QuickBooks, you'll always know how much cash you have on hand. Before repaying your aunt the start-up money she loaned you, you can hop online and check your balance—and avoid an embarrassing family blowout by giving her a check that bounces.

Besides managing your cash flow, online banking services are much more convenient than the old methods. Although you have a lot of transaction information in your account register already (from receiving payments against invoices or making payments to your vendors), matching these transactions to the ones you download from the bank tells you how much money you have in the bank—and whether someone is helping themselves to the money in your account without your permission. Or you can transfer money between your money market account and the checking account when you find yourself awake at two in the morning.

If you use online billing, you can pay bills without having to write checks, lick stamps, or walk to the mailbox. After you submit payment transactions online, the billing service either transfers funds from your bank account to the vendors or generates and mails paper checks. Online billing also lets you set up recurring bills so you can go about your business without worrying about missing a payment.

All this convenience requires some setup. QuickBooks needs to know how to connect to your bank, and your bank needs to know that you want to use online services. This chapter explains how to apply for and set up online services. With your accounts set up and your online services activated, you'll learn how to download transactions from your bank and make online payments. If you enter transactions in QuickBooks, you'll learn about matching them with the ones you download—and correcting any discrepancies.

Note: QuickBooks' Merchant Services and Billing Solutions transmit deposits and payments electronically. To find out where to learn about and sign up for these services, see the box on page 526.

Setting Up Your Internet Connection

QuickBooks uses an Internet connection for more than online banking, so chances are you've already told the program how you get online. If not, start by choosing Help → Internet Connection Setup. QuickBooks opens the Internet Connection Setup wizard. The first screen has three options, which cover the three possibilities for the state of your Internet access, as shown in Figure 22-1.

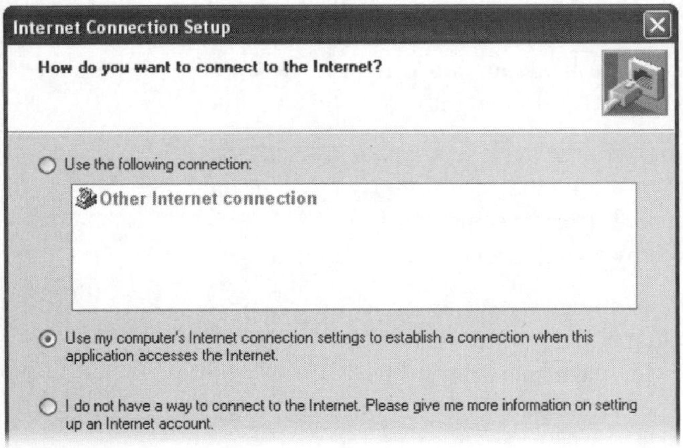

Figure 22-1:
If you see telephone icons in the "Use the following connection" box, you know that they're dial-up connections. If you dial into the Internet through your Internet Service Provider, select this option, click the connection you want to use, and then click Done. For Internet connections that are always available, including a company network, broadband, or cable, select "Use my computer's Internet connection settings to establish a connection when this application accesses the Internet." Click Next to review the connection that QuickBooks found, and then click Done.

Note: In addition to online banking, QuickBooks connects to the Internet to update your version of QuickBooks, access support and other information on the Intuit website, and run any of QuickBooks' Add-On Services (page 605).

If you don't have Internet access, don't bother choosing the third option. The additional information it promises doesn't give you anything concrete. Instead, click Cancel. Do your own homework to find an Internet Service Provider and get Internet service. When you have a connection, return to this wizard and choose the appropriate option.

When Connections Don't Appear

The dial-up connections you've configured for your computer *outside* of QuickBooks should appear in the "Use the following connection" box. If your dial-up connection isn't listed, click Cancel to close the Internet Connection Setup wizard.

Use your dial-up connection to access the Internet as if you were planning to check email. While the connection is running, reopen the Internet Connection Setup wizard, which

should now list your connection. Choose the connection, and then click Done.

If QuickBooks doesn't recognize your dial-up connection no matter what you do, don't panic. Choose the "Use my computer's Internet connection settings…" option. Before you perform any task in QuickBooks that requires Internet access, be sure to dial into the Internet outside of the program.

Setting Up Your Accounts for Online Services

Connecting your bank accounts to your accounts in QuickBooks is a lot like running a dating service: You have to prepare each participant for the relationship and then get them together.

The services you can subscribe to and the price you pay depends on your financial institution, but the services fall into one of these three categories:

- **Online account access.** This service is often free. Your bank won't admit it, but letting you check your account balance and transaction status online is cheaper than having you chat on the phone with customer service representatives.

- **Online credit card access.** You can download credit card transactions as you do checking transactions, as long as you set up your credit card in QuickBooks as a liability account (page 385) and enter individual credit card charges. Setting up a credit card as a vendor and entering only the monthly bill payment won't work.

- **Online bill paying.** This service usually comes with a fee, which is often a good deal when you consider the price of stamps and printed checks.

Note: QuickBooks' online banking works only with U.S. dollar–based accounts. If you have a bank account that uses a foreign currency, you have to handle your transactions the old-fashioned way.

Applying for Online Services

The first step in linking QuickBooks to your bank accounts is to apply for online banking services with your financial institution. If you use more than one bank, you have to apply to each one separately. If you've already started the application ball rolling, you can skip this section. If you haven't, QuickBooks helps you apply for the services your bank offers.

Choose Banking → Online Banking → Participating Financial Institutions. Peruse the Financial Institution Directory to find your bank and apply for its online services, as shown in Figure 22-2. In the Online Financial Services section, click one of the four buttons to limit the list to institutions providing that service. QuickBooks automatically selects "Any services," so you see every financial institution that the program works with. Scroll through the directory to find your financial institution. If your financial institution doesn't off the online services you want, check out Intuit's online banking services, described in the box below.

Figure 22-2:
When you click the link for your bank, you'll see its phone number and email address, the online banking services it provides, how to connect, and any special sign-up offers it has, such as a 30-day trial. An Apply Now button appears if the bank gives you the option of an online application.

When your financial institution processes your application and sends you a confirmation and a PIN (personal identification number) or password, check that the information you received is correct, like the account number. Now you're ready to set up your account for online services.

UP TO SPEED

Using Intuit's Online Banking Services

If your bank is behind the times and doesn't have an online bill payment service or online credit card access, Intuit is happy to earn more of your business. The company provides an add-on Bill Pay Service and a Quick-Books MasterCard.

Unfortunately, the Intuit website doesn't make it easy to *find* these services, though. To learn about QuickBooks Bill Pay, go to *http://quickbooks.intuit.com/product/add_ons/bill_pay.jsp*. You can find information about the Quick-Books MasterCard at *http://quickbooks.intuit.com/product/add_ons/business_credit_card.jsp*. (Or just use your favorite search engine to find "QuickBooks Bill Pay" or "Quick-Books MasterCard.")

On the Intuit website navigation bar (*http://www.quickbooks.intuit.com*), you have to choose QuickBooks → Products & Services → All Products & Services. The page that appears has information about QuickBooks editions. At the bottom of the page, to the right of the More Products and services label, click the Learn More link. Below the "Works with QuickBooks" heading, click Learn More under the Bill Pay Services label or the Business MasterCard label.

The Intuit website includes information on other services. For example, if you're interested in letting your customers pay by credit card, click Payment Solutions (page 605) on the navigation bar. To get Intuit's help paying your employees (page 361), click Payroll.

Activating Online Services for Your QuickBooks Account

When you receive a letter from your bank confirming that your online services are ready to go, you have your customer ID and your password (or PIN). Now all you have to do is set your corresponding account in QuickBooks to use these online services. The Online Banking Setup Interview wizard walks you through the steps:

1. **Choose Banking → Online Banking → "Set Up Account for Online Services".**

   In the message box that opens, click Yes to give QuickBooks permission to close any open windows. QuickBooks launches the "Set Up Account for Online Services" wizard.

   You can also start online setup in the New Account dialog box. If you create a new account and type the account number, when you save the account, the Set Up Online Services message box asks if you want to set up online services. Click Yes if you want to set it up immediately or No to do it later. In the Edit Account dialog box, click the Online Services tab to set up the service.

2. **In the "Select your QuickBooks account" drop-down list, choose the account you want to activate, and then click Next.**

   The "Select the Financial Institution for this account" screen shown in Figure 22-3 appears.

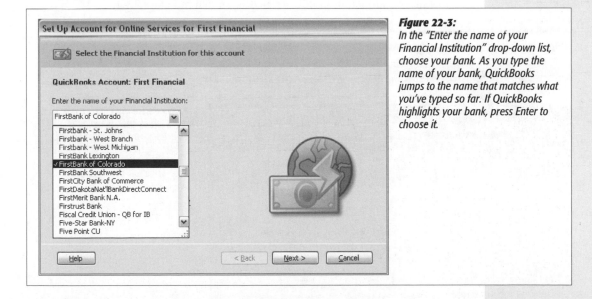

Figure 22-3:
In the "Enter the name of your Financial Institution" drop-down list, choose your bank. As you type the name of your bank, QuickBooks jumps to the name that matches what you've typed so far. If QuickBooks highlights your bank, press Enter to choose it.

3. **In the "Enter the name of your Financial Institution" drop-down list, choose your bank, and then click Next.**

   QuickBooks connects to the Internet to download info about your bank. If the program needs more information, the Account Activation Required screen appears. Select the "Yes, my account has been activated for QuickBooks online services" option, and then click Next.

4. **Fill in the Customer ID, Password, and Confirm Password boxes, and then click Sign In.**

   The Customer ID is the ID that the bank assigned to you for online services and should be on the confirmation letter from your bank.

   If you don't have your customer ID and password, click Cancel. You can repeat this process after you receive your ID and password.

5. **The next screen asks you to select the account at your financial institution. In the table, click the account you want to activate, and then click Next.**

   If you have more than one account, repeat this process to activate your other accounts at the same financial institution.

   QuickBooks and your financial institution start talking. When they're done, you'll see a screen telling you that the account is set up for online services and how many transactions it downloaded, as shown in Figure 22-4.

Figure 22-4:
The "Set Up Account for Online Services" dialog box shows how many transactions it downloaded during setup. When you click Finish, the Online Banking Center window (page 529) opens, showing the transactions you just downloaded.

6. **Click Finish.**

   That's it—you're ready to bank electronically.

An Introduction to Exchanging Data with Your Bank

Your financial institution takes the lead in controlling how QuickBooks can communicate with it. Your bank can set up this pipeline in two ways:

- **Direct connection** uses a secure Internet connection that links directly to your bank's computers. With this type of connection and a financial institution that provides the services, you can download your bank statements and transactions, transfer funds between accounts, pay bills online, and email your bank. When your financial institution uses a direct connection, you set up your fund transfers, requests for downloads, online bill payments, and emails *before* you connect.

- **WebConnect** uses a secure connection to your bank's website to download your statement information. With WebConnect, you then have to import the downloaded information into QuickBooks.

Note: Regardless of the method you use, the online balance usually isn't a true picture of your cash balance, because it doesn't show *all* transactions, such as checks you've written that the bank hasn't received.

The first step in QuickBooks online banking is exchanging data with your bank. You send any online banking items you've created, like online bill payments or transactions that have cleared at your financial institution. Connecting to your financial institution begins in the Online Banking Center (choose Banking → Online Banking → Online Banking Center), regardless of which type of connection you use.

Once you've exchanged data, QuickBooks tries to match the transactions it has with the ones you've downloaded. If it can't match some of the transactions, you step in and tell it what to do.

QuickBooks Online Banking Modes

The Online Banking Center introduced in QuickBooks 2009 had some glitches. Intuit fixed them in QuickBooks 2010, but to be on the safe side, Intuit lets you choose between the 2010- and 2008-style versions of the Online Banking Center.

Tip: You can switch between online banking modes, but you're more likely to pick the mode you prefer and stick with it. To switch modes, choose Banking → Online Banking → Change Online Baking Mode. QuickBooks opens the Preferences dialog box to the Checking section and the Company Preferences tab, so you can choose the Side-by-Side Mode or Register Mode option. When you click OK, QuickBooks closes all open windows to switch modes and discourteously doesn't reopen them when it's done.

Here's what each Online Banking Center Mode does:

- **Side-by-side mode.** The best feature of Side-by-side mode (instructions begin on page 533) is that you can match downloaded transactions to any transaction in your company file without leaving the Online Banking Center. For example, you can match a downloaded deposit to an open invoice or a paid invoice where the money is sitting in the Undeposited Funds account (page 396). Or you can simply add the downloaded transaction to QuickBooks. You can add multiple unmatched transactions to your register (something that QuickBooks 2009 online banking left out) or delete downloaded items that you've already taken care of in QuickBooks.

  Side-by-side mode also automatically creates renaming rules to rename the often inscrutable names that banks give payees. For example, if the payee for a downloaded credit card charge shows up as Conoco #123-63?#^$&*, you can edit a renaming rule so that the new name in the Payee field is, say, Conoco. From then on, QuickBooks replaces Conoco #123-63?#^$&* with Conoco.

- **Register mode.** If you thought that QuickBooks 2008's Online Banking Center was just fine, you can continue to use it. The Register mode lets you see your full account register when you're matching transactions, which is helpful if QuickBooks doesn't find a matching transaction. You can scroll through the register and correct a discrepancy that prevented the program from finding a match. In Register mode, you can create aliases to rename payees, similar to the Side-by-side renaming rules.

Note: Register mode doesn't recognize renaming rules created in Side-by-side mode, nor does side-by-side mode recognize the aliases you create in register mode.

Downloading Statements with WebConnect

If your bank communicates via WebConnect, your first steps are the same as the ones for a direct connection. In the Online Banking Center, you choose the financial institution to connect to, and then click Send/Receive Transactions (or Send/Receive for register mode). A browser window opens and displays your bank's website; use your customer ID and PIN or password to log in. On the website, click the "Download to QuickBooks" button (or one that creates a file of your transactions). Then, you can import that file (Choose Banking → Online Banking → Import Web Connect File) to load the recent transactions into your company file.

Tip: Depending on your financial institution, you don't have to go through QuickBooks to access your bank's website. Use your browser to log into the site directly. Download the file of your transactions and import it.

Creating Online Items for Direct Connections

Banks that work with direct connections can do more than those using WebConnect. Depending on which services your bank provides, you can do some or all of these tasks online:

- Receive transactions that cleared in your account

- Pay bills

- Exchange messages with your bank

- Transfer funds between accounts

You don't have to take any action to receive transactions from your accounts. QuickBooks automatically sets up a request for cleared transactions from your bank accounts every time you open the Online Banking Center. This section describes the steps in QuickBooks to set up electronic bill payments, messages you want to send to your bank, and online transfers between accounts.

Note: If you use the Online Banking Center Side-by-side mode, in the Items Ready To Send section, QuickBooks displays links (see Figure 22-5) to create online items (for the online services you've signed up for with your financial institution or Intuit).

Paying bills online

Whether you use the bill paying service that your bank provides or subscribe to QuickBooks Bill Pay service, you don't have to use any special dialog boxes to make electronic payments. Here's how you turn the three ways you make payments into electronic transactions:

- **Pay Bills.** In the Pay Bills window (page 226), in the Payment Method drop-down list, choose Online Bank Pmt.

- **Write Checks.** In the Write Checks window (page 238), turn on the Online Bank Pmt checkbox.

- **Account register window.** If you "write" checks by entering a transaction in your checking account register window (page 240), you can turn a transaction into an online payment by right-clicking it and then choosing Edit Check. When the Write Checks window opens, turn on the Online Bank Pmt checkbox and save the transaction.

When you set up a payment as an online transaction, QuickBooks adds the payments to your list of items to send. When you open the Online Banking Center window, you'll see these online bill payments in the Items Ready To Send section (Items to Send for register mode).

When you tell QuickBooks to send transactions (page 533), the program sends these electronic payments along with any of your other requests. Once the bill payment service receives your online payment information, it transfers money from your account to the vendor's account—providing the vendor accepts electronic payments. Otherwise, the bill payment service generates a paper check and mails it to the vendor.

Note: When you set your accounts up for online services, you told QuickBooks which account acts as your source of funds for the bill payment service.

Sending a message to your bank

If you have an email address for your bank, you can send messages from outside QuickBooks (that is, from your regular old email program). But when you use online banking services, your bank sends you messages that you receive in the Online Banking Center. By sending messages back through the Online Banking Center, you can see all the messages that you've exchanged (until you decide to delete them).

Choose Banking → Online Banking → Create Online Banking Message. QuickBooks opens the Online Banking Message dialog box. If you're addicted to email, you shouldn't have any trouble figuring out what to do with the following fields in the Create Online Banking Message window:

- In the "Message to" drop-down list, choose the bank you want to send a message to. QuickBooks automatically timestamps the message with the current date and time and adds your company name to the From box.

- In the Subject box, type a short but informative subject.

- If you have more than one account enabled for online services, in the Regarding Account drop-down list, choose the account.

- In the Message box, type your message or question.

- If you want to save a copy of the message, click Print before you click OK to send it.

Transferring funds between accounts

When you have two accounts at the same financial institution and they're both set up for online banking services, you can set up online funds transfers in QuickBooks.

Choose Banking → Transfer Funds as you would for a non-electronic transfer (page 393). But in the Transfer Funds dialog box, in addition to filling in the fields, be sure to turn on the Online Funds Transfer checkbox. When you save the transaction, QuickBooks adds the transfer as an item to send to your bank.

Note: Online fund transfers using QuickBooks work only with two Web-enabled accounts at the same bank. You can't transfer funds electronically using QuickBooks if the accounts are at different financial institutions. You also can't transfer funds electronically using QuickBooks if one of the accounts at your bank is set up for online services but the other isn't.

Online Banking Using Side-by-side Mode

Side-by-side mode makes it easy to see what's going on with your accounts at financial institutions. You can see online balances, downloaded transactions, and the work you have to do to match them to transactions in your company file. You can do everything to match downloaded transactions to the ones you have in QuickBooks without leaving the Online Banking Center.

Sending and Receiving

Every time you go online, QuickBooks automatically requests newly cleared transactions from your financial institution. If you've set up items to send to your bank, going online pushes those along, too. Here's what you do to send requests and receive replies in Side-by-side mode:

1. **To open the Online Banking Center, choose Banking → Online Banking → Online Banking Center.**

   The Online Banking Center opens.

2. **If you have online services with more than one bank (say, a checking account with one bank and a credit card with another), in the Financial Institution drop-down list, choose the one you want to connect to.**

   To the right of the Financial Institution heading, you'll see all the accounts you have at the institution you selected. QuickBooks automatically turns on all the Download checkboxes to grab transactions from all your accounts at that financial institution. If you don't want to download transactions for an account, turn off its checkbox.

   As Figure 22-5 shows, the Online Balance column shows your balance according to your financial institution as of the last update. The Last Update column shows the date of that last update.

   If you have any items to send to your bank (like messages you've written or online transfers you've created as described on page 532), they appear in the Items Ready To Send section. QuickBooks selects all the requests you have set up to send to your bank.

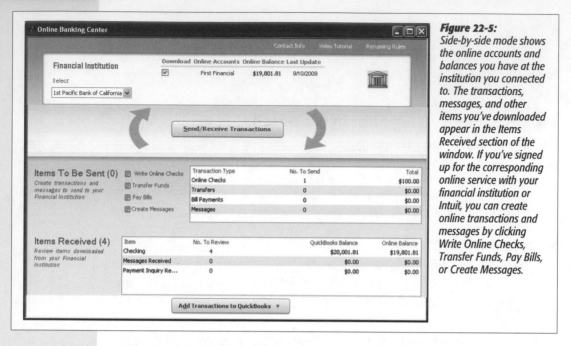

Figure 22-5:
Side-by-side mode shows the online accounts and balances you have at the institution you connected to. The transactions, messages, and other items you've downloaded appear in the Items Received section of the window. If you've signed up for the corresponding online service with your financial institution or Intuit, you can create online transactions and messages by clicking Write Online Checks, Transfer Funds, Pay Bills, or Create Messages.

3. **If you want to edit or delete any items you have to send, do that now—before you go online. Once you're connected, it's too late.**

    To edit an item like a funds transfer or bill payment you're sending, select the item in the Items Ready to Send section, and then click Edit. Make the changes you want, and then click OK. If you want to remove an item like a fund transfer you no longer need, in the Items Ready To Send section, select the item, and then click Delete.

4. **When the items you want to send are ready, click Send/Receive Transactions.**

    If you don't have any items to send, the button label says Receive Transactions.

5. **In the Access to <institution name> dialog box that appears, type your password or PIN, and then click OK.**

    You type your password or PIN so QuickBooks can communicate with your financial institution. The Online Status dialog box shows the progress QuickBooks is making communicating with your bank. When the two are done talking, the Online Transmission Summary dialog box tells you how many accounts it updated and how many transactions it downloaded.

6. **In the Online Transmission Summary dialog box, click Close.**

    The Items Received section shows the number of items received and the balances for your online accounts (see Figure 22-5).

Matching Transactions

Every time you connect to your financial institution (see page 533), QuickBooks downloads all the transactions that cleared since the last time you went online. This section describes how you match downloaded transactions using Side-by-side mode.

Note: The first time you download transactions for an online account, QuickBooks looks at transactions marked as cleared in your account register. For all subsequent downloads, the program tries to match only transactions that haven't already cleared.

After you connect, the Items Received section displays information about the transactions QuickBooks retrieved, as shown in Figure 22-5. You'll see the number of items received and your current online balances. Here's how you process the items that QuickBooks received:

1. **At the bottom of the Online Banking Center, click Add Transactions To QuickBooks and choose the account you want to work on from the drop-down menu.**

   QuickBooks opens the Add Transactions To QuickBooks window and tries to match the downloaded transactions to the ones you've already entered in QuickBooks.

   The top of the Downloaded Transactions section summarizes how many transactions the program matched on its own, how many new transactions it created, and how many transactions you have to help with. Initially, only unmatched transactions appear in the list, because those are the ones you have to work on.

2. **If you want to see matched or new transactions in the list, click the Show link to the right of the Matched or New lines.**

   In the downloaded transactions list, the status for matched transactions is set to Matched, as shown in Figure 22-6, and you don't have to do anything to them. QuickBooks automatically marks them as cleared in the bank account register (page 544).

   Transactions that the program can't match have a status of Unmatched, as you can see in Figure 22-6. The next section tells you how to handle unmatched transactions.

Note: For transactions without check numbers, QuickBooks matches a downloaded transaction with the oldest transaction of a matching amount. For example, suppose you withdrew $200 from your checking account twice last month. When you download a $200 withdrawal transaction, QuickBooks matches it to the oldest matching transaction in your register.

If QuickBooks matches every transaction, your work is done. If you open the account register (page 384) in the Cleared column, you'll see a lightning bolt for every matched transaction. If you're not so lucky, read the next section.

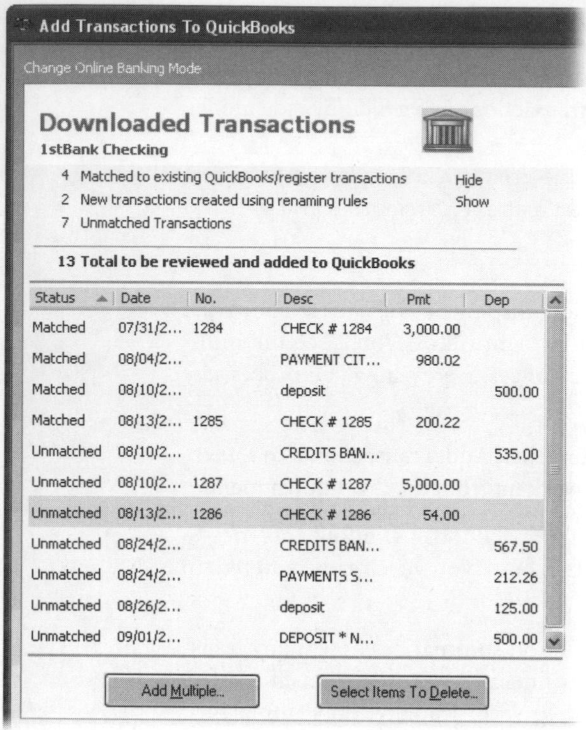

Figure 22-6:
When you click a Show link, QuickBooks displays that type of transaction in the Downloaded Transactions list and changes the link to Hide, as shown here. To display only unmatched transactions, click the Hide link to the right of the Matched line and the New line.

Note: When you reconcile an account, the mark in the Cleared column changes from the lightning bolt to a checkmark for transactions that have been reconciled.

Matching Unmatched Transactions

Unsuccessful attempts to match transactions can happen for several reasons, but the source of the problem is *almost* always a mistake or omission in your Quick-Books account register. If you forgot to record a transaction in QuickBooks before you downloaded transactions, this section tells you how to make everything match up. The box on page 542 describes other problems you might see and the steps to take to correct them.

Matching deposits

When you use the Receive Payments window to record check or credit card payments you receive, you might place the payment in your Undeposited Funds account and forget to make the deposit to your bank account using the Make Deposits window (page 354). As shown in Figure 22-7, QuickBooks can match these deposits to payments in your Undeposited Funds account or even to open invoices.

In the Downloaded Transactions list, select the unmatched deposit that you want to match (the amount is in the Dep column). The "Record a QuickBooks Deposit" pane appears on the right side of the window, as you can see in Figure 22-7. In QuickBooks, there are three ways to handle deposits. Here's what you do for each:

Note: If your bank deposit represents several checks from several customers, you can select more than one open invoice or undeposited funds entry, and add more than one item directly in the Deposit List table. Below the Deposit List, the "Difference remaining" value shows the difference between the deposit amount and the items you've selected. When the difference equals 0.00, you're ready to click "Add to QuickBooks".

- **Payments in the Undeposited Funds account.** If you used the Receive Payments window to record a customer payment you received and the money is sitting in the Undeposited Funds account (page 396), click the Undeposited Funds tab. Turn on the checkbox for the received payment that corresponds to the deposit. Click "Add to QuickBooks". If you look at your bank account register, you'll see the deposit with a lightning bolt in the Cleared cell to indicate that it's matched with a transaction downloaded from the bank.

- **Deposits for open invoices.** If you haven't recorded the received payment in QuickBooks, the money is still tied up in an open invoice, which means the money is setting in the Accounts Receivable account. To match a deposit to an open invoice, click the Open Invoices tab, shown in Figure 22-7. Turn on the checkbox for the invoice that corresponds to the deposit, and click "Add to QuickBooks".

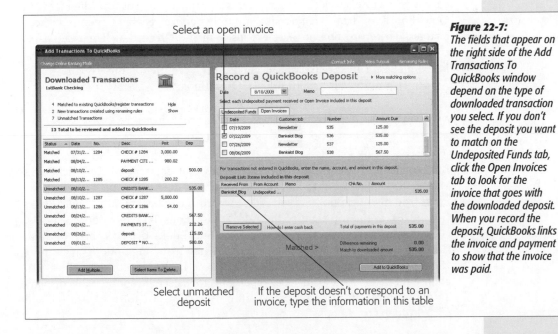

Select an open invoice

Select unmatched deposit

If the deposit doesn't correspond to an invoice, type the information in this table

Figure 22-7:
The fields that appear on the right side of the Add Transactions To QuickBooks window depend on the type of downloaded transaction you select. If you don't see the deposit you want to match on the Undeposited Funds tab, click the Open Invoices tab to look for the invoice that goes with the downloaded deposit. When you record the deposit, QuickBooks links the invoice and payment to show that the invoice was paid.

• **Other deposits.** If you receive some other type of deposit that you haven't recorded in any way in QuickBooks, an insurance claim refund, say, you can record the deposit information on the right side of the window directly in the "Deposit List: Items included in this deposit" table. In the Received From drop-down list, choose the customer or vendor who sent the money. In the account drop-down list, choose the account to which you want to assign the deposit. QuickBooks automatically fills in the Amount cell with the value from the downloaded deposit. Type a memo and check number if you want and then click "Add to QuickBooks".

Matching checks and expenses

When there's no sign of a check transaction in QuickBooks for the one you downloaded, you may have forgotten to enter the transaction (or someone's stealing from your account). Or you created a bill, but forgot to record that you paid it. Even with online banking, you don't know what your bank charges are until you download them.

In the Downloaded Transactions list, the amount of a check or payment appears in the Pmt column. A value in the No. column tells you the payment is a check. Otherwise, the payment is a bank charge or bank transaction.

In the Downloaded Transactions list, select the unmatched check or payment that you want to match. The "Record an Expense" screen appears on the right side of the window. Here's how you match checks and payments:

• **Checks or charges that aren't bill payments.** These payments include any checks you wrote, or electronic payments you made without recording a bill in QuickBooks, or bank charges like monthly service fees and bounced check charges. To record one of these expenses, in the "Record an Expense" pane, choose the name of the payee in the Payee drop-down list (or type the payee's name if it isn't in the list). Then choose the account for the expense in the Account drop-down list. Click Add To QuickBooks.

Tip: If you want to add more information about the transaction like splitting the amount between several accounts or adding a memo, click the "Show splits, memo, date, number" link.

• **Bill payments.** For downloaded transactions that correspond to QuickBooks bill payments, you need to link the payment and the bill so that the bill shows up as paid in QuickBooks. If you didn't record the bill payment in QuickBooks (page 226), at the top-right of the Add Transactions To QuickBooks window, click the "More matching options" link. QuickBooks displays three options, shown in Figure 22-8. The link changes to "Hide matching options". Select the "Select open bills to pay in QuickBooks" option. In the Vendor drop-down list, choose the vendor you paid. The "Open Bills for selected vendor" table displays all the open bills for that vendor. Turn on the checkbox for the open bill and click "Add to QuickBooks".

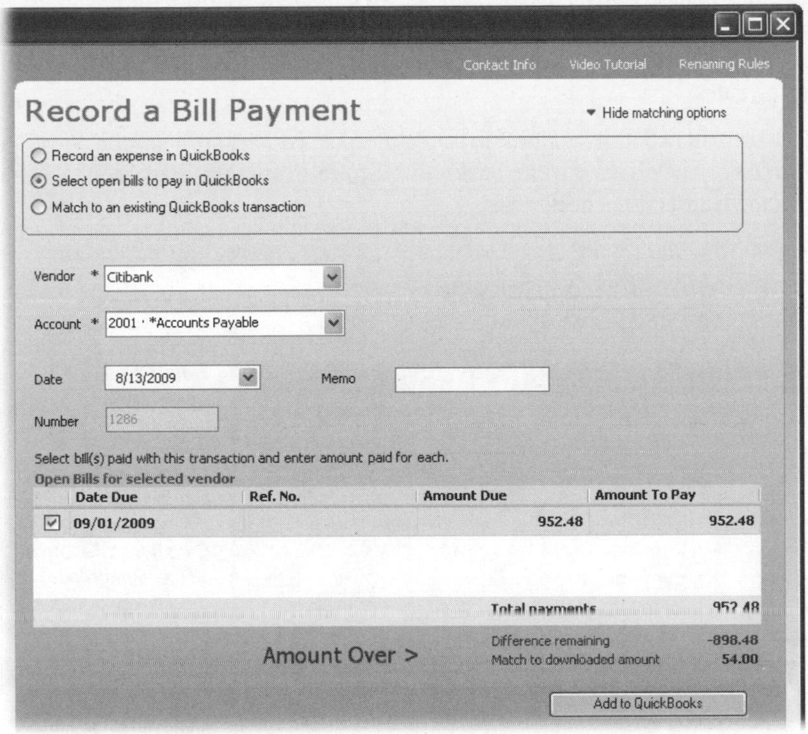

Figure 22-8:
If you wrote one check to pay several of a vendor's bills, turn on all the checkboxes for all the bills that the check covers. As you turn on checkboxes, QuickBooks updates the "Difference remaining" value to show the difference between the downloaded transaction amount and the total of the bills you selected. When "Difference remaining" equals 0.00, you can click "Add to QuickBooks" to save the match.

- **Match an expense manually.** The "Match to an existing QuickBooks transaction" option (click the "More matching options" link at top right) covers all the other bases. Say QuickBooks doesn't match an ATM withdrawal correctly. When you choose this option, QuickBooks displays the "Match to a Register Transaction" panel on the right side of the window. The values for the downloaded transaction appear in the panel. The "Unmatched transactions in QuickBooks" table shows register transactions that haven't yet been matched. For example, if you have two ATM withdrawals, you can pick the one that goes with the downloaded transaction. Then click Confirm Manual Match.

Adding Multiple Transactions

If you write only a few checks and receive a few payments each month, matching each one individually isn't too painful. But you have better things to do than match hundreds of transactions one by one. As long as you don't need to match downloaded transactions to open transactions in QuickBooks or do anything fancy like create splits, you can add multiple transactions with the Add Multiple Transactions dialog box.

In the Add Transactions To QuickBooks window, click Add Multiple. The Add Multiple Transactions to QuickBooks (Figure 22-9) opens and shows renamed, unmatched, and matched transactions. See the box on page 541 for the scoop on renaming rules.

To add unmatched transactions to QuickBooks, you just fill in the Payee and Account cells (they have a white background to indicate that they're editable) and turn on the transaction checkboxes.

When you're ready to add the transactions to QuickBooks and you've turned on all their checkboxes, click Add Selected.

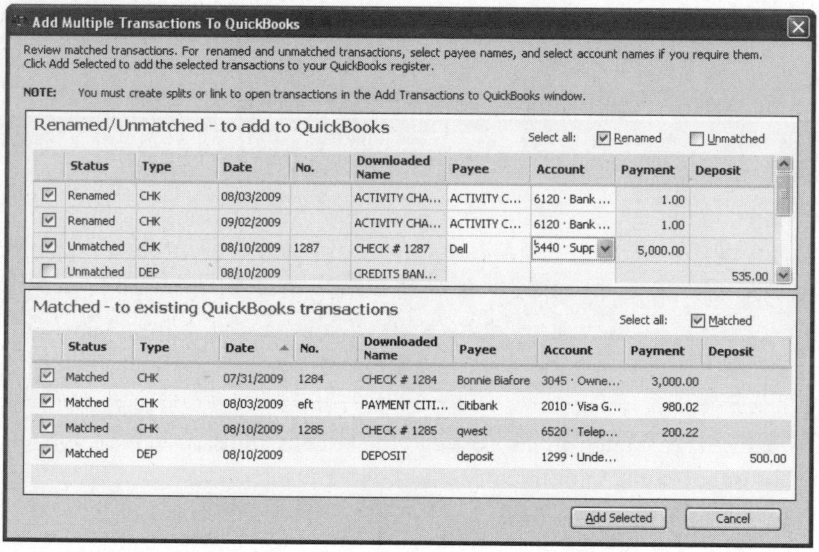

Figure 22-9:
QuickBooks automatically turns on the checkboxes for renamed and matched transactions because they're ready to add to QuickBooks. To turn on all the unmatched checkboxes, just turn on the Unmatched checkbox above the right end of the Renamed/Unmatched table. If you want to turn off all the transaction checkboxes, just turn off the appropriate "Select all" checkbox.

Deleting Downloaded Transactions

Say you've reconciled your credit card account to your statement. You go online and download transactions only to find that you've downloaded transactions you've already reconciled. You don't have to match the downloaded transactions because your account is already matched up with your bank's records, so you want to delete the downloaded transactions. In the Downloaded Transactions list, click Select Items To Delete; the Select Items To Delete dialog box opens. Here's how you can select transactions to delete:

- **Select individual transactions.** QuickBooks selects this option automatically. To select a transaction to delete, turn on its checkbox.

- **Select all downloaded transactions older than.** This option is perfect if you want to delete transactions that you've already reconciled. Type the cutoff date in the box and QuickBooks automatically turns on the checkboxes for transactions that occurred before that date.

GEM IN THE ROUGH

Renaming Downloaded Payee Names

One drawback to downloading transactions is the crazy payee names that often show up in your downloaded transactions. A gas-station credit card charge downloads with the station's ID number—*Conoco #00092372918027* or a payment to your favorite office supply store appears as *Internt PMT Have a Great Day 1429AZ#2*. You want payee names that make sense, like *Gasoline*, or are at least consistent, like *Office Supply Heaven #121*. QuickBooks' renaming rules let you replace downloaded payee names with something short, sweet, and meaningful.

QuickBooks automatically creates renaming rules whenever you change the payee name for a downloaded transaction. Problem is, the renaming rules it creates are so restrictive that they rarely help. For example, if you change the downloaded payee *Conoco #00092372918027* to *Conoco*, the renaming rule looks for the exact downloaded payee name *Conoco #00092372918027* in the future. What you want is a renaming rule that recognizes any downloaded payee containing Conoco and renames it to Conoco.

Here's how you edit a renaming rule:

1. At the top-right of the Add Transactions To QuickBooks window, click Renaming Rules.

2. In the Edit Renaming Rules dialog box, select the payee name stored in QuickBooks (Conoco in this example). On the right side of the dialog box, you'll see all the renaming rules that exist for that payee.

3. In the first drop-down list (the value is probably "Exactly matches"), choose Contains for the most flexible rule.

4. In the second box, type the value that appears in all the downloaded payee names for that vendor, Conoco in this example.

5. Click Save.

6. If you want to remove one of the existing renaming rules, click the Remove button to the right of the renaming rule boxes.

7. Repeat steps 2 through 5 to edit other renaming rules.

When the transaction checkboxes are turned on, click Delete Selected.

Note: If you're sure that the check amount you recorded is correct, change the check amount anyway. Your bank won't go back and edit that transaction. Contact your bank and work out the discrepancy. If the bank was at fault, it will issue a separate transaction to correct the error, and you can then download the corrected version.

QuickBooks can't match other types of transactions like ATM withdrawals or debit card purchases if the amounts don't match or you haven't recorded the transactions in QuickBooks.

Online Banking Using Register Mode

With Register mode, you can see your full account register, which makes it easy for you to find a matching transaction that QuickBooks doesn't recognize. You can edit transactions in the register, for example, to correct a typo that prevented the program from making a match.

Why Transactions Don't Match

If you recorded all your transactions in QuickBooks, but your downloaded transactions refuse to match up with what's in your company file, small discrepancies are probably to blame. For example, with downloaded transactions that include check numbers, QuickBooks first looks for a matching check number and, if it finds one, only then does it check the amount. The program considers check transactions matched only if both the check number and amount match. If the check already exists in QuickBooks, there are two reasons that QuickBooks can't match a check:

- **The check number in your register is wrong.** For example, if you wrote several checks at the same time, you might have entered them in QuickBooks in a different order than the paper checks you wrote out. Open the register window (in the Chart of Accounts window, double-click the name of the bank account). Find the check transaction and edit

the check number. QuickBooks might warn you about duplicate check numbers. Go ahead and use the check number. After you've edited all the check transactions, you should be back to unique check numbers.

- **The amounts on the checks don't match for some reason.** If the amounts disagree, first look at the account register to see if you typed the amount correctly, and correct it if necessary.

If transactions from the bank don't include check numbers, QuickBooks scans transactions without check numbers in your account register for matching amounts. If the program doesn't find a match, you might have forgotten to record it in the Make Deposits window (page 354) or the deposit doesn't link to a customer payment. If you work in Side-by-side mode, you can rectify these omissions as described on page 536.

Sending and Receiving

In Register mode, choose Banking → Online Banking → Online Banking Center to begin connecting to your financial institution. The Register mode Online Banking Center window is more compact than its Side-by-side sibling, as you can see in Figure 22-10.

After you send your requests, the Online Transmission Summary dialog box tells you how many transactions downloaded from your bank. Click Close. The Items Received From Financial Institution box shows the balances for your online accounts and any messages that your bank sent you.

Working with Online Items

In the Online Banking Center window (choose Banking → Online Banking → Online Banking Center), you can make changes to items to send before you go online. After you receive items from your bank, you can view them or delete them. Here's how you use the buttons in the Online Banking Center window:

- **Edit.** Before you go online, you can edit any items other than a request for a statement, for example, a funds transfer or bill payment you're sending. Select the item and click Edit. Make the changes you want and then click OK.

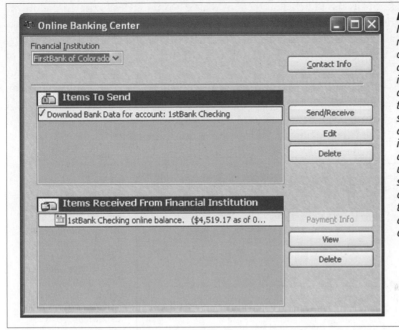

Figure 22-10:
If you have online services with more than one bank (say, your checking account with one bank and a credit card with another), in the Financial Institution drop-down list, choose one to connect to. QuickBooks automatically selects all requests (like downloading your transactions) in the Items To Send box. If you don't want to send an item, uncheck it. Click Send/Receive to send the selected requests and connect to the bank's website. In the "Access to <your bank>" dialog box, type your password or PIN, and then click OK.

Note: QuickBooks adds a request for a statement to the Items To Send list every time you open the Online Banking Center window. A statement is simply a list of the transactions that cleared in your account since the last time you retrieved information formatted in a way that QuickBooks can import.

- **Delete.** If you set up a fund transfer between accounts that you no longer need or want to remove another type of item, in the Items To Send list, select the item and then click Delete.

  You'll find that your bank is fond of sending you messages about new services or holidays. There's no reason to clutter the Items Received From Financial Institution with these messages. In the Items Received From Financial Institution box, select an item and then click the Delete button (at right).

- **View.** In the Items Received From Financial Institution box, select an item and click View to see it. When you want to match the transactions in a statement to your QuickBooks bank account transactions, select the statement and then click View.

Matching Transactions

Every time you connect to your financial institution (by clicking Send/Receive in the Online Banking Center window), QuickBooks requests a statement of all the transactions that cleared since the last time you went online. After you connect, in the Items Received From Financial Institution box, you'll see an entry for the statement QuickBooks retrieved. To view the downloaded transactions and pull them into your company file bank account, select the entry and then click View.

QuickBooks opens the Match Transactions dialog box and tries to match the down-loaded transactions to the ones you already entered in QuickBooks. If QuickBooks automatically matches transactions, the Results of Automatic Transaction Matching dialog box tells you how many. Click OK to close the dialog box. At the bottom of the Match Transactions window on the Downloaded transactions tab, the status for those transactions is set to Matched and you don't have to do anything to them. QuickBooks automatically marks them as cleared in the register. Transactions that the program can't match have a status of Unmatched, as you can see in Figure 22-11. The next section tells you how to handle unmatched transactions

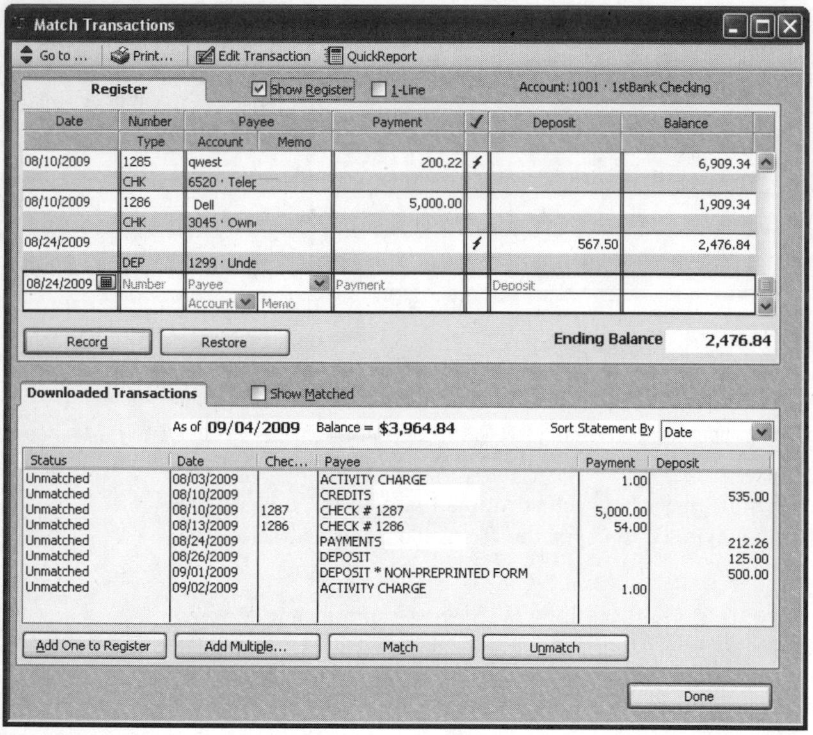

Figure 22-11:
If you dutifully enter all your transactions before you download, dozens of unmatched transactions might make you nervous. You must first turn on the Show Register checkbox (below the Match Transactions toolbar) for QuickBooks to compare the downloaded transactions to the ones in your account register.

Note: The first time you download transactions for an online account, QuickBooks looks at transactions marked as cleared in your account register. For all subsequent downloads, the program tries to match only transactions that haven't previously cleared.

If QuickBooks matches every transaction, your work is done. In the account register in the Cleared column, you'll see a lightning bolt for every matched transaction. If you're not so lucky, keep reading.

Unmatched checks

For checks that are payments for bills, you must first use the Pay Bills window to enter the transaction (page 226) so that your bills in QuickBooks show up as paid. For checks that aren't linked to bills or refunds, select the check that you didn't enter in QuickBooks and then click "Add One to Register". In the Account box, choose the account to which you want to post the expense and then click Record. This technique works for deposits that aren't linked to customer payments and bank charges.

Unmatched deposits

If transactions from the bank don't include check numbers, QuickBooks scans transactions without check numbers in your account register for matching amounts. If the program doesn't find a match, you have two options, depending on the type of transaction downloaded.

When you use Register mode, you must first record all your customer payments in QuickBooks and move deposits from the Undeposited Funds account into your bank account. If you have a deposit that doesn't link to a customer payment, you can add the transaction to the register from the Match Transactions window. In the list of downloaded transactions, select the deposit, and then click "Add One to Register". In the Account box, choose the account to post the deposit to and then click Record.

Bank charges

For charges including monthly service fees, bounced check charges, and so on, in the list of downloaded transactions, select the transaction and click "Add One to Register". In the Account box, choose the account for the charge and then click Record.

Adding Multiple Transactions

If you have several unmatched transactions that you want to add to the register, click Add Multiple. The Add Multiple Transactions to QuickBooks opens and lists all the unmatched transactions. As you can see in Figure 22-12, the top half of the dialog box lists transactions that are either ready to go or are missing an account. After you choose accounts for the transactions that don't have them, click Record.

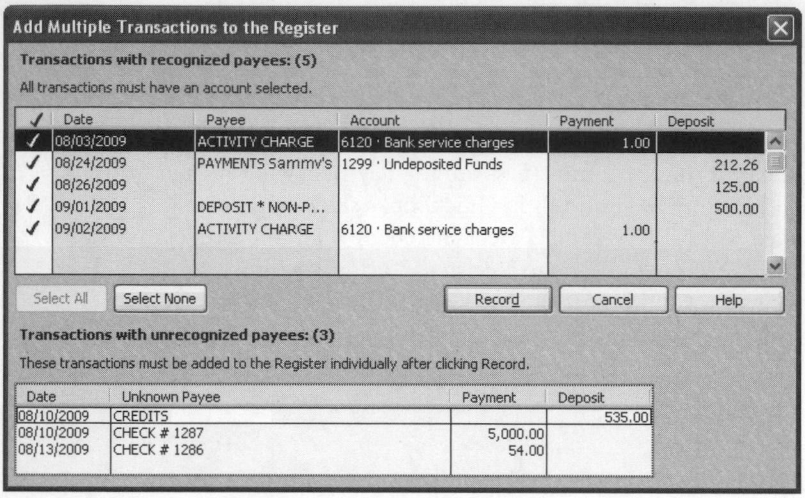

Figure 22-12:
In this window, you can't do anything for the transactions at the bottom of the window with unrecognized payees. To correct those, close the Add Multiple Transactions to the Register window. In the Match Transactions window, select each one individually and then click "Add One to Register". You can edit the payee name in the register.

Deleting Downloaded Transactions

Register mode has no way to delete transactions on the Downloaded Transactions tab. If you already reconciled your account and then downloaded the transactions, you might think you have to live with those unmatched transactions forever. With some fancy, though tedious footwork, though, you can get rid of those downloaded orphans. Here's what you do:

Scroll in the register to find the reconciled transaction that pairs with an unmatched transaction. Click its Cleared cell until the cell is blank. An Asterisk in the cleared cell means the transaction is cleared; a checkmark indicates that it's reconciled.

As soon as the Cleared cell is blank, QuickBooks automatically matches the register transaction and the downloaded transaction. You'll see a lightning bolt in the Cleared cell to indicate the match. The downloaded transaction disappears from the Downloaded Transaction tab.

Now, click the Cleared cell again until you see a checkmark. The register transaction is back to being reconciled and the downloaded transaction is gone forever.

CHAPTER 23

Configuring Preferences to Fit Your Company

An organization's approach to accounting often depends on business objectives, policies, procedures, and the industry in which the organization operates. Maybe you want inventory tracking and payroll or maybe you don't. The way you and your accountant like to work also influences your organization's accounting practices. For instance, you might prefer the simplicity of cash accounting or the more intimate pairing of income and expenses that accrual accounting (page 7) offers.

Enter QuickBooks, an accounting program with the Herculean task of satisfying every nuance of business operation and personal proclivity. QuickBooks *preferences* are configurable settings that accommodate different business styles and personal tastes. During installation, QuickBooks picks the settings likely to work for a majority of organizations. And if you set up your QuickBooks file using the EasyStep Interview (page 21), you might already have most preferences set the way you want.

But you can reset preferences to control all sorts of QuickBooks behaviors and features, such as whether you create estimates for jobs you go after or how you calculate the amount of inventory that's available. Preferences also let you turn on QuickBooks features, such as inventory and payroll. Using QuickBooks for a while can make it clear which preferences you need to change. This chapter presents all the preferences that QuickBooks has and helps you determine which settings are appropriate for you and your organization.

Note: You can toggle most preferences at any time, but you can't turn the preference for multiple currencies off once you turn it on. Before you change any preferences, back up your company file. Then, feel free to tweak and tinker with your preferences.

An Introduction to Preferences

You can't quibble over quantity when QuickBooks gives you 21 categories of preferences that control QuickBooks' behavior. Each preference category has several settings, so finding the preferences that do what you want is your biggest challenge. To view and set preferences, open the Preferences dialog box by choosing Edit → Preferences.

On the left side of the Preferences dialog box is a pane containing icons for each preference category, as shown in Figure 23-1. To display the preferences within a category, click the appropriate icon in the pane. QuickBooks highlights the icon you click to indicate that it's active.

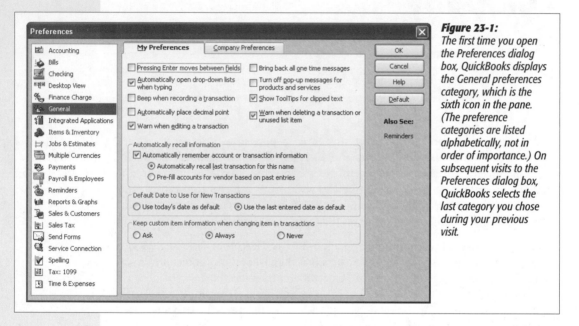

Figure 23-1:
The first time you open the Preferences dialog box, QuickBooks displays the General preferences category, which is the sixth icon in the pane. (The preference categories are listed alphabetically, not in order of importance.) On subsequent visits to the Preferences dialog box, QuickBooks selects the last category you chose during your previous visit.

To accommodate both company and personal preferences, QuickBooks includes two tabs for each category:

- **My Preferences.** As you might expect, the My Preferences tab contains options that people who log into QuickBooks can set for their QuickBooks sessions alone. For example, you can choose options in the Desktop View preference category if you want to look at multiple windows using a lurid purple color scheme (called Grappa Granite), without forcing your tastes on everyone else.

- **Company Preferences.** Some preferences have to remain consistent for everyone in an organization. For example, the IRS won't tolerate some financial reports produced using cash accounting and others using accrual accounting (see page 7 for the pros and cons of each). The preferences that appear on the

Company Preferences tab ensure consistency because they're applied no matter who in your company logs in. To make sure company preferences are set properly, only folks who log in as QuickBooks administrators (see page 630) can change the preferences on the Company Preferences tab.

Note: If you're puzzled by QuickBooks' habit of opening the Preferences dialog box to a My Preferences tab that has no preferences, rest assured that Intuit has its reasons. Only QuickBooks administrators can change settings on the Company Preferences tab. Rather than taunt the majority of people who log into QuickBooks with preferences they can't modify, QuickBooks displays the My Preferences tab. But, for most preference categories, the Company Preferences tab is where the action is.

When you click OK to close the Preferences dialog box, QuickBooks saves the changes you made in the current preference category. What if you're on an energetic mission to reset preferences in several categories? If you change preferences in one category and click the icon for another category, QuickBooks asks you whether you want to save the changes in the category you're about to leave. Make sure you save what you want by clicking one of the following:

- **Yes.** Click Yes to save the changes in the current category before switching to the category whose icon you clicked.

- **No.** Click No to discard your changes and move on to the category whose icon you clicked.

- **Cancel.** Click Cancel to discard your changes and remain in the current category so you can make other choices.

The rest of this chapter explains each set of preferences. They're listed here in alphabetical order, as they are in the Preferences dialog box. You'll also find preferences mentioned throughout this book where they apply to the bookkeeping tasks you perform.

Accounting

QuickBooks' accounting preferences control key accounting practices, such as requiring accounts in transactions, assigning transactions to classes, and closing the books at the end of a fiscal year. Accounting practices stay the same throughout a company, so the Accounting Preferences reside on the Company Preferences tab. Here's what they do:

Note: For QuickBooks Premier and Enterprise, the My Preferences tab has one preference: the "Autofill memo in general journal entry" checkbox. You keep the debit and credit sides of general journal entries linked by adding memos to the lines of the entries. Turn on this checkbox if you want QuickBooks to copy the memo you type for the first line of a journal entry to every subsequent line of the entry.

- **Use account numbers.** In the accounting world, most people follow a numbering standard, which uses ranges of numbers for different types of accounts. For example, asset account numbers (bank accounts, inventory, and so on) run from 1000 to 1999; liability accounts (credit cards, loans, and so on) appear in the 2000 to 2999 range. If you work with an accountant, she'll probably ask you to turn on this checkbox. By doing so, you can assign a number, in addition to a name, to each account you create.

Tip: When you assign an account to a transaction, such as applying your rent check to the Rent expense account, you can locate the account in the Account drop-down list by typing either the account number *or* the first few letters of the account name.

- **Show lowest subaccount only.** If you use only top-level accounts in your chart of accounts, you have no need for this behavior. But if your chart of accounts is a hierarchy of accounts and subaccounts as described on page 55, turn on this checkbox to easily identify the subaccount you've selected in an Account field, as shown in Figure 23-2.

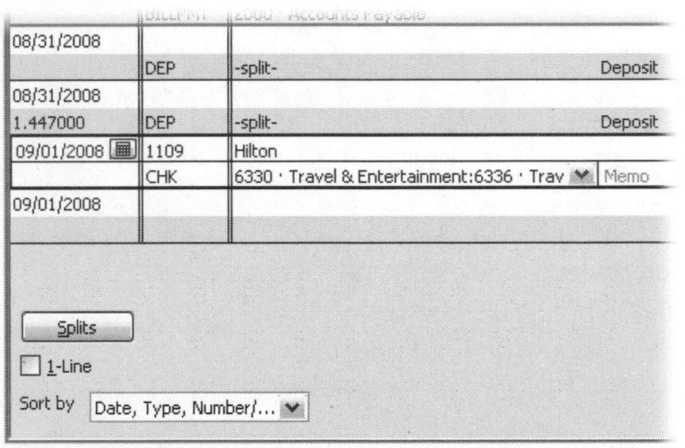

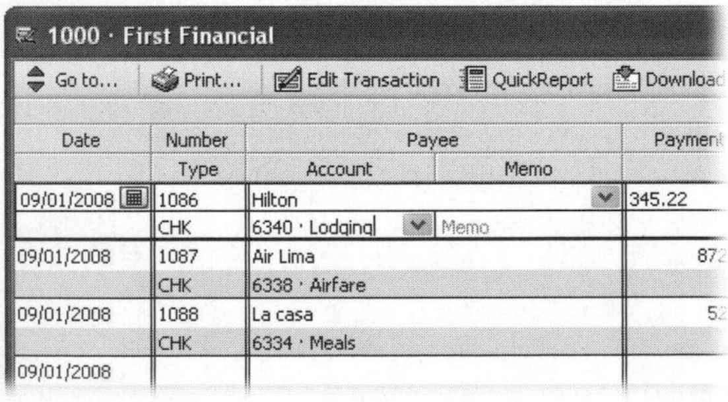

Figure 23-2:

Top: In Account fields, QuickBooks links the name of the top-level account and the name of the subaccount, separating the two with a colon. For example, the top-level account 6330 Travel & Entertainment and the subaccount 6336 Lodging become "6330 Travel & Entertainment:6336 Lodging". Because of the length of these combined names, only the top-level account is visible unless you scroll within the Account field.

Bottom: When you turn on the "Show lowest subaccount only" checkbox, the Account field shows the subaccount number and name, which is exactly what you need to identify the assigned account.

- **Require accounts.** Details help you manage your business, but they're *essential* to surviving the toughest of IRS audits. If detail isn't your strong suit, turning on this checkbox forces you to assign an account to every item and transaction you create, which, in turn, creates a trail that you, your accountant, and the IRS can follow. For example, with the "Require accounts" checkbox turned on, when you click Record without an assigned account, QuickBooks warns you that you have to enter an account. To record the transaction, in the Warning message box, click OK. Then, choose the account in the transaction Account field. Now, when you click Record, QuickBooks completes the transaction without complaint.

  If you turn this checkbox off and record transactions without assigned accounts, QuickBooks assigns the transaction amounts to either the Uncategorized Income or Uncategorized Expense accounts. For example, if you receive a payment from a customer and don't assign an account to the deposit, that income posts to the Uncategorized Income account.

Warning: If the IRS decides to audit your tax returns, you'll have to go back and move your uncategorized income and expenses into the right accounts to prove that you paid the right amount of taxes. And, if you happened to pay too little, the IRS will charge you penalties and interest.

- **Use class tracking.** When you want to track your business in more ways than accounts, customer types, and job types can offer, you can use classes (page 138) to add another level of categorization to your reports. For example, you can create classes to track the income that business units generate, regardless of which types of customers they support or the type of work they do. To activate the Class feature, turn on the "Use class tracking" checkbox, which adds a Class field in every transaction window.

- **Prompt to assign classes.** If you turn on the Class feature, your reports by class won't accurately reflect your business performance unless you assign classes to *all* your transactions. To make sure you assign classes consistently, turn on the "Prompt to assign classes" checkbox so that QuickBooks reminds you when you forget a class assignment for a transaction.

- **Automatically assign general journal entry number.** Journal entries (page 421) refer to the traditional approach to accounting, in which accountants assign credits and debits to accounts in paper-based journals. If you miscategorize a transaction, your accountant can create a journal entry to move dollars from your incorrectly assigned account to the correct account, for instance, moving company-paid health club dues from the Membership & Dues account you used to a more appropriate Employee Benefits account.

  Discussing changes that you and your accountant make to your books is much easier when you can refer to journal entries by an identifier or number. There's no reason to turn this checkbox off. With it on, QuickBooks makes sure that

---

each general journal entry has a unique number. When you create a new general journal entry (see page 421), QuickBooks increments the previous general journal entry number by one, as shown in Figure 23-3.

Note: If the previous entry number is blank, QuickBooks won't automatically assign a number to the next entry. If you notice that QuickBooks has begun to shirk its automatic numbering duties, look for a blank entry number. Add numbers to any existing journal entries without them. Then, when you add a new journal entry, QuickBooks will number the next entry as it should.

- **Warn when posting a transaction to Retained Earnings.** The program automatically turns on this checkbox, and it's a good idea to leave it that way. QuickBooks creates the Retained Earnings account to track past profits that you've retained in the company's coffers. For example, if your company earned $50,000 in 2010 and didn't distribute that money to the owners or as profit-sharing bonuses to employees, that money becomes Retained Earnings once you begin 2011. QuickBooks updates the balance in the account automatically at the beginning of a new fiscal year by transferring the previous year's net profit into it. This preference warns you before you post a transfer directly to the Retained Earning account and inadvertently create inaccurate records. (See page 449 to learn how to differentiate your most recent year's retained earnings from earlier retained earnings.)

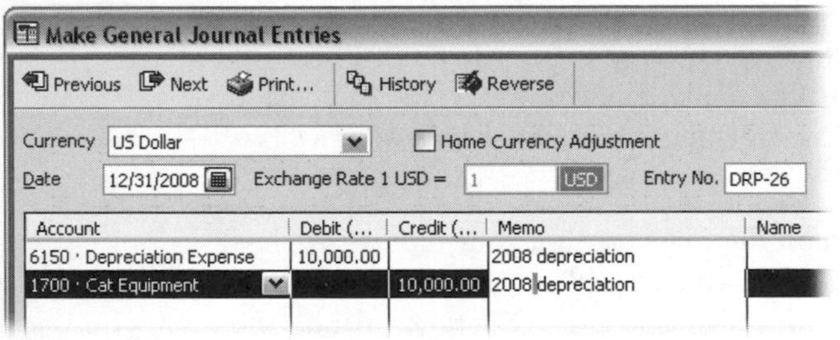

Figure 23-3:
QuickBooks follows your lead in numbering journal entries. For your first general journal entry, you can type a journal entry number, such as your initials and a sequence number (DRP-1, for example). As you create journal entries, QuickBooks increments the journal entry number to DRP-2, DRP-3, and so on.

- **Date Warnings.** If your books are up to date, then very old or very prescient dates are usually mistakes. To receive warnings for dates too far in the past or too far in the future, turn on the "Warn if transactions are _ day(s) in the past" checkbox and its companion, "Warn if transactions are _ day(s) in the future" checkbox. The boxes are set to 90 for past dates and 30 for future dates, but you can change them.

- **Closing date.** After producing the financial reports for a fiscal year and paying corporate income taxes, most companies *close their books*, which means locking the transactions so no one can change anything. By closing the books, you ensure that your past transactions continue to match what you submitted to your accountant, reported to the IRS, and communicated to your shareholders.

When you use QuickBooks, your QuickBooks company file is synonymous with your "books." Therefore, you close your books by clicking Set Date/Password and then choosing a date in the "Set Closing Date and Password" dialog box. For example, if you run your company on a calendar year and just reported and paid taxes for 2009, type or choose *12/31/2009*.

If you absolutely have to edit a transaction that happened before the closing date, you can assign a password so that you can edit, delete, or create transactions that would alter account balances. In the "Set Closing Date and Password" dialog box, type the password in the Closing Date Password and Confirm Password boxes, and then click OK. If you *have to* edit a transaction prior to the closing date, you'll first have to type the password.

Bills

The Bills category lets you specify how you want to handle the bills that vendors send you. The My Preferences tab is empty, so these settings all appear on the Company Preferences tab:

- **Bills are due __ days after receipt.** The first time you access Bills preferences, you'll find that QuickBooks has set this preference so that bills you enter show a due date 10 days after the date of the bill. For instance, if you receive a bill dated June 15, and in the Enter Bills dialog box fill in the Date field as such, Quick-Books automatically changes the Bill Due field to June 25. This value is fine in most cases. If a bill arrives that's due in a different number of days, you can change its due date in the Enter Bill window's Bill Due field.

- **Warn about duplicate bill numbers from same vendor.** Surely you don't want to pay the same bill twice, so be sure to turn on this checkbox so QuickBooks warns you that you're entering a bill with the same number as one you already entered from the same vendor.

- **Paying Bills.** If you want QuickBooks to automatically apply to your bills any credits and discounts to which you're entitled, turn on the "Automatically use discounts and credits" checkbox. For example, if you typically receive a 15-percent discount on all purchases and also have a $100 credit, QuickBooks applies these adjustments to your bill before calculating the total. When you turn on this checkbox, in the Default Discount Account drop-down list, choose the account to which you usually post the discounts you take, for example, an expense account specifically for vendor discounts.

Note: Set up the payment terms that vendors extend to you in vendor records, as described on page 147.

Checking

Checking preferences let you set company-wide settings to control the appearance of the checks your company prints through QuickBooks. On the My Preferences tab in this category, you can also set preferences for the accounts that QuickBooks selects automatically for several types of financial transactions, as shown in Figure 23-4 (top).

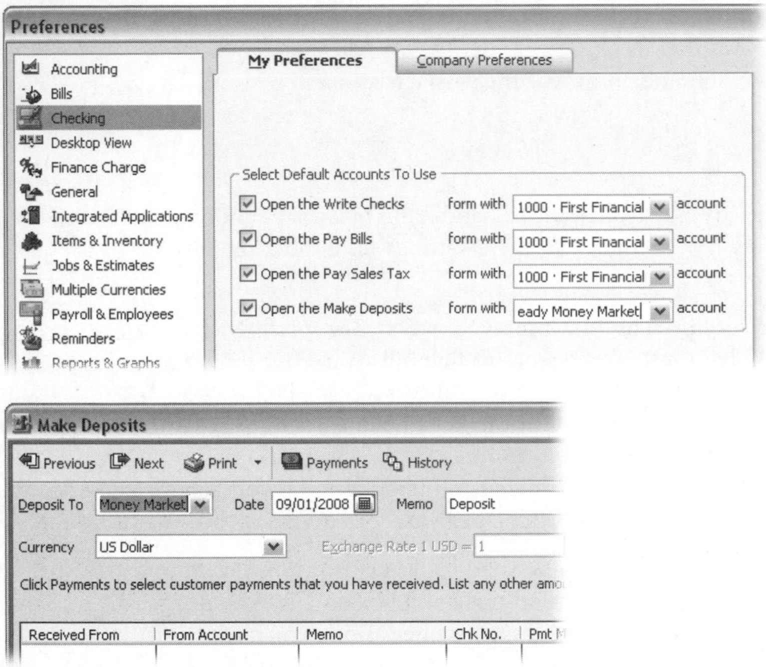

Figure 23-4:
Top: When you choose accounts in Checking preferences, you have one less field to fill in for each banking transaction. For example, if you always deposit money into your money market account, you can set your preferences so the Write Checks window selects your checking account, whereas the Make Deposits window selects your money market account.

Bottom: When you set an account preference for a transaction window, the window automatically fills in that account. You can choose a different account if the transaction is an exception to the rule.

Choosing the Bank Accounts You Use

If you have only one bank account, you can ignore the preferences for default accounts. QuickBooks automatically chooses your checking account for writing checks, paying bills, paying sales tax, and making deposits. But suppose your company has stores in several states and each store has its own checking account. Using the options on the My Preferences tab, each person who logs into QuickBooks can choose her store's accounts for banking transactions. The person in Miami wants the Florida checking account to appear in the Write Checks window, but the person in New York wants to see the Manhattan checking account. To save some time (and prevent folks from selecting the wrong account in a drop-down list), set your accounts according to the following guidelines:

- **Open the Write Checks form with _ account.** In the account drop-down list, choose the account you typically use to write checks. When you open the Write Checks window (page 238), QuickBooks automatically fills in the Bank Account field with the account you specify here.

- **Open the Pay Bills form with _ account.** In real life, paying bills and writing checks usually mean the same thing. In QuickBooks, you can enter bills you receive and pay them at a later date, as described on page 226. For this preference, choose the account you typically use to pay bills in the account drop-down list, which is often the same checking account that you chose in the "Open the Write Checks form with" preference. When you open the Pay Bills window, QuickBooks automatically fills in the A/P Account field (A/P stands for accounts payable) with the account you specify in this preference.

- **Open the Pay Sales Tax form with _ account.** If you collect sales tax from your customers (see page 263), you have to remit the taxes you collect to the appropriate tax authority, such as the state where your business is located. When it's time to send the taxes in, you open the Pay Sales Tax dialog box and create a payment. This preference sets the account that QuickBooks uses in the Pay From Account field.

- **Open the Make Deposits form with _ account.** Unlike the other options on the My Preferences tab, this preference sets up the account you typically use when you *deposit* money. For many small businesses, the deposit account and the checking account are one and the same. But some businesses deposit money into an account that pays interest, and then transfer money (see page 393) into a checking account only when it's time to pay bills. After you choose the account you use to deposit money, the Make Deposits window (page 354) automatically fills in the Deposit To field with the account you specify here, as Figure 23-4 (bottom) shows.

Setting the Way Company Checks Work

Although a company might have several checking accounts, QuickBooks assumes that company checks should look the same no matter who prints them. Most preferences on the Company Preferences tab let you set the company standard for printing checks from QuickBooks. (If you use preprinted checks and write them out by hand, you can skip these options.)

- **Print account names on voucher.** If the paper checks that you print include check stubs, you might as well turn on this checkbox. When you do, QuickBooks prints on the stub the account name for the account you used to pay the check. If you use only one bank account, printing the account name might not seem all that useful. But QuickBooks also prints the payroll item on the stub for payroll checks, and for checks used to purchase inventory, it prints the name of the inventory item you purchased—both of which can help you keep track of where your money is going.

Note: Regardless of how you set the "Print account names on voucher" preference, QuickBooks always prints the payee, date, memo, amount, and total amount on stubs.

- **Change check date when check is printed.** When you turn on this checkbox, QuickBooks inserts the date that you *print* checks as the check date, which is just fine in most situations. You can enter checks into QuickBooks over several days, but date all the checks with the day you print them. Turn off this checkbox if you want to control the check dates, for example, to defer payments for a few days by post-dating checks for the day the payees receive them.

- **Start with payee field on check.** Turning on this checkbox is a small but satisfying time-saver. If you always write checks from the same account, or you use the "Open the Write Checks form with" preference to specify an account (page 554), tabbing in the Write Checks window to skip the Bank Account field for each check transaction gets old quickly. When you turn on this checkbox, you can save one pesky keystroke each time you write a check.

  Turning on this preference also opens the Enter Credit Card Charges window with the cursor in the Purchased From box.

- **Warn about duplicate check numbers.** Not surprisingly, turning on this checkbox means that QuickBooks warns you that you're trying to record a check with the same number as one you already entered.

- **Autofill payee account number in check memo.** Just as you assign account numbers to your customers, the vendors you do business with assign your company an account number, too. Printing account numbers on the checks you write helps a vendor credit your account, even if the check gets separated from its accompanying payment slip. If you enter your company's account number in each Vendor record in QuickBooks (page 135), turn this checkbox on to print these account numbers on your checks.

Choosing Company-Wide Payroll Accounts

The two Checking preferences in the Select Default Accounts To Use section of the Company Preferences tab let you set the accounts you use for payroll. QuickBooks might seem to jump the gun by offering company-wide settings for the accounts used for payroll and payroll liabilities, but most companies centralize payroll no matter how regional other operations are. If you don't use QuickBooks payroll features, don't bother with these preferences because you'll never open the Create Paychecks or Pay Payroll Liabilities forms. (To learn how to turn on QuickBooks payroll features, refer to page 571.)

Tip: A separate bank account for payroll simplifies reconciling your regular checking account, particularly for companies with numerous employees and weekly paychecks. Otherwise, you'll have to reconcile dozens or even hundreds of paychecks each month in addition to the other checks you write.

- **Open the Create Paychecks form with _ account.** In the account drop-down list, choose the account you use to write payroll checks. When you open the Create Paychecks window (page 376), QuickBooks automatically fills in the Bank Account field with the account you specify in this preference.

- **Open the Pay Payroll Liabilities form with _ account.** From the Account drop-down list, choose the account you use to pay payroll taxes.

Choosing the Online Banking Mode

In QuickBooks 2010, you can switch between the Online Banking Center from QuickBooks 2008 and earlier and the QuickBooks 2009 version of the center. The look might be different, but the online tasks you can perform are basically the same. And you can switch between the two modes any time you want by selecting the Side-by-side mode or Register mode options. See page 529 to learn how the two modes work.

Desktop View

Each person can customize the QuickBooks desktop for herself. You can fulfill your every desktop desire with the preferences on the My Preferences tab—your choices don't affect anybody else who logs into QuickBooks. On the other hand, the Company Preferences tab includes preferences that control what appears on the QuickBooks Home page (page 35).

Window Preferences

You can keep your desktop neat with only one window at a time, or you can view multiple windows:

- **One Window.** If you're not good at multitasking or you simply prefer full-size windows, choose the One Window option so that QuickBooks displays only one full-size window at a time. Although you can open multiple windows, they're stacked on top of each other so you see only the top one. With this approach, you can switch windows by choosing windows in the Open Window List (choose View → Open Window List) or on the menu bar, choose Window and then choose the name of the window you want to display.

- **Multiple Windows.** If you like to view several windows at a time or want to size windows based on how much information they display, as shown in Figure 23-5, choose the Multiple Windows option. When you choose this option, the Windows menu has commands such as Cascade and Tile Vertically for arranging windows.

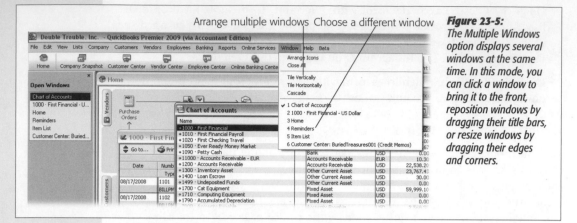

Arrange multiple windows Choose a different window

Figure 23-5:
The Multiple Windows option displays several windows at the same time. In this mode, you can click a window to bring it to the front, reposition windows by dragging their title bars, or resize windows by dragging their edges and corners.

Preferences for Saving the Desktop

On the My Preferences tab, the Desktop category gives you four choices for what QuickBooks does with the windows that are open when you exit the program. For example, if you have your windows arranged just the way you like, you can save your QuickBooks desktop so the windows open in exactly the same arrangement the next time you log in. Here's the lowdown on why you might choose each option:

- **Save when closing company.** If you typically continue bookkeeping tasks from one QuickBooks session to the next, this option saves the open windows and their positions when you exit QuickBooks. The next time you log in, Quick-Books opens the same windows and positions them where they were so you can finish entering the remaining 300 checks you have to write.

  Choosing this option adds a small delay to the time it takes QuickBooks to close. If you'd rather have QuickBooks live up to its name and close more quickly, choose one of the other desktop options.

- **Save current desktop.** If you have a favorite arrangement of windows that works well for the bulk of your efforts in QuickBooks, you can save that arrangement and display it every time you log in. To do this, first open the windows you want and position them. Open the Preferences dialog box, choose this option, and then click OK. When you choose this option, QuickBooks adds the "Keep previously saved desktop" option to the My Preferences tab.

- **Don't save the desktop.** Choosing this option displays a desktop with only the menu bar, the icon bar, the Home page, and the Reminders window. Quick-Books opens faster, and the Home page gives you fast access to the windows and dialog boxes you use regularly.

- **Keep previously saved desktop.** Once you've saved a desktop you like, this option appears on the Desktop View My Preferences tab. Choose this option so that QuickBooks opens with the desktop as it was when you selected "Save current desktop".

- **Show Home page when opening a company file.** The Home page (page 35) shows the entire workflow of your accounting tasks, as well as links to oft-opened windows like the Chart of Accounts window. Keep this checkbox turned on to see the Home page each time you log in.

- **Show Coach window and features.** The Coach can help you learn your way around the program (page 41). After you know what you're doing, turn off this checkbox to work without handholding.

- **Show Live Community.** Initially, this checkbox is turned on, which displays the Live Community window (page 656) on the right side of the QuickBooks main window. If you want the Live Community and the help it offers to stay out of sight until you open it (choose Help → Live Community), turn off this checkbox.

- **Detach the Help Window.** At long last, QuickBooks 2010 lets you position the Help window wherever you want, resize it to your heart's content, and mini-mize it—all without affecting the main QuickBooks window. QuickBooks doesn't turn this checkbox on out of the box, but you'll want to. Otherwise, when you open the Help window, it sticks to the right side of the main Quick-Books window, where it reduces your QuickBooks window space and behaves in other annoying ways. See page 654 to learn more about QuickBooks Help.

Choosing a Color Scheme

The last preference of note on the My Preferences tab is Color Scheme. The stan-dard color scheme that QuickBooks applies is neutral and easy on the eyes. If you're color blind or simply like some color to brighten an otherwise dull finan-cial day, choose one of the other built-in color schemes.

Note: The Windows Settings section at the bottom of the My Preferences tab has a Display button and a Sounds button. These buttons take you to the appropriate category of your Windows Control Panel to change your Windows settings, where any changes you make affect every program on your computer.

Setting Up the QuickBooks Home Page

Since QuickBooks automatically displays its Home page when launched, you prob-ably know that this window lets you access almost any accounting task. As you can see in Figure 23-6, the Home page has three horizontal panels for tasks related to vendors, customers, and employees. The Desktop View Company Preferences tab is where you can customize what you see here.

On the Desktop View Company Preferences tab, simply turn on checkboxes to dis-play the Home page icons for various tasks like sales receipts, statements, and pay-ing bills, as shown in Figure 23-7. These checkboxes control only whether the icons appear in the workflow on the Home page. To set preferences for features like inventory, click their links in the Related Preferences section to switch to the appropriate preference category.

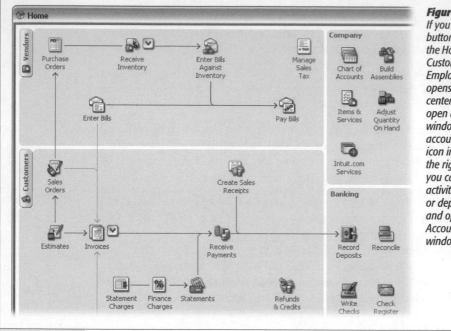

Figure 23-6:
If you click one of the buttons on the left side of the Home page (Vendors, Customers, or Employees), the program opens the corresponding center (page 36). To open a dialog box or window for an accounting task, click the icon in the workflow. To the right of these panels, you can launch banking activities (like reconciling or depositing money) and open the Chart of Accounts and Items windows.

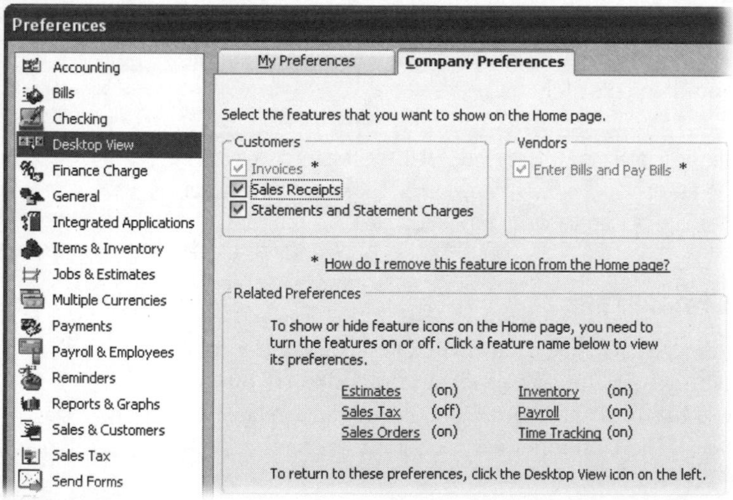

Figure 23-7:
If the checkboxes for invoices or bill payment tasks are dimmed and you want to remove those tasks from the Home page, you first need to turn off other preferences. For example, for invoices, you have to turn off the Estimate and Sales Orders preferences (in other Preference categories). Click the "How do I remove this feature icon from the Home page?" link to read a Help topic that lists the settings you need to change.

Finance Charge

If you're lucky enough to have customers who always pay on time or if you run a nonprofit organization that graciously accepts donations, you can bypass this category of preferences. But if you want to add an incentive for customers to pay on time, finance charge preferences determine your level of leniency.

Because you probably don't want each of your employees deciding how to charge customers for late payments, all the preferences in the Finance Charge category appear on the Company Preferences tab. Only someone logged into QuickBooks as an administrator can change these settings. To learn how to add the finance charges configured here to the invoices you create, see page 346.

Tip: If you plan to charge late fees, include the finance charge terms in your contracts. Your customers are less likely to complain if the added charges aren't a surprise.

Here are the finance charge preferences you can set and what they mean to your customers:

- **Annual Interest Rate (%).** Type the interest rate that you charge per year for overdue payments. For example, if you charge 18 percent per year, type *18* in the Annual Interest Rate (%) box. QuickBooks calculates the finance charge due by prorating the annual interest date to the number of days that the payment is late.

- **Minimum Finance Charge.** If you charge a minimum finance charge no matter how inconsequential the overdue amount, type that minimum value in this box. For example, to charge at least 20 dollars, type *20*. If you work with more than one currency, you still specify your minimum finance charge in your home currency. QuickBooks converts the finance charge to the customer's currency when you apply finance charges.

- **Grace Period (days).** Just like the grace period that you probably enjoy on your mortgage, the grace period in QuickBooks is the number of days that a payment can be late before finance charges kick in. In the "Grace Period (days)" box, type the number of days of grace you're willing to extend to your customers.

- **Finance Charge Account.** Choose the account you use to track finance charges you collect. Most companies create an Other Income account (page 53) to track finance charges, which are interest income.

- **Assess finance charges on overdue finance charges.** If a customer goes AWOL and doesn't pay the bill *or* the finance charges, you can get tough and levy finance charges on the finance charges that the customer already owes. If your customer owes $100 in finance charges and you assess an 18% finance charge, turning on this checkbox would result in an additional $18 a year on the outstanding finance charges alone.

Note: Most companies find it excessive to tack finance charges on overdue finance charges. Moreover, you should check the lending laws that apply to your location and business—some laws restrict your ability to charge interest on outstanding interest payments.

• **Calculate charges from.** You can calculate finance charges from two different dates, depending on how painful you want the finance charge penalty to be. Choosing the "due date" option is the more lenient approach. For this option, QuickBooks assesses finance charges only on the days that an invoice is paid past its due date. For example, if the customer pays 10 days after the due date, QuickBooks calculates the finance charges for 10 days. If you want to assess finance charges from the date on an invoice, choose the "invoice/billed date" option. If the customer pays 10 days late on a *Net 30 invoice* (meaning payment is due no more than 30 days after the invoice date), QuickBooks calculates finance charges based on 40 days—the 30 days until the invoice was due and the 10 days that the payment was late.

• **Mark finance charge invoices** "To be printed". If you want QuickBooks to remind you to print invoices with finance charges, turn on this checkbox. Invoices that you haven't printed yet appear as alerts in the Reminders window.

General

You might find it odd that the most common preferences appear in the middle of the preferences list. And it's even stranger that QuickBooks selects the General preferences category the very first time you open the Preferences dialog box. What gives? Simple—the preference categories appear in alphabetical order.

Don't bypass the General settings. They can make your QuickBooks sessions either a breeze or an annoyance. Most of the General preferences appear on the My Preferences tab, but a few apply to everyone who logs into QuickBooks.

Tuning QuickBooks to Your Liking

The following settings on the My Preferences tab can help you fine-tune Quick-Books' behavior:

• **Pressing Enter moves between fields.** In the Windows world, pressing the Enter key usually activates the default button in a dialog box, while the Tab key advances the cursor to the next field. If you press Enter in QuickBooks and find that your dialog box closes unexpectedly, this QuickBooks checkbox can provide some relief. When you turn on this checkbox, pressing Enter moves the cursor between fields in a dialog box rather than closing it. However, because Enter no longer closes a dialog box, you have to click a button to do so, such as OK, Record, Save & Close, or Save & New (depending on the dialog box). You can also press Ctrl+Enter to close a dialog box.

• **Automatically open drop-down lists when typing.** This preference makes drop-down menus spring open as soon as you type a letter in a field, as shown in Figure 23-8. You can then click the entry you want.

- **Beep when recording a transaction.** If you like auditory assurance that your software is working, turn on this checkbox to have QuickBooks beep when it records a transaction. If you grow tired of QuickBooks sounding like an arcade game, simply return to the Preferences dialog box and turn off this checkbox. (Remember, you'll hear beeps only if you haven't muted the audio on your computer.)

- **Automatically place decimal point.** When you turn on this checkbox, QuickBooks automatically places a decimal so that the last two numbers you type represent cents. For example, typing *19995* automatically becomes 199.95. (If you want to enter a whole dollar, type the decimal point at the end of the number.) Having QuickBooks place decimal points in numbers for you can be quite addictive once you get used to it, particularly if you haven't graduated to rapid-fire numeric entry on the numeric keypad of your computer—or, if you work on a laptop and haven't realized that your keyboard *has* a numeric keypad.

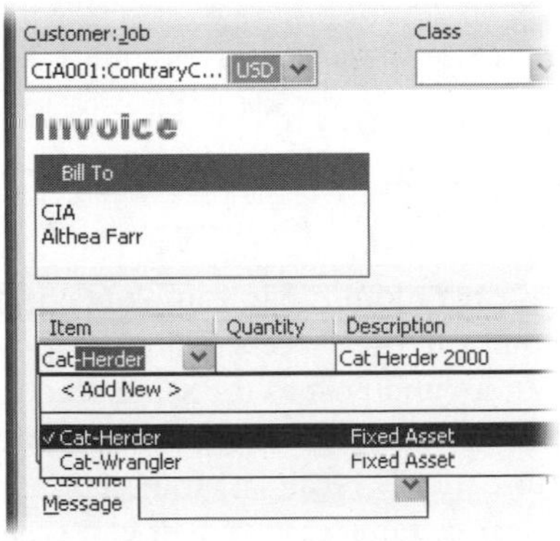

Figure 23-8:
The drop-down list appears as soon as you begin typing an entry in a field, so you can keep typing or click an entry. The list narrows down to the choices that match the letters you've typed so far (like showing Cat-Herder and Cat-Wrangler for the letters "cat"). You can also expand or contract the width of the drop-down list by dragging the bottom-right corner to show as much or as little information as you want.

- **Warn when editing a transaction.** QuickBooks turns on this checkbox automatically, which means that the program displays a warning if you edit a transaction and attempt to leave it (for instance, by clicking another transaction) without explicitly recording the change. If you inadvertently modify a check or invoice, this warning gives you a chance to exit without saving the changes.

  If you decide to turn off this feature, QuickBooks automatically records transactions that aren't linked to other transactions. However, if a transaction has links—such as a payment that links to a customer invoice—you need to record transactions after you change them regardless of how you've set this preference.

- **Bring back all one-time messages.** One-time messages instruct beginners in the ways of QuickBooks, but for experienced fans, these messages are merely annoyances. The only time you might want to turn on this checkbox is if you were overly enthusiastic about hiding one-time messages and find yourself in need of QuickBooks' mentoring once more.

- **Turn off pop-up messages for products and services.** Out of the box, Quick-Books displays its own pop-up messages about other products and services Intuit would love to sell to you. Turn this checkbox off to stop the marketing.

- **Show ToolTips for clipped text.** Text in QuickBooks fields is often longer than what you can see on the screen. For example, if you see the text "Make sure you always" in a text box, you'll want to see the rest of the message. This checkbox, which QuickBooks turns on automatically, tells QuickBooks to display the entire contents of a field when you position the mouse over it.

- **Warn when deleting a transaction or unused list item.** QuickBooks turns this checkbox on automatically, so you have to confirm that you want to delete a transaction, such as a deposit or check, or a list item that's never been used in a transaction. Caution is a watchword in the financial world. Although Quick-Books lets you delete transactions, it's a good idea to include this extra step to make sure you're deleting what you want. If you turn off this checkbox, you can delete a transaction without confirmation.

Note: Regardless of how this preference is set, QuickBooks won't let you delete a list item, such as a customer type or shipping method you use, if it's been used even once in a transaction. Learn what you've got to do to delete or inactivate list items on page 129.

- **Automatically remember account or transaction information.** Do you write similar checks or incur similar credit charges each month? Say you write checks each month from the same account for your Internet access. Those transactions include the same vendor, the same amount, and post to the same account. QuickBooks turns on the "Automatically remember account or transaction information" checkbox and selects the "Automatically recall last transaction for this name" option to make these recurring transactions easy. When you type a name in a transaction, QuickBooks fills in the rest of the fields in the transaction with the values you used in the last transaction for that name. If you select the "Pre-fill accounts for vendor based on past entries" option, QuickBooks automatically fills in the accounts you use consistently for vendor transactions. Since you can set up pre-fill accounts for vendors with other QuickBooks features (page 138), the "Automatically recall last transaction for this name" option gives more bang for the buck.

  AutoRecall has a couple of limitations you should keep in mind. You can't recall a transaction in one account if the previous transaction was in another account. In addition, you can recall transactions for bills, checks, and credit card charges only. For other transactions—such as purchase orders, invoices, sales receipts, and credit memos—you have to fill in all the fields or use a memorized transaction.

Tip: It's a rare occurrence, but if you find this automated data entry more of a hindrance than help, turn off the "Automatically remember account or transaction information" checkbox. You can still reuse transactions by memorizing them and choosing them from the Memorized Transaction List, described on page 319.

- **Default date to use for new transactions.** In this section of the My Preferences tab, choose the "Use today's date as default" option if you want QuickBooks to fill in the date field with the current date for every new transaction you create.

  If you create invoices over the course of several days but you want each invoice to reflect the first day of the month, choose the "Use the last entered date as default" option. In the first invoice you create, type the date you want for all your invoices. For subsequent invoices, QuickBooks fills in the Date field with the date you entered on the previous invoice. When you want to use a new date (after all the invoices are complete), simply type the new date in your next transaction.

Tip: When you select the "Use the last entered date as default" option, be sure to check the transaction date to make sure it's the one you want.

- **Keep custom item information when changing item in transactions.** This setting determines how QuickBooks responds when you change an item in a transaction after customizing its description. Say you add an item to an invoice, edit the description in the invoice, and *then* realize that you added the wrong item. When you choose a new item to replace it, if you've selected the Ask option in Preferences, QuickBooks asks you if you want to use the edited description for the new item. The Always option automatically applies the edited description to the new item. With the Never option, QuickBooks replaces the item immediately, using the description from the new item's record.

Company-Wide General Preferences

The Company Preferences tab includes four preferences, shown in Figure 23-9. Only a QuickBooks administrator can change these settings. Here's what these preferences do:

- **Show portions of an hour as.** You can enter hours in one of two ways—as decimal numbers that represent hours and fractions of an hour, or as hours and minutes separated by a colon, as you can see in Figure 23-9. This preference tells QuickBooks which way to display time values.

- **Always show years as 4 digits.** Turning on this feature tells QuickBooks to display all four digits of the year whether you type two digits or four. For example, if you type *09*, then QuickBooks displays 2009. Turning off this checkbox shows years as two digits.

  When you type a two-digit number for a year, QuickBooks translates numbers from 00 through 38 as years 2000 through 2038. Numbers 39 through 99 become 1939 through 1999.

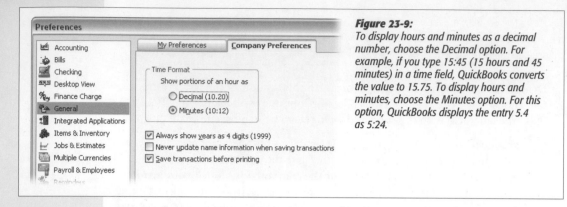

Figure 23-9:
To display hours and minutes as a decimal number, choose the Decimal option. For example, if you type 15:45 (15 hours and 45 minutes) in a time field, QuickBooks converts the value to 15.75. To display hours and minutes, choose the Minutes option. For this option, QuickBooks displays the entry 5.4 as 5:24.

Tip: When you turn off the "Always show years as 4 digits" checkbox, QuickBooks does as it's told and displays only two digits for the year. If a date field shows 40 and you want to see whether that stands for 1940 or 2040, in the date field, click the Calendar icon. The Calendar shows both the month and the full four-digit year.

- **Never update name information when saving transactions.** QuickBooks comes set so that when you change information for a name, such as a customer or vendor, the program asks if you want to replicate that change back in the original record—on the Customer:Job List or Vendor List. Possibly the only time you might want to change this behavior (which you do by turning on this checkbox) is if you use generic names, such as Donor or Member. If you receive donations and your donors want receipts with their names and addresses filled in, you don't want the names and addresses you enter on sales receipts to alter your generic donor record.

- **Save transactions before printing.** QuickBooks turns this checkbox on initially, and it's a good idea to leave it that way. It tells QuickBooks to save a transaction before you print it, so the transaction in QuickBooks is the same as the one you print. If you turn this checkbox off, you could print the transaction with one set of data and then close the dialog box without saving that data, thus making your QuickBooks books different from your paper records.

Integrated Applications

As you'll learn in more detail in Chapter 24, QuickBooks plays well with other programs, like Microsoft Excel and Access. For example, by integrating Microsoft Outlook with QuickBooks, you can easily keep your contact information synchronized in both programs. Third-party vendors create all sorts of programs that integrate with QuickBooks for tasks like document management, project tracking, creating bar codes, and so on. If you're a QuickBooks administrator, the Integrated Applications preferences category is where you control which programs can interact with QuickBooks and the extent of their interaction. For example, you can use another program to produce estimates and want to transfer the completed estimates into QuickBooks to fill out invoices and other forms.

Sometimes third-party programs alter key QuickBooks features, such as your chart of accounts and invoice items. So before you try to integrate a new program, back up your QuickBooks file. After you integrate a program, check your QuickBooks file for unwanted changes, such as new accounts or classes that you don't want. Depending on what you find, you can restore your backup, modify your lists manually, or leave things the way they are.

To access these preferences, choose Edit → Preferences and click the Integrated Applications icon. Here's a guide to setting the preferences on the Company Preferences tab to allow or restrict other programs' access to your QuickBooks file:

• **Don't allow any applications to access this company file.** The quickest way to lock down a QuickBooks file against access by other programs is to turn on this checkbox. When you do so, QuickBooks prevents integrated programs from accessing the file and also suppresses the display of screens that allow people to authorize access. If you want QuickBooks to display access screens, turn on this checkbox. Others can authorize access only if a QuickBooks administrator sets up their accounts to do so, as discussed on page 637.

• **Notify the user before running any application whose certificate has expired.** The most security conscious of administrators might turn on this checkbox to see a warning if a program trying to access the QuickBooks file has an expired certificate. But an expired certificate doesn't mean that the program has changed or has morphed into malicious code—it indicates only that the certificate has expired. For most administrators, turning off this checkbox is preferable.

• **Applications that have previously requested access to this company file.** When programs request access to a QuickBooks file, QuickBooks displays an access screen to the QuickBooks administrator who has to approve or deny access. Programs that have received approval to access your company file appear in this list. To deny access to one of these programs, click the checkmark in the Allow Access column, or select the program, and then click Remove.

Items & Inventory

The Items & Inventory preferences apply mainly to what QuickBooks does when you create purchase orders or invoices for inventory. The first checkbox is the most important: Turning on the "Inventory and purchase orders are active" checkbox tells QuickBooks that you want to track inventory, which activates the program's inventory-related features (page 465). If you turn inventory tracking on, here are the settings you may want to adjust as well:

• **Inventory and purchase orders are active.** If you want to track inventory using QuickBooks, turn on this checkbox. After doing so, you can perform inventory related tasks like creating inventory part items, producing purchase orders, and generating inventory reports. Turning this checkbox on adds icons like Purchase Orders and Receive Inventory to the Home page.

- **Warn about duplicate purchase order numbers.** Turn on this checkbox if you want QuickBooks to warn you when you're creating a purchase order with the same number as one you already entered.

- **Calculating the quantity available.** QuickBooks actually tracks two quantities for inventory items. Quantity On Hand is always the actual number of items sitting in inventory. Quantity Available can equal Quantity On Hand, but you can also tell QuickBooks to calculate the quantity available by deducting the number of items already on sales orders or used in pending builds (when you build products out of components). If you use sales orders (page 276) to track orders that haven't been invoiced, QuickBooks automatically turns on the "Quantity on Sales Order" checkbox. With this setting, QuickBooks calculates how many items in inventory are available by deducting the number of items on sales orders from the number of items on hand, which helps prevent out-of-stock items. If you turn this checkbox off, the quantity available reflects the inventory that's been invoiced and shipped, so you won't know that your inventory is low until you start filling the sales orders you created.

- **Warn if not enough inventory to sell.** If you prepare an invoice to sell more doodads than you have in stock, QuickBooks warns you—*if* this checkbox is turned on. Suppose you sell 500 quarts of sesame soy swirl frozen yogurt, but you have only 400 quarts in stock. When you attempt to save the invoice for the 500-quart order, QuickBooks displays a warning message box informing you of your shortage. But QuickBooks doesn't go any further than that. You can save the invoice, but it's up to you to order more inventory.

  Besides giving you a heads-up that inventory is low, this setting helps you keep your customers happy, since you can ask them if they want to wait for a backorder to be filled. Select the appropriate option to tell QuickBooks whether you want a warning based on the Quantity On Hand or the Quantity Available. Because Quantity Available can be lower than the Quantity On Hand, that's the safest route.

Note: In some QuickBooks Premier Editions (Accountant, Contractor, and Manufacturing & Wholesale) and QuickBooks Enterprise, you can specify different units of measure for inventory items, in case you sell wine by the bottle, by the case, and by the vat, for example. In the "Unit of Measure" section, click Enable. Then, select the Multiple U/M Per Item option. With this option selected, the Create Item and Edit Item windows include a unit of measure field, as shown in Figure 23-10.

Jobs & Estimates

If you create estimates or document job progress in QuickBooks, head to the Jobs & Estimates preferences category to set up your progress terminology and estimating features. Although QuickBooks forces nonprofits to think in terms of customers, it does let you choose the terminology you prefer for progress on a job. For example,

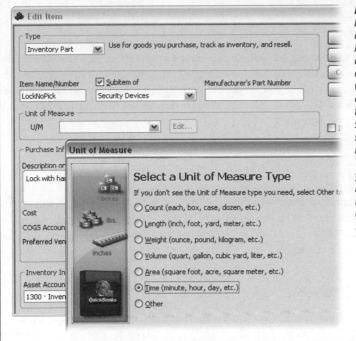

Figure 23-10:
In the "Unit of Measure" drop-down list, double-click <Add New>. The "Unit of Measure" dialog box opens to the "Select a Unit of Measure Type" screen. To use one of the built-in units, like count, length, weight, volume, area, or time, select the corresponding option and click Next. On the "Select a Unit of Measure" screen, select a measure. For example, if you select the Length option as the unit of measure type, you can select Foot, Inch, Yard, Mile, Millimeter, Meter, and Other. If you select Other on the "Select a Unit of Measure Type" screen, and then click Next, you can type a name and abbreviation for the measure, like Space Warp Area or SWArea.

if you're a professional gigolo, your terminology for a woman you didn't win over might be "TooSmart," and you can instruct QuickBooks to display that term in the Job Status field.

QuickBooks includes five fields for job status: Pending, Awarded, "In progress", Closed, and "Not awarded". Despite QuickBooks' field names, you can type any term you want for status in any of the five boxes. You can type *Waiting* in the Pending box, *Whoopie!* in the Awarded box, and *Finally!* in the Closed box. Then, when you edit a job and display the Job Status drop-down list, you can choose from these terms.

The rest of the preferences on the Company Preferences tab relate to estimates and progress invoicing. Choose any or all of the following preferences:

- **Do You Create Estimates?** This question is simple but, unfortunately, misleading. If you create estimates in a program other than QuickBooks, you still choose the No option. Only choose the Yes option if you want to create estimates in QuickBooks, as described on page 280. Selecting Yes adds an Estimates icon to the Home page.

- **Do You Do Progress Invoicing?** Also known as "partial billing," progress invoicing means that you invoice your customer for work as you go instead of billing for the entire job at the end. For example, if you're building a shopping mall, you don't want to carry the costs of construction until shoppers walk in the front door. You want to charge your client as you meet milestones. To create invoices for portions of your estimates, choose the Yes option. Then, you can invoice for part of an estimate and show how much you billed previously, as described in more detail on page 285.

If you choose the No option, you can create progress invoices from your entire estimate. After you bring the entire estimate into your invoice, remove entries until the invoice includes only what you want to bill. The flaw in this approach is that you can't show previous totals billed or compare the amount billed and remaining to your estimate.

- **Warn about duplicate estimate numbers.** Turn on this checkbox if you want QuickBooks to warn you if you're creating an estimate with the same number as one you already entered.

- **Don't print items that have zero amount.** When you produce progress invoices, you might not charge for every estimated item on every progress invoice. To keep your progress invoices tidy, suppress the items that you're not charging for by turning on this checkbox.

Multiple Currencies

If you use only one currency, you can skip this preference section, because Quick-Books automatically selects the "No, I use only one currency" option, as shown in Figure 23-11. But if you have customers who pay you in other currencies, or vendors who want to be paid in their country's currencies, you can turn on the multiple currency preference. Once you do, it's on for good. However, if you stop doing business with foreign-currency customers and vendors, you can simply skip the currency boxes in QuickBooks' windows and dialog boxes. (QuickBooks automatically fills them in with your home currency.)

To turn on multiple currencies, in the Preferences dialog box, click the Multiple Currencies icon, and then click the Company Preferences tab. Select the "Yes, I use more than one currency" option. In the "Select the home currency you use in transactions" drop-down list, choose the currency you use.

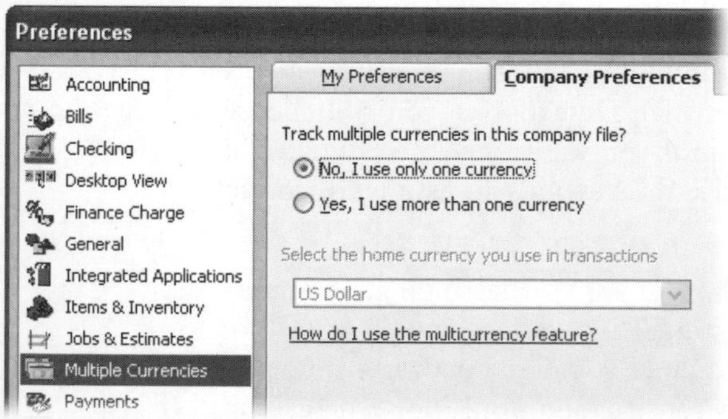

Figure 23-11:
QuickBooks sets the home currency to US Dollar out of the box, but you can choose your home currency in the "Select the home currency you use in transactions" drop-down list. In transaction windows and dialog boxes, QuickBooks initially fills in the Currency box with your home currency. However, after you set up a customer or vendor to use a foreign currency, QuickBooks automatically uses that currency instead. See page 444 for the full scoop on using multiple currencies.

Payments

QuickBooks 2010 includes one new category of preferences: Payments. The preferences for applying and calculating payments have relocated from the Sales & Customers category. However, this category also includes links you can click if you want to sign up for Intuit's credit card, paper check, or eCheck processing services.

- **Intuit Payment Solutions.** Intuit offers QuickBooks Merchant Services for processing payments from your customers, whether you want to accept credit card payments or process checks electronically. To sign up for one or more of these services, click the Get Started link for the service to open a browser window to the sign-up page.

- **Automatically apply payments.** This checkbox in the Receive Payment section is best left turned off, which means you have to manually match payments you receive to the corresponding customer invoices. When you turn this checkbox on, QuickBooks applies customer payments to invoices for you. If a payment doesn't match any of the invoice amounts, QuickBooks applies the payment to the oldest invoices first, which could mask the fact that a payment wasn't received or that a customer's check was for the wrong amount.

- **Automatically calculate payments.** This preference is also better kept turned off. When you receive a payment from a customer, in the Receive Payments window's Amount box, you typically type the amount that the customer sent. Then, as you choose the invoices to apply the payment to, you can see if the payment balances the amount the customer owes. If the customer underpaid, QuickBooks asks you if you want to keep the underpayment or write off the amount that the customer did not pay. If you turn on this checkbox, QuickBooks calculates the payment for you as you choose invoices, so discrepancies aren't readily apparent.

- **Use Undeposited Funds as a default deposit to account.** If you typically collect a few payments before heading to the bank to deposit them, turn on this checkbox so QuickBooks automatically adds payments you receive to the Undeposited Funds account. When you turn on this checkbox, QuickBooks doesn't show the "Deposit to" box in the Receive Payments window, so you have no choice but to deposit payments to Undeposited Funds. If you want a choice about whether to deposit payments right away, keep this checkbox turned off. Then, in the Receive Payments window's Deposit To field, you can choose a bank account to deposit funds immediately, or you can choose Undeposited Funds to collect several payments before you make a deposit.

Payroll & Employees

Perhaps the most annoying things about employees is their insistence on being paid. Sad to say, but using QuickBooks for payroll doesn't eliminate the need to transfer money from your company into your employees' pockets, but it can simplify the task. If you choose one of the QuickBooks payroll service options, the

Payroll & Employees preference category is command central for configuring your payroll service and how it operates. Payroll and employee preferences appear on the Company Preferences tab, so only QuickBooks administrators can set them.

Tip: If you'd rather someone else incur brain damage figuring out government payroll requirements, on the QuickBooks menu bar, choose Employees → Payroll → Learn About Payroll Options. In a Web browser window, the Intuit QuickBooks Payroll screen displays buttons to learn more. If you like what you see, you can then sign up for one of Intuit's payroll services.

On the Company Preferences tab, the QuickBooks Payroll Features area gives you three options for choosing a payroll service: Full Payroll, No Payroll, and Complete Payroll Customers. Because the option labels don't tell the entire story, this list helps you determine which one you should choose:

• **Full Payroll.** If you want to produce payroll documents such as paychecks; payroll reports; and payroll forms, including 940 (employer federal unemployment tax), 941 (employer quarterly federal taxes), W-2 (employee wage and tax statement), and W-3 (transmittal of W-2s), choose this option. Full Payroll is the option you want if you plan to calculate payroll yourself and use QuickBooks' features to produce the documents—or, if you use QuickBooks Basic Payroll, Standard Payroll, Enhanced Payroll, or Assisted Payroll to figure out payroll amounts.

Tip: If you want to allocate wages and payroll taxes to jobs, you have two choices. If you use a third-party payroll service, you can select the No Payroll option and then use journal entries to reassign payroll and payroll taxes to jobs. The other alternative is to choose the Full Payroll option and use QuickBooks' payroll features to assign payroll and payroll taxes to jobs. See page 362 for details.

• **No Payroll.** Only two situations warrant choosing the No Payroll option: you don't run payroll in any way, or you use a third-party payroll service and don't want to assign payroll amounts to job costs. If you're a sole proprietor and pay yourself by taking owner's draws, this is the right option. Likewise, if you use an outside payroll service, such as Paychex or ADP, and have no need to print payroll documents or assign payroll costs to jobs, choose this option. With this option selected, QuickBooks suppresses the appearance of payroll-related commands on the Employees menu and in the Employee Center.

Note: If you have transactions from prior payrolls and switch to using an outside payroll service, the past payroll data remains in your QuickBooks file.

• **Complete Payroll Customers.** If you use Intuit Complete Payroll, a full-blown outsourced payroll service described on page 362, choose this option. When you use Intuit Complete Payroll, you transmit your payroll data from QuickBooks to the payroll service, and then import the processed payroll transactions from the service into QuickBooks.

The Payroll & Employees preference category has plenty of additional settings, which are intimately linked to payroll and described in detail in Chapter 14. For example, you can specify the deductions and payroll items that affect every employee, and you can control the fields that appear on paychecks and paycheck stubs.

Whether you run payroll or not, here's the lowdown on the remaining employee preferences that don't relate to payroll:

- **Display Employee List by.** When your company employs only a few people, you can choose the First Name option so that QuickBooks sorts the Employee List by first names. However, if you employ hundreds of employees or you want practice remembering your employees' last names, choose the Last Name option. Regardless of which option you choose, QuickBooks prints paychecks with employee names with the first name first and last name last.

- **Mark new employees as sales reps.** If only a few of your employees act as customer contacts and receive commissions, you can reserve the Sales Rep List for them by turning off this checkbox and adding names to the Sales Rep List manually (page 144). On the other hand, if you consider every employee a potential sales rep, you can turn on this checkbox so that QuickBooks automatically adds every employee you create to the Sales Rep list, saving you a five-step process each time.

- **Display employee social security numbers in headers on reports.** QuickBooks automatically turns off this checkbox, which is preferable if you want to protect your employees' financial privacy.

Reminders

QuickBooks reminds you when to perform many of your accounting and business tasks, so you can save your brain cells for remembering more important things—like your employees' names or depositing checks. Even if you have a brain the size of a small planet, you're likely to rely on QuickBooks' reminders to nudge you when it's time to print checks or reorder inventory. And when you turn on reminders for To Do Notes, the program can give you hints about any task that you don't want to forget whether it's for a customer, vendor, employee, or yourself.

Reminders on the My Preferences Tab

In the Reminders preference category, the My Preferences tab has only one preference, but it can render all of the settings on the Company Preferences tab useless. If your short-term memory is mere nanoseconds, turn on the "Show Reminders List when opening a Company file" checkbox. That way, QuickBooks displays the Reminders list window (Figure 23-12) whenever you open your company file, and it stays open unless you close it.

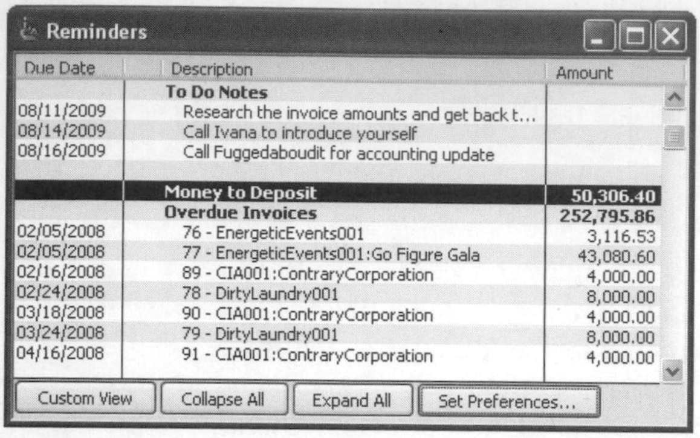

Figure 23-12:
In the Reminders Company Preferences tab, the Show Summary options tell QuickBooks to display a single reminder and the total amount of money in the Reminders window, like the "Money to Deposit" row shown here. Show List options display each transaction on a separate line, as shown below the Overdue Invoices heading. QuickBooks shows one line with the total for overdue invoices, followed by a line showing each overdue invoice.

Reminders for Everyone

The Company Preferences tab lists 14 different types of reminders, which are available only if you've turned on the corresponding QuickBooks feature. For example, if you don't use QuickBooks' inventory, the "Inventory to Reorder" reminder is dimmed. As shown in Figure 23-13, you can specify the level of detail for each type of reminder and when you want QuickBooks to remind you.

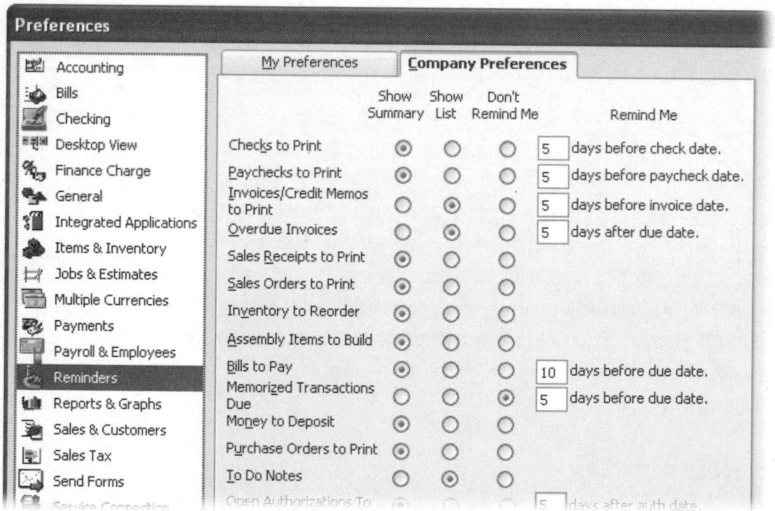

Figure 23-13:
You can choose how and when QuickBooks reminds you to order inventory, pay bills, and so on. For transactions like bills that require action by a specific date, you can tell QuickBooks how far in advance to remind you. If you don't want a reminder for a type of transaction, choose the option in the Don't Remind Me column.

QuickBooks can generate reminders for the following transactions:

• **Checks to Print.** You can queue up checks to print in the Write Checks window (page 238) by turning on the To Be Printed checkbox for each check you create. This reminder tells you that you've got checks queued up to print. You can also specify how many days' notice you want before the date you entered to print the checks.

- **Paychecks to Print.** This reminder tells you that paychecks are waiting to print. You can specify how many days' notice you want before the payroll date you entered.

- **Invoices/Credit Memos to Print.** To print invoices or credit memos in batches, as described on page 311, in the Create Invoices window, turn on the "To be printed" checkbox. Then, this reminder notifies you about unprinted invoices or credit memos. You can specify how many days' notice you want before the invoice or credit memo date you entered.

- **Overdue Invoices.** This reminder warns you about invoices that have passed their due date with no payment from the customer. You can specify how many days an invoice is late before QuickBooks reminds you.

- **Sales Receipts to Print.** If you queued up sales receipts to print as a batch (page 311), this is the reminder about printing them. QuickBooks reminds you as soon as you have any sales receipts to print.

- **Sales Orders to Print.** This preference is available only if you use QuickBooks Premier or Enterprise, and it reminds you to print sales orders you queued up.

- **Inventory to Reorder.** When you create inventory part items in QuickBooks, you can set a reminder for when you need to reorder inventory. This reminder warns you when a sales form you create reduces the number of items on hand below your reorder point. The program generates a reminder immediately.

- **Assembly Items to Build.** This preference is available only if you use Quick-Books Premier or Enterprise. It warns you when the quantity of assembled items drops below your build point (page 114).

- **Bills to Pay.** This reminder nudges you about the bills you have to pay. (Entering bills is described on page 206.) You can specify how many days' notice you want before the date the bills are due.

- **Memorized Transactions Due.** When you memorize transactions, you can specify a date for the next occurrence (page 319). This reminder tells you about recurring memorized transactions. You can specify how many days' notice you want before the date for the next occurrence.

- **Money to Deposit.** When you receive payments, you can group them with other undeposited funds (page 396), so you aren't running to the bank every five minutes as checks pour in. If you want to put your money to work as soon as possible, turn on this checkbox to receive a reminder as soon as you have any funds to deposit.

- **Purchase Orders to Print.** This reminder gives you a prod about purchase orders you haven't yet printed.

- **To Do Notes.** To-do items that you associate with customers can include dates, as described on page 93. This reminder shows you when to-do items are due.

Reports and Graphs

QuickBooks administrators can modify settings that apply to every report and graph the company produces. Each person who logs into QuickBooks can specify a few preferences for the reports and graphs she generates.

Preferences for the Reports You Generate

Here's a guide to the personal preferences shown in Figure 23-14 and the effects they have on performance:

- **Prompt me to modify report options before opening a report.** The reports you want usually require small tweaks—a different date range perhaps—so turning on this checkbox works for most people. QuickBooks automatically opens the Modify Report window when you generate a report. You can make any change you want to the report, and then click Refresh to view the results. If you turn off this checkbox and want to modify a report, on the report's button bar, click Modify Report.

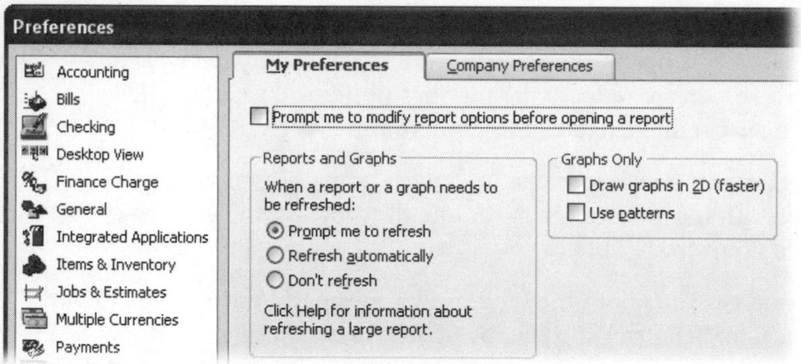

Figure 23-14:
Keeping reports up-to-date with the information in your company's QuickBooks file can be time-consuming. To accommodate the inclinations of each person who logs into QuickBooks, the preferences on the My Preferences tab control how QuickBooks updates reports and graphs.

- **Prompt me to refresh.** If your QuickBooks file changes frequently and you don't want to wait while QuickBooks incessantly refreshes every report you have open, choose this option. It's the best option if you want QuickBooks to remind you to refresh your reports when you've changed data that affects them. For example, suppose you generated a Profit & Loss report and then created a new invoice for a customer; QuickBooks would prompt you to refresh your report. Refreshing your report requires a small amount of time, so you can choose whether you want to refresh or not. When you're ready to refresh your report or graph, in the Report window, simply click Refresh.

- **Refresh automatically.** This option can be slow and disruptive to your work, particularly if numerous people are frantically changing data in the company file, as is often true as year-end approaches. However, if it's critical that your reports and graphs are always accurate, choose this option so QuickBooks automatically refreshes reports and graphs whenever the underlying data changes.

- **Don't refresh.** If you find yourself distracted by refreshes or even prompts about refreshing, choose this option. QuickBooks won't refresh your reports and graphs or remind you—no matter how significant the changes to the underlying data. When you've finished your report and graph customizations, click Refresh to generate the report with the current data.

- **Draw graphs in 2D.** If you care about time more than fancy graphics, turn on this checkbox. QuickBooks displays graphs in two dimensions, which is faster than drawing the 3D graphs that appear if you turn off the checkbox.

- **Use patterns.** When you turn on this checkbox, QuickBooks uses black and white patterns instead of colors to differentiate areas on graphs. If you turn off this checkbox, QuickBooks displays colors on color monitors or shades of gray on black-and-white monitors.

Preferences That Apply to Every Company Report

The Company Preferences tab has several preferences for the reports and graphs you generate for your company. If you're a QuickBooks administrator, use the following preferences to format reports and graphs:

- **Summary Reports Basis.** Nothing starts adrenaline flowing like financial reports that aren't what you expect, particularly when the IRS auditors are dropping by to take a peek at your company books. Be sure to choose the corresponding Cash or Accrual option so that the reports you generate reflect your financial performance accurately. If you choose Cash, your reports show income when you receive payments for income and show expenses when you pay for them. If you choose Accrual, your reports show income as soon as you record an invoice or enter a sale regardless of whether you received payment. Expenses appear as soon as you enter a bill.

Note: In most cases, when your accountant recommends cash or accrual, you choose the appropriate option, and then you can forget about it. But if you upgrade or reinstall QuickBooks, make sure that QuickBooks didn't reset your Summary Reports Basis choice.

- **Aging Reports.** You can control how QuickBooks calculates age for invoices, statements, and bills. If you choose the "Age from due date" option, QuickBooks shows the number of days between the due date and the current date. If you choose "Age from transaction date", QuickBooks shows the number of overdue days from the date of the transaction to the current date. Suppose an invoice is dated September 1 with a due date of October 1. On October 10, the "Age from due date" option shows the invoice age as 10 days, whereas the "Age from transaction date" option shows the invoice age as 40 days.

- **Reports – Show Accounts by.** Reports typically show accounts by name. If you use especially short account names, you can use the account description in reports. You can also show both names and descriptions.

- **Statement of Cash Flows.** Although QuickBooks does a great job of associating your accounts with the Operating, Investing, and Financing categories of the "Statement of Cash Flows" report, some companies are bound to require a customized cash flow report. If you're lucky enough to need a customized cash flow statement, click Classify Cash to open the Classify Cash dialog box. See page 439 to learn how to generate and customize a cash flow statement for your company.

- **Format.** Click Format to set up standards for all of your reports. For example, you can choose the information that you want to appear in headers and footers, and whether they're aligned to the left, right, or center of the page.

Sales & Customers

With the Sales & Customers preferences category, shown in Figure 23-15, you can control how QuickBooks handles the sales you make to your customers, whether it be the shipping method you choose, tracking reimbursed expenses as income, or simply finding out that you've created a duplicate invoice number.

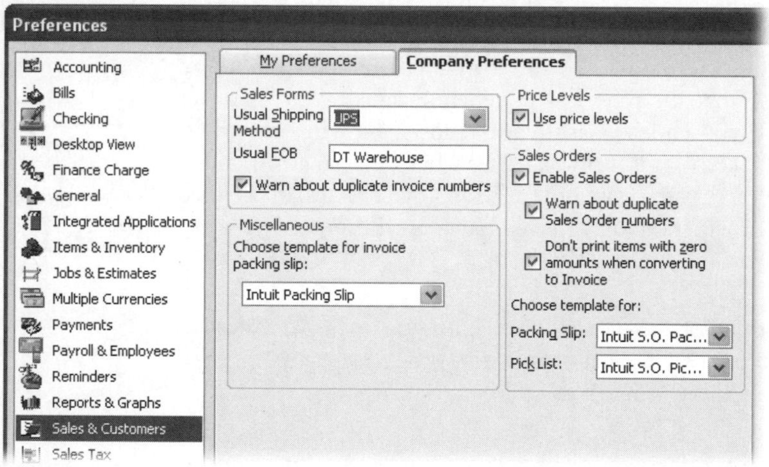

Figure 23-15:
Preferences in the Sales & Customers category affect the information that appears on invoices, as well as the account to which QuickBooks assigns reimbursable expenses.

The My Preferences tab has one set of options that tell the program what to do about outstanding billable time and expenses. Here's what each option does:

- **Prompt for time/costs to add.** If you typically bill for time and expenses, select this option. That way, the "Choose Billable Time and Costs" dialog box opens automatically when you create an invoice for a customer who has outstanding billable time charges or expenses.

- **Don't add any.** Select this option if you rarely have time or expenses to invoice and don't want to see the "Choose Billable Time and Costs" dialog box or receive a reminder that outstanding time and expenses exist.

- **Ask what to do.** This option merely adds an additional step to what the "Prompt for time/costs to add" option does. You have to tell QuickBooks whether or not to open the "Choose Billable Time and Costs" dialog box. However, if you select the "Prompt for time/costs to add" option, you can simply close the "Choose Billable Time and Costs" dialog box without adding anything to the invoice.

Here's a guide to the Sales & Customers preferences on the Company Preferences tab, all of which only QuickBooks administrators can change:

- **Usual Shipping Method.** If you negotiate a sweet deal with a shipping company and use it whenever possible, choose that company in the Usual Shipping Method drop-down list. When you do, QuickBooks fills in sales form Ship Via fields with this shipping method. If the method you want to use isn't on the list, choose *<Add New>* to open the New Shipping Method dialog box (page 149).

- **Usual FOB.** FOB stands for "free on board" and represents the location at which the customer becomes responsible for the products you ship. For example, suppose you ship products from your warehouse in Severance, CO and you use Severance as your FOB location. As soon as your shipments leave Severance, the customer becomes the official owner of the products and is responsible for them should they be lost, damaged, or stolen in transit. Type a brief description of your FOB location in this box. QuickBooks fills in the FOB field on invoices and other sales forms with this information.

Note: To keep you on your toes, the Intuit developers used a standard size for the Usual FOB text box, but you can type no more than 13 characters in the box.

- **Warn about duplicate invoice numbers.** Turn on this checkbox if you want QuickBooks to warn you when you create an invoice with the same number as one you already entered.

- **Choose template for invoice packing slip.** If you ship products to customers, you can print a packing slip with QuickBooks to include in your shipments. To specify the packing slip you want QuickBooks to use, in the drop-down list, choose the form you want. QuickBooks selects its predefined packing slip, Intuit Packing Slip, initially. You can create your own template by following the instructions on page 621. After you set this preference, when you create an invoice and choose Print Packing Slip on the Print menu (page 314), QuickBooks automatically selects the template you specified.

- **Use price levels.** You can set up multiple prices on the items you sell by setting price levels. To do this, first turn on this checkbox. Refer to page 141 and page 266 to learn how to define and apply price levels.

- **Sales orders.** To use sales orders (QuickBooks Premier and Enterprise only) to record customer orders before you create invoices, turn on this checkbox. With sales orders turned on, you can also tell QuickBooks to warn you when you create a sales order with a duplicate number. And you can tell the program to leave off any items with zero amounts when you convert the sales order into an invoice.

Sales Tax

Charging sales tax can be a complicated business, as the number of preferences on the Sales Tax Company Preferences tab indicates. If you don't charge sales tax, in the Do You Charge Sales Tax? area, simply choose the No option and move on to more important endeavors. If you do charge sales tax, you'll learn how to use the rest of the preferences as you set up sales tax items (page 126), charge sales tax on your sales, and pay sales tax to the appropriate authorities (page 244).

Send Forms

As you'll learn throughout this book, you can include a cover note when you send invoices, purchase orders, and other business forms via email, as shown in Figure 23-16. For example, if you email a purchase order, you can include details about the delivery in the note. Or, you can include a cover note along with an invoice to add some personal interaction with your customer.

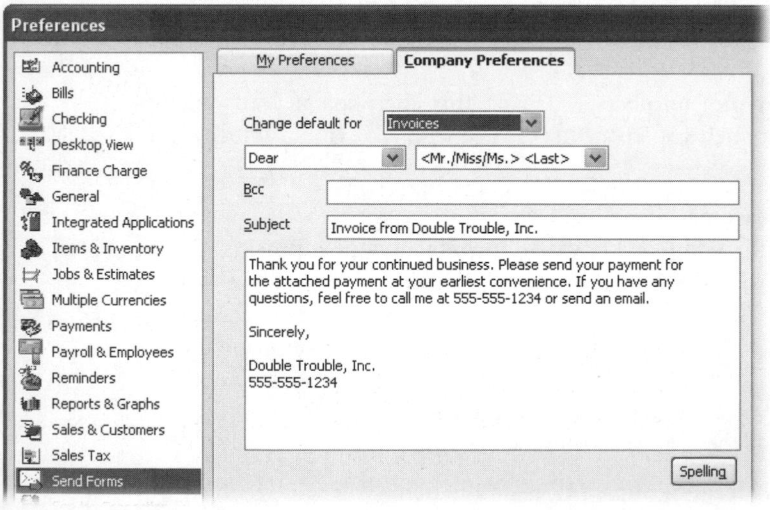

Figure 23-16:
The contents of the note that you create in the Send Forms preference category appear in the Send Forms dialog box. QuickBooks attaches your invoice or other sales form as an Adobe PDF file.

QuickBooks includes standard messages for each type of form you send via email. These messages won't win any awards for creativity, but fortunately, QuickBooks administrators can change them. You can create standard notes for invoices, estimates, statements, sales orders, sales receipts, credit memos, purchase orders, and reports. In fact, if your company has standard letters on file, you can copy and paste the contents of those letters from another program, such as Microsoft Word, into the QuickBooks cover note in the Send Forms preference Company Preferences tab.

To configure a standard note for a particular type of business form, follow these steps:

1. **To modify the note that accompanies a particular type of form, in the "Change default for" drop-down list, choose the form you want to customize.**

   For example, if you want to set up a cover letter to go with your invoices, choose Invoices in the list.

2. **To specify the salutation you want, choose one from the drop-down list.**

   Your choices include "Dear" and the impersonal "To".

3. **To specify the format for the recipient's name, choose it from the format drop down list.**

   Depending on how formal or chummy you like to be, you can choose to display the person's first name only, the first and last name, or a title and last name. For example, if you choose *<First>*, your note begins with something like "To Dana" or "Dear Dana". For more formal notes, choose *<Mr./Miss/Ms.> <Last>* to begin with "Dear Ms. Dvorak".

4. **Edit the content of the note using typical editing techniques.**

   For instance, click in the text to position the cursor where you want to add text. Drag the pointer to select text you want to replace. Double-click a word to select the entire word.

5. **To save the changes to your notes and close the Preferences dialog box, click OK or select another preference category.**

   If you make changes to notes and click another preference icon, QuickBooks displays a Save Changes dialog box. To save the changes you made, click Yes. When you email an invoice or other form, QuickBooks opens the Send Invoice dialog box (or the dialog box corresponding to the business form you're sending) with your note filled in, as described on page 315.

Note: On the My Preferences tab, QuickBooks automatically turns on the "Auto-check the 'To be e-mailed' checkbox if customer's Preferred Send Method is e-mail." checkbox. That way, you don't have to remember whether customers want to receive paperwork by email or snail-mail. If you want to send QuickBooks email using Microsoft Outlook, select the Outlook option. If you use a different program for email, select the QuickBooks E-mail option, which uses Intuit's free email service to send messages to your customers.

Spelling

The spell checker in QuickBooks isn't the all-knowing, willing-to-learn assistant that you find in other programs, but it helps you find common misspellings in most text fields. Spell checking is a personal preference: Each person who logs into Quick-Books can choose whether to use spell checking by turning on or off the "Always check spelling before printing, saving, or sending supported forms" checkbox.

If you turn spell checking on, you can also choose words that you want the spell checker to ignore. For example, you can ignore Internet addresses, words that contain numbers, words beginning with a capital letter, all uppercase words, and words with a mixture of upper- and lowercase letters.

POWER USERS' CLINIC

Service Connection Preferences

If your company uses QuickBooks services, such as online banking, QuickBooks administrators can control how people log into those services. The easiest way to learn about or sign up for these services is to choose Help → Add QuickBooks Services and then click the link for the service you want. Each person who uses QuickBooks services can control the behavior of online sessions. Security is a company-wide issue, so the options for whether to prompt for a password appear on the Company Preferences tab. Here are the service connection preferences that administrators can set and when you might want to use them:

- **Automatically connect without asking for a password**. Choosing this option automatically logs people into the QuickBooks Business Services network without a login name or password. This option is appropriate if you're the only person who accesses the network or you aren't concerned about security.

- **Always ask for a password before connecting.** Choose this option if you want everyone to provide a login name and password each time they access QuickBooks business services. This option is handy if several people access QuickBooks business services or different people have different privileges with the services you use.

- **Allow background downloading of service messages.** If you want QuickBooks to check for messages and updates when your Internet connection

isn't tied up with other work, turn this checkbox on. QuickBooks checks the Intuit website periodically and downloads QuickBooks updates or messages. If you turn this checkbox off, you can check for updates at a convenient time by choosing Help → Update QuickBooks.

If you aren't a QuickBooks administrator, you can still make some choices about your connection to QuickBooks Business Services.

On the My Preferences tab, the "Give me the option of saving a file whenever I download WebConnect data" checkbox lets you decide when you want to process downloaded transactions. Suppose you download transactions from your bank or another financial institution (page 533), but it's the end of the day and you want to process them later. If you want QuickBooks to ask you whether you want to process downloaded transactions immediately or save them to a file, turn this checkbox on. If you turn this checkbox off, QuickBooks automatically processes downloaded transactions immediately.

You can launch QuickBooks by downloading WebConnect data or by double-clicking a QuickBooks file that contains WebConnect data that you downloaded previously. When you open QuickBooks this way, you often want to continue working in QuickBooks after you process the downloaded transactions. To keep QuickBooks open after processing transactions, turn the "If QuickBooks is run by my browser, don't close it after WebConnect is done" checkbox on.

Tax: 1099

The Company Preferences tab in the Tax: 1099 preference category begins with the most important 1099 question: "Do you file 1099-MISC forms?" If you don't use 1099 vendors, such as self-employed subcontractors, or you delegate 1099 generation to your accountant, simply choose the No option and ignore the rest of the preferences in this category. If you do file 1099-MISC forms, you can specify the accounts you use to track 1099 vendor payments and the minimum amount you have to report to the IRS. To learn how to generate 1099s and set the preferences that control them, refer to page 458.

Time & Expenses

The first option in this category is whether you track time at all. If you do, select the Yes option. Then, you can choose the first day of the work week that appears if you use weekly timesheets in QuickBooks (see page 191).

The "Invoicing options" section has settings for how you handle billable time and expenses on invoices.

- **Create invoices from a list of time and expenses** If you turn this checkbox on (available only in Premier and Enterprise), the Customer menu includes the "Invoice for Time & Expenses" command. With this setting, you can view a list of all your unbilled time and expenses and select the customers you want to bill, which is described in detail on page 270.

- **Track reimbursed expenses as income.** Companies differ in their approach to reimbursed expenses, as explained on page 223. Some companies assign reimbursed expenses as income and then deduct the expenses as costs. The method you choose doesn't affect the profit you earn—the reason for tracking reimbursable expenses as income is to charge sales tax on those expenses. If you want to post reimbursed expenses to an income account, turn this checkbox on.

- **Default Markup Percentage.** Suppose you're an interior decorator and you mark up the furniture and bric-a-brac you sell by a standard percentage. When you specify your markup percentage in this text box and create a new item (page 112), QuickBooks calculates the item's sales price based on its cost. For example, if you create an inventory part for a black leather sofa and enter its cost as $10,000, a 20-percent markup results in a sales price of $12,000.

- **Default Markup Account.** To assign the income from your markup percentage to a specific account, select it in this drop-down list. You can choose an account dedicated to markup income or simply assign markup to your product-related income account.

If you charge a different markup on a few of the things you sell, then simply modify the sales price that QuickBooks calculates.

CHAPTER 24

Integrating QuickBooks with Other Programs

Most businesses use other programs in addition to QuickBooks to keep things running smoothly. You can put QuickBooks to use in many other programs studying your company's financial ratios, calculating employee bonuses based on hours worked and services sold, sending special sales letters to customers on their birth days, and so on. Similarly, other programs may contain data that would be useful to pull into QuickBooks. For example, if you use an estimating program that has all the products and services you sell in its database, there's no reason to manually enter those in QuickBooks.

QuickBooks doesn't share its most intimate details with just any program. It reserves its data for a few select programs—or the ones you tell it to play nicely with—but then it gets really chummy. For example, you can set up letters in QuickBooks to send to customers, and the program automatically opens Microsoft Word with your customer data merged into form letters and envelopes. If you use Outlook (not Outlook Express) as your contact-management tool, keeping records up-to-date is easy. By synchronizing your QuickBooks company file and your contact database, you enter changes in one place and the programs automatically copy data from one file to the other.

Programs that can read a QuickBooks company file still have to ask permission to grab QuickBooks data. The QuickBooks administrator (or other QuickBooks users that the administrator anoints) can say whether another program can have access and how much. For software that can't read a company file directly but *can* provide valuable assistance processing your financial data (such as an Excel spreadsheet that calculates financial ratios that QuickBooks doesn't), you can export and import data between programs (page 596).

This chapter describes how to integrate QuickBooks at whatever level of trust you prefer. It also tells you about add-on services that Intuit provides and how to find third-party programs that work with QuickBooks.

Mail Merge to a Word Document

Business communications are the perfect marriage of QuickBooks data and word processing. You can generate your letters and envelopes in no time by combining QuickBooks customer contact info and other data with Microsoft Word mail merge documents. QuickBooks includes dozens of ready-to-mail letters as Word documents that cover the most common business communications, from customer thank-you notes to less friendly denials of requests for credit. If nothing less than Pulitzer Prize quality will do for your business letters, you can modify the built-in letters and envelopes in Word or write your own.

The best place to start when you want to prepare letters in QuickBooks is Company → Prepare Letters with Envelopes, which displays a submenu with the following entries:

- **Collection Letters** include the invoices or statements that are overdue, and they remind customers to pay up. QuickBooks automatically pulls the overdue balance and overdue invoices from your company file.

- **Customer Letters** pull only the customer contact and address information from QuickBooks to address the letter and envelope. The rest of the letter is boilerplate for situations such as thanking customers for their business, apologizing for a mistake, or sending a contract.

- **Vendor Letters** include credit requests, disputed charges, payments on your account, and two blank templates for mailing or faxing a vendor.

- **Employee Letters** cover birthdays, sick time, vacation, and general communications.

- **Letters to Other Names** cover a hodge-podge of different recipients, so QuickBooks doesn't even try to guess what you need. The only template in this category is a blank letter with basic mail merge fields.

- **Customize Letter Templates** is a command that helps you create a brand new template, convert a Word document into a template, edit an existing template, or organize the templates you already have, as described in the box on page 587.

Creating Letters and Envelopes in QuickBooks

Though preparing any kind of letter with the QuickBooks letter wizard takes no more than a few clicks, the collection letter wizard has some extra smarts. For most letters, you can tell QuickBooks whether you want to include active and inactive names and then select the names you want to receive letters. The collection letter wizard can also filter the customer list by how late payments are.

POWER USERS' CLINIC

Customizing Letter Templates

To create, edit, or otherwise manage customized letter templates, choose Company → "Prepare Letters with Envelopes" → Customize Letter Templates. (The first time you choose this command, QuickBooks tells you it can't find the pre-installed letter templates in your company file folder and asks if you want to copy its built-in templates. Click Copy to create copies of the built-in templates in the folder with your company file. If you store letter templates in another folder on your computer, click Browse to choose the folder.) Then, in the "Letters and Envelopes" wizard, choose one of these options:

- **Create a New Letter Template From Scratch.** You can specify the type of letter you want to create and the name of the template. QuickBooks sends a blank letter template to Word along with the toolbar, shown in Figure 24-1. In addition to writing the content of the letter, you can add fields from QuickBooks to automatically fill in your company and customer or other recipient info.

- **Convert an Existing Microsoft Word Document to a Letter Template.** You can use an existing Word document as the basis for a new template.

Then, once you specify the type of letter, you can add more text or QuickBooks fields to the document as if you were creating a new template from scratch.

- **View or Edit Existing Letter Template.** You can open and edit any existing template.

- **Organize Existing Letter Templates.** When you choose this option, you can navigate through each category of template, choose a template, and then delete, duplicate, rename it, or move it to a different category.

QuickBooks stores the Word documents for letter templates in a document folder. For example, with Windows XP, your letter templates are in *C:\Documents and Settings\ All Users\Shared Documents\Intuit\QuickBooks\Company Files\QuickBooks Letter Templates*. For Windows Vista, the templates are in *C:\Users\Public\Public Documents\Intuit\ QuickBooks\Company Files\QuickBooks Letter Templates*. There's a subfolder for each category of template (Collections Letters, Customer Letters, and so on).

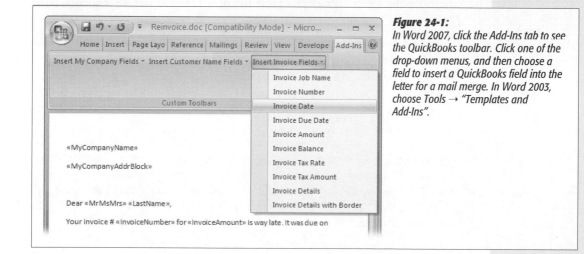

Figure 24-1:
In Word 2007, click the Add-Ins tab to see the QuickBooks toolbar. Click one of the drop-down menus, and then choose a field to insert a QuickBooks field into the letter for a mail merge. In Word 2003, choose Tools → "Templates and Add-Ins".

Here are the steps for creating letters and envelopes using a collection letter as an example:

1. **Choose Company → "Prepare Letters with Envelopes" → Collection Letters.**

   QuickBooks opens the "Letters and Envelopes" wizard and shows the recipient options for collection letters, as shown in Figure 24-2.

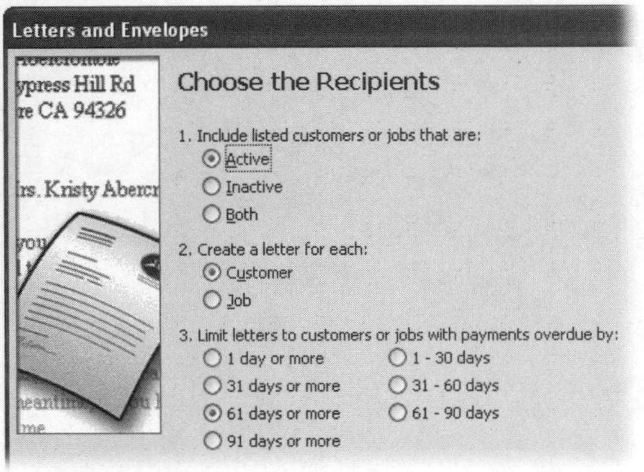

Figure 24-2:
On the "Choose the Recipients" page, QuickBooks automatically selects the option to include active customers. If you want to send letters to active and inactive customers alike, for a recall notice, for example, choose the Both option. Item 2 on the page lets you choose whether to send a letter to each customer or to the contact person for each job a customer hires you to do. For collection letters, item 3 asks you to specify how late the payment has to be before you send a letter.

Letters and Envelopes

Choose the Recipients

1. Include listed customers or jobs that are:
   - ⦿ Active
   - ○ Inactive
   - ○ Both

2. Create a letter for each:
   - ⦿ Customer
   - ○ Job

3. Limit letters to customers or jobs with payments overdue by:
   - ○ 1 day or more   ○ 1 - 30 days
   - ○ 31 days or more   ○ 31 - 60 days
   - ⦿ 61 days or more   ○ 61 - 90 days
   - ○ 91 days or more

Note: For non-collection letters, you still choose active or inactive customers and whether to send letters to each customer or each job, but those are your only choices. (The first screen you see for letters to vendors, employees, and people on the Other Names list combines the list of selected names and the options for filtering names.)

2. **After you choose the filters you want to apply for your letter recipients, click Next.**

   For collection letters, QuickBooks displays a message if any customers have unapplied credits or payments. Rather than embarrassing yourself by sending a collection letter to a customer whose payments are up-to-date, you're better off canceling the wizard and applying credits and payments before preparing collection letters.

Tip: The Open Invoices report shows unapplied credits and payments (along with open invoices). To run the report, choose Reports → Customers & Receivables → Open Invoices. To see only unapplied credits and payments, in the report window toolbar, click Modify Report, and then click the Filter tab. In the Filter list, choose Transaction Type. In the Transaction Type drop-down list, choose Multiple Transaction Types. In the Select Transaction Types dialog box, click "Credit Memo and Payment", and then click OK. Click OK once more to update the report to show only unapplied credit memos and payments.

For a quick view of one customer's transactions, open the Customer Center (on the Home page, click Customers) and select the customer on the Customers & Jobs tab. At the top right of the Customer Information panel, click the Quick Report link.

The next screen is "Review and Edit Recipients". QuickBooks automatically selects all the names that passed your filters.

3. **If you've already talked to some customers and want to remove them from the list, click the checkmarks in front of their names to turn them off.**

You can click Mark All or Unmark All to select or clear every name, respectively. If you want only a few names, it's faster to click Unmark All and then click each name you want. The recipient list is sorted by name initially, but you can select the Amount option to sort by the amount that's overdue, for instance, if you want to send letters only to customers whose balances are greater than $10,000.

4. **When you've selected the customers you want to send letters to, click Next.**

QuickBooks moves you to the "Choose a Letter Template" screen.

5. **Select the collection letter template that you want to send, and then click Next.**

QuickBooks includes three types of collection letters. The formal collection letter is a straightforward request for payment. The friendly collection letter assumes the customer simply forgot. The harsh collection letter includes the threat of turning the account over to a collection agency. The friendly and formal letters can't do any harm, but if you're considering sending harsh letters, you might want to create your own template for that communication.

To use a different template entirely, select the "Create or Edit a letter template" option. When you click Next, you can choose one of the options described in the box on page 587 (create a new template, convert a Word document, or edit an existing template).

6. **On the "Enter a Name and Title" screen, in the Name box, type the name you want to include in the letter signature block. In the Title box, type the signer's title.**

When you click Next, QuickBooks sends the information to Microsoft Word, as shown in Figure 24-3. Depending on how many letters you're sending, you might have to wait a few minutes before Word launches with your letters.

7. **After you print the letters from within Word, back in QuickBooks, the Print Letters and Envelopes screen appears. Click Next if you want to print envelopes that go with the letters you just printed in Word.**

If you don't want to print envelopes, click Cancel. The wizard closes and you're done.

8. **If you choose to print envelopes, QuickBooks opens the Envelope Options dialog box. In the Envelope Size drop-down list, choose the type of envelope you use.**

If your envelopes already include your return address, turn off the "Print return address" box. Turn on the Delivery Point Barcode if you're mailing letters in the US and want the post office bar code printed on the envelopes. When you click OK, you'll see a preview of the envelopes in Word.

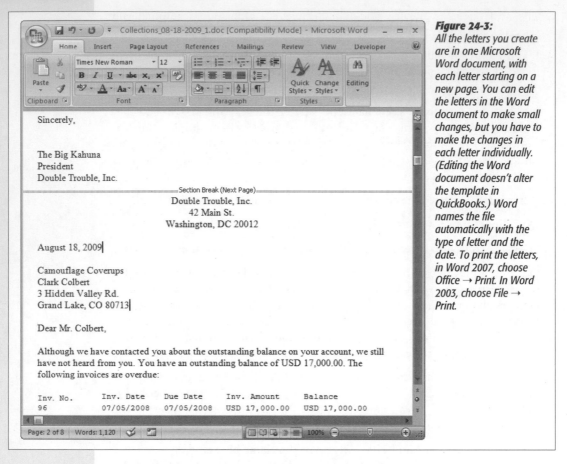

Figure 24-3:
All the letters you create are in one Microsoft Word document, with each letter starting on a new page. You can edit the letters in the Word document to make small changes, but you have to make the changes in each letter individually. (Editing the Word document doesn't alter the template in QuickBooks.) Word names the file automatically with the type of letter and the date. To print the letters, in Word 2007, choose Office → Print. In Word 2003, choose File → Print.

9. **When you've got envelopes in your printer, click OK.**

The envelope print job runs right away.

Synchronizing Contacts

If you keep information about contacts in Microsoft Outlook (2000 through 2007)—*not* Outlook Express—you can synchronize those records with your QuickBooks contact data. In addition to saving time by not duplicating data entry, synchronizing your contact info helps reduce errors. As long as you enter an update correctly in the one program, you're sure to get the right info in your other contact database. Regardless of which program you update contact information in, you can transfer any changes to the other database.

Note: The only time synchronizing doesn't apply is when you delete names. If you delete names in Outlook, QuickBooks doesn't delete them in your company file. If you really want those names gone, you have to make them inactive or delete them in QuickBooks. (Making them inactive is the best course, because deleting names can create problems, as page 96 explains.) On the other hand, if you delete a name in QuickBooks but don't delete it in Outlook, it'll reappear in QuickBooks unless you tell Contact Sync to ignore it (page 592).

Using QuickBooks Contact Sync for Outlook

If you use QuickBooks 2005 or later (and Outlook 2000 or later), you use "QuickBooks Contact Sync for Outlook" to synchronize your contact data. Although the command to synchronize is already on the File → Utilities menu, you have to install Contact Sync before you get started. Here's how to download this tool and put it to work:

1. **Choose File → Utilities → Synchronize Contacts.**

   If Contact Sync isn't installed, a message box tells you that you have to download and install it. Click OK to do just that. QuickBooks opens a Web browser to the QuickBooks Contact Sync for Outlook page (*http://support.quickbooks. intuit.com/support/tools/contact_sync*). Type the email address you used when you registered QuickBooks (page 649), and then click "Continue to Download". You can save the installation file (click Save) or run it immediately (click Run) to install the software.

   Installing is easy. First, be sure to close Outlook. Then, run the installation wizard as you do for other programs. Accept the license agreement, choose a destination folder, and then click Next or Install, and the installation begins.

2. **After you install Contact Sync, launch both Outlook and QuickBooks.**

   Log into QuickBooks as the administrator and open the company file you want to synchronize.

   In Outlook, the Contact Sync Setup Assistant appears, offering to help you import your contacts from QuickBooks into Outlook. After you click Get Started, a "Connecting to QuickBooks" message box appears while Outlook and QuickBooks introduce themselves to each other. Eventually, the QuickBooks Contact Sync dialog box opens and selects the company file that's open in QuickBooks.

Note: If you want to import contacts from a different company file, click Cancel and, in QuickBooks, open the company file with the contacts to import.

3. **Click Setup to begin the setup in earnest.**

   The Select An Outlook Folder screen appears. If you're like most people, you have only one folder for contacts, *Personal Folders\Contacts*, which the wizard selects automatically.

4. **If you want to synchronize to a different Outlook folder, choose it. Click Next.**

   The Select QuickBooks List Types To Synchronize screen appears.

5. **To synchronize all contacts, turn on the Customer, Include Customer Jobs, and Vendor checkboxes, and then click Next.**

   For each checkbox you turn on, the Setup Assistant creates a subfolder in the Outlook Contacts folder.

6. **In the "Exclude Contacts From Synchronization" screen, turn on the checkboxes for types of names you don't want to transfer back and forth, and then click Next.**

   When you turn on these checkboxes, names assigned to Outlook's Personal category or marked as Private won't transfer to QuickBooks.

7. **In the Mapping Customer Fields (Part 1 of 2) screen, change the field mapping for any QuickBooks field that doesn't point to the right Outlook field, as shown in Figure 24-4. Click Next when the mappings are the way you want them.**

   The Mapping Customer Fields screen displays the QuickBooks contact fields on the left side, along with its guesses about what Outlook fields to map to.

8. **If you turned on the checkboxes to import jobs and vendors, repeat step 7 to map job and vendor fields to the corresponding Outlook fields.**

   Chances are you'll make the same changes for jobs and vendors as you did for customer fields.

9. **In the Set Conflict Action screen, select the option for how you want Contact Sync to resolve discrepancies between Outlook and QuickBooks, and then click Save.**

   Contact Sync automatically selects the "Let me decide each case" option, which means you get to tell QuickBooks what to do if the contact in Outlook differs from the data you have in QuickBooks. If you usually update contacts in Outlook, select the Outlook Data Wins option. Select the QuickBooks Data Wins option if you usually update contacts in QuickBooks.

10. **In the "Change Settings or Synchronize Now" screen, click Setup to change any settings (you retrace your steps until you're back in the "Change Settings or Synchronize Now" screen). When you're ready to synchronize, click the Sync Now button.**

    The Contact Sync screen keeps you updated on the progress it's making. When the synchronization is done, the Contact Overview Complete screen appears, showing you how many customers and vendors it found and either matched or added to Outlook.

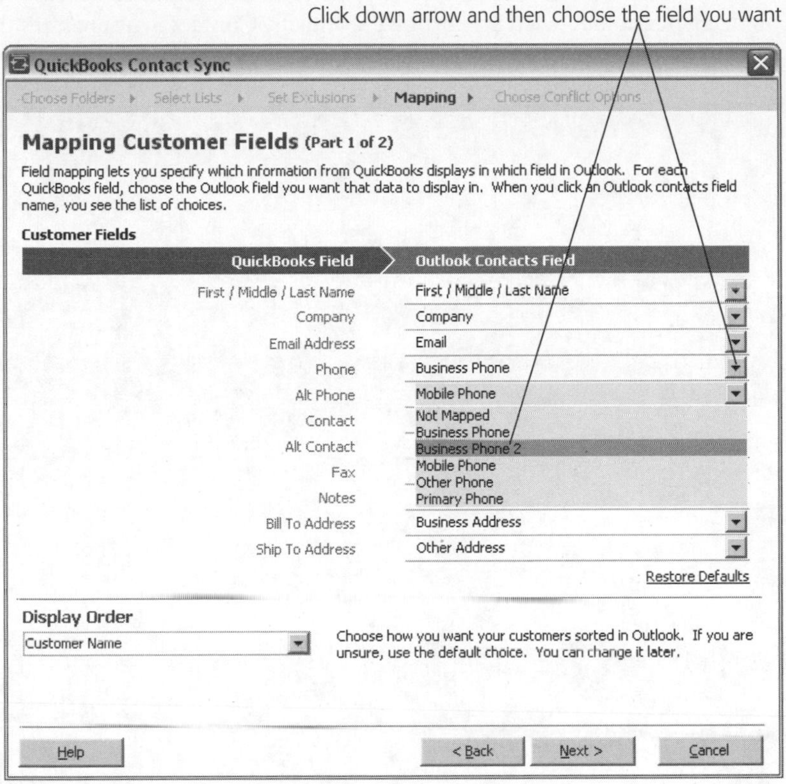

Click down arrow and then choose the field you want

Figure 24-4:
The Setup Assistant makes some astute guesses about which Outlook fields map to QuickBooks fields. However, if the selected field isn't what you want, click the down arrow to the right of the Outlook field, and then choose the correct Outlook field.

11. **When the Contact Overview Complete screen appears, click Next.**

    If contacts that already existed in Outlook don't match up to a QuickBooks list (like Customer or Vendor), the "Select Categories for QuickBooks" screen appears. You can add an Outlook contact to a QuickBooks list by selecting the contact, choosing the QuickBooks list in the "Select list for contact" drop-down menu, and then clicking Apply.

    If the contacts don't match up to a QuickBooks list because they aren't business contacts, you can tell Contact Sync to ignore them. Click the first contact and Shift+click the last contact to select them all. Then, in the "Select list for contact" drop-down menu, choose Ignore, and then click Apply.

12. **After you've selected categories for Outlook contacts, click Next.**

    In the Accept Changes screen, you can review the changes that will occur in Outlook and QuickBooks. If the changes are OK, click Accept. If you don't want to make the changes, click Cancel. If you click Accept, a progress box shows you where Contact Sync is in transferring data. The Synchronization Complete message box appears when your info is synchronized. Click OK and you're done.

From now on, you can update contact information with just one click. In Outlook, in the Contact Sync toolbar, click Synchronize Contacts. Contact Sync analyzes the changes in the two programs and updates both as necessary.

UP TO SPEED

Finding Third-Party Integrated Applications

Because QuickBooks is so popular with small businesses, plenty of companies besides Intuit develop programs to fill the niches that QuickBooks doesn't handle—or doesn't handle very well. The Intuit Marketplace website (*http:// marketplace.intuit.com*) is one place to look for third-party programs. (Most third-party programs offer free trials that last from 30 to 90 days.)

Programs listed in the Marketplace share data with Quick-Books but target different industries or services. Sure, QuickBooks has Premier editions for a few industries (see page 5); but the Marketplace offers additional software in those industries as well as accounting solutions for industries like agriculture, hotels and restaurants, transportation, and utilities. For example, the Construction area of the Solutions has programs that produce estimates more easily than QuickBooks' Construction Edition and that generate documents that conform to industry association standards—while still sharing data with your QuickBooks company file.

Intuit lists third-party programs in two ways: by industry and by business function. For example, if you're looking for contact-management software, you don't have to navigate

every industry link looking for programs. Below Find Apps, click Search By Business Need. Then, choose CRM /Sales Force Automation.

The Marketplace doesn't show you *every* third-party program that integrates with QuickBooks. If you use Google (*www.google.com*) to search for basic terms like "Quick-Books third-party applications," you'll get more than 300,000 results. Of course, if you focus your search (add "medical office," for example) you can narrow the results (to about 7,000 in this case). And, if you use all of the 10 keywords that you can enter in a Google search to describe the QuickBooks add-ons you seek, you might get a few dozen links worth investigating.

If you're familiar with websites like Download.com (*www. download.com*), try using "QuickBooks" as a keyword for a search. Download.com has dozens of programs that work with QuickBooks, some of which aren't industry-based at all but are still incredibly valuable. For example, one program scans paper documents you receive and enters the data it extracts (using optical character recognition) directly into your QuickBooks company file.

Setting Up an Integrated Application

Integrated applications don't read data from exported text files; they actually access your company file to get info. To protect your data from programs that *shouldn't* read your company file, you have to tell QuickBooks which programs you *do* want digging into your financial data.

Letting programs access your data is something you set up with preferences. Choose Edit → Preferences, click the Integrated Applications icon, and then click the Company Preferences tab, shown in Figure 24-5. Here, you can turn on the "Don't allow any applications to access this company file" checkbox to keep all programs out. But if you're reading this section, you probably want at least one program to access your QuickBooks data.

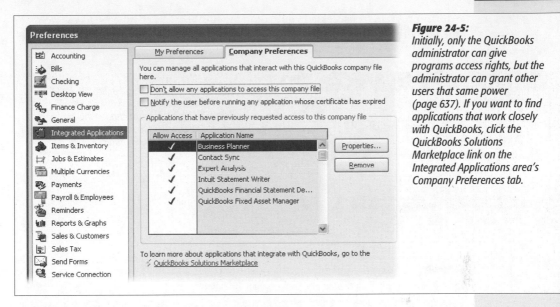

Figure 24-5:
Initially, only the QuickBooks administrator can give programs access rights, but the administrator can grant other users that same power (page 637). If you want to find applications that work closely with QuickBooks, click the QuickBooks Solutions Marketplace link on the Integrated Applications area's Company Preferences tab.

As long as the "Don't allow any applications to access this company file" checkbox is turned off, when a program tries to access your company file, QuickBooks displays an Application Certificate dialog box. If you're the QuickBooks administrator or someone else with the permission to dole out file access, choose one of the options to set the program's access to the company file. Obviously, choosing No keeps the program out. But you have three options when you want to let the program in:

- **Yes, prompt each time.** When you're letting another program access your data, this is the safest option. The program can get in only when someone with the rights to approve access says so—a small obstacle that prevents the wrong person from running the program after breaking in after hours. If someone who can approve access isn't available to say yes, the integrated application (or the person who's running it) is out of luck.

- **Yes, whenever this QuickBooks company file is open.** This option is a bit more trusting. As long as someone is working on the company file, the integrated application can access the file without asking permission.

- **Yes, always; allow access even if QuickBooks is not running.** This is by far the most lenient choice. The integrated program can help itself to your financial data even if no one with a QuickBooks login is working on the file. This option is exactly what you need if the integrated application is a resource hog that you run at night.

When you choose this option, you can specify the QuickBooks user for the login. Rather than use the login for one of your employees, you can create a QuickBooks user (page 634) specifically for an integrated application, which lets you control the type of data the program can access without affecting someone else's login.

After a program has accessed your company file, you can change its access rights in the Properties dialog box, as shown in Figure 24-6.

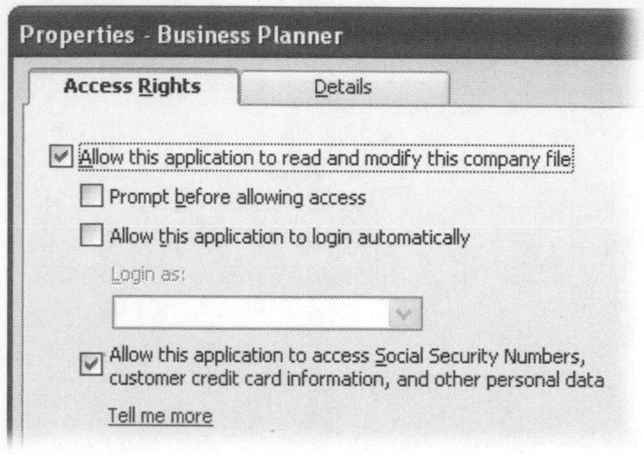

Properties - Business Planner

Access Rights | Details

☑ Allow this application to read and modify this company file
☐ Prompt before allowing access
☐ Allow this application to login automatically
Login as:
☑ Allow this application to access Social Security Numbers, customer credit card information, and other personal data
Tell me more

Figure 24-6:
On the Company Preferences tab, select the application and then click Properties. In the Properties dialog box, you can turn checkboxes on and off to remove access or change the level of access the program has. The Details tab shows the program name, the company that developed it, the version, and its certificate.

Warning: Sometimes third-party programs alter QuickBooks features, like your chart of accounts. So before you integrate a new program, back up your QuickBooks file. After you integrate a program, check your QuickBooks file for unauthorized changes, like new accounts you don't want to use. If the program made changes you don't like, you can restore your backup or modify your lists manually in QuickBooks (see Chapter 4, 5, 6, or 7, depending on the list).

Exporting QuickBooks Data

Programs that don't integrate with QuickBooks can still do things that QuickBooks can't. For example, you can export a report to Excel and take advantage of a wider range of formatting options and calculations. To get data out of your QuickBooks company file and into another program, you have three choices:

• **Export file.** You can create a *delimited text file* (that is, a file that separates each field with a delimiter like a comma or tab) that contains data from your QuickBooks file. For example, you can generate export files for QuickBooks lists, such as your Item List or Sales Tax Code List. For the named records in QuickBooks like your Customer:Job and Vendor Lists, you can produce export files that contain all your contact information or only address information.

• **Report file.** Create any report in QuickBooks and you can then export it to a file that you can use in another program. Compared to exporting an entire list, a report gives you more control over the exported information. If you want to export data from several lists or from transactions, exporting reports is your *only* choice.

• **Excel file.** Throughout QuickBooks, you can get to the same Export dialog box that you see when you export reports. For example, at the bottom of the Item List window, click Excel, and then choose Export All Items. In the Customer Center's menu bar, click Excel, and then choose either Export Customer List or Export Transactions. (The Vendor Center and the Employee Center have similar commands.)

Exporting Lists and Addresses

When you export lists to QuickBooks delimited text files, the export file (called an IIF file because of its .iif file extension) contains all the fields associated with those QuickBooks lists. Creating export files is easy, and the only choice you have to make is which lists to export. If you export several lists, the IIF file that QuickBooks creates contains every field for every list you chose.

Exporting lists to a text file

Exporting one or more lists to a delimited text file takes only a few quick steps:

1. **Choose File → Utilities → Export → "Lists to IIF Files".**

   QuickBooks opens an Export dialog box, which contains checkboxes for each list in QuickBooks from the Chart of Accounts to Customer List to Sales Tax Code List, as shown in Figure 24-7.

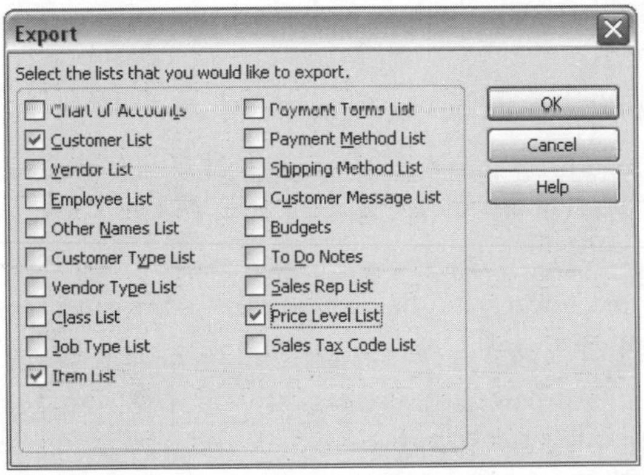

Figure 24-7:
Turning on a checkbox tells QuickBooks that you want to export all the records in that list. If you turn on more than one checkbox, the data for every list you choose gets dumped into a single export file.

2. **Turn on the checkbox for every list you want to export into the same file, and then click OK.**

   If you want to export lists into separate files, you have to repeat all the steps in this procedure for each export file you want to create. For example, if you want to export your Customer List and your Item List to two different files, repeat these steps twice through.

3. **In the second Export dialog box (which is basically a Save As dialog box), navigate to the folder where you want to save the export file and, in the "File name" box, type the name of the file.**

   Your export files are easier to find if you create a folder specifically for them. For example, you could create a subfolder called Export_Files within the folder that holds your company files.

4. **Click Save to create the file.**

When the QuickBooks Information message box tells you that your data was exported successfully, click OK to close the message box. Now, you're ready to import the file into Microsoft Excel or another program, as described later in this chapter.

Tip: Exporting QuickBooks data can help you learn the format you need to *import* data into your company file. For instance, once you've entered a sales tax code or two (using the laborious process described on page 124), you can export them. Then, in the export file, create the rest of your codes using the same format and then import that file back into QuickBooks.

Exporting addresses

With QuickBooks features to generate mail merge letters, export contact list reports, and synchronize your company file with Outlook, there isn't much reason to use the tab-delimited address files that QuickBooks produces. However, if you need a text file of names and addresses to import into another program, here's what you do:

1. **Choose File → Utilities → Export → "Addresses to Text File".**

If an Export Addresses message box appears and suggests that you try Write Letters, turn on the "Do not display this message in the future" checkbox, and then click OK to close the message box.

2. **In the "Select Names for Export Addresses" dialog box, choose the category of names you want to export, and then click OK.**

Initially, QuickBooks chooses "All names" to export all names in your company file. You can also choose categories of names, like "All vendors". To select individual names, choose "Multiple names", and then pick the names you want.

3. **In the Save Address Data File dialog box, select a folder where you want to save the exported file, type a file name in the "File name" box, and then click Save.**

QuickBooks automatically assigns a .txt extension to the file. You can now import it into any program that likes tab-delimited addresses.

Exporting Reports

If you remember all the way back to Chapter 21, you know that you can customize reports to contain just the information you want, presented just the way you want. When you want to export only *some* of your QuickBooks data or export it in a specific way, your best bet is customizing a report before you export it.

You can export a report to a comma-delimited file if that's what another program needs. If the other program is as fussy about data as QuickBooks is, making those changes in Excel is easier than trying to do the same in a text editing tool such as Windows Notepad. You can also export reports to extract some QuickBooks lists like the Item List, Customer List, Vendor List, and Employee List. Here are the different ways you can use this technique:

- **Running a report.** Start by running the report you want to export as you normally would just to view or print it (page 501). In the report window button bar, click Export. The Export Report dialog box lets you choose the file and options for the export, as shown in Figure 24-8.

- **From the Item List window.** Open the Item List window (on the Home page, click the Items & Services icon). At the bottom of the window, click the Excel button and then choose Export All Items. QuickBooks opens the same Export dialog box you see when you export a report (Figure 24-8).

- **From a QuickBooks Center.** In the Customer Center's menu bar, click Excel, and then choose Export Customer List or Export Transactions. In the Vendor Center and Employee Center, choose Export Vendor List or Export Employee List, respectively.

Figure 24-8:
If you want a worksheet with tips for working with the resulting Excel worksheet, be sure to leave on the "Include a new worksheet in the workbook that explains Excel worksheet linking" checkbox.

The Basic tab has options for where you want to save the exported report:

- The **"a new Excel workbook"** option is selected initially, which creates a brand-new Excel file for the report.

- The **"an existing Excel workbook"** option exports the report to an existing file. This option is ideal if you're planning to calculate ratios and want your most recent financial statements in the same workbook as statements for previous periods. If you export to an existing file, you can also choose options to create a new worksheet for the report or add the report to a sheet already in the workbook.

• Turning on the "Include a new worksheet in the workbook that explains Excel worksheet linking" checkbox tells QuickBooks to create a worksheet of tips. At the bottom of the Excel window, click the QuickBooks Export Tips tab and read about how to customize, update, and manage the exported reports.

The Advanced tab of the Export Report dialog box lets you set the formatting you want to transfer from QuickBooks to Excel, which Excel features you want the workbook to turn on (like AutoFit to size the columns to display all the data), and where you want the report header information stored. The "Send header to Page Setup in Excel" option copies the report header into the Excel page header. The "Send header to screen in Excel" option copies the report header into cells in the worksheet. Unless you have special requirements for your workbook, you won't go wrong keeping the choices that QuickBooks makes.

After you've selected the export file and options, click Export. QuickBooks launches Excel and copies the data in the report to the Excel workbook you specified, placing the data in the report columns into columns in a worksheet, as shown in Figure 24-9.

Importing Data from Other Programs

Importing data from other programs comes in handy mostly for generating lists in QuickBooks. However, you can also import data to generate your chart of accounts (page 46) or to load different versions of your company budget (page 489).

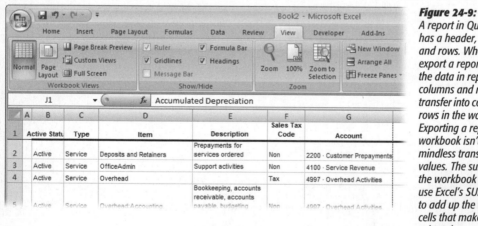

Figure 24-9:
A report in QuickBooks has a header, columns, and rows. When you export a report to Excel, the data in report columns and rows transfer into columns and rows in the worksheet. Exporting a report to a workbook isn't a mindless transfer of values. The subtotals in the workbook actually use Excel's SUM function to add up the workbook cells that make up the subtotal.

The biggest requirement for importing data is that the files be either Excel workbooks (.xls file) or delimited text files, which separate each piece of information with commas or tabs.

Importing Formatted Excel Files

QuickBooks veterans often amass all sorts of tools that they've built over the years, like Excel files set up to import information. Although QuickBooks has a wizard that shows you exactly where to put what kind of info in an Excel file, you can skip the handholding by choosing Files → Utilities → Import → Excel Files and then, in the "Add Your Excel Data to QuickBooks" wizard, clicking Advanced Import. In the "Import a file" dialog box that opens, you can import a file that's already formatted by following these steps:

1. In the Set Up Import tab, click Browse and then select the Excel file you want to import. (QuickBooks 2010 works with workbooks from Excel 97 through Excel 2007.)

2. QuickBooks fills in the "Choose a sheet in this Excel workbook" drop-down list with the worksheets from the workbook you selected. Choose the worksheet to import.

3. QuickBooks automatically turns on the "This data file has header rows" checkbox, which is the perfect choice when the first row of the Excel workbook contains text labels for the columns.

4. In the "Choose a mapping" drop-down list, choose <Add New>. Then, in the "Mapping name" box, type a name for the set of correspondences between fields and columns you're about to choose. (Once you've set up a mapping, you can reuse existing mappings by clicking Mappings and selecting the mapping you want.)

5. If you're defining a mapping, in the "Import type" drop-down list, choose the data you're importing: Customer, Vendor, Item, or Account.

6. For each QuickBooks field listed in the left column, in the "Import data" column, choose the corresponding Excel header or column name, as shown in Figure 24-11.

7. After you've mapped all the columns you want to import to QuickBooks fields, click Save.

8. In the "Import a file" dialog box's Preferences tab, tell QuickBooks how to handle errors and duplicate records. QuickBooks sets the Duplicate Handling option to "Prompt me and let me decide", so you're in complete control.

9. To review the data you're about to import, click Preview. In the Preview dialog box, in the "In data preview show" drop-down list, choose "only errors" to see rows of data that contain errors. When you select an incorrect entry, the "Details for" table shows the values you're trying to import and what the error is so you can correct it. You can also select options to skip importing rows with errors or import records and leave errors fields blank.

10. In the "Import a file" dialog box, click Import. Importing isn't reversible, so take QuickBooks up on its offer of backing up your company file before continuing.

Importing an Excel Spreadsheet

If you're familiar with importing Excel spreadsheets into other programs, importing them into QuickBooks is a snap. In fact, QuickBooks includes several Excel import templates that walk you through getting your Excel data for customers, vendors, and items into the format that QuickBooks requires. If you have a file that's already formatted to work with QuickBooks, choose File → Utilities → Import → Excel Files and then click Advanced Import. The box on the previous page tells you how to import a pre-formatted file. Here's how to use the Excel import templates:

1. **Choose File → Utilities → Import → Excel Files.**

   QuickBooks opens the Add Your Excel Data to QuickBooks wizard.

2. **Click the button for the type of data you want to import: Customers, Vendors, or Products I Sell.**

   QuickBooks opens an Excel template for the type of data you're importing, as shown in Figure 24-10.

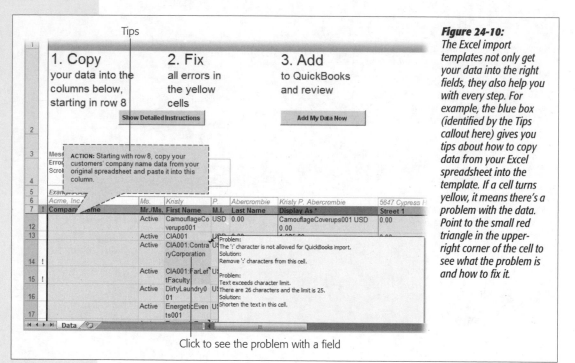

Tips

1. Copy
your data into the columns below, starting in row 8

2. Fix
all errors in the yellow cells

3. Add
to QuickBooks and review

Show Detailed Instructions

Add My Data Now

ACTION: Starting with row 8, copy your customers' company name data from your original spreadsheet and paste it into this column.

Click to see the problem with a field

Figure 24-10:
The Excel import templates not only get your data into the right fields, they also help you with every step. For example, the blue box (identified by the Tips callout here) gives you tips about how to copy data from your Excel spreadsheet into the template. If a cell turns yellow, it means there's a problem with the data. Point to the small red triangle in the upper-right corner of the cell to see what the problem is and how to fix it.

3. **After you've copied all the data from your spreadsheet into the Excel template and none of the data cells are yellow, save the spreadsheet.**

   In Excel 2007, click the Office button, and then choose Save As → Excel 97 - 2003 Workbook. In Excel 2003, choose File → Save As.

4. **In the Excel template, click Add My Data Now.**

   QuickBooks resumes control. The "Add Your Excel Data to QuickBooks" wizard shows the progress of the import. When it's done, it places green checkmarks to the left of all three steps and shows you how many records were imported. You can click the button (it says View Customer List, for example) to see the list you imported. Or, simply click Close and view your lists as you usually do. For example, to see your customer list, click Customer Center on the Home page.

Importing a Delimited File

If you're importing a Customer List, Vendor List, or Item List, don't even think about importing a delimited file. It's much easier to open that file in Excel and use the wizard described in the previous section. But if you want to import other kinds of lists or a budget, using a delimited file works just fine. QuickBooks needs to know the *kind* of data you're importing—and it learns that from special *keywords* for row and column headers. Keywords are strings of characters in a delimited text file that identify QuickBooks' records and fields. Before you import data from another program into a QuickBooks list, you need to know the correct keywords for the fields you're importing. The easiest way to see the keywords for a list is to export that list from QuickBooks and examine the keywords at the beginning of the rows and at the tops of the columns.

Deciphering keywords requires a smattering of computerese. For example, when you see the column heading Billing Address, you know instantly what kind of information you're looking at. But the only way QuickBooks recognizes the first line of a billing address is from the keyword BADDR1. Figure 24-12 explains all (showing the delimited file in an Excel spreadsheet to make the fields easier to read).

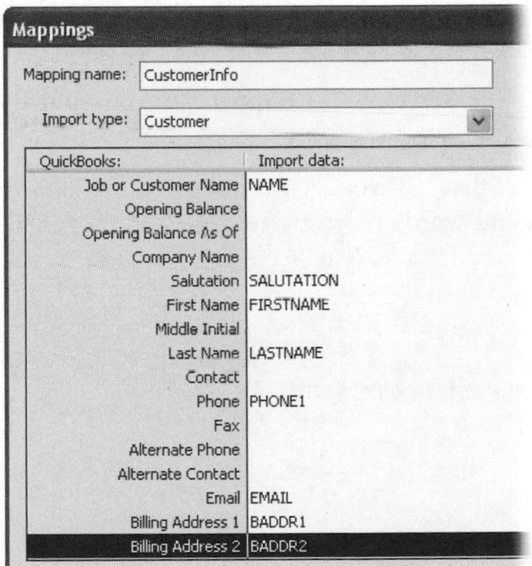

Figure 24-11:
The correct column is easy to pick when the workbook contains column headers in the first row. Otherwise, you're left to guess what kind of information Column A and Column B hold.

When you have an IIF file with the correct keywords, here's how you import it into QuickBooks:

1. **Choose File → Utilities → Import → IIF Files.**

   QuickBooks opens the Import dialog box with the file type set to IIF Files (*.IIF).

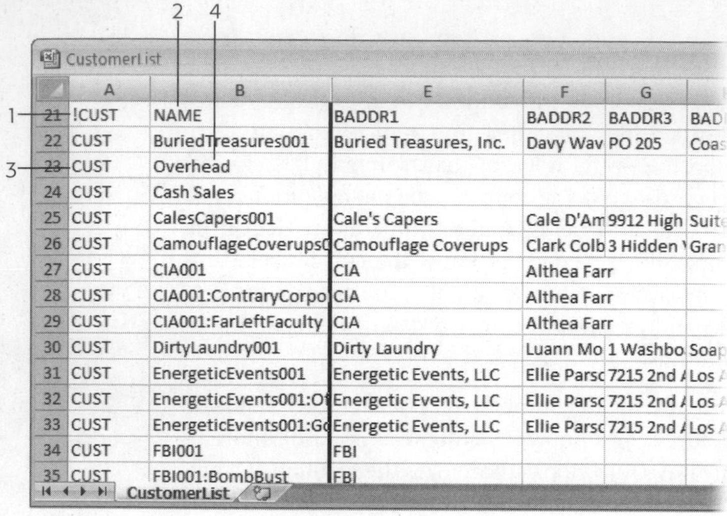

Figure 24-12:

1: In the first cell in the first row of a list, an exclamation point in front of the keyword tells QuickBooks that the data in the rows that follow are for that list. !CUST represents data for the Customer List.

2: Keywords in the other cells of the same row specify the QuickBooks field names. In cell B21, the keyword NAME identifies the values in that column as the name of each customer. In cell G21, BADDR3 identifies the third part of the billing address.

3: A keyword is the first text in the row. Each row that begins with CUST in the first cell represents another customer record.

4: The other cells in a row contain the values that QuickBooks imports into the designated fields.

2. **Navigate to the folder where the file you want to import is saved, and then double-click the filename.**

   QuickBooks displays a message box that tells you that it imported the data successfully. If you didn't set up the keywords correctly or QuickBooks ran into other problems with the data in your IIF file, it tells you that it didn't import the data successfully.

QuickBooks Add-on Services

Intuit offers several business services you can subscribe to for additional fees. The price might be worthwhile when you take into account the cost of your employees' time or—far more valuable—you being able to relax on the weekend instead of catching up on company paperwork.

To scour Intuit's business services using your Web browser, go to *http://quickbooks.intuit.com*. In the horizontal navigation bar, choose Payroll to learn about Intuit's payroll services (Chapter 14) or choose Payment Solutions to learn about accepting credit cards, debit cards, or electronic checks. On the QuickBooks Customers menu, choose Add Credit Card Processing, Add Electronic Check Processing, or Link Payment Service to Company File. Or choose Help → Add QuickBooks Services and then click the link for the type of service you're interested in, such as Payroll, Credit Cards, or Marketing Tools. Go to *http://payments.intuit.com/* to learn about all of Intuit's payment services.

Here are some other business services that Intuit offers and why you might consider using them.

- **QuickBooks Merchant Services** provides two very important features with one service. First, you get a merchant account, which is a bank account that handles credit card payments from your customers. The merchant account you get through QuickBooks accepts all major credit cards, which might mean more business for you, and it charges discounted rates you might not get from your bank. And, with a QuickBooks Merchant Account in place, you can download your credit card payment transactions directly into your company file.

  When a customer pays with a credit card, in the Receive Payments window, you enter information about the payment as usual. The only difference is that you also turn on the "Process <*credit card name*> payment when saving" checkbox. When you save the transaction, QuickBooks not only records the payment in your company file; it also transmits the payment to your merchant account and authorizes it. If customers hand you their credit cards in your store,

you can buy a card reader from Intuit that sends credit card data to QuickBooks. You don't have to be in your office to process credit card payments. Suppose you attend a trade show and you have a computer and Internet connection. You can accept credit card payments at the show and download them into QuickBooks.

- **Intuit GoPayment** (*http://payments.intuit.com/ products/basic-payment-solutions/mobile-credit-card-processing.jsp*) lets you accept credit card payments from your mobile phone if it can access the Internet. Some phones can use the GoPayment downloadable application, which makes credit card transactions even easier (see the Web page for supported carriers and phone). The service costs $19.95 per month with $0.23 charge per authorization and a $59.95 setup fee.

- **QuickBooks Billing Solution** (*http://payments. intuit.com/products/quickbooks-payment-solutions/ quickbooks-online billing.jsp*) is a medley of services, all designed to help you get payments from your customers more quickly and easily, for $14.95 a month plus tax. With this service, QuickBooks mails your invoices. In the Create Invoices window, choose the Mail Invoice command and select "Mail through QuickBooks". Invoices mailed through QuickBooks Billing Solution go to a centralized mail center, which prints customized invoices using your logo and invoice template, stuffs envelopes, and mails the invoices with remittance tear-offs and return envelopes. You can also find out whether customers have viewed invoices you email to them. Billing Solution not only reminds you about overdue payments, it also lets you email payment reminders to your customers. For that matter, customers can set up a password-protected web page for paying their invoices, viewing past billing, and submitting customer service questions.

CHAPTER 25

Customizing QuickBooks

Laid out like the workflow you use when you're bookkeeping, the QuickBooks Home page provides instant access to all the accounting tasks you perform. Among the Centers for vendors, customers, and employees, and your old friend the QuickBooks icon bar, you can take your pick of helpful shortcuts to the features you use the most.

But your business isn't like anyone else's. If you run a strictly cash sales business, you couldn't care less about customer lists and invoices; making deposits, though, is a daily event. You don't have to accept QuickBooks' take on convenience. The Home page and the icon bar come with a set of popular shortcuts, but you can add, remove, rearrange, and otherwise edit which features appear. In QuickBooks 2010, you can also add your favorite commands, windows, and reports to the new Favorites menu on the program's menu bar. This chapter covers all your options.

QuickBooks helps you get up and running with built-in business form templates. They'll do if you have to blast out some invoices. When you finally find a few spare minutes, you can create templates that show the information you want, formatted the way you want, and laid out to work with your letterhead. Create as many versions as you want. For example, you can create one invoice template to print to your letterhead and another that includes your logo and company name and address for creating electronic invoices to email. This chapter describes the most efficient ways to create forms—using QuickBooks's new form designs or using built-in templates as a basis for your own forms. In Appendix E (*www.missingmanuals.com/cds*), you can learn how to fine-tune your forms with advanced customization techniques and even start templates from scratch.

Customizing the Desktop

Everyone who uses QuickBooks can make the program's desktop look the way they want. Page 557 gives the full scoop on how you can customize the desktop to look the way you want. Here are the different ways you can make the desktop your own:

- **One window or several.** You can focus on one window at a time with the One Window option. The Multiple Windows option lets you see several windows at once.

- **Show Home page when opening a company file.** The Home page (page 35) shows the entire workflow of your accounting tasks along with popular windows and tasks like the Chart of Accounts window or writing checks.

- **Show Coach window and features.** If you want QuickBooks to help you learn how to use its features, turn on its checkbox so the Coach walks you through using the program.

- **Show Live Community.** If you have a lot of questions about QuickBooks, keep the Show Live Community checkbox turned on. With this setting, QuickBooks automatically opens the Live Community window (page 656). You can search for answers from experts or your peers. The Live Community window also has a Help tab that displays QuickBooks' Help topics.

- **Detach the Help Window.** You'll want to turn this checkbox on (new in Quick-Books 2010), because it tells the QuickBooks' Help window to play nicely with other windows on your screen (page 655). You can position it where you want on the screen, resize it, or minimize it.

- **Choosing colors.** If you want to change the color scheme that QuickBooks uses, choose one of the built-in color schemes from the Color Scheme drop-down menu.

Customizing the Home Page

The QuickBooks Home page is a chameleon that changes to fit your business's workflow. The program performs its magic by incorporating your answers from the EasyStep Interview with your company-wide Desktop View preferences, as shown in Figure 25-1. For example, if you don't have inventory, the tasks for buying, receiving, and paying for inventory are nowhere to be seen on your Home page. And if you don't have employees, the employee panel disappears. See page 559 for the full scoop on changing the icons you see on the Home page.

Fast Access to Favorite Commands

In addition to the Home page, QuickBooks has two other ways to get to your favorite features fast: the Favorites menu (new in QuickBooks 2010) and the icon bar. Out of the box, the Favorites menu is nearly empty and waiting for you to add

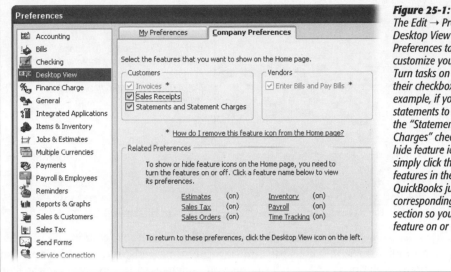

your favorite commands and reports. QuickBooks' centers and icons for other popular features fill up the icon bar from the get-go, but depending on how you like to work, those icons may languish unclicked. This section describes how to fill the Favorites menu with your favorite commands and modify the icon bar to display only the features you want.

Building Your Favorites Menu

The Favorites menu, which appears to the right of the Lists menu on the Quick-Books menu bar, has only one entry initially: Customize Favorites, which opens the Customize Your Menus dialog box. Despite the name, it lets you customize only the Favorites menu, but you can add almost any command or report to that menu.

In the Customize Your Menus dialog box, the Available Menu Items list is a directory of every feature QuickBooks has to offer. From the Lists menu through to the Help menu, every command on every menu and submenu on the QuickBooks' menu bar appears in this list. The top-level menu bar entries are aligned to the left side of the list box. Menu entries are indented, and submenu entries indented even more. Even the Reports section leaves nothing out—you can choose any built-in, customized, or memorized report in your company file.

Adding a command to the Favorites menu is easy. Select the command in the Available Menu Items list and then click Add. The command appears in the Chosen Menu Items list, as shown in Figure 25-2. Click OK to close the dialog box.

Customizing the Icon Bar

The icon bar, which appears below the QuickBooks menu bar, includes icons that take you to some of the program's popular features like QuickBooks centers,

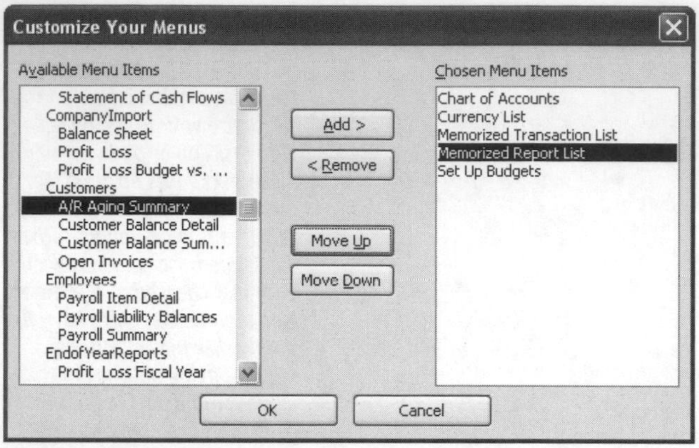

Figure 25-2:
To remove a command from the Favorites menu, select it in the Chosen Menu Items list, and then click Remove. To change the order of the entries, select the command you want to move, and then click Move Up or Move Down until the command is where you want it.

Reminders, Search, and others depending on the QuickBooks edition you use. You can modify the icon bar to add your favorite commands, memorized reports, or windows you open often. What's more, you can change the appearance of the icon bar in several ways, as described in the following sections.

Here are the basic steps for saving icon bar customizations:

1. **Choose View → Customize Icon Bar (or click the double right arrows on the right end of the icon bar, and choose Customize Icon Bar).**

   The Customize Icon Bar dialog box (Figure 25-3) opens showing the current list of icons.

Note: The icon bar has to be visible before you can customize it. If you choose View when the icon bar isn't visible, the Customize Icon Bar entry is dimmed. Choose View → Icon Bar to turn the icon bar back on, and then choose View → Customize Icon Bar.

---

2. **As described in the following sections, add other shortcuts to the icon bar, remove icons for features you don't want, edit, or change the order in which they appear.**

   The icon bar immediately shows the results of the changes you make in the Customize Icon Bar dialog box.

3. **To save the icon bar, in the Customize Icon Bar dialog box, click OK.**

Adding and removing icons

If you know which icons you want and don't want, you can make those changes in one marathon session. First open the Customize Icon Bar dialog box by choosing View → Customize Icon Bar. To remove an icon from the bar, simply select the entry in the Customize Icon Bar dialog box, and then click Delete. Adding an icon takes a few more steps:

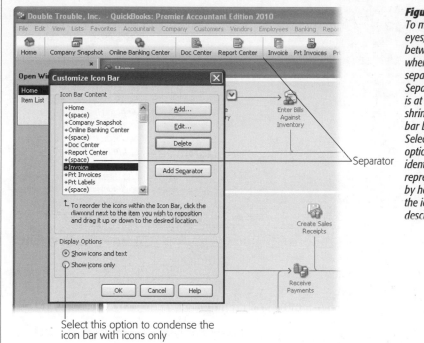

Figure 25-3:
To make icons easy on the eyes, you can add separators between them. Select the entry where you want to insert the separator and then click Add Separator. If screen real estate is at a premium, you can shrink the height of the icon bar by removing icon labels. Select the "Show icons only" option. Without labels to identify what the icons represent, you can see a hint by hovering the cursor over the icon to display its tooltip description.

Select this option to condense the icon bar with icons only

1. **In the Customize Icon Bar dialog box, select the entry where you want to insert the new icon.**

   In the Icon Bar Content list, the entries appear one below the other. This order translates into icons from the left to the right on the icon bar.

2. **Click Add.**

   The Add Icon Bar Item dialog box opens, as shown in Figure 25-4.

3. **In the list on the left, click the window or command you want to add, like Chart of Accounts to open the Chart of Accounts window.**

Tip: See page 612 to learn how to add almost any QuickBooks window to the icon bar, even if it doesn't appear in the Add Icon Bar Item list.

---

4. **Click OK to add the icon to the icon bar.**

   You don't have to close the Customize Icon Bar dialog box to see your changes.

5. **Repeat steps 2–4 to add more icons to the bar.**

   Back in the Customize Icon Bar dialog box, you can rearrange or edit (page 613) the entries.

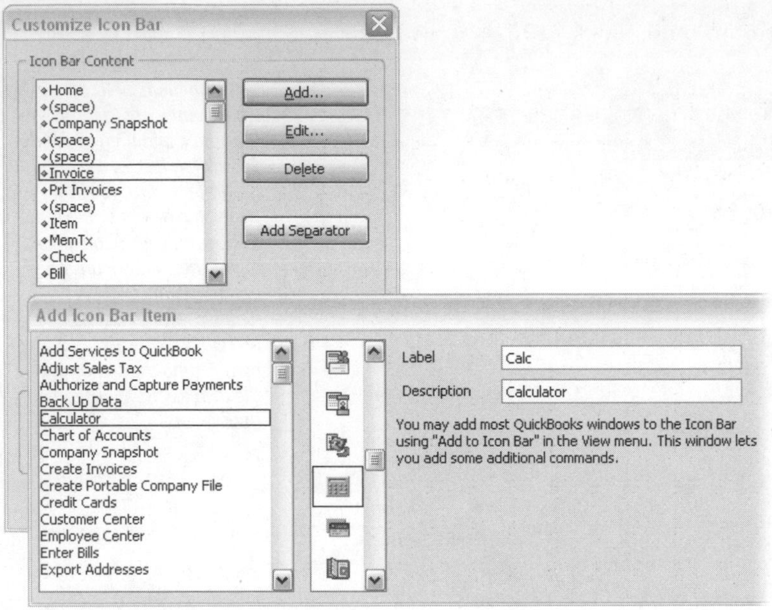

Figure 25-4:
When you click a command in the list, QuickBooks automatically selects an icon and fills in the Label and Description boxes, but you can change any of QuickBooks' choices. If you want to change the icon, label, or description, click the new icon and type the new text in the Label and Description boxes. Keep the Label text as brief as possible, so the icon doesn't hog space in the icon bar. What you type in the Description box pops up as a tooltip when you point the mouse at an icon on the icon bar.

Adding windows to the icon bar

The Add Icon Bar Item dialog box doesn't list every QuickBooks window, but that doesn't have to stop you from adding a window to the icon bar. Once you realize that you open the same window again and again, you can add an icon for that window to the icon bar without going *anywhere near* the Customize Icon Bar dialog box. Here's how:

1. **Open the window for the feature or report you want to add to the icon bar.**

   For example, you can add a window for a memorized report that you've created (an Accounts Receivable Aging Detail report, say). When you run a report, it appears in a report window.

2. **Choose View → "Add <window name> to Icon Bar", where <window name> is the name of the window you just opened, as in "Add 'A/R Aging Detail' to Icon Bar".**

   If the wrong window name appears in the command name, be sure to activate the window you want before choosing the command on the View menu. When you choose View → "Add *<window name>* to Icon Bar", QuickBooks opens the "Add Window to Icon Bar" dialog box.

3. In the "Add Window to Icon Bar" dialog box, click the icon you want to use and, in the Label and Description boxes, type the text you want for the icon's label and description.

In the icon bar, the text in the Description box appears as a tooltip when you position the mouse over the icon. Instead of using the same text for the label and description as QuickBooks does, keep the Label short and use the Description to elaborate on the window or report contents.

4. Click OK to add the window to the icon bar.

QuickBooks plunks the window at the right end of the icon bar. If you want the icon somewhere else, choose View → Customize Icon Bar, and then reposition the window in the list (page 613).

Changing icon appearance

To change an icon or its associated text, in the Customize Icon Bar dialog box, click the icon entry you want to change, and then click Edit. QuickBooks opens the Edit Icon Bar Item dialog box, which lets you change three features of each icon:

- **Icon.** In the icon list, select the graphic you want to appear on the icon bar.

  You can't demonstrate your creativity by designing your own icons. But QuickBooks doesn't care whether you choose an icon that fits the feature you're adding. For instance, an icon with a checkbook register and pen might be good for Writing Checks, but you could choose the faucet with a drip of water if you prefer.

- **Label.** If you don't like the label that QuickBooks provides or want to shorten the label to condense the icon bar, in the Label box, type your own.

- **Description.** To change the text that appears as a tooltip for the icon, in the Description box, type your own.

Changing the order of icons

If you want to group related icons, you can change the order of the icons in the icon bar and add separators to make the groups stand out. Open the Customize Icon Bar dialog box to make these changes (choose View → Customize Icon Bar). Figure 25-5 shows the process of rearranging icons.

Customizing the Company Snapshot

The Company Snapshot (page 41) is a handy timesaver that displays key statistics about your business all in one convenient dashboard window. In QuickBooks 2010, the Company Snapshot lets you choose from a dozen different views of financial status, like income and expense trends, account balances, customers who owe money, and so on.

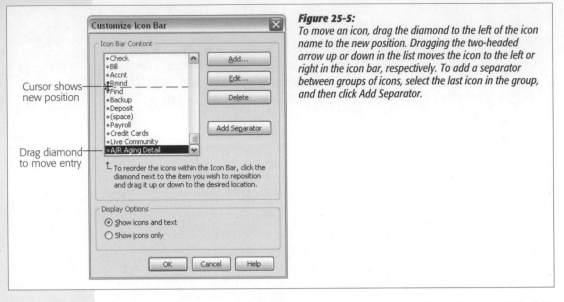

Figure 25-5:
To move an icon, drag the diamond to the left of the icon name to the new position. Dragging the two-headed arrow up or down in the list moves the icon to the left or right in the icon bar, respectively. To add a separator between groups of icons, select the last icon in the group, and then click Add Separator.

To change the views that appear in the Company Snapshot window, click Add Content in the top-left corner of the window. The "Add content to your Company Snapshot" panel appears with the name and a thumbnail of each view you can choose, as shown in Figure 25-6. Here's how you customize the Company Snapshot:

- **Add a view.** Click the Add button to the right of the view you want. QuickBooks adds it to the body of the Company Snapshot.

- **Remove a view.** Click the Close button (an X) at its top-right corner.

- **Reposition a view.** Hover the pointer over the view header; the cursor changes to a four-headed arrow. Then drag the view to its new location in the Company Snapshot.

When the Company Snapshot shows what you want, click Done to close the "Add content to your Company Snapshot" panel.

Note: In the top-right corner of the Company Snapshot, you'll see the Recommended For You view—a shameless marketing ploy. This view lists links to Intuit's add-on services like Payroll. You can't turn this view off, even if you know you don't need any other services. Even more annoying, it's always visible, refusing to yield its pole position to the views you do want.

Here is a quick introduction to the views you can choose:

- **Account Balances** shows the balances for your bank accounts, Accounts Receivable, and Accounts Payable. To choose the accounts you want listed, click the Select Accounts link at the bottom of the section. Double-click an account name to open the register window for that account.

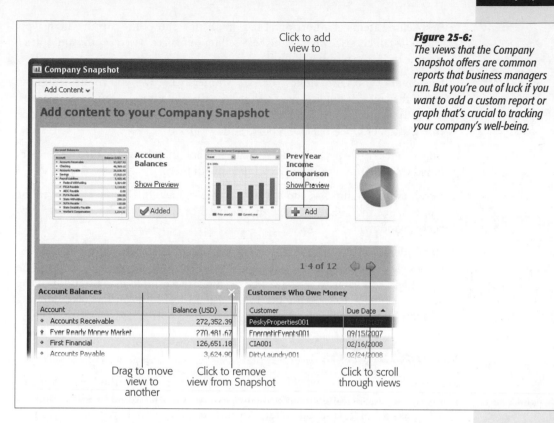

Click to add
view to

Figure 25-6:
*The views that the Company
Snapshot offers are common
reports that business managers
run. But you're out of luck if you
want to add a custom report or
graph that's crucial to tracking
your company's well-being.*

Drag to move
view to
another

Click to remove
view from Snapshot

Click to scroll
through views

- **Prev Year Income Comparison** displays a bar graph of your income with the current year in green and all previous years in blue. You can choose the type of income from the drop-down list on the left side of the view. To change the time period, choose from Monthly, Quarterly, Weekly, and Yearly in the drop-down list on the right.

- **Income Breakdown** displays a pie chart of each income account in your company file. Choose the time period you want from the drop-down list.

- **Prev Year Expense Comparison** displays a bar graph of your expenses similar to the Year Income Comparison. You choose the type of expenses and the time period you want to see from the drop-down lists at the top.

- **Expense Breakdown** displays a pie chart of each expense account in your company file. Choose the time period you want from the drop-down list.

- **Income and Expense Trend** is a bar graph of income (green bars) and expense (orange bars). Click the down arrow to the right of the date range box and choose the period you want to review.

- **Top Customers by Sales** is a horizontal bar graph that shows the top five customers based on sales volume (in thousands of dollars).

- **Best-selling Items** is a horizontal bar graph that shows the top five items you sell. You can choose whether the best-selling items are based on the amount of income or by the number of units.

- **Customers Who Owe Money** shows customers who owe you money and how much they owe. If invoices are overdue, the due date is red. Double-click a customer name to see the transactions that contribute to the customer's balance (the Customer Open Balance report window opens).

- **Top Vendors by Expense** is a horizontal bar graph that shows the top five vendors based on the amount of money you spend with them.

- **Vendors to Pay** shows vendors who you owe money to. Double-click a vendor name to see the bills that make up the balance (in the Vendor Open Balance report window).

- **Reminders** is a list of all the reminders you've set up in QuickBooks, such as to-do notes, deposits to make, bills to pay, and overdue invoices. To specify the reminders you want to see, click the Set Preferences link at the bottom of the section. Double-click a reminder to open the transaction in its corresponding window or dialog box.

Customizing Forms

Everything you do says *something* about your business—even the business forms you use. For a small company or someone with spectacularly bad taste, the built-in QuickBooks invoices and other forms work just fine. But if you want business forms that convey your sense of style and attention to detail, customized forms are the way to go.

In QuickBooks, form customization comes in several shapes and sizes, described in detail in the sections that follow:

- **QuickBooks Form Design.** The QuickBooks Forms Customization online tool is new in QuickBooks 2010 and helps you produce consistent, professional-looking business forms. Unlike a form template, which specifies everything about *one* form (content, formatting, and layout), a form design specifies form appearance; including background (like a watermark), logo, colors, fonts, and the format of the grid that holds your data. The step-by-step process is easy to follow and when you're done, you can save the design and apply it to all the forms in your QuickBooks company file in one fell swoop. From then on, you choose the forms you want to use as you would normally (page 257).

Note: Don't expect miracles from form designs. The formatting you can choose is limited. If you want to get fancy, use the customization tools within QuickBooks, which are described in the following sections and in Appendix E (*www.missingmanuals.com/cds*).

- **Basic customization.** If you don't use QuickBooks Form Design, you can make the same kinds of design changes within QuickBooks: add a logo to the form or turn company information fields on or off depending on what your business letterhead includes. Aesthetics like the color scheme and fonts are also at your command.

- **Changing fields.** To notch the customization up, you can choose the fields that appear in the form: the header, footer, and columns. You can also specify some printing options and what numbers look like. For all of these tricks, see "Additional Customization" on page 625.

- **Designing form layout.** The ultimate in form customization, QuickBooks' Layout Designer gives you full control over form design. You can add fields and images, plunk them where you want, and format them as you please. For example, you can resize and reposition fields to emphasize the balance due. To learn how to fine-tune forms and build them from scratch, see Appendix E at *www.missingmanuals.com/cds*.

Working with Form Designs

In QuickBooks 2010, it's as easy as one, two, three, four to build a design that you can apply to all your forms. Once you create a design, you save it to your online Intuit account (it's free). Then, you can apply the design to any or all of the forms in your QuickBooks company file. This section describes how to create and apply form designs.

You have two ways to open a browser window to the QuickBooks Form Design tool:

- **The Templates window.** Choose Lists → Templates to open the Templates window. Then, click Templates and choose Create Form Design on the shortcut menu. A browser opens to the QuickBooks Forms Customization screen, shown in Figure 25-7.

- **A transaction window.** If you click Customize in a transaction window like Create Invoices, QuickBooks opens the Customize Your QuickBooks Forms window with Create New Design and Apply Saved Design buttons. Click Create New Design to open a browser to the QuickBooks Forms Customization screen.

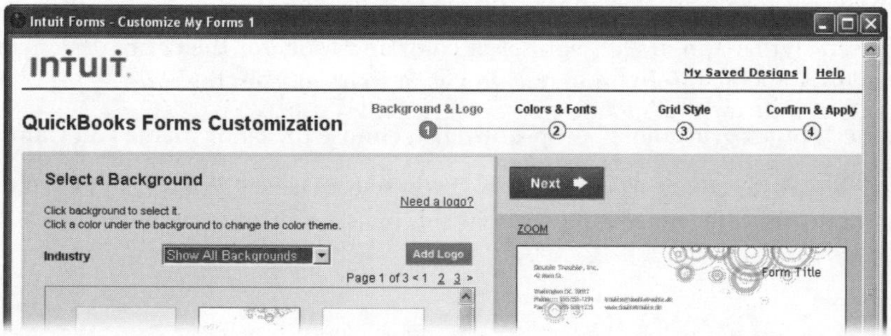

Figure 25-7:
To proceed to the next step in the design process, click Next. If you've already created a few design masterpieces, click the My Saved Designs link at the top right of the window. You can apply those designs to other forms, edit the designs, or get rid of them.

Creating a form design

There's no limit to the number of designs you can create, perfect for indefatigable entrepreneurs with several small companies to their credit. Although the form designs you create are stored online, the form templates you apply a design to still reside in your company file on your computer.

Here's how you create a form design:

1. **Open a browser to the QuickBooks Forms Customization screen. (In the Templates window, click Templates and then choose Create Form Design on the shortcut menu.)**

   The Select a Background page appears showing all the backgrounds that Intuit offers. Although Intuit has a slew of ready-made backgrounds that you can add to your design, they're a little hokey. If you want to see the backgrounds for different industries, click the down arrow to the right of the Industries box and choose an industry.

2. **Click the icon for the background you want to use.**

   If you use letterhead or simply prefer a blank background, click the Blank background icon (which appears on the first page when the Industry box is set to Show All Backgrounds). A few seconds after you click a background, it appears in the preview of your form design on the right side of the window.

3. **To add a logo to your form, click Add Logo.**

   The Logo Upload page appears. Click Browse. The "Choose file" dialog box opens to the folder that contains the images for your company file (page 623). Select the logo you want to upload and then click Open. The logo appears at the top left of the form in the preview window. (If you want to reposition the logo, see Appendix E at *www.missingmanuals.com/cds*.)

   If you've already uploaded a logo, click the "Use a previously uploaded logo" link and choose the logo. (You have to sign in to your Intuit online account to access logos you've uploaded and designs you've saved.) The Select Logo screen appears. Select the radio button for the logo you want and then click "Apply Selected Logo to Product".

4. **Click Next to proceed to step 2: Colors & Fonts.**

   The screen that appears lets you select color and fonts for the entire design and also the company information that you want to include on the form.

5. **In the "Font & grid colors" drop-down list, choose the color theme you want.**

   The choices for colors are quite basic. If you select Design Default, you'll get the colors that Intuit gives you. Or you can choose Black or several shades of gray.

6. **In the "Overall font" drop-down list, choose the font you want to use.**

   You can only choose from basic fonts when you create a form design. If you want to use other fonts that you've installed on your computer, see page 624 or Appendix E (online at *www.missingmanuals.com/cds*).

7. **To include company information in your design, turn the checkboxes for company fields on or off.**

   All the company fields (name, address, phone, fax, email, and website) are turned on initially. These fields appear at the top left of the form preview. You can change the font for your company name and address by clicking the corresponding "Change font" link.

Tip: If you turn on the "I use window envelopes with my QuickBooks forms" checkbox, the form design tool positions your company name and address so they appear in the return address window on your envelopes.

---

8. **Click Next to proceed to step 3: Grid Style. Select the option for the grid style you want, and then click Next.**

   You'll see several options for how tables in your forms appear. The grid styles specify whether columns and rows have borders around them and whether the table headings are shaded.

9. **Click Next to proceed to step 4: Confirm & Apply.**

   If you don't like what you see, click Back to return to previous steps and make the changes you want.

10. **After you review the design, click Next to save it.**

    The Apply Design screen appears and automatically selects the custom templates from your company file. If you don't want to apply the design to a template, turn its checkmark off. Click Select All or Clear All to select or deselect all the templates in the list. If you want to see all the templates in your company file, including built-in ones, click Show All Templates.

11. **To apply the design to the templates you selected, click Apply.**

    The Design Applied screen appears. Click OK to close it. Back in QuickBooks, you'll see the new template in your templates list. Look for templates whose names begin with "MyDesign", your clue that the templates have a form design applied.

12. **In the browser window, in the Save Design Online screen, type a name for the design you created and click Save.**

    By saving your design you can apply it to other forms in the future or to forms in other company files. If you don't want to save it, click No Thanks.

Managing form designs

If you've saved one or more form designs, you can use them on other forms, edit them, or delete them. Here's what you do:

Note: To apply the form design to forms in a different company file, open the company file before launching the form design tool.

1. **Open a browser to the QuickBooks Forms Customization screen. (In the Templates window, click Templates and then choose Create Form Design on the shortcut menu.)**

   Ignore the Select a Background page. The link you want is My Saved Designs.

2. **Click My Saved Designs.**

   The Saved Form Designs screen appears. Each saved design includes the name and a thumbnail of the selected background.

3. **To apply the design to templates in a company file, click the "Re-apply to Forms" link.**

   The Apply Design screen appears and automatically selects the custom templates from your company file. Choose the forms to which you want to apply the design as described on page 619.

4. **Click Edit to display the QuickBooks Forms Customization screen (page 617). Or, click Remove to delete the saved form design from your account.**

When you're done, close the browser window.

Editing an Existing Form in QuickBooks

One way to build your own forms is to start with a template that QuickBooks provides or use another customized template that you've put together. Whether you plan to make minor adjustments or major revisions, you won't have to start from scratch. To learn how to customize a template while you're in the middle of a task like creating an invoice, see the box on page 622.

Here's how you edit an existing template:

1. **Choose Lists → Templates.**

   QuickBooks opens the Templates window, which displays built-in templates and any that you've created. If you're looking for a specific type of form to start with, the Type column displays the type of form, such as Invoice or Credit Memo, as shown in Figure 25-8.

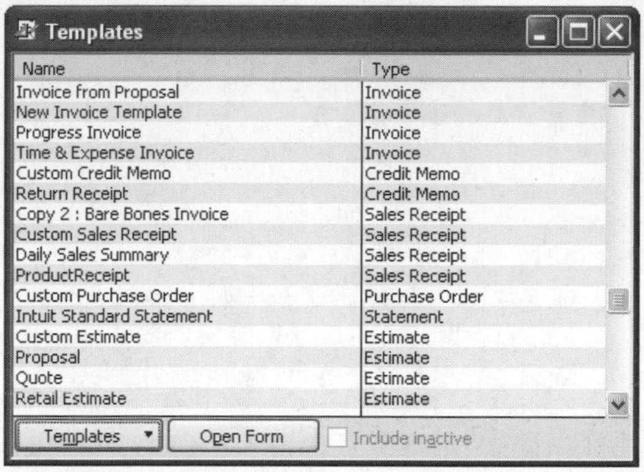

Figure 25-8:
To sort templates by type, click the Type heading. To use any form as a basis for customized forms, simply make a copy of the form first (page 627), and then edit it all you want.

2. In the Name column, click the template you want to edit, and then press Ctrl+E to open the Basic Customization dialog box.

   You can also click the template name, click Templates at the bottom of the window, and then choose Edit Template on the drop-down menu.

3. In the Basic Customization dialog box, click Manage Templates so you can make a copy of the form.

   In the Manage Templates dialog box, QuickBooks automatically selects the name of the template you're editing. Click Copy. QuickBooks automatically fills in the Template Name box on the right side of the dialog box with "Copy of: <form name>". Name the form something meaningful, and then click OK to return to the Basic Customization dialog box. This way, you can keep the edited form or go back to the original.

4. In the Basic Customization dialog box, make the changes you want.

   For basic customization, see the next section. To learn about changing the fields on a form, see page 624. And, for full layout instructions, see Appendix E at *www.missingmanuals.com/cds*.

5. When the form looks the way you want, in the Basic Customization dialog box, click OK.

Basic Customization

When you edit a form, QuickBooks serves up the most common changes right away, while the fancier options stay hidden unless you ask for them. The name of the form you're customizing appears at the top-left corner of the dialog box, just below the Selected Template label. It's a good idea to verify that the template you're about to edit is the one you want. (If you want to rename the template, see page 627.) This section walks you through your basic options.

Editing a Template While You Work

I've created an invoice and the form preview doesn't look the way I want. Is there a way to change the form without leaving the Create Invoices window?

If you're in the midst of creating a transaction and realize you need to modify the template, you can customize the form without interfering with the transaction in progress. In the transaction window (Create Invoices, for instance), make sure that the template you want to use (and modify) appears in the Template box in the top-right corner of the dialog box. If it doesn't, click the down arrow on the right side of the box, and then choose the form you want.

To customize a template, *don't* click the Customize button, which looks like a ruler with a pencil, at the right end of the window's tool bar as shown in Figure 25-9. If you do, Quick-Books 2010 pushes its new form design tool on you by opening the Customize Your QuickBooks Forms window.

Instead, click the down arrow to the right of the Customize button and then choose Manage Templates. In the Manage Templates window, click OK to open the Basic Customization dialog box (page 621). From there, you can access Additional Customization for middle-of-the-road changes (page 624) and Layout Designer for advanced customization (Appendix E).

Working on a template and an invoice at the same time can overtax a computer that's low on memory and other system resources, causing the computer to crash—taking your work with it. If your computer isn't well-appointed hardware-wise, consider finishing the transaction first, and then modifying the template. Then, you can reopen the transaction window, display the transaction you want, and then print or email it.

Note: The Basic Customization dialog box includes a Preview pane on the right side so you can see if your changes are what you want. To preview a form for a transaction like an invoice you're about to send, in the transaction window (Create Invoices in this example), click Print Preview in the top-right corner (Figure 25-9).

Adding a logo

Adding a logo to a QuickBooks template can turn plain paper into a decent-looking document, and it's the *only* way to display your company logo on a form you send as a PDF file. Here's how you add a logo to a form:

1. **In the Basic Customization dialog box, turn on the "Use logo" checkbox, and then click Select Logo.**

   The Select Image dialog box opens. The program sets the "Files of type" box to All Image Files, so you'll see any kind of graphic file in the folder.

2. **In the Select Image dialog box, navigate to the folder holding your logo file, and then double-click the filename.**

   In the Basic Customization dialog box, the filename and size appear to the right of the "Use logo" checkbox, as Figure 25-10 shows. Your logo initially appears in the top-left corner of the form.

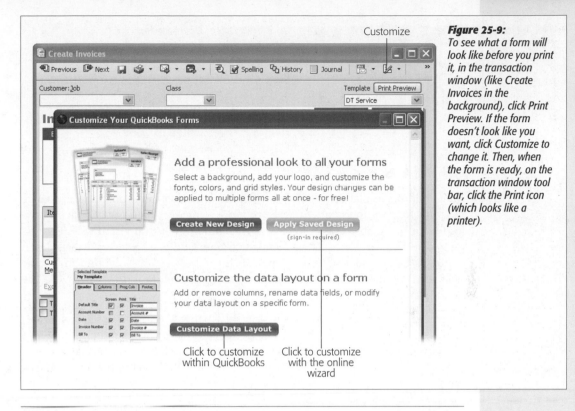

Customize

Figure 25-9:
To see what a form will look like before you print it, in the transaction window (like Create Invoices in the background), click Print Preview. If the form doesn't look like you want, click Customize to change it. Then, when the form is ready, on the transaction window tool bar, click the Print icon (which looks like a printer).

Click to customize within QuickBooks

Click to customize with the online wizard

Note: QuickBooks copies the logo file into a subfolder within the folder that holds your company file. For instance, if your company file is named *Allyoucaneat.qbw* and resides in a folder *C:\QBCompanyFiles*, QuickBooks creates the folder *C:\QBCompany-Files\Allyoucaneat - Images* and places the copy of the logo file there. If you decide to edit your original logo file, be sure to copy the edited file into the Quick-Books image folder.

---

3. **If you want to reposition the logo, do so within the Layout Designer** (Appendix E, *http://www.missingmanuals.com/cds*).

Note: After you add a logo to a template, it sometimes disappears. Don't panic—simply repeat the steps to relink the logo to the template. If the logo still doesn't appear, exiting and restarting QuickBooks usually solves the problem.

Applying a color scheme

If you're anxious to show off your new color printer, you can change the color of the lines and text on the form. In the Select Color Scheme drop-down menu, choose the color you want, and then click Apply Color Scheme. The Preview box shows the results.

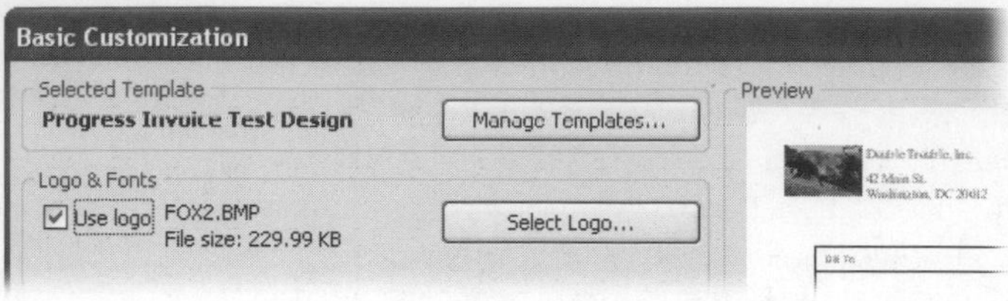

Figure 25-10:
If you print some forms on your company letterhead and send others via email, create two templates for the form—one with your logo and one without. Then, when you create the invoice or other transaction, choose the template to go with the way you plan to send the document.

Changing fonts

Built-in forms display some labels in different and larger fonts, but you can change the fonts to make them easier to read or more attractive. (You can also change the font for a single object, as described in Appendix E.) QuickBooks divides the text on a form into categories: Title, Company Name, Company Address, Labels, Data, Subtotals Label, and Total Label. The Labels category controls the font for all the field labels on the form; the Data category changes the font for the values, like the item description and price.

To change the font for a text category, in the Change Font For list, select the category, and then click Change Font. The dialog box that opens has all the usual font formatting options, just like the dialog boxes you see when you format a report (page 516). If you selected a color scheme, the font color is set to that color. Check out the Preview box to see the Technicolor results.

Including basic company and transaction information

QuickBooks automatically turns on the Company Name and Company Address checkboxes, which is perfect if you print to plain paper. If you have letterhead with your company name and address preprinted on it, be sure to turn these checkboxes off. The other checkboxes let you add your company phone number, fax number, email address, and website address. These values come from the company information you entered (choose Company → Company Information).

Note: If you're the QuickBooks administrator, you can modify the company information values right from the Basic Customization dialog box. Click Update Information to open the Company Information dialog box.

Remember the status stamps that QuickBooks adds to forms, such as PAID, which appears as a watermark on an invoice when you've received the payment? If you want to *print* these status stamps, turn on the Print Status Stamp checkbox.

Additional Customization

At the bottom of the Basic Customization dialog box, clicking Additional Customization takes you to a dialog box with several tabs for picking the fields you want on the template and when they appear. The tabs are the same for every type of form, unless you create an invoice form and have the Progress Invoicing preference turned on (page 569). Then QuickBooks adds the Prog Cols tab so you can pick the columns you want to add for progress billing. Each tab relates to a different area of the form, as Figure 25-11 shows.

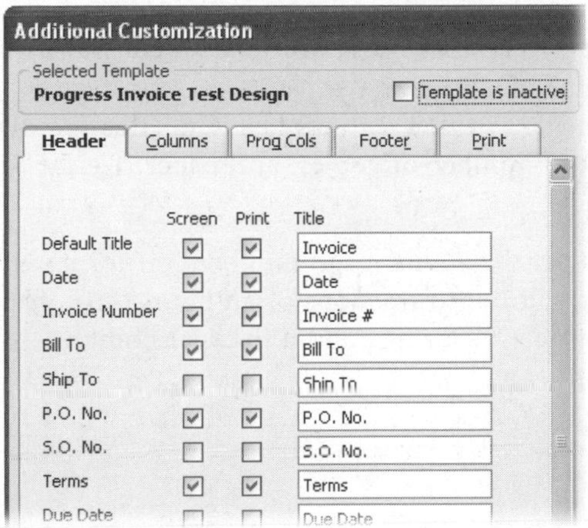

Figure 25-11:
To include a field onscreen, turn on its Screen checkbox. To print a field, turn on its Print checkbox. The Title boxes show the text that appears for the field labels. QuickBooks fills them in with either the field name or a label that identifies the type of form, such as Invoice for the Default Title field. You can edit the labels in the Title boxes.

Note: Some of the checkboxes are dimmed if a choice doesn't make sense. For example, the checkbox for displaying the Project/Job on the screen is dimmed, because the Create Invoices window (and other windows) include the Customer:Job field, which tells you the same thing.

Setting up the fields on the tabs is straightforward, but a few of them have extra features that make a complete tab review worthwhile:

- **Header.** These fields appear at the top of the form just above the table area. The more common fields like Date, Bill To, P.O. No., and Terms are turned on automatically. At the bottom of the list, you can turn on the checkboxes for custom fields you've created to include them on your forms.

- **Columns.** These fields appear as columns in the table area of a form, like the item description, quantity, rate, and amount for each line item in an invoice. In addition to specifying whether they appear onscreen or when printed, you can specify the order of the columns by filling in the Order boxes with numbers starting at 1 for the first field. If a field isn't included in the form, QuickBooks changes its Order box to zero (0).

- **Footer.** The fields that appear in the footer (the area below the form's table) include Message, Sales Tax, Total, and so on. If you want to include the total balance for a customer including both the current balance and previous balance, turn on the Customer Total Balance checkbox.

  The "Long text" box lets you add a substantial block of text on a form like a legal disclaimer or other lengthy note. If you add this field to the form and type the text in the box, the long text appears only on the printed form, not on the screen.

- **Print.** You can set up printer settings for different types of forms by choosing File → Printer Setup, selecting the form, and then choosing the settings you want (page 306). QuickBooks automatically selects the "Use *<form>* printer settings from Printer Setup" option, which uses those printer settings. But if you have a special form that doesn't follow the other templates in that category, on the Print tab, select the "Use specified printer settings below for this *<form>*" option and choose the orientation, number of copies, and paper size for just that form.

  QuickBooks automatically turns on the "Print page numbers on forms with more than 2 pages" checkbox. If you bill to fractions of an hour, turn on the Print Trailing Zeros checkbox, which adds zeros and a decimal point, so that whole number and decimal quantities all line up.

Managing Templates

Like other QuickBooks list windows, the Templates window includes commands for managing the templates you create. In the Templates window's button bar, click Templates, and then choose a command on the shortcut menu.

Besides obvious tasks like New, Edit Template, and Delete Template, there are some other helpful things you can do with your templates. The box below describes another way to get templates.

The one problem with the Templates shortcut menu is that you can't see what the templates look like. If you want to preview templates before you choose one to work on, do the following:

1. **Edit any template of the type you want (Invoices, Purchase Orders, and so on).**

   In the Templates list, select the type of template you want, and then press Ctrl+E.

2. **In the Basic Customization dialog box, click Manage Templates.**

   The Manage Templates dialog box opens, listing all the templates of the same type as the one you edited.

3. **In the Select Template list, click a template name to see a preview in the Preview area.**

   If you want to rename a template, select it in the Select Template list. Then, in the Template Name box above the preview, type the new name.

POWER USERS' CLINIC

Templates Without the Tedium

Say you find the QuickBooks built-in templates boring, but you don't have the time or design know how to put together templates of your own. You can download spiffier templates from the QuickBooks website. For example, contractors can choose invoice templates with a drill or tape measure in the background.

In the Templates List window, click Templates, and then choose Download Templates. The program opens a Web browser to the Forms section of the QuickBooks Library.

You can search for report or form templates and specify the type of report or form and even a specific industry.

Click the name of a template to view a larger sample. When you find a template you like, click Download, which saves a template export file (with a .des file extension) onto your computer. In QuickBooks' Templates window, click Templates and choose Import on the shortcut menu. In the "Select File to Import" dialog box, select the file you downloaded, and then click Open.

Copying a Template

Copying a template before you start editing it is always a good idea, in case your edits go awry and you want your original back. QuickBooks automatically names the copy "Copy of:" followed by the original template's name and then selects the new copy. To create a copy of a template, click its name in the list, and then click Copy.

You can also copy a template in the Templates window. Click Templates, and then choose Duplicate on the shortcut menu. The Select Template Type dialog box appears. As it turns out, you can choose any type of template for the duplicate, regardless of what the original template type is. In the Select Template Type dialog box, when you click OK, QuickBooks adds the duplicate template to the list with "Copy of:" in front of the original name.

Warning: If you copy a template as a basis for a new one you want to create, be sure to edit the copy's name to identify what the form does, such as InvoiceNoLogo for the one you print to your letterhead. If you copy a template as a backup in case you mangle the original, first check that the copy is what you want. The "Copy of:" that QuickBooks adds to the beginning of the template name tells you that it's a backup. After you've modified the original template and you're completely confident that the edited template is correct, you can delete the copy.

Deleting a Template

You can delete only templates that you create yourself. If you try to delete a built-in QuickBooks template, the program tells you that you're out of luck. You can hide built-in templates (page 627), if you don't want them to appear in the Templates list. To delete a template, click it, and then click Delete.

Hiding a Template (Making It Inactive)

If you want to keep a template (like an original that you've duplicated), but you don't want it to appear in the Templates list, you can make it inactive. It's just like making a customer, vendor, or invoice item inactive. To do so, in the Templates window, select the template, click Templates, and then choose Make Template Inactive. You can reactivate it by first turning on the "Include inactive" checkbox to display all templates, and then clicking the X to the left of the template name.

Exchanging Templates Between Company Files

If you want to trade form templates between company files, you can export templates from one company file and import them into another. To create a form export file, in the Templates List window, select the template you want to export. Click Templates, and then choose Export. In the "Specify Filename for Export" dialog box, navigate to the folder where you want to save the file, and in the "File name" box, type the name of the file. QuickBooks automatically sets the "Save as type" box to Template Files (*.DES).

To import a template, on the Templates shortcut menu, simply choose the Import command instead of Export. In the "Select File to Import" dialog box, double-click the template file you want to import, and you're done.

chapter 26

Keeping Your QuickBooks Data Secure

Your QuickBooks records are indispensable. They help you invoice your customers, pay your bills, and prepare your taxes, prevent you from overdrawing your checking account, and provide the information you need to plan for the future. A company file does so much, yet many companies don't take the time to keep their financial data safe and secure.

Losing data to a hard disk crash is a shock to your financial system as well as your computer's, and rebuilding your records is inconvenient, time-consuming, and—if you hire someone else like Intuit to do it—costly. But having someone embezzle the money from your accounts could send years of hard work down the drain. Protecting your QuickBooks data takes so little time that there's no excuse for not doing it. (In addition to QuickBooks security, don't forget common-sense security like locking the door to your office.)

If you're the untrusting type or simply have no one else willing to do your bookkeeping, you can skip this chapter's discussion of creating users and setting up user permissions. The administrator login is all you need to work on your company file—and QuickBooks creates *that* automatically. Although you might not let other people access your financial data, that doesn't mean that someone won't try to access it *without* your permission. Good security measures like firewalls, up-to-date antivirus software, and passwords that strangers can't guess go a long way to prevent unauthorized fiddling with your finances.

When you have several people working on your company file, security is a bit trickier. Each person who accesses your financial data is a potential problem, whether intentional or inadvertent. By setting up users in QuickBooks and specifying which areas of the program they can access, you can delegate work to others

without worrying about security quite so much. With the audit trail that Quick-
Books keeps (page 640), every transaction that's modified or deleted is there for
you to review.

Setting Up the Administrator

In QuickBooks, the administrator is all-powerful. Only that person can create new
users, assign permissions and passwords to other users, and set QuickBooks company preferences. If you use the EasyStep Interview to create your company file
(page 21), the wizard won't let you finish until you specify the user name and
optional password for the QuickBooks administrator (page 630).

Note: Although the administrator password is optional, you should set one right away. If you don't, anyone who opens your company file is logged in as the administrator, with full access to every feature of
QuickBooks and every byte of your QuickBooks data.

If you skip the EasyStep Interview, you can create, open, and close a company file
without any sign of a login screen. But behind the scenes, QuickBooks logs you in
as the administrator without a password. As soon as you try to set up additional
users, QuickBooks first asks you to specify the administrator's user name and password—which you'll learn how to do next.

Assigning the Administrator User Name and Password

When you create a company file, QuickBooks automatically creates the QuickBooks
administrator, but it doesn't require you to assign a password to the administrator.
Now that you know how important a password is, you can edit the administrator
to assign one (and change the administrator user name if you want).

Tip: If you're the only person who acts as the QuickBooks administrator and you want to transfer the
duties to someone else, create a new user and give that user access to all areas of QuickBooks (page 637).
That way, the audit trail (page 640) can differentitate changes made by you and the new administrator. In
fact, it's a good idea to create a new user using your name and use that login for most of the work you do.
Login as the administrator for tasks that only the Administrator can do.

You can use this procedure to change the values for the administrator user at any
time. Here's how:

1. **Log into the company file as the administrator.**

   Open the company file using your preferred method and then, in the Quick-
   Books Login dialog box, type your user name and password. If the administrator
   is the only user, the QuickBooks Login dialog box shows only the Password box.

2. Choose Company → "Set Up Users and Passwords" → Set Up Users. In the User List window, click Edit User.

QuickBooks automatically selects whoever you're logged in as in the User List window. The "Change user password and access" dialog box opens, as shown in Figure 26-1.

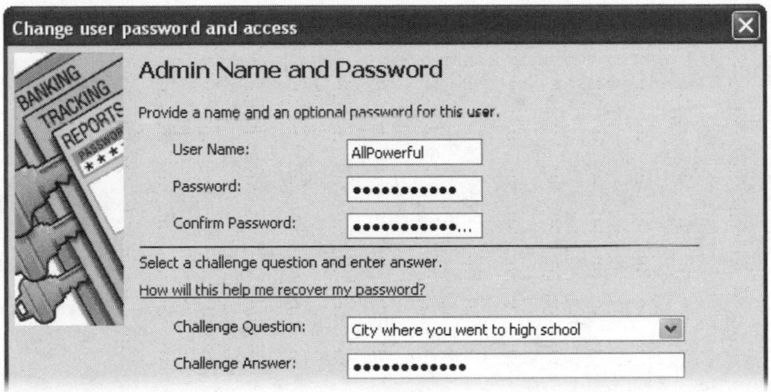

Figure 26-1:
Fill in the New Password and Confirm New Password boxes. Be sure to set up a challenge question and answer so you can reset your password if you forget it.

3. To change the administrator name, type the new name in the User Name box.

When you change the administrator name, the User List identifies the administrator by adding "(Admin)" after the user name, for example, "All Powerful (Admin)".

4. In the Password box, type the password for the administrator user. In the Confirm Password box, type the password again.

See the box on page 631 for tips for good passwords. Don't copy and paste the password from the Administrator's Password box into the Confirm Password box. If you copy a typo from one box to the other, you won't know what the administrator password is, and you won't be able to open your company file.

5. To give yourself a chance to easily reset a forgotten password, in the Challenge Question drop-down list, choose a question like "City where you went to high school". In the Challenge Answer box, type the answer to the question.

The next section explains how to reset the administrator password with the help of this challenge question. (The box on page 633 tells you how to download a tool for resetting your administrator password if you don't know the password, and either don't know or don't have a challenge question.)

6. Click Next.

The dialog box reminds you that the administrator has access to everything in QuickBooks. Click Finish to close the dialog box.

Warning: If you work on more than one QuickBooks company file, the program throws one password-related curve at you: It fills in the QuickBooks Login dialog box with the last user name you typed—whether or not it goes with the file you just opened. Say you opened the Toboggan Tours file using the user name Admin. When you open the Double Trouble file, the QuickBooks Login dialog box fills in the User Name with Admin, even if the administrator name for Double Trouble is I_Can_Do_Everything. If QuickBooks won't let you log in, make sure you're using the correct user name and password for that company file.

WORD TO THE WISE

Password Guidelines

Because the QuickBooks administrator can do *anything* in a company file, choosing a trustworthy person for that role is only your first step in preventing financial misfortune. Your efforts are in vain unless you secure the administrator's access with a good password. In fact, assigning passwords to *all* QuickBooks users is an important security measure.

Ideally, a password should be almost impossible to guess, but easy for the rightful owner to remember. It's easy to meet the first criterion by using a random combination of upper- and lowercase letters, numbers, and punctuation, but that makes the password harder to remember. And unfortunately, if people have trouble recalling their passwords, they'll write them down somewhere, shooting holes in your security. To improve your security, change your password every 3 to 6 months.

Here are some tips for creating passwords in QuickBooks that are both secure *and* easy to remember:

- Make passwords at least six characters long, and combine upper- and lowe--case letters, numbers, and punctuation. These are the same guidelines that the credit card industry uses as part of its standard for protecting customer information, as you can read on page 633. (QuickBooks passwords are case-sensitive and can include up to 16 characters.)

- Don't use family birthdays, names, phone numbers, addresses, or Social Security numbers.

- To make guessing more difficult, replace letters with numbers or punctuation that look similar. For example, replace the letter "I" with the number 1 or an exclamation point (!). Or replace the letter "s" with the number 5, or the letter "e" with the number 3.

- To make remembering easier, consider using names, birthdays, phone numbers, or addresses of people *not* obviously connected to you. For example, if no one suspects that Kevin Spacey is your favorite actor, Kev!n5pacey would be a good password (but not anymore).

Resetting the Administrator Password

If you can't remember your password and you selected a Challenge question for the administrator user, you can answer that challenge question to earn the opportunity to reset your password. Here's how to make this life-saving feature work:

1. **In the QuickBooks Login dialog box, click Reset Password.**

   The Reset Password button doesn't appear if you didn't set up a challenge question.

TROUBLESHOOTING MOMENT

What's the Administrator Password?

The time may come when QuickBooks asks you for a password you don't know. For instance, maybe the person with the administrator password left in a hurry, and you need it to open the company file. Or perhaps you're trying to open a QuickBooks file from a few years ago and the passwords you've tried don't work. If the challenge question doesn't help, first try these solutions before you resort to Intuit's password removal tool:

- The Caps Lock and Num Lock keys may not be set the way they were when you set your password. Try turning them on or off.

- Test your keyboard. Create a text document and type each key to make sure they send the correct character.

If the password is still a mystery, you can download the Automated Password Reset Tool, which lets you reset the administrator password for company files opened with QuickBooks 2006 or later. To download the program, your QuickBooks program has to be registered with Intuit (page 649).

In the QuickBooks Login dialog box, click Reset Password. In the Reset QuickBooks Administrator Password dialog box, click the "I can't remember my answer" link. In the Help topic that opens (titled "Forgotten challenge phrase answers" in case you want to search for this topic later), click the "Download the automatic password reset tool" link. On the QuickBooks Automated Password Removal Service web page, select the version you used last to open the file. Then, fill in your QuickBooks license number, first name, last name, email address, telephone number, and postal code (the ones you used to register your program so Intuit can find your registration).

After you download the program, double-click the file to run it. You choose the company file you want to reset, and then type a new password. The program only resets your password once. If you forget it again, you have to download the tool again.

---

2. **In the Reset QuickBooks Administrator Password dialog box, type the answer to the challenge question that appears, and then click OK.**

   A Password Removed message box tells you that your password, challenge question, and answer have been removed, which means your company file is no longer password-protected.

3. **Click Close.**

   QuickBooks nudges you to add a password by immediately opening the Change QuickBooks Password dialog box.

4. **Fill in the boxes as you would to edit the user. Click OK.**

   Now, when you correctly fill in the boxes in the QuickBooks Login dialog box, QuickBooks opens the company file.

Complying with Credit Card Security Regulations

If your company accepts credit cards, you probably already know that you have to comply with standards for protecting your customers' credit card information (known as the Payment Card Industry Data Security Standard). If you don't, not only is your customers' financial information at risk, but you risk paying fines for

---

your oversight. Part of the standard requires you to change your password every 90 days and to use a *complex password* (one that's longer than seven characters and has a combination of uppercase and lowercase letters and numbers). The steps to take in QuickBooks to comply with these password requirements are simple:

1. **Choose Company → Customer Credit Card Protection.**

   The Customer Credit Card Protection dialog box opens and explains a little bit about the feature.

2. **Click Enable Protection.**

   The Customer Credit Card Protection Setup dialog box opens. The fields are the same ones you see in the "Change user password and access" dialog box. The only difference is that the New Password and Confirm New Password boxes won't accept passwords that don't meet the secure password criteria.

3. **In the Current Password box, type the current password (which may not meet the criteria). Fill in the New Password and Confirm New Password boxes with a complex password.**

   QuickBooks won't accept the password unless it's longer than seven characters and has at least one number and one uppercase letter; for example, "Kath3rine."

4. **In the Challenge Question drop-down list, choose a question that you can answer in case you need to reset the password, like "Best friend's last or first name". Type the answer in the Answer box.**

   When you use password protection, QuickBooks requires you to set up a challenge question and answer.

5. **Click OK.**

   After 90 days pass, QuickBooks asks you to set a new password.

Creating QuickBooks Users

Setting up users in QuickBooks has the same advantages as setting up users in the Windows operating system or on your network—you can restrict people's access to just the financial data they need to see, and you can keep track of what they're doing. By setting up user logins for the people who work on your company file, you can:

- **Keep sensitive data confidential.** User names, passwords, and permissions (page 637) help protect both your and your customers' sensitive data from prying eyes.

- **Prevent financial hanky-panky.** By limiting each employee's access to job-relevant data and checking the audit trail for changes or deletions (page 640), you can prevent embezzlement—or catch the culprit early. These measures also help protect your data from unintentional errors by new or careless employees.

• **Let several people work in QuickBooks at the same time.** QuickBooks has no way of knowing if several people share the same user name. If you want to protect your data or identify who's doing what in your financial records, each person who accesses your company file needs a unique user name and password. If more than one person works on your company file simultaneously, you have to switch it to multi-user mode, as the box below explains.

Sharing Your Company File

Setting up several users for a company file doesn't mean more than one person can work on the file at the same time. If you want your company file to bustle with financial activity, you have to buy a copy of QuickBooks Pro, Premier, or Enterprise for *each* computer on which you want to run Quick-Books *and* switch the company file to multi-user mode.

Ever since QuickBooks 2006, multi-user mode means that you access the data in your company files through a database server. Here's how it works: When someone performs a task in QuickBooks, their copy of the program asks the database server to send information or make changes. The database server makes the changes, retrieves information, and sends it back to them—and at the same time makes sure that the changes don't conflict with changes someone else wants to make. (There's no quiz. You can concentrate on your business and let multi-user mode take care of the file sharing.)

To turn on multi-user access, choose File → "Switch to Multi-user Mode". When multi-user mode is on, the title bar of the QuickBooks window includes the text "(multi-user)(*<user name>*)" to indicate that several people can work on the file simultaneously and who is working on the file in the current session.

If you're the QuickBooks administrator but you also perform bookkeeping tasks, it's a good idea to log in as the administrator to perform the tasks that only the administrator can do. For your bookkeeping duties, log in with your other user name, particularly if you want the audit trail to record who makes transaction changes.

After you begin using your company file in multi-user mode, you soon discover that some tasks in QuickBooks like condensing your company file require single-user mode. If multi-user mode is turned on and you try to perform a single-user mode task, QuickBooks tells you that you need to switch modes.

Single-user mode also runs faster than multi-user mode, which makes it ideal if you have monumental reports to generate and a tight deadline. To switch a company file to single-user mode, first ask everyone to exit QuickBooks or perform your task when others aren't in the office. After everyone has logged off, choose File → "Switch to Single-user Mode".

Note: If company email isn't enough, you can send instant messages to other people logged into the same file. Choose Company → "Chat with a Coworker" or in the Windows system tray, double-click the QuickBooks Messenger icon (which looks like a stylized person next to a thought balloon). To chat with another user, select her name and then click Start Chat in the QuickBooks Messenger window's toolbar. To send a message to everyone logged into the company file (to ask them to log off so you can switch to single-user mode, for instance), in the QuickBooks Messenger window toolbar, choose Actions → "Send Message to Logged In Users".

Adding New Users

Only the QuickBooks administrator can create additional users. After you log in as the administrator, here's how you create other users:

1. **Choose Company → "Set Up Users and Passwords" → Set Up Users.**

   The QuickBooks Login dialog box reopens, asking you for your password. This extra request for the administrator password prevents someone from walking up to your computer while you're away and creating an account for herself. After you enter your password, the program opens the User List dialog box, shown in Figure 26-2.

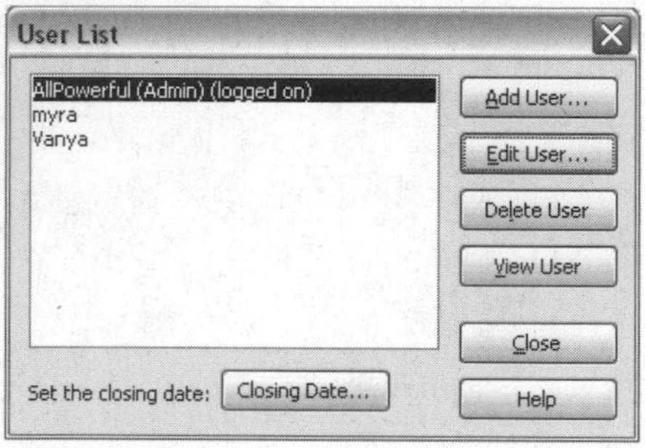

Figure 26-2:
The User List displays "(Admin)" after the name of the person who has administrator privileges. The text "(logged on)" after a username shows who you're logged in as.

2. **Click Add User.**

   QuickBooks opens the "Set up user password and access" dialog box.

3. **In the User Name box, type a name for the person to use to access the company file. And in the Password box, type a password for the person.**

   In the Confirm Password box, retype the password.

4. **Click Next to begin setting permissions, which are described in detail in the next section.**

   When you click Next to begin specifying the areas of QuickBooks that the person can access, the program selects the "Selected areas of QuickBooks" option automatically. Selecting the "All areas of QuickBooks" option instead gives this user access to *all* your financial data, as shown in Figure 26-3. That's why QuickBooks asks you to confirm that you want the person to have access to every area of QuickBooks.

Note: The external accountant user introduced in QuickBooks 2009 has access to all parts of your company file except sensitive customer information—perfect if you want to set up a QuickBooks user for your accountant or bookkeeper. To learn how to set up an external accountant user, see page 457.

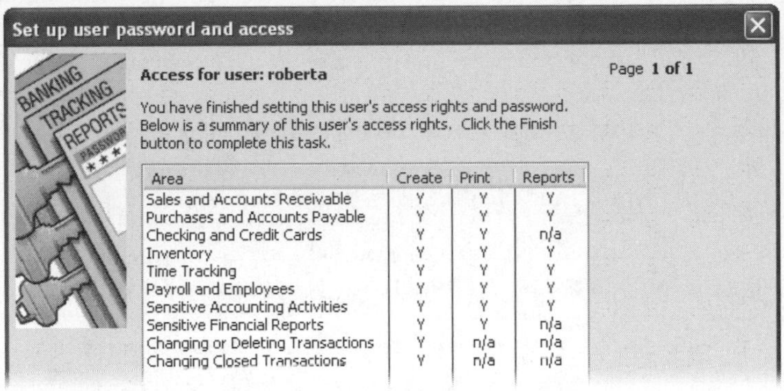

Figure 26-3:
*If you click Yes when QuickBooks
asks you to confirm this user's open
access, the "Set up user password
and access" dialog box summarizes
their access. All you have to do is
click Finish (not shown here), and
their user name appears in the
User List dialog box, ready to log
into QuickBooks.*

Resetting a User Password

Users can change their own passwords, which makes your company data even more secure. This way, users can't log in as someone else and perform transactions they shouldn't (like writing checks to themselves). To change their passwords, folks simply choose Company → "Set Up Users and Passwords" → Change Your Password. They have to type their current password and then type the new one. The administrator can change passwords and delete users if people leave the company.

Restricting Access to Features and Data

When several people work on your company file, it's safer to limit what each person can do. For example, Trusty Ted has earned his nickname, so you could set his login up with access to every QuickBooks feature, including sensitive financial reports and accounting activities. Myra Meddler can't keep a secret, but there's no one faster for data entry, so you want to make sure that she gets no further than doing the checking, credit cards, and bill paying.

If a person chooses a command and doesn't have permission for that feature, QuickBooks displays a warning message that identifies the permission needed to perform the action. In case the lack of permission was a mistake or an oversight, the warning message also suggests asking the QuickBooks administrator to grant that permission.

What the Access Areas Represent

When you tell QuickBooks that a user should have access only to selected areas of QuickBooks, you have to tell the program *which* areas the person can use. As you click Next, the "Set up user password and access" dialog box steps through one area at a time, as you can see in Figure 26-4. There's some overlap, because each area actually covers a lot of ground:

- **Sales and accounts receivable.** This area includes creating sales transactions with any kind of sales form (invoices, sales receipts, statements, and so on) and with any additional features (receiving payments, reimbursable expenses, finance charges, and so on). With sales and accounts receivable permissions, you can open the Customer Center and modify sales-related lists, such as the Customer:Job, Customer Type, and Ship Via lists, and customize sales forms. Full access includes printing and creating sales-related reports.

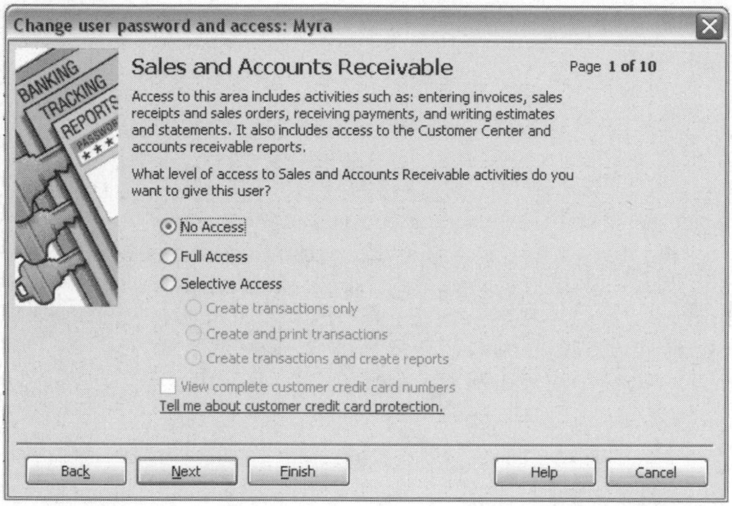

Figure 26-4:
In the upper-right corner of the "Change up user password and access" dialog box, QuickBooks shows which access page you're on. Each area of QuickBooks appears on its own page (there are nine pages of permissions). When you're done, QuickBooks displays a summary page with the features the person can access.

For the sales and accounts receivable area, selective access includes the "View complete customer credit card number" checkbox, which helps protect your customers' financial information. QuickBooks automatically turns off this checkbox, to restrict who can see a customer's full credit card information. If you don't accept credit cards, you can leave this setting as it is. Otherwise, you can turn the checkbox on for the people you trust to work with customer credit card numbers.

- **Purchases and accounts payable.** These permissions include all aspects of bills and vendors: entering and paying bills, working with purchase orders, entering reimbursable expenses and credit card charges, and paying sales tax. You can open the Vendor Center and modify purchase lists, such as the Vendor and Vendor Type lists, and customize purchase forms. Full access includes printing 1099s and reports about vendors or purchases.

- **Checking and credit cards.** Permissions in this area let people write expense checks and refund checks (but not payroll checks), enter credit card charges, and make deposits.

UP TO SPEED

Commonsense Security Measures

Your QuickBooks company file isn't the only place that you keep sensitive information. Be sure to set up your computers so that your QuickBooks data *and* all your other proprietary information are secure:

- **Back up your data regularly.** Back up your company file (page 163) and other data and store the backups in a safe place. Check that your backups save the files you want and that your backups restore without any problems.

- **Update your operating system with security updates.** If you run a Windows operating system, review the articles about the latest security updates software at *http://www.update.microsoft.com*.

- **Use antivirus software and keep it up-to-date.** These days, you need antivirus and anti-spyware

software. Because the rogues who write viruses, worms, Trojans, and spyware don't look like they're going to stop any time soon, be sure to update your antivirus and anti-spyware programs regularly.

- **Install a firewall.** An Internet connection without a firewall is an invitation to nosy nerds and criminals alike. A firewall restricts access from the Internet to only the people or computers you specify.

- **Plan for problems.** Cross-train your employees so that more than one person knows how to do each procedure in your company, including working with QuickBooks. Store the QuickBooks administrator's password in the company safety deposit box or give it to a company officer for safekeeping.

- **Inventory.** People with these permissions can maintain the inventory items on the Item List, receive products into inventory, adjust inventory quantities, work with purchase orders, and generate inventory reports.

- **Time tracking.** Time tracking permissions include the ability to enter time transactions in the weekly and single activity timesheets, import and export Timer data, and generate time reports.

- **Payroll and employees.** Payroll permissions include opening the Employee Center and the Payroll Center, writing and printing paychecks, setting up and paying payroll liabilities, using the selected payroll service, maintaining the Employee and Payroll Items lists, and generating payroll forms and reports.

- **Sensitive accounting activities.** Sensitive accounting activities don't belong to any one area of QuickBooks. Reserve these permissions for people who are not only trustworthy, but who understand how your accounting system works. With these permissions, someone can maintain your chart of accounts, make general journal entries, transfer funds, reconcile accounts, access accounts through online banking, work in balance sheet account registers, and create budgets. Other permissions include condensing data (which removes details of past transactions), using Accountant's Review, and generating the payroll report.

- **Sensitive financial reporting.** These permissions let someone print every report in QuickBooks, regardless of any reporting restrictions from the other access settings you choose. For example, someone with this kind of access can print Profit & Loss, Balance Sheet, Cash Flows, and audit trail reports.

- **Change or delete transactions.** As an extra precaution, you can give people permission to create transactions in an area, but not let them change or delete the transactions that they've created. For example, for trainees just learning the ropes, you might remove their permission to edit transactions, so they need to ask someone more experienced to make changes. An additional option lets people change transactions prior to the closing date. (Ideally, give this permission only to those who really know what they're doing—like your accountant.)

Setting Access Rights

In the "Set up user password and access" dialog box, the "Selected areas of Quick-Books" option takes you on a journey of specifying access to areas of QuickBooks. As you click Next to access each area of QuickBooks, you can give someone no access at all, full access, or the right to perform some tasks in the area, as shown in Figure 26-5.

Here's a guide to what each level of access lets people do:

- **No Access.** People can't open any windows or dialog boxes for that area of QuickBooks, meaning they can't perform any actions in that area. QuickBooks automatically chooses the No Access option. To give someone any access to an area, you have to choose either Full Access or Selective Access.

- **Full Access.** The person can perform every task in that area of QuickBooks, but not tasks reserved for the administrator user.

- **Selective Access.** When you choose this option, you also need to tell Quick-Books what the person can do (Figure 26-5).

The final page in the "Set up user password and access" dialog box summarizes the access rights that you chose for the person, as shown in Figure 26-3. The Summary screen separates access into the same categories as the Selective Access level: Create, Print, and Reports. In most cases, giving someone full access means that "Y" appears in all three columns. No access usually displays "N" in all three columns. When a permission isn't applicable to an area, QuickBooks displays "n/a". For example, there aren't any reports associated with the right to change or delete transactions.

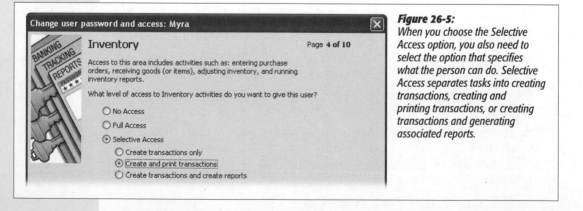

Figure 26-5:
When you choose the Selective Access option, you also need to select the option that specifies what the person can do. Selective Access separates tasks into creating transactions, creating and printing transactions, or creating transactions and generating associated reports.

Audit Trails

The audit trail feature is always turned on, keeping track of changes to transactions, who makes them, and when. You check this permanent record—the Audit Trail report, shown in Figure 26-6—to watch for unseemly activity.

You have to be the QuickBooks administrator or have permission to generate sensitive financial reports to run the Audit Trail report (choose Reports → Accountant & Taxes → Audit Trail).

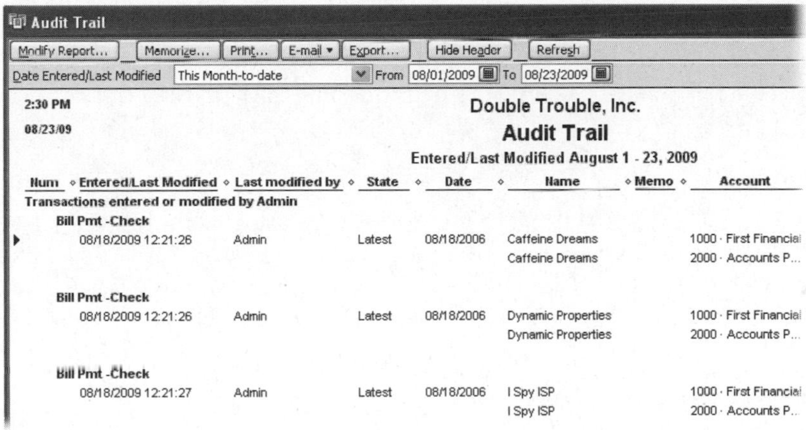

Figure 26-6:
The Audit Trail report shows every transaction that's been created, changed, or deleted. To see the details of a transaction, double-click it.

Note: The Clean Up Company File tool (page 182) removes the audit trail information for transactions that the cleanup deletes. So if you're watching transaction activity, print an Audit Trail report *first*, and, as always, back up your company file regularly.

Installing QuickBooks

QuickBooks' installation procedure seems to gain or lose a few steps—and clicks of the Next button—with each new version. Still, you only have two basic options: install the program from scratch or upgrade from a previous version. When you upgrade, you can run both versions on your computer at the same time, which is essential if you're an accountant or bookkeeper who works with company files from several different clients. But if you use QuickBooks to run your own business, there's not much point keeping two versions around. Once you open your company file in a new version of QuickBooks, it won't run in the earlier version (see the box below). Either way, this appendix walks you through the installation process.

POWER USERS' CLINIC

Installing Multiple QuickBooks Versions

If you work with clients running different versions or editions of QuickBooks, don't panic: QuickBooks versions and editions can run on the same computer *mostly* without squabbling with each other.

For example, you can run QuickBooks Pro 2009, QuickBooks Pro 2010, and QuickBooks Premier Edition 2010 all on the same machine. As long as you access each company file with *only one version* or edition of the program, you'll be fine. However, QuickBooks updates company files in two situations, which means you won't be able to use the files in the previous version or edition:

- Opening a company file in a new version updates the file to work with the new version and prevents earlier versions from opening the file. So once you open your company file with QuickBooks 2010, your accountant who's running QuickBooks 2009 won't be able to access your data.

- Opening a company file in QuickBooks Enterprise Edition optimizes the file for faster performance. Once you open a company file in this edition, the file is off-limits to QuickBooks Pro and QuickBooks Premier.

This appendix also tells you how to install QuickBooks 2010 on a company network (page 644). If, like most businesses, you have several people who can access a company file at the same time, everyone has to run the same version of Quick-Books, so prepare to spend the time installing the program on all those machines. You'll also learn where on a network you can store your company file—and which location to choose for best performance.

Note: You don't have to pay list price for QuickBooks ($199.95 for a single license of QuickBooks Pro; $399.95 for a single license of QuickBooks Premier). Your local office supply store, *www.Amazon.com*, and any number of other retail outlets usually offer the program at a discount. (If you buy QuickBooks from Intuit, you pay full price, but have 60 days to return the program for a full refund.) In addition, accountants can resell QuickBooks to clients, so it's worth asking yours about purchase and upgrade pricing. QuickBooks ProAdvisors can get you up to a 20 percent discount on QuickBooks Pro or Premier, and you'll still have 60 days to return the program for a refund.

Before You Install

Intuit recommends a 1.8 GHz processor and 256 MB of RAM for a single user of QuickBooks Pro. For a single user of Pro or Premier on Windows Vista, Intuit recommends a 2.0 GHz processor and at least 512 MB of RAM. Add another 512 MB of RAM for more than one concurrent user—but doubling the recommended RAM (2 GB at a minimum as a rule of thumb) will probably bring you closer to acceptable number-crunching speeds. You also need about 2 GB of free disk space and a 4X CD/DVD drive to install the program. (If you plan to use Google Desktop Search to search within your company file, make sure your computer is generously equipped with processing speed, RAM, and at least another gigabyte of disk space for the search index.) QuickBooks 2010 can run on Windows XP (Service Pack 2 if you want Intuit's technical support to help you), Windows 2003 Server, and Windows Vista.

If you're planning to use QuickBooks' integration features, the versions of your other programs matter, too. For example, writing letters and exporting reports requires Microsoft Word and Excel 2000 or later; synchronizing contacts requires Outlook 2000 or later.

If you have several QuickBooks users, plan on upgrading everyone's copy of QuickBooks at the same time. Once you've upgraded everyone, you can update the company file to the new software version. Then, have everyone make sure that they can open the company file with the new version of QuickBooks. (If you update the company file first, your colleagues won't be able to work in it until they have the newest version of the program.)

Note: If your QuickBooks installation and registration behave differently than described in this appendix, go to the Missing CD page at *www.missingmanuals.com/cds* for updated instructions. Or, simply follow the onscreen instructions and don't worry.

Installing QuickBooks

If you have a single-user license for QuickBooks, installing or upgrading the program is incredibly simple. Even on a network with a multiuser license, installing QuickBooks is mostly common sense. If you're installing on a computer running Windows Vista, search the QuickBooks Knowledge Base (page 658) for instructions.

Note: In previous versions of QuickBooks, the installation wizard informed you that it was installing Microsoft .Net Framework. In QuickBooks 2010, the installation goes ahead and installs this program without a word. QuickBooks 2010 uses Google Desktop for its Search feature, but doesn't install that program until the first time you use Search (page 320). Then, if Google Desktop isn't already installed on your computer, the program asks if you want to install it.

Here are the steps for installing QuickBooks:

1. **Log into Windows as a user with administrator rights.**

   Windows XP, Windows 2003 Server, and Windows Vista require administrator rights to install QuickBooks. If you're running Windows Vista, disable the firewall.

2. **Shut down any running programs, including your virus protection programs (a good idea for any installation). Then put the QuickBooks CD in your CD drive.**

   Most of the time, the installation process starts on its own, and the QuickBooks installation dialog box appears on your screen.

Tip: If the installation window doesn't appear, try using the Windows installation feature. Choose Start → Settings → Control Panel, and then double-click "Add or Remove Programs". In the navigation bar on the left, click Add New Programs. Click "CD or Floppy", select the QuickBooks CD, and then follow the onscreen instructions.

---

3. **In the QuickBooks installation dialog box, click Next.**

   The installation wizard extracts the files it needs to install QuickBooks. You'll see progress bars that give you an idea about you how long you have to wait. You'll have time to reply to a few emails and make a few calls.

4. **If the QuickBooks installation dialog box asks if you want to check for and download the latest installation update, leave the Yes option selected, and then click Next.**

   When the program finishes looking for updates, the screen tells you whether any are available. It installs any updates that it finds along with QuickBooks. On the screen that tells you whether any updates are available, click Next.

5. **When you see Welcome to QuickBooks! screen, click Next.**

   The QuickBooks Software License Agreement screen appears.

6. **After you read the software agreement carefully, select the "I accept the terms in the license agreement" option and then click Next.**

   You can proceed with the installation without *reading* the software agreement, but it's a really good idea to make sure the agreement doesn't ask for something you aren't willing to provide.

7. **On the Choose Installation Type screen, select either the Express or "Custom or Network options" option. Click Next.**

   The Express option sets up QuickBooks for single-user access (page 161) and installs QuickBooks in *C:\Program Files\Intuit\QuickBooks 2010*. If you choose this option, the installation jumps to the screen asking for the license and product numbers—and you can continue with step 9. You can change the preference to allow multiple users after QuickBooks is up and running (page 161).

   The "Custom or Network options" option lets you install QuickBooks where you want on your computer, install QuickBooks and share a company file with others, or set up the computer only to share the company file (page 650).

8. **If you're the only person who uses QuickBooks, on the "Custom and Network Options" screen, select the "I'll be using QuickBooks on this computer" option.**

   This option installs QuickBooks on your computer and sets it up for single-user access to your company file. You can change the preference to allow multiple users after QuickBooks is up and running (page 161).

   If you're going to run QuickBooks and also want to store the company file on this computer to share with other QuickBooks jockeys, select the "I'll be using QuickBooks on this computer, AND I'll be storing our company file here so it can be shared over our network" option and then click Next.

   The third and most long-winded option which begins with "I will NOT be using QuickBooks on this computer" is the one you select when you're installing the program on a computer that acts as a file server; in other words, the computer stores your company files but won't run QuickBooks (page 650).

9. **Fill in the License Number and Product Number boxes with your QuickBooks license number and product number, and then click Next.**

   The license number and product number are hard to miss—they're printed on the bright yellow sticker on your QuickBooks CD sleeve.

   As you finish typing the digits in one box, QuickBooks automatically jumps to the next box. If you're confident on the keyboard, you can keep your eyes on the yellow sticker and type all the digits for the license and product numbers without a break.

10. If you have a version of QuickBooks installed and want to upgrade that version, in the Upgrade or Change Installation location screen, select the "Replace the version selected below with the version I'm installing" option. In the dropdown list, choose the version that you want to upgrade.

    The path for your current version of QuickBooks appears below the drop-down list.

    If you don't have a version of QuickBooks installed, the Installation Location Options screen appears. The only thing you can do is change the installation location.

11. **If you want to install QuickBooks 2010 without upgrading an existing version, select the "Change the install location" option. To choose a different location, click Browse (see Figure A-1, background). Select the new folder and click OK.**

    If QuickBooks isn't installed on your computer, simply click Browse to change the installation location

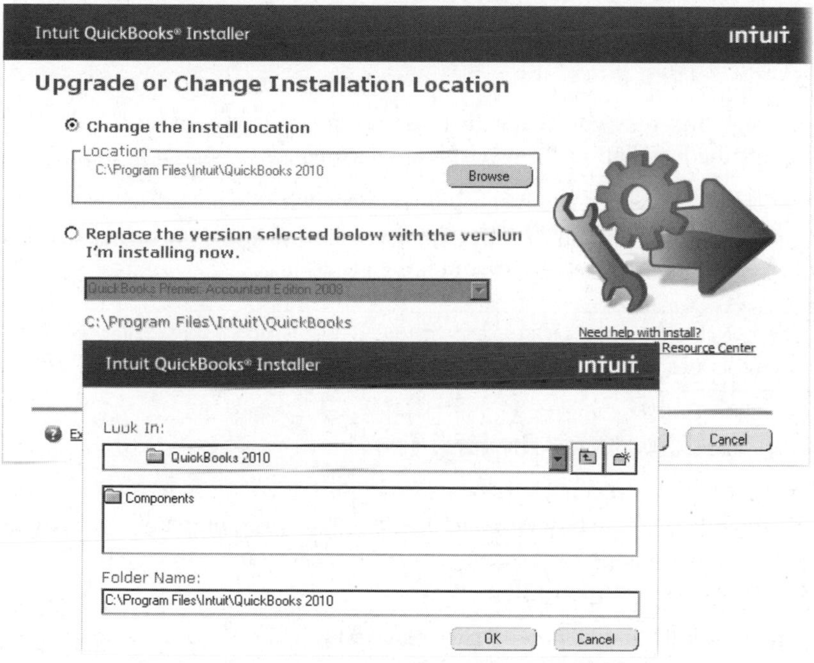

Figure A-1:
If the folder you want to use doesn't exist, click the New Folder Icon, which looks like a stylized folder with an asterisk (foreground). To view the folders one level up, click the icon that looks like a folder containing an arrow pointing up. To select a folder within the box, double-click it.

12. **When the installation location is set the way you want, click Next.**

    The "Ready to Install" screen appears with a summary of the program version, the license and product numbers, and the installation folder you chose. It also warns you that the installation could take 15 to 20 minutes.

13. If you want to change, say, the folder you're installing to, click Back until you get to the appropriate screen and make the changes. Then click Next until you're back at this screen.

Unless you like your desktop covered with shortcuts, turn off the "Add service and support icons to your desktop" checkbox. You can reach the same services from the Help menu with commands for contacting QuickBooks technical support (page 658) and ordering checks.

14. If the settings are correct, on the "Ready to Install" screen, click Install.

When you click Install, the CD starts whirring again and your hard drive makes busy sounds. The wizard shows the installation task it's performing and progress bars indicate how far it's gotten. When marketing information about new features pops up in the dialog box, you know that the installation might take some time and you can take a walk or return phone calls. (The process continues for a few minutes even after the progress bars reach the right side of the window.) But eventually, the "Congratulations!" screen appears.

15. If you're ready to get to work, click Finish.

If you want some help with QuickBooks, turn on the "Help me get started" checkbox *and then* click Finish.

16. A message box tells you that you must restart your computer. Click Yes to complete the installation. To restart later, click No.

If you asked for help, a browser window opens with links that tell you how to create or update company files, set up QuickBooks for more than one user, or point you to helpful information about the program.

Note: Even if you told the installation not to add shortcuts to your desktop, it still adds the desktop shortcut for QuickBooks itself.

Running QuickBooks for the First Time

The first time you run the new version of QuickBooks, you need to take a few extra steps after you launch the program and before you open a company file. Chapter 1 takes through launching QuickBooks and opening files for day-to-day work, but the following steps walk you through the first pass:

1. To launch QuickBooks, double-click the desktop shortcut, or choose Start → All Programs → QuickBooks → QuickBooks <edition> 2010.

2. If you're upgrading your version of QuickBooks, the program displays a dialog box asking if you want to convert your company file (page 32). In the text box, type Yes and then click OK.

The program displays a message that Automatic Update is turned on automatically, which means that QuickBooks uses your Internet connection to go online and download updates.

3. **Click OK to install updates made since the CD came out.**

When Intuit releases software *patches* for QuickBooks (small, free upgrades to the program), the Automatic Update option downloads and installs those patches for you. But many people prefer to do these updates themselves, so they don't get taken by surprise when the software changes. To learn about Quick-Books Automatic Update feature (and how to turn it off), choose Help → Update QuickBooks.

4. **In the main QuickBooks window, click "Create a new company file" to create a brand-new company file.**

If you've upgraded from a previous version, your accountant built your company file for you, or you're restoring from a backup, click "Open an existing company file". The first time you open any file in the new version, the Register QuickBooks dialog box asks you to register your software, which is the topic in the next section.

Registering QuickBooks

The Register QuickBooks dialog box doesn't appear until the first time you open a company file with the new version of the program. If you're new to QuickBooks and create a brand-new company file, the EasyStep Interview (page 21) walks you through the entire process without mentioning registration. But when you open the file you've just created or converted from an earlier version, you'll see the Register QuickBooks Now dialog box. You don't have to register QuickBooks immediately, but you'll have to eventually—the program runs for only 30 days unless you register your copy. In other words, Intuit doesn't really give you a choice in the matter.

In addition to letting you run the program you've already paid for, registration is worthwhile for a couple other reasons: You get 30 days of free callback support from the day you first register, and you'll receive any updates that Intuit releases. The price you pay is having to sit through online sales pitches for Intuit's other products.

1. **To register, make sure that you're connected to the Internet, and then click Begin Registration.**

The Register QuickBooks <edition> 2010 page appears with a phone number to call to obtain your Validation Code. When you call the number, you have to provide your license number, product number, and your telephone number to the agent.

A browser window opens to QuickBooks Registration. The first step is either creating an Intuit Account (page 29) or signing in with your Intuit account User ID and password. If you haven't provided information about you and your company before, you need to fill in a few screens of information. The fields that are required have an asterisk to the right of the field label.

2. **In the Validation Code box, type the number that the agent gives you. Click Next and then click Finish.**

    Keep a copy of the license number, product number, and the telephone number you used for registration. You'll need them if you have to reinstall QuickBooks or install it on a new hard drive.

Setting Up QuickBooks on a Network

For several people to work on the same company file from different computers, the computers running QuickBooks have to be networked together. Making this arrangement work requires a few extra—but simple—setup steps. Each user in a multiuser environment has to:

- Run the same version of QuickBooks (QuickBooks 2010, for example).

- Have permission to read, write, create, and delete in the folder in which the company file resides. A network administrator typically sets up each user for these permissions. If you're responsible for getting users set up, but you never wanted network administrator as your job title, choose Start → "Help and Support" and then, in the Search box, type "Share folder" to find the instructions for sharing a folder using your operating system.

Tip: You can simplify access to the company file folder by mapping a drive to that folder. In the Windows "Help and Support" window, search for "Assign drive."

- Have a valid license number and product number. You need a separate Quick-Books license for each computer on which you install the program.

QuickBooks Pro and Premier can handle up to five people accessing a company file at the same time. Intuit is happy to sell you more than five licenses for Quick-Books to install on other people's computers, but only five of the licensed users can work on the company file simultaneously. QuickBooks Enterprise comes with 5-, 10-, or 15-user license packs and expands the number of simultaneous users to 30.

Where to Store Your Company Files

QuickBooks 2010 has its favorite spot for company files, but you can save your files where it makes the most sense for your company. For example, if several people work on your company files simultaneously, choose your storage location to get the quickest performance (and you can read how to do that on page 651). This section explains how to choose where to store your company files.

In Windows Vista, the program automatically sets the company file folder to *C:\Users\Public\Public Documents\Intuit\QuickBooks\Company Files*. The folder for Windows XP is *C:\Documents and Settings\All Users\(Shared)\Documents\Intuit\QuickBooks\Company Files*. If you're browsing through folders, the Windows XP path shows up simply as "Shared Documents".

But you're free to choose a different folder. QuickBooks lets you store your company files anywhere you like, so you may as well keep them with the rest of your documents. It also makes sense to create a folder dedicated to just your Quick-Books files. In addition to company files, you'll probably create backup files, message templates, files that you export from QuickBooks, and files for importing into your company file. With a QuickBooks folder as a container, you can create subfolders for each type of file, as shown in Figure A-2.

Tip: If you aren't totally at ease working with files in your computer operating system, *Windows XP Pro: The Missing Manual* or *Windows Vista: The Missing Manual* will make you an expert in no time.

Storing company files on a network

If several people work on your company files, where you store the files can determine whether the people who work on them get blisteringly fast responses or nod off waiting for commands to complete. For the best performance, store company files on the network computer with the most memory, the fastest processor, the most available disk space, and—ideally—the least amount of activity. The location of your company file depends on the type of network you use:

- Peer-to-peer networks don't use dedicated file servers, so you can store your company file on any computer on the network. The computers running Quick-Books need to use Windows XP, Windows 2003 Server, or Windows Vista.

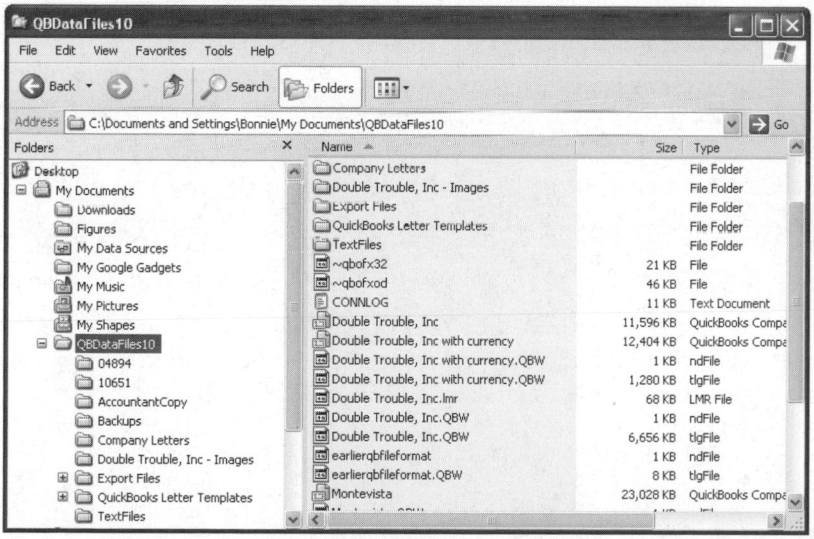

Figure A-2:
A subfolder for each type of QuickBooks-related file makes it easy to find what you want. If you save a copy of your company file at the end of each year, you can create subfolders for each year. To create a new folder, in a Windows Explorer window, first select the folder in which to create the new folder. Choose File → New → Folder, and then type a name for the new folder.

• On a client-server network, the company file typically resides on a *file server*, a dedicated computer for sharing files. Every computer on the network that has QuickBooks installed can access the company files, but one of the computers has to host multiuser access (page 646). Intuit recommends installing Quick-Books and the company files on the server, which has to run Windows XP, Windows 2003 Server, or Windows Vista.

However, in some cases, you *can't* install QuickBooks on the computer that holds the company files (if you use a Novell file server, for instance). You have to log into the computer that you want to use as the *host* and open company files in multiuser mode (page 161). When QuickBooks asks if you want this computer to host multiuser access, click Yes. This computer then plays traffic cop for several people working on the company files at the same time.

Tip: When you perform resource-gobbling tasks, like running massive reports or reconciling accounts, performance is paramount. On a peer-to-peer network, log into QuickBooks on the computer that holds the company files to perform these tough tasks. On a client-server network, use the fastest computer on the network.

Help, Support, and Other Resources

Between questions about how to do something in QuickBooks and how to handle something in accounting, you might need help almost every time you open the program. Finding answers isn't always easy, however, and online help can sometimes cause more frustration than it solves. But QuickBooks 2010's Help system has a few features that actually help. For example, when you open QuickBooks Help, it automatically shows links to topics relevant to what you're doing in the program. So if the Create Invoices window is open, the relevant topics tell you how to fill out or edit invoices, record payments toward invoices, and so on. You'll find topics with background info, troubleshooting tips, and even advice on why you should or shouldn't perform certain steps.

Another option is Live Community. As its name suggests, this help comes from fellow QuickBooks wranglers. Live Community may seem like yet another move toward self-service, but the help you receive from your colleagues is often more pertinent than what you get from Intuit. If you don't see a question and answer close to the question you have, you can post yours to the community. If you're a QuickBooks veteran, you can even answer someone else's pleas for help.

Where QuickBooks Help falls short is giving you different ways to find information. You can search for information using keywords or browse through QuickBooks' relevant topics until you find what you're looking for, but if you prefer a table of contents or an easy-to-scan index, they're nowhere to be found.

In this appendix, you'll learn your way around QuickBooks Help. But if the Quick-Books help you find isn't very helpful, you'll also learn about other resources that might do better.

QuickBooks Help

Wherever you are in the program, you can get help by pressing F1 or choosing Help → QuickBooks Help. The "Have a Question?" window opens to the Help tab and its Relevant Topics tab, which lists topics related to what you're doing, as shown in Figure B-1. The Relevant Topics feature is like a revved-up version of the How Do I? or Help buttons you used to find in QuickBooks windows and dialog boxes. Your other option is the tried and true keyword search (click the Search tab).

Note: In QuickBooks 2010, the Help window has finally learned how to play well with other windows, as the box on page 654 explains.

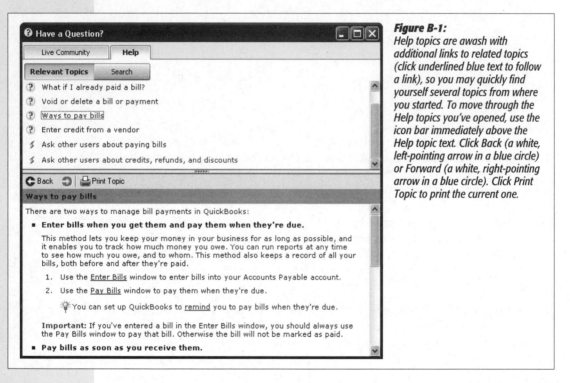

Figure B-1:
Help topics are awash with additional links to related topics (click underlined blue text to follow a link), so you may quickly find yourself several topics from where you started. To move through the Help topics you've opened, use the icon bar immediately above the Help topic text. Click Back (a white, left-pointing arrow in a blue circle) or Forward (a white, right-pointing arrow in a blue circle). Click Print Topic to print the current one.

The Relevant Topics tab in the QuickBooks Help window is smart. The topics change automatically to show help that's relevant as you click commands, display windows, or open dialog boxes. For example, when the QuickBooks Home page is active, relevant topics include "Use the Home page," "Customize the Home page by choosing which icons appear," "Show or hide the QuickBooks Home page," and so on. Then, if you click the Pay Bills icon in the Home page, the relevant topics change to things like "Pay a bill with a check" and "Ways to pay bills." When you click a topic on the Relevant Topics tab, it appears in the bottom half of the "Have a Question?" window.

Resizing and Moving the Help Window

How can I resize and position the Help window the way I want?

In previous versions, QuickBooks' Help window would glom onto the right side of the main QuickBooks window and stay there until you closed it. If you widened it to read a help topic, it stole space from the QuickBooks main window and wouldn't give it back. The Help window wouldn't yield the floor to the windows or dialog boxes you used to actually do work. In QuickBooks 2010, it's finally learned the tricks that Help windows in other programs have known for years.

To make the Help window show some manners, choose Edit → Preferences and then, in the Preferences dialog box, click the Desktop View icon. Turn on the "Detach the Help Window" checkbox and click OK.

Here's how the Help window works once you've detached it:

- **Move the Help window.** Drag the Have a Question? title bar to the new location. The next time you open the Help window it conveniently appears in the same location.

- **Resize or widen the Help window.** Hover the cursor over any border of the window until it changes to a double-headed arrow and then drag in the direction that you want the size to change. The next time you open the Help window, it opens to the size it was when you last closed it. (If you widen the Help window when it's attached to the QuickBooks main window, it narrows the main window. However, when you close the Help window, the program restores the main window to its original width.)

- **Minimize the Help window.** If you want to focus on the task at hand click the Minimize button in the upper right corner of the window. To restore the minimized Help window, click the Have a Question? button in the Windows taskbar.

The other way to find a help topic is to click the Search tab, type keywords into the text box that appears, and then click the right arrow to search for related topics, as shown in Figure B-2.

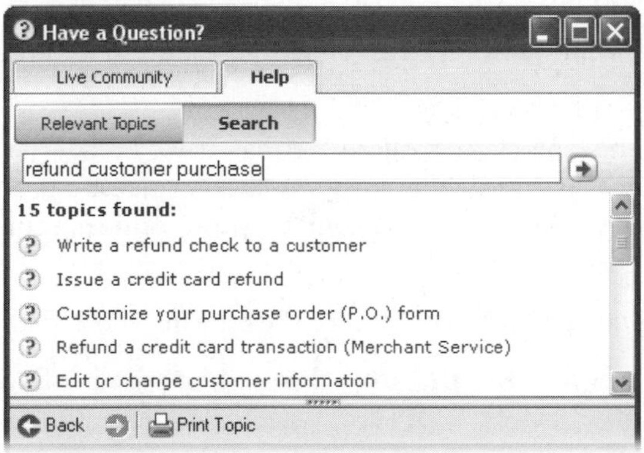

Figure B-2:
No matter how many keywords you type in the Search box, QuickBooks Help lists 15 topics that relate to those keywords. Typing more keywords doesn't narrow the results. Instead, QuickBooks finds 15 topics by including ones that relate to only one of the keywords.

Live Community

Live Community is a portal to Intuit's QuickBooks community message boards. The system is simple to use: You ask a question, and Live Community checks whether it's already been answered by someone else who uses QuickBooks. If none of the answers it finds are what you want, you can pose your question to the community. By the same token, you can post your solutions to questions that others have asked (if you know the answer). Otherwise, Live Community wouldn't be very lively.

The downside to Live Community is that you can't control the answers that the feature displays. You'll see different responses depending on how you phrase your question. And Live Community doesn't give you a way to scan all the questions that others have posted and the answers they received.

Tip: Should you want to scan existing questions and answers, see page 659 to learn how to review the QuickBooks community message boards without Live Community's help.

You have to create an Intuit User ID to use Live Community. The first time you submit a question, Live Community asks you to sign in. Click the "Create an Account" link to set up your User ID. The browser title bar begins with "https"—your clue that you're entering your information on a secure website. Type your email address, the screen name you want to use, and your Intuit user ID and password. To get a hint if you forget your password in the future, choose a security question like the name of your first pet and type your answer.

Here's how you use Live Community after you sign in:

1. **Choose Help → Live Community or click Live Community in the QuickBooks icon bar.**

    The "Have a Question?" window opens to the Live Community tab.

2. **In the box containing "Type your question here" (Figure B-3), do so and then click Ask My Question.**

    A browser window opens, showing similar questions that have already been answered, as shown in Figure B-4. Live Community searches for questions and answers that contain the same words you used in your question (omitting common words like "the", "a", and so on).

3. **If you see a question that seems similar to yours, click the blue question link.**

    When you hover the cursor over the text, the cursor changes to a pointing finger to indicate that the text is a link.

    When you click a question, the browser window displays the question and all the answers that have been posted so far. If you find your answer, click Yes to close the browser window. Otherwise, click No to return to the list of similar questions.

---

4. **If none of the questions seem relevant or you discover that the answers aren't what you want, at the bottom of the window, click Ask My Question.**

   The Live Community browser window displays boxes for the question title and question text. You can type up to 120 characters in the title box and 7200 characters in the "Your question details" box, so enter a thorough request. The "Email me when my questions receive new replies" checkbox is turned on automatically, so you'll receive an email notification when someone answers your question.

5. **Click Send My Question to publish it to Live Community.**

   If you left the "Email me when my questions receive new replies" checkbox turned on, you'll receive an email notification every time someone replies to your question. In the Live Community window, a New Reply flag pops up when someone answers your question.

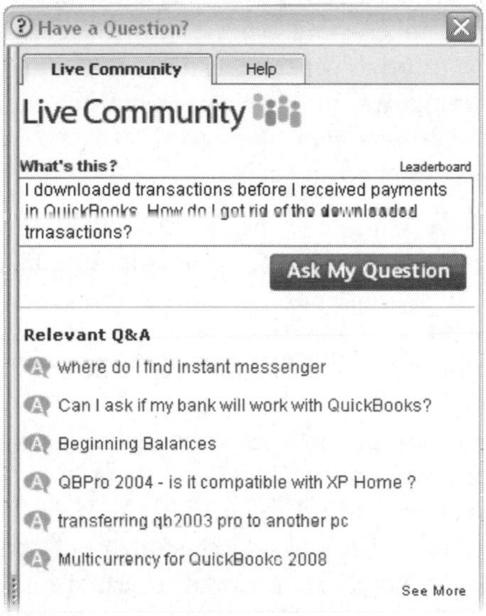

Figure B-3:
You can type your request in any format (a question, a topic heading, or a series of keywords), but a clear and complete description of your question or issue is more likely to produce a relevant answer. The question box holds up to 250 characters, but it lacks a scrollbar. To move up and down in the box, press the up or down arrow key.

6. **When someone solves your problem, click either Helpful or Solved (these options are next to your question).**

   Clicking Helpful or Solved awards point to the person who answered the question. Points aren't worth anything, although the number of points someone has can indicate whether they know what they're talking about. Clicking Solved closes the thread, which means no one can post to the thread in the future. If you want to leave a comment for the person who answered the question, post your comment first and then click Solved.

Note: At the bottom of the Live Community window, the "Give Advice, Answer a Question" section lists a few unanswered questions. If you feel like sharing, click See More to see all the unanswered questions posted to Live Community. If you see a question you can answer, click its blue title to read the complete question. If you still think you can answer the question, click Submit An Answer. Type your response in the box, and then click Submit. (If you realize you can't answer the question, click Cancel.)

Other Kinds of Help

Unsurprisingly, the first command on the Help menu is QuickBooks Help. However, commands further down on the menu may provide the assistance you want, depending on your level of experience and the way you prefer to learn:

- **Learning Center Tutorials.** Choose this command to open the QuickBooks Learning Center window and watch video tutorials about popular tasks. For example, in the QuickBooks Learning Center's navigation bar, click the Customers & Sales icon to access tutorials for creating estimates, invoices, sales receipts, statements, and payments. The tutorials generally run between 4 and 5 minutes, so don't expect in-depth training. An audio track (or optional text) explains what's going on as you see the pointer move around the screen, buttons highlight, and windows or dialog boxes open and close.

- **Support.** This command opens a browser window to the QuickBooks support Home page (you can also click the Support icon, in the icon bar—it looks like a life preserver). Front and center on the support page, you'll see the product you're using, such as QuickBooks Pro 2010. If you want support on a different edition, click the "Choose a different product" link. In the search box to the right of the "Search the QuickBooks Support site" label, type keywords and click the Search button. The web page displays articles from the Knowledge Base and answers from the QuickBooks community. The Knowledge Base is a database of detailed instructions that you won't find in QuickBooks Help. For example, you can find out how to install QuickBooks successfully on a computer with Windows Vista (page 645). Type the text you want to search for, or the error number you've received.

Tip: The way to get in touch with an Intuit QuickBooks support person isn't immediately obvious. The box on page 661 explains how.

- **Find a Local QuickBooks Expert.** If you're tired of figuring things out on your own, you can find plenty of accountants and bookkeepers who are QuickBooks experts—you'll be glad you did. Intuit has a certification program for accounting professionals, and this command opens a web browser to the QuickBooks Find-a-ProAdvisor website (*http://quickbooks.intuit.com/product/training/local_ expert.jsp*) where you can find someone in your area. ProAdvisors have passed tests to prove their QuickBooks expertise. Finding a ProAdvisor is free, but a ProAdvisor's services aren't. When you find ProAdvisors near you, ask about their fees before hiring them.

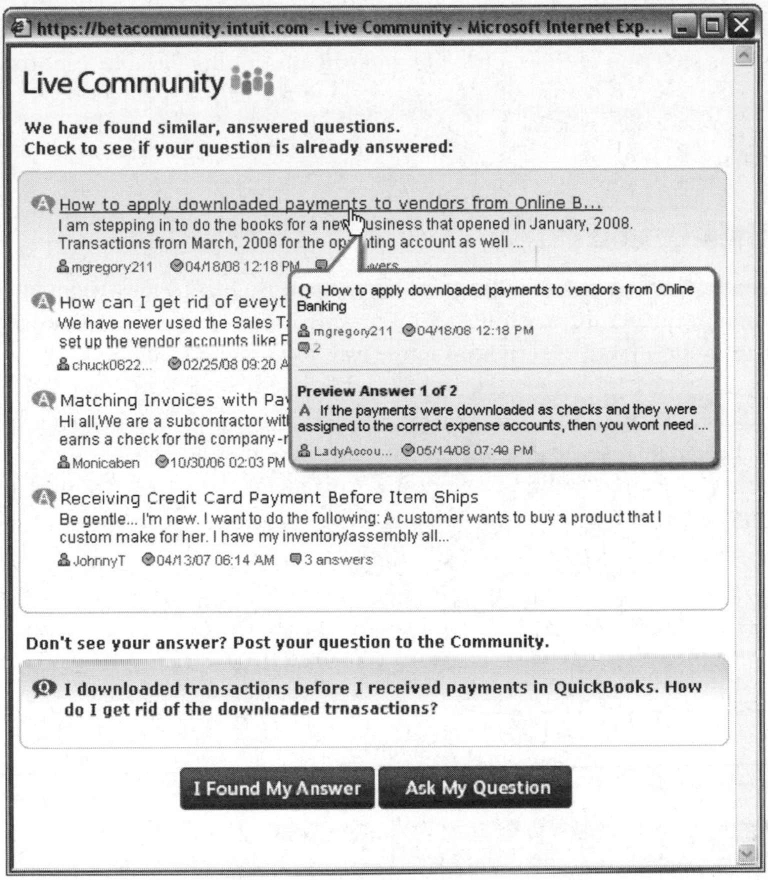

Figure B-4:
The browser lists a heading for each similar question and a portion of the full question text. When you hover the cursor over the question link, a pop-up box displays the question and a preview of the first answer.

- **Send Feedback Online.** This command won't provide instant gratification for your QuickBooks problems, although a quick rant may make you feel better. You can send suggestions for improvements to QuickBooks or QuickBooks Help. You can also report bugs that you find.

The QuickBooks Community

Live Community and the search feature on the QuickBooks Support web page both deliver answers posted to the QuickBooks community message boards. Both features rely on the words you type to find likely responses to your question. If you'd rather scan the QuickBooks community message board to see what's available, you can open a web browser directly to the QuickBooks Community web page (*http://community.intuit.com/quickbooks*). The forums are the best place to look for answers to thorny problems, especially when the issue is a combination of accounting practices and how to do them in QuickBooks.

You can click the name of one of the high-level forms, like "Paying Bills and Vendor Management", to see all the posts for that area. Or, you can find more focused material by clicking one of the subheading links like Accounts Payable Reports or Purchase Orders. Before you post a message asking for help, type keywords into the Search box and click Ask to see if anyone has already solved your dilemma, as shown in Figure B-5.

Other Help Resources

If you don't find an answer to your questions in QuickBooks Help or the Quick-Books Community forums, you can use Google to search or try an independent QuickBooks message board. Quickbooksusers.com (*www.quickbooksusers.com*) has forums for different editions of QuickBooks, including one each for QuickBooks overall, QuickBooks Pro, Premier Non-profit, and Premier Manufacturing and Wholesale. People post some gnarly problems on these message boards, but each question gets at least one reply. In some cases, you might receive several different solutions to the same problem.

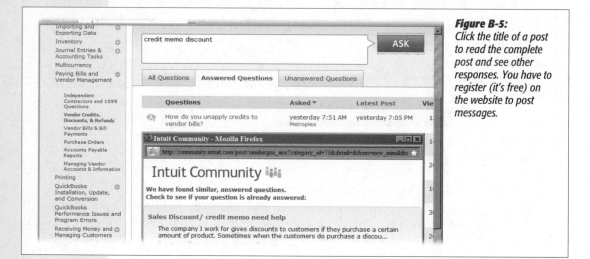

Figure B-5:
Click the title of a post to read the complete post and see other responses. You have to register (it's free) on the website to post messages.

The Quickbooksusers.com message boards are free. This site supports itself by selling data recovery services and tech support, and it also has advertising. Then again, a data recovery service might be just what you need. If you're looking for an add-on program or having problems with one, check out the site's QuickBooks 3rd Party Software Forum. When you really get going with QuickBooks, you can even prowl the QuickBooks Jobs forum.

Tip: When you receive an error message in QuickBooks, typing the message or error number into your web search engine's search box is a great way to find answers.

QuickBooks Training

Searching for QuickBooks training online yields more results than you want to surf to. You can narrow the search by including your city: "QuickBooks training Denver," for example. If you prefer to study on the Web, search for "QuickBooks training Web-based" or "QuickBooks training online" For example, Qbalance.com (*www.Qbalance.com*) offers QuickBooks training for folks at any level of experience. You can get one-on-one training with a QuickBooks expert, classroom-based training, or training on a CD. Real World Training (*www.realworldtraining.com*) offers regularly scheduled instructor-led classes in many cities around the country (or in your office), training on CD, and weekly online classes.

UP TO SPEED

Getting Answers from Intuit

Free support from Intuit is rarer than hen's teeth. But reaching someone from Intuit, whether you pay or not, has gotten a little easier. To contact support, choose Help → Support. The QuickBooks Support web page opens in a browser. In the navigation bar, click Contact Us. On the contact page that appears, you fill in your name, email address, and phone number. QuickBooks automatically fills in your license number for you. When you click Continue, you can describe your issue. Then, you'll receive a phone number and case ID. If the call is going to cost you money, the support person will tell you that.

Here is the rundown on free versus for a fee support:

*   You can obtain free support for the first 30 days after you register your software.

*   Help with installation, errors, and so on is free for 12 months after you register, if the problem has to do with installing or upgrading QuickBooks, error messages you receive, or behavior that you suspect is a bug.

*   Support plans come by the month or the year. The monthly support plan costs $79 for the first month and $39 per month after that. The first year of an annual support plan is $349. After that, support costs $299 per year. If you suspect that you'll want to call support several times, a support plan is more cost-effective. The Intuit Support website has no obvious links to find out about these plans. Go to *http://quickbooks.intuit.com/product/support/monthly_plan_financial_software.jsp* to get the full story.

*   If you are reinstalling QuickBooks and can't find your license number, under the Popular Topics heading on the Support web page (*http://support.quickbooks.intuit.com/support/Default.aspx*), click the "Find your license number" link. You enter your last name and business telephone number, and Intuit retrieves your registration record with your license number and key code.

Index

I

O

One Window option, 608
online
    backup of data, 163
    bill paying, 525, 531–532, 538
    file backup, 166
    Online Backup Service (Intuit), 166
    time tracking, 194
    training, 661
online banking services
    activating for QuickBooks accounts,
        527–528
    applying for, 525–526
    from Intuit, 526
    interface choices, 2
    methods for connecting to, 529
    online banking modes, 529–530, 557
    online items for direct connections,
        531–533
    overview, 523–524
    Register mode. *See* Register mode (online
        banking)
    setting up accounts for, 525
    setting up Internet connections, 524
    Side-by-side mode. *See* Side-by-side mode
        (online banking)
    WebConnect, downloading statements
        with, 530
open invoices, 331, 589
opening
    any company files, 30–31
    portable company files, 32
    QuickBooks, 15–16
    recently opened company files, 30
Opening Balance field (customers), 74
ordering inventory, 467
Other Charge items, 119
Other Names List, 146
**Outlook, synchronizing contacts with
        QuickBooks**, 591–594
overdue balances, finance charges on,
        347–348
owner contributions to company, 428
owners' equity, 388

P

packing slips, printing, 314
parts, turning into products, 115
passwords
    administrator, 22
    assigning administrator, 630–632
    credit card security requirements, 633–634
    resetting administrator, 632–633

    resetting user, 637
    setting login (company files), 23
    tips for creating, 632
paychecks
    building from time worked, 197
    deleting duplicate, 376
    printing, 376–378
    reissuing lost, 379
payee names, downloading, 541
paying
    bills. *See* bill paying
    sales tax, 244–248
payments
    choosing payments to deposit, 354
    designating payment information
        (customers), 77–79
    early payment discounts, 337–340
    payment deposit types, 356
    Payment items, 123–124
    Payment Method List, 149
    preferences, 571
    receiving for invoiced income, 332–335
    setting up for loans, 411–413
    ways of applying, 338
payroll
    adding transactions from outside
        services, 360–361
    applying for service, 362–363
    choosing service, 361–362
    company-wide payroll accounts, 556–557
    compensation and benefits, setting up,
        364–366
    direct deposit, setting up, 371
    duplicate paychecks, deleting, 376
    employees, setting up, 366–371
    entering historical payroll, 372–373
    lost paychecks, reissuing, 379
    overview, 359–360
    Payroll & Employees preferences, 571–573
    preparing information for company file, 20
    printing paychecks/stubs, 376–378
    running, 373–375
    selecting start date for, 367
    setup overview, 363
    summary reports, 372
    tax forms, preparing, 381–382
    taxes, paying, 378–381
    taxes, setting up, 371–372
    updating tax tables, 373
pdf files, saving reports as, 506
pending invoices for backorders, 276
**percentage charges, applying to
        invoices**, 265–266
percentage gross profits, 431
permissions, user, 638–640

Colophon

Rachel Monaghan provided quality control for *QuickBooks 2010: The Missing Manual*.

The cover of this book is based on a series design originally created by David Freedman and modified by Mike Kohnke, Karen Montgomery, and Fitch (*www.fitch.com*). Back cover deisgn, dog illustration, and color selection by Fitch.

David Futato designed the interior layout, based on a series design by Phil Simpson. This book was converted by Abby Fox to FrameMaker 5.5.6. The text font is Adobe Minion; the heading font is Adobe Formata Condensed; and the code font is Lucas-Font's TheSansMonoCondensed. The illustrations that appear in the book were produced by Robert Romano using Adobe Photoshop CS4 and Illustrator CS4.

THE MISSING MANUALS
The books that should have been in the box

Answers found here!

Most how-to books bury the good stuff beneath bad writing, lame jokes, and fuzzy explanations. Not the Missing Manuals. Written in a unique, witty style that helps you learn quickly, our books help you get things done. Whether you're looking for guidance on software, gadgets, or how to live a healthy life, you'll find the answers in a Missing Manual.

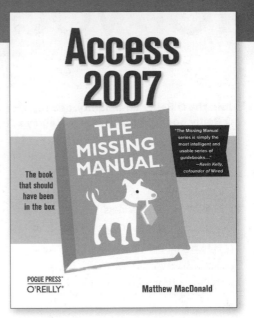

Access 2007: The Missing Manual
By Matthew MacDonald
ISBN 9780596527600
$34.99 US, 45..99 CAN

Excel 2007:
The Missing Manual
By Matthew MacDonald
ISBN 9780596527594
$39.99 US, 51..99 CAN

Creating a Web Site:
The Missing Manual
By Matthew MacDonald
ISBN 9780596520977
$29.99 US, 29.99 CAN

Your Money:
The Missing Manual
By J.D. Roth
ISBN 9780596809409
$21.99 US, 27.99 CAN

Quicken 2009:
The Missing Manual,
By Bonnie Biafore
ISBN 9780596522483
$24.99 US, 24.99 CAN

Look for these and other Missing Manuals at your favorite bookstore or online.

www.missingmanuals.com

POGUE PRESS™
O'REILLY®

Get even more for your money.

Join the O'Reilly Community, and register the O'Reilly books you own.It's free, and you'll get:

- 40% upgrade offer on O'Reilly books
- Membership discounts on books and events
- Free lifetime updates to electronic formats of books
- Multiple ebook formats, DRM FREE
- Participation in the O'Reilly community
- Newsletters
- Account management
- 100% Satisfaction Guarantee

Signing up is easy:

1. **Go to: oreilly.com/go/register**
2. **Create an O'Reilly login.**
3. **Provide your address.**
4. **Register your books.**

Note: English-language books only

To order books online:

oreilly.com/order_new

For questions about products or an order:

orders@oreilly.com

To sign up to get topic-specific email announcements and/or news about upcoming books, conferences, special offers, and new technologies:

elists@oreilly.com

For technical questions about book content:

booktech@oreilly.com

To submit new book proposals to our editors:

proposals@oreilly.com

Many O'Reilly books are available in PDF and several ebook formats. For more information:

oreilly.com/ebooks

Spreading the knowledge of innovators   www.oreilly.com

Buy this book and get access to the online edition for 45 days—for free!

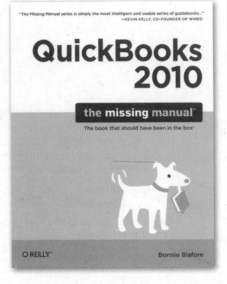